This is a comprehensive survey of the history of the church between around 900 and around 1125, considered both as a set of institutions and as a spiritual body. The emphasis of the first half is on the structures of religious belief and practice in the period between 900 and around 1050: conversion and mission; religious life and experience; the church hierarchy; rulers and the churches in their kingdoms; monasticism; currents of orthodox and heterodox thought. The second half concentrates on the revolutionary changes associated with the rise of the papacy to a new position of rulership within the church. It shows how far one can talk of a 'reform movement' and what the relations were between those who sought for a renewal of Christian life and those who wished to assert the authority of the papacy over all Christians, lay and clerical. It also does justice to the 'opposition', stressing the deep religious convictions of those who on certain issues came to oppose popes and 'reformers', and showing also how fragmentary were the advances of the 'reform movement'.

Tellenbach's survey is the book of a scholar who has been working in the field for sixty years, characterised by the freshness and the maturity of its judgements, which cuts through many fashionable theories and shows how thin is the evidence for them. No other work on the topic offers the same range, depth, and authority.

Cambridge Medieval Textbooks

THE CHURCH IN WESTERN EUROPE FROM THE TENTH TO THE EARLY TWELFTH CENTURY

Cambridge Medieval Textbooks

This is a series of specially commissioned textbooks for teachers and students, designed to complement the monograph series 'Cambridge Studies in Medieval Life and Thought' by providing introductions to a range of topics in medieval history. The series combines both chronological and thematic approaches, and will deal equally with British and European topics. All volumes in the series will be published in hard covers and in paperback.

Already published

Germany in the High Middle Ages *c.* 1050–1200
HORST FUHRMANN
Translated by Timothy Reuter

The Hundred Years War: England and France at war *c.* 1300–1450
CHRISTOPHER ALLMAND

Standards of Living in the Later Middle Ages: Social Change in England,
c. 1200–1520
CHRISTOPHER DYER

Magic in the Middle Ages
RICHARD KIECKHEFER

The Struggle for Power in Medieval Italy: Structures of Political Rule
GIOVANNI TABACCO
Translated by Rosalind Brown Jensen

The Papacy 1073–1198: Continuity and Innovation
I. S. ROBINSON

Medieval Wales
DAVID WALKER

England in the Reign of Edward III
SCOTT WAUGH

The Norman Kingdom of Sicily
DONALD MATTHEW

Political Thought in Europe, 1250–1450
ANTHONY BLACK

The Church in Western Europe from the Tenth to the Early Twelfth Century
GERD TELLENBACH
Translated by Timothy Reuter

Other titles are in preparation

THE CHURCH IN WESTERN EUROPE FROM THE TENTH TO THE EARLY TWELFTH CENTURY

GERD TELLENBACH

Emeritus University Professor of History, Freiburg im Breisgau

Translated by TIMOTHY REUTER

Monumenta Germaniae Historica

CAMBRIDGE
UNIVERSITY PRESS

Published by the Press Syndicate of the University of Cambridge
The Pitt Building, Trumpington Street, Cambridge CB2 1RP
40 West 20th Street, New York, NY 10011–4211, USA
10 Stamford Road, Oakleigh, Victoria 3166, Australia

First published 1993

Printed in Great Britain at the University Press, Cambridge

A catalogue record for this book is available from the British Library

Library of Congress cataloguing in publication data
Tellenbach, Gerd, 1903–
[Westliche Kirche vom 10. bis zum frühen 12. Jahrhundert.
English]
The Church in western Europe from the tenth to the early twelfth
century / Gerd Tellenbach: translated by Timothy Reuter.
p.   cm. – (Cambridge medieval textbooks)
Translation of: Die westliche Kirche vom 10. bis zum frühen
12. Jahrhundert.
Includes bibliographical references and index.
ISBN 0 521 43105 0. – ISBN 0 521 43711 3 (pbk.)
1. Europe – Church history – Middle Ages, 600–1500. 1. Title.
II. Series.
BR270.T4513 1993
274'.03 – dc20 92–13778 CIP

ISBN 0 521 43105 0 hardback
ISBN 0 521 43711 3 paperback

For
Marie Elisabeth

CONTENTS

ix

x   *Contents*

———— • ————

TRANSLATOR'S NOTE

———— • ————

The translation is a complete rendering of the German original, which
appeared in 1988. The bibliography and footnotes have been reworked to
conform to English practice, typographical and other small errors have
been silently corrected where noted, and the author has taken the opportunity to add two or three paragraphs in chapters 6 and 7, and to cite
additional literature in a few footnotes. Works for which an English
translation exists have been cited using the pagination of the original, and
English works used by Professor Tellenbach in German translation have
been cited using the pagination of the translation; but in these cases a
reference to the English translation or original is given in the bibliography. The work has not otherwise been revised. Professor Tellenbach
has seen and approved the entire translation, and I should like to express
my gratitude to him here for his care and attention and his many helpful
suggestions; but I alone am responsible for the errors of translation which
remain.

Timothy Reuter
Monumenta Germaniae Historica, Munich

AUTHOR'S PREFACE

In 1983 I published a draft of an introduction to this book.[1] Contrary to
my intention then, I shall not repeat what I wrote there, merely refer to
it. Only a few points necessary for the understanding of this period of
church history will be set out here by way of a prelude.

He who concerns himself with church history must be constantly aware
of the fact that it is a whole of which all isolated happenings are merely a
part; for it is determined by divine foreknowledge. However puzzling
may be the connections between its transcendental origins and destination
on the one hand and its human, sometimes all too human course on the
other, this unity is nowadays seen as a crucial element of church history
by church historians of all confessions, whatever they may understand by
the term church history. Even an author like Joseph Lortz regarded it as
fruitless 'to acknowledge the existence of certain questionable episodes in
church history and the history of theology'. It would be to diminish God's
control over history if one were small-mindedly to try to explain away its
many weaknesses, scandals, and contradictions; God rules the world and
makes human error a tool of his will – even human guilt is made use of in
this way and becomes *felix culpa*.[2]

Such a conception allows full freedom to a scholarly study of church
history. Nothing need be touched up or passed over in an apologetic
spirit. The history of the church needs no human advocate. The famous
dispute about whether the history of the church since the time of the
primitive church is to be seen as one of progress and development or as

---

[1] Tellenbach, 'Abendländische Kirche'.　　[2] Lortz, *Geschichte der Kirche*, I vii and 7.

one of decline becomes pointless, since both rise and fall are subsumed in God's plan for man's salvation.

What men think about the history of the church and of human salvation is historically determined and subject to historical change. The middle ages tended to see God's hand everywhere in earthly events. The prophetic spirit was accustomed to interpret history on the basis of the Old and New Testaments, and not just the whole course of history but individual events as well. The sacred texts were interpreted inventively and without preconceptions, symbolically, allegorically, and literally, and these interpretations were made to serve both the religious life and also quite concrete earthly interests. It was thought possible to look to the world beyond and determine God's intentions. Nowadays one is generally more modest and more cautious in interpreting the significance for the history of salvation of particular characteristics and changes in the history of the church; nevertheless, many prominent theologians and historians still occasionally risk crossing this frontier. The author of this book belongs to those who refuse strictly to draw any parallels between the visible history of the church and the mystery of divine intentions.

Historical periodisations, if they are not purely chronological, can often be of assistance to the understanding of historical connections, but they also carry the danger of arbitrary or at least one-sided interpretations. Since we nevertheless need a beginning and an end for every survey, the question arises: what could make the history of the church in the tenth and eleventh centuries a coherent period within the history of the church as a whole? To survey such a period might be justified either on the grounds that both centuries have so much in common that they appear by contrast with the periods before and after to form a unity, or on the quite opposite grounds that changes of such significance took place during them that afterwards conceptions of the nature of the church were quite different from those which had prevailed before.

There are convenient labels available for this period: 'Cluny', 'Church reform', 'Gregorianism', 'Reform papacy', 'freeing of the church from lay control'. But do these not, even where they have not simply become clichés, tend if inadequately defined to overstress certain aspects of the historical process and so to conceal more than they explain?

The subtitle of my book of 1936 – 'The church and the ordering of the world in the age of the Investiture Contest' – was already intended to refer primarily to the changes in ecclesiology. In Yves Congar's *Die Lehre von der Kirche* the fifth chapter on the reform of the church in the eleventh century has the subtitle 'the ecclesiological turning point'. In it he writes, among other things, 'The Ecclesiology of the Latin church followed the path which we shall describe: the development of papal authority, juristification, clericalisation, a challenge to secular power which brought the church to see itself as a power'.[3] And Gilles Gérard Meersseman has explained from a new perspective the changes in the relations between clerics and laymen in the life of the church.[4]

These few references may help to suggest that the second half of the eleventh century was an epoch of church history whose importance can only be understood in connection with its preconditions and its consequences. In this sense the period dealt with in this book is determined not so much by its bracketing dates of *c.* 900 and *c.* 1100, as above all by the critical era of the second half of the eleventh century and the early twelfth century.

---

[3] Y. Congar, *Die Lehre von der Kirche. Von Augustinus bis zum abendländischen Schisma* (Handbuch der Dogmengeschichte III 3c, Freiburg 1971), 60f.

[4] Meersseman, *Ordo Fraternitatis*, 241.

ABBREVIATIONS

AfD	*Archiv für Diplomatik*
AHC	*Annuarium Historiae Conciliorum*
AHP	*Archivum Historiae Pontificum*
AHVN	*Annalen des historischen Vereins für den Niederrhein*
AKG	*Archiv für Kulturgeschichte*
ALW	*Archiv für Liturgiewissenschaft*
Annales ESC	*Annales. Economies, Sociétés, Civilisations*
AUF	*Archiv für Urkundenforschung*
BDLG	*Blätter für deutsche Landesgeschichte*
BISI	*Bulletino dell'Instituto Storico Italiano per il Medio Evo*
Bouquet, *RHF*	H. Bouquet and M. Brial, *Recueil des Historiens des Gaules et de la France* (Paris 1738–)
Bresslau, *Jahrbücher Konrads II.*	H. Bresslau, *Jahrbücher des deutschen Reiches unter Konrad II.*, 2 vols. (Leipzig 1879–84)
BZ	J.-F. Böhmer, *Papstregesten 911–1024*, edited by H. Zimmermann (Vienna 1969) (cited by number)
CCM	*Cahiers de Civilisation Médiévale*
DA	*Deutsches Archiv für Erforschung des Mittelalters*
DACL	*Dictionnaire d'Archéologie Chrétienne et de Liturgie*

xvi

DHGE	*Dictionnaire d'Histoire et de Géographie Ecclesiastiques*
Dümmler, *Jahrbücher Ottos I.*	R. Köpke and E. Dümmler, *Kaiser Otto der Große* (Leipzig 1876)
Dümmler, *Jahrbücher des ostfränkischen Reiches*	E. Dümmler, *Jahrbücher des ostfränkischen Reiches*, 3 vols. 2nd edn (Leipzig 1887–8)
EC	P. Jaffé, *Epistolae Collectae, Bibliotheca rerum Germanicarum* (Berlin 1865)
EHR	*English Historical Review*
FMSt	*Frühmittelalterliche Studien*
Hirsch, Pabst, and Bresslau, *Jahrbücher Heinrichs II.*	S. Hirsch, H. Pabst, and H. Bresslau, *Jahrbücher des deutschen Reiches unter Heinrich II.*, 3 vols. (Leipzig 1862–75)
HJb	*Historisches Jahrbuch*
HZ	*Historische Zeitschrift*
Jaffé, BRG	P. Jaffé, *Bibliotheca rerum Germanicarum*, 6 vols. (Berlin 1860–9)
JE ⎫ JK ⎬ JL ⎭	P. Jaffé, *Regesta pontificum Romanorum ab condita ecclesia ad annum post Christum natum MCXCVIII*, 2nd edn by W. Wattenbach, P. Ewald, F. Kaltenbrunner, and S. Loewenfeld, 2 vols. (Leipzig 1885–8); cited as JK (to AD 590), JE (AD 590–882) or JL (AD 882–1198) and number
JEH	*Journal of Ecclesiastical History*
LThK	*Lexikon für Theologie und Kirche*
Mansi	J. D. Mansi, *Sacrorum Conciliorum Nova et Amplissima Collectio* (Venice 1757–98)
Meyer von Knonau, *Jahrbücher Heinrichs IV.*	G. Meyer von Knonau, *Jahrbücher des deutschen Reiches unter Heinrich IV. und Heinrich V.*, vols. I to V (Leipzig 1890–1902)
Meyer von Knonau, *Jahrbücher Heinrichs V.*	G. Meyer von Knonau, *Jahrbücher des deutschen Reiches unter Heinrich IV. und Heinrich V*, vols. VI and VII (Leipzig 1907–9)
MGH	Monumenta Germaniae Historica, with subseries:
BDK	Die Briefe der deutschen Kaiserzeit
Capit.	Capitularia regum Francorum
Const.	Constitutiones
Dipl.	Diplomata

Epp.	Epistolae
LdL	Libelli de Lite
SRG	Scriptores rerum Germanicarum in usum scholarum
SRG NS	Scriptores rerum Germanicarum, nova series
SS	Scriptores in Folio
Migne, *PL*	J. P. Migne, *Patrologia Latina* (Paris, 1841–64)
MIÖG	*Mitteilungen des Instituts für österreichische Geschichtsforschung*
MCSM	*Miscellanea del Centro di Studi Medievali (Mendola)*
NA	*Neues Archiv der Gesellschaft für ältere Geschichtskunde*
NSLG	*Niedersächsisches Jahrbuch für Landesgeschichte*
PBA	*Proceedings of the British Academy*
PRE	*Realencyclopädie für protestantische Theologie und Kirche*
QFIAB	*Quellen und Forschungen aus Italienischen Archiven und Bibliotheken*
RAC	*Reallexikon für Antike und Christentum*
Registrum	*Gregorii VII Registrum*, ed. E. Caspar (MGH Epistolae selectae II/1–2, Berlin 1920–3), cited by book and number
RGG	*Religion in Geschichte und Gegenwart*
RH	*Revue Historique*
RHE	*Revue d'Histoire Ecclésiastique*
RQ	*Römische Quartalschrift*
RSCI	*Rivista di Storia della Chiesa in Italia*
RSI	*Rivista Storica Italiana*
s.a.	*sub anno*: under the year
Settimane	*Settimane di Studi sull'alto Medio Evo*
Steindorff, *Jahrbücher Heinrichs III.*	E. Steindorff, *Jahrbücher des deutschen deutschen Reiches under Heinrich III.*, 2 vols. (Leipzig 1874–81)
StGrat	*Studia Gratiana*
StGreg	*Studi Gregoriani*
StMed	*Studi Medievali*, 3rd series
StMGBO	*Studien und Mitteilungen zur Geschichte des Benediktinerordens*

TRHS	*Translations of the Royal Historical Society*
Uhlirz, *Jahrbücher Ottos II.*	K. Uhlirz, *Jahrbücher des deutschen Reiches unter Otto II. und Otto III.*, vol. i (Leipzig 1902)
Uhlirz, *Jahrbücher Ottos III.*	K. Uhlirz, *Jahrbücher des deutschen Reiches unter Otto II. und Otto III.*, vol. ii (Berlin 1954)
VSWG	*Vierteljahresschrift für Sozial- und Wirtschafts- geschichte*
VuF	*Vorträge und Forschungen herausgegeben vom Konstanzer Arbeitskreis für mittelalterliche Geschichte*
WaG	*Die Welt als Geschichte*
Waitz, *Jahrbücher Heinrichs I.*	G. Waitz, *Jahrbücher des deutschen Reiches uinter König Heinrich I. 919–936*, 3rd edn (Leipzig 1883)
ZBLG	*Zeitschrift für bayerische Landesgeschichte*
ZGO	*Zeitschrift für die Geschichte des Oberrheins*
ZKG	*Zeitschrift für Kirchengeschichte*
ZRGGA	*Zeitschrift der Savigny-Stiftung für Rechts- geschichte, Germanistische Abteilung*
ZRGKA	*Zeitschrift der Savigny-Stiftung für Rechts- geschichte, Kanonistische Abteilung*

I

WESTERN CHRISTENDOM AND ITS ENVIRONMENT IN THE TENTH AND ELEVENTH CENTURIES

THE INTERNAL AND EXTERNAL SECURITY OF WESTERN CHRISTENDOM

Viewed from the standpoint of comparative history, Christendom in these two centuries seems to have been a fairly united and uniform community of faith, at least in the West, and in spite of numerous lost struggles on the margins its existence was not seriously threatened from outside.

Following the controversies between Paschasius Radbertus of Corbie and his supporters on the one hand and the theologians like Hrabanus Maurus, Ratramnus, or Gottschalk on the other over the Eucharist there were no serious disputes over dogma.[1] Not until the debate over Berengar of Tours's doctrine of the Eucharist in the middle of the eleventh century was there a revival of such disputes, and from then on early scholastic theology developed through a series of dogmatic controversies.[2] Ancient relics of paganism, residual elements of the old religions, and, still more, the continuing pagan practices of the newly converted proved hard to eradicate; but these things were not a serious threat to the Christian peoples. From the acceptance of Christianity to its internalisation,[3] to a genuine absorption of Christian faith and morality, as these were then understood, there often lay a long and winding path. Heresies occurred here and there from the eleventh century on, but in the period

---

[1] Haendler, *Frühmittelalter*, 59.

[2] See below, pp. 139 and 318–19.

[3] W, Baetke, 'Die Aufnahme des Christentums durch die Germanen', *WaG*, 9 (1943), 143; Kahl, 'Heidnisches Wendentum', 73; Lammers, 'Formen', 23–46.

under discussion they were not yet a serious danger.[4] More frequent were meaningless accusations of heresy in the course of political or ecclesiastical propaganda, but even these were not so numerous or so hate-filled as they were to become from the late eleventh century on. In general they were countered by an affirmation of the correctness of one's own belief and by accusations against one's opponent.

Apostasy from the Christian church was very rare. If a Christian converted to Judaism he became the object of intense attention.[5] It is a rare event to find Archbishop Fulco of Rheims writing that in the regions attacked by the Vikings only those who accepted paganism and the protection of the barbarians could retain their homesteads in safety.[6] The newly converted, by contrast, frequently reverted to their old beliefs in the course of pagan reactions in their newly Christianised country. The history of the spread of Christianity in England, Scandinavia, Hungary, and the Slavonic lands is full of such reverses. Here there may have been fluctuations barely visible to us, especially where political struggles allowed first one and then the other side to come out on top in rapid succession, so that for most the overwhelming priority was to anticipate the changes. The Islamic rulers of Spain and Sicily tolerated other religions of the book, as is well known, so that the Christian church in those parts was able to preserve its faith and its organisation.[7] But, as in all countries controlled by Islam, the Christians were second-class citizens and were exposed to a variety of pressures in the course of time. There were also periods of tension, with persecutions, destruction of churches, and punitive taxation, especially following acts of provocation by Christians.[8] The Spanish peninsula saw numerous Islamicisations and re-Christianisations.

Christian Europe was sorely afflicted and suffered severe damage through the attacks of various heathen peoples: Saracens, Norsemen, Magyars, and Slavs. But for a long time after Charles Martel drove off the Islamic attack in the eighth century, the heart of western Christendom was neither seriously nor permanently threatened in its existence, in

---

[4] Grundmann, *Ketzergeschichte*, 8ff.

[5] Alpert of Metz, *Libri duo de diversitate temporum*, MGH SS IV.721.

[6] *Historia Remensis* IV 3, MGH SS XIII.563; see Tellenbach, 'Thronfolge', 295 n. 286.

[7] F. Cabrol, 'Mozarabe', *DACL* XII/1, col. 390f.; de Valdeavellano, *Historia de España*, 369ff.; there were, however, Islamic groups who were less tolerant, such as the Almoravids in Spain (*ibid.*, 843); Villada, *Historia Ecclesiastica*, 29ff.; Dufourcq, 'Coexistence', 211ff.; Amari, *Storia*, 619ff., especially 627: the position of the lower orders was often so much more favourable under the Moslems in Sicily that many fled from those cities which had remained Christian, or even converted to Islam.

[8] De Valdeavellano, *Historia de España*, 439f., who speaks of a 'collective delirium'.

fact not until the Mongol onslaught in the thirteenth century. Even in northern Spain the small Christian lordships managed to survive the pressure from a culturally and politically dominant Islam in spite of all the dangers.

The most serious loss was the conquest of Sicily in the ninth century by the Aghlabites of northern Africa, completed by the fall of the last Byzantine bastion, Taormina, in 903. Under the new Fatimid dynasty (909) the Arabs made several attempts to establish a foothold in southern Italy. They sometimes managed to hold bridgeheads for several years, but were never able to establish themselves there permanently. The political and ecclesiastical arrangements in southern Italy in the tenth and eleventh centuries were complicated by the rivalries between a number of powers – the Byzantine emperor, the Lombard princes, the Arab invaders – and by the occasional incursions of the Roman pope and the western emperor.[9] Not until the coming of the Normans was the Italian south definitively freed from the influence of Islam and of the Greek Orthodox church (regarded from 1054 on as schismatic) and permanently won for western Christendom and the Roman church. In Spain, recent research has shown that from the time of Abd ar-Rahman III (912–61) there was an explosion of conversions from Christianity to Islam. At the beginning of the tenth century only a quarter of the Christian population had been converted; by 1100 the figure was 80 per cent.[10]

It has been debated whether England, Scotland, and Ireland were in danger during the Viking era of breaking away from the Carolingian and Mediterranean cultural circle in which they had previously moved and joining a Nordic one; whether there was a possibility of the North Sea's becoming a Scandinavian sea and of England's becoming Danish and pagan.[11] The behaviour of the Vikings in the Christian kingdoms they afflicted and the way in which Christianity penetrated their own country and finally came to dominate there do not suggest that this was ever very likely. When in the person of William the Conqueror the Frankicised Normans in England drove back the Danish element, which had been powerful under Cnut, the ties between England and western and central Europe were secured, while for Europe the Scandinavian north became more peripheral.[12]

---

9 This constellation of forces has to be borne in mind if a one-sided view is to be avoided; see Hiestand, *Byzanz*.
10 T. F. Glick, *Islamic and Christian Spain in the Early Middle Ages* (Princeton 1979), 33f., 42ff. and the table on 35.
11 Deanesly, *Pre-Conquest Church*, 283ff.
12 Musset, 'Relations', 82.

True, there were admittedly repeated clashes between heathens and
Christians, with great losses on both sides and sometimes annihilation for
the losers. But it was only the Christian and Islamic powers which had a
sufficiently developed social order to be able to extend their lordship on
a permanent basis, and only they as representatives of higher religions with
universal claims were in a position to proselytise among peoples with a
gentile organisation. Scandinavian, Slav, or Magyar paganism did not call
Christianity as such in question, apart from the occasional pagan reaction
in newly converted territories. Such paganisms could survive tenaciously,
but their ethnicity prevented them from becoming missionary systems of
belief.[13] In the Viking lordships in Christian heartlands like northern
France and England paganism did not survive for long, because pagans in
Christian surroundings rapidly became Christian.[14]

Saracens, Norsemen, and Magyars attacked Christian countries not to
conquer them or to make converts but to take plunder. The main motive
for the Slavs was to take revenge for attacks on them. The Christians were
often only able to stave off attacks by negotiations and economic or
political concessions. Payments of tribute were probably more frequent
than we know of. Pope John VIII bought off the Saracens; Charles the
Bald and Charles the Fat bought off the Vikings; Henry I bought off
the Magyars.[15] The treaty which Duke Arnulf of Bavaria made with the
Hungarians in 926 was probably also accompanied by payments.[16] Such
tribute-payments were the more questionable in that they merely served
to divert pagan plundering expeditions to other Christian countries. That
was not all. Christian princes allied themselves with pagans against other
Christians frequently enough. The best-known case is the alliance
between Henry II and the pagan Liutizi against the Christian duke of
Poland.[17] Already in the tenth century the pagan Slavs of Rügen had been
used as auxiliaries in the wars against the Abodrites.[18]

[13] Kahl, 'Heidnisches Wendentum', 88 and 98, draws the distinction between universal and
gentile religion; see also Lammers, 'Formen', 180f.
[14] Prentout, *Essai*, 111; Sawyer, *Age of the Vikings*, 3f.; Sawyer, *Kings and Vikings*, 137.
[15] Tellenbach, 'Thronfolge', 295 n. 286; the examples could easily be multiplied. See e.g.
H. Büttner, 'Die Ungarn, das Reich und Europa bis zur Lechfeldschlacht des Jahres 955',
ZBLG, 19 (1956), 449; G. Fasoli, 'Points de vue sur les incursions hongroises en Europe
au Xe siècle', *CCM*, 2 (1959), 29 and 31; Sawyer, *Kings and Vikings*, 196.
[16] Reindel, *Liutpoldinger*, 106ff.
[17] Hirsch, Pabst and Bresslau, *Jahrbücher Heinrichs II.*, 1.256ff.; Brüske, *Untersuchungen*, 47;
W. H. Fritze, 'Beobachtungen zu Entstehung und Wesen des Liutizenbundes', *Jahrbüch
für die Geschichte Mittel- und Ostdeutschlands*, 7 (1958), 1–38. Another well-known
example is the alliance between Byzantium and the Sicilians, already Moslems, against
Otto II; see Amari, *Storia*, 376.
[18] Wenskus, *Studien*, 194.

Italy and Spain in particular saw rapid shifts of alliances between Christians and non-Christians against enemies of their own or other faiths. In southern Italy Lombards, Byzantines, Saracens, and the rulers of the lands to the north were partners in rapidly changing coalitions.[19] Constantine VII sought to win not only Otto the Great but also the Ummayad Caliph Abd ar-Rahman an-Nasir in Cordoba for a broadly based alliance against the Abbasids in 949.[20] A Tuscan margravine calling herself 'Queen Bertha of Rome' pursued a project which similarly transcended religious boundaries.[21] In Spain, for example, Sancho I the Fat of Leòn (956–8) reconquered his capital with the help of Muslim troops and drove out his rival Ordoño IV.[22] He had had to promise the caliph ten border fortifications as a reward for the help, but on his ally's death he broke his promise. In the eleventh century as well Christians and Muslims frequently made common cause, for example in the attempt to ward off the attacks of the Almoravids.[23]

The Swedish king Olaf Tax-King had been baptised in 1008 by the English missionary bishop Siegfried, but he was king over both the Christian Gauts and the heathen Svear. Most of the warriors whom he sent to help his son-in-law Olaf the Saint to conquer Norway are said to have been pagans; Olaf allegedly refused to accept their aid. The army with which Cnut conquered England was also mostly heathen. Even Robert Guiscard's troops at the siege of Salerno in 1076 included Saracens, while the core of al-Mansur's army included both Berber contingents and Arabised Christian soldiers.[24]

It is well known that many Christian princesses of the early middle ages married heathen or Muslim rulers. And Christian nobles repeatedly took refuge temporarily or permanently among pagan peoples. Arnulf of Bavaria fled with his family to the Magyars before his advancing stepfather Conrad I, as his son Eberhard may also have done in the face of Otto the Great.[25] The best-known example is that of Wichmann, the nephew of

---

[19] Chalandon, *Domination*, 12f.; Gay, *L'Italie méridionale*, 136f.

[20] Hiestand, *Byzanz*, 207.

[21] G. Levi della Vida, 'La corrispondenza di Berta di Toscana col Califfo Mustafi', *RSI*, 67 (1954), 21ff.; Hiestand, *Byzanz*, 110ff.

[22] Lévi-Provençal, *Histoire*, 174ff.

[23] De Valdeavellano, *Historia de España*, 840; Menéndez Pidal, *Spanien des Cid*, 30ff. and 78. The Cid fought together with Christians and Muslims against his Christian opponents.

[24] Seegrün, *Papsttum*, 53; Larson, *Canute*, 163; for the Berber contingents and Arabised Christian mercenaries in al-Mansur's army see Lévi-Provençal, *Histoire*, 224, and for Robert Guiscard's Greek, Roman, and Saracen troops in the army besieging Salerno in 1076 see Chalandon, *Domination*, 244.

[25] Reindel, *Liutpoldinger*, 107ff. and 187; Hóman, *Ungarisches Mittelalter*, 126.

Hermann Billung, who even led pagans against his own Christian countrymen, and died while doing so.[26]

In spite of the harshness of these conflicts between creeds and the contemptuous judgements of Christian authors about the inferiority and indeed the repulsiveness of the heathen, one should not ignore the rich and varied opportunities for contact, even if contacts were the exception rather than the rule. In the middle ages pagans, regardless of their race and their state of development, were regarded not only as being worthy of baptism but also as being obliged to accept it.

ON THE NATURE AND SIGNIFICANCE OF CHRISTIAN MISSION IN EUROPE IN THE TENTH AND ELEVENTH CENTURIES

In the second volume of his *History of the Expansion of Christianity* Kenneth Scott Latourette described the period between 500 and 1500 as 'the thousand years of uncertainty', an interpretation assessed in a suggestive review by Ernest Benz entitled 'World History, Church History, and the History of Mission'.[27] Such an interpretation is valid only in secular terms; it is based on statistics, namely on the increases and decreases in the numbers of Christians and of the countries they inhabited or controlled. How can one assess the religious growth or decline of church or faith, things which are not open to human judgement? Such considerations may seem surprising against the background of the traditional view of mission in the period we are considering. This sees these two centuries as marking progress in the 'Christianisation' of our part of the world, a progress which has shaped Europe's development down to the present day. From the beginning of the tenth century east central Europe, eastern Europe, and Scandinavia became Christian, though in many cases there had been earlier traces of Christianity. Taking all these lands together it would be better to see the period of mission as lying between the middle of the ninth century and the early thirteenth century, for only then were the last remnants of paganism eliminated in north Europe and among the Slavs of the Elbe and Baltic regions. Taking western Christianity as a whole it is also significant that the crucial advance of the Spanish reconquista came at the beginning of the thirteenth century.

[26] On Wichmann's exiles see Dümmler, *Jahrbücher Ottos I.*, 250, 266f., 292, 387, 433.

[27] E. Benz, 'Weltgeschichte, Kirchengeschichte und Missionsgeschichte', *HZ*, 173 (1952), 1–22. K. D. Schmidt, *Grundriß der Kirchengeschichte*, 5th edn (Göttingen 1949), 49ff., wrote from the conventional point of view of European rather than global church history about the two 'great missionary victories', namely the conversions of the Germans and of the Slavs.

The acceptance of Christianity in numerous countries and regions, peoples and tribes, was seldom easy or rapid; it was mostly slow, uneven, and faced powerful and stubborn resistance and hence many setbacks. The concept of mission did not have the same connotations in this period as in the first centuries of Christianity, or in our own time. Nowhere was it a spontaneous movement from one family or community to the next, gripping souls, converting them (*metanoia* in the terminology of the early church), and filling them with an enthusiasm which itself could be passed on. Mission was rarely unintentional, unorganised. It was supported and planned by Christian princes and nobles conscious of their calling to spread the rule of Christ, by bishops and their clerical assistants or by monasteries and monks in fulfilment of the obligation to 'go forth and teach all peoples'. Christianity was inspired by the claim to be the one true religion for all mankind. Jesus Christ had appeared on earth to save men's souls for eternal life. The news of this was to be brought to those who did not yet know it. The Christian God was the only God; other beings which were called god or gods were recognised as existing, but they were devils, demons, or idols, and to serve them was not only an intellectual but also a moral error. Later interpretations saw Augustine as already having argued for the need to compel idolators, by force if necessary, in an interpretation of the phrase *coge intrare* in Luke 14: 23 which reversed its sense, though Augustine had restricted this to heretics and schismatics.[28] Gregory the Great went beyond this, and called Sardinian peasants who worshipped stones 'enemies of God', and their attitude 'guilt, sin, treachery, obstinacy'. They were to be punished by being made to pay higher dues and compelled to walk the true path.[29] Gregory could even praise 'indirect' missionary warfare.[30]

In considering the religion of heathen times a distinction has been made between mythology and a true religion. The primitive worship of natural forces in waters, trees, stones, and the stars and weather becomes confined to the lower orders with the arrival of higher religions, and there it has the role of stubborn superstition or secondary belief, as seen in the stone-worship of the Sardinians just cited. Such subliminal religious feelings, in reality more like fears, can survive for millennia, and not just among the uncultured 'people'.

The tough resistance to Christianity which we find in our period,

---

[28] See E. Fascher, 'Zur Problematik von Lc. 14.23', *Evangelische Dialoge*, 27 (1956), 12ff.; Kahl, 'Compellere', 273 n. 339.

[29] 'hostes Dei . . . culpa, peccatum, perfidia, obstinatio': *Gregorii I Registrum* 1 23 and 26, MGH Epp. 1.257f. and 261. Kahl, 'Baustein', 57ff.; Kahl, 'Altschonisches Recht', 37.

[30] *Gregorii I Registrum* 1 73, MGH Epp. 1.93; Erdmann, *Entstehung*, 8 and n. 12.

especially in Scandinavia and among the Slavs of the Elbe and Baltic, had
other roots. These peoples long had no sense of the complete otherness of
Christianity. Their gods were tribal or ethnic gods with limited areas of
authority. They could not easily understand the idea that there is only one
God who rules everywhere, especially as the missionaries and victorious
armies with whom they were confronted and who themselves still
believed in the existence of devils tended to depict the Christian God as
the most powerful rather than as the only god. One had to reckon not just
with the power of the new god but with that of the old ones as well.[31] For
this reason there were several examples of pro-Christian, even baptised
rulers who relapsed into paganism. Adam of Bremen reports of the
earliest Christian king in Sweden, Eric (*c.* 1000), that he reverted to
heathenism.[32] His son Olaf Tax-King (995–1021/2) was baptised by the
English missionary bishop Siegfried in 1008, as has already been noted,
and the Gauts largely accepted Christianity, while the Svear stuck to their
religion. When he came to destroy their chief shrine at Uppsala, the
Swedes prevented him, being still afraid of their old gods. A compromise
was reached: Olaf, should he wish to be a Christian, should take the best
part of the country and introduce Christianity there, but he was not to
force anyone to renounce the cult of the traditional gods.[33] Evidently it
was long uncertain which of the gods was the most powerful. As late as
the early twelfth century the Anglo-Danish monk Ælnoth wrote in his
'Legend of Cnut': 'It seems that the Svear and Gauts pay lip-service to the
Christian religion, as long as everything goes well and in accordance with
their wishes. But when the storms of tribulation come upon them –
harvest failure, drought, bad weather, invasion, or fire – then they
persecute the religion which they had seemingly just venerated.'[34]

This kind of fearful uncertainty is probably the main reason why the
spread of Christianity in the high middle ages was only with difficulty
crowned with final success. Besides this, the military campaigns and
demands for tribute by Christian neighbours, coupled with the harshness
of their rule once they had conquered, often gave paganism extra strength.
We can often see, moreover, how in dynastic disputes claimants would be
supported by a heathen or by a Christian party.[35] Religious differences

[31] Kahl, 'Heidnisches Wendentum', 88f.; Rehfeldt, *Todesstrafen*, 22.

[32] Adam of Bremen, *Gesta* II 28, p. 99; Seegrün, *Papsttum*, 53.

[33] Adam of Bremen, *Gesta* II 58, pp. 118f.

[34] Cited by Andersson, *Schwedische Geschichte*, 53.

[35] A well-known example is that of Svein Forkbeard, who conquered his father Harold
Bluetooth in 985 with the help of a heathen party. Harold was probably killed in the
decisive battle. See Maurer, *Bekehrung*, I. 246f. One might think also of the appalling

could easily be coupled with those of power and politics, both in civil wars and in wars with neighbouring peoples.

We do not know much about what pagans thought of the Christian religion, but they were probably predisposed by their polytheism not to regard the gods of other peoples as devilish.[36] The history of their conversion reveals the pagan Germans as comparatively tolerant, and there were not many Christian martyrs. The Germans expected their gods to punish blasphemers themselves, as many examples show. If they did not do so, their potency was called in question, something which could be exploited by Christian missionaries. Ungracious gods are always perceived as dangerous; one must seek to win the favour of one's own god in order to find help and protection against them. Christians, by contrast, always saw it as a crime to venerate gods other than the one Christian God. Heathens are gentiles, infidels, pagans, unfeeling, heretics, schismatics, apostates.

We do indeed find distinctions in medieval thought between the less and the more guilty, for example, the notion that heretics and apostates were worse than and should be dealt with more severely than heathens. Compassion and goodwill were to be shown primarily towards those who allowed themselves to be converted easily. But one should bear in mind that this whole phraseology was polemical in origin, designed for the writing of apologetic literature and hence aggressive in tone. Paganism was persecuted in west Scandinavia and in Hungary more cruelly than elsewhere after the triumph of Christianity, not because it took more reprehensible forms from a theological or ethical point of view but simply because a different missionary style had been practised in these regions from that customary in east Scandinavia or among most of the western Slav tribes.[37] The Liutizi were denounced, not just as heathens but as apostates in memory of their relapse in 983, because they put up tough resistance for centuries to Christian mission. This justified war and atrocities, culminating in Bernard of Clairvaux's phrase – which may be interpreted in various ways – of 'baptism or death'.[38] The terror used

---

struggles for the throne in Hungary in the decade following the death of Stephen I; see Hóman, *Ungarisches Mittelalter*, 256.

[36] Lange, 'Studien', 164ff. is illuminating on the nature of north Germanic polytheism, which allowed the choice of a special god. The fact that a 'duel' could take place between Christ and Thor rather than among many gods by no means implies that monotheistic thinking was at work.

[37] On the differences between the styles of mission practised in eastern and in western Scandinavia see Kahl, 'Altschonisches Recht', 26ff.

[38] Kahl, 'Compellere', 227; Wenskus, *Studien*, 157; Lotter, 'Bemerkungen', 400ff.; F. Lotter, *Die Konzeption des Wendenkreuzzugs* (Vorträge und Forschungen, Sonderband 23, Sigmaringen 1977), 10.

against heathens could not in practice be clearly distinguished according
to its intentions: first to secure the elimination of paganism and then to
bring about conversion. Neither its exponents nor its recipients were in
reality able to observe or keep to such distinctions. To deprive heathens
of their religion or cult was only possible if they were simultaneously to
be given (or have enforced on them) some kind of alternative. Or were
they to live, 'depaganised', as atheists until they deigned to accept
conversion? Such distinctions are theoretical constructs which are of little
use for understanding reality.[39]

We have already seen that in these centuries there was no permanent
front between Christianity and heathenism, even though there was often
bloody fighting and violent oppression. Just as a Christian king in Sweden
had to leave the pagan shrine at Uppsala untouched and move his ruling
seat to Sigtuna,[40] so also might Christians and heathens coexist under
Viking rule in England and Ireland. Viking armies might be made up of
heathen and Christian warriors, just as in Spain they could be composed
of Islamic Berbers and Christian Mozarabs. Even among the west Slavs,
where the conflicts between Christians and heathens were at their
bitterest, there were Christian princes ruling over populations where the
majority were heathen. The Abodrite prince Henry had to abandon the
attempt to convert his people to Christianity and content himself with
a small Christian church and a single priest in his city of Old Lübeck.
Prince Pribislaw-Henry had a small chapel in his fortification of the Brandenburg, not far distant from the temple of the three-headed god,
Triglav.[41]

We must thus reckon with the possibility of long transition periods in
which coexistence between Christianity and Islam or heathenism was
possible.[41] The most significant example is probably the history of the
Norwegian king. Hakon the Good, who was baptised and brought up in
England but could not impose Christianity on Norway and was forced by

[39] This is not directed against the well-founded distinctions made by Kahl in his works,
especially in 'Compellere'; it is simply meant to remind us of the fact that these
distinctions were applied as needed. It was not a matter of religious or legal integrity to
claim that it was justifiable to proceed more severely against the Liutizi because their
ancestors of fifty or a hundred years ago had been compelled to accept baptism. Such
a theory of apostasy was invented in order to put the blame on the enemy for the
adoption of a more ruthless style of warfare, as so often in history.

[40] See above, pp. 8f.

[41] Guttmann, 'Germanisierung', 419; Brüske, *Untersuchungen*, 17f.; Kahl, 'Heidnisches
Wendentum', 102ff.; Lammers, 'Formen', 196; Lotter, 'Bemerkungen', 417; R. Schmidt,
'Rethra. Das Heiligtum der Liutizen als Heiden-Metropole', *Festschrift für Walter
Schlesinger*, ed. H. Beumann (Vienna 1973–4), II.393 in particular.

[42] Dufourcq, 'Coexistence', 211.

the peasants there to take part in pagan sacrifices, something of which he bitterly repented on his deathbed.[43] Christians and heathens might fight side by side in Viking armies; the populations conquered by Norsemen or Saracens might remain Christian. Heathens and Christians are said to have coexisted peacefully in Hungary under Géza.[44] The conflict between German Christianity and Slavic heathenism was still undecided in Adam of Bremen's time; many phenomena have rightly been seen as showing a syncretism of heathenism and Christianity alongside the survival of unreconstructed paganism, or as signs of unresolved conflict.[45] The pagan cult in Uppsala survived up to the end of the eleventh century.[46] Besides this, there were often heathen elements below the surface of Christian populations. Johannes Canaparius noted in his *Vita Adalberti* that in the Slav lands many were Christians only in name and still followed the 'pagan cult'.[47] When the Icelanders finally accepted Christianity they did so on condition that secret heathen sacrifices as well as the practices of eating horse-meat and child exposure should remain lawful.[48] How could a pagan mind be easily persuaded that there was really only one God? The gods are powerful, and can bring either rescue or ruin. If one stood between two religions it was only logical to be concerned to win over not only the new but also the old gods and to propitiate both.

The penetration of the paganism which lay on the borders of Christianity was a long-drawn-out process, varied and unhomogenous. Christians and heathens had long had contacts in the form of trade. These may have been responsible for the appearance of traces of Christianity in pagan regions before we have any indication of mission or of political or

[43] Gerhardt, *Norwegische Geschichte*, 53ff.; Maurer, *Bekehrung*, 154ff.
[44] Hómn, *Ungarisches Mittelalter*, 156f.
[45] Kuhn, 'Fortleben', 752; Kahl, 'Bausteine', 57; see Löwe, 'Pirmin', 241, who describes for a much earlier period a syncretism of heathenism and Christianity, in Hesse and Thuringia in the eighth century. The remarks by Lange, 'Studien', 17f., are important for the principles of syncretism: 'The result of any conversion or transfer of another religion is necessarily syncretism, for the norms of thought and the religious psychology of the recipient are the means by which the transfer takes place.'
[46] Seegrün, *Papsttum*, 54; Andersson, *Schwedische Geschichte*, 54.
[47] 'ritu gentilium': Johannes Canaparius, *Vita Adalberti*, MGH SS IV.596; on 'superficial Muslims' in Islamic Spain see Dufourcq, 'Coexistence', 219.
[48] Gerhardt, *Norwegische Geschichte*, 63f.; E. Krenn, 'Christianisierungsgrund und katholische Mission in Island', *Neue Zeitschrift für Missionswissenschaft*, 4 (1948), 244; H. Kuhn, 'Das älteste Christentum Islands', *Zeitschrift für deutsches Altertum und deutsche Literatur*, 100 (1971), 4–40; on the question of the survival of older religious notions see also W. Göbell, 'Die Christianisierung des Norderns und das Werden der mittelalterlichen Kirche bis zur Errichtung des Erzbistums Lund (1103)', *Österreichisches Archiv für Kirchenrecht*, 15 (1904), 98f.

military contacts.[49] Besides traders, exiles will also have brought back an awareness of foreign lands and peoples. How much people learned of the other side in the course of offensive or defensive warfare on the other hand is doubtful. Although Christians and Muslims lived for centuries alongside one another in Spain, they did so in a state of mutual incomprehension,[50] while the notions which Christians had of Magyars, Norsemen, or even the neighbouring Slavs were often highly distorted. The Magyars had already come repeatedly into contact with Christianity in the course of their trek westwards, and when Christian missionaries occasionally penetrated the camps of Magyar raiders the doctrines they preached there were not completely unfamiliar.[51] Vikings even plundered churches and monasteries; the wars fought between Christians were brutal, but they spared churches on the whole, something the heathens did not need to do.[52]

Large numbers of Christians were carried off as prisoners of war and slaves. It has been said of the Norsemen that they took only a few women with them on their raids, and since they had great vitality and were used to having many women at home they were not able to do without them abroad either.[53] The knowledge of Christianity acquired from the women they took or from the slaves they brought home was certainly superficial; equally superficial was what ransomed slaves were occasionally able to understand and report of pagan religion.

The very fact of ransoming slaves implies negotiations. The Vikings are said to have traded in the lands they raided, and to have bought food, fodder, and horses as well as plundering them.[54] From early on they repeatedly allowed themselves to be persuaded by single payments or regular tribute to spare particular places or regions. Here again it was necessary to negotiate. Thus from the ninth century onwards powerful Christian princes came into genuine political contact with the leaders of pagan armies, and this could lead to more. The most famous and far-reaching treaty was that between Charles the Simple and the Norse chieftain Rollo at Saint-Clair-sur-Epte, by which the Norseman was granted territory around the mouth of the Seine on a permanent basis in

---

[49] F. Dvornik, *The Slavs. Their Early History and Civilisation*, 2nd edn (Boston 1959), 174; K. Schäferdieck, 'Zur Frage früher christlicher Einwirkungen auf den westgermanischen Raum', *ZKG*, 98 (1987), 149–66.

[50] Lot, *Invasions*, 44.

[51] See Hóman, *Ungarisches Mittelalter*, 147, on St Wikbert in the camp of the Magyar Bulcsu near Gembloux.

[52] Sawyer, *Age of the Vikings*, 143; Sawyer, *Kings and Vikings*, 96f.

[53] Prentout, *Essai*, 249; Jones, *Vikings*, 230 n. 1.

[54] W. Vogel, *Normannen*, 231ff.

return for his promise to accept baptism and to defend the region against
pagan marauders.[55] For a long time there was follow-up immigration by
pagan Scandinavians, and it was only gradually that Normandy was
completely Christianised, Romanised, and feudalised, becoming in the
process a French feudal state which was in the eleventh century to gain
the upper hand over the Scandinavian element in England (itself also now
Christian) and thus exercise decisive influence on the position of the
island kingdom within western Europe.[56]

Treaties like that with Rollo were also concluded with other Norse
leaders, for example under Louis the Pious and Lothar I with relatives of
the Danish petty king Heriold, baptised in 826. These held Frisian territories and seem to have commuted between their colony in the Frankish
kingdom and their homelands as well as between Christianity and
paganism.[57] Charles III also gave the sea-king Gottfried Frisian territory in
the treaty of Asselt in 882, in return for their promise to accept baptism
and drive off invaders;[58] Gottfried was even given Lothar II's daughter
Gisela as a wife. Shortly afterwards, however, the emperor had him and
his entourage assassinated, regardless of whether they were Christian or
heathen.[59] The Danish settlement in Frisia thus had no lasting consequences. It was otherwise with the treaty made between the Anglo-Saxon
king Alfred the Great and the Norse prince Guthrum at Wedmore in 878
after Alfred had defeated the invaders at Edington. Guthrum withdrew
from Wessex, accepted baptism and took the name Æthelstan.[60] The
regions controlled and settled by the Danes in eastern England north of
the Thames were a factor of great significance not only in English history
but also in that of the Scandinavian conversion. Eric Bloodaxe, after he
had been driven out of Norway by his brother Hakon the Good, had to
accept baptism along with his household when he received Northumbria

[55] Prentout, *Essai*, 124f., 183f., 249f.; Douglas, 'Rollo', 417ff.; Douglas, 'Rise of
Normandy', 101ff.; H. W. Goetz, 'Zur Landnahmepolitik der Normannen im
fränkischem Reich', *AHVN*, 183 (1980), 9ff.

[56] Douglas, 'Rollo', 429ff.

[57] W. Vogel, *Normannen*, 85, 224f.; Lot, *Invasions*, 143.

[58] W. Vogel, *Normannen*, 290ff.; Musset, 'Relations', 66ff.; Musset, 'Naissance', 75–
130.

[59] Tellenbach, 'Thronfolge', 287.

[60] W. Vogel, *Normannen*, 261, 411; Musset, 'Relations', 64ff.; Jones, *Vikings*, 223f.; Loyn,
Vikings, 59; Loyn, *Anglo-Saxon England*, 51, notes that in the tenth century the territories
of the Norse rulers were subordinated to the Anglo-Saxon king and Christianised. F. M.
Stenton, 'The Scandinavian Colonies in England and Normandy', *TRHS*, 4th series 27
(1945), 1ff., stresses the contrast between Normandy and the Danish settlements in
England, while Douglas, 'Rollo', 428, points to the parallels between the cases of
Guthrum and Rollo.

from the hands of King Æthelstan (925–39) sometime around 935 and took up his seat at York.[61]

Thus in France, in the lands around the mouths of the Scheldt and the Rhine, in England, Scotland, Ireland, the Hebrides, the Orkneys, and the Shetlands there were countless Norse settlements, some short-lived, some long-lived, where heathenism came into contact with Christianity. Such contacts were simultaneously political, economic, military, and religious. The mediatory function of these settlements was all the more important in that their links with the mother country remained intact for generations. New impulses were provided by later heathen immigrants and returning Christians, until Svein Forkbeard (956–1014) and his son Cnut the Great (1018–35) could rule both Christian England and Christian Denmark.[62]

All these contacts made it possible for the Christian faith and Christian way of life to influence heathens and heathen peoples; but how this happened is mostly unknown and unknowable. Besides the involuntary influences on paganism which went with the contacts just mentioned there were also planned actions carried out with the intention to convert. But we cannot discern much in the way of unified and coherent methods of missionary activity; it has even been doubted whether the Ottonian 'missionary church' had a model. However, it is often possible to distinguish according to whether the missionary work among heathen peoples and tribes was directed from outside or came from within and was carried through by a native instance. The Christianisation of a people can be brought about surprisingly quickly, at least at a superficial level, in those regions where the prince already has considerable and politically unifying power, as for example in Bohemia under Wenceslas, Boleslav I, and Boleslav II, or in Poland under Miesco I; in the north as well much depended on the will and the power of the king. The ups and downs of the conflict between old and new religions lasted in Denmark until Gorm the Old (d. 950) set up a united kingdom, so that his son Harold Bluetooth (950–86), with the support of Otto I and help from the church province of Hamburg–Bremen, was able to complete in all essentials the Christianisation of his country.[63]

Just how much things depended on the king can be seen from the counter-example of the Norwegian king Hakon Sigurdson (961–95). As a pretender he had found refuge and help in Denmark. Harold Bluetooth had forced him to accept baptism and provided him with Christian priests

[61] Gerhardt, *Norwegische Geschichte*, 51; Seegrün, *Papsttum*, 45.
[62] Larson, *Canute*, 52ff. and 104ff.
[63] Maurer, *Bekehrung*, 1.189; Gerhard, *Norwegische Geschichte*, 56.

for his return to Norway. But he parted from them while still on the journey and restored the temples of Thor in Norway.[64] Perhaps he thought that he would not be able to succeed as a Christian; as we have seen, Hakon the Good before him had failed in the face of resistance by the free peasantry.[65] Not until Olaf Tryggvason (995–1000) and St Olaf Haraldson (1015–30) was heathenism ended. The establishing of a strong and unitary royal power and Christianisation went hand in hand, and they were both pushed through with what was often remarkable cruelty. In Sweden the stabilisation of a kingship over all of Sweden and the conversion to Christianity came about later and more slowly, and so less violently. Olaf Tax-King (995–1021/2) was himself a Christian and the Gauts followed him in this. But the Swedish kulaks resisted, and were even able to put pressure on the king. Even Olaf's heirs and successors were not able to establish either their royal power or the acceptance of Christianity fully, so that it was not until about 1100 that Sweden became a genuinely Christian country.[66]

The tough resistance to Christianity shown by the Slavs around the Baltic and Elbe has also been explained in terms of the parallelism between their archaic religion and their social conditions. The Liutizi were a confederation of small tribes; like the Abodrites, they had princes, but none seems to have been able to create a permanent concentration of political power.[67] As early as Otto the Great's time we hear of a prince of the Hevelli, Tugumir, who had become a Christian while in German captivity, had then handed over the principal seat of his territory, Brandenburg, and subsequently held it under German overlordship.[68] The country was seemingly only superficially Christianised, and even this did not survive the uprising of 983. Around the middle of the eleventh century it seemed that the Christian Abodrite prince Gottschalk would establish sole rule over his people together with their conversion to Christianity. But in 1066 he was killed together with many Christians, both priests and laymen; the kingdom he had put together broke apart and the Slavs who had submitted to him reverted to a great extent to

---

[64] Maurer, *Bekehrung*, I.185ff. and II.509; Wolf, *Olav Tryggvason*, 19ff.; Gerhardt, *Norwegische Geschichte*, 83ff.; Seegrün, *Papsttum*, 49ff.; Kuhn, 'König und Volk', 6f.

[65] See above, pp. 10–11f., and n. 43.

[66] Andersson, *Schwedische Geschichte*, 52. For parallels in Hungary see Hóman, *Ungarisches Mittelalter*, 164ff.

[67] Brüske, *Untersuchungen*, 70; Fritze, 'Beobachtungen', 30f.; H. Ludat, 'Elbslawen und Elbmarken als Problem der europäischen Geschichte', *Festschrift für Friedrich von Zahn*, ed. W. Schlesinger (Cologne 1969) I.42ff.; Kahl, 'Heidnisches Wendentum', 85f. and n. 46.

[68] Kahl, 'Heidnisches Wendentum', 86; Dümmler, *Jahrbücher Ottos I.*, 103.

heathenism.[69] We have already mentioned his son Henry (d. 1127), who lived a modest existence in his city of Old Lübeck, more or less tolerated as a Christian, and the Christian prince Pribislaw-Henry, threatened on all sides in Brandenburg.[70]. It was not until the time of Henry the Lion and Albert the Bear that heathenism was eliminated in these regions.

It would thus seem that a more unified royal power was on the whole more favourable to Christianity than decentralised polities consisting of free communities of peasants or small aristocratic lordships. This can perhaps be explained by saying that the Christian faith transcended borders and was in principle everywhere the same, just as the Christian cult tended towards uniformity; this had a unifying effect on human and political communities just as did the other great religions. Pagan gods and cults, by contrast, tended to be tied to regions or localities. The god who is venerated here or there is content with the boundaries of his power, though he does not tolerate their violation.[71]

If we examine the behaviour and feelings of the Christian peoples towards their pagan neighbours we find that from the second half of the ninth century at the latest fear of danger and attack outweighed any offensive tendency, either in the sense of using military force to make the heathens submit or of spreading the Christian faith. Saracens, Norsemen, and Magyars were on the offensive; between the Slav pagans and their Christian neighbours there was a to and fro of offensive and defensive warfare, with many reprisals. The Christian church as the community of all Christians needed in the first instance protection, peace, safety, preservation of its freedom, submission to its God. It is these things which the liturgical prayers, greatly extended in the ninth and tenth centuries, concern themselves with: *defensio, protectio* against the wildness of the barbarian nations, *pax ecclesiarum, securitas, libertas, devotio Christiana*.[72] Christian princes and armies were thought of as being there above all for the *protectio* and *defensio* of churches and the peace of Christian peoples. It was for this that God's help was invoked. Naturally, effective defence could often be provided only by offensive operations, which led to brutal annihilation of Norse groups in France, bloody wars in England and Ireland, including such shocking events as the 'Danish vespers' of 1002, in which Æthelred II had all Danes, whether heathen or Christian, killed, and the fluctuating campaigns against Saracens and Magyars in Italy and in

[69] Guttmann, 'Germanisierung', 419; Brüske, *Untersuchungen*, 77; Kahl, 'Heidnisches Wendentum', 81ff. On the Nakonids see also Lammers, 'Formen', 45.

[70] Kahl, 'Heidnisches Wendentum', 102ff.

[71] A characteristic example is offered by Kahl, 'Heidnisches Wendentum', 97f.

[72] Tellenbach, 'Reichsgedanke', 52ff.

the lands north of the Alps.[73] German armies conducted countless campaigns on enemy territory along the eastern frontier, as well as some on the Danish borders. Neighbouring territories could be dealt with using familiar and normal techniques to establish a loose but stable overlordship: treaties, secured by sacred oaths and hostages; tribute payments; garrisons on both sides of the border. There was no clear distinction between defence of one's own land and expansion into others.[74] The 'Ottonian march system', which in spite of many setbacks paved the way for permanent expansion of the German kingdom, is probably the most impressive demonstration of such methods. Determination to win heathens for Christianity was by no means always and everywhere the same and self-evident. Otto I and Otto III certainly displayed it more strongly than Henry II and his successors. The majority of the bishops of the high middle ages did not see mission as a pressing task, and they were hardly in a position to carry it out. Many lay nobles on the German eastern frontier had even less interest in mission, especially as heathens could be more easily exploited than could Christians.

It may well be asked whether there were any purely missionary wars in the tenth and eleventh centuries, that is, wars, whose sole or at least primary purpose was to win people for Christianity and hence for their own eternal salvation and to save them from eternal damnation. It is difficult to find clear signs of this before the time of the crusades, and even here such ideas were mixed with the tendency to see paganism as an offence in itself and its reactions against Christianity as a punishable crime,[75] though this was counteracted by another quite different train of thought common within Christianity, which saw the terrible losses inflicted by pagans as divine punishments for the sins of Christendom itself.[76]

The ecclesiastical organisation of pagan or semi-pagan regions revealed a mixture of secular and ecclesiastical politics and genuine missionary consciousness in the way it treated both the needs of the present and the planning of the future. The Ottonian foundations of bishoprics and arch-bishoprics in the Slav and Danish border regions were a complement to political and military measures of protection, but were at the same time intended to perform genuinely missionary functions. In spite of the variety of his motives in the foundation of the new bishopric at Bamberg

---

[73] Larson, *Canute*, 39; Gerhardt, *Norwegische Geschichte*, 69; Loyn, *Vikings*, 87f.

[74] Tellenbach, 'Zusammenleben', 2ff.

[75] See above, p. 10.

[76] So for example Thietmar of Merseburg, Wipo, Burchard of Worms, Adam of Bremen; cf. Kahl, 'Compellere', 257ff.; Lippelt, *Thietmar*, 170 and 193ff.

Henry II's intention of carrying out mission and improving pastoral care should not be underestimated.

Missionary plans and measures taken by outside potentates were seldom of decisive importance for the success of missionary work among heathen peoples in the tenth and eleventh centuries, even though their services were praised by hagiographers and propagandists. Charles the Great's decisive mixture of piety and brutality was for a long time to find no imitators; only in the twelfth century was it to be repeated on a smaller scale by such figures as Henry the Lion, Albert the Bear, Bernard of Clairvaux, and others.

The rival claims of ambitious princes, metropolitans, and bishops tended to lead more to fruitless ecclesiastical disputes than to genuine missionary progress. The famous controversies of the ninth century, such as that between Nicholas I and Byzantium in the conversion of the Bulgars and Croats or that between Byzantine, Roman, and east Frankish missionaries in the Moravian empire, were to find pendants in the period which followed. German and Byzantine missions clashed in Russia, but also in Hungary, Norway, and Iceland.[77] Occasionally a clash between John XIII and Otto I over Magdeburg's role as a missionary centre for the Slavic territories has been posited, even a papal claim to an independent missionary policy in the east; we shall return to these hypotheses later.[78] The difficulties experienced by Otto in founding the province of Magdeburg are well known. The territorial integrity of the bishopric of Halberstadt and the province of Mainz were more important to those concerned than the success of the mission. Later there were rivalries between Magdeburg and Posen on the one hand and the newly founded archbishopric of Gnesen on the other hand, and then between Würzburg and Bamberg in Henry II's reign, as well as between Hamburg–Bremen and Magdeburg over the mission to the Slavs on the lower Elbe and the Baltic coast. There were also lively and varied rivalries between English and German missionaries in Scandinavia, which, however, gradually emancipated itself after the failure of Adalbert of Bremen's plan for a northern patriarchate.

---

[77] Stöckl, *Slawenmission*, 82ff.; Beck, *Orthodoxe Kirche*, 103ff.; K.Onasch, 'Denkwürdigkeit und Problematik der byzantinischen Slawenmission', *Theologische Literaturzeitung*, 88 (1963), 641 and 656; K. Onasch, *Russische Kirchengeschichte*, 3ff.; L. Musset, *Les Peuples scandinaves au moyen âge* (Paris 1951), 124; F. Dvornik, *Byzantine Missions among the Slavs* (New Brunswick, N.J. 1970), 24ff. on Croatia, 37ff. on Serbia, 130ff. on Rome and the Moravian mission. G. Moravšik, *Die byzantinische Kultur und das mittelalterliche Ungarn* (Sitzungsberichte der Preußischen Akademie der Wissenschaften zu Berlin, Phil.-Hist. Klasse 1955, 4).

[78] On John XIII see below, pp. 71f.

The foundation of bishoprics and churches in pagan or semi-pagan territories was merely a precondition for full conversion. What was crucial was to win competent and self-sacrificing clerics, bishops, and priests. We hear again and again of requests for the sending of clerics by converted princes or princes willing to receive conversion. Often the prince engaged himself personally. Olaf Tryggvason and Olaf the Saint of Norway are said to have destroyed heathen shrines with their own hands and punished recalcitrant pagans with executions, maimings, and sentences of exile.[79] There were heathen martyrs as well as Christian ones.[80] The Abodrite prince Gottschalk, killed in 1066, himself preached in Slavonic.[81] The Icelander Stefnir is a good example of tough missionary methods. At the urging of Olaf Tryggvason he returned to his home country, but his own relatives rejected him. 'Then Stefnir became angry and began with his companions to break the temples and altars and burn the images of idols.' But the Icelanders stopped him. They did not kill him, but, significantly, passed a law at the following Allthing against blasphemy. Stefnir had to return unsuccessful to Norway.[82]

But many missionaries tried to follow the example of the apostles in their behaviour. They went to pagan lands with the support of their own princes and bishops, sought support there from the powerful, provided them with instruction in the Christian religion and sought to convince them. If it was possible they preached about God as the creator of heaven and earth, a god more powerful than any of the gods in whom their audience believed. Like the apostles they are said to have worked miracles. It could be counted as a miracle when they destroyed a pagan shrine, as Boniface did the Donar oak in Fritzlar, without being destroyed by the god supposed to be present there. The Danish king Harold

---

[79] See Wolf, *Olav Tryggvason*, 24ff., who notes that Harald Finehair had already proceeded with great brutality against the free peasantry. In Olaf's case religious motives were added to the political ones. On the connection between the development of a large-scale ethnic unit and the victory of a supreme god which existed even in the heathen period see K. D. Schmidt, *Germanische Glaube und Christentum* (Göttingen 1948), 69; Rehfeldt, *Todesstrafen*, 98. See also Gerhardt, *Norwegische Geschichte*, 59; Seegrün, *Papsttum*, 50.

[80] Wolf, *Olav Tryggvason*, 26; Gerhardt, *Norwegische Geschichte*, 59; specific examples are cited by Vesper, 'Machtgedanke', 138, so that the opinion of Lortz, *Geschichte der Kirche*, 201, that the Germanic mission witnessed Christian martyrs but no heathen ones, must be corrected.

[81] See above, p. 15, and Kahl, 'Heidnisches Wendentum', 82, who draws attention to the preaching of Olaf Tryggvason and Henry III.

[82] Maurer, *Bekehrung*, 373ff. on Stefnir; on Stefnir and Dankbrand see also Lange, *Studien*, 191; Kuhn, 'König und Volk', 1–11; Kuhn, 'Fortleben', 172; Düwel, 'Bekehrung auf Island', 288.

Bluetooth is said to have been hostile to Christianity until he was moved to accept baptism by a fire miracle worked by the missionary Poppo. The legend, which is also recounted of other missionaries, relates how the holy man was able to wear a glowing iron glove without harm or to survive having a garment soaked in wax burnt off his body.[83] Once missionaries had found enough supporters they built churches and celebrated the liturgy there using beautiful robes and utensils and many candles, with genuflections, chants, and so on. All this could make a deep impression on the converted and unconverted alike. The names of the missionaries are often not recorded, but the long series from the ninth century includes Ebo of Rheims, Gauzbert of Osnabrück, Halitgar of Cambrai, Ansgar and Rimbert of Hamburg–Bremen, and the Slav apostles Cyril and Methodius. It was continued in the tenth century by Adalward of Verden, Unni of Bremen, Adalbert, the first bishop of Magdeburg, Wolfgang of Regensburg, Boso of Merseburg, Adalbert of Prague, Dankbrand and Stefnir in Iceland, and in the eleventh century by Gaudentius of Gnesen, Anastasius/Ascharicus of Gran, Brun of Querfurt, and Günther the Hermit. Many of these suffered martyrdom.

It has often been pointed out that these first missionary successes must have been very modest ones.[84] The new faith might be accepted for quite opportunistic reasons, and even where genuine religious feeling was at work it was often very superficial, primitive, and lacking in deeper understanding. The missionaries were often unable to make themselves understood because of language difficulties, and for that reason they were scarcely able to convey the fundamentals of the religion to their new converts. Everything depended at first on baptism. It was said of the Northumbrian sea-king Guthrum that 'in essence he admitted one more god to his pantheon and allowed Christianity the fullest privileges within his dominion'.[85] Baptism was only the first step; follow-up work was

---

[83] On this legend and its transmission see C. Freiherr von Schwerin, 'Das Gottesurteil des Poppo', *ZRGGA*, 58 (1938), 69ff.; Lammers, 'Formen', 32 n. 29; and Vesper, 'Machtgedanke', 128ff., though on p. 141 he concludes 'that the dominant role played by the concept of power in the conversion reports of the Icelandic sagas is either to be ascribed to a Christian reinterpretation of events which in fact occurred quite differently or else is explained by their literary character'. Rehfeldt, *Todesstrafen*, 99, notes the basis of tolerance in a lack of religious sensibility.

[84] According to Claude, *Magdeburg*, 155f., no more than the observation of the most important rites was possible, while Rehfeldt, *Todesstrafen*, 99, sees conversion less as a religious experience and more as a political event and a change of cult. Kahl, 'Bausteine', 70f., notes that the former institution of the catechumenate had decayed. Both Lotter, 'Bemerkungen', 44f. and Claude, *Magdeburg*, 13f. point to the lack of knowledge of Slav languages amongst the clergy.

[85] Jones, *Vikings*, 223. The Hungarian Geza considered himself rich enough to be able to afford two gods: Hóman, *Ungarisches Mittelalter*, 157.

urgently needed.[86] Often this too did not penetrate deeply, especially if the few priests available did not understand the local tongue or were inadequately educated or if their utensils and books were insufficient for the performance of the liturgy. It was still worse if they could not support themselves or were threatened by pagans seeking revenge.

Nevertheless, baptism was not just a formal and external action. The baptised were now implanted within the church; and it was the church which performed the follow-up work. The main thing here was not doctrine but life within the church over a long period. The reception of the Eucharist and other sacraments; the celebration of feasts; the discipline of penance; the veneration of the saints; the prayers for the living and the dead: all these things made the baptised in the course of years, even of generations, into Christians like all others. To have prepared the way for this process and set it in motion is the historical and religious significance of the often very earthly and imperfect actions of kings, bishops, and clergy.

[86] Kahl, 'Bausteine', 75; Kuhn, 'Fortleben', 380; baptism is the constitutive factor, and to be baptised is to be a Christian.

2

THE CHURCH AND ITS
MANIFESTATIONS ON EARTH

—————— • ——————

Between the end of the ninth century and the decisive events of the
eleventh there were hardly any serious, deeply divisive conflicts within
Christianity. The Trinitarian disputes of late antiquity and the early
middle ages were long forgotten; the echoes of Adoptionism concerned
theologians and synods only briefly. The old struggles between Rome and
the eastern patriarchates, Constantinople in particular, which flared up
from time to time, hardly concerned most Christians either in the West
or in the East. The controversies of the ninth centuries about the
Eucharist and their consequences also hardly touched most Christians;
they were confined to narrow channels.[1] There was a general consensus
about the nature of the church, and its daily liturgical life was in practice
carried out in an impressive and essentially uniform manner, in spite of
manifold peripheral variations. Nor were the roles of clergy and laity
within the liturgy a matter of dispute, though they underwent some
changes in this period.

Everywhere bishoprics and parishes formed the most significant
context for the life of the church, which was a comparatively uniform one
even though their internal formation had occurred at different times and
under different circumstances and even though wars had occasionally led
to breaks in continuity. The units above the level of the diocese, provinces
or metropolitan districts, were gradually introduced everywhere, but their
significance and coherence were very uneven both temporally and

---

[1] See above, p. 1.

geographically. Primacies and apostolic vicariates remained in general merely plans, and where they were realised this was only a temporary phenomenon, apart from the primacy of Rome within Italy. From the end of the eighth to the early twelfth century there were no ecumenical councils or general councils of comparable status.[2] Sacral kingship at this time enjoyed an undisputedly ecclesiastical function and dignity. The position of the Roman church as the mother church of Christendom, of the pope as the highest bishop and patriarch, were undisputed, as was the religious conception of his status. Even Gelasius I's definition of the relationship between *sacerdotium* and *regnum* was undisputed, especially as he defined priestly superiority there unambiguously and decisively in purely eschatological terms: 'in as much as they will have to give an account for the kings of men themselves at the last judgement'.[3] The most likely looking field of conflict was, from the time of the appearance of the Pseudo-Isidorian forgeries in the middle of the ninth century, the question of the relationship between the powers of bishops, metropolitans, and pope. But for about two centuries it remained latent; alive, but seldom prominent. However high the pope's spiritual standing may have been, his jurisdictional and ecclesiastical effectiveness was unstable and discontinuous. Apart from a few episodes, there can be no question, before the middle of the eleventh century, of there having been a planned papal government of the church which might have intervened even in distant countries.

For the Christians of the tenth and eleventh centuries the church was, as it had been for their ancestors, the kingdom of God, which had begun with the appearance of Christ on earth and would be completed with the second coming on the last day. Essentially therefore the church was an eschatologically conceived phenomenon; this world is comprehended in the next. The church is both heavenly and earthly; its existence is thus fundamentally and permanently spiritual and its nature perceived primarily by intuition. Although the church had long been defined doctrinally, it was still easier to conceive of it through metaphors such as kingdom, body, bride of Christ, or mother of Christendom than through the systematic concepts found from the twelfth century onwards.[4] Canon

---

[2] The Fourth Council of Constantinople of 869 was the last recognised in both East and West. The next ecumenical council was the First Lateran Council of 1123, which after the schism of 1054 was seen as ecumenical only in the West.

[3] *Epistolae Romanorum pontificum*, ed. Thiel, 349, c. 2.

[4] H. Lietzmann, *Geschichte der alten Kirche*, 3rd edn (Berlin 1969), II, 42: 'The Ekklesia is not the sum of all individual earthly congregations but a suprasecular body, which includes everything which belongs to Christ and is a member of His Body'; Congar, *Ecclésiologie*, 98.

law already had a long history behind it full of both productive and unpro-
ductive periods, in which for the most part old principles were quoted and
subjected to minor variations, even when this produced inconsistencies
and contradictions. The external regulation of the life of the church was
not yet comprehensive and not controlled in a unitary fashion by any
authority.

The church is most evidently present in the liturgy, since to participate
in and be affected by the liturgy renews the presence of Christ and of
the salvation he brought. In divine service the church is the congregation of Christians, their 'we', as Yves Congar has put it.[5] In the
consciousness of the early church, the whole of the church is present in
each individual church as a whole, for Christ is with her: 'for where two
or three are gathered together in my name, there I am with them'
(Matthew 18: 20). Christianity was present in the cathedral church and in
the king's chapel, just as it was in a village church and in a modest
oratory, both during the solemn celebration of mass and during simple
prayer.[6]

The unity of the church as a whole and in its parts, whether visible or
invisible, can only be discussed in terms of its eschatological orientation,
that is, with a view to that kingdom that is not of this world. It never
occurred to anyone that this did not include all Christians, those in
distant lands, in Asia or Africa. No one in England or Italy or any other
western country would have excluded in their thought the Christians of
Constantinople or Egypt from the community.[7] Up to the middle of the

---

[5] Congar, *Ecclésiologie*, 64; in a similar sense R. Schulte, 'Die Messe als Opfer',
Liturgiegeschichtliche Quellen und Forschungen, 35 (1959), 113.

[6] O. Linton, *RAC*, 4, vol. 913; K. Stendhal, *RGG*, 3, 3rd edn, cols. 1296–1326 and
LThK, 6, cols. 167–83; H. Dombois, 'Der Kampf um das Kirchenrecht', *Die Katholizität
der Kirche*, ed. H. Asmussen and W. Stählin (Stuttgart 1957), 291f.; H. de Lubac,
Méditation sur l'Eglise (Paris 1953), 114: 'Never does she deserve her name more than
when in a given place the people of God gather around their pastor to celebrate the
Eucharist. It is no more than a cell of the whole body, but the body as a whole is
virtually present. The Church is in various places, but there are not diverse Churches';
Congar, *Ecclésiologie*, 63.

[7] This sense of unity, often only vaguely felt, continued to exist in the tenth and early
eleventh centuries and to speak of the western church is to ignore it. See E. H.
Kantorowicz, 'The Problem of Medieval World Unity', in his *Selected Studies* (Locust
Valley, N.Y., 1965), 76–81, especially 81: 'Medieval World Unity, as conceived in East
and West, is primarily eschatologic and its reality is identical with the Lord's real
presence in the sacraments'; on the terminology 'western/eastern' or 'occidental/
oriental' church see W. Aymans, *Das synodale Element in der Kirchenverfassung*
(Münchener Theologische Studien, III 30, Munich 1970), 20.

eleventh century the church history of the West and East constituted a unity, even if the links in reality were loose and far from continuously present.[8] Indeed, the relations between the churches in Italy and Greece were often closer than those of the Italian with the Spanish or even the English churches, and certainly closer than those with the emerging churches of Scandinavia. Even after the schism of 1054 Christianity and the Christian church in the whole world have a common history. In opposition to this notion stands the more rigorous view that it is only those churches who obey the pope who belong to the church. Gregory VII made his claim to jurisdiction simultaneously a matter of faith, and thus completed the dogmatic identification of the papal church with the universal church. All that was left beyond that was a purely spiritual unity.

In the tenth and eleventh centuries Latin was the common liturgical language in the west, though here and there Anglo-Saxon and Slavonic were used, not without provoking some protests. The venerable texts were valid and authoritative even when they were misspoken or not properly understood by some members of the congregation. It is reported of the youth of the great Anglo-Saxon preacher Ælfric that he received his training in the rudiments of theology from an old priest who did not know the distinction between the Old and the New Testament.[9] Baptism was valid even when the formula was spoken erroneously, 'in the name of the fatherland, the daughter, and the holy spirit',[10] and the commemorative prayer of a bishop did not lose its value if he prayed for 'male and female mules' instead of 'male and female servants'.[11] It was of no concern for the essential aspects of the life of a congregation or for its essence as a part of the church universal if the building in which it gathered and the property associated with the church belonged to another bishop, a monastery or collegiate church, a cleric or layman, or was even divided up among various owners.[12] Such things, purely contingent and subject to change over time, did not touch the church at its heart.

---

[8] On the relationship between the Greek and the Roman church see Beck, *Orthodoxe Kirche*, 116; the story told by Einhard, *Vita Karoli Magni*, c. 27, ed. O. Holder-Egger (MGH SRG, Hanover 1911), 31, about Charles the Great's alms 'beyond the seas' is noteworthy in this context.

[9] Deanesly, *Sidelights*, 41.

[10] 'in nomine patria et filia et spiritus sancti': *Vita Bonifatii auctore Otloh*, ed. W. Levison (MGH SRG, Hanover 1905), 169.

[11] 'mulis et mulabus' instead of 'famulis et famulabus': *Vita Meinwerci episcopi Patherbrunnensis*, ed. F. Tenckhoff (MGH SRG, Hanover 1921), 107.

[12] Häussling, *Mönchskonvent*, 79.

PARISH AND DIOCESE, CHURCH PROVINCES AND SYNODS

The ecclesiastical units which had most vitality and were most clearly defined were the diocese and the parish. For centuries they had been the centrepoint of the religious, social, legal, and economic life of Christendom. The parish has been termed the basic ecclesiastical unit, the bishopric the most vital element in the period.[13] The parish was certainly fundamental for the common religious life, the diocese equally so for hierarchy and jurisdiction. The bishop stood at the head of the clergy of his diocese by virtue of the powers of consecration and jurisdiction he possessed; the parish congregation was the place in which most of the Christian's life within the church took place. Here he was baptised, celebrated divine service, participated in the Eucharist, submitted to church penance, made offerings and paid fees, prayed with others for temporal and eternal salvation, hoped for the intercession of his fellow Christians both before and after his death, and found his last resting-place. Such congregations have been termed 'miniature Christianities' (*de petites Chrétientés*).[14]

They had emerged from the episcopal churches and communities. The legal separation of the property and identity of the parish from that of the diocese was a process which lasted centuries and took varying forms in the different Christian countries. The nature of the bishoprics, the relation between the bishop and the individual churches in towns and rural areas, the form of his influence, and the extent to which there were layers of church government in between, as well as the relations between the occupants of old-established parish churches and those of new ones and also with lesser churches within the parish, developed in the course of the tenth and eleventh centuries in different countries, even in different regions within western Christianity, into a complex variety which should make us wary of generalisations.[15] Throughout our period, however, one very important characteristic remained a constant: no one was to be bishop in two dioceses, and no diocese could rightfully have more than one bishop. Should two bishops lay claim to a diocese then they were antibishops, of whom at most one could be the real occupant of the office.

In the course of the wars with Norsemen, Saracens, and Magyars in the

---

[13] Barlow, *English Church 1000–1066*, 242: 'In all the western kingdoms of Christendom the most vital unit in the church was the bishop's parish or diocese', Addleshaw, *Beginnings*, 3: 'But the parish does not function on its own. It is a subdivision of a wider unit, the diocese, ruled by its bishop, the ordinary.'

[14] Imbart de la Tour, *Paroisses rurales*, 6ff.

[15] Kloczowski, 'Structures', 446.

ninth and tenth centuries bishoprics were laid waste in many countries either temporarily or permanently. Where Arab rule became permanent many were never re-established, though the network of dioceses continued to exist in part in Sicily and Spain under these lords with a different faith.[16] In England and in west and northern France there were interruptions of episcopal series; in the course of the tenth century almost all of the bishoprics here were restored, though occasionally with new sees. Numerous bishoprics were founded in the missionary regions of north and east Europe; as a consequence of pagan reactions many of these were abandoned, though not wholly given up, by their bishops. Here too there were often transfers of sees, sooner or later. It was felt to be a scandal when a bishopric like Merseburg was given up just because its bishop Gisilher had become archbishop of Magdeburg under Otto II; but Merseburg was restored under Henry II. There were occasional disputes and doubts about diocesan boundaries,[17] but it was very difficult to make permanent changes to the territorial substance of old-established bishoprics. Otto the Great had to spend years of patient effort to persuade the bishop of Halberstadt to give up those parts of his diocese which were needed for the founding of the archbishopric of Magdeburg. Henry II had to spend just as much energy and to make substantial recompense to the bishop of Würzburg to make his new foundation at Bamberg possible. Missionary bishops tended to have vaguely defined spheres of influence; often it is only much later sources which give us some idea of how and when these were transformed into fixed diocesan boundaries. In the more densely populated countries where Christianity was of long standing, Italy, southern Gaul, and Spain, the dioceses were comparatively small; in northern Gaul, England, Germany, and in the lands to the north and east they were large, and this did not change much even when the population grew.

Within the dioceses there was a general tendency in the tenth and eleventh centuries towards restoration of old churches and foundation of new ones in both town and country, once the second wave of invasions had died away; there was a close connection here with the slow growth of population as a result of internal colonisation.[18] Originally the parish was comparatively extensive; it could be an overall unit which

---

[16] Villada, *Historia Ecclesiastica*, 47ff.; de Valdeavellano, *Historia de España*, 816; Amari, *Storia*, 629.

[17] Mehr, *Navarra und Aragon*, 30: 'Seemingly it was easier to tear them from the hands of the Moors than subsequently to mediate between the bishops and abbots haggling over diocesan boundaries'.

[18] Imbart de la Tour, *Paroisses rurales*, 88; Toubert, *Structures*, 716; Godfrey, *Church*, 309f.

comprehended smaller churches, oratories, and chapels, and included many settlements great and small, even isolated homesteads or groups of homesteads. If churches were built there they could be serviced by the parish priest or the parish clergy under him, until such time as they acquired a cleric or a clerical community of their own.

The motives behind church foundations varied and are often not clearly discernible. Property-owners might found churches or chapels near their own residence or at central points on their estates either from religious need, or as a display of their power, or out of concern for their dependants, or with the intention of cashing in on church dues.[19] The great distance from the parish church must often have led the inhabitants of distant settlements or colonists who were engaged in clearing new land to build churches or chapels of their own. The veneration of a saint, the occurrence of a miracle, the finding or acquisition of a relic could all lead to the foundation of a church. In many parts of western Europe this was also the consequence of an increase in the population. Often attempts were made to secure parish rights for such newly established churches, which means that the old super-parishes, the *pievi* in Italy or minsters in England, lost most if not all of their privileged position. In parts of France and Italy this may have been the result of changes in the structure of lordship. In France the castellans emancipated themselves from comital control; in Italy the great vassals from that of the margraves. Castle-building or *incastellamento* often led to the building of chapels in or near the castle, which subsequently became parish churches. Castles could produce new forms of settlement. Both these and older settlements could simultaneously become church congregations and groupings organised for mutual protection and the cooperative ordering of their internal life.[20] The multitude of rival parish churches could lead to centrifugal tendencies which had to be counteracted in the interest of the unity of the diocese.[21]

---

[19] Lemarignier, *Gouvernement*, 86; Duby, *Société*, 215, 230ff. In explaining the motives of church founders Imbart's warning about earlier centuries is still important: 'finally, let us not forget the people, this huge anonymous worker, this immense crowd of believers of whom history hardly speaks'. Although Kurze, *Pfarrerwahlen*, 448ff., stresses the reciprocal influences of parish and secular community he comes to the conclusion that neither in towns nor in the countryside were parochial elections the norm in central Europe.

[20] Lemarignier, *France médiévale*, 109ff.; Duby, *Société*, 101ff. and 141ff.; Violante, *Società Milanese*, 136 (1st edn); Violante, 'Monachesimo', 173ff.; Toubert, *Structures*, 855ff. (with the title 'De la plebs publique à l'église centrale').

[21] Imbart de la Tour, *Paroisses rurales*, 52ff.; Musset, *Peuples Scandinaves*, 141ff.; G. Forchielli, *La pieve rurale. Richerche sulla storia della costituzione della chiesa in Italia e particolarmente nel Veronese* (Rome 1931), 83.

For this purpose new offices were created, and later on fixed districts to go with them; the bishop needed these in order to fulfil his duties in the more densely populated and finely organised – hence at times more fragmented – diocese. The archdeacon was at first a functionary who was immediately subject to the bishop within the episcopal city. Later, dioceses came to have several archdeacons, each of whom had a fixed part of the diocese as the district within which he held office. The *archipresbyter*, the archpriest, had control over several parishes and the clergy associated with them. The rural deans, found in western France from the ninth century but not until the eleventh century or later in Germany and other countries, with a few isolated examples, had similar functions. Archpriests and rural deans were generally incumbents of a parish.[22]

The office of parish priest included exalted tasks and duties. He and his assistants had above all to dispense the sacraments of baptism and the Eucharist, to impose penances and present penitents to the bishop for reconciliation, and to carry out the last unction. The priest heard confessions, performed the various benedictions in use, presided over divine service; he was supposed to preach and to hold a school. He accepted the offerings made at divine services with celebration of mass, and the 'surplice fees' for the performance of burial and other rites; he collected in tithes, a part of which he was supposed to retain for himself, and other dues, where these were customarily paid by the members of his parish, such as Peter's pence. Here he probably acted as the bishop's agent. He was responsible for equipping the church with the utensils needed for performing the liturgy, and for the working of the land assigned to him as the endowment of his office. He was responsible to the bishop for his parish; he received the chrism from the bishop and had to attend the diocesan synod. He had to pay a fee for the chrism and another, the *synodaticum*, to the bishop as head of the synod, and to pay the costs of putting up the bishop and his entourage when they came to his parish on a visitation.

The bishop had the supreme power of consecration. He alone could consecrate churches, altars, cemeteries and chrism, abbots, priests, and clerics; together with the bishops of his province he could even consecrate other bishops and the archbishop. He was the spiritual head of the clergy and laity of his diocese. He taught them the articles of faith and the norms

[22] Feine, *Kirchliche Rechtsgeschichte*, 204, gives the literature for Germany from 1914; Lemarignier, 'Institutions', 19f.; Lemarignier, *France médiévale*, 75; Duby, *Société*, 84; Deanesly, *Sidelights*, 145ff.; Godfrey, *Church*, 391ff.; Brett, *English Church*, 211ff.; Barlow, *English Church 1000–1066*, 184ff.; Barlow, *English Church 1066–1154*, 48ff. and 136.

applying to the Christian order and duties, as well as moral precepts. In the Carolingian era several bishops had drawn up _capitula episcoporum_ or had them drawn up.[23] The most well known are those of Bishop Theodulf of Orleans,[24] the so-called _Collectio Anselmo dedicata_ (c. 885) and the _Libri duo de synodalibus causis et disciplinis_ of Regino of Prüm (d. 915).[25] Regino's second book is a compilation from older writings, in particular the penitential of Pseudo-Bede, which is primarily concerned with penitential practice. Here and elsewhere there is a close connection between this and both royal and episcopal capitularies;[26] the already ancient tradition of books of penance influenced these capitularies, whose provisions were in turn taken over by later regulations about morality and penance. Both isolated regulations and collections tended to repeat older provisions _in extenso_ and without much system, over and over again. The 'reform' demands of the Carolingian period were much the same as those of the eleventh century: opposition to simony of all kinds; denunciations of infringements of the ancient but rarely observed rules on priestly celibacy; prohibitions of interventions by either clerics or laymen in areas which did not concern them.

A continuity in episcopal and conciliar legislation can be observed from the ninth to the eleventh century. It has often been assumed that _capitula episcoporum_ and related writings did not have such a wide circulation in the tenth century as before and after. Admittedly, we do not find in this period such comprehensive collections as those of Regino of Prüm on the one hand and of Bishop Burchard of Worms (c. 965–1025) on the other.[27] But a number of observations and the results of recent research on manuscript transmission have made us more cautious. The manuscript tradition of the episcopal legislation of Bishop Theodulf of Orleans dating from the tenth and eleventh centuries, for example, is considerable,[28] and the tenth century did in fact see the production of works like the

---

[23] A. Werminghoff, 'Capitula episcoporum s. VIII et IX', _NA_, 26 (1901), 665ff.; Fournier and Le Bras, _Histoire_, 112ff.; de Clercq, _Législation religieuse_, 1.259ff.

[24] Brommer, 'Bischöfliche Gesetzgebung', 1–120.

[25] Fournier and Le Bras, _Histoire_, 35ff., 364ff., 414ff.

[26] Poschmann, _Abendländische Kirchenbuße_, 89.

[27] Fournier and Le Bras, _Histoire_, 88.

[28] Brommer, 'Bischöfliche Gesetzgebung'; Brommer, 'Rezeption der bischöflichen Kapitularien', 113–60; Brommer, 'Benedictus Levita', 145ff.; Brommer, 'Die Quellen der "Capitula" Radulfs von Bourges', 27–43; Sauer, 'Theodulfi Capitula'; Sauer, 'Wulfstans Handbuch', 341–84; R. Pokorny, 'Zwei unerkannte Bischofkapitularien des 10. Jahrhunderts', _DA_, 35 (1979), 487–513; G. Picasso, 'Campagne et contadini nella legislazione della chiesa fino a Graziano', _Medioevo rurale. Sulle traccie della civiltà contadina_, ed. V. Fumagalli and G. Rossetti (Bologna 1980), 381–97.

capitulare of Bishop Atto of Vercelli (d. 961),[29] the *De contemptu canonum* and *Synodica* of Bishop Rather of Verona and Liège, and the *Collectio canonum* of Abbo of Fleury.[30] The synodal sermon *Fratres presbyteri et sacerdotes*, which has been called a 'handbook of canon law on the official duties of the parish clergy' was even incorporated into the *Pontificale Romano-Germanicum* drawn up in Otto I's time.[31] The fact that the first great canon law collection, the *Decretum* of Burchard of Worms, could draw on an unbroken tradition is a confirmation of the continuity already mentioned.[32] Nevertheless, it is improbable that such capitularies or books were actually in the hands of the parish clergy in thousands of parishes, and still more doubtful whether their provisions were regularly observed.

In order to instruct, control, and when necessary to judge clergy and people, bishops were supposed to hold regular diocesan synods.[33] By and large these concerned themselves with local or regional affairs.[34] They were genuine church assemblies, but the decisions lay in the hands of the bishop; the assent of the participants did not, as it did with the great councils, imply that they represented the whole church; it was more like the usual consent given to rulers at assemblies.[35] It is hard to say how regularly diocesan synods were held in practice, and the differences across periods and countries were probably considerable. Complaints that the practice was neglected were not infrequent.[36] A recent study has turned up twenty-seven mentions of diocesan synods for France in the period between 888 and 987, though the provinces of Auch, Dol, Embrun,

[29] Migne, *PL* 134, cols. 27–52. On its sources see Wemple, *Atto of Vercelli*, 38ff.; on p. 175 she rightly notes that 'a comparison of Atto's, the Frankish bishops' and the Gregorian reformers' programs demonstrates moreover that there was a continuous canonical tradition running from the ninth to the eleventh century'. The other tenth-century writings mentioned here are also witness to this continuity, though the warnings of Fuhrmann, *Pseudoisidorische Fälschungen*, II.442 should be noted.

[30] Rather's *Synodica*: Migne, *PL* 136, cols. 551–68; *Die Briefe des Bischofs Rather von Verona*, ed. F. Weigle (MGH Die Briefe der deutschen Kaiserzeit 1, Weimer 1949), pp. 124ff., no. 25; Abbo of Fleury, *Collectio Canonum*, Migne, *PL* 139, cols. 473–508.

[31] *Le pontifical Romano-Germanique*, ed. Vogel and Elze, III.256ff., no. 80 c. 51. See Lotter, 'Kanonistisches Handbuch', 1–57.

[32] On the *sermo synodalis* among the additions to Burchard's *Decretum*, see Meyer, 'Überlieferung', 141–83.

[33] Barion, *Synodalrecht*; de Clercq, *Législation religieuse*.

[34] Pontal, *Status synodaux*, 33.

[35] On the significance of consent see Barion, *Synodalrecht*, 91ff.; Barion distinguishes clearly between diocesan, provincial, national, imperial, and papal synods, although he notes on p. 172 that the middle ages made no distinction between different kinds of synod. Boye, 'Synoden Deutschlands', 131–284, has a similar classification; Pontal, *Statuts synodaux*, 20, rightly warns that 'all such distinctions are somewhat artificial'. See Fransen, 'Papes', 204.

[36] Barion, *Synodalrecht*, 38.

Rouen, and Tarantaise have left no records of synods at all for this period.[37] An older catalogue of synods in Germany lists only sixteen diocesan synods between 922 and 1059. Of course, we must assume that our records are very fragmentary.[38] But there remains nevertheless a question-mark over the relationship between normative law and legal reality, in other words an uncertainty about how far we can deduce from statutes and their provisions the existence of regular synods, and how far the reality of ecclesiastical life and custom corresponded to such law. All too often recent research has deduced past reality (and judged it favourably or unfavourably according to taste) simply from what happens to have come down to us in the form of legislation.

Not only did the Christian people, both lay and ecclesiastic, come to the bishop; he came to them. He journeyed through his diocese on visitations, and had the right to claim food and lodging for himself and his entourage and their horses. The episcopal right of command allowed him to exercise ecclesiastical jurisdiction and impose punishments such as penitential prayers, fasts, pilgrimages, or excommunications.[39] It became customary at different times in different places for him to be represented by archdeacons who were each responsible for a part of the diocese.[40] In Germany this came to be normal practice between the tenth and the twelfth century. The episcopal court of visitation (*Sendgericht*) developed its own procedures which included sworn jurors – clerics at first, but as early as the ninth century also laymen of good reputation – who 'presented' punishable offences in their district.[41] From the Carolingian period onwards the same defects were complained about and the same norms of Christian life proclaimed, a sign of how much human frailty the church had to cope with. Priests who refused to dispense the sacraments and parishioners who did not know to which parish they belonged were probably the exception.[42] The abuses of the proprietary church, which we

---

[37] Schröder, *Westfränkische Synoden*, 45ff.; on the provinces mentioned above see p. 39.
[38] Boye, 'Quellenkatalog', 45–96. The only Italian diocesan synod mentioned there (p. 53) is one held in Padua in 955.
[39] Feine, *Kirchliche Rechtsgeschichte*, 216ff. with the literature mentioned there, especially G. Flade, *Die Erziehung des Klerus durch die Visitationen bis zum 10. Jahrhundert* (Zurich 1933).
[40] A. Amanieu, 'Archidiacre', *Dictionnaire de droit canonique* I (Paris 1935), cols. 948–1004; A. Fransen, 'Archidiakon', *LThK* I (1957), cols. 524ff.; Feine, *Kirchliche Rechtsgeschichte*, 203f. and the literature cited there on France, England, Hungary, Poland, and Italy.
[41] A. M. Koeniger, *Die Sendgerichte in Deutschland* (Munich 1907), I (all published); A. M. Koeniger, *Quellen zur Geschichte der Sendgerichte in Deutschland* (Munich 1910); Poschmann, *Abendländische Kirchenbuße*, 127.
[42] Godfrey, *Church*, 307; Lemarignier, 'Etudes', 68 n. 19 following Ordericus Vitalis, *Historia ecclesiastica* III 2, ed. Le Prévost, II.26.

shall return to, meant that there were poor priests who had to give more attention to working church lands than to their spiritual duties, especially as they were burdened with numerous dues and had to take care that their parishioners provided them with the minimum necessary to live on. Besides devout, responsible, and learned bishops there were also others who were more concerned to gain and enjoy riches, to participate in politics, or simply to conduct very mundane quarrels than to exercise their high spiritual office.[43] We hear that at times no diocesan synods were held for years on end and that the priests only travelled once a year to the bishop's court to collect the chrism and pay their dues. Even then they did not always have personal contact with the bishop. There were numerous complaints, which may or may not have been justified, about the harsh demands made in connection with the obligation to provide hospitality to the bishop on visitations. Since bishops might possess property and dependants, even churches and monasteries in other dioceses, there were occasionally clashes between neighbouring bishops. Archbishop Lanfranc of Canterbury complained at some time before 1087 to Bishop Stigand of Chichester that the latter's archdeacons had extorted monies from clerics on Canterbury possessions within the diocese of Chichester. Up until then he (Lanfranc) had, contrary to the usual practice, instructed these clerics to attend the Chichester synods, reserving only judicial cases for himself. Now, however, he insisted on the return of the monies paid, and he had instructed his priests outside Kent not to attend the synods of either the bishop of Chichester or any other bishop. They were henceforth permitted only to collect the chrism from their diocesan bishop.[44] Lanfranc may here have been exploiting his position as metropolitan, but the conflict was essentially one between two diocesans.

Parishes and dioceses had – in spite of the numerous variations across time and space as to their size, the numbers of their inhabitants, their internal organisation, and the social composition of their clergy – essentially the same characteristics as far as the dignity of their religious functions and their hierarchical organisation was concerned. This is not true to the same extent of the next level up in the hierarchy, the province.[45] The metropolitan, who from the tenth century onwards normally held the title of archbishop, had no higher orders than did any other bishop. But he had a special relationship to the pope, who was

[43] Böhmer, 'Eigenkirchentum', 351; Godfrey, *Church*, 324; Barlow, *English Church 1000–1066*, 186; Barlow, *English Church 1066–1154*, 24.

[44] Böhmer, 'Eigenkirchentum', 301.

[45] Fundamental, though it stops at the ninth century, is Lesne, *Hiérarchie épiscopale*; see also Kemp, *Aspects*, 27ff.; Kempf, 'Primatiale und episkopal-synodale Struktur', 27–66.

recognised as the earthly head of the church, and this was expressed by the
conferral of the pallium (though even after the Carolingian period this
might be granted to other important bishops as well on occasions).[46] It was
his duty to supervise the bishops of his province and to arbitrate or judge
in any cases of conflict which might arise between them. Normally he was
only active in this capacity when asked to do so by one of the parties. His
powers were not undisputed. Hincmar of Rheims had had opponents
among the episcopate in the ninth century, and the Pseudo-Isidorian
decretals could be used to restrict the rights of the metropolitan in favour
of bishops. Besides this, the metropolitan might find himself in rivalry
with the king, particularly if the king took his theocratic office especially
seriously. Whether a metropolitan was able to carry out his functions
depended to a large extent on his powers of persuasion, his effectiveness,
and his tact. Some tried in the tenth and eleventh centuries to acquire a
papal vicariate or a primacy over a larger region, but such pretensions
were almost all short-lived and ineffectual, apart from the recognition or
toleration of more or less empty titles.[47] Can we really assume that
Archbishops Frederick and William of Mainz sought a primacy in
Germany, even though it was at the time quite unthinkable that the other
archbishops would have submitted to them or their successors?[48] Adalbert
of Bremen's plan to found a patriarchate in northern Europe was artificial
and impracticable.[49] In Anglo-Saxon and early Norman times Canterbury
had the primacy over the whole of England, though it could not maintain
this in the twelfth century.[50] We can also speak of a primacy of Rome
within Italy, though the frictions which arose out of this between
Rome and the churches of Milan and Ravenna in particular only faded
away after the gradual rise of the papacy to a new role within the church
from the middle of the eleventh century onwards. The resistance to a level
of the hierarchy above the metropolitan came from bishops, theocratic
rulers, and then from a strengthened papacy, which had no interest in the
existence of a powerful intermediate instance in church government.

[46] Lesne, *Hiérarchie épiscopale*, 94; Feine, *Kirchliche Rechtsgeschichte*, 119 and 231ff.; T. Zotz,
   'Pallium et alia quaedam archiepiscopatus insignia', *Festschrift für Berent Schwineköper*, ed.
   H. Maurer and H. Patze (Sigmaringen 1982), 155–75.
[47] Foreville, 'Royaumes', 272. It is not clear whether Erchanbald made a fresh attempt at
   the end of the tenth century to renew the vicariate for Gallia and Germania bestowed by
   John VIII in 876 but never realised. See Kempf, *Handbuch*, 173, 331; on the planned
   vicariate of Ansegis of Sens see also Arnaldi, 'Papato, arcivescovi e vescovi', 41ff.
[48] Büttner, 'Mainzer Erzbischöfe', 1–26, where it is noted (p. 26) that there are no signs of
   any claims to a vicariate in Hatto's pontificate; Lotter, *Brief*, 89f.
[49] Fuhrmann, 'Patriarchate' (1955), 120ff.; Fuhrmann, 'Provincia constat', 389ff.
[50] Foreville, *L'Eglise et la royauté*, 40 and 48.

The size of church provinces and the number of suffragans in them varied greatly between the western European countries. Apart from the sprawling Roman province there were a number of important ones in Italy such as Milan, Ravenna, Aquileia, Grado, and Benevento, to which were later added a number of others in the south. France had nine provinces,[51] the east Frankish or German kingdom six, the kingdom of Burgundy seven, while England only had two, the archbishoprics of Canterbury and York (the latter had at first no suffragans). Scotland was a hierarchy without a head, in spite of repeated attempts by York to exercise metropolitan powers there. The situation in Ireland fluctuated, though Armagh had a nominal supremacy. Hungary had two provinces, Poland only the one enormous province of Gnesen,[52] and the Scandinavian kingdoms were later to have only one province each. The numbers of their suffragans varied just as much. The Roman province was by far the largest with fifty to sixty mostly small bishoprics.[53] Canterbury had eighteen suffragans. In Germany Mainz was the largest province, with fifteen suffragans including the largest German diocese, Constance; Trier was the smallest, with three. In France, Tours, Rheims, Auch, and for a time Narbonne had numerous suffragans, though Narbonne was reduced in size after the restoration of Tarragona under Urban II.[54] Tours only had a few suffragans once the Breton province was set up under Dol, until Innocent III restored the old provincial organisation.[55]

The possibility of making the authority of the metropolitan a reality depended not just on the personality of the holder but on a number of historically determined contingencies. If a king or prince saw himself as protector of the churches in his country a metropolitan might either make a name for himself by opposing him or exercise considerable influence in cooperation with him. Metropolitan activities might be curtailed by the proximity of the pope in central and northern Italy in those periods when the pope was not hampered by his own regional opposition. Since in most of France, especially in the south and west, the archbishops, just like the bishops, were sons, brothers, or other relatives of the regionally dominant

---

[51] Counting Tours and Dol twice. The summary offered by Schröder, *Westfränkische Synoden*, 4, includes the Burgundian provinces as well.

[52] Foreville, 'Royaumes', 285 and 290; Kloczowski, 'Province ecclésiastique', 437ff.

[53] The most reliable survey is provided by the first five volumes of *Italia Pontificia*, which note which bishoprics had breaks in continuity and which belonged for a time to Rome or Milan or Ravenna.

[54] Foreville, 'Royaumes', 297f.; Vincke, *Staat und Kirche*, 358f.; Guillemain, *Origines*, 374–407.

[55] Foreville, 'Royaumes', 284f.; Kaiser, *Bischofsherrschaft*, 114ff.

ducal, comital, or vicecomital families,[56] they were scarcely able to exercise much influence ex officio over their suffragans; it depended in general on the relationships between the families concerned.

There were canon law norms which demanded that provincial councils should be held periodically, and there were some attempts to comply with these. But provincial councils can be found only here and there, and their deliberations and decisions did not differ greatly from those of diocesan synods. They were often summoned to deal with a particular problem or dispute; only rarely before the middle of the eleventh century was there the intention of examining the state of the church and of issuing new legislation for it, let alone of dealing with questions involving the faith. It is hard to fit them into a systematic classification of church synods. Neighbouring metropolitans or bishops might take part in provincial councils, as might abbots, clerics, and laymen from outside the province. Thus the archbishop of Rouen was present at the synod of Rheims in 900, at which the murderers of Archbishop Fulco were condemned,[57] and also at the Rheims provincial council held at Trosly in 909, about which we are fairly well informed.[58] The boundaries between such extended provincial synods and those in which the king and his clerical and secular entourage participated are hard to determine. Apart from this there were hardly any councils held by metropolitans at which at least a few of their suffragans were not present, either because they were genuinely unable to come or simply because they did not want to.[59] The traditional classification of synods into diocesan, provincial, national or imperial, and papal has recently been called into question, with much justification. If for the 137 years between 922 and 1059 only nineteen provincial councils can be found in Germany and nine in Italy, then even if we allow for gaps in the evidence this shows either that such councils were indeed rare or that the classification used in the counting is questionable. The latter seems more likely when the participants in such councils are examined more closely.[60] It is still more

---

[56] The fragmentation of the greater part of the western and southern French church is impressively documented by Kaiser, *Bischofsherrschaft*.

[57] Migne, *PL*, 132, col. 673. On the murdered archbishop see Schneider, *Erzbischof Fulco von Reims*.

[58] Schmitz, 'Konzil von Trosly', 332–434.

[59] Schröder, *Westfränkische Synoden*, 6.

[60] Boye, 'Quellenkatalog'. Provincial synods seem to be particularly frequent in the province of Rouen, a fact probably explicable in terms of the closed nature of Normandy, which meant that 'foreign' bishops only rarely appeared at a council. See Foreville, 'Synods', 19–40; Foreville, 'Royaumes', 303ff.; Vicaire, 'Pastorale', 79 stresses the changes in synodal practice in the area he has studied around the middle of the

dubious to call large councils held in Germany 'national' synods and large ones held in Italy 'imperial' synods. What was common to all synods, however we classify them, was their desire and their claim to be led by God and the Holy Spirit, aspirations reflected in countless preambles to synodal decrees and to the liturgies according to which they were conducted and which were part of their essence. Synods and councils were, as we can see from both their form and their content, in the first instance divine services; it was only their agendas which made them also bodies which took decisions about administrative and legal questions. A vivid picture of how they worked can be gained not only from the detailed accounts of particular synods but also from the *ordo Romanus qualiter consilium generale agatur* (Roman order for the holding of a general council) in the *Pontificale Romano-Germanicum*. We may cite one of its prayers as a particularly characteristic example: 'Almighty and eternal God, who has promised with Thy Holy Word that wherever two or three are gathered in Thy name that Thou wilt be among them, have mercy on our gathering and enlighten our hearts in Thy mercy, so that we may not deviate from the treasure of Thy pity but hold fast to the right way of Thy justice.'[61] The postulate that a true and valid council was divinely inspired repeatedly showed itself.[62]

THE SIGNIFICANCE OF KINGDOMS AND PRINCIPALITIES
FOR THE FORMATION OF PARTICULAR CHURCHES
The question

The whole church is the spiritual unity of all the christened, organised in a hierarchical order in the community of bishops including the highest bishop, the bishop of Rome. But it is also present in the particular churches: parish, diocese, province. These units, moreover, possess clear legal, social, and geographical boundaries, in spite of their participation in the universality of the church. We thus have the question whether in the tenth and eleventh centuries there existed organised units which were larger than single church provinces. The old patriarchates and the primacies or vicariates, in the west mostly originating in special

eleventh century: 'the southern councils had been purely local or at best provincial', whereas from the time of Gregory VII onwards they were determined by events in Rome.

61 *Ordo romanus qualiter concilium agatur generale*, in Vogel and Elze, *Pontificale Romano-Germanique*, III.272, no. 79, c. 16. On the great age of these texts see Munier, 'Ordo Romanus', 288f.

62 Barion, *Synodalrecht*, 175, in spite of his rejection of the well-known theses of Rudolf Sohm.

circumstances and hence of a transitory nature, have already been mentioned. When we speak of a German, French, English, or Saxon church it should be immediately apparent that we are not talking about ecclesiastical or hierarchic units but about geographical, historical, and political nomenclature. Strictly speaking there was, for example, no church in Italy, and consequently no Italian church history. There were only Christian churches in Italy and their history. The totality of the churches in Italy did not form a unit, either in a religious or in a legal sense. They existed, as did the church outside Italy, in the form of parishes, bishoprics, metropolitans, and of course as a manifestation of the church in general as well. This must be remembered precisely because there can be no question of changing a terminology which is long established and has become indispensable, even if it is somewhat artificial.

On the other hand we need to consider carefully whether and to what extent independent lordships – kingdoms or principalities – could create or consist of ecclesiastical units. It is all the more necessary to think about this because such lordships did not just function in a purely secular manner or bind together parishes, bishoprics, and provinces only superficially. They too had a teleologically determined existence by the standards of theocratic, ecclesiastical norms. The monarch was in a special way a member and a functionary of the church; he was not just like all other Christian laymen, but was a 'mediator between clergy and people'.[63] The antithesis of church and state has long been recognised as an anachronism, though a long-lived one, when applied to the early middle ages. The 'church' was not yet so institutionalised as to be capable of expressing a collective will, of acting politically towards other organisations or persons. And a 'state' as a counterpart in the modern sense also did not exist. Rulers by the grace of God were still, in a quite different fashion from other laymen, persons and functionaries within the church.

The influence of rulers within the church in the tenth and eleventh centuries was based on both old and new elements. Many of the attributes of the Christian Roman emperors, Constantine and his successors, were still visible. The kings who founded kingdoms on the territory of the *imperium Romanum* took over within their territory the imperial function of caring for the church, not just in the sense that they protected the material basis of the church's existence, but also in that they mediated in its internal disputes, appointed to bishoprics, summoned and participated in church councils, and determined canon law. It was not just a case of kings adopting imperial prerogatives in their own interest; it soon became

---

[63] 'mediator cleri et plebis': Vogel and Elze, *Pontificale Romano-Germanique*, III.257 no. 25.

clear that the churches themselves were dependent on cooperation with some kind of superior instance. Rulers like Theoderic the Great, though Arian, were called on by Catholic churches, while as late as the tenth century in Spain even Islamic emirs and caliphs appear to have participated in church life, in a sense as the successors to the Visigothic rulers.[64]

It was long believed that the Germanic notion of royal or aristocratic charisma, that is to say of primitive magic powers associated both in theory and in practice with medieval kingship, played a part here, but this has recently been called in question.[65] What cannot be denied is the high, in effect charismatic status of king and nobility in the early middle ages, still apparent in the tenth and eleventh centuries. But this can hardly be separated from the totality of kingly and princely rulership, which was shaped decisively in its theory and in its practice by the church. The king is ordained by God to protect the churches and the Christian people. The idea of kingly rule as an office held by the grace of God was, as in the whole of the early middle ages, unproblematic and unchallenged in the tenth and early eleventh centuries, and its 'supernatural aura' continued to exercise the popular imagination as long as monarchy lasted.[66] Major works of twentieth-century scholarship have been devoted to Christian rulership; we may here name Fritz Kern's unsurpassed study on kingship by the grace of God and the right of resistance,[67] Marc Bloch's book on royal healers, the writings of Ernst Kantorowicz,[68] the work done on *ordines*, especially by Michel Andrieu,[69] and the comprehensive studies by Percy Ernst Schramm and his circle on rulers' insignia and the symbolism of state.[70]

These works have shown with ever-increasing clarity that royal government in our period did not just consist of winning, increasing, and maintaining power, of more or less ethically determined politics; it was the creation of order in a world where the sacred and the profane were ultimately undivided. The king was legitimated by God's will; his actions were carried out in his capacity as God's agent. This applied especially to his concern for peace, which was to be maintained both externally against heathens and the putative opponents of God's will, and internally through the maintenance of Christian order. The life of the ruler with the church

---

[64] Villada, *Historia Ecclesiastica*, 79; de Valdeavellano, *Historia de España*, 376; Menéndez Pidal, *Spanien des Cid*, 26; Lévi-Provençal, *Histoire*, 223, 286.

[65] Tellenbach, 'Thronfolge', 239ff.

[66] Bloch, *Rois thaumaturges*, 20.   [67] Kern, *Gottesgnadentum*.

[68] Kantorowicz, *Laudes regiae*; Kantorowicz, *The King's Two Bodies*; Kantorowicz, *Selected Studies*.

[69] Andrieu (ed.), *Pontifical Romain*.

[70] *Herrschaftszeichen* and many other publications.

and of the church with him stood at the core of rulership.[71] As a person
he participated in the whole church, wherever he might be, whatever
church feast he might take part in. If in the churches of his land prayers
were said for him and for the earthly and eternal salvation of his kingdom,
his family, and his army, then these were not just services rendered; they
were actions on which he depended, and we would today call them 'acts
of state'.[72] Government consisted of the liturgy of royal election, unction,
and coronation, of the celebration of the high church feasts – Christmas,
Easter, Whitsun – at places of special ecclesiastical importance, of ecclesiastical ceremonial at the entry of the king in towns, palaces, cathedrals, or
monasteries,[73] of the singing of the royal *laudes* on numerous occasions.[74]
The legal dispositions in royal charters were made in God's name and the
documents were dated by the year of the Lord's Incarnation. The life of
the itinerant royal court was largely determined by the ecclesiastical year.
The royal insignia had a religious significance: crown, throne, Holy
Lance. They usually existed in multiple copies; but each copy was, as far
as possible, hallowed by the presence of relics. They were thus, like all
liturgical and ceremonial acts, symbols in the sense understood in the high
middle ages, at once reality and sign, sources and means of power for the
king.[75]

However, it should be noted that the Christian lordships of the early
middle ages were not all equal at all times in the extent to which they
were filled with religious and ecclesiastical significance; neither the
influence of the king on the life of the church nor the role of the higher
clergy as advisers of the king were constants. The variation can be seen
most impressively in the nature and extent of royal participation in
appointment to the highest ecclesiastical office, that of the bishop. So long

[71] But see for example Häussling, *Mönchskonvent*, 357: 'If it is true that the liturgy performed
by the Carolingian royal chapel was a matter of state importance, because it demonstrated
political rule and continually reestablished it'; a demonstration of how difficult it is for
conventional thinking to grasp the point that all the ruler's functions were supposed to
be performed in the service of God.
[72] Tellenbach, 'Historische Dimension', 208.
[73] H. W. Klewitz, 'Die Festkrönungen der deutschen Könige', *ZRGKA*, 28 (1939), 48–96;
Kantorowicz, *Laudes Regiae*, 97ff., who talks of a 'festival itinerary'; C. Brühl,
'Fränkischer Krönungsbrauch und das Problem der "Festkrönungen"', *HZ*, 194 (1962),
265–326; C. Brühl, *Fodrum, Gistum*, index s.v. 'Festkrönungen', 'Festtagsorte'; H. M.
Schaller, 'Der heilige Tag als Termin mittelalterlicher Staatsakte', *DA*, 30 (1974), 1–24;
Tellenbach, 'Kaiser, Rom', 233f.
[74] Kantorowicz, *Laudes Regiae*, 13.
[75] Schramm, *Herrschaftszeichen*, II.492ff. and 519f. on Hungary; P. E. Schramm, 'Die
Geschichte Polens im Lichte der Herrschaftszeichen', in *L'Europe aux IXe–XIe siècles*
(Warsaw 1968), 363.

as an anointed king took part in the nomination, election, or confirmation
of the bishop the bishoprics could never be absorbed completely by the
feudalisation of the church. Thietmar of Merseburg described it as
improper that Duke Arnulf of Bavaria should have been able to appoint
the bishops in his duchy, and argued that Christ had set bishops under the
rule of 'those who alone through the glory of unction and the crown are
set above all morals'.[76] True, certain forms appropriate to the non-
vassalitic benefice had come to be used for the high churches from the
late ninth century. From this point it gradually became the norm for
a bishopric to be bestowed by the handing over of the episcopal staff.
Not until the end of the tenth century did this act come to be called
investiture, and the regular use of the term is still later.[77] Nevertheless, it
was only where the person bestowing the bishopric was not an anointed
king, as in large areas of France, that the bishopric became simply a
proprietary church. For this reason the ability of kingdoms to form
ecclesiastical units of some kind was also very varied. Concept such as
'imperial church', 'national', or 'regional' church in the tenth and
eleventh centuries denote very disparate phenomena. This is very evident
if we compare the 'imperial' or the 'English' church on the one hand with
the churches in France, Burgundy, or Italy on the other hand, where one
can speak of national churches only with considerable reservations, if at
all.

France and Spain

The sacral character of kingship was established earliest and most fully in
Carolingian west Francia, in what was to become France. In a development of Carolingian political theology, unction and coronation of the
king at Orléans in 848 and at Metz in 869 took definitive liturgical shape.[78]
It is worth noting that these earliest rites were restricted in their
significance to the royal dignity in Aquitaine and Lotharingia respectively,
in other words only to parts of the kingdom claimed by Charles the
Bald, not to the whole of it. Only in 877 in Compiègne was Louis the
Stammerer crowned and anointed for the whole of his kingdom.[79] It was

---

[76] *Chronicon* I.26, p. 34; see Tellenbach, *Libertas*, 74 and 107f. with n. 27, where a further
anecdote is cited from Rodulfus Glaber, in which the belief is attributed to Henry III
that in the moment of investiture Christ himself worked through the king, an anecdote
also discussed by Mayer, *Fürsten und Staat*, 75.

[77] Hinschius, *Kirchenrecht*, II.529, n. 2; Stutz, 'Lehen und Pfründe', 220, n. 2; Feine,
Kirchliche Rechtsgeschichte, 250f. and n. 15.

[78] Schramm, *König von Frankreich*, 16ff. and 25ff.

[79] *Ibid.*, 54ff.

around this time that the so-called 'west Frankish *ordo*' for the anointing of the king was composed; this represented a complete liturgification of king-making. Like a bishop, the king was anointed with chrism and received insignia such as ring and staff accompanied by formulae and prayers. The term 'episcopalisation of the king' has even been used.[80] But the king remained *mediator cleri et plebis*, a mediator between clergy and people. He was consecrated, but had no power to consecrate; neither then nor later was such a power either claimed or exercised by a secular ruler. This should be borne in mind in the face of the tendentious complaints of a much later period about the real or supposed interventions by the 'crown' in the sphere of influence of the 'priesthood'. Besides, king-making had been churchified but not clericalised; representatives of all the members of the church, laity as well as clergy, participated in differing roles in the ceremony.

The king of France did not rule over the church; he was himself a part of it. He sat enthroned, surrounded by bishops, counts, and other lay magnates; together with them he took decisions of all kinds and celebrated church feasts; he summoned synods and was present at them, as did Robert the Pious in Chelles in 1008 together with the archbishops of Sens and Tours and eleven other bishops, whom he called *episcopi nostri*. The synod was *synodus nostra*.[81] Prayers were said for the king, for his family, and for his kingdom; charters were dated by the years of his reign, even in distant parts which he never visited. The kings, both Carolingian and Capetian, exercised decisive influence on episcopal elections and practised investiture – not, however, in the whole of France, only in those regions where their lordship was a reality.[82] In the tenth century France was divided by the rivalry between Carolingians and Capetians. The kings were scarcely able to secure more than an acknowledgement of their overlordship from the great vassals.[83] The king

---

[80] Lemarignier, *Gouvernement*, 26; Lemarignier, *Institutions*, 42.

[81] Duby, *Frühzeit*, 4: 'The ruler was part of the church': Lemarignier, *France médiévale*, 66: 'Kingship was an institutional power because a power within the church'; Lemarignier, *Institutions*, 45, on the synods held by Robert the Pious; Kienast, *Deutschland und Frankreich*, 125ff. on the synods of Saint-Basle, Mouzon and Chelles: on p. 127 n. 302a it is stressed that by contrast with Germany it was not customary for the king to preside over the synod. We shall discuss the German king's self-restraint later.

[82] Dhondt, *Etudes*, 48: 'royal authority over the church, royal intervention in episcopal and abbatial elections rapidly decreased and in the end disappeared altogether'; Kienast, *Deutschland und Frankreich*, 1.35, calculates that Hugo Capet installed bishops in 14 of the 77 French dioceses, and Louis VII in 25.

[83] *Ibid.*, III, appendix III, 658ff., where Kienast supports Ferdinand Lot in his famous controversy with Jacques Flach in arguing that the territorial princes of the tenth to the twelfth century were indeed vassals of the crown.

was present as a ruler only in parts of the former west Francia; the number of royal charters declined, and according to Lemarignier none was issued for a recipient in Languedoc, which might be termed a 'region of royal absence', between 987 and 1108.[84] One should bear in mind the often-quoted remark made by Abbo of Fleury after he came to be abbot of Réole, shortly before his death: he was, he said, more powerful than the king of France here, where no one feared the latter's power.[85]

Thus in the tenth and eleventh centuries the French kings did not bind the church provinces together to form a more comprehensive unit, and it is hardly possible to talk of a French national or regional church in this period. Charles the Bald had tried to preserve something of the Carolingian imperial church in his failed attempt to establish the primacy of Sens. In the early Ottonian era we find echoes of a 'pan-Frankish' church, particularly at the synod of Ingelheim, which, with the help of Otto I and some French bishops intervened in the archbishopric of Rheims in favour of Louis IV and his candidate. But such things became less and less common, though one should bear in mind the influence exercised over parts of the French church by Archbishop Bruno of Cologne from Lotharingia, and in the reverse direction King Lothar's ultimately unsuccessful attempt to take Aachen. In the end there were only a few remnants of such transregnal links, for example the bishop of Cambrai, who was a prelate of the Reich but a suffragan of the archbishop of Rheims.[86]

Even provincial boundaries were affected by royal weakness. The archbishop of Tours, for example, lost most of his suffragans to the church province of Dol, which had been created by Breton independence and recognised by the papacy from the time of Hadrian II onwards.[87] Equally characteristic was the demand by the duke of Aquitaine to have the diocese of Limoges transferred from the province of Bourges to that of Bordeaux.[88] It has even been said of the French church provinces that they atrophied, leaving only the diocese as a unit, though this is not equally true of all parts of France.[89] In the regions where the weak king still counted for something the metropolitans were able to call on him. In those regions less close to the king in the west and south, and in northern Spain, the provinces tended to splinter as a consequence of the rivalries

[84] Lemarignier, 'Institutions', 50; Lemarignier, *Gouvernement*, 30, 41; Kienast, 'Wirkungs-bereich', 529–65, especially the impressive summary on p. 552.
[85] Aimo, *Vita Abbonis*, Migne, *PL* 139, cols. 387–414.
[86] Kienast, *Deutschland und Frankreich*, 152.
[87] Duine, *Métropole de Bretagne*, 13ff.; Foreville, 'Royaumes', 283ff.; Kaiser, *Bischofsherrschaft*, 114ff.
[88] Lemarignier, 'Institutions', 10.   [89] Lemarignier, *France médiévale*, 56.

between ecclesiastical and secular magnates, and there was little apart from
the title to distinguish the archbishops from their suffragans.

There are some signs of ecclesiastical initiation-rites for the greatest and
most important French princes, even of insignia used for the purpose,
such as ring, sword, crown, or golden diadem.[90] None apparently was
anointed with chrism.[91] A Norman *officium ad ducem constituendum*[92] and
an Aquitanian order for a ducal coronation[93] survive in late manuscripts;
they have the form of the liturgical texts used at the coronation of
emperors and kings, and include the same sequences of prayers. For
Brittany there are also some reports of coronations of the Breton princes.[94]
As elsewhere, princes and even counts sometimes used royal devotion-
formulae in their charters: *dei gratia, divina favente clementia*, etc.[95] Their
rulership took on certain theocratic elements: they were often referred to
as *sanctus*[96] and at the high church festivals or on arrival in cities they were
greeted, as were kings, by the singing of *laudes*.[97]

It is worth noting that Normandy was identical with the church
province of Rouen,[98] and Brittany with that of Dol.[99] The duchy of
Aquitaine consisted essentially of the provinces of Bordeaux and Auch.[100]
If one can risk talking of a Norman, Breton, or Aquitainian church this is
yet another sign that French kingship, in spite of its undisputed sacrality
and its feudal overlordship, was not able to bring the churches of France
together as a unity. That became possible only much later, at a time when

[90] Tellenbach, 'Herzogskronen', 68ff.; Hoffmann, 'Fürstenweihen', 92–119.

[91] Bloch, *Rois thaumaturges*, 497; Fawtier, *Histoire*, 32; Hoffmann, 'Fürstenweihen', defines
the precedence of the king precisely on p. 88 by saying that he alone was anointed with
the oil from the holy amphora. We should not, unlike Kienast, *Studien*, 120, deduce from
the fact that the king might send insignia or invest with them that the appointment took
on a purely secular character by virtue of this.

[92] *Benedictional of Archbishop Robert*, ed. W. H. Wilson (Henry Bradshaw Society 24,
London 1902), 157ff.; see Bloch, *Rois thaumaturges*, 497ff.

[93] Bouquet, *RHF*, XII.541; see Schramm, *König von Frankreich*, 129ff.

[94] *Ibid.*, 25.

[95] Kienast, *Herzogstitel*, 409ff., where the great number of variants should be noted;
Foreville, 'Synods', 19–40; further Fauroux, *Recueil*, 85, 95, 103ff., 137, 151.

[96] Kienast, *Deutschland und Frankreich*, Appendix, especially p. 682.

[97] Kienast, *Studien*, 99; Schramm, *Geschichte des englischen Königtums*, 31 and Appendix 8;
Kantorowicz, *Laudes regiae*, 166, to be read with the qualification made by Hoffman,
'Langobarden', 152ff.

[98] Kaiser, *Bischofsherrschaft*, 160ff., where on p. 171 there is even talk of a Norman ducal
church; Fauroux, *Recueil*, 103, with the subscription of the count-duke preceding that of
the archbishop of Rouen; Kienast, *Studien*, 98ff.

[99] Hoffmann, 'Fürstenweihen', 110.

[100] William V of Aquitaine is termed 'totius Aquitaniae monarchus' by Ademar of
Chabannes. See Higounet, *Histoire de l'Aquitaine*, 173ff.

a revived kingship was able to present itself as the sanctified pinnacle of the political system and subordinate the princes, whose position lacked theoretical definition and hence legitimation, more closely to itself.[101]

In general the influence of Spanish princes on the churches of their territories was similar to that of the French ones. Here too they were occasionally given theocratic rank.[102] Count Ramon Borell issued a charter with the high-sounding title 'Raimund by the grace of God count and marquis and inspector to the bishops who by God's gift pertain to our rule'.[103] As a rule they controlled appointments to bishoprics.[104] Count Bernard Taillefer of Besalù made a journey with his son to Rome in order to procure from Pope Benedict VIII a bishop of his own for his territory.[105] Hence the term territorial bishopric which has been used of the Spanish principalities, though the term 'territorial church' has preserved its inverted commas when used of them. It was even possible for princes to concern themselves with metropolitan provinces which transcended these territories. Margrave Borell I of Barcelona tried to get Pope John XIII to restore the province of Tarragona.[106] French archbishops also intervened in Spain. Archbishop Wifred of Narbonne, who had bought his own church for a high price, spent much money on buying the bishoprics of Urgel, Gerona, and Elna for his brothers.[107]

Burgundy

Of the two Burgundian kingdoms, only the Welf kingdom of Upper Burgundy survived, greatly enlarged, following the death of Louis the Blind of Provence and Hugo of Arles's renunciation of his claims to Provence in 933. Both in the manner of their foundation and in the form of their government they resembled the theocratic style current in the other Carolingian successor-kingdoms.[108] The election of Boso in Manteille in 879, at a synod attended also by laymen, was carried out in liturgical forms, and with divine inspiration (*nutu Dei*).[109] There is no doubt

---

101 Werner, 'Untersuchungen', 269.
102 Menéndez Pidal, *Spanien des Cid*, 52; D. Gudiol, *La Iglesia en Aragon durante el siglo XI* (Publicaciones de la seccion de Zaragoza 4, Sarragossa 1951), 17ff.
103 'Raimundus gratia Dei comes et marchisus et inspector episcopis dante Deo nostre ditione pertinentibus': Mundó, 'Moissac', 555.
104 Kehr, *Navarra und Aragon*, 10.
105 Vincke, *Staat und Kirche*, 254ff.; Kehr, *Katalanischer Prinzipat*, 19.
106 Vincke, *Staat und Kirche*, 257, 346ff.
107 Mundó, 'Moissac', 560; Vincke, *Staat und Kirche*, 254ff.
108 MGH Capit. II.305ff., no. 284; Poupardin, *Provence*, 97; Böhm, 'Rechtsformen', 11ff.
109 MGH Capit II.376, no. 289; cf. Poupardin, *Provence*, 156 n. 4.

that he was subsequently crowned and anointed; his son Louis was elected
crowned and anointed in a similar fashion at Valence in 890.[110] A
Burgundian order for the crowning of a king, known only from a much
later manuscript, has been convincingly dated to the end of the ninth
century and connected with the events of Manteille.[111]

We have only sparse information about the elevation of the first king
of Burgundy, Rudolf I, but it is said that he had himself crowned in Saint-
Maurice-d'Agaune.[112] We know nothing about Rudolf II's accession, but
Rudolf III says in a charter that he was elected and crowned in the
cathedral of Lausanne, as his father Conrad had been.[113] The emperor
Conrad II was elected and crowned in Payerne in 1033. In 1038 he
conferred the rule of the kingdom on his son Henry III in Solothurn.
Here there is no reference to election or coronation, but there was at least
a divine service held in the church of St Stephen, 'which is held to be the
royal chapel at Solothurn'.[114]

Although the Burgundian kingdom had from the start an unambiguous
religious and political basis, it never developed into a closed homogenous,
or even clearly defined sphere of rule. It has rightly been described as
remarkable that the kingship remained 'acknowledged without question'
in the great fiefs 'and was able to make its presence felt fitfully, not least
because of the loyalty of the archbishops of Lyon and Vienne'.[115] By
contrast, it has been said of the Salian period that the region from Lyons
down to the Mediterranean scarcely preserved any memory of once
having been part of a kingdom.[116] As in France, the kings had a crown
domain, though on a much smaller scale, around Lake Geneva and the
edges of the Alps, besides regions where they could occasionally exercise
influence and regions which ignored them completely.

Of the seven church provinces of the kingdom there was royal
influence of a more or less continual kind only in that of Besançon with
its suffragans of Lausanne and Basle. All the suffragans of the archbishop
of Lyons lay outside the borders of the kingdom.[117] It is significant that
the archbishop of Tarantaise was present at the election of Boso, but that
his suffragans of Sion and Aosta were not, just as the archbishop and

[110] MGH Capit. II.376 no. 289; cf. Poupardin, *Provence*, 156 n. 4.
[111] Eichmann, 'Königskrönungsformel', 516; Böhm, 'Rechtsformen', 27.
[112] Poupardin, *Bourgogne*, 11, n. 3.
[113] *Ibid.*, 66 n. 2.
[114] 'quae pro capella regis Soloduri habetur': Bresslau, *Jahrbücher Konrads II.*, II.70, 324; Steindorff, *Jahrbücher Heinrichs III.*, I.43f.; Jacob, *Bourgogne*, 33.
[115] MGH Dipl. Burgund. no. 4.
[116] Büttner, 'Friedrich Barbarossa', 81.
[117] Poupardin, *Bourgogne*, 311ff., 301 n. 2 and 4, and 376.

bishops of the province of Embrun were also absent.[118] Only for a few bishoprics did the king invariably influence appointments, and as in France one must distinguish between royal and seigneurial bishoprics. As in France the bishops were generally members of the leading families. In Burgundy there were some large synods with participants from several provinces, and in the course of the Peace of God movement there were several synods at which bishops from both Burgundy and France took part.[119] The king by the grace of God played little part in this, and the fact that he could not bring the churches of his large and sprawling kingdom together was the consequence of the limitations of his religious, political, and financial power.

Italy

The Italian peninsula not only had a still more fragmented structure of authority than France or Burgundy, but also one whose fragmentation was extremely unstable. More than any other land of the period it lay open to intervention by foreign powers: the Aghlabites and Fatimids in north Africa and Sicily; the Burgundian princes; German dukes and kings; Magyar invaders; Norman conquerors and late-comers. Kings, popes, and Lombard princes as well as lesser potentates always had to reckon with Byzantium as well, which had a foothold on the peninsula until the fall of Bari in 1071 and always offered asylum to Italian emigrants.[120] Its influence fluctuated unpredictably in many parts of Italy. The land itself lacked strong and permanent political centres which could provide some continuity of orientation. There were some significant personalities among the popes of the period, who commanded respect from those near at hand and enjoyed a high reputation abroad, but even these could be eliminated from the game overnight by trivial shifts in the regional balance of power. The *regnum Italiae* with its ancient capital at Pavia should have provided a core of stability; but, as Liudprand of Cremona wrote, the Italians, like their predecessors in the former Lombard kingdom, always preferred to have two rulers so that they could restrain the one by fear of the other.[121] Berengar I had to face five antikings in the course of seventeen of the twenty-six years of his rule: Arnulf, Wido, Lambert, Louis III, and Rudolf II of Burgundy. Their power was often

---

[118] Poupardin, *Provence*, 109f.

[119] Poupardin, *Bourgogne*, 301ff.

[120] Gay, *L'Italia méridionale*, especially 437ff. (Pandolf von Capua), 469ff. (Argyros); Mor, *L'età feudale*, I, especially 238ff. and 545ff.

[121] *Antapodosis*, I.37, ed. J. Becker (MGH SRG, Hanover 1915), 27.

greater than his. The Burgundian claimant continued to be a threat for the first six years of the reign of Hugo of Arles and his son Lothar, a period also marked by the intervention of Duke Arnulf of Bavaria in 934–5.[122] Of the twenty-two years from Otto I's first intervention in Italy until his death, only the last four were free from rivals: Berengar II of Ivrea and his son Adalbert could not be wholly neutralised for the other eighteen, and they remained a threat which could not be overlooked, especially in view of their contacts with Byzantium. Arduin was able to maintain his position as antiking for twelve of the twenty-two years of Henry II's reign.[123] The three Ottos spent rather more than sixteen years out of fifty-one in Italy, nearly a third of their reigns; Henry II and the first two Salian rulers spent only six years out of fifty-four, a ninth in other words, beyond the Alps. If one considers the fact that the *praesentia regis*, or at least the need to reckon with it, was the basis of rulership in this period, the significance of these figures becomes apparent.[124] There were only rudimentary institutions through which the absent king could carry out government, and the parties or personalities on whom he depended often turned out to be unreliable. Rapid changes of front and betrayal were the normal order of things; loyal margraves and counts were the exception, loyal bishops and abbots hardly the rule.

The royal dignity was based, in Italy as elsewhere, on the theocratic notion of kingship as office. The king was a consecrated figure imbued with divine grace and as such had a firm place in the spiritual and worldly order of things. Of the tenth-century kings it was probably only those who had not previously been consecrated elsewhere who were crowned and anointed: Berengar I, Wido and Lambert, Hugo and Lothar, Berengar II of Ivrea, and Adalbert.[125] Later both Henry II and Conrad II were crowned in Pavia and Milan, presumably as a counter-weight to the coronation of the antiking Arduin,[126] while it is recorded of both Otto III and Henry III that a gesture was made to the Italians by letting Italian bishops assist at their coronations as king in

---

[122] Hartmann, *Geschichte Italiens*, III/2, 198; Mor, *L'età feudale*, I.139f.

[123] *Ibid.*, 525, 549. His support was limited, however; only Bishop Petrus of Como, Otto III's archchancellor for Italy, had defected to him. See Fleckenstein, *Hofkapelle*, II.160.

[124] Tellenbach, 'Kaiser, Rom', 231–53, especially the tables on 250f.

[125] A. Kroener, *Wahl und Krönung der deutschen Kaiser und Könige in Italien (Lombardei)* (Diss. Freiburg 1901); K. Haase, *Die Königskrönungen in Oberitalien und die 'eiserne' Krone* (Diss. Strasbourg 1901); E. Eichmann, 'Zur Geschichte des lombardischen Krönungsritus', *HJb*, 46 (1926), 517–31.

[126] Hirsch, Pabst, and Bresslau, *Jahrbücher Heinrichs II.*, I.306; Bresslau, *Jahrbücher Konrads II.*, II.122; A. Kroener, *Wahl und Krönung*, 46ff.; K. Haase, *Königskrönungen*, 30.

Germany.[127] Royal government took similar forms to those found in other kingdoms. The kings played a certain role in the appointment of bishops. The Ottonians and Salians frequently appointed Germans to bishoprics, though one should not exaggerate the importance of this for the consolidation of their rule: the proportion of non-Italian bishops has been estimated at a quarter for the reign of Henry III and at a sixth for the reigns of his two predecessors.[128]

It can hardly be maintained that the kings succeeded in turning Italy, even that part which they ruled directly, into an ecclesiastical unity, an 'Italian church'. There were frequent conflicts and disputes over rank between the provinces, and conflicts or at least tensions between kings and bishoprics. The synods held by both pope and emperor had the largest attendance from Italian archbishoprics and bishoprics. Such assemblies, which were rare, were notable events for the Italian church, though the attendance at them by German or Burgundian bishops was poor. We have lists of participants for a few of the synods. A synod at Ravenna in April 967 was attended by Pope John XIII, Emperor Otto I, the patriarch of Aquileia, the archbishops of Ravenna and Milan, the bishops of Minden and Speyer, and by no fewer than fifty-one Italian bishops.[129] For the synod held in St Peter's on 6 November 963, at which John XII was deposed in Otto I's presence, Liudprand of Cremona names as participants, besides the archbishops of Milan and Ravenna, two from Saxony, one from Francia, three from *Italia*, eight from Tuscany, twenty-five *a Romanis*, as well as fifty high ecclesiastics from the city of Rome itself.[130] Here we presumably have a synod of the Roman diocese and church province, with a few additions from the rest of Italy and from Germany, just as elsewhere 'foreigners' might also take part in provincial synods. When John XII returned a few months later and held a synod at the same place in February 964, which condemned the previous synod as uncanonical, the Roman church province was represented by essentially the same names, while the external participants were of course absent.[131] The first two Salian rulers held well-attended synods which had more participants from Germany and Burgundy than those of the tenth

---

[127] Uhlirz, *Jahrbücher Ottos II.*, 197; Uhlirz, *Jahrbücher Ottos III.*, 9; Steindorff, *Jahrbücher Heinrichs III.*, 1.15, writes of a large imperial assembly at which Rome and Italy were also represented.

[128] Schwarz, *Besetzung*, 5.

[129] BZ no. 415f. and 420; Manaresi, *Placiti*, 50ff. no. 155.

[130] BZ no. 31; Liudprand of Cremona, *Historia Ottonis*, c. 9, ed. J. Becker (MGH SRG, Hanover 1915), 164ff.

[131] BZ no. 347; MGH Const. 1.352 no. 380.

century.[132] The great church feasts were often the occasion for conflicts between the metropolitans of northern Italy, as at Conrad II's coronation in 1027 and at the first major synod held by Clement II in 1047.[133] Even when pope and emperor acted together they might meet with episcopal resistance, as in the case of Bishop Alderich of Asti, nominated by Henry II in 1014 and consecrated by Pope John XVIII; Archbishop Arnulf II of Milan forced him by a military expedition to submit to Milan.[134] Conrad II failed throughout his reign to subordinate Archbishop Aribert of Milan, who was accused of conspiring with Count Odo of Champagne.[135] The popes, though recognised in principle as head of the church, were unable to establish any effective supremacy over the Italian church provinces other than Rome, and so it is impossible to talk of a unity of the Italian churches, of an Italian territorial church.

The east Frankish/German kingdom

After the death of Louis the Child and the failure of Conrad I's attempt to win back Lotharingia, the unity of the churches of the eastern kingdom was severely disturbed; even its church provinces were affected in their ability to act as fixed units which determined the ecclesiastical life of the country. In 895 the council of Tribur had been able to assemble the majority of the kingdom's bishops for the last time: the archbishops of Mainz, Cologne, Trier with all its suffragans except Toul, the Salzburg suffragans Freising and Regensburg, the Besançon suffragan Basle, as well as the bishop of Bremen, whose status as a suffragan of Cologne was still a matter of dispute.[136] But from 911 on Cologne, together with its suffragans on the left bank of the Rhine, Liège and Utrecht, belonged to

---

[132] Whether Henry III was present at Clement II's first synod in early 1047 is uncertain, but at all events a throne stood prepared for him at the pope's right hand (Steindorff, *Jahrbücher Heinrichs III.*, 1.319). We do know who took part in a synod which met on the king's instructions at Pavia on 25 October 1046 (see MGH Const. 1.24 no. 48): twenty-nine Italian, two Burgundian, and eight German archbishops and bishops (Steindorff, *Jahrbücher Heinrichs III.*, 1.307f.).

[133] Bresslau, *Jahrbücher Konrads II.*, 1.149: between the archbishops of Ravenna and Milan; Steindorff, *Jahrbücher Heinrichs III.*, 1.120: between the same two and the patriarch of Aquileia as well.

[134] BZ no. 1031; Arnulf of Milan, *Gesta archiepiscoporum Mediolanensium* 1.18, MGH SS VIII.11.

[135] Bresslau, *Jahrbücher Konrads II.*, 11.232f. and 236f.; after Aribert, who had been entrusted to Patriarch Poppo of Aquileia, had been able to escape, there was also a conflict with Poppo.

[136] MGH Capit. 11.196ff. no. 252, especially the list on pp. 210f. and the subscription-list on p. 246.

Lotharingia, which was west Frankish; the east Frankish border divided it from its Saxon suffragans, Minden, Osnabrück, Münster, and Bremen. It is uncertain which of the bishops of the east Frankish kingdom really took part in the famous and much-discussed council at Hohenaltheim in 916. We know only those who were certainly not present: the Saxon suffragans of Cologne and Mainz, and the bishop of Strasbourg, who was a protégé of Charles the Simple. It is unlikely that the recently blinded bishop of Speyer was present. It is certain that Archbishop Heriger of Mainz was there, and it was probably his doing that Bishop Peter of Orte was there as papal legate. The bishop of Worms was presumably there, since he was entrusted with the task of bringing to justice those who had carried out the attack on the bishop of Speyer.[137] The location suggests that it was expected that Bavarian bishops would attend, but it is quite uncertain who really came.[138]

Of the twenty-two bishops of the east Frankish kingdom in office in 916, twelve are mentioned in Conrad I's diplomata: two of them four times, one thrice, five twice, four once.[139] Ten are not mentioned, including seven Saxon ones. Since Adalward of Verden was in Conrad's entourage in 916, it is possible that he appeared in Hohenaltheim; whether this was with Duke Henry of Saxony's approval or against his will is not known. Nevertheless, at least nine of the twenty-two east Frankish bishops were not at Hohenaltheim, and we do not know whether it was a substantial gathering or not. The texts have rightly been much studied and frequently quoted, but the commonly held thesis of an alliance between Conrad I and the bishops against the dukes who were in the process of consolidating their power does not have much support from the evidence.[140] On the contrary, Conrad's reign was characterised by an extreme lack of cohesion between province and diocese.

At first this did not change under Henry I either. It is an anachronism to interpret Henry's refusal of the unction offered by Archbishop Heriger of Mainz as a reaction to the 'pro-ecclesiastical' policy of his

[137] MGH Const. I.618 no. 433. The absence of the Saxon bishops can be deduced from c. 30 and that of the bishop of Strasbourg from c. 29; on Richwin of Strasbourg see E. Dümmler, *Geschichte des ostfränkischen Reiches*, 2nd edn (Leipzig 1888), III.593.

[138] C. 41; Lintzel, *Hoftage*, 61, thinks it probable that the 'order to hold the synod at Hohenaltheim was issued by Conrad I . . . who did not take part in it'. Here too we can only speculate.

[139] The figures which follow are derived from Hauck, *Kirchengeschichte Deutschlands*, III.981ff., and the diplomata of Conrad I in the MGH edition.

[140] BZ no. 43 and the literature cited there, in particular the studies by M. Hellmann and H. Fuhrmann.

predecessor.[141] Henry felt himself to be a son of the church just as much as any other king or duke, and there is nothing to suggest otherwise. It is hardly plausible to suppose that he had no house or court clerics in his entourage. His relationship with the archbishop of Mainz was untroubled. The fact that he only took over one of Conrad I's notaries says little when one remembers that only two diplomata survive from his first three years, and only nine from the first six. It is part of the tendency he showed more generally in the early years of his reign not to hold a court on a large or regal scale.[142]

Nevertheless, he was surrounded by bishops (including Heriger of Mainz) and counts at the meetings with west Frankish kings in Bonn (921) and Coblenz (922).[143] After he had come to terms with Duke Arnulf of Bavaria the whole of the province of Salzburg continued distant from the king, while the province of Cologne on the other hand was reunited following the acquisition of Lotharingia. The archbishops of Mainz, Trier, and Hamburg together with six Mainz suffragans and two Cologne suffragans appeared at the synod of Erfurt in 932.[144]

In spite of the brilliance of his consecration and coronation in Aachen, Otto I had difficulty in maintaining and consolidating his rule until the mid 950s. The defeat of the rebellion by Duke Arnulf's sons and the installation of Arnulf's brother Berthold led in 938 to the end of the special position of the Bavarian church. The Ottonian and early Salian kings had responsibility for the church and control of church appointments throughout their kingdom, which is not true of the rulers discussed earlier.[145] Nevertheless, bishops as well as dukes took part in the conflicts

---

[141] The idea that Henry I broke the traditional links between king and 'church' on which Conrad I had relied so much, and that he at first tried to rule without 'the church', was restated by Erdmann, 'Ungesalbter König', forcefully and with new arguments. I raised objections to the argument when the article was still in manuscript; in 1979 after having reflected on the matter for decades I suggested that Henry's rejection of unction could be accounted for by the doubts he had had at first about how far the kingship which had been offered him by some of the bishops and the peoples could be realised; see Tellenbach, 'Thronfolge', 244 n. 22.

[142] Fleckenstein, *Hofkapelle*, II.6 and 12.

[143] MGH Const. I.I, no. 1; 627ff. no. 434.   [144] *Ibid.*, II no. 2; Fischer, *Politiker*, 20ff.

[145] Dümmler, *Jahrbücher Ottos I.*, 79; Reindel, *Liutpoldinger*, 183ff. no. 93; for a time it was assumed that the dukes who succeeded him also participated in episcopal elections, but nothing is known about this for certain, either as a matter of right or as one of custom. See Fleckenstein, *Hofkapelle*, II.113. That Tagino, who was presented by the clergy of Regensburg but rejected by Otto III, was also the candidate of Henry IV of Bavaria, as Fleckenstein supposes, is probably right: Regensburg was a ducal residence and Tagino afterwards became the duke's chaplain. But this does not prove that the duke had preserved a general right of nomination in Bavaria. Nevertheless, magnates probably

which followed – at Breisach in 939 Archbishop Frederick of Mainz himself as well as the bishops Ruthard of Strasbourg and Adalbero of Metz.[146] Although Frederick and Ruthard were released from captivity in the summer of 940 and restored to office,[147] the Mainz metropolitan was suspected of complicity in the rebellion by Otto I's brother in 941 and still more in 951, when he withdrew from the court at Pavia together with Otto's disaffected son Liudolf, with whom he celebrated Christmas at Saalfeld (the ominous place where the rebellion of 939 had begun).[148] Bavarian bishops, including Archbishop Herold of Salzburg, were also suspected of not being wholly reliable in the rebellion by Liudolf and Conrad of Lotharingia.[149] A Bavarian bishop, Abraham of Freising, together with Henry of Augsburg, sided with Duke Henry the Quarrelsome of Bavaria against Otto II;[150] and as late as the end of Henry III's reign Bishop Gebhard III of Regensburg, the emperor's half-uncle, led the dangerous Bavarian uprising of 1055 along with the deposed Duke Conrad of Bavaria and Duke Welf III of Carinthia.[151]

Quite apart from such severe crises, which were rare, there were other conflicts between kings and bishops. Mostly it was a matter of episcopal or archiepiscopal rights, particularly in connection with the founding of the archbishopric of Magdeburg, where Otto I met with resistance from his son William of Mainz and Bishop Bernard of Halberstadt. The dispute about episcopal rights over the monastery of Gandersheim

---

exercised an influence on the appointment of bishops fairly frequently, as did the margrave of Meissen for the bishopric of Meissen, for example. See Schlesinger, *Kirchengeschichte Sachsens*, I.89f., and, on the participation by Henry II and Conrad II in episcopal elections, T. Schieffer, 'Heinrich II. und Konrad II.', 395f. and 405f.

[146] Dümmler, *Jahrbücher Ottos I.*, I.88ff.

[147] *Ibid.*, 105; Norden, *Erzbischof Friedrich von Mainz und Otto der Große*; Fischer, *Politiker*, 116ff. The variation in the judgements of current scholarship on Frederick's behaviour can be found already in the writings of contemporaries. The continuator of Regino, who was not ill-disposed towards Frederick, says 'sicubi vel unus regis inimicus ermersit, ipse se statim secundum apposuit', *Reginonis abbatis Prumiensis Chronicon cum continuatione Treverensi*, ed. F. Kurze (MGH SRG, Hanover 1890), 168, *s.a.* 954. Ruotger closes an intensive discussion of contemporary opinions, *Vita Brunonis*, c. 20, ed. I. Ott (MGH SRG NS, Berlin 1951), 15, with the words: 'Nos interim haec Dei iuditio relinquimus.'

[148] Dümmler, *Jahrbücher Ottos I.*, 116, 215ff. It is noteworthy that Frederick was taken back into royal favour on both occasions, on the first by taking the Eucharist as a proof of the purity of his intention, and on the second by offering to take the same test.

[149] *Ibid.*, 229, 248.

[150] Uhlirz, *Jahrbücher Ottos II.*, 53ff.; on the treasonable activities of the archbishops Aribert of Milan and Burchard III of Lyons see below, p. 56. Bishops Dietrich of Verdun and Wazo of Liège aroused Henry III's displeasure by being too conciliatory towards Duke Godfrey of Lotharingia. See Steindorff, *Jahrbücher Heinrichs III.*, II.21ff.

[151] *Ibid.*, 318f.

between Archbishop Willigis of Mainz and Bishop Bernward of Hildesheim led to a severe disturbance of the relations between the archbishop and Otto III.[152] The union of the bishopric of Merseburg with the archbishopric of Magdeburg as a result of the translation of Bishop Gisilher from Merseburg to Magdeburg long weighed on the life of the church. Gisilher could only just keep his head above water during the reigns of Otto III and Henry II, right up to his death; and immediately afterwards Merseburg was restored.[153] The foundation of Bamberg also created friction, for Bishop Henry of Würzburg, the distinguished brother of Archbishop Pilgrim of Cologne from the Bavarian family of the Aribonids, was unwilling to accept a diminution of his diocese, and the promised elevation of his bishopric to an archbishopric could not be carried out.[154] The king was able to frighten the less-well-born Bishop Gundechar of Eichstätt, whose diocese was also affected by the new foundation, into compliance.[155]

The behaviour of the episcopate was not uniform, especially in the cases of disputed succession to the throne. On the news of Otto II's death Bishop Folkmar of Utrecht is said to have released Henry the Quarrelsome, whose gaoler he had been. Archbishop Warin of Cologne handed over the newly crowned boy Otto III to Henry; the archbishops of Trier and Magdeburg as well as several bishops, especially those from Bavaria, gave their support to him. It was above all the careful but energetic opposition by Willigis of Mainz and Duke Bernard of Saxony which decided the course of events in favour of the empresses and Otto III.[156] The rivals for the throne in 1002 and 1024 also had supporters among the bishops. This was not opposition to the king based on principle or political calculation, but merely support for one or other of the claimants.

[152] BZ no. 249; Giesebrecht, *Kaiserzeit*, III.888; Jaffé, *BRG* III.347; Dümmler, *Jahrbücher Ottos I.*, especially 273 n. 2; Büttner, 'Mainzer Erzbischöfe', 16ff. On the Gandersheim dispute BZ nos. 929, 945, 957, Uhlirz, *Jahrbücher Ottos III.*, 346ff. and 382ff.; Hirsch, Pabst, and Bresslau, *Jahrbücher Heinrichs II.*, I.185, II.1ff., 66 and the epilogue between Aribo and Godehard, III.254. On the archiepiscopal synod in Gandersheim and the over-turning of its decisions see below, pp. 59–60.

[153] BZ no. 598ff., 616, 786, 846, 862; Uhlirz, *Jahrbücher Ottos II.*, 158ff., Uhlirz, *Jahrbücher Ottos III.*, 234 and 284ff.; Hirsch, Pabst, and Bresslau, *Jahrbücher Heinrichs II.*, I.274.

[154] BZ no. 1022 and 1023; MGH Const. I.59 no. 29; Hirsch, Pabst, and Bresslau, *Jahrbücher Heinrichs II.*, II.59ff.; H. Zimmermann, 'Gründung und Bedeutung des Bistums Bamberg', *Südostdeutsches Archiv*, 10 (1967), 35–49.

[155] Hirsch, Pabst, and Bresslau, *Jahrbücher Heinrichs II.*, II.84f., following *Anonymus Haserensis* c. 25, MGH SS VII.260: 'cave ne unquam tale quid audiam ex te, si vel episcopatum vel gratiam meam velis retinere'. See T. Schieffer, 'Heinrich II. und Konrad II.', 406.

[156] Uhlirz, *Jahrbücher Ottos III.*, 12ff.

Personal or ecclesiastical motives may have played a part, but it is more likely that the behaviour of the bishops was governed simply by the calculation that support for the successful candidate would be rewarded. For our purposes it is instructive to note that the bishops' decisions did not fall unanimously along the lines of church provinces; neither the personal authority nor the office of the metropolitan was sufficient to secure this.

It would hardly lead to more generalised insights if we were to list further disturbances in the relationships between king and bishops, especially since we often know nothing or at least too little about the nature and origins of such disturbances. We know, for example, that Henry II's brother Bruno, a canon at Hildesheim, took part in 1003 in the uprising of Margrave Henry of Schweinfurt and fled to Bohemia and Hungary after the rebellion failed. Henry II and Bruno were reconciled in early 1004 and after Bruno had been chancellor for a year he was elected bishop of Augsburg. Nevertheless we hear of his being exiled again in 1024, before becoming one of Conrad II's most influential episcopal advisers.[157] Still stranger is the account by Thietmar of Merseburg of Adalbert of Magdeburg's incurring Otto I's deep displeasure by receiving Duke Hermann Billung with royal honours in his city and leading the duke to the cathedral by the hand while all the bells of the city were being rung. According to Thietmar, Otto as a punishment forced Adalbert to present him with as many horses as he had bells rung and candlesticks lit for the duke.[158]

In general it is not the comparatively rare conflicts but a cooperation which frequently reached the level of personal friendship which is rightly thought of as having been characteristic of relations between king and bishop in the Ottonian and early Salian period. The alliance between king and the bishops was not, as was long taught, directed against the 'lay' nobility. Occasionally dukes and bishops united against the king, as in the first third of Otto I's reign. Much more frequently they were united in their will to support the king; for the lay nobles, founders of churches and monasteries, were just as much governed by Christian ideals as kings and bishops, in spite of revelations of weakness which were human and indeed all too human. We have also seen that kings were generally ready to compromise and were willing to forgive bishops even open infidelity. It was the exception in Germany when Duke Henry I of Bavaria had

---

[157] Hirsch, Pabst, and Bresslau, *Jahrbücher Heinrichs II.*, I.263; III.289; Bresslau, *Jahrbücher Konrads II.*, I.25 and 118.

[158] Thietmar, *Chronicon* II 28, 74f. See now G. Althoff, 'Das Bett des Königs in Magdeburg', *Festschrift für Berent Schwineköper*, ed. H. Maurer and H. Patze (Sigmaringen 1982), 141ff.

Archbishop Herold of Salzburg blinded (probably without Otto I's knowledge or consent); and it was equally unusual that Conrad II should have died without being reconciled with Archbishop Aribert of Milan and his three fellow-conspirators, the suffragan bishops of Piacenza, Cremona, and Vercelli, or with Archbishop Burchard of Lyons, who was also accused of high treason.[159] Otto I and Henry II showed themselves surprisingly patient and respectful of their opponents in the course of the conflicts to which the foundation of Magdeburg and Bamberg led. It must have been an impressive spectacle when Henry II fell at the feet of the bishops at the synod of Frankfurt in 1007 to beg for their consent to the foundation of the bishopric of Bamberg; even after this he showed patience and a remarkable willingness to make concessions in order to reconcile Henry of Würzburg to the new foundations. Phrases like 'the church under the rule of the state' or 'in the power of laymen' are anachronistic, influenced by the events of the age which followed, in which the 'church' was said to have been freed from 'secular' domination. The bishops had a good deal of freedom, and the rulers could scarcely be said to have imposed a heavy yoke on them.

The term 'imperial church system' has been used for the tenth and eleventh centuries;[160] but what was the 'imperial church' at that time?[161]

---

[159] Bresslau, *Jahrbücher Konrads II.*, II.232ff., 265ff., 421 and n. 2; Steindorff, *Jahrbücher Heinrichs III.*, I.46, 84f., 134; T. Schieffer, 'Heinrich II. und Konrad II.', 405.

[160] Santifaller, *Ottonisch-salisches Reichskirchensystem*. His definition on p. 10 makes use of the concepts 'church' and 'constitution' in a manner which appears rather problematic. The 'strange relationship between religion, church and state' seems to us to have been unsystematic in many ways; see also Kehr, *Vier Kapitel*, 24: 'not a closed organisation'. See the recent clarification by Reuter, '"Imperial Church System"', 347–74.

[161] This term is now established and can probably not be eliminated; but it should at least be noted that its use is not without problems. J. Haller, *Das Papsttum: Idee und Wirklichkeit* (5 vols., 2nd edn, Stuttgart 1950–3) II/2, 498 (n. to II/1. 261ff.) is one of the few who reject it completely: 'That a "System" or an organisation of the German imperial church existed at all would first have to be proved; I can find no trace of such a thing.' The judgement of Schlesinger, *Kirchengeschichte Sachsens*, I.247, is noteworthy: 'It is better not to speak of an imperial church to which the bishoprics belonged. An organisation of this kind, forming a closed group, a part of the universal church while at the same time independent and possessing its own identity, corresponding territorially to the German kingdom, did not exist.' Nitschke, 'Ziele Heinrichs IV.', 52 and n. 75 also expresses doubts about an 'imperial church system'. Fleckenstein, *Hofkapelle*, II.120 and n. 8 is conscious of the problem, and seeks to use the term 'imperial church' as a juristic one, citing in support the formulation used in the Concordat of Worms, which refers to the bishoprics and imperial monasteries. He continues his discussion in 'Zum Begriff', 61–71, where he acutely distinguishes (69f.) between a narrower and a broader sense of the concept; see also his formulation in 'Hofkapelle und Reichsepiskopat', 119 n. 8. Köhler, *Bild des geistlichen Fürsten*, 21, describes the kingdom of the Ottonian period as being

The churches which were taken into the service of the kingdom and in return endowed with land and 'public' governmental rights which in the last resort remained the property of the 'kingdom'? It was not the 'church' which was endowed but a number of churches. This was done in the only way possible in the economic and social system prevailing at the time: by using feudal forms for the transfer of rights and property. The churches worked by prayer and divine services for the well-being of the king, his army, and all Christians; in effect they did the same when they gave hospitality to the royal court, when they supplied the king with money or food, when they helped to maintain the peace at home and abroad in person or by sending their feudal contingents, when ecclesiastics advised the king and his representatives or acted as diplomats. It was their relationship to the king by the grace of God, to the king who held an office divinely conferred on him, which made the churches into an 'imperial church'; and this was possible because the kingdom was a kingdom of the church, and had in the last resort and in principle the same function as they did.

Church provinces were supposed to unite a number of suffragan bishoprics into larger and higher units, something which can be said to have happened only to a limited extent. But all the bishoprics of the kingdom were united by their links with the sacral person of the king, anointed as he was with holy oil, neither layman nor cleric but *mediator cleri et plebis*, and this more effectively than the ties of the provinces.[162] The king was assigned to the bishops and the bishops to the king. He could celebrate divine service in the court chapel, but equally well in any other church, and he did it with his court ecclesiastics; in the eleventh century this was often done in cathedrals, at least for the high feast of the church. The royal chapel concentrated the life of the church within the kingdom; it was not a counterpart to the 'imperial church' but together with the

'essentially congruent with the spiritual kingdom'. See also Köhler, 'Ottonische Reichskirche', 141–204.

162 On the royal canonries see the early and much-admired article by A. Schulte, 'Deutsche Könige, Kaiser, Päpste als Kanoniker an deutschen und römischen Kirchen', *HJb*, 54 (1934), 137–77. Fleckenstein, 'Rex canonicus', 57–71 and *Hofkapelle*, II.231ff., took up the discussion again. Groten, 'Von der Gebetsverbrüderung', 1–34, rejects previous views and shows that royal canonries do not go back to Henry II (Schulte) or even Otto III (Fleckenstein) but only as far as Conrad III. Neither participation in a prayer-confraternity nor in a chapter was exclusively royal, nor were such things signs of royal sacrality, which was based on quite different premisses. But see the objections to Groten raised by H. Fuhrmann, 'Rex canonicus – Rex clericus?' and by H. Boockmann, 'Eine Urkunde für den Damenstift Obermünster nin Regensburg', both in *Festschrift für Josef Fleckenstein* (Sigmaringen 1984), 321 n. 1 and 211ff. respectively.

king helped to make the churches of the empire something which we may
call, with reservations, the 'imperial church'.

It was not a closed or omnipresent organisation. Nor did it release the
individual churches from their ties with the universal church, which
transcended all partial unities and was the only true spiritual unity of the
church. What held it together was the right of the king to take part in the
appointment of bishoprics, though here there were variations across time
and between rulers. In Germany such participation was a royal monopoly
after the special rights of the Bavarian duke were ended by the death of
Duke Arnulf and the rebellion of his sons.[163] Other princes exercised
influence here and there, but it was the king who decided. He could take
account of the candidate elected or requested by the cathedral chapter but
he did not have to do so. He could accept a member of the cathedral
chapter proposed to him or pass him over in favour of another cleric. The
importance of the royal chapel for recruitment to the episcopate can
scarcely be overestimated; its history has been traced in an important study
by Josef Fleckenstein for the period up to the death of Henry III. The
capellani grew from modest beginnings to become the most significant
group of clerics in the king's entourage; they were mostly drawn from
the high nobility, and such exceptions to this rule as there were were
usually explicitly noted. They were chosen by the king and by his
relations and intimate counsellors on the basis of birth but also of talent
and education.

Whereas the *capellani* of the Carolingian period were continuously at
court and were maintained by it, it became customary in the Ottonian
period for them to become or remain members of cathedral chapters or
collegiate churches.[164] This did not affect all such churches evenly;
capellani are found in about a dozen, notably Aachen, Mainz, Hildesheim,
and Magdeburg.[165] It was the positions they had in these churches which
provided them with their income, and they lived partly at court and partly
in residence in the churches, when they were not travelling on other
duties. In the course of the eleventh century the circle of churches was
greatly extended. The regions at first favoured were joined by others, so
that by the time of Henry III's reign there was a reasonably even
distribution across the Reich.[166] The *capellani*-canons were an important
link between the king and the high clergy in the individual churches,
between the court and the churches of the duchies. It was thus not just
through the unity of faith and liturgy but also politically that the churches
fostered the unity of the kingdom. The fact that the king had the decisive

[163] See above, p. 52 n. 145.   [164] Fleckenstein, *Hofkapelle*, II.118ff.
[165] *Ibid.*, 132ff.   [166] *Ibid.*, 278f.

word in the appointment to bishoprics meant that the episcopate acquired a supra-ethnic and supraregional character. He had at his disposal as a nursery the royal chapel, which itself was supraregional in its personnel; besides this, it was customary for the great noble families, including that of the king, to dedicate sons to a clerical career, either as members of the royal chapel or as dignitaries of cathedral chapters or collegiate churches, with good chances in either case of a bishopric.

The royal assemblies were always attended by high ecclesiastics; the synods and councils were usually attended by lay members of the high nobility. At those assemblies at which the king was present he had the last word, and the sources occasionally speak of his having presided over a synod.[167] It is noticeable, however, that such an expression normally seems to have been avoided. By contrast it is frequently said that he took counsel with archbishops, bishops, abbots, and prominent laymen, that decisions were taken in his presence, or that he had issued edicts in the presence of bishops and with their consent.[168] The king's presence gave added weight to a synod or council. The names of the participants enable us to assess the importance of such an assembly. The king will scarcely have taken part in a mere diocesan synod, but where important matters were at stake the bishop normally called on his colleagues in neighbouring dioceses to give their opinion. Provincial synods, as in other countries, were not confined to the bishops of the province concerned. So-called 'national' or 'regnal' synods never included the entire episcopate of the kingdom, and did not exclude Burgundian or Italian bishops. Where the king was present it was his will and his authority which were decisive, often even in those cases, which will be discussed shortly, where the pope or a papal legate presided. A good example is the synod of St Sebastiano in Pallara at Rome, held on 13 January 1001. This can definitely be termed a Roman provincial synod, if the expression is permissible, in which twenty bishops from the country around Rome took part, together with a few from *Italia* and *Tuscia* and three from Germany.[169] The synod dealt with the complaint of Bishop Bernward of Hildesheim about the claims of Archbishop Willigis over the monastery of Gandersheim, which the metropolitan had recently defended at a turbulent provincial synod at

---

[167] See for example the Frankfurt synod of September 1027. The *notitia* made of the synod by Godehard of Hildesheim (MGH Const. 1.86 no. 40) says 'in generali Franca-navordensi concilio, presidente imperatore Conrado cum episcopis XXII et abbatibus octo cum numerosa cleri plebisque frequencia'.

[168] The phrase used both in *regesta* and in the literature: 'under the presidency of King N.', is frequently wrong. It is advisable to check; often it turns out that the king had, at least formally, observed the independence of the council.

[169] BZ no. 929. *Thangmari vita Bernwardi episcopi* c. 22, MGH SS IV.768f.

Gandersheim itself.[170] The question posed by Pope Silvester II, how such an assembly should be termed, was answered by the participants at the Roman synod, after they had withdrawn for consultations, with the term *scisma consilians discordiam* (a schism counselling discord). This was one of the few significant cases where a council explicitly disavowed another council. The Saxon priest Frederick, later to become archbishop of Ravenna, was to travel to Germany and hold a synod at Pöhlde in June 1001. At this synod there were turbulent discussions, probably accompanied by violence, as a consequence of which the legate suspended the archbishop.[171] This was hardly a conflict between pope and 'German church', however, rather one between the young emperor and the most distinguished German archbishop, whom Otto III had thrown over in favour of his friendship with Bernward of Hildesheim, although he owed him so much. The main source stressed that Silvester II presided at the synod (*praesidente domino Gerberto apostolico cum imperatore*), but where the king or emperor was present it was his will that determined events, even if the proprieties were formally observed. Besides this the pope himself was a friend of Otto III, to whom he owed so much that he was concerned to fulfil Otto's wishes as far as possible, particularly as in this case the rights of the papacy were not affected one way or the other. It was not until 1007 that Henry II could persuade Archbishop Willigis to be reconciled with Bernward, and the pope played no part in this.

England

It has been observed that conditions in England in the tenth and eleventh centuries are more properly compared with those in Germany than with those in France or Italy.[172] That is not to say that England did not have its own peculiarities. England was a much smaller kingdom, which was only unified in the course of the tenth century. The distances from royal court to the regions and bishoprics were trivially small compared with those found in the Reich. England had only two church provinces, and Canterbury was so much more important than York that it is possible to talk of a unification of the *ecclesia Anglicana* of a king which in Germany was only provided and maintained by the king's position over the six church provinces.

---

[170] See above, n. 152.
[171] Uhlirz, *Jahrbücher Ottos III.*, 379.
[172] Barlow, *English Church 1000–1066*, 98f.; Loyn, *Structures*, 88 and 92; Moorman, *Church in England*, 47ff.; for parallels between the imperial church and the state church which the Normans transferred to England see Cantor, *Church, Kingship*, 27f.

The unification of England was the work of the kings of Wessex. Alfred the Great had managed to preserve a core area of Anglo-Saxon England. His son Edward the Elder (901–24) and his grandson Æthelstan (925–39) were able to win back the lost territories, so that under Æthelstan coins were struck with the inscription *rex totius Angliae*.[173] But already under Æthelstan's sons Edmund (939–46) and Eadred (946–55) there were new uprisings by the Danes in York which were all the more dangerous in that not only lay magnates but also Archbishop Wulfstan I of York submitted to a pagan king; Odo of Canterbury, by contrast, remained a loyal adviser and assistant to the king throughout.[174] Under Eadred Wulfstan was deprived of his office for a time, but he was restored before the king's death.[175] Yet for the early tenth century it is hardly possible to say that the ecclesiastical unity of the Anglo-Saxon kingdom was created above all by the church itself.[176]

In the comparatively peaceful reign of King Edgar (959–75) the various Anglo-Saxon peoples grew closer together and the integration of the Scandinavian immigrants made further progress. One expression of this was the famous scene in which the king was rowed by eight kings on the River Dee as a symbolic acknowledgement of his overkingship.[177] The important pontificates of Dunstan of Canterbury (960–88), Oswald of York (971–92), and Æthelwold of Winchester (963–84) fell largely in his reign.[178] There has been much talk of reform or of reformation in connection with the English church in the tenth century. The notion of reform implied is not usually precisely defined, a point to which we shall return later. Alfred the Great's successors showed both piety and responsibility in their treatment of the churches of their country. Their main energies were devoted to the defence of the realm, but Edward the Elder founded the New Minster in Winchester and Æthelstan the New Minster in Exeter; they saw the prayers of the church as important, and Æthelstan's veneration for relics is well known. Entries in German *libri*

---

[173] Deanesly, *Pre-Conquest Church*, 253ff.; Hunt, *English Church*, 298f.

[174] *Ibid.*, 309f.

[175] Deanesly, *Pre-Conquest Church*, 272ff.

[176] Kempf, *Handbuch*, 257, may be accepted in spite of this, when he argues that the rise of the Anglo-Saxon kingdom could hardly have succeeded without the cooperation of the church. But it does not seem fair to say that the kings took up the reform of religious and ecclesiastical life for this reason alone. Their actions were determined in the first instance by the responsibility held by a Christian ruler, not by political rationality.

[177] Schramm, *Geschichte des englischen Königtums*, 23. The fact that this symbolic service did not become a tradition is probably the result not, as Schramm thinks, of the disintegration of royal overlordship but of its consolidation. See also Oleson, *Witenagemot*, 2.

[178] Deanesly, *Pre-Conquest Church*, 305; Godfrey, *Church*, 298ff.

memoriales, which are connected in part with the conclusion of the marriage alliance between his sister Edith and Otto I, have allowed new insights into the nature of this king's piety.[179] In tenth-century England there were many ruined churches to be rebuilt and new ones to be built; the life of the church needed ordering and raising to a new level. The leading ecclesiastics came largely from famous Benedictine monasteries like Glastonbury and Edington. They often had links with the monastic movements of the continent. By replacing secularised communities of clerics by communities of monks following a strict discipline they renewed the monastic character of English church life, which already had a long tradition and was to have a long future.

On Edgar's death his sons Edward and Æthelred were respectively fifteen and ten years old. After Edward's murder in 979 the kingdom was reunited under Æthelred, still a minor, who ruled from 979 to 1013 and then again briefly until his death in 1016. Dunstan retired to Canterbury; his influence and that of the other monastic ecclesiastics grew smaller. New attacks by Danes and Norwegians seemed to produce a renewal of the old misery; it was the dark hour of the 'Danish vespers', when the Anglo-Saxon king ultimately had to flee to France from the conqueror Svein Forkbeard.[180]

But the Danish rulers, Svein (1013–14), Cnut (1017–35), Harold (1035–40), and Harthacnut (1040–2) regarded themselves as kings of England. They were Christians, and adopted without hesitation the ecclesiastical functions carried out by their predecessors. We know most about the long reign of Cnut, with his church building, his legislation, his influence on the appointment of bishops, his endowment of monasteries, his devout pilgrimages, and his participation in the commemoratory prayers of churches even outside his kingdom.[181]

Cnut had married Emma, the widow of the Æthelred whom he had defeated, a daughter of the duke of Normandy. Her son by her first marriage, Edward, had spent a part of his youth in France. Her son by Cnut, Harthacnut, who had no children of his own, recalled his step-brother to England and it was by his will that Edward succeeded him. Edward the Confessor (1042–66) married Edith, the daughter of the powerful Earl Godwin of Wessex and sister of the Harold who was to lose

---

[179] These entries have long been the subject of scholarly enquiry. See K. Beyerle, 'Die Gebetsverbrüderung der Reichenau', in *Die Kultur der Abtei Reichenau* (Munich 1925), I.291ff. and above all K. Schmid, 'Neue Quellen', 191ff. and 'Thronfolge', 110 and 116. Clark's explanation, that Bishop Coenwald's legation was concerned above all with political aims, was refuted by Schmid, 'Neue Quellen', 199.

[180] Deanesly, *Sidelights*, 281; Godfrey, *Church*, 308.

[181] Hunt, *English Church*, 339.

his kingdom and his life at Hastings in 1066.[182] Although there were
tensions between a native and a Norman faction it could be said that in
1066 England possessed more organic unity than in 1042.[183]

It is not recorded that the Danish rulers of England were either
anointed or crowned.[184] Since unction had been the norm for the Anglo-
Saxon rulers of the tenth century, however, and since in Dunstan's time
special *ordines* had been drawn up for the ceremonial of royal accession, it
is probable that here also the Danish rulers followed the traditions of
the house of Cerdic.[185] The English royal consecration and coronation
followed Frankish and east Frankish models. As in these, the English king
is a *mediator cleri et plebis*, which gave him his special character and dignity;
he is not a mere layman like all the other unconsecrated.[186] It was this that
gave him his rights over the church, and like the German ruler the English
king had a monopoly of appointments to bishoprics.[187] No one disputed
this with him, though as in Germany there were not infrequent clashes
between the powers on the spot, the cathedral chapter or the local
magnates with their influence (*de facto* if not *de jure*) on the one hand, and
the king and the court on the other. One of the most significant cases of
this kind occurred in 1050 when Canterbury fell vacant. The monks
wanted one of their own number as successor, a relative of Earl Godwin,
who supported the monks. The king and his court, however, supported
Robert of Jumièges and had him translated from London to Canterbury.[188] In England as well as in Germany the king's decisive influence on
episcopal elections helped to consolidate church unity, and here also the
king often selected the bishops from among the court clergy. An English

[182] Barlow, 'Edward the Confessor's Early Life', 225–51; Barlow, *Edward the Confessor*, 65.
[183] *Ibid.*, 287: 'By 1066 the kingdom had more organic unity than it had possessed in 1042.'
[184] Hunt, *English Church*, 391, describes Cnut's consecration by Archbishop Lifing as probable; Barlow, *Edward the Confessor*, 54 n. 2, stresses the silence of important sources on the matter.
[185] P. E. Schramm, 'Die Krönung bei den Westfranken und Angelsachsen von 878 bis um 1000', *ZRGKA*, 23 (1934), 151–82; Schramm, 'Ordines Studien III: Die Krönung in England', *AUF*, 15 (1938), 305–91; *Geschichte des englischen Königtums*, 12ff.
[186] Barlow, *English Church 1000–1066*, 32; 'the office of emperor when revived by the Carolingian and then the Saxon Kings was more an ecclesiastical than a secular institution', and 54: 'To liken the king's coronation to the ordination of a priest and to make of the king a kind of ecclesiastical person was, of course, a commonplace idea'; Moorman, *Church in England*, 47f. On the adoption of the Anglo-Saxon coronation *ordines* and unction, as well as of 'priestly powers and a sacred right' by William the Conqueror see Cantor, *Church, Kingship*, 30.
[187] Hunt, *English Church*, 315; Barlow, *English Church 1000–1066*, 109; Barlow, *Edward the Confessor*, 79; Darlington, 'Ecclesiastical Reform', 415: King Athelstan makes regulations 'with the advice of my archbishop Wulfhelm and my other bishops'.
[188] Hunt, *English Church*, 404ff.; Barlow, *Edward the Confessor*, 104f.

peculiarity was the high proportion of former monks among the episcopate: for the eighteen dioceses, 67 out of 116 bishops in the period between 960 and 1066 are known with certainty to have been monks, and the proportion was probably higher. In the two or three generations before the conquest most of the bishops were monks: nine of the fifteen appointments made by Cnut, for example, though Edward the Confessor showed a preference for court clerics in the first half of his reign.[189]

Ecclesiastical legislation of all kinds was formulated in gatherings of clerics and laymen, which the king summoned and from which he asked for counsel without being bound by it. The mixed composition of the witan was typical of royal assemblies in Europe as a whole, as was the king's presence at synods. It is characteristic that there was a formula for a mass *pro rege dicenda tempore sinodi*. The synod or council with the king present were characteristic expressions of the consciousness of a national church which saw itself as being simultaneously a particular and the universal church.[190]

Northern and Eastern Europe

In the lands of northern and eastern Europe, which were long not reached by missionaries and subject to pagan reactions until well into the eleventh century, the churches were so dependent on the protection of the king or prince that this naturally led to the formation of a kind of national church. There was a monarchic and theocratic strain of thought similar to that found in England and Germany.[191] The king himself was of course a member of the church universal, and it was from this fact that his functions in the church were theoretically derived. Without his assistance no mission could be carried out and no dioceses set up. He was the most important founder of churches and monasteries; he took the important

---

[189] Godfrey, *Church*, 309 and 386; Barlow, *Edward the Confessor*, 59; Cantor, *Church, Kingship*, 32: in 1090 half of the bishops and abbots had been royal chaplains.

[190] Liebermann, *National Assembly*, especially p. 64; Mitteis, *Staat*, 85f.; Barlow, *English Church 1000–1066*, 107 and 137ff.; Oleson, *Witenagemot*, 91ff., where the importance of the witan in various areas of political life is stressed.

[191] Cantor, *Church, Kingship*, 29, considers it possible that there was a historical connection between the 'church-state system' in Normandy, England and the Scandinavian kingdoms. On p. 12 he stresses: 'The Christian Norwegian kings of the eleventh century maintained complete control over the church in their territory.' On Scandinavia see, besides the works of Gerhardt, Andersson, and Seegrün, also Nylander, *Kirchliches Benefizialwesen*, 40 and 45; on Poland see Völker, *Kirchengeschichte Polens*; on Hungary see Hóman, *Ungarisches Mittelalter*.

decisions in the presence of ecclesiastical and secular magnates. His entourage contained clerics who enjoyed his confidence and sooner or later something like a royal chapel grew up. In the selection of bishops his influence was decisive, and they were often taken from the 'royal chapel' or from monasteries particularly favoured by the king.[192]

Although church provinces were established comparatively early in eastern Europe, the solitary Polish metropolitan or the two Hungarian archbishops[193] were more assistants than rivals to their ruler. Provincial councils which might have taken a stand against him were inconceivable. In northern Europe the provinces of Lund, Trondheim, and Uppsala were not created until the twelfth century. The attempts at subordinating the Scandinavian bishoprics to German church provinces were successful only in part and only for a time. Archbishop Adalbert of Bremen's plan for a patriarchate failed in the end. Scandinavian bishops were often consecrated abroad, as in 1022 when Archbishop Ethelnod of Canterbury consecrated the bishops Gerbrand of Roskilde, Bernard of Schonen, and Reginbert of Fünen.[194] Harold Hardrada, king of Norway, is alleged to have said, 'I do not know who is archbishop or ruler in Norway besides me, Harold', commenting on Bremen's claims. But not even this royal 'archbishop' claimed to be able to consecrate bishops; Norwegian bishops were anointed in England or Aquitaine or, later, Rome.[195]

THE POPE: IDEAL AND REALITY[196]

Kings were able to draw in varying degrees on a belief in the sacrality of their dignity and in the ecclesiastical character of their rule to unite the churches of their countries. Yet none was able to unite the national churches in a way which represented the spiritual universality of the church, not even the emperor, the universality of whose rule was in any case more a matter of ideology than of reality. The frequently used terms *regnum* and *sacerdotium* are abstractions, not historical phenomena, which can be perceived acting in reality only at a great distance from their fundamental and universal significance. For this reason talk of a conflict

---

[192] Völker, *Kirchengeschichte Polens*, 22; Kloczowski, 'Province ecclésiastique', 440; Bardach, 'L'Etat Polonais', 292f.; Hóman, *Ungarisches Mittelalter*, 173, 192ff.

[193] See above, p. 35.   [194] Seegrün, *Papsttum*, 58.

[195] Gerhardt, *Norwegische Geschichte*, 81f.

[196] This section is based on Tellenbach, 'Zur Geschichte', with some additions and some compression. In particular I have only summarised the results of the accounts of the various conflicts in which popes were involved, and used footnotes only to identify literal quotations and as an apparatus to the additions.

between *regnum* and *sacerdotium* or of individual instances of such conflicts is bound to be vague, even empty.

In the tenth and early eleventh centuries the religious universality of the church found its primary earthly expression in the belief that the pope was the highest member of Christianity after Christ Himself.[197] Theologically and spiritually the pope was the highest priest, the head of the church. Christians displayed deep reverence for St Peter and his representative. He was the bishop of Rome, which itself was seen as the most reliable guardian of doctrinal truth. In the West as in the East the pope was regarded up until the schism of 1054 as the first of the patriarchs. In the middle ages there was a unanimous and untroubled belief in the dignity of his high office. This was maintained even on those occasions, rare enough before the middle of the eleventh century, where conflicts arose between the pope and others.

In most Christian countries the pope was an exalted figure, almost a figure of legend; in general, little was known about what he was really like, or about what went on in Rome.[198] The Christians in Moslem Sicily are said almost to have forgotten the pope, and those of Moslem Spain had no contact with Rome. The churches of Byzantium and of Rome coexisted, apart from brief periods of friction, in a state of 'mutual lack of interest',[199] even though the Byzantines played an important role in the politics of central Italy, in which the Roman church was of course also involved, a role which at times threatened Rome. But even northern Italy was very distant from Rome, let alone the transalpine countries, the British Isles, Scandinavia, or eastern Europe. How could a government of the church based on Rome have existed?

It is customary in recent historiography to talk of the 'papacy' from a very early date as an instance which ruled the church and in doing so pursued a 'church policy' of its own extending beyond the pontificates of individual popes, controlling and directing the remaining members of the hierarchy, laying down regulations and norms, defining and planning its relations with patriarchs, archbishops, bishops, and abbots as well as with emperors, kings, and princes, and administering its wealth, the territories, and patrimony, in a rational fashion. This is to a large extent an anachronistic projection of a later state of affairs into an earlier period.

---

[197] 'summum post Christum totius christianitatis membrum': Jaffé, *BRG*, III, 347, William of Mainz's letter to Pope Agapetus II of autumn 955. In principle the pope was certainly something else and something more than simply the first among the bishops, long before the middle of the eleventh century; see on this Goez, 'Papa qui et episcopus', 59.

[198] Hoffmann, 'Von Cluny', 170: 'the authority of the pope within Christendom north of the Alps had virtually vanished'.

[199] Beck, *Orthodoxe Kirche*, 127.

Anachronistic notions about the state of the early and high middle ages have in the twentieth century been exposed and corrected; we now stress the gradual emergence of a modern, objective, and suprapersonal form of state organisation with its own administrative apparatus, means of coercion and rational policy. A similar corrective is necessary for the history of the papacy. What were the tasks of the papacy, as perceived at the papal court before the middle of the eleventh century, and which of these were actually taken up? In what ways was it possible for it to exercise influence on individual churches, and what means and coercive methods were available to it to do so?

We should never forget how easily people and communities could avoid being ruled by authority at that time, simply because given the transport facilities available they could be reached only with difficulty or not at all. Authority could often be silently ignored. There could be no question of a pope's having been present outside his own church province or the papal patrimony. Between the pontificates of John VIII (872–82) and Leo IX (1043–54) only one pope crossed the Alps: Benedict VIII, who was received with full honours by Henry II in Bamberg in 1020 and celebrated Easter with the emperor there in a demonstration of their common high office in Christendom. The visit also displayed the close alliance between them; undoubtedly the coming campaign against the Greeks and their allies in southern Italy was discussed. Pope and emperor travelled together as far as Fulda; they met again on Henry's south Italian expedition early in 1022 and they appeared together once more at a council in Pavia.

There were indeed papal assistants and representatives in the form of legates, who could be empowered by the pope to act on his behalf in distant lands, but these cannot be regarded as a method of continuous government before the middle of the eleventh century. For the 150 years which preceded we know of a total of about fifty such legations; even allowing for huge gaps in the evidence there can still not have been many. As a rule legates had specific tasks to fulfil, and returned to Rome after carrying them out. Some journeyed to Byzantium, others to Russia, Dalmatia, Croatia, Hungary, and Bulgaria. Legates and messengers to the German kings are mentioned comparatively frequently, though often these only had the task of asking for help against rebellious Romans. Legates were thus by no means always concerned with the papal government of the church as such; on the other hand there were indeed legations which were intended to bring the pope's weight of authority to bear on difficult ecclesiastical problems. To the extent that we hear anything at all about the names and ranks of legates, we hear of bishops of the province of Rome or clerics (very occasionally laymen) of the *sacrum palatium Lateranense* or of the Roman regions. It was a rare exception when an archbishop of Milan or an archbishop of Ravenna appeared as a legate. The papal entourage of the period included virtually no foreigners, as far as we know; it was a provincial affair.

Both the popes and their entourages were primarily concerned with the church and its situation in Rome, in the Roman church province and neighbouring districts. Besides this they had to administer and exploit the *patrimonium Petri*, which required continuous attention to central Italian conflicts and politics, full of trickery and violence. The most important popes took part in planning and carrying out wars, as did for example John X against the Saracens and Benedict VIII against Byzantine attacks. Within Rome and central Italy they could pursue political plans and decisions of their own. Information about changing affairs was available; it was both possible and necessary for them to act on their own initiative, for it would not have been sufficient merely to have reacted to hostile or friendly interventions from outside.

By comparison, a planned intervention in the life and norms of the church in more distant countries, a church policy based on the popes' own initiative, was before the middle of the eleventh century possible only to a very limited extent, and rarely attempted. For almost all of the small number of legations already mentioned we can show that they were set in motion by requests from outside. The spiritual authority of the pope was so high that help was indeed expected from him in disputes and difficult decisions; confirmations of possessions and declarations of protection were also sought after, though the popes could only offer spiritual, not material support. However, it should be noted that the number of papal privileges issued in this period was not high. In the tenth century it was roughly a fifth of the number issued in the eleventh century, and within the eleventh century twice as many were issued in the second half as in the first. More privileges went to distant countries than to Italian churches; but as a rule these were issued at the request of the recipients and not on the pope's own initiative. From the ninth century onwards a *bibliothecarius* was solely responsible as a member of the *sacrum palatium Lateranense* for letters and privileges; for the actual work of drawing these up it was enough to use the *notarii* or *scriniarii* of the Roman city regions. A *notarius et scriniarius sacri palatii Lateranensis* appears for the first time under John XV; around the end of the tenth century we find first a *cancellarius* and then a *cancellarius sacri palatii Lateranensis*.[200] The high-

---

[200] Elze, 'Sacrum Palatium Lateranense', 38; on the papal chapel, 47f. and Elze, 'Die päpstliche Kapelle im 12. und 13. Jh.', *ZRGKA*, 67 (1950), 143ff. and in particular S. Haider, 'Päpstliche Kapelle', 38–70.

ranking office of *bibliothecarius* continued to exist. Benedict VIII conferred it as an honour on various bishops, in the case of Archbishop Pilgrim of Cologne (1021–36) even on a German one. The old curial script[201] continued to be employed in papal charters alongside the charter minuscule gaining acceptance elsewhere in western Europe. There were chancellors, but no chancery or 'writing-office'; the notaries continued to be drawn from the city of Rome. It is clear, however, that the small circle of those who dealt with the pope's correspondence had their own scribal and cultural traditions, and that notaries were aware to a greater or lesser extent of the contents both of previous privileges and of canon law collections.[202] The documents and earlier charters necessary for the drawing up of charters were provided by those who sought them either for themselves or for their clients; it was these too who took the charters back from Rome to their recipients. The popes and their assistants were dependent on the facts with which they were provided;[203] they were hardly ever in a position to judge whether they were acting impartially or not or were being deceived by forged claims.[204] This could lead to quite mistaken decisions, or in the course of disputes to victory for those who had the more powerful advocates of their case or were better able to secure a favourable hearing for themselves with gifts.[205]

The way in which popes often took up positions which varied according to the information they were provided with and to the political influences they were subjected to, without any consideration of their own interests, was seen at its crudest in the Rheims schism, which began on the death of Archbishop Seulf in 925 and was ended only at the synod of Ingelheim in 948. Here there was a scandal when the delegate of the deposed archbishop, Hugo, produced a mandate from Pope Agapetus II which restored Hugo to Rheims and declared his opponent Artold – in whose favour the synod had just decided – deposed.

---

[201] Klewitz, 'Cancellaria', 44–79; Jordan, 'Entstehung', 97–152; Jordan, 'Päpstliche Verwaltung', 111–55; Pásztor, 'Curia Romana', 490–504.

[202] *Ibid.*, 499.

[203] Fuhrmann, 'Pseudoisidor in Rom', 15–66; note p. 48, where it is shown that it was possible to choose from among several collections, but also p. 62: 'this incident makes abruptly clear how we attribute too much to the popes of the time and their collaborators if we assume that they had a sovereign command of the legal texts'.

[204] So for example a certain Balduin, excommunicated by Adalbero of Rheims, was able to secure a hearing from Pope John XV by deceit (in the archbishop's opinion): Gebert, ep. 113, ed. F. Weigle (MGH Briefe der deutschen Kaiserzeit 2, Weimar 1966), 141 = BZ no. 663.

[205] Tellenbach, 'Zur Geschichte', 168ff.

The mandate had been given to him by precisely that papal *datarius* Marinus who was present in Ingelheim as a papal legate. From that day to this there has been talk of forgery, calumny, false pretences. But the matter is probably simpler than that. The mandate was issued on the basis of information which had been taken from a letter of the bishops of the province of Rheims, and this contained a wholly one-sided account of the dispute in Hugo's favour. After the mandate had been issued, Otto I's influence and that of the German episcopate led, as so often, to a change of position in Rome. Influence should not be understood as pressure or control by the German and French kings, however. Pope Agapetus II could allow himself a few years later to turn down Otto I's request to be received in Rome and granted the imperial crown, even though the king was present in northern Italy with an army. Pressure from Alberic of Rome, the local lord of the city, was more important than a wish expressed by a ruler who was still distant. In the tenth century and the first half of the eleventh the slogan 'the papacy under imperial rule' is quite simply wrong; and even for the following period it is misleading. The notion of pope and emperor as heads of the Christian world represents an ideological construct rather than reality; there can be no question of any opposition of principle between the two offices before Henry IV. He was not crowned emperor until 1084, and then only in a very questionable manner: in what sense did he represent the 'empire'?

In the tenth century the political history of the popes was determined less by their connections to distant bishops and princes than by the politics of the city of Rome and its hinterland. After two popes had been murdered in 903 there followed what by the standards of the time was a long period of quiet. In 928 John X, whose successful pontificate with its major victories against the Saracens made him probably the most important pope of the century apart from Silvester II, was imprisoned and in the following year murdered. In 936 John XI, the half-brother of the lord of the city, Alberic, who was a great patron and friend of Abbot Odilo of Cluny, was imprisoned. The fact that in the period up to Otto I's intervention things went fairly well for the remaining popes can be ascribed to the dominance of Alberic's grandfather Theophylact – *vestiarius*, consul, and senator, his wife Theodora, and his daughters Marozia and Theodora. In Alberic's own time – he was the son of Marozia and of Margrave Alberic of Spoleto – Rome was more or less stable.

The Ottonian period saw a series of conflicts between Roman factions which are difficult to make sense of. The deposition, restoration, and renewed deposition of John XII were of no fundamental importance for the history of the church.[206] John, a son of Alberic, had become unacceptable to Otto and to certain Roman circles both by his way of life, which was excessive, and by his connections with King Adalbert, which were treasonable. It is worth noting that none of the popes of the Ottonian period could really be certain of avoiding imprisonment, exile, and murder in spite of their generally good relations with the German emperors, who could intervene helpfully in Roman politics. A brief survey will help to make this clear and at the same time underline the weakness of imperial control over Rome, often overestimated. Leo VIII (963–5): once exiled; John XIII (965–72): imprisoned, fled; Benedict VII (973–74): imprisoned, murdered; Boniface VII (974–81/2): twice exiled; Benedict VII (974–83): once exiled; John XIV (983/4): imprisoned, murdered; John XV (985–96): fled to Tuscany; Gregory V (996–9): once exiled; Silvester II (999–1003): driven out together with Otto III. After the death of Otto III the popes were once again generally undisputed, since first the Crescentii and then the counts of Tusculum, from whose family three popes in succession were drawn, were able to establish a firm grip on the city. Henry II was present in Rome for only four weeks of the whole of his pontificate, and Conrad II for only three; they were neither willing nor able to do much for the popes, nor were there any fundamental differences between emperors and popes in the period from 1002 to 1039.

Received opinion is that there were serious tensions between Otto I and John XIII which arose in the course of the foundation of Magdeburg and the planning of the Slav mission.[207] But to suppose that John XIII had refused to cooperate with Otto's plans and developed an independent papal missionary policy in rivalry with the imperial one is hardly tenable. We have already spoken of the dependence of the popes on imperial help, and this was particularly true of John XIII. In October 963 he had been elected by the Romans in the presence of the bishops sent by Otto I, Otgar of Speyer and Liudprand of Cremona. As early as December of that year he was captured and beaten up by his opponents, and then imprisoned first in the Castel Sant'Angelo, then in the Campagna. After some months he was able to flee and beg help from Otto. In the autumn of 966 he moved on Rome, accompanied by imperial troops, and in November fear of the emperor made the Romans receive him. At the beginning of 967 Otto came to Rome and punished the rebels. In the

---

[206] The deposition, return, and renewed banishing of this pope were scarcely of fundamental importance in the history of the church; BZ nos. 312 and 318f., and see Zimmermann, *Papstabsetzungen*, 81ff.

[207] Tellenbach, 'Zur Geschichte', 175ff.

spring pope and emperor travelled via Spoleto to Ravenna, where they
celebrated Easter together on 31 March. They spent April in and around
Ravenna, where they held a number of judicial assemblies and synods; it
was in these weeks of cooperation that the decisions about Magdeburg
were taken.

Can it really have been at this time that the pope thwarted the
emperor's pet plans for Magdeburg and asserted his own superior rights in
questions of missionary policy in eastern Europe? The emperor who is
supposed to have been 'angered' at this stayed with the pope in Ravenna
well into May; they issued a joint invitation to Otto II to celebrate
Christmas with them at Rome. This all three of them did, and the pope
crowned the young king as emperor, by no means the norm while his
father was still alive. What has evidently happened is that a picture of the
popes as pursuing a deliberate and calculated policy with a consistent
theoretical justification has been projected back from the twelfth and
thirteenth centuries into the tenth, where it has completely clouded
perceptions of the contradictions inherent in contemporary political
realities: high ideals, with only restricted possibilities of realising them at
a distance, coupled with continual existential threats from near at hand.

The fact that the popes and their entourage in the *sacrum palatium
Lateranense* were almost completely absorbed by the demands and needs
of their own province, of the city of Rome, of the *patrimonium Petri*, and
of the often anarchic neighbouring provinces, was probably one of the
main reasons why their contacts with the bishops and churches of distant
countries remained intermittent. It has been said that the imperial bishops
linked their rights far more with the ruler than with the pope; but they
had no other choice. The pope was too far away and too lacking in power
to give them much in the way of political or material support. Their
connections with him were not very institutionalised. From early on the
pallium, a liturgical symbol of high ecclesiastical office, and the privileges
associated with it, which determined when it could be used, offered an
opportunity to make contact by letter or in person. Often it was
customary to journey in person to Rome to receive it, and in the course
of the tenth and eleventh centuries it became the exclusive preserve of
archbishops. The claim that it was only after having received the pallium
that metropolitans had the right to consecrate suffragan bishops was
occasionally made, but it was not until later that the pallium came to have
legal significance. Bishops and laymen brought (and received) gifts when
they visited the papal court; so did those prelates who came for the
pallium, a practice which led to an obligation to pay pallium fees, about
which there were disputes from an early date.

Apart from the pallium we do not hear much at this time of papal activities in distant church provinces or dioceses, nor, in spite of the widespread reverence for the pope, of bishops' taking any great notice of them in their spiritual activities or their jurisdictional practice. The contacts between popes and bishops in the monastic sphere, the papal protection and exemption from the normal jurisdiction of the diocesan bishop granted by some papal privileges, will be discussed later; here it should be noted that the initiative for such grants normally lay not with the popes but with the monastery or with its founder and patrons. Rarely do we hear of conflicts between popes and bishops, not least because the distance between them meant that there were normally no opportunities for friction. There were a few exceptions, however, and even questions of principle were raised in the course of some of these incidents.

This could be said, for example, of the well-known Gandersheim dispute, in which Silvester II supported Otto III, whose passionate friend-ship with Bernward of Hildesheim led him to break with Archbishop Willigis of Mainz; it could also be said of the measures taken against Arnulf II of Milan by Benedict VIII and Henry II or of the excommuni-cation of Aribert of Milan, deposed by Conrad II, by Benedict IX. The appeal of Countess Irmingard of Hammerstein to the pope against the verdict of emperor and episcopate on the lawfulness of her marriage led to a real conflict between Benedict VIII and a substantial part of the German episcopate. A Mainz provincial synod in Seligenstadt issued a brusque prohibition: such appeals were only to be made with the permission of the diocesan bishop. The pope protested against such a denial of his judicial supremacy, while the emperor apparently remained inactive. Although the conflict remained unresolved as a result of the death of both pope and emperor which followed, it raised questions of principle not normally touched on at that time.

The sharpest attacks on papal authority which we know of in the tenth and early eleventh century were made in the course of the Rheims schism between the Carolingian archbishop Arnulf and Gerbert of Aurillac, whom Hugo Capet wished to appoint to the see. John XV did not at first have anything to do with the dispute; it seems that the Empress Theophanu led him to support the Carolingian candidate. King Hugo's party protested at this and went so far as to declare null and void any addition to canon law made by a Roman pope which should contradict the decrees of the church fathers. But the problems touched on in the course of this dispute, the relationship between papacy and episcopate or between pope and council, were not taken up; the questions remained unresolved and interest in them dwindled.

The conflicts with external bishops, archbishops, and rulers were, as we have seen, hardly ever due to Rome's taking the initiative and meeting with resistance; almost always the intervention by the pope or his representative had been requested by an external party. Even this kind of intervention was hardly numerous, not surprisingly in view of the distance between pope and regional episcopate. Privileges and papal letters were also almost invariably sought by their recipients or beneficiaries, who largely determined their content. Rome was generally held to be the centre of the church, but it was not a centre in the sense that it exercised influence through custom and practice, through established routines of control, or through corrective reactions to what Rome itself perceived as deviations from norms which it considered to be authoritative. The contacts ran first from periphery to centre, and only secondarily and in consequence from centre to periphery. Even this was only possible because of the immense prestige which the Roman church enjoyed within the Christian world. Although the transmission of this prestige through the spread of Roman liturgical practices was by this time a thing of the past – in the liturgical exchanges of the tenth and eleventh centuries Rome was if anything an importer rather than an exporter – there was still subjectively the feeling that in liturgical practice Rome, the head of the church, was being imitated. Princes and bishops journeyed to Rome not so much in order to deal with questions of organisation, jurisdiction, or church policy as to see the representative of St Peter and to pay him reverence. Countless pilgrims streamed into the Holy City. These included devout penitents, those who hoped to have their wishes realised by fulfilling a vow of pilgrimage, and those who wanted to participate in divine services in Roman churches and thus feel themselves to be in a special sense members of the universal Christian community. Under the leadership of knowledgeable guides one proceeded to the graves of the saints in order to pray. Rome was the city with the greatest number of relics and the most powerful relics. If at all possible one tried to secure some. The pope often gave relics in return for the rich presents bestowed on him, and these were received with joy and thanks. Others bought relics; even the theft of relics was common, and could be seen as *pia fraus*, devout deception.

Thus although the organisational unity of the various particular churches – parishes, dioceses, provinces, and 'national churches' – under the pope was still a very loose one, the devout veneration of the vicar of St Peter and the Holy City expressed, as we have already remarked, the unity of the church on earth more tangibly than anything else could do.

3

THE MATERIAL EXISTENCE OF THE
CHURCHES AND THE CLERGY

•

Even in the time of the early church, when Christians still anticipated the Lord's return in the immediate future, the question of how the communities' material needs were to be met presented itself nevertheless. It became ever more pressing as the numbers of the faithful grew and the Lord's return was delayed. There was a need for rooms to meet in and for money, either to acquire liturgical utensils, lights, and the food for common meals, or to support brothers and sisters in need, or to lay out and decorate cemeteries and church buildings. To send information to befriended communities or to travel to them also cost money. When the bishops and their helpers ceased to be able to support themselves from the fruits of their labours, the communities had to provide for them.

From the beginning it was laid down that all the faithful should, if possible, bring their offerings to the altar during divine service. These were then to be accepted and divided out. But quite apart from such consumable income the communities could through gifts and testaments also become owners of money, houses, and property, and hence could dispose not only of income which had to be spent immediately but also of more permanent forms of wealth.

Wealth always has a secular character; even when it is owned and used by churches it is subject to the legal and economic constraints of its time. In financial as in other matters we must speak with Jean François Lemarignier of an 'interpenetration' of church and Roman society in the

late antique period;[1] Gonzalo Martinez Diez has pointed to a similar
interaction for the late medieval era and noted that 'the decisive and
determining factor was the socio-economic infrastructure within which
the church developed in these centuries'.[2] The same was true of the
period from the eighth to the eleventh centuries; one should not be led
astray by later ideologies and ecclesiologies into seeing the state of affairs
at the end of our period as a decline simply because it no longer matched
up to the demands of a rapidly changing new era.

At first it was the diocese which was the unit of property-holding, and
only the bishop was empowered to administer property. He provided for
the churches and clerics in his city and its surroundings. The clergy of the
churches and oratories outside the city resided with the bishop; they were
maintained by him, and even when they lived at some distance from him
they remained in close contact with him. This was only practicable in the
Roman or Romanised countries with many cities, however, where the
diocese based on a central city remained fairly small. In the much larger
new dioceses such arrangements could not be made to work, particularly
once the number of churches grew. The great majority of oratories,
churches, and monasteries were built not by diocesan bishops but by
others, who then became the owners of the church building and its
endowment. The majority of country churches belonged to the royal
fisc. But other wealthy landowners also built churches or chapels for
themselves, their families, and their dependants. As early as 742 Carloman
laid down that each count was to have a priest with him who could
judge those who confessed their sins and impose an appropriate penance.[3]
Landowners will equally have wished to have a priest for their residences;
those who had several residences needed a priest for each. This is true
both of secular magnates and of bishops, monasteries, and collegiate
churches. Occasionally parishes themselves founded churches; here and
there wealthy priests did so as well. Parish churches gradually acquired
rights over their own property, and at the same time all the 'proprietary'
churches represented special forms of property; as a result, the diocese

---

[1] Lemarignier, *France médiévale*, 34. This process was accompanied by considerable
    difficulties, however. See Lesne, *Propriété ecclésiastique*, 2f.
[2] G. M. Diez, *El patrimonio eclesiástico en la España Visigoda* (Universidad Pontificia de
    Comillas, Facultad de derecho canónico. Publicaciones Anejes e Miscellanea Seria
    Canónica 2, Comillas 1959), 71; Congar, *Laie*, 46: 'Church and clergy have an existence
    within history and within society and make use of the means provided by their social and
    temporal context to achieve their religious aims'.
[3] MGH Capit. I.45 no. 19 c. 1 (Charles the Great, 769). H. Mordek has been kind enough
    to inform me that this capitulary is of disputed authenticity; but the sentence is already
    found in Carloman's genuine capitulary of 742 (MGH Capit. I.25, c. 2).

came to have a more and more decentralised form of property organisation.[4]

We may posit a number of different reasons for the creation of
proprietary churches. To provide dependants with churches may have
made it easier for secular or ecclesiastical lords to control them, and by
having offerings and fees paid to their own churches they avoided the
diversion of resources away from their estates. The right to present the
bishop with a cleric as candidate prevented unwelcome intrusions from
outside. The owner of the proprietary church had rights over its revenues,
so far as these did not come directly to the parish priest and other clerics.
But political and financial motives were scarcely the principal ones behind
the construction of proprietary churches, which after all represented a
considerable investment and would generally have cost more than they
brought in if the purpose for which they were ostensibly built was taken
at all seriously. The main motive for the foundation of churches and
monasteries was faith: 'the institutions themselves had their roots in
belief'.[5]

Such good intentions were nevertheless often not fulfilled. Both
ecclesiastical and secular landlords frequently failed to present the priests
who served their churches to the diocesan bishop for consecration, and
the latter could often be equally negligent in fulfilling his duties. The
priest was often not given the prescribed minimum endowment, so that
he starved and was unable to pay the prescribed dues to the bishop. The
unfree were supposed to have been emancipated before they were
consecrated as priests, and the priest was supposed to possess the knowledge and qualities necessary for his office; these requirements too were
not always met.[6]

The Carolingian proprietary church legislation of the eighth and ninth

---

[4] Still fundamental for the history of the proprietary church system are the writings of
Stutz, especially *Benefizialwesen, Eigenkirche als Element*, 'Lehen und Pfründe', 'Kirchenrecht'. Stutz's doctrine of the Germanic origin and nature of the proprietary church has
not gone unchallenged. Feine, *Kirchliche Rechtsgeschichte*, 160ff., defends the idea of the
Germanic character of the institution against theories which see its origins in estate
lordship; note especially his references to the lines of development on p. 164. From the
ninth to the twelfth centuries the proprietary church was the norm in western Europe,
even in the newly converted countries. The origins of the institution were accounted for
in this period either not at all or in a distortring fashion. Besides the large-scale
possession of churches by kings, rich noble families, bishops, and great monasteries
there were a few parish or collective churches. See Feine, 'Genossenschaftliche
Gemeindekirche', 171–96; H. F. Schmid, 'Gemeinschaftskirchen', 1–61; Hartmann,
'Rechtlicher Zustand'.

[5] Imbart de la Tour, *Paroisses rurales*, 38 and 143; Lemarignier, *Gouvernement*, 86.

[6] On the nature of this manumission see below, p. 89.

centuries tried to deal with all such abuses and breaches of the rules.[7] It
was laid down by kings in capitularies, by councils in canons, and by
bishops in *capitula episcoporum*,[8] which found their way into collections
such as those of Ansegis, Regino of Prüm, or Burchard of Worms. Old
regulations were frequently worked over, and identical provisions were
often to be repeated in the following centuries. The norms laid down for
proprietary churches did not constitute a section or block of legislation of
their own; they were mixed in with general regulations for the life of the
church and for the duties of bishops, priests, and laymen. Comparatively
little attention was paid to whether kings, bishops, abbots, or laymen were
the owners of the churches. The main question was the preservation of
the traditional organisation of the diocese as laid down by canon law and
of the spiritual authority and competence of the bishop in the face of an
expanding proprietary church system. Where these demands were realised
churches belonged to two separate legal spheres: they were subject both
to the ecclesiastical authority of the diocesan bishop (as in the early
church, though with some restrictions) and to the power of their clerical
or lay owner. Proprietary churches are often condemned out of hand as
being incompatible with the church's constitution as defined in canon
law.[9] In reality they were like so much else, absorbed into and regulated
by canon law; one cannot separate proprietary church law and the
provisions of canon law which went with it. Where canon law provisions
were violated, so was the law governing proprietary churches; one must
distinguish between the law and its abuse.

When a church was founded the bishop had to satisfy himself that the
prescribed conditions had been fulfilled before consecrating it. Its
financial basis had to be assured – in the case of parishes this meant a
minimum endowment of a hide. The bishop had to consent to the
appointment or deposition of the priest, and he alone was empowered to

---

[7] See above, p. 30; Stutz, *Benefizialwesen*, 222f., stresses that we are dealing here with the
regulation and not the elimination of the proprietary church.

[8] *Contra*, Hartmann, 'Rechtlicher Zustand', 241, who stresses, against the views of Stutz,
that canon law by no means absorbed the proprietary church system completely. Krause,
'Papstwahldekret', 49, also emphasises the distinctions very sharply: 'And yet proprietary
church law had determined the organisation of the church for centuries, and that in a
much more powerful fashion than did the canonical precepts set out at length and
restated at the synod.' But are we not dealing here with the differences between legal
norms and legal reality? One must bear in mind when assessing the historical significance
of the proprietary church what Häussling, *Mönchskonvent*, 79, rightly points out: 'The
ideal implicit in the celebration of the Eucharist is not affected at all by the proprietary
church.'

[9] The references in this note and those which follow are taken as typical examples from a
few particularly significant capitularies, here MGH Capit. II.12 no. 191 cc. 4 and 1.

consecrate him.[10] The priest had to have been emancipated previously if unfree, since traditional canon law laid down that the exalted duties of a priest could not be carried out by a 'vile and servile person'. On the other hand the bishop was not supposed to reject suitable and useful persons whom laymen presented to him.[11] He or his deputy had not only the right but also the duty to supervise the church, regardless of whether the church's owner was another bishop, an abbot, a layman, or a community. That included controlling whether the cleric did what he was supposed to in respect of divine service, in respect of building maintenance and the provision of lighting for the church, and in respect of showing his lord due reverence.[12] Churches were not supposed to be divided, but the more flexible provision was occasionally made that they could be if the heirs were willing to maintain and honour the church in accordance with the bishop's prescriptions. If they refused to do so it was a matter for his judgement whether he allowed the church to continue to exist as a church or removed the relics from it. He was also supposed to keep an eye on the fabric of the church; if this was damaged he or his representative was to investigate whether carelessness or incompetence on the part of those responsible had led to the damage.[13] It was also laid down that bishops were not to be a burden to priests and congregations on their visitations, nor to neglect the clergy of their diocese, nor to reside in remote places.[14] There were to be no ordained clerics not subject to a diocesan bishop. No priest was to celebrate the Eucharist on his own, or to tempt members of another parish to come to him.[15]

Ulrich Stutz noted at the beginning of this century that the Carolingian norms continued valid in the following centuries and were hardly added to.[16] The same is true of the general legislation with which they were interwoven. Synods and collections of canon law repeated them up to the middle of the eleventh century in stereotype fashion, without concerning themselves much with the origins of such provisions or with the question, hardly resolvable by the means available, of whether they were genuine

---

[10] MGH Capit. I.356 no. 173; II.35 no. 196 c. XV (18).

[11] MGH Capit. II.33, no. 196 c. VIII (11).

[12] MGH Capit. II.12 no. 191 cc. 2 and 3.

[13] MGH Capit. II.32ff., no. 196 c. V(8), c. XIII and XIV (16 and 17).

[14] MGH Capit. II.121 no. 228 c. 18.

[15] MGH Capit. II.190 no. 249 c. 17.

[16] Stutz, 'Eigenkirche, Eigenkloster', 369: 'The second period of legislation on proprietary churches brought nothing new to set against this; since the episcopate was able to hold on to what had been achieved in the first period only with difficulty, it confined itself essentially to the repetition of older precepts.' See also the summary in Tellenbach, *Libertas*, 217f.

or false. They continued to be relevant, not least because they were often ignored, as they had been in the Carolingian period. The distance between legal theory and practical reality continued through the centuries; one should not leap to speak of 'reform' just because traditional legislation reappears in the decrees of synods, in charters or collections or canon law. The most famous programmatic demands of 'Gregorian reform', the condemnation of 'simony' and of 'clerical marriage', were not new. The way in which such demands were transformed, extended, and applied in practice will be described more extensively later. The reforms of the tenth century were in general simple and straightforward. Wars and pagan incursions had led in many countries to the ruin of churches; whole villages had been more or less depopulated. Impoverished priests were forced to feed themselves by agricultural labour; monasteries were deserted; homeless monks wandered far and wide; even some bishoprics remained unfilled.[17]

In the course of the tenth century the afflicted countries and regions recovered, some sooner, some later. The population began to increase once more; villages were rebuilt or, in the case of clearances, newly founded. Church reforms still consisted largely in restoring ruined churches and building new ones, in securing proper training for the priests to be appointed, in the refounding or founding of monasteries, in the renewal of church life in cathedral cities, where bishop, chapter, and collegiate churches took up their tasks once more, and in the reintroduction of the *vita communis* in collegiate churches where this was possible. Above all, both greater and smaller churches had to be provided with an adequate financial backbone; for impoverished churches could provide neither proper liturgical services nor the basis for their clergy to lead a regular life.

The means at the disposal of both greater and smaller churches consisted partly of landed property, and partly of tithes, gifts, and offerings by the faithful, paid either in kind or in money. Landed property might mean estates with a home farm at the centre and dependencies; it might also mean individual peasant holdings, meadows, fields, pieces of woodland, fisheries, mills, smithies, even proprietary monasteries and churches. How could income be won from such property, which was often scattered? The holding associated with the parish church would normally have been

---

[17] Richer, *Gesta Senonensis ecclesiae* c. 17, MGH SS xxv.278 ('De Adelhardo misero abbate'): 'victu quippe deficiente et vestitu decreverunt more rusticorum agricultores fieri, ut ita saltim possent inopem defendere vitam'. For England see for example Godfrey, *Church*, 254f.; Deanesly, *Pre-Conquest Church*, 252f., where it is said that Alfred the Great was in such straits that the churches could not be rebuilt.

worked by the priest himself together with his family and a few servile labourers. More distant pieces of land which had been given to the church could not be managed in this way; the lords of churches had to lease them out using the forms customary in the region and period. This was one way in which church property might come into lay hands. A monastery could certainly manage its own garden and the farms in the vicinity of the monastery, but here again more distant property complexes, estates, and churches had to be rented out in customary fashion. The rents came either to the churches concerned or to the monastery itself. The same can be said of the property which belonged to bishops, cathedral chapters, and collegiate churches. Bishops often owned not only proprietary churches but also proprietary monasteries, either in their own or in other dioceses. These owed their bishop various services, spiritual, economic, and military. Bishops and abbots needed armed warriors both for their own protection and to perform the military service they owed, and these received vassalitic benefices just like their equivalents in the service of kings or secular magnates. In short, the property of both greater and lesser churches was exploited in the same contemporary forms as was that of kings or magnates. Bishops and abbots had, like these, to provide their spiritual and secular officials and assistants with land, castles, or proprietary churches; and the holders of such things exploited them by granting out land as fiefs or on lease. A proprietary church might be given to a count or to a monastery, either of whom would then take on the duties and rights of a proprietary owner, including presenting candidates for the priesthood of the church to the diocesan bishop, cashing the dues owed to the lord or even taking the entire revenues of the church and merely providing a salary for the priest. It has been assumed that such a 'feudal-isation' of the church set in at different points in different parts of Europe. For most of France and Italy the expression 'church of the first feudal age' has been used by contrast with the 'prolongation of the Carolingian church' in those regions where, as in Germany, royal France, or Normandy, a 'central government' either survived or was newly estab-lished.[18]

Apart from the profits from property, church had both regular and irregular forms of income. If a bishop was lord of a market he made

---

[18] Stutz, 'Eigenkirche, Eigenkloster', 273; Imbart de la Tour, *Paroisses rurales*, 142; Lemarignier, 'Institutions', 6f.; Lamarignier, *France médiévale*, 192; Violante, *Società Milanese*, 142 and 154 (1st edn); Violante, *Pataria Milanese*, 116: 'One needs to bear in mind that if society became feudal the *societas Christiana* could not take on a quite differ-ent character'; Boyd, *Tithes*, 56 and appendix 1, 252ff. on 'The Literature on the Private Church'. Cluny was by no means a revolutionary mine within feudal society, according to Fechter, *Cluny*, 44.

money out of it. In France and Italy the trade carried out by privileged
episcopal merchants brought in substantial sums. From the earliest times
the faithful had offered oblations, usually small gifts in kind or money, at
divine service. Probably more significant financially were gifts, which
might consist either of money, consumables, or land, and often carried the
obligation of prayer for the soul of the giver or his relations and of saying
mass and feeding paupers on the anniversaries of their deaths.[19] Among
the most important sources of income were tithes, which had been made
compulsory by Carolingian legislation and had to be paid by all the
faithful to their parish churches. The obligation had originally been a
personal one, but gradually it came to be linked with land: whoever was
in possession of land was then bound to pay its tithes.[20] The obligation to
pay tithes had to be reiterated countless times. In some regions of Europe
the income from tithes was divided into three parts, but more usually into
four: one of these parts came to the bishop, the others to his clergy, to the
poor, and to the church fabric respectively. In the case of proprietary
churches it was the owner who disposed of the last three parts. The bishop
received fees from priests when they collected chrism, and at synods and
courts of visitation. They were also obliged to give hospitality to the
bishop and his entourage when he went on visitation; but there are
complaints from an early date that bishops no longer fulfilled their duty of
travelling round their dioceses preaching and confirming but instead
demanded the commutation of the obligations of hospitality into other
payments.[21]

The acts of the synod of Tribur (895) noted once again that it had
become customary in many places to pay for receiving chrism, baptism,
even the Eucharist. The synod denounced and cursed what it saw as the
seed of 'simoniacal heresy', and laid down that in future nothing should
be demanded for consecrations, chrism, baptism, burial, or communion;
Christ's free gifts should be freely dispensed. The synod gave a lengthy
justification based on quotations from the Old Testament of why all
Christians were forbidden to sell 'earth to the dead' or deny burial. 'You
have received freely from God; give freely thereof for His sake' was the
principle to be followed, unless the relatives and friends of the dead

---

[19] For a characteristic early example see Capitula Pistensia (869), MGH Capit. II.33f., no.
275 c. 8: 'Ut presbyteri parochiani suis senioribus debitam reverentiam et competentem
honorem atque obsequium secundum suum ministerium impendant . . . et illi pro
senioribus suis orare et seniores illorum sacra officia et divina mysteria puro corde per
illos suscipere possint.' See in general below, pp. 105–6, 127ff.

[20] On the origins of church tithes see Stutz, 'Karolingisches Zehntgebot', especially 197 and
222f.

[21] MGH Capit. II.247 no. 252 c. 5.

person were willing to make a voluntary donation for God's sake and for the redemption of the dead person's soul. Similar provisions are found in the acts of the synods of Meaux and Paris in 845 and 846,[22] which cite a letter of Pope Gregory the Great. The pope had allowed that voluntary gifts for candles made by heirs and relatives might be accepted, but had explicitly forbidden demands for such gifts.[23] One's impression is that the voluntary gifts to which Gregory I restricted offerings had already in the Carolingian era become a custom which could easily turn into compulsory fees. Admittedly, later synods also threatened those priests with anathema who sold chrism, baptism, and burial, as did for example a synod which met in 1036, again in Tribur.[24] But by this time the 'idea of payment for services' which Georg Schreiber showed to have been at the root of twelfth-century church life had already become standard. All spiritual services from baptism through to the last unction and burial were paid for by 'surplice fees'.[25]

Not only the income from landed property, including churches, but also revenues of this kind, in particular tithes, could be leased or given out as a fief. This too was an adaptation to the forms of economic organisation characteristic of an agricultural society based on lordship. How else indeed could property and revenues be exploited, once they exceeded what was necessary for their owners' own consumption and for building up a reserve for times of famine? Leases and fiefs of all kinds almost invariably entailed gifts by their recipient to the owner of the property. When a peasant holding changed hands a fixed payment of this kind was made; so also when secular and ecclesiastical owners of churches appointed a new priest.[26] Vassals brought honorific gifts to their lord when they were given their fiefs, and received them from him as well. This is probably how we should see the origins of the gifts made by bishops on their appointments, who in their turn received privileges or confirmations of privileges. Transactions which we could call sale and purchase were found at times

---

[22] 'Gratis accepisti a deo, gratis da pro eo': MGH Capit. II.206f. no. 252 and 221f., c. 15f. (Tribur); *ibid.*, 415 no. 293 c. 72 (Meaux).

[23] *Registrum* VIII 356, MGH Epp. II.37.

[24] MGH Const. I.89 no. 44. See on this Böhmer, 'Eigenkirchentum', 301–53.

[25] Schreiber, 'Abgabenwesen', 442; Schreiber, 'Segnungen', 290; Schreiber, 'Gregor VII', 77, where there is even an account of 'the mass as a means of bringing in dues'; Böhmer, 'Eigenkirchentum', 321: 'nothing was free'.

[26] Imbart de la Tour, *Paroisses rurales*, 254; Schreiber, 'Abgabenwesen', 445; Schreiber, *Kurie und Kloster*, II.50; Lemarignier, *France médiévale*, 67; Lemarignier, *Institutions*, 62ff.; Böhmer, 'Eigenkirchentum', 322, thinks that such payments had their positive side for the clerics who served in proprietary churches; it was not possible to take the churches away from them so easily.

in southern France and occasionally elsewhere. The most famous example was the case of Wifred, the son of the count of Cerdaña, who bought the archbishopric of Narbonne for 100,000 shillings and procured the bishoprics of Urgel, Gerona, and Elne for three of his brothers by paying large sums.[27] Later, as lay appointment of bishops, abbots, and priests came to seem objectionable, such examples were, exaggeratedly, treated as the norm in polemics.[28] For kings it was not so much presents as other things which determined their decision in favour of a candidate: *fidelitas* to both Christ and the king, family and kinship, political and personal connections.[29] It might happen that a poor bishopric was to be given a blood transfusion by the appointment of a rich bishop, made in the justifiable expectation that he would make his church the heir to some of his wealth. Of course, kings' attitudes varied. But one should not underestimate the importance of the kings' view of themselves as acting in the service of the Lord of the church when they appointed bishops. Often their decisions were the result of prayers or dreams. When the bishop of Regensburg died in 940, Otto I is said in Thietmar's account to have travelled there and to have been warned in a dream to give the bishopric to no one other than the first person he should meet on the following morning. In the first glimmerings of dawn the king came with a few companions to St Emmeram, knocked on the door and was received by Gunther, the venerable *custos* of the monastery. Otto looked at him, went first to pray, and then asked Gunther: 'What will you give me, brother, for the episcopal office?' The old monk smiled and answered: 'My boots'. The king then recounted his dream to all present in the church of St Peter, and by the advice of clergy and people made Gunther bishop.[30]

Historians and charters tell us much about disputes over ecclesiastical property, more indeed than about disputes between laymen over property, which is perhaps a result of the richness of church archives. Often the invasions and depredations of powerful laymen are denounced; churches and monasteries are depicted as the victims of their deplorable greed and arbitrariness.[31] But devout laymen are equally often depicted as the benefactors and founders of churches and monasteries, and church

---

[27] Vincke, *Staat und Kirche*, 254ff.

[28] Barlow, *English Church 1000–1066*, 112ff.

[29] Political considerations are particularly visible in the appointments to bishoprics in imperial Italy; see Schwarz, *Besetzung*.

[30] Thietmar, *Chronicon*, II 26, p. 70; for the appointment of Gero as archbishop after a dream see *ibid.*, II 24, p. 68.

[31] Yet Duby, *Société*, 165, quite rightly speaks of an exaggeration of aristocratic excesses by ecclesiastical writers.

lands did indeed come to a great extent from donations by kings and by greater and lesser laymen. At times such gifts, especially those to monasteries, seem to have impoverished lay families.[32] Such pious wastefulness led in parts of France in the second half of the tenth century to a social crisis among the political élite. Often heirs were unwilling to recognise the gifts made by their ancestors, and made their claims more or less forcibly known.[33] But leaving this aside many of the accusations and the defensive measures taken by the church were entirely justified. It should not be overlooked, however, that laymen also fought many struggles both in court and with the sword over lands and lucrative rights. We also hear much about disputes between bishops and other bishops, cathedral chapters, collegiate chapters, monasteries, or parishes over lands and revenues of greater or lesser importance. It is said of bishops that they were more concerned for power and wealth than for their high office; that they gave church property in benefice to the relatives with whose help they had secured office; that they plundered monasteries, particularly in the vacancy between the death of an abbot and the election of a new one; and that they mulcted the country clergy with their excessive demands.[34] Otto III accused bishops and abbots at the synod of Pavia in 998 of abusing church lands which they gave to certain persons in benefice, not for the profit of the church but for the sake of money, kinship, or friendship.[35] In 1039 Juthail acquired the metropolitan see of Dol from Duke Alan of Brittany by paying for it, and made extensive gifts of church property, as was common practice at that time.[36] Monasteries, it was complained, also did not perform the services they owed their bishops and reduced the already scanty incomes of the priests of the churches they owned;[37] these in their turn neglected their duties, stayed away from the diocesan synod, and were in arrears with their payments. How far such complaints and warnings had an effect is difficult to say. Certainly they encouraged many people, from the bishop down to the peasant who owed tithes, to meet their obligations; on the other hand one cannot help noting the increasing contrast between the demands of canon law and customary practice. In general we may say that between the eighth and

---

[32] Lesne, *Propriété ecclésiastique*, 169; Godfrey, *Church*, 308; Duby, *Société*, 68ff., on the impoverishment of the laity.

[33] As one example among many see F. W. Oediger, 'Adelas Kampf um Elten', *AHVNR*, 155–6 (1954–5), 76ff.; see also Schreiber, 'Kluny und die Eigenkirchen', 96ff. and 117.

[34] Lemarignier, 'Institutions', 68: 'bishops more preoccupied with their territorial lordships than with matters of religion'.

[35] MGH Const. I.50 no. 23.

[36] Duine, *Métropole de Bretagne*, 7ff.   [37] Böhmer, *Eigenkirchentum*, 344.

the twelfth centuries it probably became more customary to take payment for spiritual services and that the life of the church became more dominated by economic considerations.

The material basis for the existence of churches and clergy varied greatly across countries, periods, and levels of the hierarchy. Bishoprics and the great monasteries and canonries were fairly rich.[38] Their incomes allowed them to provide help in times of famine, which were frequent, by opening up the reserves stored in their barns and stalls. They were in a position to take on the duty of caring for the poor and sick and for pilgrims. The highest ecclesiastical offices, bishoprics, abbacies, canonries, and other dignities in cathedral and collegiate chapters were financially attractive even for the children of the nobility, though to an extent which varied from land to land. The German and French bishoprics were prosperous or wealthy, and in Italy we do not hear of poverty, whereas some at least of the bishoprics in England, which had a fair number for its size, were only modestly endowed.[39] Naturally, a period with no sense of statistics does not allow us any great precision here. Even so valuable a source as the list drawn up by Otto II after the battle of Cotrone, laying down the numbers of armed mounted soldiers to be sent to him by ecclesiastical and secular lords in Germany, must be treated with caution;[40] for we do not know how many troops those concerned had already sent, nor the extent to which the list took account of the situation on the home front (for example, that on the borders) in drawing up the demands. Still, although no secular prince had to send more than forty armed soldiers, Cologne, Mainz, Augsburg, and Strasbourg had to send one hundred; Salzburg, Trier, and Regensburg seventy; Liège, Verdun, Würzburg, Fulda, and the Reichenau sixty; Eichstätt, Lorsch, and Weißenburg fifty; Chur, Freising, Worms, Ellwangen, Hersfeld, Prüm, and St Gallen forty. With all due caution we may still see in these figures a confirmation of the high economic, political, and military potential of the ecclesiastical elite confirmed in general by the course of German medieval history.

The financial situation of the papacy is very unclear for the tenth and early eleventh centuries.[41] Its revenues from land, from the administration of the patrimonium, from coinage, tolls, and justice were considerable,

---

[38] Lesne, *Propriété ecclésiastique*, 370ff.

[39] Darlington, 'Ecclesiastical Reform', 399, names as one reason for pluralism – that is, for holding more than one bishopric at the same time – the poverty of at least one of them; see Godfrey, *Church*, 387.

[40] MGH Const. I.362 no. 436.

[41] Jordan, 'Päpstliche Finanzgeschichte', 62: 'it will probably never be possible to write a clear account of the earliest history of papal finances'.

but uncertain in view of fluctuations in the political situation in central and southern Italy.[42] Nevertheless, John VIII was able to raise a Saracen tribute of 25,000 silver mancuses, an enormous sum,[43] although it probably included substantial payments from the property and from the treasure of the individual churches. The military operations conducted by popes of the tenth and eleventh centuries also suggest a certain financial solidity. Troubles in Rome and the Campagna constantly endangered the financial independence of the popes and of the personnel of the *sacrum palatium Lateranense*.[44] Payments of special taxes by foreign princes, for example by the rulers of Poland and England, were considerable but irregular.[45] The papal properties beyond the Alps probably did not bring in much, and nor did the yearly gifts made in token of subjection by those monasteries which belonged to the papacy or were under its protection. More important were the valuable gifts made by pilgrims to Rome, which were reciprocated by donations of relics from Rome's rich treasures. Pallium-payments, which had developed from gifts into fees, probably brought in something, as did payments for privileges.[46]

Contemporaries complained that much could be achieved in Rome by payments. In a famous letter of Archbishop William of Mainz it is claimed that Otto I's ambassador Abbot Hadamar of Fulda had boasted that for a hundred pounds he could bring as many pallia as he wished back from Rome.[47] Cnut is later said to have complained bitterly to John XIX about the extortionate demands for payment made to his archbishops when they followed ancient custom and came to the apostolic see to collect their pallia. It was decided that this should not happen in future.[48] But the same

---

[42] Duchesne, *Premiers temps*; T. Hirschfeld, 'Das Gerichtswesen der Stadt Rom vom. 8.–12. Jahrhundert, wesentlich nach stadtrömischen Urkunden', *AUF*, 4 (1913), 419–543; Hartmann, 'Grundherrschaft und Bürokratie', 142; Hartmann, *Geschichte Italiens*, II/1, 141; II/2, 112; Halphen, *Etudes*; Kölmel, *Rom und der Kirchenstaat*, 18ff.; Hiestand, *Byzanz*, 26; Toubert, *Structures*, 906ff.

[43] MGH Epp. VII.85 no. 89.

[44] After the collapse of the empire the popes were free from imperial control but also from imperial protection. See Dupré-Theseider, 'Ottone I e l'Italia', 98f.; this was in effect already true from the death of Louis II onwards.

[45] C. Daux, *Le Denier de St. Pierre* (Paris 1907), 11f. and 19; D. Jensen, *Der englische Peters-pfenning und die Lehnssteuer aus England und Irland an den Papststuhl im Mittelalter* (Diss. Rostock 1903); E. Maschke, *Der Peterspfennig in Polen und dem deutschen Osten* (Leipzig 1933), especially 17f.; W. E. Lunt, *Financial Relations of the Papacy with England to 1327* (Cambridge, Mass. 1939), 3ff., 22ff., 68ff.; Barlow, *English Church 1000–1066*, 295ff.; Godfrey, *Church*, 388.

[46] C. B. Graf von Haake, *Die Palliumsverleihungen bis 1149* (Diss. Göttingen 1898); Lesne, *Hiérarchie épiscopale*, 94; Feine, *Kirchliche Rechtsgeschichte*, 119, 231, 365.

[47] Jaffé, *BRG*, III.349 no. 15.

[48] *Ex Florentii Wigorniensis Chronicon Chronicarum*, MGH SS XIII.126.

pope asked Bishop Peter of Gerona about the possibility of ransoming captives; and the bishop offered to provide the means to ransom thirty, provided that the pope gave him a pallium, at that time the prerogative of metropolitans.[49]

When Abbo of Fleury journeyed for the first time to Rome in order to have the privileges of his monastery confirmed, he is said by his biographer Aimon to have found in John XV a profit-hungry and in all his activities thoroughly corrupt pope, but to have reported of Gregory V, whom he found as an exile in Spoleto, that the pope had treated him well and not sought to make money.[50] Gerbert of Aurillac reports that in 990 a delegation from the council of Senlis, which sought Rome's confirmation of its deposition of Archbishop Arnulf of Rheims, was out-bribed by the proctors of the other side, who made rich presents including a magnificent white horse.[51] At some points popes in financial straits probably did find gifts really important. When relations with Byzantium were good, subsidies came from there to Rome. In 1007 the Jew Jacob bar Jekutiel came from Rouen to John XVII, complained about persecution of Jews, and secured a papal mandate which laid down excommunication for all who killed Jews. He offered 200 pounds in coin, 7 gold pieces for the legate, and 100 silver pieces and 12 horses for the costs of the journey.[52] When Leo IX entered Rome at the beginning of 1049 for his enthronement on 12 February, he is said to have found no provisions of any kind for himself and his entourage. All the money that had been brought from Germany had been spent on travel costs and alms. According to Leo's biographer they were debating whether to leave Rome again when an embassy from Benevento arrived with gifts so rich that the worst financial straits were eased for the time being.[53] The administration of the pope's finances was so hand to mouth and so lacking in plan that such crises could easily occur, especially after vacancies.

The financial situation of the isolated country clergy probably also varied from country to country and period to period, but in general it was a modest or even a needy one. The office of parish priest was therefore probably not a very attractive one materially. Lords often told off serfs to

[49] Kehr, *Katalanischer Prinzipat*, 22.

[50] Aimo, *Vita Abbonis*, Migne, *PL* 139, col. 401f.; on Farfa see Sackur, *Cluniacenser*, 350 n. 3.

[51] *Acta concilii Remensis* c. 27, ed. A. Olleris, *Ouvres de Gerbert* (Clermont 1867), 203ff.; Gerbert von Aurillac, ep. 217, ed. J. Havet, *Lettres de Gerbert* (Collection de textes pour servir à l'enseignement de l'histoire 6, Paris 1889), 205; BZ no. 693.

[52] BZ no. 1018.

[53] Wibert, *Vita Leonis* II 3, Migne, *PL* 143, col. 496.

be priests of their churches.[54] True, the provision that the unfree were to be emancipated before being made priests was repeatedly promulgated, but it was by no means always observed. The *presbyter venerandus* Baldmunt, who was originally a serf from the *familia* of the monastery of Kempten, was emancipated only in 926 by King Henry I at the request of Arnulf, duke of Bavaria.[55] He must thus have been appointed priest while still servile. What could happen to such people is shown by the fact that the synod of Ingelheim forbade lay owners of churches to beat their priests or to oppress them and do them injustice.[56] One must in any case ask how much the *libertas* of such priests was worth. The last canon of the synod of Hohenaltheim of 916 dealt at length with the problem. The starting point was the case of a lord who selected one of his serfs, had him educated, gave him his *libertas*, interceded with the bishop to have him made a priest and, following the precepts of the apostle, furnished him with clothing and upkeep. Should such a priest refuse in pride to celebrate mass for his lord, observe the canonical hours, sing the psalter and 'obey him right-fully' (*ei iuste obedire*) on the grounds that he was a free man and did not want to be or become the free dependant of another lord, the holy synod condemned this and laid down that he was to be excommunicated until he should see reason and obey his lord. Should he remain obstinate he was to be denounced to the bishop who had ordained him, degraded from the priesthood, and become once again the serf of the man who had been his lord when he was born.[57] Here again it is clear how relative was the medieval concept of freedom. *Libertas* by no means excluded dependence or the obligation to do spiritual or material services to a lord or pro-tector.[58] The acts of the synod of Tribur (895) even complain that certain laymen were so unjust towards their priests that they demanded a part of their movable property on their death, just as they demanded part of the property of dead serfs; priests were to be able to dispose freely of two-thirds of their movables, with one-third going to their church.[59]

The economic position of the country clergy meant that the enforce-ment of clerical celibacy was fraught with difficulty. The demand for sexual abstinence had been linked from apostolic times with the expec-tation of parousia, participation in the coming kingdom of God. It was thus a part of monastic asceticism. For priests it was a consequence of God's presence in the Eucharist which they celebrated. This required

[54] Stutz, 'Eigenkirche, Eigenkloster', 323; Barlow, *English Church 1000–1066*, 186.
[55] MGH Dipl. Henry I, no. 10.   [56] MGH Const. I.15 no. 6 c. 5.
[57] MGH Const. I.626f. no. 433 c. 38.
[58] Tellenbach, *Libertas*, 21f.; Tellenbach, 'Servitus', 232f.
[59] MGH Capit. II.248 no. 252, *canones extravagantes* no. 6.

their purity, and as in many other religions sexual intercourse was considered to make its participants impure. Canons of councils and penitentials laid down numerous regulations on the subject, graded in severity according to the place of the delinquent in the ranks of the church hierarchy.[60] Only gradually did such provisions come to be observed. Even in the early middle ages bishops were generally unmarried (with numerous exceptions), and to a large extent they did indeed observe the regulations as to which women might live with them in the same household.[61] The ancient problem was most easily solved for those clergy who lived in *vita communis* in large clerical communities. But a country cleric who was so poor that he could scarcely afford male and female servants was dependent on the help of wife and children in order to wring from the parish lands enough from which to live and to pay the dues to the bishop.[62] Moreover he had to take care to see that his family was provided for after his death, either by putting savings aside or by having one of his sons appointed in succession as 'hereditary priest'.[63] This was the origin of 'hereditary churches', which were tolerated by bishops, so long as the priest trained one of his sons for spiritual service and fulfilled his financial obligations. Nevertheless, they carried the risk that church property might be alienated. There was a tendency for free or freed priests to take free women as wives, in order to win freedom for their children and leave them a free inheritance. This must have occurred frequently enough, to the detriment of the churches concerned, for churchmen to seek a remedy. In the early eleventh century in particular they did this by laying down that the children of priests were serfs of the church, even when they had issued from unions with free women.[64]

---

[60] H. Chadwick, 'Enkrateia', *RAC* 5, col. 362; A. Oepke, 'Ehe I', *RAC* IV, col. 659ff.; H. Barion, 'Zölibat', *RGG*, 3rd edn, col. 1923f.; Hödl, *Lex continentiae*, 325–44.

[61] Lesne, *Propriété ecclésiastique*, 254; for an example see the council of Augsburg, MGH Const. I.19 no. 9, cc. 1, 4, 11.

[62] Böhmer, 'Eigenkirchentum', 312ff.

[63] *Ibid.*, 327ff.

[64] MGH Const I.62 no. 31; 70ff. no. 34; Violante, *Pataria Milanese*, 11.

4

RELIGIOUS LIFE AND THOUGHT

—— • ——

It has become customary to speak of the faith or piety of the people or of the masses and to posit a distinction between this and the religious notions of the educated, in particular of the clergy and the lay élite. According to this view popular religiosity was suffused with archaic, numinous, pre-Christian elements, which had long been excluded from the church by the early councils and popes. As an example of this we need only mention the veneration of stones, trees, and waters, or the fear of witches and demons. Credulity in respect of the legends of the saints, of miracles, and of the effects of relics is also often taken to be a sign of 'popular' religion. More recently there has been a cautious reaction against this view, seen for example in the following quotation from Raoul Manselli (though he too is concerned with 'popular religion' in the middle ages): 'it would in our opinion be a fundamental methodological error to conceive of popular religion as having been something quite different from learned religion'.[1] It is indeed an error to separate popular religion

---

[1] Manselli, *Religion populaire*, 14 n. 4; E. Delaruelle, *La Piété populaire au moyen-âge* (Turin 1975), also makes reservations, as for example on p. 529: 'not necessarily, for one often has the impression that clerics and knights, even princes and bishops did not have a noticeably more refined piety than that of the people'. See also Demm, 'Rolle des Wunders', 316: 'Most bishops were locked into popular magical conceptions'. The old provision that bishops and clerics of all grades who consulted magicians were to be deposed was frequently repeated; see for example Atto of Vercelli, *Capitulare*, Migne, *PL* 134, col. 137. A discussion of the book by R. and C. Brooke, *Popular Religion in the Middle Ages. Western Europe 1000–1300* (London 1984), which appeared while the German version of this book was being printed, was no longer possible; see provisionally below, pp. 100–1.

or popular piety from a theoretically more or less enlightened religion. How could medieval religion have been differentiated according to social position or education? To suppose that it could is to project the ideas of the Enlightenment back into the middle ages.

Of course, many aspects of the belief, doctrine, and liturgical practice of Christianity are a component of religion in general; others can be traced to the customs of specific peoples in pre-Christian times or to a profound or more superficial understanding of the Bible and the church fathers. But the religious beliefs and needs of the peasant scarcely differed in this respect from those of the upper classes (including those of the clergy, whether poor or educated); much that we now see as a remnant of paganism or as naive or primitive can be found just as easily in lay and ecclesiastical élites. The 'official' religion of the liturgy and the life with the sacraments may often have degenerated into a shallow traditionalism at all levels of society; but it always contained within itself the possibility of its own revival.

It is surprising how varyingly the state and effectiveness of theological studies in the early and early high middle ages have been judged by scholars of the highest rank in our time. On the one hand one finds statements about the theological dark ages between Gregory the Great and Anselm of Canterbury, or about a theological nadir at the end of the eighth century;[2] it has been claimed that the theological problems of the Carolingian era were restricted only to learned polemic, with Gottschalk alone achieving the level previously attained by Bede and the 'powerful' Boniface. On the other hand it has been claimed that the period from the sixth to the eighth centuries was one of great liturgical creativity, and the period from the ninth to the eleventh centuries has also been seen as one in which the development of the liturgy was very much alive, though more so in some countries than in others. Admittedly the tendency towards learned controversy or systematic thought was not a strong one between the ninth and eleventh centuries.[3] The differing conceptions of transubstantiation propounded by Hrabanus Mauris and Ratramnus of Corbie on the one hand and by Paschasius Radbertus on the other continued to give impulses to thought in the tenth and eleventh centuries until they took on new life and a new precision of expression in the controversies surrounding the doctrines of Berengar of Tours.[4] There was no shortage of 'learned' theologians in the tenth and early eleventh century. In the question of the Eucharist there was undoubtedly a certain tendency towards syncretism, in so far as the dogmatic problem was even

---

[2] Angenendt, 'Religiosität und Theologie', 29.
[3] Neunhäuser, 'Gestaltwandel', 170f.   [4] See above, p. 1.

perceived.[5] In general the fairest view of the theology of this period is to see it as practical rather than speculative theology. As such, as the proclamation of the true faith, as exposition of the sacred page and of the church fathers, it had a considerable effect. It was practised without much regulation from above, using techniques which had been developed much earlier for expounding the Bible according to its literal, allegorical, and historical senses. These were employed with enthusiasm in the service of an eschatological view of the world to show parallels between the Old and New Testaments and to provide prophecies and warnings for one's own time.

Preaching was expected not just of bishops and abbots but also of parish priests. Burchard of Worms (d. 1025) recapitulated in his canon law collection the older injunctions to the priest to preach.[6] He did so in what is an extensive text, almost a sermon in itself, and one could well imagine that a priest might impress his congregation simply by repeatedly reading it aloud. At the beginning the fundamental articles of faith are to be proclaimed, belief in 'the one omnipotent God, Father, Son, and Holy Ghost, the eternal and invisible who created heaven and earth, the seas and all that is therein; that divinity, substance and majesty are one in the three persons of the Father, the Son, and the Holy Spirit'. Thereafter the remaining sentences of the creed are to be expounded, the doctrine of the last judgement, of those sins and crimes which will be visited with eternal punishments, but also of the love of God and one's neighbour, of belief and hope in God, humility and patience, chastity and abstinence, mildness, mercy, alms and the confession of sins, and the duty to forgive those who trespass against us their trespass as laid down in the Lord's Prayer.

The effects of divine service in rural churches on the broad mass of the rural population, the majority of all Christians, have also been judged very variedly in modern times. From early on in the missionary period in Scandinavia candles, incense, purple stoles, chant and bells are supposed to have made a great impression.[7] For peasants and knights alike in England the ecclesiastical sphere was allegedly the quintessence of all things beautiful: the church buildings themselves; the liturgical utensils; the priests who could read English and sing in Latin; and so on.[8] By contrast it has been asked: 'what could this superstitious rural population,

---

[5] Geiselmann, *Eucharistielehre*, 283f. and 407f.; de Lubac, *Corpus Mysticum*, 117ff.

[6] *Decretorum Collectio* II 59ff., Migne, *PL* 140, col. 636: for corresponding texts see *Ansegisi Capitularium* I 76, MGH Capit. 1.404f.; *Reginonis abbatis Prumiensis libri duo de synodalibus causis et disciplinis ecclesiasticis* 1.204ff., ed. E. Wasserschleben (Leipzig 1840), 103.

[7] Gerhardt, *Norwegische Geschichte*, 63.   [8] Deanesly, *Sidelights*, 328.

which crowded around the church door and heard Latin being spoken at
a distance and watched the priest's gestures, have understood of the
gospel? What could the poor have expected of a clergy which was drawn
from the serfs of the great estates, of parish priests who had themselves to
plough their fields to feed their wives and children and soon forgot what
they had learned?'[9] In another author we read that 'the tedium of all these
sermons should not allow us to forget that their monotonous drip helped
to form some of the deep structures of our society, both in its annual
rhythms and in its sexual morality'.[10] The reality was probably even more
varied and differentiated than these imaginative portraits put together by
knowledgeable scholars familiar with the sources. It is certain, however,
that over generations and centuries men's religious feelings and thoughts
were deeply moulded by experiences and patterns of behaviour which at
first seemed strange, then were half understood, only to become more and
more habitual in the end. One should not forget how powerful in all
religious are ancient customs and socially prescribed rituals. But even the
most fossilised practices can once again become free and alive with
charisma.

The centre of all devotion was the belief in God's presence in the
sacraments as performed in the liturgy. Just as God had become man in
Christ, so the boundary between heaven and earth was conceived of as
permeable. Admittedly, the part played by the people in the celebration
of the Eucharist had declined long before the tenth century.[11] The priest
normally stood with his back to the congregation, rarely as in former
times *versus populum*.[12] The canon of the mass, which in the eighth
century had been said as a quiet prayer, was now softly spoken by
the priest; the prayer of the congregation, which had been stressed
in Carolingian capitularies, had become less important. The subtle
expositions of learned theologians were probably not really understood by
most priests and laymen of all classes. But the central and simple theme of
the unity between Christ and His church and hence between Christ and
those present (even if they only stood at the church door) in the congregation, and the indispensability of this unity for one's salvation were
recognised consciously or unconsciously; even the idea of losing
membership of this community was a frightening one. The individual's

---

[9] Duby, *Frühzeit*, 91.

[10] Boglioni, *Culture populaire*, 29: 'the tedium of all these sermons should not make us
forget that their monotonous rain formed some of the deepest structures of our society,
from the calendar to sexual morality'.

[11] G. Nickl, *Der Anteil des Volkes an der Messliturgie in Frankreich von Chlodwig bis Karl den
Großen* (Innsbruck 1930), 72; T. Klauser, *Liturgieschichte*, 101.

[12] Nussbaum, 'Standort', 414.

own life was in practice bound up with the more or less comprehended liturgies of baptism, confirmation, penitence, and unction of the sick, which marked fateful moments in the life of the Christian and his nearest and dearest. The presence of Jesus Christ in all these actions was perceived as a mystery, even as a miracle. But the miracle of the Eucharist is not perceptible by our senses. To support faith the assistance of other miracles was drawn on, according to Ambrose by analogy with two other great miracles, those of the Creation and the Incarnation.[13]

The sacrament of consecration made bishops and priests instruments of the Deity. Through them he was omnipresent in the dispensing of the sacraments, and he conferred on them much of its power to bless. The consecration of churches and of chrism was reserved to bishops, but the other consecrations could be performed by all priests, some even by clerics in deacon's orders. The great number of benedictions was increased still further between the ninth and eleventh centuries;[14] as a rule the sacramentaries of the period include a large number of them. There were blessings of, among many other things, churches and chapels, altars, bells and liturgical utensils, holy water, cemeteries, brides and bride-grooms, fields, flocks, bread, the weapons of Christian warriors, the sick, travellers and pilgrims, even the objects used in ordeals. The counterpart to the power of blessing was the power to conjure and drive out evil spirits by exorcism. It is evident that this whole area of blessings and exorcisms was full of elements of archaic religiosity.[15] The most questionable aspect of the syncretism between archaic and Christian religion was that found in the theory and practice of the ordeal. This tried provocatively to tempt God and to misuse him for aims which were sometimes harmless, and sometimes appalling, for gaining power and annihilating opponents. In this area least of all can we speak of a special kind of 'popular religion'.

That the invisible, the numinous, the divine, and the demonic can intervene in the visible world, and that such intervention is determined by the way men behave, is a belief common to all religions.[16] A sharp

---

[13] De Lubac, *Corpus Mysticum*, 298. Von Harnack, *Christus praesens – vicarius Christi*, 419, also termed the presence of Christ in the sacraments 'the greatest miracle known to the history of religion'.

[14] Schreiber, 'Abgabenwesen'; 'Segnungen'.

[15] The power to bless corresponded to the power to curse; see Little, 'Formules monastiques de malediction', 377–99.

[16] Ordeals and the belief in them are a dark chapter in the history of all religions; see Nottarp, *Gottesurteile*, especially 155ff.; Nottarp, *Gottesurteilstudien*; Leitmaier, *Kirche und die Gottesurteile*, offers a pointed analysis of the originally magical conception of the world from which the ordeals sprang.

division between this world and the transcendental regions beyond it, a
humbly devout or helplessly anxious agnosticism in respect of all that lies
beyond death are modern attitudes which would have been incomprehensible and unbearable to ancients and primitives alike. Christians, even
if they believe themselves to be living in an intermediate time of
unpredictable length, are conscious of the coming of God's kingdom; in
part they try to live like the Lord's disciples in the early church, and in
part they remain rooted in earthly doings, awaiting the end of the world
in hope and fear. The temporal life is always lived with a view to eternal
life. The basic premise both of the church and of the individual Christian
is eschatological. One may be lost to mere worldly things, troubled by
sinfulness and guilt, but the aid of the heavenly powers seems to be
attainable through penance, prayer, and good works, and the powers
intervene of their own accord in the world below. The miraculous
transcendence of the boundary between heaven and earth, between God
and man, is visible first of all in Christ's humanity, then in his presence in
the sacraments, and then in the power of bishops and priests to bless.[17]
After numerous controversies the theological doctrine had been
established that it was his power alone which was at work in their
blessings; the efficacy of the gifts of the spirit was not dependent on the
personal worthiness of the priest who dispensed them.[18] One should recall
that the church prayed for the living and for the dead, for their eternal
salvation, in so far as they had not already achieved it as saints and
martyrs. Christianity formed a unity beyond the grave.[19] Visions, dreams
and warnings offered premonitions of the world beyond, and poetic
fantasy provided pictures and interpretations which amounted in effect to
maps of the next world.[20] The fundamental sense of closeness between
heaven and earth, characteristic of many religions, was intensified in

[17] Nussbaum, 'Standort', 414: 'In the liturgy in the basilica, heaven and earth, visible and
invisible are united with one another'; Pascher, *Liturgie der Sakramente*, 7ff.; Congar,
Ecclésiologie, 259: 'eschatology is already overcome within the church, for the Christian
life of the faith and the sacraments is already *in mysterio* the life of the next world'.
[18] Among the voices for and against see for an early example Odo of Cluny, *Collationes*
I 21, Migne, *PL* 133, col. 533: 'Non ergo melior est baptismus per manus cuiuslibet sancti
hominis quam per manus peccatoris, quoniam qualiscumque baptizator sit, Jesus est qui
baptizat.'
[19] Tellenbach, 'Historische Dimension', 202ff. and the literature cited there; see also
O. G. Oexle, 'Der Gegenwart der Toten', in *Death in the Middle Ages*, ed. H. Braet and
W. Verbeke (Louvain 1983), 19–77.
[20] Tellenbach, 'Historische Dimension', 204ff. and the literature cited there; see also
C. Carozzi, 'La Géographie', 423–81; P. Dinzelbacher, *Mittelalterliche Visionsliteratur*
(Spoleto 1989); P. Dinzelbacher and D. Bauer (ed.), *Volksreligionen im hohen und späten
Mittelalter* (Darmstadt 1990).

Christianity to an experience of God's miraculous intervention in the course of Christendom on earth, moving in hope and fear towards the last judgement. The short earthly life of man was lived under the shadow of the question of his eternal fate, to an extent which can hardly be exaggerated. Life was dominated by a longing for aid and for rescue from death. It was this which produced prayers and prayer-confraternities; from this among other things originated the expectant waiting for miracles, the deep willingness to recognise and venerate martyrs and saints as beings who could intercede with God for His mercy on sinners and at the same time be close to men in the form of their relics.[21]

As it was throughout the middle ages, Christian history in the tenth and eleventh century was moved by miracles, frequently and profoundly.[22] Of course the sensational appearance of phenomena which were thought to be unnatural or supernatural played a great part, and there was a belief in the possibility of magical or demoniacal sorcery. Belief in these things as such did not count as superstition, only their confusion with true miracles, which could be worked by God alone.[23] The historical signifi-cance of miracles was as manifestations of the intervention of divine omnipotence in the world. It is hardly possible to categorise the countless reports of miracles, however sophisticated the classification scheme. It can hardly be denied that there was a belief, even if only in the form of an unconscious mental reservation, in the possibility of archaic magic. But how was one to distinguish between magic and divine miracle-working? Matthew 9: 33–4 told the story of how Christ had driven the devil out from a dumb man and restored his speech to him: 'and the multitudes marvelled, saying, It was never so seen in Israel. But the Pharisees said, He casteth out devils through the prince of the devils.' For miracles to be perceived there must be wonder at things which have never been seen or heard of. One and the same phenomenon can become a miracle through the belief in divine intervention or sorcery by assuming that devilish or some other kind of numinous power was at work. Councils sought to set limits to what was perceived as an excessive addiction to miracles.[24] But why should those priests who sought to fight fires in a church with the altar-cloth on which the Eucharist rested be called 'most stupid' (*stultissimi*) when it was a commonplace of hagiographical literature that

---

[21] It would have been logical to recognise this as a deviation from the doctrine that revelation had come to an end since the death of the last apostle. See J. Ratzinger, 'Das Problem der Dogmengeschichte in der Sicht der katholischen Theologie', *Arbeits-gemeinschaft für Forschung des Landes Nordrhein-Westfalen*, 139 (1966), 18.

[22] Finucane, 'Use and Abuse', 1–10.

[23] Grant, *Miracle and Natural Law*, 127.

[24] Council of Seligenstadt (1023), MGH Const. I.637 no. 437 c. 6.

fires consumed everything but left the host or the altar untouched?[25]
There were gestures and signs used to ward off demons and disasters.[26]
Among the holy objects used in the liturgy which could perform
miracles, the bread and wine of the Eucharist were the holiest,[27] since the
flesh and blood of the Lord, and so his complete presence, consecrated
them.[28] It was thus held to be just as reprehensible to reconsecrate them
as it was to rebaptise.[29] It is recorded that a spider fell into the chalice after
consecration, and that the priest knew of no other remedy than to drink
the holy blood with the spider, which then reemerged when he had his
blood let that evening.[30] Eucharistic miracles, especially those concerning
healing, were transmitted in thankful veneration. God and the saints
could also make their will known through natural events. Rome is said
to have been struck by an earthquake in 1021; this was seen as a sign of
divine anger over the mocking of the cross by Jews, and when Pope
Benedict VIII had the Jews executed the earthquake ceased.[31] The
veneration of the holy cross spread everywhere in the high middle ages,
and that of the *volto santo*, the 'Holy Face of Lucca', probably began at this
time.

Saints were capable not just of helping men to save their souls but also
of rescuing them in a thousand different earthly predicaments and of
granting their hearts' desires. Fantasy was here at work in pictures and
poetic narratives. One example of the saint as helper of those who desired
children must suffice. A noble Alsatian lady had prayed to St Odilie for
children, but had given birth only to girls. The saint appeared in a dream
to the desperate mother and advised her to turn to St Verena in Zurzach:
'she, not I, has power to give sons and daughters to those who pray
for them'. The lady followed this advice and was blessed with twin
boys.[32]

---

[25] See for example Browe, *Eucharistische Wunder*, 679; Demm, 'Rolle des Wunders', 330;
    Tellenbach, 'Translation', 611.
[26] We may point to the cross and the gesture of making a cross. See Nicholas I, epistola 82,
    MGH Epp. VI.438: when wood is made into a cross 'suscipiens autem omnimodo
    venerandam similitudinem, sacra est et daemonibus terribilis, propter quod in ea
    figuratus est Christus'.
[27] Browe, *Eicharistische Wunder*, 93ff.
[28] *Ibid.*, 199f.
[29] *Ibid.*, 64.
[30] Grant, *Miracle and Natural Law*, 153: 'Guiding the course of nature and of history by
    frequent interventions in the "natural" order of events'.
[31] BZ no. 1229; Adémar von Chabannes, *Chronicon*, III 52, ed. J. Chavanon (Collection de
    textes 20, Paris 1897), 175 and 206.
[32] K. Schmid, 'Heirat, Familienfolge, Geschlechtsbewußtsein', *Settimane*, 24 (1977), 124;
    see on this the pilgrimage made by the parents of Bishop Benno II of Osnabrück,

The veneration of saints and martyrs began early. Frantisek Graus has shown convincingly that the origins and dissemination of their cults were due not primarily to the historicity of their martyrdom or to the genuine deeds of the virtuous, but to the literature of the legends of the saints.[33] The veneration of saints often began on a small, local or regional scale; either it died out or it was kept alive and often spread far and wide by the legends.[34] Some great saints existed only in legends. Such writings might be tendentious propaganda, aimed at increasing the fame of a church, a monastery, or a place, and we know of examples of jealous rivalries over the possession of saints. But they were able to have their effect only because of the fundamental need to see the saints as mediators between this world and beyond and between God and men in need of mercy, for they were normally credited with the power to 'intercede' with God and to work miracles. By contrast with the magical and pagan concept of miracle the Christian aspect of this has rightly been described as a 'triangular relationship between God, the miracle-worker and the miracle-receiver'.[35] In spite of the part played by the writers of legends the cults of saints were generally of spontaneous origin, without direction from above. There is occasionally a reference to episcopal measures against abuse, but there were no formal procedures. Not until the late eleventh century did the popes concern themselves with the control of the cult of saints. The first papal canonisation, that of Bishop Ulrich of Augsburg in 993, was due to the initiative not of John XV but of an Augsburg delegation.[36] Only from the time of Leo IX onwards did this gradually change, when the pope had moved from being the spiritual head of the church to being truly its ruler and director.

The cult of the saints was made more powerful by the veneration of their relics. The grave or body or parts of the body of the martyr or saint brought about his presence and gave hope that he would give assistance. The role played by icons in the East was played in the West by relics,

---

G. Tellenbach, 'Die Stadt Rom in der Sicht ausländischer Zeitgenossen (800–1200)', *Saeculum*, 24 (1973), 19.

[33] Delehaye, *Sanctus*, 74ff. and 109; Delehaye, *Origins*, 208ff.: 'The saints who never existed'; T. Klauser, 'Christlicher Märtyrerkult, heidnischer Hexenkult und spätjüdische Heiligenverehrung', *Arbeitsgemeinschaft für Forschung des Landes Nordrhein-Westfalen*, 91 (1960), 30f.

[34] Graus, *Volk, Herrscher und Heiliger*, 39ff., 62ff., 302. Graus seems to me to underestimate religious needs, which are present as he rightly says (p. 32) not just in the 'people' but in all Christians.

[35] Delehaye, *Sanctus*, 184; de Gaiffier, *Etudes critiques*, 475ff.; Demm, 'Rolle des Wunders', 302.

[36] T. Klauser, 'Liturgie der Heiligsprechung', especially his list of canonisations from 993 onwards, 229ff.; R. Klauser, 'Zur Entwicklung', 90ff.; Mascard, *Reliques*, 92ff.

though here too the saints could be present in their pictures.[37] The
faithful are repeatedly reported to have seen the statues of saints weeping,
sweating, bleeding, or even speaking. The acquisition of relics was
pursued with vigour. They were much sought after as gifts and as objects
of trade, and were stolen by the most respectable and distinguished
persons and their representatives, a practice which led to the development
of a complete casuistry of relic theft, *pia fraus*.[38] The majority of the
customers of relic traders and thieves were kings, prelates, and members
of the high nobility.[39] Those who did not have a great saint or a large
collection of relics at home set out for Jerusalem, Rome, or Santiago de
Compostela or goals nearer home to seek the help of the saint. Whether
near at home or further away it was customary to make lavish presents to
him, and the dangerous pilgrimage was an effective means of both doing
penance and acquiring merits. The intercession of the saints could be
implored for earthly assistance; their relics might be decorated with gold,
silver, and precious stones, but there was no hesitation in showing
disappointment if their help was withheld. Indeed, on occasions the saint
would be punished for his failure. His coffin or his relics would be taken
from the altar and placed on the ground in the ritual known as *humiliatio
sancti*, forbidden by the second council of Lyons in 1274.[40] It has been well
observed that relics were 'the main channel through which supernatural
powers could have an influence on the needs of daily life. The normal
mortal could see them and handle them, although they belonged not to
this transitory world but to eternity.'[41]

The belief in miracles, saints, and relics, their veneration in the hope of
help both in this world and in the winning of eternal life permeated all
levels of Christendom. Here and there we find some reservations, a
tendency to set more weight on love of God and of one's neighbour, or
to place prayer higher as a human means of achieving salvation.[42] Some

---

[37] Congar, *Ecclésologie*, 314 n. 21: 'what icons were in the East, namely the presence on earth
of celestial beings, relics were in the Germanic world'.
[38] Fichtenau, 'Reliquienwesen', 60–89; Delehaye, *Sanctus*, 196ff.; Dupré-Theseider,
'Grande rapina', 420–31; Tellenbach, 'Translation', 608ff.; Geary, *Furta Sacra*; see on
this M. Heinzelmann's review in *HZ*, 232 (1981), 402ff.; Hermann-Mascard,
Reliques.
[39] Geary, *Furta sacra*, 68.
[40] Geary, 'Humiliation', 42; Geary, 'Coercition des Saints', 145–61; Little, 'Morphologie'.
[41] R. W. Southern, *Western Society and the Church in the Middle Ages* (Harmondsworth
1970), 30.
[42] R. Klauser, 'Zur Entwicklung', 88ff.; when Demm, 'Rolle des Wunders', 330 and 342,
speaks of a negative or hostile attitude to miracles in the case of Otloh of Bamberg, this
is probably a misunderstanding. Otloh merely refuses to perform miracles himself and
refers those seeking wonders to saints and relics.

were cruder than others in their dealings with relics, but this was hardly a question of social rank or of education. Sigebert of Gembloux records how Pope John XIII healed a count in Otto I's entourage, who had become possessed, by hanging St Peter's chains round his neck. At first two bold Roman clerics brought false chains, which had no effect; then the pope commanded in anger that the genuine ones should be brought. Bishop Dietrich of Metz, a great collector of relics, was struck by this and tried to acquire the chains for himself; his fervent prayers at least secured him a present of a piece of them from the pope. Pope, emperor, bishop, and the monk of Gembloux must presumably all have been convinced of the miracle-working power of relics.[43] Similar stories were retailed through the centuries. Occasionally there was some resistance to the more excessive expressions of imagination or relics of ancient superstition, but even the cruder notions of saints, miracles, and relics were not an expression of the piety of the 'people' or the 'masses'; they were rather the expression of a spontaneous longing for extraordinary manifestations of the saint from whom one expected help on earth and salvation in the world to come.[44]

MONASTICISM: A LIFE DETERMINED BY THE NEXT WORLD AND ITS INFLUENCE ON THIS ONE

The significance of monasticism was probably at its greatest and most varied within the life of western Christianity between the ninth and the end of the eleventh centuries. Its history was in essence a continuation of the eastern and western monasticism of late antiquity and the early middle ages, and it laid the foundations for the great orders of the high and late middle ages which shaped the course of western history. Monasteries and communities of clerics and hermits set the tone in the spirituality of the whole church, in education and art, in the transmission of culture in particular, in agriculture and the social structures based on it. Over and above this they were, willingly or unwillingly, participants in the political life of kingdoms and principalities, though to an extent which

---

[43] Sigebert of Gembloux, *Vita Deoderici* c. 16, MGH SS iv.474f.; *Chronicon, s.a.* 969, MGH SS vi.351; BZ no. 461; see Fichtenau, 'Reliquienwesen', 85f. and Dupré-Theseider, 'Grande rapina', 428. Amatus, *Ystoire de li Normant* viii 79f., ed. O. Delarc, 352, tells of a deadly serious belief in relics shown by two famous princes a century later: Robert Guiscard demanded a tooth of St Matthew from the vanquished Duke Gisulf of Salerno. Gisulf had a tooth broken from the mouth of a dead Jew, but the deception was uncovered and he had to hand over the 'genuine' tooth.

[44] Deanesly, *Pre-Conquest Church*, 336: kings venerated saints and relics just as much as did peasants.

102 The western church

varied with time and place. But whatever they managed to achieve rested on the spiritual conception of monasticism, as treated and reflected on in what was seen then and has been seen by its modern students as a 'theology of monastic life'.[45]

The true reason for choosing the life of a monk was the idea of divine vocation, a kind of charismatic talent for ascetic concentration. There followed a decision to be converted and to do penance. This often arose out of a general sense of human guilt rather than from any specific experience of sin, from a leaning towards a common life, a life in a community of brotherly love, a life of contemplation not of action, coupled with a concentration on the life beyond death, the eternal life with Christ following the promised resurrection. The models for this way of life were the apostles and the communities of the early church on the one hand and the future as then conceived of on the other; it was rooted in the desire to be as close as possible both to Christ's own times and to his eternal kingdom.[46] Christ's kingdom is not of this world, which neither can nor should have any great significance. One renders unto Caesar the things that are Caesar's. Monasticism occasionally reflected an ancient Christian attitude of protest against those fellow Christians and their institutions which had allowed themselves to become too concerned with the things of this world.[47] By contrast, the true monk showed a certain indifference towards the here and now.[48] Even to try to correct the world's weaknesses and failings was to risk diverting attention from the true goal and ending in sin and confusion. The question of whether the relationship of the monk and monastic institutions to the world was to be a more irenic one or a more aggressive one is a problem which has permeated the whole history of monasticism, and it was much discussed in the tenth and eleventh centuries in particular.

It is one of the most remarkable phenomena in the whole of history that in the high middle ages to many members of the highest and wealthiest or at least prosperous strata of society, who had the best chances of enjoying earthly pleasures to the full, renounced them. Taken over the whole of the West it must at times have amounted to thousands in each

[45] Leclercq, 'Monachisme', 437–45.
[46] K. Hallinger, 'Le Climat des premiers temps de Cluny', Revue Mabillon, 45–7 (1955–7), 120, 124: 'To be a monk is to realise the Pentecostal church; to be a monk is to anticipate the life to come'; Leclercq, 'Idéal monastique', 231: 'Monasticism is the extension of Pentecost.'
[47] Hallinger, 'Geistige Welt Clunys', 437; G. Le Maître, 'Pour une théologie de la vie monastique', Théologie, 49 (1961), 9ff.
[48] Tellenbach, Libertas, 32ff. with nn. 44 and 45; de Valous, Le Monachisme Clunisien, part 2.

generation. It is rare to hear that either old-established or newly founded monasteries had difficulty in finding fresh recruits. The flow of new candidates was particularly impressive in those places where the rules of monastic life had been restored to their ancient strictness, imposed more rigorously or even redefined more severely. Even hermits living in solitude, chastising themselves to the limits of what was possible, found imitators and followers who revered them. We must assume that the main motive for the choice of a monastic life was always the eschatological ideal of monasticism, even if this may have lost something of its driving force in the course of a long life or was mixed with other motives from the start. The parents of those who were dedicated to monasteries as children will have thought not only of the salvation of the child oblate concerned and the help in prayer which could be given to the other members of the family, but also more opportunistically of avoiding an excessive fragmentation of the family inheritance.

In a monastic community there were comparatively few who as abbots or holders of other offices enjoyed a spiritual responsibility and a position of power which might satisfy earthly or human needs and which they exercised over the rest of the community and within the environment of the monastery in defence of its religious, financial, and political interests. They alone were the direct recipients of the veneration felt towards their community and its salvation-bringing powers by laity and clergy alike. It is hardly possible to calculate precisely how many did so, but at least a part of the monastic population lived a life genuinely cut off from the world. Some might occasionally have an opportunity to participate in the active life, as administrators of monastic property and revenues, as witnesses of legal transactions or in journeys made on behalf of their abbot. It will be easier to estimate the degree to which monks kept in contact with their families and relatives when the prosopographical studies of monasticism currently being undertaken have progressed further. But in the monastery itself the emphasis was on spiritual contemplation, which with luck corresponded to the monk's own inclinations and was not felt as a tedious restriction. It could be enriched when monastic leisure gave the suitably talented monk the opportunity to read sacred writings or write liturgical and theological treatises or practice theological and literary meditation or artistic creativity.[49] Asceticism could spring from the longing for the peace and quiet needed to prepare oneself for the heavenly Jerusalem. But we should also be realistic: it could equally lead to excesses rooted in

[49] Moulin, *Vie quotidienne*, 27ff., on the long day of the religious; de Gaiffier, 'L'hagiographie et son public', 148, on the monk as reader; Leclercq, 'Was Cluny an enemy of culture?', 172–82.

impatience or ambition and to petty jealousies and quarrels about trivial matters.

There is an immense literature about monasticism and monasteries. Its main concern is with the contact between monasticism and the world and with monasticism's effects on the world. It deals with the history of foundations and founding families and of monastic possessions, their acquisition, preservation, and exploitation. In connection with these it deals with the charters, scriptoria, and libraries of monasteries, with the relations with princes and lords in the immediate vicinity or further afield, and with bishops and other monasteries. Much space is often devoted to abbots, to their origins and to their actions inside and outside their monastery, and to selected monks whose reputation, whether due to noble birth or to special achievements in asceticism, art, scholarship or even on occasion missionary work, had spread beyond the monastery. The study of liturgy, monastic customs, and religious attitudes has thrown light on the internal life of monasteries.[50]

Little is known about the individuality of most monks. That is a logical consequence of their decision to withdraw from the earthly world of history. Only recently has it gradually become possible to build up a picture of religious communities and convents through the study of commemorative prayer and the liturgical writings which this produced;[51] techniques have been developed which have made it possible to study these sources critically and make them speak.[52] We are slowly coming to know more about thousands of these previously unknown monks: what they were called, when they joined their monastery, whether they received holy orders and if so which, when they lived and died. Their names and dates often tell us something of their origins, and hence of possible connections with the founders and patrons of their monastery.[53]

---

[50] A short and precise account of *Libri memoriales* and necrologies as sources is given by K. Schmid in *Mittelalterliche Textüberlieferung und ihre historische Aufarbeitung. Beiträge der Monumenta Germaniae Historica zum 31. Historikertag, Mannheim 1976* (Munich 1976), 76–85.

[51] A decisive change in the direction of enquiry has been brought about by the researches of K. Schmid, J. Wollasch, and their collaborators. See on this Schmid and Wollasch, 'Gemeinschaft der Lebenden und Verstorbenen', 367–405. The two scholars have founded a collective work with the title *Societas et Fraternitas*; see the programmatic article with the same title, *FMSt*, 9 (1975), 1–48.

[52] D. Geuenich, 'Der Computer als Hilfsmittel der Namen- und Sprachsforschung', *Freiburger Universitätsblätter*, 51 (1976), 33–45; G. Althoff, 'Zum Einsatz der elektronischen Datenverarbeitung in der historischen Personenforschung', *Freiburger Universitätsblätter*, 52 (1976), 17–32.

[53] These methods were used to prepare the monumental work *Die Klostergemeinschaft von Fulda im frühen Mittelalter*, ed. K. Schmid (with G. Althoff, E. Freise, D. Geuenich,

But it is the inevitable result of their own intentions that the historian often has to content himself with learning how they prayed for the salvation of their own souls, of those of their fellow-monks and of the other people who were in some way connected with them.

It would not be quite accurate to assume that monks, in renouncing the *vita activa*, including the Christian care of souls, restricted themselves to a concern for the salvation of their own souls.[54] The service of the sacraments by the monastic community was by its nature a part of the service performed by the church universal. Just as the church building and its ornaments served the glory of God, so did the liturgy, which took ever more elaborate and ceremonious forms. In their prayers monks implored God for protection, prosperity, and peace for Christian princes and peoples even on earth, and hence the service of those who realised the Christian life at its purest always had a political element. The lives of those who had resolved to despise earthly things (*terrena despicere*)[55] set standards for all those Christians who did not lead the monastic life; in particular the norms for the clergy serving the holy sacraments came more and more to be modelled on the life of monks. Not to follow these models was increasingly a matter for silent or even noisy reproach.[56] The greatest value was set on the prayers said by monks for the eternal salvation of all living and dead; the contemplation of the last judgement, the fear of eternal death, the hope of God's mercy and of eternal life stood above all

F. J. Jakobi, H. Kamp, O. G. Oexle, M. Sandmann, J. Wollasch, and S. Zörkendörfer), 3 vols. in 5 (Münstersche Mittelalter-Studien 8, Munich 1978) as well as the editions in the *Libri memoriales et Necrologia Nova Series* of the MGH; see most recently the fundamental study by Wollasch and his collaborators, *Synopse*. As an example of the kind of historical results to be expected from such researches see K. Schmid, 'Auf der Suche nach den Mönchen im mittelalterlichen Fulda', in *Von der Klosterbibliothek zur Landesbibliothek*, ed. A. Brett (Stuttgart 1978), 125–62, and J. Wollasch, 'Wer waren die Mönche von Cluny vom 10.–12 Jahrhundert?', in *Mélanges Jacques Stiennon* (Brussels 1982), 663–78.

[54] Thus the penance performed by monks was done on behalf of all Christians. See Chenu, 'Moines', 79: 'traditionally monastic life had been considered primarily in its character as penance, even as an institute of public penance'. On the problem see W. Schatz, *Studien zur Vorstellungswelt des frühen abendländischen Mönchtums* (Diss. Freiburg 1957), 96f. and 229; Leclercq, 'Idéal monastique', 236: 'Monasticism has as its mission the applying of remedies to the evils from which the world and the church suffer.'

[55] J. Pascher, '"Despicere terrena" in den römischen Messorationen', in *Kyriakon, Festschrift für Johannes Quasten* (Münster 1970), II.876–85; M. Bernards, 'Nudus nudum sequi', *Wissenschaft und Wahrheit*, 14 (1951), 148ff.; Bultot, 'Mépris du monde', 219–28; G. Olsen, 'The Idea of the Ecclesia Primitiva in the Writings of the Twelfth-Century Canonists', *Traditio*, 25 (1969), 61–86.

[56] Chenu, 'Moines', 68: 'the most complete and perfect Christian is the monk, the Christian who is dead to the world'.

earthly and transitory things. The prayers were bound up with the performance of penance. Many entered monasteries to make amends for sins which troubled their conscience. Others took on penance voluntarily for themselves and for others. With this were linked acts of charity for the monastic community or for the salvation of the souls of people whom one had taken under one's protection: the feeding of the poor, the care of the sick, the provision of hospitality to strangers and pilgrims.

The idea that only God's mercy could free from sin and only his inscrutable decision could lead to eternal life was also present; hence everything that was done by the consecrated members of the church was done in their capacity as God's representatives, whether it was in receiving confession, in imposing penitence, or in reconciling sinners. But religious feelings are not consistently logical; hence it was believed that people could influence God's decisions by prayer and good works. The vision of St Pianone recorded by St Jerome reported that Pianone had seen how an angel wrote the names of monks who approached the altar in a book, but not of all monks.[57] Those excluded were in a state of mortal sin. Thereafter the saint exhorted them to penitence and he wept with them until their names too were entered in the angel's book. Such things were recorded repeatedly, often in curiously calculatory forms, as in the norms laying down how many psalms were to be said daily or weekly or annually. It became necessary to set restrictions on the numbers of silent masses, about which Petrus Damiani complained that they sacrificed the Lord on the altar for the advantage of the individual, though he had suffered on the cross for the salvation of the whole world.[58]

There was a widespread belief that prayers and acts of penance and of Christian charity were merits in the sight of God, which could be performed on behalf of others both alive and dead. This could lead to such crude practices as the action of the rich sinner who divided the penance laid on him between himself and a hundred dependants, so that none was greatly burdened.[59] In general, however, the aid of prayers and of related good works was accepted in devout gratitude and with the intention of imitating monastic life as far as one's own strength allowed. The aid of

---

[57] Odo of Cluny, *Collationes* II 32, Migne, *PL* 133, cols. 577f.; see Capitani, 'Motivi di spiritualità cluniacense', 18 and n. 1.

[58] *Opusculum* XXVI.2, Migne, *PL* 145, col. 501.

[59] Poschmann, *Abendländische Kirchenbuße*, 56f. and 196 on the idea of the dangers of the arbitrary use of penance and of the priestly power to bind and loose; Duby, *Société*, 61, on the idea of 'purchasing salvation'; for an appreciation of the medieval notion of merits see K. H. Holl, *Gesammelte Aufsätze* (Tübingen 1938), II.32.

prayers was sought from those monks especially whose purity of life allowed one to suppose that God looked on them with favour. Such an attitude can be seen in a letter of Henry III's in which he begged Hugo of Cluny to act as godfather to his son: 'Which man who knows the right way would not hope for your prayers and those of your monks? Who would not strive to hold fast to the indissoluble bond of your love, you whose prayer is all the purer in that it is remote from worldly deeds, all the worthier in that it is near to God's sight?'[60] Hope and gratitude were expressed not only in words but also in gifts which were intended to make it possible or easier for the monks to perform acts pleasing to God; we shall return to this aspect.

It is characteristic that it was seen as possible to join together in common prayer and mutual enjoyment of the merits which these gained with God. This can already be seen in the prayer confraternities entered into by bishops and abbots at Attigny, Altötting, and Dingolfing in the second half of the eighth century;[61] in the *libri memoriales*, primarily of the ninth and tenth centuries but also begun or continued in later centuries; then above all in necrologies, calendar-based lists containing the dates of the deaths of the members of the religious community itself and beyond this of many individuals both lay and spiritual who were associated in fraternity, of popes, kings, bishops, priests, and nobles.[62] Such specific prayer-confraternities went beyond the universal petitions of prayer for all Christians whether living or dead. What is still more noticeable is the gradation of services performed for the dead according to their rank. It is understandable that for the salvation of the soul of a dead person a monk should sing many psalms, a bishop or priest celebrate many masses, a king or duke feed many poor people. But how are we to explain the fact that far more masses were to be said for a dead bishop than for a dead priest? Was it because his high office exposed him to greater temptations? Or because bishops in their capacity of teachers 'watch over your souls, for which they must give a reckoning' (Hebrews 13: 17)?[63] Prayer-confraternities could extend far beyond the walls of monasteries. They could include bishops, priests, clergy, and laity. Associations of priests were presumably always prayer-confraternities as well; but there were also confraternities which consisted to a great extent of lay persons, both men

---

[60] MGH Dipl. Henry III., no. 263.

[61] K. Schmid and O. G. Oexle, 'Voraussetzungen', 71–122.

[62] See above, nn. 50 and 53, and also Oexle, 'Memoria und Memorialüberlieferung', 70–95.

[63] On these problems see Tellenbach, 'Historische Dimension', 211; even if one follows Häussling, *Mönchskonvent*, 112, in saying that figures are 'means of expression not payments', the difference still remains.

and women, who gave each other mutual support in acts devoted to the care of the dead.[64]

Of course, monasteries could degenerate. In times of war monastic churches and buildings might be destroyed, monks might suffer material want to such an extent that they had to work with their own hands to win the bare necessities of life, which naturally meant that monastic discipline and the fulfilling of spiritual duties suffered. At the other end of the scale, growing prosperity led to monks who could not in the long run stand the sacrifices, hardships, and monotony of monastic life with its daily repetition of prayers, psalm-singing, and fasts; they associated with laymen or left the monastery and wandered around. Many abbots were also excessively concerned for their revenues, their comfort, and their power.

Here and there and from time to time such things will certainly have occurred. Nevertheless we must ask whether there were really so many decayed monasteries in the tenth and eleventh centuries as enthusiastic contemporaries and historians in our own time have liked to make out. Certainly not a few monasteries in those countries affected by warfare were completely ruined; certainly the piety of the monks occasionally slackened; certainly they sometimes fell into need after losing battles for properties and revenues. But their opponents were by no means always 'the laity'; often it was bishops, other monasteries, and dependent clerics with whom they had to deal. Complaints about the greed of laymen are one-sided at the least, for what laymen were able to steal from churches had all been granted to these churches by laymen. It was after all not the business of the clergy to create revenues for themselves, but rather to let themselves be provided for by devout laymen so that they could carry out their exalted service. If the institutions of proprietary church and monastery were responsible for so much damage as has often been maintained, usually in a rather stereotyped fashion, then one would have to blame not only lay but also clerical owners. Monastic owners may indeed have exploited their monasteries – sometimes because they themselves were in need – but most of them had a great interest in seeing that their monasteries were so endowed and internally ordered that they were able to fulfil their spiritual purpose.[65] Even the participation of lay monastic

[64] See below, pp. 130f. nn. 154ff.

[65] As an example of the prevailing schematism see P. Schmitz, *Geschichte des Benediktiner-ordens* I (Einsiedeln 1947), for example p. 85 on proprietary churches and proprietary monasteries in the eighth and ninth centuries as 'the main cause of monastic decline', or p. 105 on the alleged opposition of clergy and laity: 'even though the synods protested repeatedly, the magnates simply imposed their will on the clergy they hated'. See against this Fechter, *Cluny*, who points to the gifts of churches to Cluny by the laity (pp. 29ff.) and to the positive attitude taken by Cluny towards the nobility (p. 69).

proprietors in the election of abbots did not have to be disadvantageous, for often enough it was they who insisted on choosing the most devout and intelligent candidates, who would then be consecrated by the bishop, whose rights were normally respected.[66]

There have always been 'monastic reforms'. What was understood by this varied greatly, and needs to be clarified from case to case. It might simply mean, as it often did in the tenth century, repairing or rebuilding the churches and buildings of the monastery, gathering up the monks who had dispersed in the face of want, putting the material basis of the monastery on a sound footing, winning an important abbot, who could restore the monastery and provide the leadership needed for a genuinely monastic life.[67] Such a 'reform monastery' might acquire a high reputation and lead others to imitate its patterns of monasticism. The older monasteries included many which were regarded as eminent and venerable, such as St Gallen, the Reichenau, Fulda, Corvey, Glastonbury, Saint-Denis, Nonantola, Bobbio, and many others; these were by no means decayed, but continued traditional monasticism. The tenth century was no period of general monastic decline, but on the contrary one in which many important monastic centres were set up and spread: Cluny, Brogne, Gorze, Saint-Vanne, Einsiedeln, Camaldoli. Their monasticism was so famed that old monasteries were reorganised after their example and new ones founded on their pattern. Important abbots were summoned by princes to reform their monasteries: Odo of Cluny was called by the *patricius* Alberic to Rome, Gerard of Brogne by the count of Flanders and by the king of England to their countries.[68] A further possibility was to ask for an abbot or a few monks from one of these centres, even the entire team of monks necessary to start off a convent. This established connections between the centre providing assistance and the reformed or newly founded monasteries which might last a long or only a short time. Such 'filiations' should not, however, be thought of as permanent

---

[66] The rights of the diocesan bishop were generally respected, whether the monastic proprietor was a layman, an external bishop, or an abbot.

[67] Especially in recent English scholarship the tenth century is depicted as an era of reform for both monks and the churches. See for example John, 'The King and the Monks', 61–87, or the subheadings in chapter 14 of Deanesly, *Pre-Conquest Church* and in chapter 4 of her *Sidelights*. But there are stereotypes in the description of reform and decline in other countries as well.

[68] On Odo's monastic activities in Rome see G. Ferrari, *Early Roman Monasteries* (Studi di Antichità Christiana 23, Rome 1957), 230ff.; G. Antonelli, 'L'opera di Odone di Cluny in Italia', *Benedictina*, 4 (1950), 19ff.; on Brogne see J. Wollasch, 'Gerard de Brogne und seine Klostergründung', *Revue Bénédictine*, 70 (1960), 62–82, 224–31.

groupings.[69] Even the monastic rules which were adopted were usually changed in the course of time. The monastery which had provided the initial example might retain a certain authority, but permanent cooperation or regular visitation were not yet normal practices. Even more lasting and firmer groupings did not yet constitute 'orders' in the strict sense.[70] The Cistercians in the twelfth century were the first to organise themselves as an order. The connections between the Cistercian daugter monasteries and their famous mothers really were binding and permanent, and the 'filiation' was an essential part of Cistercian organisation. The abbots of mother houses visited their daughter houses regularly; all abbots came each year to the general chapter in Cîteaux, which issued statutes and modifications to them which were binding on all houses. This institutionalisation, characteristic of both the secular and the spiritual life of the twelfth century, was a model for older and younger forms of monasticism alike.

Orders can be clearly distinguished from each other and do not overlap. The monastic groupings of the tenth and eleventh centuries did not have such sharp boundaries. There were centres from which impulses of renewal and intensification went out to other monasteries, to abbots and monks, to the laymen and bishops who helped to support monastic life by founding, patronising and venerating monasteries. A list of such centres would include among others Gorze, St Maximin in Trier, Einsiedeln, Hirsau, Siegburg, Brogne, Saint-Vanne in Verdun, Fécamp, Stavelot, Fleury, Saint-Benigne in Dijon, Saint-Victor in Marseilles, Camaldoli, Vallombrosa, and Fruttuaria. What held together each of these circles was a matter of historical contingency: the authority of a founder or of a living abbot of the central monastery; the will of monastic proprietors and supporters both episcopal and lay; monastic ideals and customs. All these things mattered much more than legal conditions or constitutional subordination.[71]

Concern to realise the monastic ideal as fully as possible led to rivalries between streams of monasticism which were played out on the fields of

69 The lines of filiation constructed with great scholarship by Hallinger in *Gorze und Cluny* suffer from not taking this into account. The fact that a monk of a famous monastery was called to become abbot of another need not imply any long-term connection between the two houses. As a corrective to exaggerated ideas of the influence exercised by reform connections see e.g. Lippelt, *Thietmar*, 194 n. 8, who cites Hallinger, 1,620 n. 16, to the effect that Thietmar was a 'personality formed by Gorze'.

70 Such more or less fixed groups are often inaccurately termed 'orders', though even Cluny adopted the constitution of an order only after the Cistercians had provided a model. Hoffmann, 'Von Cluny', 167, also talks of Cluny's 'formation of an order'.

71 Great stress is often put on the differences between the Consuetudines, whether these concerned matters of religious and historical importance or only details which seem to us from this distance merely trivial (see Duby, *Frühzeit*, 183). But before the late eleventh

penance, liturgy, and *caritas*, as well as of asceticism as seen in clothing,
fasting, and manual labour. Each tended to see its own customs as
exemplary and to encourage their introduction in other monasteries as a
part of 'monastic reform'. There might even be jealousies and disputes.[72]
In the course of the eleventh century monastic reform increasingly came
to imply such changes of observance. Noteworthy here was the wise
restraint shown in the famous reply given by the monks of Monte Cassino
to the question of Abbot Hartwig of Hersfeld: there were many and
varied customs everywhere, which did not conflict with the Rule. All
were good and useful. 'For this reason we cannot wonder sufficiently why
some in rough arrogance and in proud contempt presume without
reflection to substitute an admittedly good custom for another which is
perhaps just as good, if not better!'[73] Yet this happened, and could be
praised as monastic reform.[74]

   Related to similar movements of monastic renewal and yet fundamentally different from them was Cluniac monasticism. Its essential
characteristics have been set out by Joachim Wollasch, basing himself on
existing scholarship and on the new insights won by his own research; his
work has revealed new problems to be solved.[75] According to Wollasch
Cluny was not essentially different from other monastic impulses and
circles which sought to realise the life of the apostles and the primitive
church and concentrate on the coming kingdom of God. But Cluny
distanced itself from the world in a new way in order to carry out this
intention. This was what the founder, Duke William of Aquitaine, and
the early abbots intended when they gave the monastery to the pope, not
so that he could rule over it but so that he could protect it.[76] It was clear
to all participants that papal protection from such a distance could only be
spiritual in nature. Cluny was thus left to its own devices; it was under no

----

century it seldom came to hostile rivalries, 'clashes of reform ideals', as it was later to do
between Cluniacs and Cistercians.

[72] 'Clashes of reform ideals' are one of the main themes of Hallinger, *Gorze und Cluny*.

[73] MGH Die Briefe der deutschen Kaiserzeit III.13, no. 1; see Hoffmann's remarks in
Dormeier, *Monte Cassino*, 18. For this reason one should not divide monasteries into
'reformed' and 'unreformed', nor speak of the demand that a monastery should
introduce 'reform'. There was not just a single and constant reform, but rather many. See
J. Vogel, 'Zur Kirchenpolitik', 167.

[74] Restrictions on or the elimination of the rights of the laity might come to be added to
the notion of monastic reform in the eleventh century; see below, pp. 293ff.

[75] Wollasch, *Mönchtum*; Wollasch, 'Reform und Adel'.

[76] In the literature it is often ignored that in spite of the famous formulation in the
foundation charter (A. Bernard and A. Bruel, *Recueil des Chartes de l'abbaye de Cluny* (Paris
1876), I.124 no. 112) Cluny was not a papal monastery; the ties between Rome and the
Burgundian monastery are often seen as closer than they actually were.

lordship, no concrete and legally effective protection, nor did it have anyone who was obliged to look after its interests. It was shaped by the need to stand in the world protected only by its religious reputation, asking and negotiating but if possible avoiding conflict. This became all the more difficult as the sphere of influence of the Burgundian abbey grew.

There were parallels for the fact that even its first abbots stood at the head of several monasteries. But the number of the monasteries and priories which in some fashion belonged to Cluny in the tenth century was already greater than that of any other monastic circle, and that was at a time when its range was narrower than later under Odilo or Hugo. The difference between the two centuries can be impressively demonstrated cartographically, though the extent of Cluniac expansion in the eleventh century has occasionally been exaggerated: it would be better not to speak of Cluniac imperialism.[77] What united the Cluniacs was the *ordo cluniacensis*, which has been happily defined as 'the Cluniac way of monastic life'.[78] The notion has thus little to do with the kind of orders which became common from the twelfth century onwards. The 'Cluniac way of monastic life' could be shared by monasteries which legally were subject to a king, a bishop, or a noble layman. The renunciation of proprietary monasticism was not the precondition for the introduction of Cluniac monks and practices. The 'Cluniacs' were thus a very varied phenomenon 'above the level of political and ecclesiastical complications'. The picture becomes still more blurred when we consider that a link with Cluny might be only a temporary one, just as was possible with other streams of monasticism. The old notion of the independence of each monastery occasionally surfaced, and the *ecclesia Cluniacensis* was flexible enough to allow a fair amount of latitude to groups within it.[79]

---

[77] De Berthelier, 'L'Expansion de l'ordre de Cluny', 320f.; see also P. Cousin, 'L'Expansion Clunisienne sous Saint Odilon', in *A Cluny, Congrès scientifique* (Dijon 1950), 186ff.; it has at times not been sufficiently taken into account that it was only under Odilo that the numbers of Cluniac priories began to grow significantly, as noted rightly by Bulst, *Untersuchungen*, 217, and that the real leap forward came under Hugo. Jakobs, 'Cluniacenser und Papsttum', 651 speaks of a 'Christian European rule' and on p. 658 describes the *ecclesia Cluniacensis* as a 'church within a church'. On the tendency to strengthen existing spiritual ties by adding juristic ones see Wollasch, *Mönchtum*, 171. On Navarre and Aragon see Kehr, *Navarra und Aragon*, 9 and also Segl, *Königtum und Klosterreform in Spanien*, 12, against an exaggerated estimate of Cluniac influence in Spain. Note in particular his remarks on p. 218: 'For the *perfectio ordinis* it sufficed to introduce and practice Cluniac customs. There was no need for any change in legal status.' Hirsch, 'Untersuchungen', 421, had claimed the opposite.

[78] Wollasch, *Mönchtum*, 154.

[79] *Ibid.*, 151, where Fleury is seen as a representative example of Odo's not always having wanted to change the legal status of a monastery which he had reformed; see also Wollasch, 'Reform und Adel', 286.

In the eleventh century Cluniac self-understanding was determined
ever more by the notion of the community of all those who had made
their profession to the abbot of Cluny himself. Already under Abbot
Odilo all archbishops, bishops, abbots, and monks were to be entered as
nostre congregationis monacus (a monk of our congregation), regardless of
their status and place of death. Many of the dependencies where Cluniac
monks lived were directly subject to the abbot of Cluny and ruled by
priors. These and the commended monasteries were often visited from
Cluny. The abbots themselves travelled a lot. Abbot Odo, who at the
request of the *princeps* Alberic concerned himself with a number of
Roman abbeys, is said to have been in Rome six times in six successive
years.[80] The abbots of the eleventh century aroused some hostile criticism
as a result of their many journeys, on which they were accompanied by
countless monks and a substantial baggage-train. It is difficult to make out
how much of this was justified; the satirical account by Bishop Adalbero
of Laon, in which Odilo gave his monks ridiculous armaments and set out
will a million of them (*millia mille viri*) against the Quirites, on each camel
ten, on each donkey two, and on each gazelle three, is certainly grossly
exaggerated.[81] How seriously we should take the accusations against
Cluny – relaxation of monastic discipline, involvement in the affairs of the
world, and striving for power by its abbots – is hard to say. What speaks
against them is the overwhelming veneration of Cluny and the Cluniacs
by popes, emperors, kings, bishops, and nobles who had high religious
standards and set great hopes on it both for their earthly fortune and their
eternal well-being.

The relations between the popes and Cluny in the tenth and eleventh
centuries are a matter of dispute; in our opinion they are too often judged
in terms of quite inappropriate categories of ecclesiastical power-politics.
As early as 1957 a warning was rightly pronounced against seeing Cluny
as a kind of early Jesuit order.[82] Cluny could not have meant much to the
popes of the tenth century. Their political and jurisdictional activities
were confined essentially to central Italy and to the Roman church
province; their occasional interventions in the affairs of more distant
churches and monasteries normally occurred only when they were asked

---

[80] See above, n. 68.
[81] Sackur, *Cluniacenser*, II.97 on verse 145 of Adalbero of Laon, *Carmen ad Robertum regem*,
verses 142ff., ed. G. H. Hueckel, *Les Poèmes satiriques d'Adalberon* (Bibliothèque de la
Faculté des Lettres de l'Université de Paris 13, Paris 1901) or ed. C. Carozzi (Les
Classiques de l'histoire de France au moyen âge 32, Paris 1979), 10; on this edition see
the review by G. Silagi, *DA*, 37 (1981), 853.
[82] C. Courtois in the discussion on Lemarignier, 'Structures monastiques', 537: Cluny was
not a papal order in the sense that the Jesuits were.

to intervene.[83] Even the privileges of protection were probably granted at the request of those who received them, and they did not in any case provide much protection. Hardly ever did a pope take the initiative in fostering 'monastic reform' of whatever tendency in any European country. It is significant that up until the middle of the eleventh century papal and royal protection were quite compatible with one another. The pope, under whose protection a monastery like Cluny stood, could even go so far as to ask the king of France for protection for his 'own' monastery.[84]

Recent scholarship has found the institution of monastic exemption, that is, emancipation from the spiritual jurisdiction of the diocesan bishop and direct subjection to the papacy, difficult to assess. The popes are supposed to have made use of exempt monasteries in a planned action aimed at bringing their claims of universal episcopacy to bear; the monasteries wanted exclusive dependency on Rome in order to counteract episcopal interventions and demands. In France in particular it has been suggested that there was a fragmentation of diocesan structure through the increase in the numbers of exempt monasteries, in particular by Cluny and its dependent houses; this has been seen as a parallel to the fragmentation of the county by the lordship of the castellans.[85] In this way exemptions gradually paved the way for the papacy's rule over the whole church.[86] Exemption, however, was by no means a rigid and clearly

---

[83] See the contribution by François Masai to the discussion on Lemarignier, 'Structures monastiques', 53of.: papal power at that time was 'spiritual, perhaps all too exclusively spiritual'. Taken in this sense we may also agree with Cowdrey, *Cluniacs*, 15 n. 15, when he warns us not to underestimate papal prestige.

[84] See already Hirsch, 'Untersuchungen', 369. H. Appelt, 'Die Anfänge des päpstlichen Schutzes', *MIÖG*, 62 (1954), 111, notes the 'purely ecclesiastical roots of the apostolic see's universal duty of protection'; see Szaivert, 'Entstehung', 287, for the commendation of Cluny to the protection of King Rudolf of France, JL 3578 = Migne, *PL* 132, col. 812. On this compare Semmler, 'Traditio', 18: 'Papal protection was still an extension of royal *defensio* and even the *traditio* of a royal *monasterium* to St Peter was less important than the king's rights of protection and lordship', and p. 33, where he speaks of 'complementary papal protection' under Otto I.

[85] This opinion is widely held but cannot be demonstrated from the sources. See e.g. Duby, *Frühzeit*, 135: 'the Cluniac movement was decidedly antiepiscopal . . . it fragmented the diocese at the same time as the independent castellans were fragmenting the county'. Violante, 'Monachesimo', 3–67, comes to similar conclusions for Italy: 'the disintegration of the diocese', as does Cowdrey, *Cluniacs*, 71. Such theses depend on exaggerated ideas about the coherence of dioceses and the firmness of episcopal control over them before exemption began to be common.

[86] Kehr has pointed out repeatedly and quite rightly that in the tenth and early eleventh century the pope did not normally intervene on his own initiative. See e.g. *Navarra und*

defined legal institution. If only because some monks were laymen and some clerics, the functions of the diocesan bishop in respect of monasteries were ambiguous.[87] The restrictions placed on the bishop by exemption might affect his rights to dues, his jurisdiction, or his power to consecrate. Any of these things might be granted to a monastery by papal privilege.[88] We need to remember that those privileges which are brought together under the heading of exemption were concerned not so much with protection of monastic forms of life as with protection from the material demands of bishops. The bishop and his entourage were expensive guests, and his activities as consecrator or judge also cost money. Exemption of a monastery was in the first instance a financial privilege.

But did such privileges have to lead to conflict with diocesan bishops? We know of remarkably few such cases. Only under John XIX did Cluny come into conflict with its diocesan bishop of Mâcon, who was supported by the provincial synod of Lyons.[89] If one considers the immense

Aragon, 4ff. and *Katalanischer Prinzipat*, 7, where on p. 11 the thesis of the destruction of the diocese through exemption is contradicted.

[87] Szaivert, 'Entstehung', 389, draws distinctions between the legal consequences of the different kinds of privileges often summarily called 'exemptions': the right to choose any bishop to perform consecrations; forbidding the bishop to celebrate mass within the monastery without having been invited to do so; prohibitions against excommunicating monastic dependants or holding synods in monasteries. Szaivert stresses that the realisation of such privileges in practice was a gradual one. The proposal by W. Schwarz, 'Jurisdictio und Conditio', 79f., that the institution should be called emancipation, not exemption, is an illuminating one: 'monasteries did not seek liberation from the normal exercise of episcopal power but protection against its abuse'. Szabó-Bechstein, 'Libertas Ecclesiae', 187f., also distinguishes between complete exemption and partial exemptions.

[88] It was already noted by A. H. Blumenstock, *Der päpstliche Schutz im Mittelalter* (Innsbruck 1890), 24, that monastic privileges grant freedom more readily from having to pay dues to the bishop than from his power of consecration or freedom of election. Could bishops themselves as well as popes occasionally grant exemptions, as the bishop of Ivrea did for Fruttuaria? See Bulst, *Untersuchungen*, 133.

[89] Hessel, 'Cluny und Mâcon', 516ff.; Letonnelier, 'L'Abbaye exempte', 93; see Diener, 'Verhältnis Clunys zu den Bischöfen', 234ff., where one should note in particular that Gauzlin accepted the pope's intervention in favour of Cluny and after his resignation in 1030 became a monk there himself. But note also Odilo's conciliance towards Gauzlin's successor Walter; see, besides Letonnelier, L'Huillier, *Vie*, 134. According to Cowdrey, *Cluniacs*, 44, it was not here a question of Odilo's having shown monastic conciliance, but rather of necessity in view of the cool relations between Cluny and Benedict IX. But we know nothing about these relations. Mehne, 'Cluniazenserbischöfe', has made substantial progress using necrologies. On the close links between Monte Cassino and the bishops, in spite of the events in Rome in 1123, see Dormeier, *Montecassino*, 79f. See now further the fruitful study by U. Winzer, 'Cluny und Mâcon im 10. Jahrhundert', *FMSt*, 23 (1990), 154ff.

opportunities for friction provided by Cluny and its huge network of dependencies and the countless bishops in whose dioceses they lay, that is very remarkable. It will be possible to answer the question of the relationship between Cluny and other exempt monasteries on the one hand and the episcopate on the other when prosopographical studies have been carried further. It has long been noted that many bishops, especially in France, were former Cluniac monks.[90] More precise assessments will be made possible by the epoch-making studies of Cluniac monasticism now under way with the help of electronic data processing, which allows a comparison of all known sources with the records of necrologies, which are only in this way becoming accessible to critical scholarship.[91] Remarkable results have already been achieved for Cluniac monks, which promise a better basis for judging the answers to the questions posed above. In the meantime it is as well to warn against positing a general Cluniac anti-episcopalism, which seems to be something of an invention of modern scholars.[92]

One should also ask whether 'exemption' really had such a tendency to fragment the diocese as has been supposed. If the bishop no longer had any functions of spiritual jurisdiction or coercion within the exempt monasteries and its dependence, then he was admittedly deprived of the dues owed in this connection but he was also spared a good deal of friction, as was the monastery. If the exempt monastery acquired the right to have all consecrations of abbots, monk-priests, churches, chapels, altars, cemeteries done by a bishop if its choice this might be more problematic. However, one should remember that Cluny was always able to find other

---

[90] See provisionally Diener, 'Verhältnis Clunys zu den Bischöfen', 321, and the not very convincing objections offered by Violante, *Monachesimo*, 56ff. and n. 95. Capitani, 'Immunità vescovili', 529, offers a curious construction of an opposition between Cluny and the bishops: 'without this necessarily signifying hostility to the bishops, still less a programmatic hostility'. See already against this Schreiber, 'Gregory VII', 118, who noted that Cluny was on good terms with the episcopate and that its relations with bishops had often been seen quite one-sidedly in terms of exemption disputes. Schreiber, 'Mönchtum und Wallfahrt', 171 warns against assuming that bishop and *coenobium* were rigidly in opposition.

[91] Wollasch, Heim, Mehne, Neiske, and Poeck, *Synopse*; Wollasch, 'Reform und Adel', 291, on bishops as Cluniac monks and monks as bishops; Mehne, 'Cluniazenserbischöfe', 268ff.

[92] Semmler, *Siegburg*, 214, thinks that the reform movements of Cluny and Fruttuaria renounced their antiepiscopal aims under the influence of the archbishop of Cologne and became the 'episcopal monastic reform movement of Siegburg'. There are many parallels for this; but the 'antiepiscopalism' cannot have been so deeply rooted if monks from Cluny or Fruttuaria were so easily prepared to give it up.

bishops who willingly performed its consecrations when it did not wish to make use of its own diocesan bishops (perhaps because these demanded excessively high fees for their activities). There can thus be no question of there having been a general antagonism between Cluny and the 'episcopate'. The well-known disputes with the bishops of Mâcon should not lead us to assume that this was the normal pattern within the *ecclesia Cluniacensis*. Why should the abbot not have freely chosen and rewarded the diocesan bishop in many, perhaps in most cases, so long as relations with him were untroubled? Here too we may hope for clearer insights into the problem in the future.[93]

It is widely supposed that the popes sought and received aid from monasteries in building up their universal rule over the church and forcing it through against the opposition of lay princes and the episcopate, and granted them protection and exemption as a reward. Such monasteries in turn sought the protection of the holy see against all external threats. The alliance between Roman church and the privileged 'reform monasteries' was an early indication of the great turning-points to come, which from the middle of the eleventh century led to the epoch-making extension of papal rule over the church, to the recognition of the status due to the pope within the church, and to the moral renewal of the clergy.[94]

It must be asked, however, whether the popes of the tenth and early eleventh centuries thought in terms of a continuous papal leadership, control, and discipline of the church either as something possible or as something desirable. Such things had occurred up to then only as episodes or under special circumstances. Were they capable of conceiving of the 'papacy' as possessing such jurisdictional power, given its regional horizons and the frequent condition of political and material bankruptcy in which the popes found themselves? Was it really because the popes were not able to exercise their due rights that 'the church' groaned under the yoke of 'the laity'?

And what could the Cluniacs have done for the popes in practice, at least before the middle of the eleventh century, popes who could at that

---

[93] Mehne, 'Cluniazenserbischöfe', 288f.
[94] See above, n. 86. A characteristic example of the widespread but anachronistic notion of a papal policy which sought to set up a counterweight to episcopal power in the monasteries which enjoyed exemption and papal protection can be found in Hirsch, 'Untersuchungen', 387. Hoffmann, 'Von Cluny', 199, takes a similar line: 'Monastic reform and monastic exemption placed a huge reservoir of power at the papacy's disposal'; so does Cowdrey, *Cluniacs*, e.g. p. 58: 'Cluny was a principal bulwark of the papacy in promoting the reform of the church.'

time hardly have thought of putting the ideas of Pseudo-Isidore into practice? It has been shown that the monk Bertram copied a manuscript of Pseudo-Isidore in Cluny on the orders of Abbot Odilo, but equally that the Pseudo-Isidorian decretals remained unknown 'in the whole Cluniac literature' and that Cluny refused to make any use of them in the monastic sphere.[95] It is also worth noting that Abbot Abbo of Fleury made no use of them in his well-known canon law collection, although he must have known them from his participation in the synod of Saint-Basle, dealt with elsewhere.[96] However, the question at issue there was not the relations between the rights of popes, bishops, and monasteries, and the Cluniacs were not themselves a party to the dispute, which was one between Archbishop Arnulf of Rheims, deposed by King Hugo, and Gerbert of Aurillac, his rival for the archbishopric. Abbo of Fleury was a supporter here of Arnulf's cause, not Cluny's;[97] Fleury was close to Cluny but had already at that time begun to go its own way.[98] Arnulf's party, calling on Pseudo-Isidore, turned to Pope John XV, but so also did the party of king and bishops, which was equally interested in papal support. The pope took no initiative in the matter, which was evidently one of indifference to him. The fact that he decided in favour of Arnulf and against Gerbert was evidently the result of changes in the French political constellation and still more of the wishes of the imperial court and the German episcopate.

Like Cluny and the Cluniacs the other important monastic groups of the western church were principally concerned with the fullest possible realisation of the monastic ideal. They were prepared to work together with all who called on them for help or whose support seemed useful: popes, kings, bishops, nobles. What was at issue was the elimination of degenerate forms of monastic life in individual monasteries, the attainment of still higher degrees of ascetic perfection, and the deflection of encroachments by spiritual and secular partners on monastic property and rights. Leading personalities of the monastic movements won or sought after influence on kings and princes in all countries, without this leading to serious controversies.[99] Before the revolution in Rome under

---

[95] Fuhrmann, *Pseudoisidorische Fälschungen*, III.757ff. and on Bertram's manuscript 766ff.

[96] *Ibid.*, 1.231 n. 127 and III.760.

[97] Tellenbach, 'Zur Geschichte', 176, which is also relevant for what follows.

[98] See above, n. 79.

[99] A famous example is the anger shown by St Nilus about the cruel treatment of the antipope Johannes Philagathos by Otto III and Gregory V. Significantly, what was at issue here was not ecclesiology or church politics but a lack of Christian mercifulness.

Henry III they could not have been tools of a universal papal government of the church, not least because the popes, as we have noted, were restricted in their horizons and played a role more spiritual than jurisdictional.

As of old, the monks of individual monasteries and of monastic groupings were in the tenth and early eleventh century more conciliatory than aggressive towards their clerical and lay fellow-christians.[100] They lived apart from the world in humility and had no idea of making monks out of all men.[101] As a rule monasteries owned churches just like other proprietors; large monasteries often owned many churches. It was evidently the exception for monks to act as the priests in these churches.[102] Normally they were served by priests who had the same kind of relationship to the monastery as the priests of lay or episcopal proprietary churches did to their proprietors. Normally the abbot chose the priest and presented him for confirmation to the diocesan bishop. The priest had to make his payments, apart from those due to the diocesan, to the monastery. We do not have much detailed information about this; but churches were given to monasteries with the explicitly declared intention of increasing their revenues.[103] It would be interesting to know if the priests of monastic proprietary churches had to make special gifts or payments of fees to their abbot and lord, as was customary in comparable churches.[104]

It needs to be carefully considered how far monasteries and monastic groupings took any notice at all of the personal morality, the economic practices or the educational shortcomings of the priests or secular clergy attached to their churches. Up until the early eleventh century they seem to have had no great interest in a 'reform' of the secular clergy, that is, in

---

[100] Leclercq, 'Monachisme', 454, stresses that it was primarily by example that monks sought to reform the clergy. See by contrast, Duby, *Trois ordres*, 174: 'the arrogant and conquering Cluny'.

[101] Violante, *Monachesimo*, 66, speaks of a Cluniac 'panmonastic ideal', a notion which would need precise exposition. Note also Wollasch, *Mönchtum*, 170, who says that at the beginning of the twelfth century the Cluniacs claimed to be a church, a monastic church, in themselves.

[102] Schreiber, 'Gregor VII.', 52ff.: in Hugo's time the idea of monks taking on pastoral care was still rejected except in emergencies; p. 56: pastoral care was mostly performed by small houses with close ties to their immediate surroundings. See Zerfass, *Laienpredigt*, 103ff.; the assumption by Wollasch, *Mönchtum*, 169f., that the popes disposed in the monasteries of immense reserves of priests who were celibate and independent of any worldly lordship applies, as he himself makes immediately clear, only to appointments to bishoprics, not to the question of pastoral care.

[103] This idea is expressed in countless charters of donation.

[104] See above, p. 83 and n. 26.

changes in the prevailing conditions.[105] Even later, as the movement against 'simony' and 'nicolaitism' got under way, the different monastic tendencies reacted in very different ways. Italian hermits, and groups connected with them such as the Camaldulensians and in particular the Vallombrosans were noteworthy for their reforming zeal. They relaxed the old ideals of flight from the world and propagated their beliefs outside the monastery with enthusiasm. Special note should be taken of them in the context of the history of monastic preaching.[106]

No doubt monastic piety had long-term effects on the thoughts and actions of clerics and laymen. Their life of abstinence and poverty was seen as an imitation of the apostles and of the early church, and they could thus serve as an example to many. Those who served the altar and the care of souls could not better sanctify themselves for their exalted task than by living in a monastic fashion. By setting an example in this way monasticism had always had an influence on the secular clergy, though not a constant one.[107] It would seem, for instance, that the reform of clerical communities was independent of the example of particular monasteries or monastic customs, orientating itself directly on the ideals of the primitive church.[108]

Colleges of clerics living a more or less monastic life serviced cathedrals and the greater town churches, sometimes country churches as well, especially in the centres of castellanies in France and Italy.[109] Charles

---

[105] There is no reason to suppose that monasteries were exceptionally zealous in demanding that priests who served their numerous proprietary churches should remain celibate and observe the existing provisions about women living in the house of priests, or that they paid special attention to the prescriptions that spiritual functions should be performed without payment. What Hallinger, 'Geistige Welt Clunys', 440f. calls the 'extraclaustral reform aspirations' of Odo is nothing more than the common demands of the time, made with greater or lesser success in treatises and the canons of synods. The interest thought by Hoffmann, 'Von Cluny', 173f., to have been shown by Odo in the reformation of the secular clergy was scarcely peculiar to reform monasteries in general or to Cluny in particular.

[106] Miccoli, *Chiesa Gregoriana*, 61ff.; Goez, 'Toscana', 205–39; on monastic preaching Zerfass, *Laienpredigt*, 124ff.

[107] Chenu, 'Moines', 61; Häussling, *Mönchskonvent*, 143; Miccoli, *Chiesa Gregoriana*, 255ff.

[108] Dereine, 'Vie commune', 398 n. 6: 'We have nowhere found any traces of Cluniac influence among those who promoted a reform based on strict poverty'.

[109] K. H. Schäfer, *Pfarrkirche und Stift im deutschen Mittelalter* (Kirchenrechtliche Abhandlungen 3, Stuttgart 1903), 113ff.; J. Siegwart, *Die Chorherren- und Chorfrauengemeinschaften in der deutschen Schweiz vom 6. Jh.–1160. Mit einem Überblick über die deutsche Kanonikerreform des 10. und 11. Jahrhunderts* (Freiburg im Breisgau 1962), 92ff.; Lemarignier, 'Aspects', 19-40, where a distinction is made between the small canonries in castles and the larger collegiate foundations.

Dereine, to whom we owe important insights into the history of canons, the members of these spiritual communities, talks of a 'Carolingian epoch' of the history of canons, which he makes begin in 750 and end, signifi-cantly, in 1050.[110] This was the period in which the rule for canons of Louis the Pious's time set standards which were first established, then violated, and then restored.[111] In the cathedral chapters there was a gradual division between the property of the bishopric and the chapter (*mensa episcopalis, mensa capituli*); the property of the collegiate churches was divided into prebends for the individual canons.[112] Ideally, canons were supposed to live a common life in the same house with a refectory and dormitory, almost like monks.[113] But something was gained even when canons still had houses, incomes, and property of their own, provided that they still at least met regularly in a common house and demonstrated their membership of a community in the way they exercised their spiritual functions, especially prayer. On the observance of the common life depended to a large extent the observance of other ancient precepts: those governing celibacy and relations with women as well as those which prohibited the acquisition of spiritual gifts and offices in return for money.[114] It is probably accurate to speak of a coexistence of decadence and reform in this period.[115] Many chapters rose and fell; the near-monastic forms of the religious life might be taken seriously for a time, then almost disappear. 'Secularised' canons were often blamed for concerning themselves more with weapons, hunting, and women than with their spiritual duties. But conditions varied greatly with time and place, and some historians have warned against speaking in too general terms about the decadence of the clergy in this period.[116] In spite of all the shadows which fell on the face of the church in this period as in others, one should show more caution than has been usual before positing a particularly severe degree of corruption for the period preceding the middle of the eleventh century.

---

[110] Dereine, 'Chanoines', cols. 353–405.

[111] Semmler, 'Mönche und Kanoniker', 111: 'the divergence between the spirituality of canons and that of monks was to last for centuries'.

[112] Lemarignier, *France médiévale*, 79.

[113] Chenu, 'Moines', 63: 'the common life was the great remedy against clerical decadence'.

[114] Toubert, 'Vie commune der clercs', 13; on the fundamental distinctions between the spirituality of monks and that of canons see Leclercq, *Spiritualité*, 120ff.

[115] Leclercq, Vandenbrucke, and Bouyer, *Histoire de la Spiritualité*, 124: 'a coexistence of decadence and reform over two centuries'.

[116] Dereine, 'Chanoines', col. 371; see the quotation below, p. 161 n. 91.

CHRISTIAN 'ESTATES'

'Estates' are by their nature always parts of a whole. Christians are 'all one in Christ Jesus' (Galatians 3: 28). From the very beginning this faith was the basis for accepting social stratification in this world and the next together with the mutual solidarity of all those who believe in Christ and accept God's will. How the stratification was seen as a whole was admittedly varied and contradictory, from the time of the apostles through the whole of the middle ages at least. Eschatalogical and secular criteria intermingled and influenced each other: 'The religious hierarchy is based on a combination of historical foundation and a deliberate indeterminacy in religious matters.'[117] The grades of the hierarchy represent, as Father Congar has put it, both a 'spiritual anthropology' and a 'sociological ordering', without a sharp distinction being made between the two.[118]

The disciples must have found it both disturbing and hard to imagine when Jesus explained to them how differently 'they which shall be accounted worthy to obtain that world, and the resurrection from the dead' would live: they 'neither marry, nor are given in marriage' (Luke 20: 35). Thus even the distinction between man and woman will become irrelevant. In that world many will be the first who are here the last, and vice versa (Matthew 19: 30; Luke 13: 30). Jesus's answer to the naive and this-worldly request made by the mother of the two sons of Zebedee, John and Jacob, that Christ should grant that both should sit at his side in his kingdom, must have seemed quite alien to the disciples and it would have been barely comprehensible that worldly conceptions and gradations should lose their validity in the next world.[119] The answer left deep traces, nevertheless, for it became an unquestioned conviction that the bearers of tiaras and mitres, crowns and diadems would be measured by the same scales as all other men of high and low degree.[120] God is no respecter of persons.

That by no means implies that all the saved and baptised are equal in this earthly life. Even in the fraternal community of the early church there were more distinguished and more menial members, though not quite in the manner of the world where lords have power, but rather 'whosoever will be great among you, let him be your minister'; a paradoxical reversal of normality was required, which could not be maintained in earthly reality. For the real world the apostle advised Christians that

---

[117] H. Dombois, *Hierarchie. Grund und Grenze einer umstrittenen Struktur* (Vienna 1971), 13.
[118] Congar, 'Laiques', 84, 89.
[119] It must have been a shock for them that not even he was able to fulfil their request.
[120] See Tellenbach, 'Irdischer Stand', 1–16.

everyone should 'abide in the same calling wherein he was called'; 'for he that is called in the Lord, being a servant, is the Lord's freeman: likewise also he that is called, being free, is Christ's servant' (1 Corinthians 7: 20ff.). These words were used to justify slavery, unfreedom, and every kind of social distinction for as long as society was organised into estates.[121] In the early history of the church, when Christ's return was expected imminently, such an attitude reflected an indifference to this world, which survived most intensely in a world itself gradually becoming Christian in the forms of 'flight from the world' and asceticism.[122] This tension between trying to change the world and trying to flee from it has survived in Christianity to the present day.

Already in the first centuries of Christianity the two great bodies of clergy and laity had been formed within the church; the first consisted of those whose consecration made them able to dispense the sacraments and because of their task of leading their flock would have to give an account to God at the last judgement for all those entrusted to them. This gave them an undisputedly superior rank in the present life. But though the dispensation of the sacraments was their prerogative, the laity were equal in being able to receive them, and both estates were 'one in Christ'.

From the time of Constantine the Great the clergy acquired numerous secular privileges: exemption from taxation; to a large extent their own courts; exemption from the obligation to do military service.[123] Paul's phrase 'A soldier on active service will not let himself be involved in civilian affairs' (2 Timothy 2: 4) was quoted thousands of times in the middle ages and understood both as a privilege and as a restriction. In reality the clergy gradually became involved in the life of this world common to all through both giving and taking. There were repeated attempts to revive the state of affairs of the early Christian church; repeatedly, they lost momentum.

Monasticism, both coenobitic and eremitical, held on to the ideal of indifference to the world found in the early church.[124] Originally it was a lay institution, but by the high middle ages it had become clericalised. Those monks who received holy orders became ever more numerous, and even those not in orders were distinguished from the laity by their way of life. The laity had a lower status than that enjoyed by clerics and

---

[121] Hence well beyond the end of the middle ages.
[122] Tellenbach, *Libertas*, 32 and *passim*.
[123] Feine, *Kirchliche Rechtsgeschichte*, 71, 129.
[124] Tellenbach, *Libertas*, 54; Leclercq, *Spiritualité*, 123: 'While the spirituality of monks had a primarily eschatological orientation, the exhortation here was directed towards building the church on earth.'

monks. The laity were receivers, not dispensers of sacraments and they did not flee from the world but rather sought as far as possible to lead a Christian life within the world.[125] Originally the strict monks regarded both clergy and laity as the world; then clerics and monks became estates within the church competing for the highest rank.[126]

Whether one counts monks among the laity or among the clergy, the two estates determined the structure of the church community. But increasingly, fundamental distinctions were made. In an attempt to determine religious ranks and values, Christians were divided according to their manner of life into the married, the abstinent, and the chaste (*uxorati, continentes, virgines*). According to the Apostle Paul (1 Corinthians 2) this corresponded to the gradation good, better, best.[127] But such labels did not do away with the essential distinction between clergy and laity. Reference to men's functions within the church on the other hand led to the well-known trichotomy of *oratores, pugnatores,* and *laboratores* (prayers, fighters, and ploughers).[128]

This 'functional trichotomy' has been termed a scheme of thinking or of interpretation.[129] It was intended to describe the social reality of Christian society, though on closer inspection it became difficult to fit everything into this scheme. The dichotomy between clerics and laymen, who had simple and obvious characteristics, remained much less problematic and retained its validity whatever further distinctions were made. The move towards subdivisions of the lay estate was understandable, if one thinks of the enormous contrasts between nobles, free, and unfree; between riches, a sufficiency, and bitter poverty; or between the life with and the life without manual labour, with or without weapons. The ability to fight conferred by suitability and by training led to the granting of a special status to those who seemed to be called to protect the church and defend the Christian people, while all others had to provide the *oratores* and the *pugnatores* with the fruits of their labours.

---

[125] According to Cassian a monk had to flee from women and bishops. See the quotation in Hofmeister, 'Mönchtum und Seelsorge', 216.

[126] Congar, *Laie*, 25, 'It [the position of the laity] is that of Christians who achieve sanctity in the life of this world'; but p. 35: 'the life in the world is from a Christian viewpoint a compromise'.

[127] Abbo of Fleury, *Liber apologeticus*, Migne, *PL* 139, col. 463ff., with the comparison *bonus, melior, optimus* set against the comparison layman, cleric, monk. See Oexle, 'Funktionale Dreiteilung', 26; Rouche, 'De l'orient', 31–49.

[128] Congar, 'Laiques', 83ff.; G. Duby, 'Guerre et société dans l'Europe féodale; ordonnancement de la paix', in *Concetto, storia, miti e immagini del Medioevo*, ed. V. Branca (Florence 1973), 449–82; Duby, 'Aux origines', 183–8; Duby, *Trois ordres*; Oexle, 'Funktionale Dreiteilung', 1–84.

[129] Oexle's phrase implies a reservation which we shall stress still more in what follows.

It is significant and characteristic that there was no attempt to divide the clergy in this way. For there was hardly less difference between rural parish priests and many lesser clerics on the one hand and bishops, cathedral canons and abbots on the other than there was between peasant and count. The lesser clergy were often former serfs who were – usually – emancipated so that they could receive ordination in accordance with the requirements of canon law. They often had to work just like peasants, and their education was modest.[130] High ecclesiastics by contrast were generally of noble origin, had attended monastic or cathedral schools with greater or lesser success, were well or at least adequately provided for, and were accustomed to command lesser clerics and their lay servants.[131] They lived like lords exercising power over greater or lesser spheres of influence.[132] The fact that the whole of the clergy still constituted a single group in such sociological classifications was a logical consequence of its sacred orders and functions, which stamped its members with a common mark which determined their characteristics much more than did any mere differences of wealth and rank.

The duality of powers which had already emerged in the Roman empire and had even been claimed by Pope Gelasius I, in a formulation which established a tradition, as determining the relationship between the head of the laity, the *regnum*, and the priesthood, dominated thought up until the eleventh century. Alongside it we find from the tenth century, at first only in isolated instances, the schema of three functions already mentioned. The fragmentary nature of the sources makes it difficult to say when the idea arose. It is first found in the writings of Alfred the Great at the end of the ninth century, then not again in England until more than a hundred years later in the writings of the monk Ælfric, who was abbot of Eynsham from 1005 until his death in 1020 and a correspondent and associate of Bishop Wulfstan of Worcester and York.[133] On the continent the first reference to a threefold division within the church is found in the work of Abbot Abbo of Fleury (d. 1004), who had spent many years in

---

[130] See above, pp. 89–90; Barlow, *English Church 1000–1066*, 254 and 277; Barlow, *English Church 1066–1154*, 218; J. le Goff, 'Culture clericale et traditions folkloriques dans la civilisation mérovingienne', *Annales ESC*, 22 (1967), 718.

[131] According to C. Brühl, 'Die Sozialstruktur des deutschen Episkopats im 11. und 12. Jahrhunderts', *MCSM*, 8 (1974), 50, 'no simple priest ever became bishop'.

[132] Köhler, *Bild des geistlichen Fürsten*, 11, rightly notes that there were indeed bishops devoted to their spiritual task 'but also very many for whom politics was an end in itself which was pursued with pleasure'. Bishops generally came from noble families, but their office often stamped them; see the acute observations by Lippelt, *Thietmar*, 28 and 53.

[133] Oexle, 'Funktionale Dreiteilung', 33 and 39ff.; on Rather of Verona, in whom we can see traces of this notion in spite of certain deviations, see *ibid.*, 38 n. 233.

England and had contacts with numerous important personalities on the island, without our being able to say precisely whether or how he could have acquired such ideas there. The most famous example of such a division is found in the curious satirical piece written by Bishop Adalbero of Laon (d. 1030), the *Carmen ad Robertum regem*. Here too it is uncertain where he got the idea from, which once again shows the fragmentary nature of the tradition, which was as yet by no means widespread.[134] The schema was known to Bishop Gerhard of Cambrai (d. 1051), and probably its dissemination is connected with the early peace of God movement. In the course of the eleventh century we find references to the trichotomy here and there, for example, by Radulfus Glaber, Humbert of Silva Candida, and Bishop John of Cesena.[135] Only in the twelfth century did it become more common, though it still did not predominate.[136] In the face of increasing social differentiation, the expansion of town and burgher life, new forms of life practised by teachers and students, merchants and artists, as well as by religious movements, the schema represented reality still less accurately than it had done in the previous period, and was still more of an abstraction.

The allocation of functions to the three estates was very generalised; there were borderline cases, and the three groupings overlapped in many ways.[137] Monastic life entailed manual labour on the land, in the garden, house, cellar, and church, above all in scriptoria and building sites; these were often presented as asceticism and good works, but they also had an economic aspect which should not be underestimated. The rural clergy had to work the lands attached to the church and administer revenues, tithes, rents, and altar revenues as well as paying dues, just like peasants. Bishops and the canons of high churches administered and exploited both large and small estates in exactly the same ways as secular lords did with their property and fiefs, either by demesne farming using unfree dependants, or by giving them out as knightly or peasant holdings.[138]

Peasants performed less military service in the high middle ages, but

---

[134] *Ibid.*, 19ff. The consequences which have been drawn from this difficult text for the behaviour of the Cluniacs, for example already by Erdmann, *Entstehung*, 61ff., are not in my view acceptable. On Gerhard of Cambrai see Oexle, 'Funktionale Dreiteilung', 43; Duby, 'Gérard', 35f. and 58f.

[135] On John of Cesena see A. Samaritani, 'Gebeardo di Eichstätt, archievescovo di Ravenna 1027–1044 e la riforma imperiale di Ravenna delle chiese in Romagna', in *Studi di Liturgia, agiografia e riforma medioevali* (Analecta Pomposiana 3, Pomposa 1967), 137ff.

[136] Oexle, 'Funktionale Dreiteiling', 50f.

[137] Rouche, 'De l'orient', 33, on Duby.   [138] See chapter 3 above.

there were always unfree serving in the followings of noble or ecclesiastical lords, in arms as well.[139] How often the peasantry in the vicinity of a battlefield took part in the fighting is hard to say. They played an impressive part in the battle of Melrichstadt in August 1078, where among other things they killed Archbishop Werner of Magdeburg. At about the same time large forces of armed peasants along the Neckar tried on Henry IV's behalf to prevent the advance of the south German dukes; they were crushingly defeated, and the survivors were killed or cruelly maimed.[140] It is well known that bishops and abbots quite frequently took part in campaigns in the high middle ages, leading their vassals either in royal armies or on their own military enterprises. The archbishop of Magdeburg just mentioned was not the only member of the episcopate who lost his life in war.[141] Most of them, however, seem to have fallen in battle against the heathen: Magyars, Slavs, and Saracens.

The functional division of society was disturbed most by the western European peace movements of the late tenth and the eleventh centuries, the peace and truce of God. Here we need only point out that peace often enough had to be protected by force. We hear of 'parish militias' or 'diocesan armies', in which it was not only the knights, who were supposed to do the fighting according to the schema, who actually did so. In a battle at Cher in 1038, in which the troops of Archbishop Aimo of Bourges were defeated by Odo of Déols, 700 clerics are said to have been killed.[142]

Monks, as we have noted, received higher orders ever more frequently. Whether ordained or not their principal function was that of praying, and in the high middle ages they were automatically counted among the *oratores* just like the clergy. Their ascetic life meant in the eyes of their contemporaries that their intercession with God and the saints was particularly efficacious. Their meritorious works – regular feeding of the poor, help in times of famine, the care of the sick – made it possible to hope that God would hear their prayers. Prayer-confraternity with them was eagerly sought after and rewarded with rich gifts. Kings, bishops, and rich nobles founded monasteries for their own salvation and that of all Christians, in which they and their relatives and descendants were to be buried. The Christians of the neighbourhood also sought burial in the monastic church or in its vicinity.[143] Besides prayers, masses were said with great devotion, care, and regularity; many of these were said specially

---

[139] See the ninth-century example cited by Tellenbach, 'Thronfolge', 286 and n. 230.
[140] Steindorff, *Jahrbücher Heinrichs III.*, II.142 and 146.
[141] Poggiaspalla, 'La chiesa e la participazione dei chierici', 233–47.
[142] Hoffmann, *Gottesfriede*, 104ff.   [143] Schreiber, 'Gregor VII.', 54.

for the soul of the monastic community, its founders and benefactors.[144] Pastoral care on the other hand was not the monks' duty, apart from that necessary for the convent itself; with a few exceptions it was a monopoly of the diocesan clergy. Monks, like all laymen, could baptise in emergencies, and their presence at the deathbed was desired by many.[145] By contrast, preaching, other than in the monastic church, was the exclusive preserve of the pastoral clergy.[146] But already in the eleventh century there were monk-preachers from the congregations of Vallombrosa or Hirsau who travelled through near and distant regions.[147] They in particular were driven on by the great issues of the century: the condemnation of real or supposed simony, the battle of the popes against German kings. Whether monks or laymen could preach was to become one of the most disputed areas of church life in the following century. Here we need only note that the exclusive right of the bishop to consecrate was not disputed in any monastic movement, even in those which sought exemption from the power of their own diocesan bishop; among the laity it was disputed only by those who followed explicitly heretical movements and rejected the church.

If monks came to assimilate their status to that of the clergy, while respecting the most fundamental function of the latter group, their way of life had deep influence on both clerics and laymen. Many laymen, especially high-ranking ones, eagerly imitated the ascetic life of the monks; many finished by entering a monastery, while others lived like monks, so far as this was compatible with their worldly occupations. Christians who had had penances imposed often settled near a monastery, and others who had not might live as voluntary patients under the direction of a venerated abbot.[148] The monastic renunciation of property, the common life of monks in chastity and obedience were an impressive example to the clergy. Where the 'reform' of the clergy was taken seriously it was the 'apostolic' life which the monks appeared to practice which was the model.[149]

Common prayer united not just the clergy and laity of all ranks who took part in it within a church, but all Christians, wherever they lived. The liturgy has a universal character. It could also, however, be the basis for more restricted communities. Monastic convents and colleges of cler-

---

[144] See above, pp. 105–6.
[145] On baptism see below, p. 131.   [146] See above, p. 119 n. 102.
[147] See Tellenbach, '"Gregorianische Reform"', 104 n. 25, 106 n. 32 and also below, p. 000.
[148] G. G. Meersseman and E. Adda, 'Pénitents ruraux communautaires en Italie au XIIe siècle', *RHE*, 49 (1954), 343–90; Meersseman, *Ordo Fraternitatis*, 1.70ff.; Duby, *Trois Ordres*, 180.
[149] See below, chapter 5.

ics could come together to commemorate their living and dead members in prayer, and also take their friends and benefactors into their communion. Now that it has become possible to use ever more effective methods to study memorial sources, *libri memoriales* and necrologies, it is not only the religious communities, previously known only as collections of uninformative names, whose historical development, growth, and decline is becoming visible; we have come to know much about the owners of these names, about the length of time they belonged to the convent or college, about the clerical orders they held, about their origins.[150] It had long been known that such long lists of names included groups of relatives and office-holders drawn from close at hand and far away. Important results are to be expected from electronic data processing, which can link the prosopographical material contained in charters and in historiographical and literary sources with the vast quantity of names contained in the memorial sources. Already we can say that prayer communities included men of all ranks: high and lesser clergy, abbots and monks, laymen from the king down through the high and lesser nobility, and even servants.[151] Here at least we find *oratores*, *pugnatores*, and *laboratores* forming communities based on their overriding common characteristic, that of having been baptised.

But here too a certain functional division was visible. Within prayer communities, priests had the task of celebrating mass for the salvation of all, the clerics and monks not in priestly orders had to sing psalms, the laity had to feed the poor and make gifts of land or money.[152] The *pugnator* was thus like any other layman an *orator*, but in a manner different from that of the clergy. His special function of fighting to protect the church had long been recognised liturgically; from the tenth century, the warrior, his weapons and banners were liturgically blessed. This Christianisation of the arms-bearing part of the laity represented its recognition as one of the three Christian orders and it was part of the origins of knighthood and its ideology.[153] The formula 'the clergy pray and the layman gives' is too simple. For even though the laity's part in divine service was constantly being reduced, it retained important functions. The reception of the sacraments was an activity in the deepest sense of the word, and even in prayer the layman participated in litanies and by being present.

For a number of decades now scholarship has devoted increasing

---

[150] See above, p. 104 nn. 51ff.   [151] See below, nn. 155–7.

[152] Tellenbach, 'Historische Dimension', 208f.

[153] Erdmann, *Entstehung*, Appendix 1, 326; Fleckenstein, 'Abschließung des Ritterstandes', 263ff., notes that the estates were not closed castes; Oexle, 'Funktionale Dreiteilung', 46.

attention to corporatively organised associations of various kinds. As early
as the ninth century we find corporations of priests, and these become
more common in the following centuries. These were something
different from the colleges of priests in cathedral chapters or other
individual churches. They can probably be seen as guild-like associations
of clerics within a town, a diocese or a still-larger region. Sometimes they
accepted the membership of various lay persons, even of women; in some
associations the laity might be in the majority. Since religious aims were
always pursued along with profane ones we find that even here there were
priests and clerics among the members. These associations are most easily
identified when we find lists of their members in liturgical manuscripts or
when they have left statutes. The current state of research does not yet
allow us to distinguish between and compare conditions in different
countries, hence we cannot yet formulate conclusions valid for the history
of the church as a whole. P. Meerssemann had already put together a
considerable body of material for many European countries between the
tenth and the twelfth centuries,[154] more recently there have been cautious
but forceful studies of the clergy of the diocese of Constance by Karl
Schmid[155] and attempts to determine the nature of such associations and
their relationship to guilds by Otto Gerhard Oexle.[156]

Here we need offer only a few examples in the context of our
consideration of how the well-known scheme of the three orders corresponded to social and ecclesiastical reality. In the diocese of Constance
it appears to be questionable whether 'a strict division between clerics
and monks or between cathedral and urban clergy and rural clergy' is
possible.[157] The guild-like confraternity of S. Appiano in Valdelsa has left
us a comprehensive set of statutes from the tenth century which has
survived in a version from the eleventh. 'The association consisted of
laymen of both sexes, probably the notables of the region, and of clerics
from various churches in the valley of the Elsa.'[158] The list of 113
members of the *societas Sancti Mauritii* in Tours was copied from an older
manuscript dating from the middle of the eleventh century and had a
further fifty-three names added to it. Most were lay persons, male and
female; some of these are identifiable as members of the families of
clerics. Many were servants. But there were also some clerics. The

---

[154] Le Bras, 'Confréries', 310–63; Meerssemann, 'Klerikervereine', 1–42; Meerssemann,
Ordo Fraternitas, 1.70ff.; Meerssemann, 'Storiografia', 39–62; P. Michaud-Quantin,
'Universitas. Expression du mouvement communautaire dans le moyen âge latin',
L'Eglise et l'Etat du Moyen-Age, 13 (1970), 90ff. and 179ff.

[155] K. Schmid, 'Konstanzer Klerus', 26–58.

[156] Oexle, 'Mittelalterliche Gilden', 203–26; Oexle, 'Liturgische Memoria', 323–40.

[157] K. Schmid, 'Konstanzer Klerus', 48.   [158] Meerssemann, 'Storiografia', 55ff.

attractive suggestion has been made that we are dealing with a group drawn from the archbishop's *familia*, which came together by his leave but not by his orders.[159] So far no sign has been found of any tension between ecclesiastical authority and such associations, apart from warnings against excesses in the course of the regular guild feasts. Whether we can conclude from this that they were 'consensual parishes' outside the normal diocesan hierarchy seems all the more doubtful in that even in the period which followed, where any violation of the real or supposed rights of the clergy and of the diocesan constitution was the subject of fierce polemic, no voices were raised against such *societates*, so long as their orthodoxy remained beyond doubt.[160]

We can see repeatedly that the functional 'tripartition of Christian society' was an abstraction which corresponded to reality only in a general sense and only partially. The partitions were porous at many points, and there was not a rigid sense of caste, as is sometimes supposed by modern sociologists, who contrast this with the conditions prevailing in their own area of study.[161] All Christians prayed, both laity and clergy; the laity, but increasingly also clerics, fought; most laymen but also many clerics worked. Only the clergy was unambiguously distinguished from all other Christians, not in its peripheral characteristics but in its central function, by virtue of possessing the power to consecrate. No Christian disputed that only bishops and priests could dispense the sacraments, apart from baptism. Where individual leaders or whole strata in religious movements held themselves empowered to dispense the sacraments or to do without the sacraments altogether they had separated themselves from the church; they were heretics.

Even the king, who as *mediator cleri et plebis* was more than a layman, who according to the theocratic conception of office was directly responsible to God, still received the sacraments from priests; they ordained and anointed him, but he himself ordained no one. No king ever attempted to do so or to claim to be able to do so. Only those who had been ordained could bless. It is important to emphasise this, because in the great disputes to come the accusation was often made against kings that they had usurped specifically clerical functions; yet it was common to

---

[159] Meersseman, *Ordo Fraternitatis*, I.99ff.; see the decisive contribution by Oexle, 'Liturgische Memoria', 325ff.
[160] Le Bras, 'Confréries', 454; whether we can say, as does Oexle, 'Mittelalterliche Gilden', 214, that 'the guilds were communities based on consent and hence contrasted with the parishes created by ecclesiastical division and ordination' needs further investigation. Is it really to be supposed that the members of such guilds emancipated themselves from the normal parishes?
[161] *Ibid.*, 222.

priests and kings that they had to render an account to God at the last judgement for those entrusted to them.[162]

Dogmatic controversies were, as far as we know, rare in the tenth and eleventh centuries. Kings do not appear to have intervened in them. Occasionally a court might take a position on liturgical questions under the influence of theologians there.[163] Here a remarkably conciliatory attitude could be revealed, as for example with Henry II, who originally wanted to have Bishop Gerhard of Cambrai consecrated at Bamberg according to the German rite, but abandoned the idea when it was objected that this was the prerogative of the archbishop of Rheims. The king agreed, but gave the bishop a pontifical to take with him so that he could receive episcopal ordination not according to 'the rite of the Charleses' but following the normal practice of the Reich.[164] The role played by rulers in councils needs investigating from case to case, but it should not be claimed that they were accustomed to impose their will on the episcopate. As a rule solemn forms were employed which expressed the mutual respect felt by king and council fathers.

It should be noted that the extent of royal influence on the church varied from country to country.[165] It was everywhere considerable, because the royal dignity had a quasi-priestly character and the king helped to uphold the church and was a central figure in it. According to a widely held conviction the ruler had a decisive voice in the election and appointment of bishops. If one bears in mind the rule of canon law, according to which the bishop was to be chosen by the clergy and people of the episcopal city, the king could still be seen here as the head of the people everywhere, and something more than that. It was not normally thought to be reprehensible that the king should give the bishop the insignia of his bishopric.[166] Nevertheless, it is worth noting that even before the middle of the eleventh century a distinction was occasionally made between the holy office and the earthly possessions of a church. This made it possible to defend the sale and purchase of a church, which would otherwise have been simoniacal; and it also made it possible to defend the

---

[162] Those who like E. Werner, *Zwischen Canossa und Worms. Staat und Kirche 1077–1122* (Berlin 1973), 61, claim that the Ottonians and Salians arrogated priestly rank to themselves, must be contradicted.

[163] Hauck, *Kirchengeschichte Deutschlands*, III.523; T. Klauser, *Liturgiegeschichte*, 79 and 203, citing B. Capelle, 'L'introduction du symbole à la messe', in *Mélanges J. de Ghellinck* (Gembloux 1952), II.1003–27.

[164] *Gesta episcoporum Cameracensium* III 2, MGH SS VII.466; see Hirsch, Pabst, and Bresslau, *Jahrbücher Heinrichs II.*, II.322f.

[165] See above, pp. 37–8.

[166] See below, p. 169.; Tellenbach, 'Gregorianische Reform', 107.

practice whereby the investiture of a church was conferred by a layman, which was what the king was in the opinion of the critics of current practice.[167]

It has not so far been much noticed by scholarship that lay princes sometimes intervened in the relationship between a monastery and its diocesan bishop. In general it was the pope alone who was entitled to confer privileges on a monastery which might be summed up in the broad notion of exemption:[168] freedom to make use of any bishop, not just the diocesan bishop, for the consecrations within the monastery; forbidding the diocesan bishop to enter the monastery unless invited by the abbot; restrictions on the jurisdictional powers of the bishop over members of the monastery. Such cases seem, however, to have been the exception; how rare or frequent they were needs further research. The most interesting examples known so far come from the history of the important abbot, William of Dijon, whose monasticism was an example to many. At the foundation of Fruttuaria, the famous family monastery, the Italian antiking Arduin of Ivrea took part and in cooperation with the diocesan bishop and at William's request granted the monastery exemption. This initial legal status did not last long. When Henry II intervened in Italy and forced Arduin to retreat Fruttuaria was made over to him; shortly afterwards the pope confirmed its exemption and granted it protection. When Duke Richard II of Normandy handed over the monastery of Fécamp to William unusual arrangements were also made.[169] The duke granted Fécamp, following the model of Cluny, the right to choose freely the bishop who was to consecrate the abbot. This was a decisive diminution of the rights of the archbishop of Rouen, in whose competence such decisions lay.[170]

German rulers also seem occasionally to have shaped the relationship between monasteries and diocesan bishops, probably more at the urging of the monasteries concerned than on their own initiative. When Otto III acquired the monastery of Pomposa by exchange in 1001 he laid down that the abbot was to be ordained by the bishop of Commacchio. If the bishop were to become a burden to the abbot because of his demands for payment or of any *potestas humana* the abbot was to turn to the archbishop of Ravenna, and should he meet with similar difficulties here he might make use of any other bishop. This privilege was confirmed by Henry II

---

[167] *Aimoni vita Abbonis* c. 10, Migne, *PL* 139, col. 598: 'Huiusmodi emptores quasdam velut telas aranearum texunt, quibus se defendunt, quod non benedictionem sed res Ecclesiarum emunt.'
[168] See above, p. 114 nn. 85f.
[169] Bulst, *Untersuchungen*, 115ff., 220ff.   [170] *Ibid.*, 150ff.

and Henry III.[171] Henry II issued a charter for the monasteries of
S. Salvatore on Monte Amiata and S. Antimo, who had succeeded in
convincing the king that the clergy of their proprietary churches had from
time immemorial paid them tithes which were claimed by the bishop of
Chiusi for himself and his canons. Henry decided the dispute in the
monasteries' favour and made the bishop promise to consecrate the
churches without payment of any kind.[172] It was equally unusual when
the same king granted Abbot Romuald of the imperial monastery of
Biforco the right to summon a bishop of his choice to perform
consecrations.[173]

If such actions seem strange, that should serve to remind us that kings
were not accustomed to intervene unthinkingly in the internal affairs of
the church; in general, imperial law respected the autonomy of the life of
the church within its dioceses and parishes. For this reason as well, the
phrase 'the church under lay power' should be seen for what it is: an
exaggeration.

---

[171] MGH Dipl. Otto III, no. 460; Henry II, no. 473; Henry III, no. 145.
[172] MGH Dipl. Henry II, nos. 129, 369. San Sepolcro in Noceati received similar unusual
privileges; Bresslau deals with the question of authenticity at length in the edition.
[173] MGH Dipl. Henry II, no. 463. Miccoli, *Chiesa Gregoriana*, 61, also noted that this
diploma contained unusual privileges: 'he obtained an important diploma in his favour
from Henry II, which exempted him from all worldly jurisdiction, and also, a fairly
singular provision for an imperial diploma, from the jurisdiction of the ordinary'.

5

THE BEGINNINGS OF THE REVOLUTION IN CHURCH HISTORY

The question whether the ground was prepared in the first half of the eleventh century for the changes which took place within the church and Christianity in the second half can be answered only cautiously and incompletely. The changes took place at different times in the lands and regions of western Europe with differing preconditions. What we can know is dependent on highly incomplete and not always reliable information. In consequence we are often faced with casual observations and can thus offer no more than suppositions.

If the authors of the late tenth or early eleventh centuries mentioned an increase in church-building this can be interpreted simply as an expression of increases or shifts in population, which are known from other sources. The imaginative Rodulfus Glaber reported enthusiastically that after the millennium the world clothed itself in a white robe of churches.[1] We can observe that an internal colonisation accompanied population increase in a number of western countries from the middle of the tenth century onwards: this meant clearing woods, marshes, and river beds for agriculture. Many new settlements and estates arose, and fortifications were built. The initiative for these new settlements generally came from ecclesiastical and secular landlords. The consequence was that people were no longer prepared to put up with distant parish churches and sought a chapel or church of their own. It may be that the thought of

---

[1] Rodulfus Glaber, *Libri Historiarum Quinque* III 13, p. 62.

economic gain played a part, but so did religious wishes, as is suggested by
contemporary interest in the acquisition of relics and in the veneration of
saints.

We may in general assume that the increase in the size and density of
the population was accompanied by a growth in trade and transport. In
large areas of France and Italy towns of all sizes developed, and this was
accompanied by changes in the social structure of their inhabitants. The
price of land rose. We can perceive new structures of noble and ecclesiastical lordship in the countries of Europe, which in this preterritorial and
precommunal phase of social organisation rapidly crystallised and
achieved a certain coherence in their jurisdictional hierarchy and their
control over their dependants as well as a certain autonomy *vis-à-vis* their
neighbours and superiors.[2] In France this led to a fragmentation of former
princely and comital powers, whereas in Italy the margravates represented
new forms of political organisation, and in Germany royal authority long
remained effective. But everywhere feuds remained what they had always
been, a legitimate means of redress for real or supposed injuries and of
acquiring rights which were claimed. Large-scale warfare was rare in this
period, but small feuds, disputes, and tensions were endemic. This is true
not just of France in the late tenth and eleventh centuries. The 'disorder'
of the period has, however, been exaggerated, mainly because it has not
been soberly compared with reports for other periods and places. The
preferred method of pursuing feud was to damage those who were
obliged to provide the opponent with dues and rents. This often affected
others, in particular the recipients of tithes, who had nothing to do with
the dispute in question.[3] We hear frequently of ravaging of fields, destruction of harvests, driving off of herds, burning of houses; the consequence
was desperate need. Feuds belonged, like droughts, floods, hard winters,
and plagues, to the normal afflictions of mankind. They were seen as
God's punishment, either for man's guilt in general or for specific sins and
crimes recently committed; any observer of such events had no difficulty
in calling any number of these to mind. In all churches God was prayed
to for help against this evil.

The high incidence of feud and the lack of law and order came to be a
torture for men of all classes in parts of France and neighbouring lands
where power was at its most fragmented in the tenth and eleventh
centuries. Many of them, rich and poor, high and low, secular and
ecclesiastic, came together at synods and councils to pray for peace. It was

---

[2] See Tellenbach, 'Erforschung des hochmittelalterlichen Adels', 318–37, especially 324ff.
   on the structural changes of the tenth and eleventh centuries.
[3] Töpfer, *Volk und Kirche*, 97.

God who was to bring this about by reconciling or punishing the quarrelsome and the evil-doers; hence the term 'peace of God'.[4] The peace movement of the time had strong religious impulses behind it, expressed in pilgrimages and in the veneration of saints and relics, divine services, sermons, and synodal liturgies. Since it was the bishops who had to summon synods it is they who are generally seen as the initiators of the peace treaties. In these, secular and ecclesiastical lords pledged themselves to restrict feuds, to protect certain groups of persons, to observe the right of asylum or even to settle their disputes amicably. Closer examination makes it apparent that the initiative often proceeded from the great secular princes; their cooperation was at all events indispensable.[5] The intermediate and lesser prelates and lords also had to take part if the efforts for peace were to be successful.[6] The obligation to peace was reinforced by sacred oaths, for whose breach God's punishment was threatened. Even on earth, both spiritual and secular coercion were to be applied. The peace-breaker was to be excommunicated; should he be given shelter in spite of this the place concerned was to be laid under interdict.[7] If necessary, or if it seemed to the opponents of the real or supposed peace-broker to be necessary, bloody feuds were on occasion pursued. Then as now, peace was to be brought about by war. The opponents of peace were always in the wrong and the usual epithets were applied to them: robbers, highwaymen, thieves, arsonists, murderers. It is probable that there were indeed such people among the hungry peasantry and impoverished petty nobility. Since the written accounts on the whole come from clerics the *malefactores* are of course invariably laymen, which is naturally not a wholly mistaken point of view: even ecclesiastical lords pursued their feuds as a rule through their vassals and other laymen.[8]

As we have noted, the French peace movements were an expression of religious emotion, and that not just for the great masses of the lower

---

[4] R. Bonnaud-Delamare, 'Fondement des institutions de paix au XIme siècle', *Mélanges Louis Halphen* (Paris 1951), 20f.: the peace 'represented on earth a form of God's glory'.

[5] There are numerous examples in Hoffmann, *Gottesfriede*, especially 15ff. and 31ff.; even though the great peace meetings frequently took place at provincial or diocesan synods their mixed secular and ecclesiastical character is often clear: see Mackinney, 'The People and Public Opinion', 181–206, who stresses the populistic nature of the movement.

[6] T. Körner, *Juramentum und frühe Friedensbewegung (10.–12. Jahrhundert)* (Berlin 1977), 83 n. 5; Fechter, *Cluny*, 95 and 98, notes the low participation in the movement.

[7] Hoffmann, *Gottesfriede*, 28f.

[8] The punishment of 'peace-breakers' occasionally had to serve as an excuse for imposing ecclesiastical punishments or for military measures against neighbouring lay or ecclesiastical lords in the course of disputes about secular possessions; see Töpfer, *Volk und Kirche*, 15, 93.

orders of society. Beyond this it should not be forgotten that the peace and truce of God were a phase in the history of the restriction of feud; they belong to the prehistory of the *Landfriede* (territorial peace).[9] Feud was, as we have already mentioned, a legal method of self-help which got out of hand where there were no really powerful instances capable of deciding disputes, justly or unjustly. There was still a long way to go before the formation of the modern state with its monopoly of legitimate coercive force.

As far as we know, the peace movements showed no tendency to be critical of abuses in the churches within the regions they affected. They cannot be said to have opposed the prevailing form of economic organisation of the churches, that of the proprietary church, or the role of the laity within the church, or concerned themselves with the morality of the clergy. Conditions in Rome were not discussed critically at even the greatest of the peace councils, and the popes in turn hardly had any influence on the efforts for peace and the religious enthusiasm which accompanied them.[10] In general it is hard to demonstrate any immediate connection between these peace movements and 'church reform'.

The heretical groups which appeared here and there in Europe from the turn of the millennium onwards were of a quite different nature. It is unclear whether they arose quite spontaneously or were the product of local influences. We do not need to discuss them more closely here;[11] but it is important to note the unrest which they produced among both clergy and laity. Their deviations from the faith, their criticism of the clergy and of church life were signs of a religious fervour not known in earlier centuries, as equally were the fanaticism, popular fury, and intolerance with which they were persecuted. But here also there was no immediately visible connection between them and 'church reform'; and once again, no one in Rome concerned himself with them. These emotions, however violent they might have been at times, had little effect theologically or ecclesiastically.[12]

---

[9] E. Wadle, 'Heinrich IV. und die deutsche Friedensbewegung', *VuF*, 17 (1973), 170ff.

[10] The first pope who concerned himself with the peace of God was Leo IX. See Hoffmann, *Gottesfriede*, 217f. and 231; Mackinney, 'People and Public Opinion', 200ff.; L. Sittler, 'Papst Leo IX und der Gottesfriede im Elsass', in *Saint Léon: Le pape Alsacien*, ed. L. Sittler and F. Stintzi (Colmar 1950), 121, where it is stressed that Leo did not organise the peace himself.

[11] Grundmann, *Ketzergeschichte*, 8.

[12] The fanatical and cruel persecution of heretics was occasionally criticised by high ecclesiastics; see for example Grundmann, *Ketzergeschichte*, 9 n. 5, and *Registrum* IV 20, p. 328.

By contrast the eucharistic doctrine of Berengar (*c.* 1010–88), archdeacon in Angers and *scholasticus* in Tours, aroused great attention, at least among high ecclesiastics and churchmen. Berengar took the more Augustinian position of Hrabanus Maurus, Gottschalk the Saxon, and the monk Ratramnus of Corbie, according to which Christ's body was present as a mystery in the mass. Abbot Paschasius Radbertus of Corbie by contrast had drawn more on Ambrose and revolutionised the older doctrine of the Eucharist by teaching the real presence of the historical body of Christ in the sacrament; in the controversies of the ninth century his position triumphed, modified by some explanatory interpretations.[13] The theology of the tenth and early eleventh centuries experienced comparatively few controversies,[14] but the Augustinian tradition was in retreat. Berengar, in taking up the doctrines of the Augustinians of the ninth century, was faced with a more-or-less syncretistic eucharistic doctrine, which in the course of opposition to him was transformed into a crude realism, as in the case of Humbert of Silva Candida.[15] Humbert's doctrine was regarded as authoritative in the eleventh century and Berengar could not prevail against it. In spite of his high reputation as a theologian he came increasingly to be regarded as a heretic. Among his opponents was Abbot Lanfranc of Bec, the later archbishop of Canterbury, who denounced Berengar to Pope Leo IX. Leo was the first pope for a long time to concern himself with such questions. The archdeacon of Tours was excommunicated by a Roman synod in 1050 and was also condemned by a council in Vercelli shortly afterwards.[16] The conflict dragged on for decades until it was ended by Gregory VII. But it had no effects on the great contemporary events within the church.[17] The

---

[13] See above, p. 1 nn. 1 and 2; Ladner, *Theologie*, 14ff.; Geiselmann, *Eucharistielehre*, 292ff. and 315ff.; Macdonald, *Authority and Reason*, 94; Capitani, 'Studi per Berengario', especially p. 170: 'It has been possible to show how the theories of Paschasius Radbertus revolutionised the treatment of the sacraments with their powerful insistence on the concept of the real presence'.

[14] *Ibid.*, 84ff. on the doctrine of the Eucharist from Odo of Cluny to Fulbert of Chartres.

[15] *Ibid.*, 169, 'How much more did Humbert insist on this terminology of the crudest realism.' See also pp. 115, 155.

[16] Steindorff, *Jahrbücher Heinrichs III.*, II.121ff. and 131ff.

[17] See below, pp. 318–19; there has admittedly been no shortage of modern attempts to demonstrate through artificial constructions a close connection between Berengar and the general developments within the church. See for instance Ladner, *Theologie*, 14ff. What can one say of a sentence like the one there on p. 21: 'Presumably Berengar's original motive was one of revulsion against the raw capernaitical and stercoritical conception of the Eucharist that was widespread among the masses at the time, a clear expression of that "fleshy" period, against which the men of the church reform were also reacting'?

question of the real presence of Christ in the Eucharist was to become important for quite different reasons, but only after the validity of the ordinations of simoniacs and schismatics had been called in question.[18]

It was probably in Italy that people first began to object in a more than purely conventional fashion to uncanonical behaviour by ecclesiastics, to their greed and corruptibility and their disregard for the requirement of celibacy. Hermits and groups of hermits who themselves led a strictly ascetic life found many to listen to their penitential preaching. The monastic communities of Camaldoli and Vallombrosa showed a stronger tendency to try to influence the world than was found in the original ideals of monasticism. From an early date there were probably links between these circles and the Milanese Pataria, a movement which was both socially and religiously motivated; these links certainly date to a time before people in Rome had begun in a comprehensive manner and with a conscious programme to try to change those conditions in the church which were seen as unsatisfactory or degenerate. It would be a difficult task for the popes to give these movements their support and at the same time to keep them under control.[19]

In some general sense the social and religious movements of the period before the middle of the eleventh century were certainly part of the pre-conditions for the events which followed; but we cannot claim that there is a clear and calculable causal nexus. The political and economic changes of the period took place regionally, with considerable time-lags between the different regions. It is no doubt possible to see an intensification of religious consciousness as a whole, but this was very uneven. The various heretical movements may equally be seen as a sign of growing religious activity,[20] but they too as a rule seem to have been confined to one locality and to have had little or no contact with each other; it was rare that they extended beyond the borders of a single church province or territory.

[18] The importance for the conception of the sacraments of the famous discussion about the validity of simoniacal orders can hardly be overestimated. Can the unworthiness of the dispenser prevent the sacraments from being effective, or is Christ so exclusively the real dispenser that the ecclesiastic becomes a mere *minister secundarius* and hence of no importance? As we know, doctrinal development decided against Humbert's interpretation.

[19] See above, p. 120 and n. 106, and Tellenbach, 'Gregorianische Reform', nn. 25 and 32.

[20] Grundmann, *Ketzergeschichte*, 2; Töpfer, *Volk und Kirche*, 42: 'In the last resort the pilgrim movement, heresy and monastic reform are only varying aspects of the same fundamental tendency'; Manselli, 'Christianitas medioevale', 133: 'For this Christianity heresy represented a vital force, a dynamic aspect, acting now as goad, now as reins, but always as a restless, sometimes even a polemical conscience.'

The life of the church took place, apart from the universal communities of the spirit and of liturgy, within parishes, dioceses, provinces, and countries. Mutual influences were rare,[21] though in this respect monastic circles were from an early date something of an exception. These, as we have seen, did indeed have a powerful influence on religious consciousness, without having specific aims for the church as a whole; we have already mentioned the exceptions. Rome was not yet an effective force either within the external organisation of the *ecclesia toto orbe diffusa* or in establishing closer and more continuous contacts between its members.

THE POPES AND THE EMANCIPATION OF THE ROMAN CHURCH FOLLOWING THE SYNODS OF SUTRI AND ROME (1046)

The depositions of three allegedly simoniacal popes at synods held in Sutri and Rome in December 1046 belong to the most spectacular events of the eleventh century. The sources for these events present much that is contradictory or unbelievable, and modern scholarship was for long unable to reach an interpretative consensus; recent studies of the sources by Franz-Josef Schmale have produced a more reliable interpretation.[22]

Henry III probably had no very clear ideas about the state of the Roman church when he set out for Italy in the late summer of 1046. In Piacenza in November he met Pope Gregory VI, who may even have been invited by the king; he was certainly honourably received by him.[23] Was this because there was as yet no suspicion of simony against Gregory VI or was it more a question of a general uncertainty in the application of the concept of simony? On 20 December the famous synod met at Henry's instigation in Sutri; Gregory VI presided and Henry attended. Silvester III appeared, and was declared in orderly proceedings to have forfeited the papal dignity. Apparently there were then difficult discussions about whether Gregory VI had himself been guilty of simony. It is significant that the pope seems at first to have sincerely held the

---

[21] On the call to make a truce of God which was sent by Odilo of Cluny and several bishops between 1037 and 1042 to Italy see Hoffmann, *Gottesfriede*, 85, and also Mackinney, 'People and Public Opinion', 196ff.

[22] Borino, 'Elezione', especially p. 223, where he describes the notion that Henry III found three popes in office as 'a manner of speaking', and p. 229, where he says that there had long ceased to be a schism; Schmale, 'Absetzung', which cites, discusses, and supersedes the older literature.

[23] K. Schmid, 'Heinrich III. und Gregor VI. im Gebetsgedenken von Piacenza des Jahres 1046', *Verbum et Signum*, 2 (1975), 37–97; Schmale, 'Absetzung', 100 n. 163; the assumption of R. Schieffer, 'Heinrich III.', 108, that Henry followed less a predetermined plan than the needs of the moment, seems acceptable.

opinion that it was not simoniacal to have used money to persuade Benedict IX, who had a bad reputation, to resign, and then to have accepted election himself.[24] Once again we find, as perhaps in Piacenza, uncertainty about what constituted simony. Gregory VI was evidently unable to persuade the synod to accept his view. However, its members left to Gregory himself, the pope who might not be judged by any man, the decision about his future; he resigned of his own free will.[25]

In Rome Benedict IX, who had not appeared before the synod, was deposed. On 24 December Bishop Suidger of Bamberg, the first non-Roman and non-Italian pope since Silvester II, was elected as Pope Clement II at the king's proposal and was consecrated on the next day; he in turn immediately consecrated Henry III and Agnes emperor and empress. In order to underpin the new world order, which had been taken up consciously and was generally welcomed, the last of the previous popes still alive was exiled to Germany.[26]

Henry III's motives in general, his aims in his dealings with the popes and the Roman church, can only be a matter for cautious surmise.[27] The king had succeeded to his father Conrad II in 1039 at the age of twenty-two, and had thus already ruled for seven years when he set out in September 1046 for his first Italian expedition. It is certain that he intended to rule in Italy and received imperial coronation in Rome just as his predecessors had done.[28] There are many indications that Henry III lived still more than other kings did with a sense of responsibility for the holy church and was more touched than other rulers by the religious

[24] Tellenbach, 'Gregorianische Reform', 102. The protocol of Halinard's election as arch-bishop of Lyons in 1046 published by B. de Vregille, 'Dijon, Cluny, Lyon et Rome. A propos de deux documents sur Halinard de Sombernon', *Annales de Bourgogne*, 31 (1959), 23f., fits in with this: among the signatories we find S. *Gregorii papae* alongside S. *Henrici* and S. *Hugonis archipraesulis*. Johannes Gratianus must have been acknowledged as pope at that time. Holtzmann, 'Laurentius', 209, calls the archipresbyter Johannes Gratianus the most prominent representative of the reform party in Rome; but see below, p. 158.
[25] Schmale, 'Absetzung', 85f., but see already Borino, 'Elezione', 323ff. and Zimmermann, *Papstabsetzungen*, 128f.
[26] We do not know who advised him, but it can be said with certainty that the measures of Sutri and Rome could not have been taken without his agreement.
[27] The overestimation of his Italian and imperial policy is widespread; see by contrast the sober assessment by Tellenbach, 'Kaiser, Rom', 321ff.
[28] On Henry III's alleged plans see Borino, 'Elezione', 316, as well as his deductions on 332f., 340f. and 372ff. Against what Kehr, *Vier Kapitel*, says about Henry's ecclesiastical system see Tellenbach, *Libertas*, 209. Recently Jakobs, 'Cluniacenser und 'apsttum', 651 has revived the view that Henry III wished to 'draw the universal episcopacy [of the papacy] into the service of the empire'. C. Violante, 'Aspetti della politica Italiana di Enrico III prima della sua discesa in Italia', *RSI*, 64 (1952), 157–76, 293–314, gives a balanced view.

movements of his period. Before his time mercy had generally counted as a kingly virtue, but there are more reports about Henry's mercifulness than is usual.[29] The archbishops of Milan and Lyons, who had been condemned for infidelity and high treason by his father, were evidently soon restored to his grace.[30] Perhaps he had been influenced by the peace of God movements of France and Burgundy, even before his marriage with Agnes, the daughter of the duke of Aquitaine; these movements made frequent use of 'indulgences', that is, the granting of mutual forgiveness by persons at enmity with one another. Henry is several times recorded as having forgiven his enemies and as urging those present at assemblies to do likewise: in 1043 at Constance and Trier; in 1044 following his victory over the Hungarians at the battle of Menfö.[31] By contrast he took deviations from the true faith very seriously, as can be seen in his hanging of heretics at Goslar.[32] The account given by Rodulfus Glaber of the speech he made against simony at the synod of Pavia in October 1046 may contain some elements of historicity, since the rather more reliable Wipo also reports that Henry never received a penny for any ecclesiastical office he conferred.[33] We shall see shortly that many later sources and modern accounts give an exaggerated impression of the extent of simony in the tenth and eleventh centuries, and it was probably an increase in polemical zeal rather than in the phenomenon itself which meant that we hear more and more about it from the middle of the eleventh century onwards.[34] Henry III and his entourage seem to have been affected by this zeal. The king can hardly have acquired the tendency in Germany, or even from much admired ascetics like the hermit Gunther or from the Cluniacs; it is more likely that he was influenced by

[29] Henry II forgave Margrave Henry of Schweinfurt (Thietmar of Merseburg, *Chronicon* VI 13, p. 290), and at the request of Archbishop Aripert of Mainz Conrad II forgave 'omnibus quod adversus illum deliquerant' (Wipo, *Gesta Chuonradi* c. 3, p. 20ff.).

[30] Steindorff, *Jahrbücher Heinrichs III.*, 1.81, 134f.

[31] On Henry III's indulgences in Constance, Trier, and on the battlefield at Menfö see *ibid.*, 155, 195 and 209; on the general indulgence on his deathbed see Meyer von Knonau, *Jahrbücher Heinrichs IV.*, 1.17. By chance we hear of a further indulgence which Henry is said to have granted on the occasion of his coronation, only because Godfrey of Lotharingia was excluded from it; Steindorff, *Jahrbücher Heinrichs III.*', II.323 n. 2. Note T. Schieffer, 'Heinrich III.', 58: Henry did not adopt the practice of the French peace of God movement. Laudage, *Priesterbild*, 138 n. 68, erroneously sees in Henry's indulgences an indication that the king claimed to be able to forgive sins like a priest. There is no mention of this in the article he cites by M. Minninger, 'Heinrichs III. interne Friedens- maßnahmen und ihre etwaigen Gegner in Lothringen', *Jahrbücher für westdeutsche Landes- geschichte*, 5 (1979), 39.

[32] Steindorff, *Jahrbücher Heinrichs III.*, II.166.

[33] Rodulfus Glaber, *Libri Historiarum Quinque*, V.5, 133ff.

[34] See the next section of this chapter.

Italian monks and hermits with whom he came into direct or indirect contact there.[35]

It is doubtful whether simoniacal practices in Rome were what principally determined Henry's actions. Was the simony of Gratian/ Gregory VI still unknown to him six weeks before Sutri, or was it that the concept of simony was still fuzzy?[36] There is much to be said for the view that his main concern was to neutralise the rival Roman factions and liberate the mother church of Christianity, a sign of his desire to make peace which can be seen elsewhere as well. For this reason he wished to extricate the Roman church from its local and regional ties; to this end he decided to nominate Suidger of Bamberg, who was recognised as a worthy and reliable bishop, and to agree with the Romans to accept the dignity of *patricius*, which implied the right of participating in future papal elections. The *principatus electionis* conceded to Henry was intended to exclude future upsets at papal elections.[37] In the period from then up to Henry's death three German bishops were elected peacefully as pope on Henry's nomination after the early death of Clement II: Damasus II, Leo IX, and Victor II. His relations with them were characterised by amicable cooperation, especially in ecclesiastical questions, in the protection of the papal patrimony and the upholding of papal and imperial rights in southern Italy. One gets the impression that the emperor wanted his help to enable the popes to become more independent and himself wished to step into the background after Sutri and Rome.[38] During the

[35] On Henry III and the hermit Gunther see MGH Dipl. Henry III, no. 25: 'idem Guntherus pro meritorum probitate amicabiliter usus est nostra familiaritate'; on Gunther see H. Grundmann, 'Deutsche Eremiten im Hochmittelalter', *AKG*, 45 (1967), 73ff. The most impressive demonstration of Henry's veneration for Cluny and Abbot Hugo is the letter, MGH Dipl. Henry III, no. 263. But Cluny was by no means at the forefront of the fight against simony as were for example the Vallombrosans; see above, p. 119 n. 105, and Violante, *Pataria Milanese*, 7, on Henry's connections with Umbrian monasteries and hermits; see also J. E. Gugumus, 'Der heilige Abt Guido von Pomposa (970–1046)', *Archiv für mittelrheinische Kirchengeschichte*, 23 (1971), 9–19.
[36] See Tellenbach, 'Gregorianische Reform', nn. 18f.
[37] Steindorff, *Jahrbücher Heinrichs III.*, 1.506ff.; T. Schieffer, 'Kaiser Heinrich III.', 62f.
[38] Tellenbach, *Libertas*, p. 209; Vollrath, 'Kaisertum und Patriziat', 36ff. explains the Salian patriciate in terms of Henry III's renunciation of imperial rights in Rome. Szabó-Bechstein, 'Libertas Ecclesiae', 100, sees no fundamental opposition to Henry III's rule over the church under Leo IX, but Hoffmann, 'Von Cluny', 188f., talks of a 'deep opposition' to Henry III. He admits that Leo was personally loyal, but sees even in Leo's reservations about the election (the need for the consent of clergy and people) a fundamental antagonism to the king's church policy. In his view the reservation was a reaction to Henry's rejection of Halinard of Lyons, who had been nominated by the Romans. But this is inaccurate; it was Halinard himself who rejected nomination; see Steindorff, *Jahrbücher Heinrichs III.*, II.53, with the sources.

expedition of 1046 to 1047 he spent only a month in Rome, before campaigning together with Clement II in southern Italy; he then returned to Germany without visiting Rome again. It was not until eight years later that he came again to Italy for seven months, and again he did not visit Rome.[39]

Henry's position in western history has been obscured by the theory-bound constructs of modern historiography.[40] He is supposed to have tried to draw the inner revival experienced by Christianity in the course of its contemporary reform into the service of his empire and to have attempted to preserve the old duality of ecclesiastical and secular rule under the leadership of his own secular rule. Yet the notion of an internal revival of Christianity is a distinctly problematical one from an ecclesiological point of view; and above all, what did 'reform' mean at that time? Was Henry himself not just as much an example of internal revival, which was hence hardly something he could have taken over from outside? What was that hostility to simony, which he felt more strongly than most men in his lifetime and which was only later, after conceptual extension and polemical misinterpretation, to have fundamental political consequences? And what sort of unity was it which he is supposed to have sought to preserve? The empire had long ceased to be a universal body even in theory. In Henry's time there were no widespread differences of opinion about the customary and highly differentiated relationships between clerics and laymen in the churches of all the western European countries. He could not foresee what was to happen in the two decades following his death; there were no signs of a conflict between empire and papacy in his lifetime, nor of a general shift within Christendom, even in its peripheral regions.

In the history of the papacy Henry III's reign was a first phase in its rise. The Roman church was to be emancipated from the pressures of local and regional powers, and led first by important German bishops, later by leading personalities from Italy and France. The popes Leo IX and Victor II, who were able to rule for at least a few years, both repeatedly crossed the Alps to meet the emperor or to hold councils in Germany and France.[41]

[39] *Ibid.*, 1.323ff., II.297ff.; on the controversy about whether Conrad II and Henry III invested the Norman princes see Kehr, *Belehnungen*, 7 n. 4 and p. 11.
[40] Ladner, *Theologie*, 6off. and especially 78ff.
[41] Leo IX stayed north of the Alps for more than twenty months and in southern Italy for about the same length of time; the rest of his pontificate was divided roughly equally between Rome and north or central Italy. Victor II spent more than a year in Germany, rather more in central and southern Italy, rather less in Rome. The great synods of both popes were more comprehensive both in their subject-matter and in those who took part than the synods of their predecessors.

In cooperation with the emperor they began to build up a papal government over the church of a kind not previously seen. The question was
whether the new order would survive Henry's death; as was seen, there
were serious dangers to be overcome in the period which followed.

It was to be of decisive importance that Leo IX gathered a circle of
influential and for the most part non-Roman ecclesiastics around him,
who supported and advised him. Not only were they influenced by
him; they in turn gave new impulses to papal activity. Among the first
members of this group were monks from France and Lotharingia: Azelin
of Compiègne, cardinal bishop of Sutri; Humbert of Moyenmoutier,
bibliothecarius of the Roman church and later cardinal bishop of Silva
Candida; Peter of Tusculum; Hugo Candidus from Rémiremont,
cardinal priest of S. Clemente; Frederick, the brother of Duke Godfrey of
Lotharingia, deacon and chancellor of the Roman church and later
cardinal priest of S. Crisogono and abbot of Monte Cassino. From the
time of Leo XI's first journey to Rome onwards Hildebrand, subdeacon
of the Roman church, probably belonged to the papal entourage. Among
Leo's closest associates we find Archbishop Halinard of Lyons, who
accompanied the pope on his travels and represented him in Rome, the
primicerius Udo from Toul, who was *bibliothecarius* and chancellor in
Rome, the provost Petrus Damiani of Fonte Avellana, later cardinal
bishop of Ostia. This circle gradually grew and took on new members.
From Victor II's pontificate at the latest it included Desiderius, son of a
south Italian Lombard prince, who was abbot of Monte Cassino from
1058, his friend Alfanus, archbishop of Salerno, John, cardinal bishop of
Velletri and Boniface, cardinal bishop of Tusculum.[42]

The emergence of a separate collective leadership alongside the pope,
even though this as yet had no fixed rights and functions, was probably
the most important consequence of Leo IX's pontificate, a second phase
in the rise of the papacy. This body developed a powerful continuity and
was able to renew itself, with the result that it could continue in existence
across the pontificates of individual popes. The Roman church now had
an instance with some weight of its own which could act independently
of the factors which had dominated papal history: the nobility, clergy, and
people of Rome, the Roman kings and emperors, and even the popes

---

[42] The Lotharingian and Burgundian origins of many of Leo IX's assistants has often been
remarked on. See especially Hoffmann, 'Von Cluny', 186f., who goes so far as to
suppose that 'the ideas which were to revolutionise the world originated in Burgundy
and Lotharingia, and not in Rome'. On Halinard see Klewitz, 'Entstehung', 134ff.:
Halinard of Lyons even resided in Rome as the pope's deputy while Leo was called to
Hungary; Steindorff, *Jahrbücher Heinrichs III.*, II.181, 219; Kuttner, 'Cardinalis', 172ff. See
the summary by Ganzer, *Auswärtiges Kardinalat*, 6ff.

themselves. From these beginnings the college of cardinals was in the decades which followed to develop into a 'senate of the Roman church'.

The extension of papal influence beyond Rome and its environs and the Roman church province produced changes in old-established Roman church institutions. The leading members of the clergy, the cardinal bishops and cardinal priests (the priests of the titular churches who had up until then been responsible for divine service at the Lateran basilica and in the titular churches on a weekly roster), became less important for the divine service and spiritual life of the individual Roman congregations and turned into assistants of the popes in their manifold regional and supraregional obligations. Corresponding to this were changes in the hierarchy of officials. The old advisers of the popes, the *iudices de clero*, who were closely connected with the city's governing élite, came to be confined to judicial functions.[43] Already in the first half of the eleventh century the influence of western diplomatic practice had led to the setting up of a special bureau under the chancellor which was primarily responsible for the political correspondence. But as early as the pontificate of Benedict IX the offices of librarian and chancellor were combined. Besides the charters written on papyrus in the papal curial script appeared parchment charters written in western charter minuscule which were gradually to replace them; alongside the notaries of the Roman regions appeared the palace notaries, who accompanied the popes on their journeys. Old and new offices and officials coexisted in the second half of the century. The changes in and multiplications of papal functions, and the general tendency towards a fixed regulation of administration produced 'the emergence of the Roman curia'.[44]

The process of emancipation of the Roman church from the rule of the Roman nobility, which had begun in the time of Henry III and Leo IX and was supposed to be assured by the definition of the emperor's participation in papal elections, was by no means assured; nor was the development of an autonomous circle of clerics as an institution which supported and advised the popes. This was to become clear in the papal elections which followed the death of Henry III. The old model of 'canonical election' could mean practically anything which suited dominant interests. 'Clergy and people' of the episcopal city, the electors recognised by canon law, are anonymous masses; as in all collectives there have to be leaders and led, decision-takers and consenters, though these

---

[43] Jordan, 'Entstehung', 105f.; Kuttner, 'Cardinalis', 175ff.; Pásztor, 'Curia romana', 494f.

[44] Jordan, 'Entstehung', 104; Pásztor, 'Curia Romana', 500.

can normally not be identified with certainty on the basis of the sources available – all we can do is make cautious guesses.[45]

The election of Abbot Frederick of Monte Cassino, who was allegedly in Rome 'by chance' when the news of Victor II's death reached the city, cannot be completely clarified, though it certainly did not conform to the arrangements made in 1046, unlike those which preceded it.[46] Those with whom Frederick held his discussions on possible candidates before the election were *clerici quam cives* (clergy and citizens); those who took part in his election on 3 August 1057 were described much later by Leo of Ostia as 'all the cardinals together with the Roman clergy and people' or by Bonizo as 'the Roman clerics accompanied by the acclamation of the people', which hardly allows us to make out those who took the lead.[47] The election ignored the rights of the *patricius* promised to Henry III. It may be assumed that there was no intention of depriving his heir of these rights, but in the dangerous situation prevailing there were good arguments against delaying the election too long, which is what a request for confirmation from the German court would have entailed. At what point a Roman embassy sought and received the regent's agreement to the election and whether this had been preceded by a protest from the imperial court against the infringement of royal rights is a matter of dispute, which can hardly be settled definitively.[48]

When Stephen IX, mortally ill, left Rome nine months after his election he must already have experienced powerful resistance there. The journey to his brother Godfrey of Lotharingia in Florence was perhaps more of a flight. The majority of the cardinal bishops fled from the city, in so far as they were still there, on the news of his death.[49] The majority

---

[45] Fundamental on the concepts of *electio canonica* and the 'freedom' of ecclesiastical elections before the changes of the second half of the eleventh century is P. Schmid, *Kanonische Wahl.*

[46] Meyer von Knonau, *Jahrbücher Heinrichs IV.*, 1.31 n. 15; according to the *Gesta episcoporum Cameracensium* III.37, MGH SS VII.480, it would appear to have been a question of concern more for peace than for 'church reform'.

[47] Leo of Ostia II 94, MGH SS XXXIV.352f.; Bonizo, *Liber ad amicum* v, MGH LdL I.590.

[48] Meyer von Knonau, *Jahrbücher Heinrichs IV.*, 1.35 with n. 21 and 53 with n. 55; *Annales Altahenses s.a.* 1057, p. 54: 'Fridericus cognomine Stephanus, a Romanis subrogatus, rege ignorante, postea tamen electionem eius comprobante.' Krause, 'Papstwahldekret', 61 n. 108 assumed against Hauck, *Kirchengeschichte Deutschlands*, III.672f., that the empress protested. See D. Hägermann, 'Zur Vorgeschichte des Pontifikats Nikolaus II.', *ZKG*, 81 (1976), 352 n. 22.

[49] Petrus Damiani, *Epistolae* III 4, Migne, *PL* 144, col. 291: 'nobis omnibus eiusdem urbis cardinalibus episcopis reclamantibus, obsistentibus et terribiliter damnantibus'; Leo of Ostia II 99, MGH SS XXXIV.356.

of the cardinal priests on the other hand seems to have remained in Rome. It may be that Roman nobles had taken over the leadership in the events which followed. They had only two of the seven cardinal bishops on their side when one of these, John of Velletri, was elected as Pope Benedict X on 5 April 1058 in an election which – like many other papal elections – is depicted in the sources as tumultuous. John was enthroned by the archpriest of Ostia in place of the cardinal bishop, who had fled. How far the clergy and people of Rome were terrorised by the nobles and how far they gave their consent freely cannot be determined, as it cannot be for the majority of papal elections.[50] Of the leading ecclesiastics, only Cardinal Bishop Rainer of Palestrina and the chancellor and librarian Lietbuin (a German who had been taken into papal service by Leo IX)[51] are mentioned as being on Benedict's side. The electors of Benedict X had ignored the instruction of Stephen IX to delay the election until Hildebrand's return from his embassy to Germany; but in so doing they infringed neither law nor tradition, for popes did not designate their successors. However, they did quite clearly pass over the right of the German king to participate in the election agreed in 1046. Nevertheless, Benedict X was for months the undisputed pope, and even after an opposition to his pontificate had formed he resided in Rome up to the end of 1058.

Meanwhile Hildebrand, who had halted in Florence on his return from his embassy when he heard news of the events in Rome, had selected Bishop Gerhard of Florence as a rival candidate in agreement with the cardinal bishops who had fled. This time more caution was shown; the agreement first of Duke Godfrey and then of the German court was secured. At the end of the year Gerhard was elected in Siena as Pope Nicholas II. Five of the seven cardinal bishops were present, but cardinal priests are not mentioned.[52] After money and rhetoric had created a favourable climate of opinion for Nicholas in Rome it became possible to drive Benedict X out of the city, probably in January 1059, with the aid of Duke Godfrey. Yet the modalities of Nicholas's election once again did not correspond with the traditional forms of a papal election, in particular because the election occurred outside Rome, because it was performed by a group of persons who had not yet come to have a dominant role in papal elections, and because

---

[50] Klewitz, 'Entstehung', 136 and 208 no. 11a; Pásztor, 'Curia Romana', 500.

[51] Pásztor, 'Pier Damiani', 326f.

[52] Krause, 'Papstwahldekret', 71, rightly calls it remarkable that only four cardinal priests were present at Nicholas II's Easter synod of 1059: 'We do not know whether the mass of 28 cardinal priests supported Benedict.'

the greater part of the clergy and people of Rome did not participate.[53]

Benedict X remained a threat to his opponents for a time, operating
from noble fortifications like Passerano and Galera. This danger led to a
decisive change in the policy of Nicholas II's curia towards the Normans.
Southern Italy had always been a region which demanded close attention
from the popes, who had to defend their own interests there against
rival powers: Saracens; Byzantines; Lombards; on occasions the Roman
emperors; and, from the beginning of the eleventh century, Normans.[54]
It is disputed whether Henry III invested the Norman princes or not.[55]
Leo IX was defeated in battle against them, Victor II's attitude is unclear,
and Stephen IX began to take up the struggle against them energetically
once again.[56] In 1059 came a decisive change, perhaps under the influence
of Abbot Desiderius of Monte Cassino. Norman troops were used
successfully on several occasions against the Roman nobility and the
antipope; Richard of Aversa and Robert Guiscard became vassals of the
Roman church. It is certain that they were brought into play with the
intention of defending the independence of the Roman church against
local powers;[57] it cannot be determined whether they were also thought
of as a future counterweight to the German ruler. Nevertheless, it must
have become clear at the empress's court that the papal enfeoffment of the
Norman princes touched on imperial rights and claims in southern Italy.[58]

---

[53] On the credibility of the *Annales Romani*, *s.a.* 1059, MGH SS v.470f., see Meyer von
Knonau, *Jahrbücher Heinrichs IV.*, 1.119 n. 3.

[54] Deér, *Papsttum*, 35 n. 51.

[55] Kehr, *Belehnungen*, 7f. n. 4 and p. 11 denies it, against Steindorff, *Jahrbücher Heinrichs III.*,
1.327; L. von Heinemann, *Geschichte der Normannen in Unteritalien und Sizilien* (Leipzig
1894), 1.108; Erdmann, *Kaiserfahne*, 885ff., and C. Erdman, 'Kaiserliche und päpstliche
Fahnen im hohen Mittelalter', *QFIAB*, 25 (1933–4), 4. Kehr stresses that the sentence
'Rainulfum quoque ipsius Waimarii suggestione de comitatu Aversano investit' (Leo of
Ostia II 63, MGH SS xxxiv.292 ll. 14f. and 28ff.) is a later addition by Peter the
Deacon; see Deér, *Papsttum*, 23ff.

[56] Steindorff, *Jahrbücher Heinrichs III.*, 1.248ff., 294ff. and Meyer von Knonau, *Jahrbücher
Heinrichs IV.*, 1.77f.; in all these disputes the Normans sought to legitimise their conquests
by securing papal suzerainty, while Leo IX and Stephen IX sought to force back the
foreign adventurers who had done such damage to the patrimonium Petri and to Monte
Cassino; see Kehr, *Belehnungen*, 10.

[57] *Ibid.*, 15: 'At that time Rome needed help against Benedict X, the pope of the Roman
aristocratic party, Richard needed the legalising of his rule *vacante imperio*.'

[58] Probably it was thought in Rome that German help could no longer be counted on after
the death of Henry III and Victor II. Kehr hardly discusses the significance of the alliance
between pope and Normans for the relations between the papacy and the German court,
and merely notes in passing on p. 11: 'thus what was left to the Normans was to come
closer to the popes in Rome, with whom they shared the common aim of driving out

The reorganisation of the Roman church begun under Henry III and
Leo IX had been called in question since the death of Stephen IX. The
circle around Nicholas II must have recognised this. The Roman synod
of April 1059 was marked by a decisive attempt to secure and extend the
ground that had been won. The well-known papal election decree of
1059 was intended to make a repetition of the events of the previous year
impossible. By making the cardinal bishops the primary electors and the
cardinal priests participants the complete autonomy of the Roman
clerical élite was laid down for the first time. Friedrich Kempf rightly saw
that the real purpose of this was to create a supreme instance within the
hierarchy to deal with papal elections.[59] The weight of the remaining
members of the clergy and of the lay elements, in particular of the Roman
nobility, was to be reduced decisively. But the election decree was
evidently new law. Even the idea that the cardinal bishops were to take
on the same position *vis-à-vis* papal elections as metropolitans had *vis-à-vis*
the elections of their suffragans was new.[60] How far this law would prove
itself in practice remained to be seen. The legislation of 1059 did not
provide a new model for episcopal and abbatial elections. The old notion

or subjugating the Saracens and the same hostility to the orthodox emperors of
Byzantium and to the German king', Holtzmann, 'Papsttum, Normannen,', 70, is struck
by the bold and self-evident way in which the pope laid claim to lands which did not
belong to him at all. Deér, 'Papsttum', 44, thinks that it is hardly conceivable that
Nicholas and Hildebrand had no knowledge of the claims of the western empire to
Apulia and Calabria, while Kempf, *Handbuch*, 416 n. 4, is very reserved: 'it is by no means
certain that Nicholas wanted simply to exclude an imperial overlordship over the former
Lombard principalities'.

[59] Kempf, 'Pier Damiani', 86 and 88f., though I cannot follow him when he says that the
authors of the decree were no revolutionaries; Alberigo, 'Origini', investigates in detail
the ideas present in the early period of the renewed institution of the cardinalate (but see
below, pp. 322–4 with nn. 74–86).
[60] The extensive literature on the papal election decree which has appeared since the time
of P. Scheffer-Boichorst and A. Michel has been synthesised and taken further by H. G.
Krause, 'Papstwahldekret', yet in spite of many illuminating conclusions a number of
doubts have remained, with the result that the discussion has continued: see Stürner,
'Salvo debito'; Stürner, 'Königsparagraph'; Stürner, 'Papstwahldekret'; H. Grundmann,
'Eine neue Interpretation des Papstwahldekrets von 1059', *DA*, 25 (1969), 234ff.;
D. Hägermann, 'Untersuchungen zum Papstwahldekret von 1059', *ZRGKA*, 56 (1970),
157–93. More recently Jasper, *Papstwahldekret* has offered quite new insights, especially
on the dating and intention of the falsified version of the decree; see his summary, 87f.,
and further R. Schieffer, 'Rechtstexte und Reformpapsttum', in *Überlieferung und
Geltung normativer Texte des frühen und hohen Mittelalters*, ed. H. Mordek (Sigmaringen
1986), 51ff.; W. Stürner, 'Das Papstwahldekret von 1059 und seine Verfälschung', in
Fälschungen im Mittelalter (MGH Schriften 33/2, Munich 1988), 157–90; H. G. Krause,
'Die Bedeutung der neuendeckten handschriftlichen Überlieferung des Papstwahldekrets
von 1059', *ZRGKA*, 107 (1990), 89ff.

of 'free election', which by no means excluded the participation of external elements but did stress the principle, often violated, that those who objected (*invitis*) should not have a spiritual head imposed on them against their will and in particular not someone from outside their own community, long remained partially in force in bishoprics and monasteries. Only much later was the old participation by clergy and people acknowledged in a transformation and definition of their roles in elections, by recognising in the course of the twelfth century the rights of the cathedral chapter to exercise that initiative without which elections had never been possible.[61]

There has been much discussion in recent scholarship of the rights assigned to the son of the *patricius* of 1046 in the preparation of Nicholas's own election and in the papal election decree. Before the election there were negotiations with the imperial court and with Wibert, the royal chancellor for Italy. The formulations in the papal election decree were cautious and avoided taking the obvious step of explicitly confirming to Henry IV those rights which Henry III had acquired with the patriciate in 1047.[62] In the second main source, the *Disceptio synodalis* by Petrus Damiani, the 'king's advocate' refers to the 'principal role always to be played by the king in the election of the pontiff to be ordained', while the 'defender of the Roman church', significantly, mentions the privilege which was to be allowed to Henry only vaguely.[63] Was it intended to leave room for varying interpretations by curia and imperial court?[64] At

---

[61] P. Schmid's clarification of the medieval notion of election is helpful, but the assumption (*Kanonische Wahl*, 110, 128) that the papal elections from that of Stephen IX on paved the way for a new notion of *electio canonica* is quite false. The group entrusted with the initial decision, the cardinal bishops, by no means established itself immediately, and similarly the papal election was not to come to act as a model for other ecclesiastical elections for a long time. The electoral rights of the whole college of cardinals, and correspondingly of the cathedral chapter, were a product of the increased institutionalisation which set in from the later eleventh century; cf. Krause, 'Papstwahldekret', 33, who in n. 15 cites G. von Below, *Die Entstehung des ausschließlichen Wahlrechts der Domkapitel mit besonderer Rücksicht auf Deutschland* (Historische Studien 11, Leipzig 1883); see further K. Ganzer, 'Zur Beschränkung der Bischofswahl auf das Domkapitel in Theorie und Praxis im 12. und 13. Jahrhundert', *ZRGKA*, 57 (1971), 22–82 and 58 (1972), 166–97; R. Schieffer, *Die Entstehung von Domkapiteln in Deutschland* (Bonner Historische Forschungen 43, Bonn 1976).
[62] MGH Const. I.540 no. 382 c. 6; see Krause, 'Papstwahldekret', 273.
[63] MGH LdL I.80.
[64] I follow Krause, 'Papstwahldekret', 85ff. in as much as he assumes a somewhat reluctant recognition of imperial rights up to the election of Gregory VII, but in spite of his arguments on pp. 98ff. I would still like to suppose (see *HZ*, 158 (1938) 136ff.) that, as

all events allowances were made in Rome for the current situation: in the difficult struggle against the antipope the curia neither wanted nor was able to risk an affront to the regency court. Hence the elastic text of the decree, with its references to the *debitus honor* and respect reserved to the young king, which were nevertheless presented as papal concessions, just as the young king's successors were allowed only those rights which the apostolic see had conferred on them. It is hard to suppose that such vagueness was not intentional. For the time being there seem to have been no differences of opinion or conflicts, but it should not be overlooked that the curia's alliance with the Normans had increased its self-confidence and that it probably neither expected help from nor feared intervention by the regency government. It may very well be true that the young king was intended to keep his rights, formally. However, no one had thought of paying much attention to these at the time of Stephen IX's election; it was not until a dangerous position developed in 1058 that they were recalled once more. At all events the initiative in papal elections was to be wrested from Roman aristocratic circles, but after the deaths of Henry III and Victor II an emperor or king was no longer indispensable for this: there was now a circle within the Roman church which claimed the decisive role for itself. It is this shift in the centre of gravity during the pontificates of Stephen IX, Nicholas II, and Alexander II which must be borne in mind when we consider relations between the curia and the imperial court.

At the end of Nicholas's pontificate a severe conflict broke out between the two, whose causes, starting-point, and history have not been definitively clarified, in spite of all attempts by scholars to do so. The royal chancellor for Italy, Wibert, attended the papal Easter synod in 1060, which is thus presumably the *terminus a quo* for these events; that in its turn rules out the election decree as the immediate cause for the breach. Equally improbable are steps supposed to have been taken by the imperial court against the pope at the instigation of Archbishop Anno II of Cologne; Anno was on good terms with pope and curia at that time. The most probable explanation is the old one, that it was papal policy in southern Italy and towards the Normans which led to discontent in

one might expect, no notice was taken in Rome of the rights assigned to Henry III in 1047 (as was claimed by the king's representative in Damian's *Disceptio synodalis*). Instead, a formula was used which needed interpretation. Zimmermann, *Papstabsetzung*, 147 n. 15, also thinks, in spite of Krause, 'that in the decree of 1059 there was deliberately no trouble taken over a clear formulation of the rights of the *patricius*'; in the same sense Jasper, *Papstwahldekret*, 5 and n. 14.

Germany.[65] The conflict reached such a point that the papal legate, the cardinal priest Stephen of S. Crisogono, was not received by the imperial court; whether this éclat occurred before or after the death of Nicholas II is, however, unclear.[66]

The cooling of relations between the curia and the regency government was to have dangerous consequences following the death of Nicholas II in July 1061. Once again the tensions between the leading members of the curia and the Roman opposition became acute. This time Nicholas II's opponents acted more intelligently. They sent an embassy to Germany under the leadership of Count Gerard of Galera, the most longstanding supporter of Benedict X. How large their party was we do not know. The only clerical member of the embassy mentioned was the abbot of the important monastery of S. Andrea in Clivo Scauri. The members of the legation recognised Henry explicitly as *patricius* of the Romans, by contrast with the election decree of 1059; they brought him the insignia of the office – cloak, ring, and golden diadem – and they requested the nomination of the future pope. They thus reverted unambiguously to the patriciate of 1047, for it had become clear to them that their own forces were not sufficient to prevail against the non-Roman curia. But it turned out that the curia had by now developed into an institution capable of acting against the Roman opposition and taking measures without calling on the royal government. Its members moved fairly rapidly and secured the consent of Bishop Anselm of Lucca to his nomination. They also made sure of their Norman allies; Anselm was elected and consecrated under Norman protection in September 1061 as Pope Alexander II. Petrus Damiani claimed that the election followed the modalities laid down in the election decree of 1059, but some of his other statements allow doubts about this; they also make clear just how close a civil war was and how turbulent the situation in Rome had become.[67]

---

[65] See Krause, 'Papstwahldekret', 128: 'The immediate circumstances and connections remain unclear because of the poverty of the sources.' He tends (pp. 130ff.) to assume a move by German bishops against Nicholas II, referred to by Petrus Damiani and much later by Benzo of Alba and Cardinal Deusdedit. The cautious conjecture by Krause about a conflict between Anno of Cologne and the German episcopate and Nicholas II has been taken up by Jenal, *Anno von Köln*, 166f. Scheffer-Boichorst, *Neuordnung der Papstwahl*, 123f., had already noted Anno's good relations with Nicholas II in 1059; as late as 1067 Anno was to refer to the pope with great respect. Scheffer-Boichorst saw the curia's policy towards the Normans as the cause of the breach.

[66] The literature has assigned various dates to this éclat between the time immediately after the promulgation of the election decree and the vacancy following the death of Nicholas II in July 1061. Krause, 'Papstwahldekret', 132, holds the later date to be more probable; the older scholarship is cited *ibid.*, 133 n. 25.

[67] MGH LdL I.81.

Four weeks after the election an assembly at Basle rejected Alexander II and elected Bishop Cadalus of Parma as Pope Honorius II.[68] The schism which thus began continued with ups and downs for both sides until it was ended by the decisions of the synod of Mantua in 1064.[69] Although Cadalus still had supporters, he was in the end able to hold out only in his own city of Parma. Alexander II and his supporters had had to survive years of struggle, but these had substantially increased their influence in the western church. By contrast the king's standing had suffered as a result of the vacillations of the regent, Anno of Cologne, and by the open opposition by Anno's nephew Bishop Burchard of Halberstadt to the decisions taken at Basle.

By the time of the election of Hildebrand/Gregory VII in April 1073 there seems to have been no serious opposition left in Rome. The new pope stressed this in his first letters, in which he described the events of the election to a few important correspondents: 'On [Alexander II's] death the Roman people remained, quite against its custom, so peaceable and allowed us so to hold the reins of counsel in our hand that it is quite evident that this occurred through God's mercy.'[70] Hildebrand, who was from 1061 at the latest the most influential papal adviser, especially in all decisions involving finances and practical politics, could not have doubted that his turn had come. For this reason he advised that a decision about the election should be taken only after three days' fasting and prayer. But immediately after the funeral ceremonies in the Lateran basilica there was a great tumult and the people swept forward; they pressed Hildebrand like madmen. In his letters Gregory breaks off his account at this point. From the work of Bishop Bonizo of Sutri written about 1085 we learn further details: clergy, men, and women shouted 'Hildebrand Bishop!'; Hildebrand, alarmed, tried to reach the pulpit to calm the people; Hugo Candidus reached it before him to deliver a flaming speech advocating Hildebrand's election, and all the clerics called out as was customary 'God has chosen Pope Gregory'; following this the people dragged Gregory off

---

[68] Goez, 'Rainald von Como', 476f. speaks of the empress as having at first taken the side of Honorius II. But it is rather more than that, namely the official decision of the regent – who certainly intended to act in favour of 'reform', not against it. Fuhrmann, *Deutsche Geschichte*, 70, thinks that already at this period the German episcopate was divided; but there is no evidence of this.

[69] The main source, the *Annales Altahenses*, s.a. 1064, p. 65, says that Anno accused Alexander II of simony and of making an alliance with the Normans, *Romani imperii hostes*. The pope cleared himself with an oath, though he stressed that he could be neither accused nor judged, and said that he would speak with the king personally about the accusation concerning the alliance with the Normans.

[70] *Registrum* I 1 and 3, pp. 3, 5; see on what follows Goez, 'Erhebung', 119–44.

to the church of S. Pietro in Vinculis and enthroned him there against his will.[71] Bonizo's account is made more credible by a letter of Gregory of April 1073 which shows him on friendly terms with Hugo Candidus.[72] A contemporary official protocol of the election gives a picture of a regular and formally unobjectionable procedure, though it makes clear that the election degree of 1059 was not followed. The tumultuous act was evidently seen as an 'election by inspiration',[73] something which had always been regarded as an expression of the divine will.[74] Once again the rights of the king as *patricius* were ignored. It was once more impossible to secure royal consent to the election but it was now seen as superfluous even to try to do so; it is highly uncertain whether even an *ex post facto* announcement of the election was sent to Henry. Henry IV accepted the situation. As early as August or September 1073, at a time when he was hard pressed by his German opponents, he wrote a humble letter to Gregory, whose election no one contested as irregular until years later.[75] Henry's legate, the royal chancellor for Italy, Bishop Gregory of Vercelli, probably attended Gregory's consecration as bishop in June 1073.

The papal election provisions of 1046–7 and 1059 were obsolete from now on, though they were often to be cited and interpreted according to taste in the disputes which followed. From the second quarter of the eleventh century there were not only rival urban factions and external powers influencing the papacy and papal elections; there were also

[71] *Liber ad amicum* VII, MGH LdL I.601.

[72] *Registrum* I 6, p. 9.   [73] *Registrum* I 1, p. 1.

[74] P. Schmid, *Kanonische Wahl*, 151ff.; see p. 157: 'where the Holy Spirit is seen to act, no law is binding' and p. 158: 'when the Holy Spirit acted, the papal election decree was not valid; the electors took no notice of its provisions, and nor did Gregory and Bonizo'; see also Goez, 'Erhebung', 141f. I cannot accept the interpretation of two accounts of the election given by C. Schneider, *Sacerdotium*, 28ff.: it is impossible to say anything about Gregory's 'Epiphany-experience of God's power'. But it is unthinkable that this highly sophisticated report should have been composed 'spontaneously'. It is a theological and rhetorical masterpiece, hardly calculated to reveal 'experiences'. It is stamped by old traditions and customs of prayer, preaching and writing; how much of it can be immediate religious experience?

[75] Bonizo, *Liber ad amicum* VII, MGH LdL I.601, says that the election was notified to the court and gives incredible additional details. Caspar, *Registrum* I 9, p. 15 n. 1 is not prepared to accept this as certain, by contrast with the view taken by Meyer von Knonau, *Jahrbücher Heinrichs IV.*, II.210 n. 28 and others, though he does think that Gregory of Vercelli was present. Haller, *Papsttum*, II/2, 517 in a note to II/1, 343 says categorically: 'To Henry himself Gregory did not send a single line until his submission in the autumn of 1073.' Henry's letter of August or September 1073 is *Registrum* I 29a, 47ff.

institutions in the process of consolidation, the curia and the college of cardinals, on which the papacy could base itself. Papal elections gradually acquired a new consistency through the exclusive right of the cardinals to elect. Nevertheless, in the centuries which followed the popes still had to defend themselves repeatedly and with difficulty against both rebellions in the city and interventions from outside; divisions within the college of cardinals and then the conciliar movement of the later middle ages were still more dangerous. The emancipation of popes from the pressure of the old powers in the eleventh century by no means freed them from all earthly threats, to which they continued to be subject. Both before and after the great changes in the eleventh century the papacy had to develop its immense ecclesiastical and political influence on a very uncertain and unreliable base.

'CHURCH REFORM'

The 'church reform movement' of the eleventh century has been called 'the force which shaped the era'.[76] But what in reality was the church reform movement? Did it have a clear programme which remained valid and constant over a longer period of time? Did it have a single aim or a series of different motivations? What changes occurred over the period? How and when did it take on historically significant shape? Did it meet with resistance? Were there 'reformers' or 'friends of reform'? Was there 'a' or 'the' party of reform, or were there separate reform parties in the different regions and localities who confronted opponents of reform and were joined or deserted by indifferent or opportunistic groups and individuals? Were the attitudes of all reformers always and everywhere the same? Was 'reform' so monolithic that one had to accept or reject it as a whole, or was it possible to adopt a more positive or more negative position towards individual reform demands? In what ways were ecclesiastical and non-ecclesiastical motivations mixed in reform efforts?

Differentiated questions and reflections are not wholly absent in the rich literature on the subject, but the extent to which the simplified, the self-evident, and the unreflective have dominated the concept and the history of 'church reform' is very noticeable. Schematic notions derived from the Lutheran reformation or Tridentine reform or from the modern relationship between state and church as well as from such things as school or tax reforms seem to have overlaid our understanding of the extremely

---

[76] T. Schieffer, 'Kaiser Heinrich III.', 68.

complex reality of the high middle ages. We must try cautiously and patiently to get back to the reality itself.[77]

Those who approach the subject without preconceptions will experience a certain sense of helplessness when dealing with the monographs and syntheses on the subject. What church reform in the eleventh century really was is usually defined so inadequately that one can only describe it as an empty formula.[78] The word 'reform' has been used to form a whole range of composite words and phrases: reform movement, reform impulses, reforming zeal, reform attitudes, reform aims, reform intentions, reform questions, reform ideas, reform views, reform tasks, reform proposals, reform functions, the crisis of reform, reform pastoral care, reform papacy, reform centre, reform region, reform province, reform party, friends or enemies of reform, reform tradition, reform architecture, regional reform, Roman, Ravennatese, Italian, or imperial reform, reform in Lorraine or in Bari, early reform, post-Gregorian reform, the will to reform, reform periods, a reforming environment, a reform itinerary, friendly or hostile to reform, anti- or unreforming. This immense vocabulary is often confusing and conceals more than it reveals because it has no concrete reference and is vague and imprecise as to what is really to be understood by reform. A few selected examples may help to show this more clearly.

Walther Holtzmann held that Archbishop Laurentius of Amalfi, who died in Rome in 1049 and whom he identified in a remarkable display of scholarship with the monk of the same name from Monte Cassino, was a member of that Roman circle of early reformers to which Hildebrand may have owed his first initiation into ecclesiastical politics.[79] According to Holtzmann he had close contacts with the leaders of the Roman reform party, whose most distinguished member was the archpriest Johannes Gratianus (Gregory VI). Now there were certainly opponents of the

---

[77] Only rarely do we find expressions of scepticism, as for example in K. Schmid, 'Adel und Reform', 299 'the notion of reform which says either a lot or a little'; a noteworthy exception is offered by E. Wolgast, 'Reform', *Geschichtliche Grundbegriffe*, ed. O. Brunner, W. Conze, and R. Koselleck (Stuttgart 1982), V, 317: 'the church reform of the eleventh and twelfth centuries was above all monastic reform'. For a rare attempt to define church reform as a whole see the suggestive remarks in R. Schieffer, 'Gregor VII. – Ein Versuch über historische Größe', *HJb*, 97–8 (1978), 93f. H. Zimmermann, 'Die "Gregorianische Reform" in deutschen Landen', *StGreg*, 13 (1989), 263ff., investigates the origins and content of the concept.

[78] These phrases of the 'reform vocabulary' are all taken from scholarly literature, which there would be no point in citing fully here. Reform is generally taken to be self-evidently progressive and positive; the idea that history has also known *reformationes in peius* hardly raises its head, and modern scholarship is thoroughly 'reform-friendly'.

[79] Holtzmann, 'Laurentius', especially p. 226.

Tusculans in Rome, but it is pure hypothesis that there were early reformers there, and not even hypothetically can we say anything about the aims and content of such a reform.

Benedict VIII has been termed a reform pope, and it has even been supposed that it was on his initiative that the synod he held jointly with Henry II at Pavia in 1022 was summoned.[80] There is no basis for this view in the sources. And do the canons issued there on liaisons between unfree priests and free women and on the unfreedom of their children really deserve the name of 'eleventh-century church reform'? What was essentially at issue was preventing material losses for the church. Elsewhere we find the term 'reform pope' applied to Gregory VI; since we know very little about him, it is easy to produce hypotheses.

In an early work Gerhard Ladner called Victor II 'unreforming'.[81] This is said of a pope of acknowledged worthiness, the trusted collaborator of Henry III (who is supposed without question to have been a protagonist of 'reform'), perhaps only because no epoch-making synods were held during his pontificate. But the councils he did hold continued the work begun by Leo IX; the circle of helpers brought together by Leo IX consolidated its position during his pontificate; and he seems to have fostered his successor Stephen IX, at that time cardinal and abbot of Monte Cassino, to an unusual extent.

The reaction against reform in Rome is said to have set it under the antipope Benedict X, though John of Velletri is known to have been a member of the group of leading cardinals. This has even led to the hypothesis that Benedict X was not the same person as the 'reform cardinal'; John of Velletri is supposed to have died and to have had an 'anti-reforming' successor.[82] But were Benedict X's electors really against 'reform demands'? Or is 'church reform' simply to be defined as any opposition to the influence exercised by Roman aristocratic circles on papal elections? That would surely be too simple.

The assumption that the empress Agnes and the 'court' broke with

---

[80] Violante, *Società Milanese*, 160 and 171; Toubert, *Structures*, 1033 n. 2.

[81] Ladner, *Theologie*, 180.

[82] Schmidt, *Alexander II.*, Appendix, 78ff.; Meyer von Knonau, *Jahrbücher Heinrichs IV.*, II.92, had already expressed the opinion that the election of Benedict X severely hindered the party of church reform. But one should not see all conflicts as having had their origins simply in an opposition between friends and opponents of reform. Can we really explain the support given by the counts of Tusculum to Benedict and Honorius by saying 'that both popes were anti-reformers'? See Hoffmann, 'Petrus Diaconus', 3 and 6. The empress Agnes set up Cadalus of Parma, although she was a 'friend of reform'. The relations between the counts of Tusculum and Montecassino, a papal stronghold, were friendly; see *ibid.*, 60.

reform by having Honorius II elected at Basle in 1061 is quite simply grotesque.[83] Can this really be true of Agnes, the Aquitanian wife of the 'reform emperor' and later Gregory VII's supporter through thick and thin? No one has shown that Honorius II was not also against simony and for priestly celibacy. This shows once more the unreflective way in which any opposition, for whatever reason, to the ultimately victorious Roman curia can be termed 'anti-reforming'. We could produce many similar examples of inconsistency resulting from lack of conceptual clarity.

The Christian idea of reform has a long history, which has been dealt with for the patristic era in a fundamental study by Gerhard Ladner.[84] From the doctrines of the gospels and the Pauline writings onwards the idea of reform was connected with the human individual, with his renewal in God's image and likeness (*ad imaginem et similitudinem Dei*). In the early middle ages that was also the idea behind monastic *conversio*.[85] Ladner noted that there were crucial changes in the eleventh century. The Gregorian era was fired by the idea of a reform of the church in the sense of the mystic and hierarchic body of Christ.[86]

Yet it is significant that Gregory VII himself only rarely used the word *reformare* and never the word *reformatio*: *reformare* occurs just four times in all of the 350 letters preserved in his register, and here always in connection with the reform of individual churches – the archbishoprics of Dol and Ravenna, the monasteries of Montmajour and Saint-Marie-de-Grasse. Even so, there is an echo of the idea of the reform of the whole church.[87] In the first millennium, by contrast, the notion of altering the universal church through the planned actions of men was hardly thinkable; such changes were reserved for the guiding hand of Jesus Christ.

Of course, damage to the earthly existence and the earthly institutions of the church by the sinful hands of men was possible, and it was bewailed fearfully. Where it was thought to be happening men tried to counteract it and to call for self-renewal. In all periods of church history there have

---

[83] Schmid, *Kanonische Wahl*. 137: 'It [the court in Basle] broke with reform, in order to be able to carry out its own policies all the more decisively.' Nor can I follow the interpretation of the schism of 1061 offered by T. Schieffer, 'Cluny', 62. Boshof, 'Bischof Altmann', 320, also thinks that Agnes lost 'contact with church reform'; in a similar vein Lück, 'Anno', 11. All these constructions are unsupported.

[84] Ladner, *Idea* and see Ladner, 'Erneuerung', *RAC*, 6 (1966), 240–75; see also K. Repgen, '"Reform" als Leitgedanke kirchlicher Gegenwart und Vergangenheit', *RQ*, 84 (1989), 5ff.

[85] Ladner, *Idea*, 423; see also p. 61 n. 61 and the passages cited there.

[86] 'Gregory the Great and Gregory VII', 1–27; G. B. Ladner, 'Terms and ideas of Renewal', in *Renaissance and Renewal in the Twelfth Century*, ed. R. L. Benson and G. Constable (Oxford 1982), 1–33.

[87] *Registrum* IV 4 and 5, pp. 300ff.; VIII 12, pp. 531f.; IX 6, pp. 581ff.

been voices which in warning tones have depicted current times as ones of decline from original ideals. It is hardly possible for a historian to achieve an objective moral judgement on the Christians of former times; that is best left to the highest judge. It seems to me both just and justified by the evidence to talk of contradictory tendencies for the tenth and eleventh centuries: 'towards decadence and a movement of reform' (Jean Leclercq); 'permanent reform' or 'reform of the reform' (P. Toubert); 'Christian history as an unbroken process of reformation'.[88] One is reminded of Karl Holl's remark: 'we are faced with the curious fact that rise and fall always occur simultaneously'.[89]

Recent historiography, however, has been dominated by the idea that the church reform of the eleventh century was preceded by a period of particularly degenerate conditions which provoked a powerful reaction. As an example we may cite the outraged exclamation of the historian of the Benedictine order, Philibert Schmitz, on the period which followed the dissolution of the Carolingian empire: 'it is as if from then on the world had lost all morality'.[90] The cliché of a corrupt church offers the historians of 'church reform' an impressive backdrop on which to project their praise of the renewal which followed.[91] But one will probably hesitate to posit mechanistically those forms of human frailty and sinfulness which have been influential at all times in history as the driving force behind the move to reform the church and the world. We have already talked of the multifaceted monastic reform of the tenth and eleventh centuries.[92] This is to be clearly distinguished from what is normally termed 'church reform' in this period.

The aims and supposed achievements of the church reform movement according to received opinion were these: to eliminate the widespread practice of cohabitation by clerics of all grades with women, either as marriage or concubinage; and to attack simony, that is the granting and receiving of spiritual gifts, especially the sacraments, in return for material payments or favours. Such offences against both old and new legislation

---

[88] Leclercq, *Spiritualité*, 123f.: 'for two centuries decadence and reform coexisted'; Toubert, *Structures*, 789; Dickinson, *Later Middle Ages*, 36.

[89] Holl, *Gesammelte Aufsätze*, II.30.

[90] P. Schmitz, *Geschichte des Benediktinerordens* (Einsiedeln 1947) I.127. Lesne, *Hiérarchie épiscopale*, 5, also posits an 'excess of abuse' which led to the reform of the eleventh century; Mor, *L'età feudale*, II.277ff. is equally pessimistic.

[91] Dereine, 'Chanoines', col. 371 warns against generalising condemnations: 'In order to get an accurate picture of the situation one must mistrust the simplistic judgements of the Gregorian reformers'; see also Rossetti, 'Matrimonio', 547: one need not believe all the accusations directed against the scandalous way of life of the clergy.

[92] See above, pp. 109ff.

by councils, popes, bishops, and kings were in all probability indeed widespread. It is hard to say, however, whether they were more common in this or that country or period than in others. The cohabitation of clerics with women was long defended as an old-established custom; and the accusation of buying and selling spiritual gifts was also met by considered argument.

The judgement frequently made that the clergy was morally degenerate in the tenth and eleventh centuries is based on modern moral categories, which themselves, incidentally, no longer carry universal assent. The requirement that clerics should not marry was not one of the original principles of Christianity, and it took various forms. Church councils, Carolingian capitularies, episcopal regulations, and works on canon law repeated the demand in a noteworthy display of continuity.[93] They laid down precisely how those who were already married before they received higher orders should consort with their wives, and how close their relationship with women living in the same house might be. But all these regulations were frequently ignored, in particular by the impoverished rural clergy, who needed their families as labour power in order to be able to exist at all.[94]

How many clerics lived together with women – either married or unmarried – before the middle of the eleventh century, is of course impossible to determine statistically in spite of the rich evidence: was it 30 per cent or 80 per cent?[95] And what was the distribution of the practice among the various orders? Then as now, much that was forbidden or morally disreputable was denounced in exaggerated terms.[96] On the other hand there were often attempts both to disguise reality and also to conduct such relationships as honourable marriage. At a time when the popes were beginning to increase pressure on the episcopate to enforce clerical celibacy, a *scholion* of Adam of Bremen's history records how Archbishop Adalbert of Bremen addressed his clergy in the

[93] H. Barion, 'Zölibat', *RGG*, 3rd edn, VI (1968), cols. 1923ff.; H. Barion, 'Enkrateia (Christlich)', *RAC*, 5 (1962), cols. 349ff., especially 363f.; Hödl, 'Lex continentiae', 325–44; M. Boelens, *Die Klerikerehe in der Gesetzgebung der Kirche* (Paderborn 1968); J. Coppens, *Sacerdoce et célibat* (Bibliothecae Ephemeridum Theologicarum Lovaniensis 28, Gembloux 1971); Rossetti, 'Matrimonio', 491ff.; Schimmelpfennig, 'Zölibat', 2ff.

[94] See above, pp. 89f.; Plöchl, *Kirchenrecht*, 166ff.; Kempf, *Handbuch*, 390: 'It [the idea of celibacy] was too exalted to be understood by them or by a good part of their flocks.'

[95] The summaries given by Mirbt, *Publizistik*, 239–60, on the spread of clerical marriage around the middle of the eleventh century are impressive, but do not give any idea of the statistical relationship between the celibate and the incelibate; see Rossetti, 'Matrimonio', 502.

[96] *Ibid.*, 509.

following terms: 'I warn and command you to abstain from the pestiferous communion with women, or, if you cannot do so, which would be a counsel of perfection, then at least to observe the bonds of matrimony according to the motto: if not chastely, then at least carefully.'[97]

Clerical marriage was viewed even less favourably than clerical concubinage, because of its effects on church property. Married priests tried to leave their churches to their sons, and thus make them into 'hereditary priestly churches', or at least to pass church lands on to their children.[98] Bishops and synods reacted against this with the provision that the children of priests by unions with free women should become unfree dependants of their father's church, so that the church's income should not be reduced. A synod at Goslar in 1019, at which Emperor Henry II was present, had already considered this aspect of the matter, without going into the problem of clerical marriage in general.[99] The synod held by Benedict VIII and Henry II in Pavia in August 1022 tried to go further: it repeated the prohibition of clerical marriage, but then went into details only on the question of the children of such marriages with free women, repeating and emphasising the provision that these should become unfree. There are moving complaints in the synodal acts about the severe losses to church property through the alienations made by such children. The pope declared that he would not at this time speak of the problem of the sons begotten by free priests on free women, although these were also born outside the law; the matter was put off to a future synod.[100] In effect the synod had got no further than that

---

[97] 'si non caste, tamen caute': *Gesta Hammaburgensis Ecclesiae Pontificum*, Scholion 76, p. 173; see on it Robinson, 'Pope Gregory VII and Episcopal Authority', 109. See Rossetti, 'Matrimonio', 527f.; 'the indulgence of the hierarchy had no juristic basis, merely a social one: it would not have been possible to act otherwise without refusing communion to an enormously high number of sinners'.

[98] B. Bligny, *L'Eglise et les ordres religieux dans le royaume de bourgogne aux XIe et XIIe siècles* (Paris 1960), 20: 'the marriage of churchmen was still more disgraceful than their concubinage'; Rossetti, 'Matrimonio', 502. See above, pp. 90f.

[99] MGH Const. I.62 no. 31; Hirsch, Pabst, and Bresslau, *Jahrbücher Heinrichs II.*, III.213: 'The matter was discussed, as far as we know without priestly marriage seeming to be objectionable in any way.'

[100] MGH Const. I.70 no. 34; Kempf, *Handbuch*, 287, observes accurately: 'it was not a question of the internal reform of the church but of the preservation of church property, which could all too easily pass to the children of clerical marriages'. Benedict VIII and Henry II did not hit on a quite new answer to the problem here. We find the same provisions, based on older consiliar canons, for example in Abbo of Fleury, *Collectio canonum* 40, Migne, *PL* 139, col. 496. I cannot follow Laudage, *Priesterbild*, 52 and 86f., who has a tendency to see very early signs of reform in his assessment of Benedict VIII. He himself after all terms the canons of Henry II's period 'seemingly timeless formulations'.

held at Goslar; in spite of this Benedict VIII has been termed a 'reforming pope', and Pavia a 'reform synod'.[101] Henry II and Robert II are said to have counted on Benedict VIII in their deliberations at the meeting at Ivois in August 1023 at which they declared their intention to come together with the pope and with the bishops from both sides of the Alps at Pavia, in order to consult about the peace of the church and about how Christianity, 'which suffers from so many sins', might be better aided; but what was intended remains unclear.[102]

From the middle eleventh century onwards there seems to have been increasing feeling against the infringement of the prohibition of clerical marriage. Here and there outrage was expressed over 'whoring' by clerics, without much distinction being made between marriage and concubinage. The aggression expressed reached its peak with the Patarenes of Milan, but the popes and their entourages from the time of Leo IX and his successors also proceeded with increasing severity against 'dissolute' clergy. Symptomatic of these developments are the writings of Petrus Damiani, which show a remarkably detailed knowledge of male sexuality and its various 'perversions', including homosexuality and sodomy.[103] It is startling to find that he knows about the cruel and archaic practice of infibulation at all, though it is probable that his recommendation of it to incontinent clerics was intended rhetorically rather than

---

[101] So for example Violante, *Società Milanese*, 160; on p. 171 he ascribes the initiative for the synod of Pavia to Benedict VIII, but what can we know with certainty about this? Toubert, *Structures*, 1033 n. 2, says that Benedict VIII was 'already a reforming pope'; see the counter-arguments of Hoffmann, 'Kirchenstaat', 25.

[102] 'quae tot lapsibus patet': *Gesta episcoporum Cameracensium* III 37, MGH SS VII.480; C. Pfister, *Etudes sur le règne de Robert le Pieux* (Bibliothèque de l'école des hautes études 64, Paris 1885), 369: 'Henry II dreamed of nothing less than carrying through a general reform of the church in the spirit of Cluny under the direction of the pope.' We do not know much about what Robert and Henry dreamed, but the 'spirit of Cluny' and the 'direction of the pope' are certainly Pfister's dreams.

[103] Petrus Damiani, *Opsculum VII. Liber Gomorrhianus ad Leonem IX. Romanum Pontificem*, Migne, *PL* 145, cols. 159–90; *Opusculum XVII. De caelibatu sacerdotum ad Nicolaum II. Pontificem*, Migne, *PL* 145, cols. 379–88. In the case of Petrus Damiani we can see personal opinions as we rarely can elsewhere, in spite of all his learning and his conventional and artificial rhetoric. It is thus possible to perceive behind ideals of sexual continence the effects of overstressing these ideals on a man capable of extremes of asceticism. On Little, 'Personal Development of Peter Damiani', 317–41, see H. E. Mayer's review, *DA*, 34 (1978), 226. But Little's attempt must probably be taken seriously, in spite of all one's criticisms. See also Schimmelpfennig, 'Zölibat', 40: 'Propagandists of compulsory celibacy like Petrus Damiani accepted that clerics would indulge in secret sexual pleasures.'

practically.[104] In this phase the accent lay on the religiously based ideal of
celibacy: he who handled the holy sacraments should lead a clean life and
keep himself pure for his high service.[105] As early as 1059 Nicholas II
forbade the hearing of masses said by priests known with certainty to have
concubines or to be secretly married. Following a decree of Leo I on the
chastity of clerics the synod forbade those who took or kept a concubine
to sing the mass or to read the gospels and epistles. He should not remain
in the presbyterium together with those who observed these precepts;
and so on.[106] In Nicholas's later synodal legislation of the same year
nicolaitism (the infringement of the requirement of abstinence) is termed
heresy.[107] Heresy is surely a deviation from the true faith? The reason for
this identification was that obstinate disobedience to the legislation of
synods and popes was now seen as such a deviation. Nicolaitans and
simoniacs were now lumped together as heretics and thus fell under
excommunication.[108]

From the pontificate of Gregory VII at the latest the demand for
clerical celibacy came to take on political significance.[109] The pope
insisted that the bishops should enforce it, but these met with outraged
resistance within their dioceses. They tried at first to steer a middle course
between the two sides by taking only half-hearted measures, which in
turn only increased papal zeal. Lampert of Hersfeld gives an impressive
account of clerical indignation: the man (Gregory VII) must be seen as a
heretic with a mad dogma. He forgets the word of Holy Scripture
(Matthew 19: 11–12) and of the apostle (1 Corinthians 7: 9) that it is
better to marry than to burn. Should he continue to insist on his view
then they would sooner give up their priesthood than their marriages.
Then he, who despises men, may see how he can secure angels to lead the

---

[104] Petrus Damiani, *Opusculum XVII. De caelibatu sacerdotum*, Migne, *PL* 145, col. 379:
'Nuper habens cum nonnullis episcopis maiestatis auctoritate colloquium, sanctis
eorum femoribus volui seras apponere, tentavi genitalibus sacerdotum, ut ita loquar,
continentiae fibulas adhibere'.
[105] Even though the economic considerations stressed by E. Werner, *Zwischen Canossa und
Worms*, 59, were important, the religious and ecclesiastical ones should not be underestimated.
[106] MGH Const. I.547 no. 384 c. 3.
[107] MGH Const. I.548 no. 385: 'Ad communem utilitatem Deo propitio canonice
disposuimus inter caetera de Nicolaitarum haeresi, id est de coniugatis presbyteris,
diaconibus et omnibus in clero constitutis.'
[108] *Epistola de vitanda missa uxoratorum sacerdotum*, c. 1, which cites Gregory's Lenten synod
of 1078, MGH LdL III.2; G. Fornasari, *Celibato sacerdotale e 'autoscienza' ecclesiae* (Udine
1981), tries to distinguish between simony and nicolaitism, but on p. 55 stresses that
heresy in the eleventh century had not yet received a 'clear and unequivocal definition'.
[109] Meulenberg, *Primat*, 26 and 80.

people within the church of Christ.[110] Clerical resistance long remained obstinate. Siegfried of Mainz met with bitter opposition; Altmann of Passau was threatened by outraged clerics and was in mortal peril.[111] There were numerous propaganda pamphlets in defence of clerical marriage and of the sons of priests.[112]

One may thus say that the demand for clerical celibacy in the eleventh century was indeed a part of the ecclesiastical 'reform programme'; but it was neither new nor more easily enforced than in earlier periods. To get at least a rough idea of how effective such demands were in practice we need to examine the situation in the twelfth century. On the one hand resistance to the prohibition continued. Bernard of Abbeville, the founder of the order of Tiron (d. 1117) was almost lynched when he preached in favour of clerical continence and according to a report by Ordericus Vitalis, enraged priests' concubines wanted to stone John of Avaranches, archbishop of Rouen (1067–75).[113] But in the course of the decade marriages of this kind, at least those of the clergy of the higher grades, which were declared null by the Second Lateran Council, came to be rarer, though there were considerable differences between the various lands.[114] At a time when Abaelard, living in Paris, knew that his marriage to Héloïse meant an end to his ecclesiastical career, married clergy were still common in England.[115] It is hardly possible to make out how far clerics evaded the prohibition by practising monogamous concubinage. Giraldus Cambrensis's *bon mot* that God had taken sons away from bishops but the devil had given them nephews occurs in all sorts of variations, but it refers to the exception rather than the rule.[116] On the

---

[110] Lampert, *Annales, s.a.* 1074, p. 199; for the resistance of the clergy of Cambrai and Noyon to the command of celibacy which Hugo of Die renewed on 15 January 1078, see MGH LdL III.573ff., and Robinson, 'Pope Gregory VII and Episcopal Authority', 111, 130.

[111] Meyer von Knonau, *Jahrbücher Heinrichs IV.*, II.559; Hauck, *Kirchengeschichte Deutschlands*, III.780f.; Boshof, 'Bischof Altmann', 322. On the resistance of the bishop of Constance see *EC* 8 and 9, p. 528.

[112] See for example MGH LdL III.588ff., a *tractatus pro cleri conubio*, and E. Dümmler, *Eine Streitschrift für die Priesterehe* (Sitzungsberichte der königlich-preußischen Akademis zu Berlin, Phil.-hist. Klasse 1, Berlin 1901); but see on this the work by Fliche cited in the next note.

[113] C. N. L. Brooke, 'Gregorian Reform in Action', 11 n. 33; A. Fliche, 'Les versions Normandes du rescrit d'Ulrich', *Revue des sciences réligeuses*, 5 (1925), 15.

[114] According to Hóman, *Ungarisches Mittelalter*, 315f., the synod of Gran demanded that King Coloman should only make married priests bishops with the consent of their wives.

[115] C. N. L. Brooke, 'Gregorian Reform in Action', 19.

[116] Giraldus Cambrensis, *Gemma ecclesiastica*, II 27 ed, J. S. Brewer, *Giraldi Cambrensis Opera* (Rolls Series, London 1862), II.304.

other hand the rigorous demands for clerical celibacy made in the second half of the eleventh century had proved unenforceable.[117] It is hardly possible to say whether they had produced any decisive changes in clerical morality. The demands in themselves had widened the gap which already existed between clergy and laity, and to this extent they contributed to the clericalisation of the church. That is probably the main significance of this programme, which disturbed so many people.

A second aim and significant achievement of 'church reform' is generally held to have been the elimination or reduction of simony, which was seen by contemporaries as a sin and a heresy and by modern historians as a sign of extreme corruption.[118] The original and essential notion of simony implied giving and taking of money or presents for the gifts of the spirit, in particular for the dispensing of the sacraments: baptism; confirmation and the chrism given by the bishop to perform this; penance; last unction; burial; the ordination of priests and bishops in particular; the consecration of churches and cemeteries; the conferring of the pallium, which entitled its holder to receive episcopal consecration; and benedictions of all kinds.[119] The purchase of all these things had from the time of the early church been repeatedly condemned by councils, popes, and rulers, and the prohibitions included in collections of canon law. As a typical example we may mention the condemnation of this kind of simony at a synod held by Pope Benedict VII in 980 at which Otto II

---

[117] Böhmer, *Kirche und Staat*, 287; Schimmelpfennig, 'Zölibat', 19: 'Still more than in the time of the reform popes a discrepancy arose between the ever more strict formulations of legal theory on the one hand and the practice of the church on the other', and p. 39: 'the programme of celibacy put forward by the reform popes and their successors was largely a failure, at least in the middle ages'. On canonistic theory see Hinschius, *Kirchenrecht*, I/2, 154: 'The legislation of the twelfth century had the effect of reducing the wives of clerics in higher orders to the status of concubines in a legal sense, but that eliminated neither the licentiousness of the clergy nor the custom of entering publicly into marriages even though these were in church law null and void'; Böhmer, 'Eigenkirchentum', 20: 'And why? because there was a conviction that celibacy would mean continence or at least offer some guarantee of continence on the part of the servants of the altar. Just how illusory this was was soon to reveal itself'. Prosdocimi, *Chierici e laici*, 105–22; J. Gaudemet, 'Gratien et le célibat ecclésiastique', *StGrat*, 13 (1967), 341–69; J. Gaudemet, 'Le Célibat ecclésiastique. Le droit et la pratique du XIe au XIIIe siècles', *ZRGKA*, 68 (1982), 1–33. If church reform is understood as the elimination of nicolaitism and simony then there can be no question that this was 'carried through' in the second half of the eleventh century, as assumed by Toubert, *Structures*, 816, for the dioceses of the Roman province; see Hoffmann, 'Kirchenstaat', 15.

[118] The discussion here presupposes what was said above, pp. 75ff. on the economic basis of the church in the middle ages.

[119] See above, pp. 82–3 and 87 with nn. 47 and 48.

was present.[120] No one sought to defend or justify simony in this basic sense, and all were agreed that it was a grave sin.[121] But the church had long become caught up in the web of earthly life, including its economic organisation, and this brought with it, with or without simony, dangers for its spiritual existence. Medieval Christianity was never able to escape the ensuing dilemma.[122]

It is a mistake to suppose that simony was particularly favoured by the position of the laity within the life of the church. In the nature of things only clerics could receive rewards for the gifts of the spirit already mentioned, for only they could on the basis of their ordination grant such gifts: no clerics, no simony. Those who made such payments on the other hand might be either clerics or laymen: an archbishop, for example, who paid to receive the pallium from the pope; a cleric, who paid for priestly ordination; or a layman who paid for the burial of a relative or for a benediction.

It has often been stressed that simony was rife around the middle of the eleventh century. According to Petrus Damiani, when Leo IX wanted at the Roman synod held in 1049 to declare all simoniacal ordinations invalid there was a tumult not only among the priests present; even the majority of the bishops declared that in that case almost all churches would be deprived of their priests and the celebration of mass would be prevented everywhere, to the confusion of the Christian religion and the despair of the faithful.[123] Damiani said of Henry III that he and God had torn Christendom from the insatiable jaws of the dragon of simony by cutting off all its heads.[124] Humbert of Silva Candida claimed that simony had been rife from the time of the Ottonians up till that of Emperor Henry, the son of Conrad. He had to some extent prevented so great a sacrilege from staining himself and the churches of his kingdom, though much still remained to be eliminated.[125] Petrus Damiani claimed that God

---

[120] Vicaire, 'Pastorale', 108, stresses the continuity in this legislation, though on p. 310 he notes a break in it; see also Wemple, *Atto of Vercelli*, 175, and BZ no. 585.

[121] Mirbt, *Publizistik*, 367; an exception is drawn attention to by S. Hellmann, 'Anecdota aus cod. Cusanus C 14 nunc 37', *NA*, 30 (1904), 17–33, which is not just the usual monotonous polemic and is prepared to deal with concrete circumstances, in which purchase may be accepted if carried out with good intentions (see p. 25). On this see Hoffmann, 'Ivo', 396 n. 14; Benson, *Bishop Elect*, 205 n. 15.

[122] On the principle see Gilchrist, *Church and Economic Activity*, 6: 'Thus, if the spirit of Christianity urged all men to despise wealth, common sense and canon law compelled the clergy to retain and protect the property of the church. This then was the dilemma of the Church in the Middle Ages.'

[123] *Liber gratissimus* c. 37, MGH LdL I.70.

[124] *Ibid.*, c. 38, p. 71.

[125] *Adversus Simoniacos* III c. 7, MGH LdL I.206.

himself worked against the evil of simony through the Holy Spirit,[126] and according to Andreas of Strumi, writing much later, Johannes Gualberti wrote to Bishop Hermann of Volterra (1064–77?) that it was God in his mercy who had removed and destroyed the heresy of simony.[127] Yet simony had been indignantly condemned before the times of Henry III, Leo IX, Damiani, and Humbert, and there can be no doubt that it occurred wherever corruption was possible, that is, everywhere where religion and its cult were touched on by financial interests. In spite of everything said to the contrary we cannot tell whether it had increased in the period immediately before the middle of the eleventh century,[128] though there does seem to have been an increase in the indignation with which it was greeted. There is much to be said for the supposition that the concept of simony was also broadened at this time.

As we have already noted, churches were among the most important forms of property, and both ecclesiastical and lay owners derived benefits from them through the dues paid by clerics and through shares in tithes and oblations. Newly appointed clerics seem to have paid a kind of appointment fee to the owner of the church.[129] Certainly there were excesses and abuses, but it is probably an unjustifiable generalisation to talk generally of the buying and selling of churches in this connection. Since the ecclesiastic had to receive consecration from the diocesan bishop and be ordained by him, the payments did not essentially concern the forbidden sale of the gifts of the spirit, but rather the building and the property of the church, which were conferred by the proprietor of the church – the diocesan bishop himself or another bishop, a monastery or collegiate church or a lay owner. Abbots had to be consecrated by a bishop, who was either the diocesan or, in the case of monasteries with special privileges, a bishop of their own choice. The transfer of the monastery's property was a matter for its ecclesiastical or lay proprietor. Bishops were consecrated by their archbishop and the bishops of their province. In the period of theocratic rulership the bishopric was conferred by king or prince. The new abbot or bishop would normally, in

---

[126] *Opusculum V*, Migne, *PL* 145, col. 95.

[127] *Vita s. Johannis Gualberti* c. 67, MGH SS xxx.1093.

[128] P. Palazzini, 'Influssi Damianei ed Umbertini nell'azione e legislazione dei papi pregregoriani contro la simonia da papa Clemente II a Nicolo II', *Atto del II° convegno del Centro di Studi Avellaniti* (Fonte Avellana 1978), 7, says truly enough that 'it was not a new problem or one peculiar to the eleventh century, being rather one of those shadows which recur throughout the history of the church'. Yet he then continues: 'But in the tenth and eleventh centuries it reached really disturbing proportions.' How do he and the many others who write in a similar vein propose to prove such statements?

[129] See above, p. 83 n. 26.

conformity with the customs of the time, bring gifts for the proprietor of the monastery or the prince, which in turn would be matched by counter-gifts in the form of privileges and still richer counter-gifts. In some countries, particularly southern France, there does seem to have been a regular trade in bishoprics.[130]

Since, however, installation by the owner of the church or monastery in the case of churches, or selection or consent by the owner in the case of abbots, or investiture by the ruler in the case of bishops were all more important in practice than the purely ecclesiastical act which followed, the boundaries between ordination and consecration on the one hand and installation or investiture on the other hand tended to become blurred. Even installation or investiture counted as simoniacal if money or presents were given and received; thus the original concept of simony was gradually extended.[131] There are some indications in the sources that people had long been aware of the dangers of a simoniacal interpretation. When in 1017 Benedict VIII agreed to the plan to erect a bishopric in Besalù (a plan which fell through, incidentally), he laid down that each new bishop was to be consecrated by the pope and to give the pope a pound of gold after consecration. The papal notary knew very well what counted as simony, and carefully drafted the formulation 'not for the consecration but in token of due obedience'.[132] People knew how to avoid connecting gifts with consecrations, which would have been simoniacal in the old sense of the term.

In the writings of Abbo of Fleury we can already find a very explicit statement of the controversy: there is almost nothing connected with the church, which after all belongs to God alone, which is not sold for a price – bishoprics, priestships, and deaconships and the other lesser orders, archdeaconries and deaconries, provostships, treasurerships, baptism, burial and the like. 'And these traders are accustomed to offer the casuistical answer that they do not buy the blessing which one receives through the grace of the Holy Spirit, but simply the *res ecclesiarum* or the property of the bishop, though it is evident that in the Catholic church the one cannot exist without the other. Or can there be fire without fuel?[133] Here we can already find all the arguments produced with the

---

[130] But one should be careful about negative generalisations; see above pp. 83–4.

[131] For the extension of the original notion of simony see H. Fuhrmann, 'Papst Gregor und das Kirchenrecht', *StGreg*, 13 (1989), 134 n. 24, and W. Goez, 'Riforma ecclesiastica – riforma Gregoriana', *StGreg*, 13 (1989), 170f.

[132] 'non pro consecratione, sed pro debita oboedientia'; see Tellenbach, 'Gregorianische Reform', 162 and n. 14.

[133] Abbo of Fleury, *Liber Apologeticus*, Migne, *PL* 139, col. 466; see on this Hoffmann, 'Ivo', 395.

same tendency by Humbert of Silva Candida in his theory of privileges. The monk Wido had already made a similar claim explicitly in his letter of *c.* 1031 to Archbishop Aribert of Milan: he who claims that it is not the consecration but the material things which go with it which are sold, knows nothing. No concrete church (*corporalis ecclesia*) can have its being without the corporal and material things which go with it, just as the soul cannot exist in time without the body.[134] Petrus Damiani made similar comments on the interpretation offered by those who claimed that it was not simoniacal to buy bishoprics so long as one received consecration for nothing. Whoever, Damiani replied, buys a church for a price, also buys the consecration to which he is entitled by acquiring the church.[135]

Both the defenders of a distinction between the spiritual character of a church founded on its consecration and its property and those who maintained that the two formed a unity like body and soul offered a fairly subtle argumentation which would have been unknown in the days of the early church. The problem of the relationship between temporalities and spiritualities, which was perceived as such here and there from an early date and used to defend both traditional forms of appointment to churches and the dues and gifts associated with these, was at first probably not grasped in wider circles. In his *Vita Romualdi* Damiani concedes that hardly anyone in the whole of the empire in Romuald's time had known that *simoniaca haeresis* was a sin.[136] In the *Liber gratissimus* we find a similar passage: that on which all are agreed is taken to be a norm or even to be something laid down by law.[137] Even Humbert noted bitterly that this greatest of sins was so ancient that it alone counted as canonical and not that which canon law laid down in reality.[138] But can it ever have been really unknown that the giving and taking of money for the reception of the sacraments was a sin? The reality was seldom as simple as this. People had grown used to traditional favours in connection with spiritual services, rewards for the conferring of ecclesiastical offices by bishops, abbots, or laymen and for the investiture of bishops and abbots by kings, princes, or the ecclesiastical proprietors of monasteries. What was needed to make these unacceptable was a development of the concept of simony, which came in the course of

---

[134] MGH LdL 1.6.

[135] *Epistolae* I 13, Migne, *PL* 144, col. 218ff.

[136] Ed. G. Tabacco (Fonti per la storia d'Italia 94, Rome 1957), 75f.; 'Per totam namque monarchiam usque ad Romualdi tempora, vulgata consuetudine, vix quisquam noverat Simoniacam heresim esse peccatum.'

[137] c. 27, MGH LdL 1.56.

[138] *Adversus Simoniacos* III 11, MGH LdL 1.211.

time to be defined more precisely and to be extended from its original sense.[139] The history of the concept of simony and its practical applications needs closer study.[140] The grotesque extensions of the concept that were possible can be seen in the twelfth century, when payments for the entry of a dependant into a monastery could be termed simoniacal.[141]

In the agitated polemics of the eleventh century simony became the principal crime of whomever happened to be one's opponent; what the 'simonist' had in reality paid or received was ignored without any qualms. Only round figures were mentioned; invariably these are too high to deserve credence. Petrus Damiani himself denounced Pope Benedict X, who as cardinal had belonged to the core of the reform group, as a simonist. Why? 'Because he was enthroned at night, surrounded by hordes of armed men who robbed and rioted, although all we cardinal bishops of the City protested against this, resisted it and cursed it.' Did it already count as 'simony' in 1058 to be elected against the will of the majority of the cardinal bishops, who had recently come to consider themselves as the decisive element in the curia? Or was it money which made the difference? 'Then he resorted to the detestable weapon of coin; money was handed out to the populace in the quarters, alleys and streets; people ran through the arch of the venerable St Peter and henceforth hardly anything could be heard in the city, which had become the workplace of the evil-doer Simon, other than the sound of hammers on anvils.'[142] From then on popes and antipopes accused each other of simony: Alexander II and Honorius II (Cadalus); Gregory VII and Clement III (Wibert); and so on. We may well believe that each of these had indeed distributed money to his supporters – this had long been a traditional part of the ceremony practised on the entry to the city of popes, kings and distinguished guests, and it was to remain so. There was simply uncertainty as to what constituted simony. We have already noted

[139] E. Hirsch, 'Der Simoniebegriff und eine angebliche Erweiterung deselben im 11. Jh.', *Archiv für katholisches Kirchenrecht* 86 (1906), 8, in spite of many correct observations offers the view that the concept of simony in the eleventh century remained essentially constant and in conformity with the previous tradition.

[140] Gilchrist, 'Simoniaca Haeresis', 209–35, is helpful; see especially p. 211: 'few canonists and certainly none of the principal legislators, the popes, expounded in detail their ideas on simony'.

[141] J. H. Lynch, *Simoniacal Entry into Religious Life 1000–1260* (Columbus 1976), 68; Schreiber, *Kurie und Kloster*, II.17: grants, exchanges, and purchases of proprietary churches only later came to count as simoniacal with the curia, and p. 50: a sum for repurchase is simoniacal.

[142] Petrus Damiani, *Epistolae* III 4, Migne, *PL* 144, cols. 291f.

this in the case of Gregory VI.[143] It has rightly been asked whether the bishops present at Leo IX's synod of 1049 in Rheims were clear about what was to be considered as simony.[144] It was termed simoniacal when the bishop of Chiusi demanded the *cathedraticum* twice a year instead of just once;[145] and at the election of Rudolf of Rheinfelden in Forchheim in 1077 the papal legate warned those princes who wished to make their consent dependent on conditions: such an election would be not pure but stained with the poison of simoniacal heresy.[146]

In contemporary and in later historical writings those opposed to the cause supported by the author were denounced as simonists without scruple or regard for the facts, which was all the more pernicious in that simony was regarded as heresy, as deviation from the faith.[147] A particularly crass example of the unrestrained partisanship practised in such judgements can be found in the history of the two legates, Cardinal Bishop Peter of Albano and Bishop Udalrich of Padua, whom Gregory VII sent from the Lenten synod of 1079 to King Henry and the Saxons. At this time the relations between Gregory and Rudolf of Rheinfelden and the Saxons were strained, for Gregory maintained his position of impartiality between the two claimants to the throne, and the Saxons were bitterly dissatisfied both with him and with his legates. Bruno made the accusation that the two legates had come frequently to each of the parties and promised first the Saxons and then their enemies apostolic blessing and taken as much money as they could get 'in Roman fashion'.[148] In other writings the legates were also accused of having taken

---

[143] See above, pp. 141–2f., and also Gilchrist, 'Simoniaca Haeresis', 214: 'In the eleventh century the term *simoniaca* had no exact theological or canonical meaning'; R. Schieffer, 'Heinrich III.', 106, speaks of the 'accusation of simony, a cheap one at that time'.

[144] Capitani, 'Immunità vescovili', 167.

[145] Alexander II JL 4657 = *Italia Pontificia* III.233 no. 30 = Migne, *PL* 146, col. 1347 no. 63; see Schmidt, *Alexander II.*, 202.

[146] *Brunos Buch vom Sachsenkrieg* c. 91, p. 85. W. Schlesinger, 'Die Wahl Rudolfs von Schwaben zum Gegenkönig in Forchheim', *VuF*, 17 (1973), 85, in arguing that the legate conceived of the royal dignity as a spiritual office, takes the concept of simony more seriously than it deserves. See Jakobs, 'Rudolf von Rheinfelden', 88f. and n. 10.

[147] O. Hageneder, 'Die Haeresie des Ungehorsams und das Entstehen des hierokratischen Papsttums', *Römische historische Mitteilungen*, 20 (1978), 33; Zimmermann, *Papstabsetzungen*, 174: 'In the specific cases it is scarcely possible to judge how justified the charge of simony was, but it is very evident how dangerous it was.' One should for this reason show a good deal of caution about all reports of simony, especially when specific sums are named and still more when these are round figures.

[148] *Brunos Buch vom Sachsenkrieg* c. 116, p. 109.

bribes.[149] It is probable, however, that they simply accepted gifts on their visits, as was customary, the one no more and no less than the other. After they had begun their journey home, laden with rich gifts, the bishop of Padua is supposed to have travelled on alone to Rome and delivered a report favourable to Henry IV. Allegedly he was exposed as a liar by a monk of the Rudolfine party and deposed from office by the pope, whereupon he returned home in deep contrition.[150] In the meantime Cardinal Peter arrived in Rome and reported on his legation; there is of course no mention of the fact that he too had received gifts. He, who in his youth had survived the legendary ordeal by fire against Bishop Petrus Mezzabarba of Florence,[151] might be accused of corruption in Saxony, where he was not well known, but not in Rome. The slanders are all directed against Udalrich of Padua. We can see this in the account of his murder. He is supposed to have been again on his way to Rome on Henry's behalf (unthinkable if the pope had actually driven him in ignominy from office). He who had been bribed so often with presents now allegedly intended to bribe others; but one of his entourage stabbed him to death with a lance.[152] We have here yet another example of an ordeal whose outcome favoured one's own party, of an unscrupulously partisan account which made use of the notion of simony.

Later historians were equally willing to accuse the opponents of the papacy and the curia of simony. These include Guibert of Nogent, who exaggerates the position in Rome before 1046 and terms Archbishop Manasses of Rheims, who was deposed by Gregory VII after a long dispute, a simonist, though contemporary sources know nothing of this. In reality Manasses simply defended his rights as metropolitan against what he saw as encroachments by the pope and his legate Hugo of Die.[153] It is

---

[149] Hugo of Flavigny, *Chronicon* II, MGH SS VIII.451 on both legates: 'corrupti muneribus a sententia et proposito gravitatis apostolicae deviaverunt'. J. Vogel, *Gregor VII. und Heinrich IV.*, 142ff., deals with this legation, and notes (p. 169) that Berthold of the Reichenau also distorts our view of it.

[150] Berthold, *Annales*, s.a. 1079, MGH SS V.322.

[151] Tellenbach, 'Gregorianische Reform', 104 and n. 25; Goez, 'Toscana', 233, in my view gives too much weight to the pamphlets of the bishop's opponents.

[152] Berthold, *Annales*, s.a. 1080, MGH SS V.326: 'ad infernum corruptissimus quam repente Dei iudicio praecipitatus'. What these disputes were really about will be shown below, p. 245 n. 221; the thesis propounded by Borino, 'Odelrico', 63ff., that the king was the cheater and Gregory VII the cheated cannot be sustained. Although the spiteful judgements on the bishop of Padua are partisan and unprovable, something of them has stuck, as so often, in the accounts of recent scholarship: see Meyer von Knonau, *Jahrbücher Heinrichs IV.*, III.243, Morrison, 'Canossa', 123.

[153] *De vita sua sive monodia* I.11, Migne, *PL* 156, col. 855 or E. Labande (Les Classiques de l'histoire de France au moyen âge 34, Paris 1981), 64; Capitani, 'Figura del vescoco',

Guibert who offers the malicious anecdote that Manasses is supposed to have said 'the archbishopric is quite a good thing, if only one did not have to say mass for it'.[154] The standard of morality current in the Anglo-Saxon church seems to have been particularly good; yet later Norman chroniclers ascribed simoniacal practices to earlier bishops in spite of this.[155] William of Malmesbury denounced all kinds of people as simonists, including Bishop Herbert of Norwich and above all Archbishop Stigand of Canterbury, who as the representative of the Anglo-Saxon party had been unable to maintain himself in office after the conquest, though his conduct of office had aroused no complaints.[156] Even his successor Lanfranc was suspected by Eadmer of simony.[157]

Around the middle of the eleventh century new kinds of objection came to be made to practices which had been current for centuries in the church. Here it was no longer a question of real or supposed abuses as it was with the neglect of the law on celibacy or with simony in its narrower sense; these were things which had long been condemned and fought against. What was now being objected to was rights and functions of laymen within the church, which were derived in part from the idea of the theocratic rulership of the king by the grace of God, and in part from the rights of laymen as church proprietors.[158]

There was no dispute about the fact that the clergy led and the laity

184; Williams, 'Manasses of Reims', 802–24; Robinson, 'Pope Gregory VII and Episcopal Authority', 126.

[154] *De vita sua* I.10, Migne, *PL* 156, col. 855 or ed. Labande, 64: 'Bonus ait, esset Remensis archiepiscopatus, si non missas inde cantari oporteret.'

[155] Dickinson, *Later Middle Ages*, 56; Darlington, 'Ecclesiastical Reform', 400ff.

[156] Cantor, *Church, Kingship*, 33f.; Deanesly, *Sidelights*, 108; Barlow, *English Church 1000–1066*, 80, 112; Darlington, 'Ecclesiastical Reform'; p. 420 and n. 2; on Stigand's pluralism see Goez, 'Papa qui et episcopus', 53ff., though pluralism was otherwise not uncommon in England.

[157] Cantor, *Church, Kingship*, 46f.; Donizo, *Vita Mathildis* I.16, MGH SS XII.373, even calls Boniface of Canossa a simonist; Grégoire, 'Pomposa', 8f.: it was nothing new to accuse one's opponents of taking bribes in the era of 'church reform'; see above, p. 88 with nn. 50 and 51.

[158] Laudage, *Priesterbild*, in a book full of ideas and insights, has tried to account for the emergence of such reservations by talking of a movement of priestly renewal (p. 121), a new ideal of priesthood (pp. 130, 269), a forward-looking view of the priesthood (held by Burchard of Worms), a new conception of priesthood and of the priestly office (pp. 211, 269, 283), a return to the fundamentals of the priestly office (p. 317) and even to the salvation-bringing function of the sacraments (p. 81), as well as a revaluation of the priestly duty of dispensing the sacraments (p. 114). One asks oneself with surprise whether the priesthood had not long been defined so fundamentally and uncontroversially that people hardly dared to risk novelties or changes. What was to be changed was the morality and the way of life of those who held spiritual office, as humans, and also the relationship of the world to such high office.

were led as far as this applied to the most central part of the life of the church, the dispensing and receiving of the sacraments. An awareness that churches were the property of God alone and not of any earthly persons can sometimes be found, though no practical consequences were drawn from this. Occasionally in the tenth and early eleventh centuries there had also been protests when the king was thought to have exceeded his competence. Atto of Vercelli and Rather of Verona objected to the appointment of bishops and abbots by the king; Thietmar of Merseburg disapproved of the deposition of Pope Benedict V by Otto I; Wipo equally disapproved of Conrad II's behaviour towards the archbishops of Milan and Lyons. We may even ask whether the much-cited criticisms by Bishop Wazo of Liège of Henry III's ecclesiastical politics and of the form of the deposition of Widger of Ravenna, and the opposition by the anonymous *Auctor Gallicus* to Gregory VI's deposition should not be seen as further isolated expressions of misgiving in this tradition, rather than as something new.[159] Their objections to the idea of the king's sacral character and their stress on the idea that he was a layman are noteworthy, however, as are Wazo's openness and the malice of the *Auctor Gallicus* ('that emperor hateful to God').[160] Whether these authors were aware of each other, whether they had contemporaries who shared their opinions or were mere isolated exceptions, is hard to make out. It is improbable that they had any influence on the measures taken and the opinions expressed in Rome a decade later.

In the system of proprietary churches the duties and rights of clerics and laymen had not differed in essentials up to the middle of the eleventh century. There would long be no question of a struggle against the institution of the proprietary church as such. There was no new legislation about the countless monasteries and churches owned by other churches, and even church property in lay hands was not yet called in question in principle.[161] But from now on no cleric was to receive a church from the hands of a layman, either for payment or gratis. The right of a layman to confer a church on a cleric was thus decisively called in question, even if he should conform to older legislation on the proprietary church by respecting the rights of the bishop, and money and presents were neither offered nor accepted and hence no simony was present. This was the

---

[159] Tellenbach, *Libertas*, 115, 126f., 124f.

[160] 'iste imperator Deo odibilis': see *ibid.*, 73 n. 29 and p. 107 n. 26; MGH LdL 1.8ff. There is a new edition by H. H. Anton, *Traktat*; see most recently Szabó-Bechstein, 'Libertas Ecclesiae', 125ff.

[161] Boyd, *Tithes*, 115: 'whatever the reasons may be, the Lateran Synods until 1078 showed a certain reserve on the subject of the lower churches and their revenues'.

meaning of the lapidary sixth canon of Nicholas II's April synod of 1059: 'that no cleric or priest should receive a church in any manner from a layman, either freely or for payment'.[162] The formulation was so general that it applied to all churches, from the bishopric down to the rural chapel. In the third book of Cardinal Humbert's *Against The Simoniacs*, probably written shortly beforehand, the principle was applied explicitly to the bestowal of bishoprics by kings and princes. This had the consequence on the one hand that princes were there seen as mere laymen, who did not possess even a trace of a 'quasi-clerical' character, and on the other hand that the indivisible unity of the invisible grace of the Holy Spirit and the visible manifestation of the church was maintained vigorously and decisively. If a prince conferred a bishopric then he allegedly conferred everything: the lands of the church as well as the episcopal authority in matters of jurisdiction, consecration, and pastoral care.[163] Contemporary practice stood everything on its head; the first were last and the last first. The man appointed by the king went to the metropolitan not as someone who was still to be judged and examined but as one who was to judge him. What he demanded and required was a mere service, all that still remained of the metropolitan's rights: prayer and consecration.[164]

Up to now the writings of the famous cardinal and the synodal decrees of Nicholas II have been ascribed an epoch-making significance; they have often been seen as the first prohibition of 'lay investiture'. Rudolf Schieffer has questioned this in an acute and learned book.[165] He has even expressed doubts about a connection between these two critical voices of 1057–9 and the prohibitions of investiture which certainly were issued by Gregory VII. His thesis that the question of investiture did not by any means play such an important role in the conflict between popes and kings as has often been ascribed to it, and in particular that it was not the decisive factor in the breach between Gregory VII and Henry IV in 1076, is convincing.[166] His criticisms of the conclusions of older scholarship lead to the insight that it is often necessary in scholarship to be content with

---

[162] MGH Const. 1.547 no. 384 c. 6; Humbert, *Adversus Simoniacos* III.9, MGH LdL 1.208: 'Nam sicut clerici a laicis etiam intra parietes basilicarum locis et officiis, sic et extra separari et cognosci debent negotiis.'

[163] *Ibid.*, c. 1, p. 199; on similar ideas, held long before Humbert, see above, pp. 170f.

[164] *Ibid.*, c. 6, p. 205.

[165] R. Schieffer, *Entstehung*, 42ff.; see on this especially the review by F. Kempf in *AHP*, 20 (1982), 409ff., who continues to uphold the idea of a prohibition in 1075, still more forcefully argued in *AHP*, 21 (1983), 162.

[166] R. Schieffer, *Entstehung*, 153ff. Although I find his revision of the investiture question illuminating, I would explain the causes and significance of the changes within the church and the Christian world otherwise. See especially below, chapter 8.

possibilities or even with a *non liquet*; even his own cautiously advanced solutions often have the nature more of hypotheses which must be taken seriously than of firm conclusions.

The question of the origins of the prohibition of lay investiture has a larger context, that of a slow change in the conception of the laity's role within the church. If we ask how fundamental doubts about the rights of laymen in appointments to bishoprics, churches and church offices, and to monasteries came about, it is necessary to go back to the time of Humbert and Nicholas II. As we have seen, it was already customary from the tenth century onwards to meet attacks on traditional or questionable practices in connection with the bestowal of churches which were suspected of being simoniacal by offering the view (or excuse) that money and favours were nothing to do with the church and its spiritual functions but concerned church property alone. The theoretical distinction between spiritualities and temporalities was thus made from an early date.[167] The arguments produced in defence of transactions which were alleged to be simoniacal must before Humbert's time have been offered to uphold the practice of laymen's giving churches and church office. We can deduce from his writings that there was such a discussion, for Humbert rejects such ideas sharply.[168] We may thus suppose that objections were raised to the giving of churches by laymen from quite an early date.

The demand for free episcopal elections by clergy and people of the episcopal city, which was made ever more forcefully from the time of Leo IX onwards, and the forceful insistence on the old formula that no one should have a bishop imposed on them against their will, already carried the logical implication of a restriction of the rights of those empowered to name bishops and abbots at their pleasure, though not yet a rejection of such rights in principle. For bishoprics it was only the rights of 'laymen', in other words of kings and of princes with a quasi-regal position, which were affected; for monasteries the restriction applied to their owners, to kings, bishops, abbots, counts, and so on, and hence not just to laymen. Occasionally it might happen that a king did not accept the person elected in the episcopal city and instead sent a bishop he had nominated. This was usually followed by negotiations and by the fulfilment of the king's wishes; once that had been done, consecration could follow. Even during the regency of Anno of Cologne we find such decisions, as for example with the nomination of Werner, Anno's brother, in the place of Siegfried, whom the church of Magdeburg had elected in

---

[167] See above, p. 170.   [168] See above, p. 171.

1063.[169] Later, Henry IV was without difficulty able to push aside Wigold, elected by clergy and people of Augsburg, and the church of Augsburg accepted his candidate. We should probably know nothing about Wigold if he had not later been invested by the antiking and consecrated by Archbishop Siegfried of Mainz, an exiled supporter of Rudolf's, without being able to establish himself in Augsburg.[170]

After the death of Henry III there seem to have been more and more serious conflicts in connection with episcopal elections. It was once again Anno of Cologne who as regent in 1066 had his nephew Conrad chosen and consecrated archbishop of Trier at court without regard to the wishes of clergy and people. This time the inhabitants of Trier were so outraged at the infringement of their rights of election and the disregard for their wishes that the new archbishop was ambushed on the way to his see and murdered.[171] The inhabitants of Constance also put up fierce resistance when Henry IV nominated Charles, the provost of the church on the Harsburg, as the new bishop instead of their own candidate, the canon Siegfried. The result was a long-drawn-out and complicated dispute which occupied Alexander II, Siegfried of Mainz, and the king. The bishop-elect himself put an end to it. Henry IV denied personal involvement in any simoniacal transaction. Charles also denied all the charges made against him, but he returned his ring and staff of office, citing the provision of Celestine I that no one should become bishop against the will of his subjects.[172] One of the key demands of Leo IX's time was thus acknowledged. This did not affect the king's right of investiture, however, for the new bishop, Otto, was named and invested by the king in 1071 without any objection or intervention by the pope.

---

[169] Meyer von Knonau, *Jahrbücher Heinrichs IV.*, 1.352ff.

[170] Meyer von Knonau, *Jahrbücher Heinrichs IV.*, III.63f. and 122f.

[171] Meyer von Knonau, *Jahrbücher Heinrichs IV.*, 1.499 and 503ff.; Lück, 'Anno', 18, though I cannot see any connection with the disputes of the investiture contest.

[172] Meyer von Knonau, *Jahrbücher Heinrichs IV.*, II.1, 28f. and 78ff., where the case is carefully assessed on the basis of the unusually detailed and full principal source, the protocol of the Mainz synod of August 1071, Codex Udalrici no. 37 = Jaffé, *BRG*, v.70. Robinson, 'Zur Arbeitsweise', 99f., gives an unacceptable account: credence is given only to the Constance party hostile to the king and bishop, and everything which might speak for the accused is left out of account. See also Robinson, 'Bible', 65, where the same thesis is repeated with still less caution, though this criticism is not directed against the interesting conjectures about the role of the scholasticus Bernhard in the dispute. Fleckenstein, 'Heinrich IV.', 230, notes in connection with the Constance affair that the resistance of the local clergy to royal nominations was stronger in the 1070s than it had been in the time of Henry III. But this development had already begun during the regency period, and one can hardly make the king, who was only fifteen to twenty years old, responsible for it. The prestige of the royal office had simply declined under the regents. See also Fleckenstein, 'Hofkapelle und Reichsepiskopat', 122ff.

The most famous example of increased tensions over royal nomination of bishops is the disputes in Milan during the period of the Pataria.[173] In these we can see particularly clearly how in episcopal elections the new tendency within the church to apply canon law strictly was mixed up with the quite temporary and even secular interests of regional and local groups. Milanese parties who sought support from the pope or the king produced or intensified tensions between these two in ways which could not have been predicted. In Milan the old archbishop, Wido of Velate, resigned in favour of his protégé Godfrey, who was invested by the king but could not establish himself. Wido and Godfrey were excommunicated by Alexander II for this practice, which was highly questionable from the point of view of canon law, probably in 1070. At the beginning of 1072 the Patarenes under their leader Erlembald elected a certain Atto in the presence of the papal legate, Cardinal Bernard, but on the same day Atto was violently compelled by their opponents to abdicate. Here for the first time the royal right of investiture was ignored by one party in the city, acting in the presence of a papal legate, and upheld by the other. There was a decisive intensification of the conflict between curia and court when Godfrey, after a long delay, was consecrated in Novara by Milanese suffragans at the king's request. At the Lenten synod of 1073 Alexander II reacted to this by threatening several of the king's counsellors with excommunication, perhaps even by excommunicating them. The Milanese question overshadowed relations between Gregory VII and Henry IV, and was one of the main causes of the breach of 1076.[174]

Not until the time of Gregory VII were bishops consecrated according to the will of the pope without having previously received royal investiture. The delaying of the consecration of Anselm II of Lucca in 1073 did not yet represent a change in principle, for it was probably due to the fact that Henry's contacts with the excommunicated counsellors had made his standing a questionable one. At all events Anselm was invested by the king before the pope consecrated him.[175] By contrast, when Philip I of France refused to accept the election of Landricus as bishop of Mâcon, Gregory VII instructed Archbishop Humbert of Lyons to consecrate him in spite of this. Because this instruction was evidently not complied with, Gregory performed the consecration himself in Rome in early 1074.[176]

---

[173] Meyer von Knonau, *Jahrbücher Heinrichs IV.*, II.29ff., 175ff., 196ff.; Keller, *Mailand*, 343ff.; R. Schieffer, *Entstehung*, 104ff.

[174] See below, pp. 233f.

[175] *Registrum* I 21, p. 34; Hugo of Flavigny, *Chronicon* II, MGH SS VIII.411; R. Schieffer, *Entstehung*, 112 n. 22; on this case and the ones which follow see Scharnagl, *Begriff*, 25ff.

[176] *Registrum* I 35, 36, 76, pp. 56ff. and 107f.

Hugo of Die also seems to have been consecrated at this time in Rome without having received investiture beforehand.[177] If the Patarenes had ignored royal rights of investiture in 1072, Gregory himself only a little later seems to have been determined to consecrate bishops-elect or to have them consecrated without prior investiture; for the time being this was confined to special cases.

The decisive change followed shortly after this: the prohibition of investiture before consecration. It probably cannot be determined with certainty when such a prohibition was first issued. The Milanese chronicler Arnulf says unambiguously of the Lenten synod of 1075: 'The pope holds a synod in Rome and publicly forbids the king to hold any rights in connection with the bestowal of bishoprics, and he removes all laymen from the investiture of churches.'[178] This report, from an author of accepted reliability, remains an isolated one. There is no trace of any reaction by the royal court to the formal promulgation of the alleged prohibition, although Henry IV must in the first instance have been the person affected by it, especially as his counsellors were excommunicated or threatened with excommunication at the same synod, something which again was ostentatiously ignored by the king.[179] Did the court not learn of the prohibition which Arnulf reported, or did it simply not comprehend it? Relations between the curia and the royal court do not even seem to have worsened appreciably after the Lenten synod.[180] Schieffer, who has cautiously evaluated the absence of any echo of the prohibition of early 1075 and examined the investiture practice of the following years, dated a general prohibition of investiture for the whole church to the Roman autumn synod of 1078.[181] Here such a prohibition was indeed promulgated, categorically, without evasions, in detail and with the explicit provision of excommunication for those who

---

[177] *Registrum* I 69, pp. 99f.; Hugo of Flavigny, *Chronicon* II, *s.a.* 1074, MGH SS VIII.412.

[178] Arnulf, *Gesta archiepiscoporum Mediolanensium* IV 7, MGH SS VIII.27.

[179] *Registrum* II 52a, pp. 196f.; in this short report there is no prohibition of investitures, but we do find the sentence of excommunication against the five members of the 'familia regis Teutonicorum'. See R. Schieffer, *Entstehung*, 114ff., where although it is denied that a prohibition of investitures was issued in 1075, it is admitted (p. 146) that 'the Lenten synod of 1075 made a ruling which affected the practice of investiture'. See also p. 147: 'In as much as the Lenten synod of 1075 made changes in traditional practice of investiture, these must evidently have been measures which were not immediately and obviously recognisable or recognised as a prohibition.' But it should be noted here that later undoubted prohibitions also did not always produce violent reactions.

[180] *Ibid.*, 124f., as well as 135 and 149f.; we shall have to return to this psychological interpretation of Gregory's supposed assessment of Henry IV's behaviour in the summer and autumn of 1076; see below, p. 232.

[181] R. Schieffer, *Entstehung*, 171.

contravened the decree. It is formulated in quite general terms: 'at the hand of an emperor or king or of any lay person, man or woman'.[182] Nevertheless there is a series of indications in other sources that there must have been a prohibition of or at least a general decree against lay investiture before the autumn of 1078.[183] The excuses made by the bishops Gerhard of Cambrai, Huzman of Speyer and the patriarch Henry of Aquileia, who received investiture from Henry in 1076 and in the two years which followed, and excused themselves by saying that they had not known of such a prohibition, suggest very strongly that one must have existed.[184] The strongest indication is the very categorical canon issued by a legatine council held under Hugo of Die on 15 January 1078, especially since this repeats comments made by a synod of September 1077 which in turn are cited in a letter of Archbishop Manasses of Rheims.[185] Here already, long before Gregory VII's autumn synod of 1078, a decree laid down that no bishop, abbot, priest, or other member of the clergy should receive the gift (*donum*) of a bishopric, abbey, church, or piece of ecclesiastical property, but rather that a bishop should receive his church from his metropolitan, and an abbot, priest, or lesser cleric from his bishop. The penalties which followed were laid down for those laymen who resisted these canonical decrees (*decretis canonicis resistentes*). An attempt has been made to characterise this canon issued at a French synod as particular church law (as opposed to general church law); but neither the wording nor the content make such an interpretation seem particularly plausible.[186] Provisions applying to the appointment of bishops, abbots, and clerics must be valid for the whole church, even if in practice they were not observed and enforced everywhere.

However one decides the question of the origins of the prohibition of investiture and its gradual application, there are two wider issues which arise for the church history of the eleventh century: first, how and when

[182] *Registrum* VI 5b c. 3, p. 403.
[183] The 'earliest indirect reference to the decree of the Lenten synod' (of 1075) was identified by Caspar in *Registrum* II 55, p. 200 n. 2, and a further one in *Registrum* III 3, p. 247 n. 3. But both passages can easily be explained as a warning to fill ecclesiastical offices in accordance with the canons, that is, without simony. One can, however, hardly deny that Gregory's famous letter to Henry IV of 8 December 1075 (*Registrum* III 10, 266 n. 2 and 3) contains a reference to a prohibition of investiture, though R. Schieffer, *Entstehung*, 137 offers a different explanation.
[184] *Registrum* IV 22, p. 330 (12 May 1077); V 18 p. 381 (19 March 1078); Meyer von Knonau, *Jahrbücher Heinrichs IV.*, III.179f. and n. 10 (11 February 1079).
[185] Mansi XX, col. 498; Manasses's letter, which quotes the synod of Autun, is preserved by Hugo of Flavigny, *Chronicon* I 2, MGH SS VIII.419; see Scharnagl, *Begriff*, 33, and W. Schwarz, 'Investiturstreit', 290ff.
[186] Thus R. Schieffer, *Entstehung*, 168ff., with a not very convincing argument.

the reaction to lay influence within the church came about; second, what part the prohibition of investitures played in the breach between Gregory VII and Henry IV and in the subsequent development of relations between the papacy and the secular powers. The second question will be dealt with in the chapters which follow; the first can be answered shortly here.

The earliest texts which formulated Gregory's prohibition of investiture contained precisely what had been promulgated by Nicholas II in 1059 in a concise and very general form and before that had been set out in theory by Humbert of Silva Candida in a passionate and energetic justification of his views. Humbert's work, which impresses us so much, did not circulate widely and only had a very restricted manuscript transmission. Schieffer thinks that 'strictly speaking it has not even been proved that Hildebrand/Gregory VII took note of Humbert's exposition'.[187] Nicholas II's prohibition also had few echoes and seemingly very little practical effect at first. It was, however, repeated by Alexander II in an encyclical letter perhaps dating from 1063 which set out once again the synodal decrees of his predecessor.[188] There are no further traces of this letter from the years which follow, but we find at least one in the acts of a synod held at Gerona in 1078, which say: 'we know indeed that churches do not belong to the laity, but where these cannot be wholly taken from them we forbid them at least to take the oblations', and so on.[189] Humbert's work is supposed to have remained 'a dead letter'.[190] But can it be perhaps that the thoughts expressed in it remained alive and effective? In the history of ideas it is not possible to work only on the basis of those continuities demonstrable in written tradition, especially where less than two decades lie between impulse and effect. Is it conceivable that Hildebrand/Gregory VII, who from the time of Leo IX belonged together with Humbert to the leadership circle around the popes until Humbert's death in 1061, could have known nothing of or had forgotten Humbert's thoughts, given that from the middle of his pontificate it was precisely Humbert's demands that he took up, promulgated, and enforced with militant energy? It seems more plausible to us to characterise the pontificate of Alexander II and the earlier years of Gregory VII as ones in which the papal reaction to the continuing practice of royal investiture of bishops within the imperial church could

---

[187] *Ibid.*, 44.

[188] Concilium Romanum (1063), c. 6, Mansi XIX, col. 125.

[189] Mansi XX, col. 519, c. 13.

[190] See already J. Haller, *Papsttum*, II/1.379; R. Schieffer, *Entstehung*, 207, calls it a 'fact that the potentially explosive theories of the cardinal remained a dead letter for twenty years'.

best be characterised as one of '*de facto* toleration coupled with reservations in principle'.[191] What could this reserve have been based on, if not on more or less subconscious thoughts and intentions which ran parallel to those expressed by Humbert and Nicholas? The appearance of these writings is highly significant in itself, as an early symptom of tendencies which were slowly developing, even if for the time being they were not yet active at the level either of literary treatise or church policy.[192]

[191] Carozzi, 'D'Adalbéron', 83, stresses the link between Humbert and Gregory VII: 'When Gregory VII wrote his two letters to Hermann of Metz later or drew up the Dictatus Papae he was only following the path graced by Humbert of Moyenmoutier.'
[192] R. Schieffer, *Entstehung*, 103.

6

GREGORY VII (1073–1085)

·

Until the middle of the eleventh century the history of the Roman church had had a largely provincial character, with occasional periods of wider significance.[1] The general theoretical recognition of the pope's religious supremacy was not even sufficient to enable him to exercise jurisdiction in his own ecclesiastical province, let alone in the whole of Italy. The churches in the localities led their own life and could easily avoid being dominated by the head of the church in a politically divided land. Often it was only with difficulty that the popes could retain or recover the possessions of the Roman church. Besides periods of weakness and dependence on local and distant powers there were also times when the popes took on a leading political and military role in Italy. We may concede that such political activities were seen as means to spiritual ends, but they showed repeatedly that the popes were not able to exist as purely spiritual leaders even in their own immediate sphere. The typical duality of spiritual and political and material existence which is characteristic of the church on earth appears as a dilemma to the religious mind even at the highest level of Christendom.

After the decisive events of Henry III's reign the Roman church began to extend its influence over the churches in the localities, but gradually and by no means continuously; there were advances and retreats. Side by side with this went a transformation of the group of assistants available to

---

[1] See above, pp. 65f.

the pope. The tendency to institutionalisation found at the time to a greater or lesser extent in all European countries also affected the papacy. Suprapersonal ideas gradually came to prominence, as they did in royal, princely and communal administration and government. These were very long-term developments.[2] But it is no coincidence that from the second half of the eleventh century the objective term *papatus* begins to be found in the sources, alongside *pontificatus*.[3] It is only from this point that one can talk seriously about a history of the 'papacy'. Before then it had not been an institution in the later sense; the papacy was on the one hand a term for the theoretical position within the universal church of the bishop of Rome as Peter's successor and on the other hand for the historical life and activity of the individual popes.

The development of papal claims to practical leadership of the church from Leo IX's time on did not affect all countries or national and diocesan churches at the same time and with the same force. Since the Christian kingdoms and the churches in them were closely linked with each other, the questions of papal primacy and of papal authority over kings, princes, and communities can only be considered together. If popes wanted to intervene in the affairs of the regions and localities they had to consider the position there as a whole. If, for example, a bishop considered unsuitable was to be disciplined and a conflict with him threatened to develop, the curia had to assess soberly his relations with the ruler, with the neighbouring bishops, with the clergy of his diocese, especially those of the cathedral chapter, and with the inhabitants of the cathedral city, as well as weighing up his financial backing and the power of his relatives.[4] It was impossible to stick to one's own ecclesiology and policy with no concessions. The pope and his assistants were inevitably drawn into many matters which had very little to do with their spiritual, moral, and disciplinary intentions. In order to achieve his own goals, the pope had to take account of the intentions of those whom he needed for his purposes. He needed to support allies whose aims were for him of no importance, and who in their turn had little sympathy for his opinions and preconceptions. We shall see, for example, how alien to one another were

---

[2] Cf. Tellenbach, 'Vom karolingischen Reichsadel', 69ff.; Beumann, 'Transpersonale Staatsvorstellungen', 185–224.

[3] I hope to return to this question elsewhere.

[4] There are many examples of this; one might think of the cases dealt with in the text. Bishop-elect Charles of Constance, Bishop Hermann of Bamberg or Archbishop Manasses of Rheims were all deposed not because they were rightly or wrongly accused of simony or other offences but because they had too many enemies and too few supporters.

Gregory VII and his Saxon supporters.[5] In general we shall need to investigate the relations between Gregory VII and the very varied groups of Gregorians, to see what linked and what divided them.

A papacy which saw itself as called to lead Christendom was thus compelled to take account of temporal matters which were only indirectly of consequence, either positive or negative, for the road to salvation. The history of the papacy, and indeed of the church itself, therefore encompassed religious events, spiritual service, the formation of a hierarchical order, but also a concern to secure its material existence and defence against hostile interference. To maintain and increase the income of the Roman church, to preserve and defend a 'papal state' in an embattled world, to establish peace and security in central Italy, could all take on a higher meaning in the light of the idea of the divinely willed papal role in the universal church and the Christian world. But the diplomatic manoeuvring required, the concern with finances, the need for armaments and military interventions all made it difficult at times to see all measures both great and small as always being concentrated on the single high aim.

Step by step from the time of Henry III and Leo IX the papacy took on a greater weight within the Christian world in its striving to realise its claims to leadership in a religious, dogmatic, legal, and political sense. This was by no means a linear development affecting all the particular churches equally. The second half of the eleventh century saw repeated setbacks for the papacy which at times sapped its energies. Its activities were felt strongly in some countries, in others weakly or not at all. The emergence of a new ecclesiastical and political authority in Rome was only gradually taken on board in the world beyond. And where its unwanted interventions were noticed at all they were often ignored or politely evaded. The popes had little power, no compelling authority; spiritual punishments were, viewed externally, of uncertain and restricted effectiveness. Papal activity was forced to concentrate on specific issues, to be elastic both in attack and in defence, to shift between intransigence and flexibility even in controversies involving matters of principle. In spite of all this there were decisive changes in the period between the pontificates of Leo IX and those of Urban II and Paschal II. The radical principles of Humbert and Gregory VII were hardly ever realised; but even the compromises which were achieved transformed the Christian world.

The pontificate of Leo IX (1049–54) was a prologue to the rise of the papacy which surpassed in power and dynamism the scenes which immediately followed. Leo, born a count of Egisheim, belonged to the

highest aristocracy of the empire. He was related to the emperor and
linked with him in many ways, in a shared religious outlook but also in
a conviction of the pope's dignity and vocation. As bishop of Toul he
was a member of the imperial episcopate, with which he remained in
community and largely in agreement after he had become pope.[6] He was
one of the bishops who took canon law seriously; he was imbued with
contemporary piety like Archbishop Halinard of Lyons, who was close to
him, or Abbot Hugo of Cluny. His own way of life was unblemished, and
he tried to take steps against the moral laxity of the clergy. He can be
shown on many occasions to have demanded the free election of bishops
by the clergy and people of the episcopal city, in particular in the course
of his own elevation as pope, when he is said on his arrival in Rome to
have had a formal election carried out retrospectively.[7] In the few years of
his pontificate he summoned eleven synods, almost twice as many as his
predecessors had managed in a quarter of a century. They served the
purpose of gathering the bishops, clergy, and important laymen of a large
region around him so as to impress on them the requirements of canon
law, in particular the bans on clerical marriage and on simony, which had
often been promulgated but were only imperfectly observed. Even Leo
seems here to have met occasionally with passive and even active
resistance. In February 1053 there was a dangerous tumult at a synod in
Mantua, and the pope was unable to get his rigorous demands accepted.
It is probably characteristic of the man that he nevertheless forgave the
leaders of the riot.[8]

Leo could not be active everywhere in the few years of his pontificate.
Apart from Germany and Burgundy he sought to make papal primacy felt
in France. As an Alsatian and as bishop of Toul he was presumably well
acquainted with conditions there, and an extension of papal influence to
the west with the backing of the emperor and the imperial episcopate
seemed likely to be successful. Hence in 1049 he accepted the invitation
by Abbot Herimar of Saint-Rémi, Rheims, to consecrate his new
monastic church, and he took the opportunity to invite the king and the
bishops of France to a great council there. He himself arrived on

[6] On Leo's monastic policy see, besides the still valuable work by R. Bloch, 'Die
Klosterpolitik Leos IX. in Deutschland, Burgund und Italien', *AUF*, 11 (1930), 176–257,
the accurate observation by Fried, 'Laienadel', 393, that it was more characteristic of a
German prelate acting on a large scale than of an ecumenical ruler of the church. Hirsch,
'Untersuchungen', 397, offered quite different views, even wanting to contrast a 'papal
church' with an 'imperial church'.
[7] At least according to Wibert, *Vita S. Leonis* II 2, ed. Watterich, I.149. Bruno of Segni in
his later *Vita* of Leo gave these actions a revolutionary colouring.
[8] Steindorff, *Jahrbücher Heinrichs III.*, II.233f.

29 September, the first pope to visit France since John VIII in 878. But the French king Henry I, who at first had been cooperative, asked the pope to postpone visiting his kingdom.[9] According to Leo's biographer Wibert, men at court had suggested to the king that the dignity of the kingdom would be destroyed if he allowed papal authority to rule there.[10] It was probably not just an excuse when the king announced a campaign against Count Geoffrey Martell of Anjou at this time, and summoned the bishops of the crown demesne to serve on it. Nevertheless, he was perhaps grateful for a plausible excuse to avoid meeting the German bishop and Roman pope, especially since his honourable guest's intentions could be predicted from his previous activities.

The council in Rheims, attended by German, Burgundian, Norman, and northern French prelates but only sparsely by those of the Capetian dioceses, was indeed a continuation of previous synods. But it proceeded more aggressively than either the earlier or the later ones. The archbishops and bishops present were urged to confess whether they had participated in simoniacal practices. Many could deny having done so with a clear conscience, but others were embarrassed. The bishop of Nevers resigned his office, but received it again from the pope's hands. Hugo of Langres fled during the council and was deposed, though he was later restored to office. Leo himself named a successor for the deposed bishop of Amiens.[11] The bishops who had not appeared were excommunicated and deposed, though only a few were mentioned by name. Among these, Drogo of Beauvais was soon restored and remained in office until his death during the pontificate of Nicholas II.[12] The tribunal at Rheims was for a long time the most impressive intervention by any pope in the affairs of a territorial church. Leo was here by no means a rigorist, and displayed a remarkably conciliatory attitude in many cases. The king was not so much attacked as ignored; in his turn he did not react to the proceedings. It was the exception when Henry deposed an abbot who had gone to Rome without his permission in order to secure absolution from excommunication.[13] Both king and pope pursued their own interests, but they put up with not being able to get their own way all the time.

Much remains unclear about the attitudes of the participants. Many of

[9] *Anselmi monachi Remensis historia dedicationis ecclesiae S. Remigii (Itinerarium Leonis IX.)*, Watterich, I.113–27, gives the most vivid account.
[10] *Ibid.*, 115: 'Regni sui decus annihilari, si in eo Romani Pontificis auctoritatem dominari permitteret.'
[11] W. Schwarz, 'Investiturstreit', 264ff.; Becker, *Studien*, 36ff.
[12] *Ibid.*, 45.
[13] *Ex chronica coenobii s. Medardi Suessionensis, s.a.* 1049, Bouquet, *RHF* XI.367 (for Abbot Rainold of Saint-Médard); W. Schwarz, 'Investiturstreit', 266 and n. 1.

the charges in contemporary propaganda against the corruption and vice
of the churches have survived in historical writing up to the present day.
One has the impression that money and gifts played a role which was long
established in the tradition of the French church, perhaps more so even
than in Germany or England. But there seems to have been uncertainty
as to what really constituted the sin of simony.[14] In three sessions the
council reached a number of decisions, which were summarised in twelve
canons. Its primary importance lay, however, in the way in which the
papal primacy had been demonstrated within France. One detail worth
noting is the excommunication of the bishop of Compostela: he had
taken the title of 'bishop of the apostolic see', which Leo saw as appro-
priating a dignity which belonged to him alone.[15]

A few days after the French council another one was held in Mainz,
which presented quite a different picture. The emperor was present with
his following. The pope's own entourage was even larger than it had
been at Rheims, besides which all the German archbishops and nearly all
their suffragans appeared. The usual legislation on simony, clerical
marriage, and church discipline was issued; in general it seems to have
been a harmonious occasion. Bishop Sibicho of Speyer was able to
defend himself convincingly against the accusations brought against
him, and as was normal several internal ecclesiastical disputes were
settled.[16]

We hear little of tensions between Leo IX and the German episcopate.
True, there is an anecdote about a divine service held by Leo and
Archbishop Liutpold of Mainz at Worms on 26 December 1052, at which
there was temporary discord. A deacon of Mainz, Humbert, sang a
reading during the mass, which caused some Romans in the pope's
entourage to take offence. When Humbert failed to react to warnings, the
pope degraded him on the spot. But the archbishop forced Leo to retract
his decision. If the story is true, it does not seem that the pope bore
Liutpold any malice; on the contrary, he conferred further honours on
him.[17] By contrast, there was a more serious clash between Leo and
Archbishop Hunfrid of Ravenna at the synod of Vercelli, known otherwise for the decisions taken there against Berengar of Tours, but this
seems to have been over a question of property and jurisdictional rights,

---

[14] See above, p. 123 with n. 15 and p. 173 with nn. 144ff.
[15] Menéndez Pidal, *Spanien des Cid*, 161; de Valdeavellano, *Historia de España*, 674.
[16] Steindorff, *Jahrbücher Heinrichs III.*, II.96. But even this German bishop was not accused
   of any of the fashionable sins of the time.
[17] *Ibid.*, 188f. Such differences of opinion on the correct liturgy are not without parallel; see
   Klauser, *Liturgiegeschichte*, 29.

not of ecclesiastical discipline. The conflict was settled at the beginning of the following year.[18]

Leo and Henry III had frequent and lengthy meetings. On a number of occasions they gave each other support, as for example at their meeting in Lotharingia in the summer of 1049, when the pope excommunicated the leaders of the rebellion there, Duke Godfrey of Lotharingia and Count Baldwin of Flanders. In the summer of 1052 Leo hurried from southern Italy to Germany in response to an appeal by King Andrew of Hungary and persuaded Henry III to abandon the siege of Bratislava and make a treaty with Andrew, though the latter soon broke it.[19] In spite of this pope and emperor journeyed together through southern Germany for several weeks. Leo IX practised itinerant rulership, just like the other important rulers of his time.[20] He remained in Rome for periods of only a few weeks or months. His stays in central and northern Italy did not last nearly as long as those north of the Alps and in southern Italy. In the last year of his life he spent ten months without interruption in southern Italy, a region which claimed all his energies and brought him severe disappointment.[21]

It was here that the various forces of the Mediterranean world met in shifting constellations: the disunited Christianity of East and West; the Islam of north Africa, Sicily, and Spain; the Byzantine empire; rebels in Apulia; Saracen princes; the native lordships exercised by popes and Lombard princes. Added to this were irregular and uncalculable interventions by the distant emperors of the Romans, and from the second decade of the eleventh century immigrants from Normandy, who were militarily of great importance. Leo IX spent more time and energy on this region than on any other. Even today it is hard to assess his actions and those of his entourage; many of the decisions and measures contradicted one another. It is difficult to explain what calculations or feelings led him, in contrast to his predecessors and also to Emperor Henry III, to make enemies of the catholic Normans and to seek an alliance against them with the Byzantine emperor Constantine IX Monomachos (1043–58), only to contradict this by allowing an embassy to Byzantium under Cardinal Bishop Humbert of Silva Candida in 1054 to make a major issue out of a secondary question of ritual and thus not only wreck his alliance but create the epoch-making breach between the Roman and the Greek

---

[18] Steindorff, *Jahrbücher Heinrichs III.*, II.130f.

[19] *Ibid.*, 83f. and 181f.

[20] On the pope's impressive itinerary see *ibid.*, Appendix III, 452ff.

[21] Deér, *Papsttum*, 35 n. 151: 'Southern Italy was the battleground in the struggles between the great powers of the time.'

church.[22] Henry III had given the pope a free hand in the southern fringes of the empire by making over to him the duchy of Benevento *vicariationis causa*, but he did not provide the military support the pope had wished for. The defeat of the papal troops at Civitate near Fortore and his own capture by the Normans spelt catastrophe for Leo.

It is hardly possible to distinguish between religious, ecclesiastical, and political elements in Leo's actions in southern Italy. There was probably always an intention to defend papal possessions and rights of jurisdiction, in particular the abbey of Monte Cassino, which had suffered especially under the tensions between Lombards and Normans. It is also likely that he intended by his policy to free the Holy See from the constrictions of local Roman and regional forces. Leo carried out his conciliar programme in southern Italy with the same intensity as elsewhere, encouraging reform and acting as judge just as he had in Rome, Rheims, or Mainz. In the brief span of his pontificate he sought to strengthen the ecclesiastical organisation of Campania, Apulia, and Calabria.[23] The unfortunate conflict between Humbert and the patriarch of Constantinople, Michael Cerullarios, can be set in the context of the realisation of the papal claim to primacy; however sceptical one may be about the immediate significance of this conflict, it remains true that it had important long-term consequences.

In the course of a pontificate of rather more than five years Leo IX intervened jurisdictionally, ecclesiastically, and politically in the life of many countries and national churches with an intensity which had not been known before. For at least ten years after his death the papacy's activities were continued in this style, but with some restriction. It is worth noting that six months separated the election and the consecration of Victor II (1055–7); he must have hesitated about whether to accept the office. His pontificate lasted only a little more than two years after that, of which a good ten months fell in the period immediately after Henry III's death, in which Victor's attention was absorbed by the affairs of the empire. It became immediately apparent how important it was that the

---

[22] We must agree with Beck, *Orthodoxe Kirche*, 142, when he observes: 'Reform did not just mean the struggle against simony and clerical marriage but also making the pope's claims to primacy and property prevail.' But Leo IX's policy in southern Italy was marked by miscalculations and contradictions; see Nicol, 'Byzantium', 8ff.

[23] H.-W. Klewitz, 'Studien über die Wiederherstellung der römischen Kirche in Süditalien durch das Reformpapsttum', *QFIAB*, 25 (1934–5), 108; P. Herde, 'Das Papsttum und die griechische Kirche in Süditalien vom 11. bis zum 13. Jahrhundert', *DA*, 26 (1970), 7, 12; neither the Normans nor the popes pursued a systematic Latinisation of the Greek church in southern Italy, and there was an open or tacit recognition of papal primacy. On the schism of 1054 see J. J. Ryan, 'The Legatine Excommunication of Patriarch Michael Cerularius (1054) and a New Document from the First Crusade Epoch', *StGrat*, 14 (1967), 13–50, and E. Petrucci, 'Rapporti di Leone IX con Constantinopoli', *StMed*, 14

pope could no longer rely on the support of a well-disposed emperor, as Leo had been able to do.[24] Stephen IX (1057–8) was under pressure from hostile Roman circles throughout his pontificate, and died after only nine months. Nicholas II (1059–61) was hampered during the two-and-a-half years of his pontificate by the schism caused by the antipope Benedict (X), and devoted most of his energy to relations with the Normans, with the result that the regency government in Germany became hostile to him. Alexander II (October 1061 to April 1073) needed several years at the beginning of his pontificate to overcome the challenge from the antipope Cadalus and settle the conflict with the regency government.[25] Although it was only at the synod of Mantua in 1064 that the pope really established himself, he seems already before that to have intensified his external relations. Hildebrand was probably the driving force during his pontificate, and there was a renewed determination to make the papal primacy a reality, a tendency which was strengthened under Gregory VII.

There are only a few bits of evidence for the ecclesiastical policy of Victor II and Stephen IX, some of them of doubtful authenticity. Victor held a great council in Florence at Whitsun 1055, at which, allegedly, the old prohibitions of simony and clerical marriage were renewed in the presence of the emperor, a number of bishops were deposed, and Archbishop Wifred of Narbonne excommunicated. The reports of the synod are coloured by the harsh attitudes of a later period; Bonizo's more precise claim that the bishop of Florence was among those deposed is demonstrably false.[26] It was in Victor's pontificate that Hildebrand carried out a legation to France, where he presided over a synod which dealt with the case of the archdeacon Berengar of Tours. Later legends claimed that here also Hildebrand deposed a bishop. Travelling in the company of Abbot Hugo of Cluny, Hildebrand is said to have turned suddenly to the abbot and vehemently denied the charge which he was able to read in the abbot's mind 'that I had deposed that bishop more out of overweening pride than out of zeal for God'.[27] The little that is reported of Stephen IX

(1973), with the older literature cited there, especially p. 831, as well as E. Petrucci, *Ecclesiologia e Politica di Leone IX* (Rome 1977), 65ff.

[24] The impotence of the imperial government is rightly pointed to by Deér, *Papsttum*, 96ff. Whether or not corruption played a part should be judged more cautiously than he does. Even money, mentioned in some of the sources, could not have persuaded the court to intervene in Italy. See the failed attempt by Archbishop Hilderich of Capua, Meyer von Knonau, *Jahrbücher Heinrichs IV.*, 1.238 and 264. Barlow, *English Church 1066–1154*, 274 observes acutely that the Normans were not just tools of the popes but also the reverse.

[25] See above, pp. 154f.   [26] Steindorff, *Jahrbücher Heinrichs II.*, II.305f., especially 306 n. 3.

[27] 'me magis episcopum illum causa iactantiae quam zelo Dei deposuisse': Paul of Bernried, *Vita Gregorii Septimii Papae*, Migne, PL 148, col. 45; Bonizo, *Liber ad amicum*, VI, MGH LdL 1.592.

also comes mostly from later sources, though it does seem credible that he took measures at a number of synods in Rome against clerical and incestuous marriages, against monks' holding private property, and – in defence of the Roman liturgy – against the Ambrosian chant of Milan.[28]

During the pontificate of Nicholas II papal influence on the church seems to have intensified once more; at any rate the sources are richer and rather more reliable than for the previous period. The two Lateran synods of 1059 and 1060 were marked by an energetic assertion of church policy. The new policy towards the Normans led to papal synods at Benevento and Melfi, at which the usual canons were issued.[29] There seem also to have been specific decisions affecting south Italian church organisation. Here the impulse came from the papacy itself, influenced, it may be assumed, by Abbot Desiderius of Monte Cassino. Papal intervention in Milan, on the other hand, was initiated by Milan. The bitter struggles between Archbishop Wido and a part of the citizenry with the Patarenes led to the sending of a Milanese embassy to Rome, to which Nicholas II responded by sending Petrus Damiani and Bishop Anselm of Lucca as legates. Petrus has left an important report on the legation.[30] Many of the Milanese were agitated by the appearance of the legates, seeing in their presence a diminution of the dignity and the established rights of the church of Saint Ambrose. Dangerous riots broke out, which Damiani was able to quell by a long speech in which he set out the prerogatives of Saint Peter and the rights of Saint Ambrose. After this the archbishop and the clergy were compelled to renounce simony and clerical marriage; most clerics were restored to their office after accepting penances. The pressures on the established church in Milan and in Lombardy must have been considerable; this is confirmed by the fact that the archbishop and seven of his suffragans obeyed the summons to attend the Easter synod of 1059.[31]

Among the lands north of the Alps Nicholas devoted particular attention to France and continued Leo IX's attempts to influence events there. But he showed remarkable restraint. Objections to Archbishop Gervase of Rheims were withdrawn, perhaps on the advice of Hildebrand, perhaps also out of consideration for the king. He

---

[28] Meyer von Knonau, *Jahrbücher Heinrichs IV.*, I.73.   [29] *Ibid.*, 145f.

[30] *Opusculum V. Actus Mediolani de privilegio Romanae ecclesiae ad Hildebrandum S. R. E. cardinalem archidiaconum*, Migne, *PL* 145, cols. 89–96; Arnulf, *Gesta archiepiscoporum Mediolanensium* III 14, MGH SS VIII.21: the populace raised a tumult 'non quidem gratia Widonis, sed Ambrosiani honoris', see H.-D. Kahl, 'Der Chronist Arnulf von Mailand und das Problem der italienischen Königsweihen im 11. Jahrhundert', in *Historische Forschungen für Walter Schlesinger*, ed. H. Beumann (Cologne 1974), 430f.

[31] Keller, *Mailand*, 324ff., 338ff.

deposed several bishops, but tolerated their restoration. The cardinal priest Stephen, who was legate in France in 1060, showed equal moderation. The relationship with King Henry I was conventional and distant, which allowed Nicholas to avoid or ignore conflicts, as it had Leo IX.[32]

In general the old distance between the papacy and the separate countries continued; contacts were irregular and concerned specific issues. After Nicholas's death Archbishop Stigand of Canterbury journeyed to Rome to receive the pallium. This was motivated by a traditional devotion to the prince of the apostles; Roman affairs and the question of who was pope were a matter of complete indifference to him, so that he seems to have had no hesitation about accepting the pallium from Benedict X.[33] Relations with Germany were closer. The first contact with Archbishop Anno of Cologne was purely conventional: at Anno's request the pope issued privileges for two Cologne churches.[34] Archbishop Eberhard of Trier's dispensation from oaths he had taken under duress was also granted at the request of the beneficiary.[35] The demand of the empress Agnes that Archbishop Siegfried of Mainz should receive the pallium was refused. Both the tone and the content of the letter, written by Petrus Damiani on behalf of the cardinal bishops, are noteworthy.[36] It contained the inaccurate claim that it was ancient custom for the recipient to come to Rome in person for the pallium, a rule to which there had been, to say the least, many exceptions. Here we can see signs of a new line, a more determined accentuation of papal primacy. In this context we should also note the refusal under Alexander II of comparable requests by Archbishop Richer of Sens and by Patriarch-elect Ravengerus of Aquileia.[37] In Richer's case the refusal was justified with the mysterious claim that it was necessary to avoid simony. Was this an attempt to stop payments from the pallium from falling in part or completely into the wrong hands? But the relationship between the curia and the regency government does not seem to have been seriously

---

[32] W. Schwarz, 'Investiturstreit', 267ff.; Becker, *Studien*, 46, calls the relations between Nicholas II and Henry I 'though not particularly warm or friendly, nevertheless not poor or hostile'. Above all there was no question of an investiture dispute at this time.

[33] See above, p. 175.

[34] Meyer von Knonau, *Jahrbücher Heinrichs IV.*, 1.161.

[35] *Ibid.*, 179f.

[36] Petrus Damiani, *Epistolae* IV 4, Migne, *PL* 144, cols. 412f.; on Alexander II and the grants of pallia see F. Herberhold, 'Die Beziehungen des Cadalus von Parma zu Deutschland', *HJb*, 54 (1934), 95ff.

[37] Loewenfeld, *Epistolae*, 41 no. 76; 43 no. 81. See also P. Ewald, 'Die Papstbriefe der Britischen Sammlung', *NA*, 5 (1880), 338 no. 51.

disturbed until early 1060. At the beginning of the year the new archbishop of Mainz could still be invested and consecrated in the presence of the papal legate Anselm of Lucca at Altötting in customary fashion.[38] There was evidently no sense as yet that this traditional procedure was problematic in any way. And Nicholas's great Easter synod of 1060 was attended by Wibert, the royal chancellor for Italy. It was not until May or June 1060 that the papal legate Stephen was humiliated at the royal court.[39] The brusque rejection of the legate shows that the bishops and counsellors in the empress's entourage must have perceived some elements of papal policy as hostile. It is not certain, but it is probable, that it was the pope's dealings with the Normans which were seen as injuring royal rights and interests. After this pope and curia seem to have undertaken no further activities in Germany. Nicholas was pressed ever harder by his old enemy, Count Gerard of Galera, and was forced to leave Rome before his death; it is in connection with this that we hear of dissensions between Nicholas and the archbishop-elect of York.[40]

From the time of Alexander II onwards there was a noticeable increase in the effectiveness of papal legates in France, which was much greater than that which can be observed in other countries. The important legations by Petrus Damiani, which dealt principally with the conflict between Bishop Drogo of Mâcon and the abbey of Cluny, and by Cardinal Hugo Candidus, who was active in southern France at the beginning of his important legation to Spain, fell in the year 1063, and hence a year before the synod of Mantua, at which Alexander was able to defeat the antipope.[41] Cardinal Stephen appeared again in northern France in 1062 and took part in a number of councils as judge and mediator.[42] In 1064 and again in 1072 (here perhaps on the return journey from his second legation to Spain) Hugo Candidus appeared once more in southern France. Also in 1072, Cardinal Bishop Gerald of Ostia began his legation in France, which took him to Spain as well and lasted into the early part of Gregory VII's pontificate. Other legates are

[38] Meyer von Knonau, *Jahrbücher Heinrichs IV.*, 1.173; Schmidt, *Alexander II.*, 65, conjectures that he had already discussed the Norman question.

[39] See above, p. 154.

[40] On their return his legates are supposed to have been attacked by Gerard of Galera and robbed. The later report by William of Malmesbury, *De Gestis Pontificum Anglorum* III, ed. N. E. S. A. Hamilton (Rolls Series, London 1870), 251, makes the leader of the embassy say angrily to the pope: 'Parum metuendam a longinquis gentibus eius excommunicationem, quam propinqui latrunculi deriderent.' Probably many people thought in similar terms about the pope in the middle ages.

[41] T. Schieffer, *Legaten*, 66ff. and 74ff.

[42] *Ibid.*, 76ff.

known from Alexander's pontificate, including Bishop Ermenfred of Sion, who was active in Normandy as well as in England.[43]

In France, where the king's influence was limited and there was a general shortage of effective judicial instances, there was a real need for papal authority, and the legates had a promising field of activity. In general they confined themselves to dealing with conventional cases of merely regional significance, and did little that was novel or sensational. Naturally they repeated the usual prohibitions of simony and clerical marriage, but as reminders rather than startling innovations. During the pontificate of Alexander II no other land saw so many more-or-less successful attempts to judge episcopal elections and installations as uncanonical and hence void. Elected bishops of Soissons, Orléans, and Chartres were deposed (though only after struggles lasting years), and a bishop of Le Mans was installed against the will of Count Geoffrey of Anjou.[44] The dispute over the archbishopric of Tours took a rather different course. King Philip had nominated and invested Rudolf of Langlais in 1068, evidently against the will of a substantial part of the electorate. Rudolf's opponents persuaded the pope to reject Rudolf and deny him the pallium, but the king remained firm. In 1073 the pope yielded, and the archbishop was able to receive consecration. In such conflicts it was crucial whether the king held fast to a disputed candidate or dropped him. It has been said of France at this time that it was typical 'that conflicts over episcopal appointments here never led to a real breach between pope and king'.[45] Both sides alternated between firmness and conciliation; there is as yet no question of the pope's having tried to enforce a clearly defined state of canon law as a matter of strict principle.

Two of Alexander's legates proceeded from France to Spain. One of them, Gerald of Ostia, extended his stay there into the pontificate of Gregory VII. He met with resistance from the Spanish episcopate, which led to some difficulties for the new pope.[46] Hugo Candidus's activities had decisive consequences for the lands of the Pyrenean region; up until Alexander's pontificate these had hardly been touched by papal influence, whereas there was an old tradition of contacts with Catalonia as part of Gallia.[47] One of the principal papal aims was to establish Roman liturgy and eliminate the old Mozarabic rite. This was bitterly resisted in Navarre and León. Three bishops were sent with liturgical manuscripts to Rome,

[43] *Ibid.*, 80ff.
[44] W. Schwarz, 'Investiturstreit', 270; Becker, *Studien*, 38ff.
[45] *Ibid.*, 49.
[46] T. Schieffer, *Legaten*, 86.
[47] Kehr, *Navarra und Aragon*, 4ff.; Kehr, *Katalanischer Prinzipat*, 13.

in order to defend the local liturgy. It was pointed out to Alexander that an earlier Pope John had already examined the Spanish rite and given it his approval.[48] The pope is supposed to have confirmed the orthodoxy of the rite at a Roman council held in 1065 or in 1069. Strange legends grew up around this dispute. It was claimed that a judicial duel had been fought on the issue, in which the Roman champion had been defeated. Another report claims that a Roman and a Mozarabic manuscript had been laid side by side on a bonfire; the Mozarabic codex leapt out of the flames and was undamaged, whereas the Roman manuscript was burned.[49] There is a corresponding, though less hostile, story told by the Milanese Landulf the Old about the dispute over the Roman and Ambrosian liturgies. According to this it was agreed that the two codices should be laid side by side, and that the first to open of its own accord should be accepted as orthodox; both opened simultaneously.[50] In northern Spain the Roman rite was able to establish itself rapidly from the time of Alexander II and Hugh the White in spite of these difficulties. It was accepted in 1071 in Aragon, and in 1076 in Navarre, Castile, and León, while Catalonia, with its links with France, had never practised the Mozarabic rite.[51]

The activities of the legates in northern Spain were not restricted to enforcing acceptance of the Roman liturgy. As in other lands they worked on their journeys and in their synods for the rule of canon law, for the prohibition of clerical marriage and simony. They were also active in establishing closer relations between important monasteries and the Holy See and in securing privileges for them.[52] Still more significant was Rome's increasing involvement with the struggles of Spanish and French knights against Islam. Hugo Candidus was probably already active in 1063 in preparing the plans which led to the capture of Barbastro in the following year. though the town could not be held.[53] Towards the end of his pontificate the pope and his archdeacon Hildebrand gave their support to the campaign by Count Ebolus of Roucy, which was noteworthy for being governed by a treaty with the curia: the count was to hold his conquests as a vassal of St Peter.[54] The legate, Cardinal Bishop Gerald of

---

[48] Kehr, *Wie und wann*, 9f.; Säbekow, *Päpstliche Legationen*, 26.

[49] C. Cabrol, 'Mozarabe', *DACL*, XII/1, col. 396; Lerner, *Hugo Candidus*, 25.

[50] P. Lejoy, 'Ambrosien', *DACL*, I, cols. 1373–442.

[51] Kehr, *Wie und wann*, 13; Kehr, *Navarra und Aragon*, 15; Kehr, *Katalanischer Prinzipat*, 28.

[52] Lerner, *Hugo Candidus*, 31ff.; Kehr, *Wie und wann*, 11.

[53] Erdmann, *Entstehung*, 124f.; I owe to T. Reuter a reference to A. Ferreiro, 'The Siege of Barbastro', *Journal of Medieval History*, 9 (1983), 135, who shows that the view I had accepted from Erdmann, that Alexander II had granted the first papal crusading indulgence to the participants in the expedition against Barbastro, is untenable.

[54] *Ibid.*, 140f.

Ostia, and the papal subdeacon who accompanied him, Rainbald, were also concerned with the undertaking. Hugo Candidus was active elsewhere in a number of ways. It is probable that he suggested the journey of the young King Sancho Ramirez of Aragon to Rome in 1068. Here Sancho commended himself to Saint Peter, handed over his kingdom and promised 'services', though this action had no immediate practical consequences; only after a gap of some twenty-five years did the king renew the donation to Urban II and undertake, probably in lieu of the promised services, to send 500 gold mancuses a year as a feudal rent.[55]

In the case of England as well one can perceive a certain expansive tendency on the part of the curia from Alexander II's time. The country had been up until then distinctly distant from Rome. No king since Cnut had made a pilgrimage there. Only the archbishops of Canterbury had continued to follow old tradition by collecting the pallium from Rome. There was a fair number of Norman bishops at Leo IX's council at Rheims, and a small English contingent, consisting of a bishop and two abbots.[56] No accusation of simony was made against the Normans and Englishmen. The objection on the grounds of consanguinity to the marriage between Duke William of Normandy and Mathilda of Flanders was of some importance, but Abbot Lanfranc of Bec was able to mediate. The doubts about the marriage were dropped after William had agreed to found two monasteries as a penance.[57] During the reign of Edward the Confessor England was probably visited by a number of legates, and in Alexander's pontificate we have the legation of Bishop Ermenfred of Sion.[58]

Recent English scholarship has pointed out that the accusations made by Norman chroniclers against the Anglo-Saxon church were confused and ill-founded; none of the bishops in office in 1066 had been guilty of simony.[59] William the Conqueror did not at first even wish to remove Archbishop Stigand of Canterbury. The latter, however, was guilty of pluralism, besides which he represented the old régime and had the victorious curia of Nicholas II against him.[60] Only later was his case invested with deeper theological or canonical significance. Other bishops were deposed in the years that followed, but none because of opposition

---

[55] Kehr, *Wie und wann*, 14f.; Lerner, *Hugo Candidus*, 27; Erdmann, *Entstehung*, 342f.

[56] Barlow, *Edward the Confessor*, 149.

[57] Steindorff, *Jahrbücher Heinrichs III.*, II.91; Lemarignier, 'Etudes', 138, 140.

[58] Tillmann, *Legaten*, 12.

[59] Darlington, 'Ecclesiastical Reform', 401 n. 4; Deanesly, *Sidelights*, 108: 'the accusations of simony made by Norman chroniclers against the old English bishops mostly seemed confused and illfounded.'

[60] Darlington, 'Ecclesiastical Reform', 398; see above, p. 175 and n. 156.

to the demands of 'reform'. Stigand's successor Lanfranc was closely linked with William. King and metropolitan together guarded the political and ecclesiastical autonomy of England against popes and papal legates.[61]

The curia does indeed seem to have had far-reaching plans for the country. Alexander II took the side of the Normans against King Harold. Harold may have been excommunicated; William's cause was implicitly declared just by the papal banner conferred on him.[62] Gregory VII was later to declare emphatically that he had been the initiator of this policy in his predecessor's time.[63] And it is evident that he here pursued aims similar to those of the popes in respect of the Norman princes in southern Italy or of the kingdom of Aragon. While the curia under Alexander II was active in western Europe, planning, acting, and staking new claims, its contacts with northern and eastern Europe were still sparse. The letters of Alexander II to the Danish king Svein Estridson, to Danish bishops, and to the Norwegian king Harold Hardrada were all written in connection with the plans of Adalbert of Bremen to establish a new patriarchate for himself.[64]

Relations with the countries within the empire took a course of their own, with conspicuous differences between Germany, northern Italy, and southern Italy. The schism between Alexander II and Honorius II which broke out in October 1061 allowed neither of the popes to exercise much influence at first.[65] The most powerful magnates of the empire seem to have continued divided in their judgement of the papal question, or perhaps to have regarded it as being of no importance in their affairs. In 1068 Archbishop Anno and Duke Otto of Bavaria journeyed to Italy as royal legates.[66] Even these men, who favoured Alexander II, overestimated their room for manoeuvre in respect of a pope they regarded as legitimate: they judged it permissible to meet the antipope and were

---

[61] F. Barlow, 'A View of Archbishop Lanfranc', *JEH*, 16 (1965), 170: since Lanfranc had left Italy before the revival of the papacy he never paid serious attention to the new papal programme; Barlow, *English Church 1066–1154*, 60: 'for the king through thick and thin'; Cantor, *Church, Kingship*, 31: 'From a cautious pro-Gregorian position Lanfranc was advancing in the closing years of his pontificate toward an openly anti-Gregorian stand.'

[62] Böhmer, *Kirche und Staat*, 83; Erdmann, *Entstehung*, 139f.

[63] *Registrum* VII 23, pp. 409ff.

[64] Hauck, *Kirchengeschichte Deutschlands*, III.661; Gerhardt, *Norwegische Geschichte*, 81f.; Seegrün, *Papsttum*, 71ff. See JL 4471ff., Loewenfeld, *Epistolae*, 38 no. 68 for Alexander II's letter to Harold Hardrada.

[65] See above, pp. 154f.

[66] The differing positions of Archbishops Adalbert and Anno can be seen from the letter from the archbishop of Cologne to Alexander II, probably written in the summer of 1068, printed by Giesebrecht, *Kaiserzeit*, III, 1257 no. 4.

compelled to do humble penance for their action.[67] It was only from around 1068 that the curia acquired full freedom of action in Germany. Before that it was still primarily concerned to win support and to avoid giving offence, and it was hardly in a position either to state or to enforce 'reform' demands.

The first occasion when it was able to act effectively in an individual case was in 1069, when Henry IV, aged nineteen, wished to annul the marriage of three years before to Bertha of Turin. At the suggestion of the king's entourage Petrus Damiani came as legate to Germany and was able to defuse the crisis, which was essentially unpolitical and not linked with matters of current concern, at a synod in Frankfurt in the autumn.[68] Alexander's second intervention in 1070 was also in response to an appeal from outside, this time from circles in Constance which had rejected the bishop nominated and invested by the king, Charles.[69] We have discussed this case above; it was particularly noteworthy in that papal curia and royal court clashed over an episcopal appointment to a degree previously unknown.[70] This was an anticipation of the contemporary and much more significant affair in Milan.[71]

In 1073 the pope intervened in the dispute between Bishop Gebhard of Prague and his brother, the Bohemian duke Vratislav, and Bishop John of Olomouc. The bishop of Prague sought to unite the diocese of Olomouc with his own and employed great brutality in his attempts to do so.[72] The duke turned in anger to the pope, who ordained a legation to Bohemia, probably at the Lenten synod of 1073 shortly before his death; once again this was a reaction not an initiative. The affair dragged on into the pontificate of Gregory VII and took on a more fundamental significance when the archbishop of Mainz complained that the pope had infringed his rights as metropolitan.[73] This was an early sign

---

[67] The increased self-confidence of the pope and the contempt shown for the king can be seen from the fact that the king's legates were only allowed to present themselves after making a *humillima satisfactio*, *Annales Altahenses*, *s.a.* 1068, p. 74.

[68] Meyer von Knonau, *Jahrbücher Heinrichs IV.*, I.612ff., with an aberrant judgement on Henry's alleged moral rootlessness. Henry's real behaviour can be gauged fairly well from the letter from Siegfried of Mainz to Alexander II, Codex Udalrici no. 34 = Jaffé, *BRG*, v.64ff. Henry's admission that he had nothing with which to reproach Bertha is very telling.   [69] See above, p. 179 and n. 193.

[70] See in particular the *Acta synodi Maguntinensis*, Jaffé, *BRG*, v.71 (August 1071), 'Et quod rex potestate iubebat, Romanus pontifex auctoritate prohibebat.'

[71] See below, pp. 203f.

[72] Meyer von Knonau, *Jahrbücher Heinrichs IV.*, II.190ff.

[73] Codex Udalrici no. 40 = Jaffé, *BRG*, v.84: 'Debuit namque iuxta decreta canonum ad nos primum causa deferri, et ille, ad concilium vocatus, intra provinciam inter fratres suos audiri'; Gregory's reply is *Registrum* I 60, p. 87.

of clashes between the claims of a revitalised curia and of metropolitans.

Alexander's activities in Italy were not noticeably governed by
consideration for the German king and future emperor. There was talk of
plans for an imperial expedition to Italy, but there was as yet nothing
definite in the way of policy which could be counted on. The conflict
over Milan, then just beginning, was the exception. The legal, political,
and religious bases for the papal claims have been subject to varied
judgements in recent literature,[74] a reflection not least of the lack of
clarity shown by the papacy at the time.

The Normans had played at Alexander's election the role agreed on
in 1059, by clearing the way with the sword for the new pope's
enthronement. But these allies soon withdrew, leaving the pope
unprotected. Norman troops as well as Duke Godfrey were involved in
the battles in the city in 1063, but it is not known which of the Norman
princes sent them, and they may have been mercenaries. Count Roger,
the brother of Robert Guiscard, sent presents to Alexander II after his
victories in Sicily out of reverence for the head of the church. The
Norman princes had numerous conflicts among themselves. While
Richard of Capua dared in 1066 to attack papal territory, his son-in-law
William of Montmirail, who had abandoned him, was made defender of
the southern part of the papal state and received a banner – *vexillum sancti
Petri* – from the pope, a symbol which could sustain both a religious and
a legal interpretation.[75] In 1067 Duke Godfrey of Lotharingia, the most
important magnate in central Italy, undertook a campaign on behalf of the
pope against the aggressive Richard of Capua, but without success. In the
same year Alexander and Hildebrand journeyed to Apulia. They held
synods in Melfi, Salerno, and Capua, once again combining spiritual with
political activity.

In central and northern Italy the curia was chiefly concerned with
Margravine Bertha of Tuscany and her husband Godfrey of Lotharingia,
and with Margravine Adelheid of Turin. The pope's tactics were flexible.
He showed conspicuous spiritual clemency in his dealings with the lady
of Turin, who had dealt with Lodi with notorious cruelty;[76] together with
the duke of Lotharingia he supported Bishop Petrus Mezzabarba of

---

[74] Kehr, *Belehnungen*, 8: Nicholas II and Alexander II take on the position of the German
    king *vacante imperio*; Erdmann, *Kaiserfahne*, 885: usurpation of imperial rights; similarly
    Deér, *Papsttum*. Others see the rights as having been derived from the Donation of
    Constantine.
[75] Erdmann, *Entstehung*, 119.
[76] Meyer von Knonau, *Jahrbücher Heinrichs IV.*, 1.632.

Florence, accused of simony by the monks of Vallombrosa and an excited population.[77] His relations with Godfrey, who was for years his principal if not always a wholly reliable supporter, became strained when Godfrey permitted himself contacts with (though never recognition of) the hated antipope. Ecclesiastics like Archbishop Henry of Ravenna were also excommunicated when they consorted with Cadalus. It is characteristic of the contemporary situation that the Ravennatese continued to support their archbishop, even though this brought them in their turn under the ban. Only after Henry's death were they released by Petrus Damiani, acting as papal legate, and they appear to have shown deep gratitude for this.[78]

Already under Alexander II the pope's actions in the Milanese conflicts had led to events of major significance and consequence. But even here the curia was not to start with active on its own initiative. Petrus Damiani and Anselm of Lucca had already gone to Milan as legates of Nicholas II, at the request of both parties.[79] Through the Patarene Erlembald, who received a banner of St Peter from Alexander around 1065, closer ties with the Patarenes were created.[80] In 1066 Archbishop Wido was excommunicated, which led to outraged rioting at Whitsun. Both the archbishop and the Patarene leader Ariald were struck down in the cathedral; Ariald was forced to flee, and was then betrayed and murdered.[81] Once again a papal legate mediated. The conflicts continued, however, until Wido, sick of the struggle, resigned in favour of the Milanese cleric Godfrey. Although this was strictly contrary to canon law, the new candidate received investiture at the royal court. However, the Milanese did not accept him, and he was excommunicated by the pope along with the former archbishop, who died in August 1071. At the beginning of 1072 Erlembald had the cleric Atto elected in the presence of the papal legate Bernard, thereby breaking promises previously made and ignoring the king's right to consent.[82] This produced immediate and violent reactions. Many Milanese wished to avoid conflict with the king. Atto was compelled by the opponents of the Patarenes to take a solemn oath to renounce the see of Saint Ambrose. A Roman synod, by contrast,

---

[77] Tellenbach, 'Gregorianische Reform', 104 and n. 25. Petrus became bishop around 1060, see Y. Milo, 'Dissonance between Papal and Local Reform Interests in Pre-Gregorian Tuscany', *StMed*, 20 (1979), 73. He must thus have held office for years before the attacks of the Vallombrosans on him began.

[78] Meyer von Knonau, *Jahrbücher Heinrichs IV.*, II.164 n. 95.

[79] See above, p. 149 and nn. 30 and 31.

[80] Erdmann, *Entstehung*, 129.

[81] Meyer von Knonau, *Jahrbücher Heinrichs IV.*, I.563f.

[82] Keller, *Mailand*, 344f.

declared this oath invalid and confirmed his election. Godfrey, meanwhile, was consecrated by Milanese suffragans at Novara on the king's
orders, in spite of the fact that he was still excommunicated.[83] In consequence, several of the king's counsellors were threatened with or
sentenced to excommunication at the Roman Lenten synod in 1073,
shortly before Alexander's death. This gave a new and previously
unknown sharpness to the conflict between pope and king, for there can
be no doubt that the papal measures were in reality aimed at the king
himself and not just at his entourage. Of course there was talk of simony,
as by then had become customary in such disputes. But there were no
concrete accusations that the counsellors had been bribed, and if *adulatio*
alone was to count as simony this was an accusation which could always
be made against courtiers.[84]

In the conflict between papal and royal curia there were to begin with
no conflicts of principle as far as the prevailing conditions in the church
or its members were concerned. The king did not defend simony (the
notorious Milanese tariff for the consecration of clerics, for example)[85] or
corruption which went beyond the scale of presents then customary. The
question of clerical marriage probably scarcely concerned him. There was
also no issue of principle arising from these appointments to high
ecclesiastical office. The king had made very questionable use of his right
of investiture in Milan. In attacking this, the pope was not attacking the
right in general, but rather its abuse in a particular case. However, the use
of excommunication (or the threat of it) against those responsible was a
sign that the pope was making new and more extensive use of his
spiritual prerogatives than before, and hence also that the differences were
beginning to become more than casual frictions and to take on an
ecclesiological dimension.

The details are not always clearly visible, but it is likely that
Archdeacon Hildebrand was the decisive influence at the curia during the
last years of Alexander II. Papal government already showed traces of the
style which was to become evident in his own pontificate. One is tempted
to ascribe Alexander's attitude in the dispute over Charles of Constance
to Hildebrand, still more so the measures taken in the course of the
Milanese schism.[86] The excommunication, threatened or realised, of

[83] Meyer von Knonau, *Jahrbücher Heinrichs IV.*, II.196; Arnulf, *Gesta archiepiscoporum
Mediolanensium* IV 3, MGH SS VIII.26: 'accepto a rege mandato'.

[84] Remarkably, Meyer von Knonau, *Jahrbücher Heinrichs IV.*, II.198, does not doubt the
substance of the accusations of simony; but simoniacal advisers ought to have displeased
the pious empress.

[85] Petrus Damiani, *Opusculum V*, Migne, *PL* 145, col. 95.

[86] See above, p. 179 with n. 172 and p. 194 n. 31.

Henry's counsellors at the Lenten synod of 1073 showed the same previously unheard-of boldness which was to characterise Gregory as pope. In 1080 he was to remind William of England of how he had defended the Norman conquest of England in 1066, before the beginning of his own pontificate.[87] Papal policy at that time was already determined by expansionist aims, though these turned out to be unrealisable.

GREGORY VII AND THE BISHOPS[88]

From the middle of the eleventh century the papacy, always acknowledged in theory as the centre of the church, took on increasing weight in practice compared with the regional divisions of the church – bishoprics, national churches, diocesan, provincial, and national councils, at first slowly, then with gathering speed. Nevertheless, one should not visualise this process as having been even and homogenous. Papal intervention was still far more frequently set in motion from outside, provoked by the parties in dispute or by churches and monasteries seeking help, than by the curia's own initiative. Still, the greater frequency with which papal decisions were sought was in itself a sign of a growing recognition of the papal plenitude of power. Two points should not be overlooked, however. The intensity of papal intervention (or the intensity with which this was sought) varied greatly among the Christian lands of the West. And with growing recognition came growing resistance, which took various forms. Some simply used the old-established method of playing deaf; some glibly promised an obedience which they then did not perform; and some defended themselves openly against claims which they saw as an aggressive infringement of their own rights.

Gregory lived and acted in an unshaken consciousness of his own divine vocation. He was certain that as the representative of the Apostle Peter he represented the true ruler of the church on earth. Whether this was possible even in principle was a question which did not in the least concern his decisive, unphilosophical, and essentially straightforward character. This accounts for the lordly tone of his dealings with Christians of all classes, the frequent sharpness of his speech and the remarkable

---

[87] *Registrum* VII 23.

[88] The references in brackets used in the text of this and subsequent sections are to the Register of Gregory VII (ed. E. Caspar, MGH Epistolae Selectae 1, Berlin 1920–3). The letters in the *Epistolae Collectae* edited by Jaffé are cited as *EC* and number; I refer to Jaffé's edition (*Biblioteca rerum Germanicarum*, Berlin 1865), II.520–76, as it is the one cited in most of the literature, but the new edition by H. E. J. Cowdrey, *The Epistolae Vagantes of Gregory VII* (Oxford 1972) must also be consulted; see H. Fuhrmann's review in *DA*, 30 (1974), 250f.

decisiveness he showed, even though he weighed up decisions carefully.[89] He was quick to threaten and to carry out punishments against those who resisted or disobeyed or who broke the laws of the church, even if their crimes were commonplace ones. Only exceptionally was he in a position to apply physical force, but he certainly regarded excommunication, the withdrawal of eternal salvation, as the most severe threat possible. He was little concerned for others' opinions. 'We are well aware', he wrote to the Tuscan margravines Bertha and Mathilda after the first year of his pontificate, 'that men judge and think very variedly of us: in respect of the same cases and judgements some think us cruel, others all too mild. We can give them no truer or more appropriate answer than that of the Apostle: "But with me it is a very small thing that I should be judged of you, or of man's judgement"' (I 77).

Gregory's opinion of the state of the church was probably even worse than the gloomy conventional formulae he used. He could offer bitter criticism of bishops, while his praise or recognition seldom went beyond conventional phrases. Characteristic is a letter from the beginning of 1074 to the patriarch Sigehard of Aquileia: 'You know, we believe, how much the church is everywhere battered by stormy waves and through ill fortune and negligence has come near to being shipwrecked and submerged' (I 42). Long before the conflict with the German king, far from the schism and the dangers of the last years of his pontificate, he was writing in a letter to Hugh of Cluny: 'I can find scarcely any bishops who were elected and live according to the canons, who lead the Christian people in love and not in worldly striving. And among the secular princes I know none who prefers God's honour to his own, or justice to gain' (II 49). The letter which cited Siegfried of Mainz, the highest-ranking bishop of the empire, together with six of his suffragans to the Lenten synod of 1075, closes with a sentence which seems tinged with irony: 'Do not be surprised at the fact that we have invited more from your province than from others. For yours is larger than the others, and in it there are several whose reputation is not to be praised' (II 49). One of these was Bishop Werner of Strasbourg, though it had been said in his praise that he had obeyed Alexander II's summons, alone among all the bishops of Germany, of whom it is said that many not only live in the sins of the flesh but also tainted by the shame of simony (I 77).

The pope had various means of controlling and influencing the regional churches. Gregory VII made energetic and extensive use of these as no pope had done before him. He issued friendly invitations or stern summonses to high ecclesiastics to attend synods, especially the Lenten

---

[89] Caspar, 'Gregor VII. in seinen Briefen', 23.

synods in Rome. Metropolitans were to appear in Rome to collect their pallium. It is characteristic of the distant attitude of the English church to Rome during his pontificate that his exhortations to Lanfranc of Canterbury on this remained unsuccessful (VI 30; VII 1). Quite apart from this he could urge archbishops to make frequent visits, as in the case of Anno of Cologne (I 19). Legates were sent into the regions with specific duties. England, admittedly, was closed to them.[90] Nor were they allowed into Normandy, whereas France was otherwise an area where legates were particularly effective compared with Germany and Italy. Permanent legates from the native episcopate such as Hugo of Die and Lyons or Amatus of Oloron played an important role here for years on end.[91]

Gregory frequently referred to bishops as *frater* or *confrater* and as *coepiscopus*.[92] This terminology was for him self-evident, and reflected his acknowledgement of the theological significance of the episcopal consecration they had in common. But his attitude was that of a superior issuing commands, who might occasionally praise but who much more often criticised, who handed out tasks and instructions and made programmatic declarations. For him, the bishops were tools and assistants in the government of the church. As was customary, he delegated to them judgement or arbitration in disputes which had been brought before him by the parties concerned. He demanded that they intervene when the oppression or robbery of churches or clerics came to his attention. When bishoprics fell vacant he issued instructions or advice to the clergy and laity entitled to elect, and he monitored the observance of canonical principles in elections. We even have a case where he showed concern about whether a bishop was able to carry out his office in view of his presumed senility (V 19).[93] He forced bishops to act in cases of clerics who had dealings with women and in cases of simony. He was often dissatisfied because of their laxity or their disobedience. He even wrote to Archbishop Gebhard of Salzburg, one of his most loyal supporters, that he deserved to be censured for his laxity in the matter of clerical chastity, since he had up to the present apparently not followed the decisions of a

[90] Tillmann, *Legaten*; Dickinson, *Later Middle Ages*, 54; Barlow, *English Church 1000–1066*, 111, 289; Barlow, *English Church 1066–1154*, 165f.

[91] T. Schieffer, *Legaten*, 68ff.; W. Schwarz, 'Investiturstreit', 287f. and 308; Becker, *Studien*, 56.

[92] H. F. Caspers, 'Was bedeutet im Zeitalter Gregors VII. die Bezeichnung coepiscopus?', *ZRGKA*, 22 (1933), 336ff.; against Kehr's views it is shown here that the term did not denote a grade in the hierarchy (examples pp. 340ff.). See also Capitani, 'Immunità vescovili', 194f.

[93] Archbishop John of Rouen; see Caspar, 'Gregor VII. in seinen Briefen', 382 n. 3 and *Registrum* VI 35 (20 April 1079).

Roman synod which he had attended (I 30).[94] At the end of 1074 and the
beginning of 1075 in particular the pope multiplied the warnings issued to
German prelates, who were placed in an acutely embarrassing situation by
the resistance of their diocesan clergy. Gregory appears to have been
aware that the position in other countries was similar. He commanded the
inhabitants of Lodi to assist their bishop, Opizo, against simony and
nicolaitism, thus following the example of the Patarenes in mobilising the
laity against the clergy (II 55). A significant parallel to this can be found in
a letter to Bishop Josfried of Paris, the royal chancellor, in which Gregory
wrote that the bishop was to instruct all the bishops of France on apostolic
authority that they should remove those priests who continued in
shameful libertinage from the service of the altar completely: 'And should
you find the bishops lukewarm in this matter and those who have usurped
to themselves the name and office of holy orders for the above-mentioned
crimes, all the people must be prohibited from accepting the sacraments
at their hands in future' (IV 20). In similar vein he turned to German
princes: to Count Adalbert of Calw (II 11); to Count Robert of Flanders
and his wife Adela (IV 10, 11); and most impressively to Rudolf of
Rheinfelden and Berthold of Carinthia. He warned them, regardless of
what the bishops might say or not say, that they should prevent simonists
and Nicolaitans from celebrating the holy mysteries, using force if
necessary. 'And if they should babble anything against you, saying that
this is not your office, answer them that they should not threaten your
people's salvation and your own because of the duty of obedience laid
upon you, but should come to us to dispute the matter' (*EC* 9 and 10).[95]

Although one has the impression that his opinion of many of the
bishops was a distinctly sceptical one, it must be noted that the strictness
of Gregory's principles was governed by realism. He rarely took steps
against bishops, even those whom he held to be harmful. He was
ready and willing to grant forgiveness for offences where the offender
confessed, and frequently tempered harsh judgements made by his legates.
Only in cases of open or concealed resistance was he unbending, for

---

[94] Besides that to Gebhard see the letters to Anno of Cologne (*Registrum* II 25), Sigehard of
Aquileia (II 62), Burchard of Halberstadt (II 66), Werner of Magdeburg (II 68), and later
also Huzmann of Speyer (V 18).

[95] Just as the Patarenes stirred up the laity against simoniacal and unchaste priests to the
extent of encouraging a 'liturgical strike', so Gregory, although in general he set clerics
high above the laity, occasionally mobilised the latter against the former. See on this
Violante, *Pataria Milanese*, 188; Miccoli, *Chiesa Gregoriana*, 159 n. 147; Meulenberg,
Primat, 92 and 126. See also H. Fuhrmann, 'Papst Gregor und das Kirchenrecht', *StGreg*,
13 (1989), 133: 'It is also clear that he was not much concerned about the danger of
destroying hierarchical structures'.

here he saw a flouting of papal authority. Even here he normally took really firm measures only in those cases where he was certain that he could carry them through successfully with the help of local opponents of the rebellious bishop. Only in a remarkably small number of cases did excommunication and deposition actually lead to the removal of bishops, and it is significant that the numbers varied greatly from regional church to regional church.

With an eye to William I Gregory repeatedly showed himself conciliant towards Norman prelates. At the king's request he sent back the case of Bishop Evenus of Dol, who had been condemned by papal legates, for renewed investigation by Bishop Hugo of Die (IV 17 and V 22); he restored Bishop Arnald of Le Mans (VII 22 and 23); and he commanded his legates to restore certain Norman prelates to their offices in view of the fact that the king had shown himself tolerable and honourable compared with other kings. Gregory took the opportunity, however, to mention that the king was not so devout in many respects 'as we would wish it' (IX 8). A letter of 1079 to the papal legate Hubert shows a bitter helplessness towards William. The Roman church has in truth much to complain of about him. Of all the kings, even heathen ones, he is the only one who is not ashamed to keep bishops and archbishops from the threshold of the apostles (VII 1). The cooperation between king and episcopate in England, and in general also in Normandy, was so close that Gregory could hardly hope to intervene from outside.

This was not true of France as a whole, which was divided politically and ecclesiastically. Even in the region under Capetian control the bishops found little support from their king, and this was still more true of the bishops elsewhere and of the great feudatories. Even episcopal solidarity offered little resistance to the combination of local opponents and distant interventions. In no other land were so many bishops condemned by pope, legates, and synods as in France. Nevertheless, many of these succeeded in keeping their position and in achieving restoration and forgiveness.[96] One has the impression that the French episcopate offered more room for Gregory to exert his influence than that of any other country. Mostly this was less a question of the often-cited struggle against abuses within the church as a whole than of the recognition of apostolic authority; in countless individual cases this had been usurped to the bishop's own advantage, an infringement which Gregory found unbearable.

---

[96] For the details it is sufficient to refer to the full and critical studies by W. Schwarz, 'Investiturstreit', and Becker, *Studien*; the summary characterisation of the French investiture contest given by Sprandel, *Ivo*, 116ff., is very much to the point.

In general most bishops sought to avoid conflicts and were prepared to make concessions. Neither king nor bishops insisted stubbornly or rigorously on the preservation of the ruler's old-established rights of investiture, and the pope was also not intransigent as far as the realisation of his principles was concerned. True, Gregory VII had few enthusiastic supporters of his 'reform policy' in France. Hugo of Cluny showed him great goodwill and respect for his office, but as a Cluniac he had his reservations, which will be discussed later.[97] Native legates served him with greater rigour of principle, in particular Hugo of Die and Lyons, whose harshness Gregory often had to moderate. It is particularly note-worthy that Gregory had to suspend the sentences of excommunication and deposition passed by Hugo at a turbulent council at Poitiers at the beginning of 1078 (v 17),[98] though these did have the effect that many of the outraged bishops appeared before the pope to justify themselves and complain about the legate. The significance of these journeys has been compared with that of Canossa for developments in Germany, 'though here, and that is very characteristic for France, it was not the king but the prelates who crossed the Alps'.[99] The result was that in March 1078 the judgements passed by Hugo of Die on the archbishops Manasses of Rheims, Hugo of Besançon, Richer of Sens, Richard of Bourges, Rudolf of Tours, and on Bishop Josfried of Chartres were sent back for a renewed hearing. In fact the cases were not taken up again.

The most stubborn resistance to Gregory came from the most prominent representative of the French churches, Archbishop Manasses of Rheims (1069–80). Here 'reform demands' played no part.[100] Manasses did not defend lay investiture in the traditional sense; he complained to the pope that two of his suffragans had consecrated a third, Rodulf of Amiens, who had received investiture at the hands of the king, although they had been present when the papal legate Hugo had promulgated the papal decrees prohibiting investiture by laymen.[101] The conflict between Manasses and Gregory began early in the latter's pontificate over the abbey of Saint-Rémi, Rheims (I 13, 52; IV 20). It became an open one when Manasses refused to submit to the judgement of papal legates, claiming to be subject only to the pope in person. His declaration of

[97] He was probably the only person in France towards whom the pope occasionally became warm and trusting in tone.

[98] W. Schwarz, 'Investiturstreit', 292f.; Becker, *Studien*, 65f.

[99] W. Schwarz, 'Investiturstreit', 300.

[100] *Ibid.*, 290ff.; Becker, *Studien*, 71ff.; J. R. Williams, 'Manasses of Reims', 804–24. I. S. Robinson, 'The Friendship Network of Gregory VII.', *History*, 63 (1975), 17, calls both Manasses of Rheims and Wibert of Ravenna 'friends of reform'.

[101] Bouquet, *RHF* XIV.611 no. 76 (1077).

obedience was contained in a letter of complaint in which he also said 'we are no Lombards'.[102] The legatine question was a critical one for Gregory (VI 2). It was while these issues were being decided that the Burgundian archbishop of Lyons was made primate of Gallia, and hence the superior of the French church provinces of Rouen, Tour, and Sens, a measure which was certainly intended to weaken the position of the archbishop of Rheims.[103] Because Manasses did not keep the promises he had made at the synod of 1078 he was deposed at a synod held by Hugo of Die at the beginning of 1080, a sentence confirmed by the pope at the Lenten synod of 1080 (VII 20). Astonishingly, Manasses really was forced to give up Rheims (VIII 17, 18, 20). The king let him drop and the episcopate did not raise any serious objections.[104] There was no French national church with the collective will to resist; above all, the proud Manasses had many enemies. In general it can be observed that where a bishop really was removed the decisive role was played by opposition forces in the episcopal city or in the diocese. Manasses's fall did not, however, bring about a decisive change in the relationship between the pope and the French episcopate. It is characteristic that Manasses's immediate successor was Bishop Halinard of Laon, appointed at the request of the king, who took years before he could be persuaded to accept another candidate.[105]

As we have just seen, Manasses of Rheims used the phrase 'we are no Lombards' when stressing the willingness of French bishops to comply with papal wishes.[106] Gregory himself had written as early as the summer of 1073 to the margravines Bertha and Mathilda 'you know, dearest daughters of St Peter, how openly the bishops of Lombardy dare to defend and favour the heresy of simony in that they have blessed or in reality cursed the heretic Godfrey, who for this has been excommunicated and anathematised, and have under the cloak of ordination set up a cursed heretic' (I 11). It was indeed true that more bishops of northern and central Italy opposed Gregory than supported him. This was less a difference of principle than a result of contingent ecclesiastical and political circumstances: the echoes of the Cadalan schism; the conflict in Milan; reaction against the Patarenes; relations with Henry IV. The pope used the fullness of his judicial power energetically against those who deserted him and remained disobedient; but it is remarkable how difficult

---

102 Becker, *Studien*, 67 and n. 87; MGH BDK v.182 no. 107.
103 W. Schwarz, 'Investiturstreit', 304ff.; Becker, *Studien*, 70f.
104 W. Schwarz, 'Investiturstreit', 310ff.; Becker, *Studien*, 72; Sprandel, *Ivo*, 122 speaks of coalitions of local powers with the pope against the king, but such coalitions could also be directed against the bishop, as Manasses's case shows.
105 W. Schwarz, 'Investiturstreit', 316.
106 See above, n. 102.

he found it to ensure that those Italians whom he had deposed and excommunicated were really driven from their sees. Even Cadalus of Parma could not be removed. The majority among clergy and people must have supported him; his successor Eberhard was at first a supporter of Gregory, but showed considerable reserve. In 1079 he was censured by Gregory for capturing the abbot of the Reichenau (VI 18); he subscribed the sentence of deposition passed against Gregory in Brixen,[107] and as a supporter of Wibert of Ravenna took part in the battle of Sorbera against the margravine of Tuscany shortly before his death.[108] Dionysius of Piacenza, to take another example, was present when Cadalus was made pope. He was driven out of his episcopal city for a time by Patarenes, but in 1073 he dared to appear before Alexander II when he accompanied the archbishop-elect Wibert of Ravenna to Rome for consecration.[109] In April 1074 Gregory wrote to his female friends, who had expressed dissatisfaction with his conciliatory attitude, that he had conceded to Dionysius and other Lombard bishops only the right to confirm children (I 77), which meant in other words that he was reserving judgement on them. In March 1075 he announced to the inhabitants of Piacenza that their bishop was deposed and ordered them to proceed to a new election (II 54). Dionysius was not much bothered by this, and offended the pope by taking Archbishop Udo of Trier and the cardinal bishop Gerald of Ostia prisoner.[110] Like Eberhard he subscribed the sentence of Gregory's deposition at Brixen in 1080, and shortly before his death he was to be found among Henry IV's entourage in Rome.[111] A further example is Roland of Treviso. He was the Parmesan cleric who brought the decisions of the synods of Worms and Piacenza to Rome in 1076 and aroused fierce indignation amongst Gregory's followers.[112] He was among those bishops who were condemned at the Lenten synods of 1078 and 1079 (V 14a and VI 17a); he subscribed at Brixen in 1080: and as late as 1089 he is found acting as bishop.[113]

There were certainly other Italian bishops who were loyal to Gregory, but there was little change in the parties up to the time of the Wibertine schism. After that things became more confused. The entries in the episcopal lists can be assigned the labels 'imperial' or 'papal', sometimes in

[107] MGH Const I., 120 n. 70.
[108] Meyer von Knonau, *Jahrbücher Heinrichs IV.*, III.565.
[109] Meyer von Knonau, *Jahrbücher Heinrichs IV.*, II.200 n. 24, following Bonizo.
[110] *Ibid.*, 736, 769.
[111] As n. 107.
[112] *Registrum* v 14a, c. 3: 'Qui pro adipiscendo episcopatus honore subdolus factus legatus inter regnum et sacerdotium scisma facere non aborruit.'
[113] Schwarz, *Besetzung*, 61.

alternation, sometimes with a rival from each camp competing for the bishopric. But before that we have little evidence of attempts to seek reconciliation with Gregory or of bishops changing parties, and since the pope's supporters were hardly as determined as those in France and Germany we can hardly suppose that he had much success in realising his ecclesiastical policies in Italy.[114]

Gregory does not seem to have had much confidence in the German episcopate at the beginning of his pontificate. We have already noted how often he issued warnings and censures because the decisions of the Roman synods were observed only laxly or not at all. Some of the recipients of warnings were those who are generally thought of as 'reformers': Gebhard of Salzburg (I 30); Anno of Cologne (II 25); Burchard of Halberstadt (II 66). Even Burchard had to listen to the reproach: 'since you have failed up till now we shall drive away your sleepy dullness and wake you with the goad of criticism'. The letter to Otto of Constance was phrased still more brutally: 'as we have heard, you have relaxed the reins of lust for the orders of the church, the chaste, the abstinent and the married, so that those who have joined themselves with women remain in their vice and those who have not yet done this need have no fear of your prohibitions'. At the same time the pope wrote to the inhabitants of Constance, great or small, cleric or lay, to say that he had asked their bishop to drive out simony and control the chastity of the clergy, that he had cited Otto to appear at the Roman synod, and that they should refuse to obey him should be be continue obstinate (*EC* 8 and 9). This was not the only example of the pope's requesting help from the laity, as has already been shown.[115]

Among the German bishops who were summoned with Siegfried of Mainz to the Lenten synod of 1075 were – apart from Otto of Constance – Werner of Strasbourg, Henry of Speyer, Hermann of Bamberg, Embricho of Augsburg, and even Adalbero of Würzburg (II 29). The three bishops of Strasbourg, Speyer, and Bamburg were suspended by the synod, at which they did not appear (II 52a). Already in the autumn of 1074 the pope had entrusted Archbishop Udo of Trier with the investigation of charges against Bishop Pibo of Toul, who had been accused of

---

[114] Even Thedald of Milan (*ibid.*, 82ff.) was able in spite of having been excommunicated and anathematised several times to maintain his position until his death, which fell on the same day as Gregory's. Very instructive for the way in which bishops maintained themselves in cities torn by party struggles is the description by Arnulf, *Gesta archiepiscoporum Mediolanensium* v 9, MGH SS VIII.31, of the friendly greeting given to the papal legates Anselm of Lucca and Gerald of Ostia by the Milanese populace. The archbishop could do nothing to prevent this, yet his own position remained unshaken.

[115] See above, p. 208.

simony and concubinage (II 10). In early 1075 Bishop Theodwin of Liège was also warned about simony and instructed to take steps against those clerics in his diocese who did not observe celibacy (II 61). It was only because of his old age and because Bishop Hermann of Metz had intervened on his behalf, wrote Gregory, that he had spared him.[116]

The tensions between the pope and members of the German episcopate, already discernible under Alexander II, increased in number and intensity under Gregory. Gregory's mistrust of some of them led him to summon them to synods in a manner which such distinguished clerics must have found not only unaccustomed but distasteful. The summonses were often not followed, usually with threadbare excuses which provoked the pope to still more extreme claims of obedience. As has been noted, things went as far as suspensions and excommunications. The Lenten synod of 1076 responded to the repudiation of Gregory by members of the German episcopate with the excommunication of two archbishops and twenty-four bishops as well as of Henry IV (III 10a).[117] In view of this it is remarkable that from the beginning of Gregory's pontificate up to the schism of 1080 only one German bishop actually lost his office. Some died before the sentences passed on them could take effect. Many were able to secure absolution in the course of 1076; at Canossa Liemar of Bremen, Werner of Strasbourg, Burchard of Lausanne, Burchard of Basle, and Eberhard of Naumburg were absolved along with Henry IV.[118] In the years that followed no German bishop was to be either suspended or excommunicated; even those who had accepted royal investiture before consecration in contravention of the pope's prohibition were allowed to excuse themselves without difficulty.[119] It was not until 1080 that there was a general excommunication of all of Henry's supporters.

Only a single German bishop was clearly deposed for simony, and accepted his sentence after long resistance: Hermann of Bamberg. Gregory had energetically pursued Hermann's removal after the suspension at the Lenten synod of 1075. Hermann is said to have secured his bishopric in 1065 by making large payments to members of the royal

---

[116] 'Ratione igitur iustitiae his de sententia in te esset animadvertenda, sed parcimus propter senilem aetatem et quia carissimus frater noster Herimannus Mettensis episcopus, tuae ecclesiae filius, te multum apud nos excusavit.' If Gregory could write in this tone to a bishop who had held office for twenty-seven years, the feelings of many German bishops towards the pope become understandable; it is necessary to remember this when trying to understand the events of January 1076.

[117] 'Qui sua sponte eius scismati consentiendo subscriberunt', MGH Const. I.120 no. 70.

[118] Meyer von Knonau, *Jahrbücher Heinrichs IV.*, II.762.

[119] See above, p. 184 and n. 182.

court; 'all Germany was convinced of this, and rightly so'.[120] The pope
had sent Cardinal Bishops Hubert of Palestrina and Gerald of Ostia as
legates to Germany in 1074 to hold a reform synod.[121] As Henry IV had
summoned his Easter assembly to Bamberg the legates, who intended to
proceed against the bishop of Bamberg, refused to take part. In Bamberg
Bishop Hermann was repudiated by the other bishops, especially by
Liemar of Bremen; at a subsequent meeting in Nürnberg it was thus
possible to restore concord between king and legates. When Hermann
was suspended at the Lenten synod of 1075 he was given a period of grace
until the first Sunday after Easter to make his submission. He is said to
have reached the vicinity of Rome before turning back and sending the
pope costly gifts (III 1–3). By July things had gone so far that he was
removed from office and a new election ordered. On 30 November the
king appointed his successor, who was consecrated by Siegfried of Mainz.
Hermann finally gave up, retired to the monastery of Schwarzach,
submitted to the pope, and received absolution from him.[122]

The fall of the bishop of Bamberg, however justified it may have
seemed and however rigorously it was carried through, left some
questions open. Hermann, previously *vicedominus* of the church of Mainz,
had returned in the summer of 1065 from a pilgrimage to the Holy Land
with his archbishop to become the successor of Bishop Gunther, who had
recently died. Not until 1070, five years later, was he summoned to Rome
by Alexander II along with Anno of Cologne and Siegfried of Mainz,
presumably like these in order to answer for his laxity in proceeding
against simony in his diocese. But he was able not only to defend himself
but also to receive the pallium, to which the bishops of Bamberg were
entitled.[123] He was one of the most influential bishops at Henry IV's court
and was active within his own diocese as a monastic reformer. According
to Lampert of Hersfeld it was precisely this which led to sharp conflicts
with the Bamberg clergy. It was not until December 1074, after he had
been bishop for nine years, that he was summoned once again to Rome
(II 29), where he was suspended at the Lenten synod of 1075 (II 52a). From
1074 the accusations of simony raised against him grew ever louder, and
it was this which lost him his bishopric. The basis of the accusation is

[120] Erdmann, *Briefliteratur*, 232f., though I cannot overcome my reservations about the interpretation he offers there and in Appendix 6.
[121] *Ibid.*, 227–44, for a detailed account of the attempts to hold a council.
[122] Meyer von Knonau, *Jahrbücher Heinrichs IV.*, II.541ff.; the absolution p. 544.
[123] *Ibid.*, 4; see the illuminating discussion by R. Schieffer, 'Die Romreise deutscher
Bischöfe im Frühjahr 1070', *Rheinische Vierteljahrsblätter*, 35 (1971), 158ff.; Schieffer casts
doubts on Lampert's account of a summons, a common journey made by the three
prelates and a concrete suspicion of simony.

reported by Lampert of Hersfeld, writing in 1077–8, and by Bruno, writing in 1082, by which time the former bishop had long been branded by public opinion as a simonist. He is said to have spent huge sums to buy his bishopric in 1065; but it is hard to say whether we should accept this as a hard core of truth in what is otherwise a collection of fantastic gossip. Lampert's lively and novelistic account shows how the bishop, who had made himself very unpopular in Bamberg, fell into disrepute.[124] It remains suggestive that he was the only German bishop who not only enjoyed a reputation as a crude simonist but was also deposed for this. Gregory VII seems to have considered not only Hermann but also other German bishops as simonists in 1074; for he wrote to the Tuscan margravines 'many have been summoned there who are polluted not only by the crimes of the flesh but also by the infection of simony' (I 77).

Hermann of Bamberg's case shows that even before the great conflict of 1076 the German episcopate could display a closed front, at least to the world, against simonist excesses of the kind ascribed to Hermann. At least in this respect there were no open differences between the pope and the German church at the end of 1075, though such transactions may still occasionally have taken place. Generally, the pope's lordly tone was suffered in silence or responded to with conventional expressions of devotion. It is hard to say what such proud ecclesiastical lords actually thought, but there were signs of opposition and resentment at least amongst some of the German metropolitans.

Already under Alexander II the Bohemian duke Vratislav had complained to the pope about the violence used by his brother, Bishop Gebhard (or Jaromir) of Prague, against Bishop John of Olomouc. The cardinal deacons Bernard and Gregory were sent to Bohemia to deal with the affair, but the bishop of Prague refused to appear before them unless his metropolitan and the bishops of the province of Mainz were present.[125] After Alexander's death, which followed shortly after these events, Siegfried of Mainz complained bitterly to Gregory VII that a charge against one of his suffragans had been dealt with in Rome without his knowledge and that the legates had violated his rights.[126] Gregory rejected the archbishop's complaint as presumptuous. The affair of Gebhard was treated gently at the request of Margravine Mathilda, but

---

[124] Lampert offers in his *Annales*, s.a. 1075, pp. 203–10 a coherent and lively version of events; he dealt with the facts in his usual fashion, that of a teller of tales who knows only good and evil. It is impossible to reach certainty on the question of Hermann of Bamberg's guilt, but the observations above suggest doubts about previous attempts at interpretation, including those of C. Schneider, *Sacerdotium*, 81ff.

[125] Meyer von Knonau, *Jahrbücher Heinrichs IV.*, II.192ff.

[126] Codex Udalrici no. 40 = Jaffé, *BRG*, v.85.

nevertheless a letter was sent on the matter to Duke Vratislav in early 1074 (I 78). Although there were to be further frictions, Gebhard remained in office until his death in 1094.

It was regarded as a scandalous action and rejected as such when on 16 October 1074 Gregory VII ordered Archbishop Udo of Trier to investigate the charges laid against Bishop Pibo of Toul in a denunciation made by the *custos* of Toul cathedral (II 10). Pibo was accused of having sold both churches and church offices, hence of simony, and of having lived in sin with a woman. The archbishop, a distinguished noble from the house of the counts of Nellenburg, answered with unusual sharpness and openness.[127] He had had Gregory's letter read out before more than twenty bishops (probably in Strasbourg, where Henry IV celebrated Christmas in 1074). All were outraged, and found it particularly unacceptable that the complaint by a Toul cleric should have been the occasion for Gregory's commission. It was hardly a sign of apostolic moderation that Gregory should have used such offensive expressions as *exepiscopus* and *lupus* in a case which had not been decided. In spite of this he, Eberhard, had investigated the matter. The accuser had not been able to utter a word, while Pibo had been able to demonstrate his innocence completely. 'We would ask your excellency, in whose honour and service we have exerted ourselves', the letter concludes with sarcastic courtesy, 'not to trouble us with such requests in future, for we can neither bear such burdens ourselves not find others who are willing to share them with us.' Udo had also raised fundamental objections of principle against the pope's manner of proceeding. Gregory had demanded that he should collect the clergy of Toul together and order them under the threat of anathema to say what they knew about the bishop's appointment and his manner of life. That meant, as Udo put it, arming sons against their fathers and turning the laws of devout obedience upside down.

The issues raised by Archbishops Siegfried of Mainz and Liemar of Bremen in their resistance to the reform synods which the papal legates, Cardinal Bishops Hubert of Palestrina and Gerald of Ostia,[128] were to hold at the pope's request in Germany in 1074–5 were still more fundamental. Both Siegfried and Liemar were summoned in December 1074 to the Lenten synod of 1075 (II 28, 29). The archbishop of Bremen was even temporarily suspended from office; he was accused of having prevented the legatine council. At the Lenten synod there followed definitive suspension and excommunication. A letter from Liemar to

---

[127] MGH BDK v.38 no. 17; on Udo of Trier and Liemar of Bremen see C. Schneider, *Sacerdotium*, 97ff.

[128] Meyer von Knonau, *Jahrbücher Heinrichs IV.*, II.380; Erdmann, *Briefliteratur*, 238ff.

Bishop Hezilo of Hildesheim from early January 1075 reveals his views
more clearly. The legates had demanded that he and Siegfried give their
consent to the synod, but they had done so on their own authority, not
on that of the pope. The two archbishops had implied that they could
only accept this command with the agreement of their fellow-bishops.
'These men, angry and ill-advised, presented me with the choice of
fulfilling their will as regards the synod or of coming to Rome to answer
for my actions. Now the pope summons me to Rome in anger and
suspends me from office . . . This dangerous man wants to order bishops
to do his will as if they were his stewards; if they have not done everything as he wishes either they must come to Rome or they are suspended without judgement.'[129] The legatine council was a failure, but the
indignation on both sides remained great. As late as September Gregory
wrote to Siegfried of Mainz about those who had demanded a postpone-
ment of the council he had announced (III 4). These tensions between the
pope and the German episcopate and their origins in fundamental
differences of opinion about the relationship between pope and bishops
must be borne in mind when considering the éclat at Worms in January
1076.[130]

GREGORY VII AND THE RULERS OUTSIDE THE EMPIRE

In a letter to King William I of England Gregory wrote that the royal
dignity should be ruled by God and then by apostolic care and ordering.
He kept here within the bounds of the Gelasian doctrine of the two
powers. The holders of apostolic and priestly power will be called to
answer for Christian kings as for all other Christians before the divine
judge and will have to give an account of their charge. It follows that the
king must obey him unquestioningly ('could or ought I not to care
diligently for the salvation of your soul; could you or ought you without
peril to it . . . not obey me without delay?' [VII 25]). There is a similar
justification of the pope's *universale regimen* in a letter to the Danish king,
Svein Estridson (II 51), and another letter to the Norwegian ruler Olaf III
speaks of *universalis cura* (VI 13). In his letters to rulers Gregory in fact drew
frequently on the repertoire of papal claims.

But the possibilities of exercising a universal *regimen* were very limited.
There were only intermittent contacts with more distant kingdoms,

---

[129] MGH BDK v.33ff. no. 15.
[130] See Goez, 'Erhebung', 120, and also Goez, 'Rainald von Como', 490, though the
German episcopate did not reject all intervention by the apostolic see but in the first
instance the dominance of papal legates as did Manasses of Rheims.

which normally occurred when the king had approached the pope on his own account.[131] Gregory wrote to the king of Norway that his people lived at the ends of the earth (II 53). At the beginning of 1075 he wrote to the king of Denmark that legates who had been sent to him had given up the dangerous journey because of the disturbances in Germany and returned to Rome (II 51). The letters to the kings of Scandinavia dealt essentially with questions of mission and with the means of instructing the newly converted. There were not many such letters, though pilgrimages to Rome by Scandinavians may have provided further opportunities for contacts. Christianity was in these parts wholly dependent on the kings. Pagan superstition still had to be combated and Christian doctrine transmitted, while the problems more usual elsewhere – the relationship between king and episcopate, the economic basis of the churches, the celibacy of priests – played hardly any part.[132] Gregory planned to bring up one of Svein Estridson's sons as a *defensor Christianitatis* and to endow him with a rich kingdom in the Mediterranean (II 51). He wrote to the Russian king Isjiaslav-Demetrios that he had given his son Jaropolk, who had come to Rome, his kingdom as a gift from St Peter (II 74). The duke of Poland was warned around the same time to restore to the Russian king what he had taken from him, and Gregory announced the sending of legates who would assist him in setting up the ecclesiastical organisation of his country, in particular in discussing the question of a metropolitan province (II 73).[133] Gregory asked King Michael of Serbia to send Bishop Peter of Antivari and the archbishop of Ragusa to Rome so that a dispute between the archbishops of Spalato and Ragusa could be settled, and announced in the same letter the grant of a banner and of a pallium (V 12).[134] He warned a vassal of King Zwonimir-Demetrius to refrain from attacking the king (VII 4).[135] Even an Islamic ruler, En-Naser of Mauritania, can be found among Gregory's correspondents. He assented to the request by this non-Christian ruler that he should consecrate Archbishop Servandus, whom he commended to clergy and people of the city of Bougie (III 20 and 21).[136]

Relations with all these rulers were free from conflict. In Spain one can still sense echoes of the disputes about the Mozarabic and Roman

---

[131] See now the impressive survey by R. Schieffer, 'Gregor VII. und die Könige Europas', *StGreg*, 13 (1989), 189ff.

[132] See in particular *Registrum* VII 21, p. 498 (1080) addressed to the Danish king Hakon, which refers to superstitions about witches and weather.

[133] V. Meystowicz, 'L'union de Kiew avec Rome sous Grégoire VII', *StGreg*, 5 (1956), 96ff.

[134] C. Jireček, *Geschichte der Serben* (Gotha 1911), I.212.

[135] F. Sišik, *Geschichte der Kroaten* (Zagreb 1917), 304.

[136] Caspar, *Registrum*, 286 n. 1.

liturgies. Alfonso VI of León was singled out for praise in 1081 because he had secured the acceptance of the Roman rite (IX 2). There do not seem to have been serious tensions arising out of ecclesiastical abuses in the north Spanish kingdoms.[137] Characteristic of the conciliatory attitude shown by both sides was the understanding reached between the pope and Sancho I of Aragon over the succession to the bishopric of Huesca (II 50) or that with Alfonso VI over the restitution of Bishop Paulus Muñoz of Oca, whom the papal legates Gerald of Ostia and Raimbald had deposed as a simonist (I 64 and 83).

Gregory's main concern in his relations with the kings and pretenders of Hungary was his claim that the kingdom was a fief held from St Peter. The internal affairs of the Hungarian church do not seem to have been a matter for dispute; at all events they did not produce any papal intervention.[138] His letter to the *iudices* of Sardinia by contrast shows deep displeasure: they had become more distant from the pope than the peoples who lived at the ends of the earth, though he concedes that they had slipped from his grasp because of the negligence of his predecessors, as a result of which the love which had existed between the popes and the people of Sardinia since times of old had cooled (I 29).

Gregory respected William the Conqueror, though he was sometimes disappointed in him. The king had skilfully avoided having to make England a fief of St Peter after the model of the Norman principalities in southern Italy.[139] He controlled the English church firmly together with Archbishop Lanfranc of Canterbury; he allowed neither the English bishops to journey to Rome nor papal legates to visit his kingdom.[140] When Hugo of Die and Amatus of Oloron excommunicated Norman prelates Gregory ordered them to release them from the sentence: the king was not so devout as Gregory might wish but because he did not destroy or sell churches, because he saw to the maintenance of peace and justice for his subjects, because he refused to make a pact against the apostolic see, though urged to do so by enemies of Christ's cross, because he forced priests to renounce their wives and laymen to give up under oath the tithes they had usurped, he had shown himself more tolerable and more honourable than other kings (IX 5). Gregory presumably thought it

---

[137] Vincke, *Staat und Kirche*, 255ff.; Gregory VII tolerated the king's influence. By contrast there was resistance by the Spanish episcopate to the papal legate, Gerhard; See Säbekow, *Päpstliche Legationen*, 20.

[138] *Registrum*, II 13, 63, 70; IV 25; VI 29. On Gregory VII. see Hóman, *Ungarisches Mittelalter*, 279, and on the toleration of the traditional church arrangements *ibid.*, 315ff.

[139] See above, p. 207.

[140] Barlow, *English Church 1066–1154*, 60ff. and 70; Cantor, *Church, Kingship*, 30ff.: no successor was recognised in England after Gregory's death.

was wiser to show restraint towards William, especially as the Wibertine schism had already started when he wrote.[141]

Although the influence of the pope and his assistants was great in France, his direct contacts with the king were few. Philip I occurs only twice in Gregory's register as the recipient of letters (I 75 and VIII 20), though he is mentioned frequently. The tensions between king and pope were at no point entirely eliminated, though both at the beginning and the end of Gregory's pontificate a certain conciliatoriness can be observed. At the end of 1074 Gregory wrote about the king with unheard-of severity. A letter to the French episcopate of September 1074 scourges the intolerable abuses: 'your king, who should not be called king but tyrant, is the chief origin of all this'. The raising of a high tax from foreign merchants visiting a fair aroused Gregory's especial anger: Philip had taken huge sums of money from them like a robber. Gregory wished the world to know, so that no one should continue in ignorance or uncertainty, that should Philip not come to his senses in the face of the punishments threatening him Gregory would with God's help seek by any means possible to remove the kingdom of France from his rule (II 5). Two further letters with similar contents were sent in November and December, in which Philip was referred to as 'king of France, nay, ravening wolf and unjust tyrant' (II 18 and 32). These pronouncements have been termed 'stage thunder'.[142] Philip was threatened with excommunication at the Lenten synod of 1075 (II 52a), but the threat never really touched him. Neither side was prepared to let things come to a head.[143] There were a number of disputes about the king's role in episcopal elections, in which each side was prepared to tolerate the other's gaining the upper hand. The battle against simony was a matter not just for the king but also for the high nobility, lay and ecclesiastic, while the king could not do much about clerical celibacy. Philip was hardly a suitable partner with whom to reach a fundamental clarification of the relations between pope and king. The only question of principle raised in France was that of the defence of the prerogatives of metropolitans against the powers of papal legates, which was what led to the downfall of Manasses I of Rheims.[144]

The neighbouring region of southern Italy required a greater investment of political skill, material and personal involvement than all the more distant lands together. The Normans, who had once been crucial assistants

---

[141] On the use of the schism as a lever see Barlow, *English Church 1066–1154*, 275.

[142] Kienast, *Deutschland und Frankreich*, 179.

[143] Becker, *Studien*, 54 and also p. 78.   [144] See above, pp. 210f.

in the emancipation of the papacy, had soon become unreliable allies or dangerous opponents. As early as the beginning of 1074 Robert Guiscard moved against Benevento,[145] which Gregory countered by a sentence of excommunication, pronounced at the Lenten synod of 1074 on 13 March (185a). It was to be repeated on several occasions as a response to slights and attacks. The reconciliation between Robert and Richard of Capua allowed each to make further conquests. At the end of December 1077 Salerno fell and Duke Gisulf had to flee first to Capua and then to Rome, where he remained as an emigré.[146] At the same time as these campaigns there were attempts at reconciliation, in which Abbot Desiderius of Monte Cassino played an important role. Not until the summer of 1080 did they bear fruit. At the end of June the duke renewed his feudal oath and the pope in return invested him with his lands once more (VIII 1a and 1b). The relationship between Gregory VII and the Norman princes is more a part of the history of the papal state than of the history of the church. Fundamental questions about the relationship between secular and ecclesiastical power were not on the agenda. The pope, who claimed a *regimen universale* as part of his office, must have been disturbed to find that the Norman prince lived as an excommunicate for more than six years without apparently being either troubled in his conscience or disturbed in his political activity by this.[147]

GREGORY VII AND HENRY IV

Relations with the young king who ruled over the kingdoms of Germany, Burgundy, and Italy and who was intended to receive the imperial crown from the pope like his forefathers were strained from the beginning. Gregory, as Hildebrand, had been familiar with the question from the time of the regency government, and was probably the man in Alexander's entourage most responsible for the unusually severe measures taken against the young king.[148] The cause lay in the bitter conflict between the two parties in Milan about the succession to the archbishopric. It had been both politically and canonically a very questionable action of Henry's to allow himself to be persuaded by his court to invest the subdeacon Godfrey at the request of the resigning archbishop Wido.[149] What was at issue was not even new ideas about the royal right

---

[145] Meyer von Knonau, *Jahrbücher Heinrichs IV.*, II.340.
[146] Meyer von Knonau, *Jahrbücher Heinrichs IV.*, III.85ff.
[147] Deér, *Papsttum*, 79. [148] See above, pp. 204–5.
[149] Precisely when before 1071 is uncertain. See Meyer von Knonau, *Jahrbücher Heinrichs IV.*, II.102, n. 15.

of investiture in general; only the Milanese radicals ignored these, though with some support from the papacy. But it must have seemed threatening to the pope that suffragans of Milan were willing to participate in the subsequent consecration of the newly invested archbishop. The pope had few friends in the high nobility and the episcopate of imperial Italy, and many were indifferent to him. It was a long-standing tradition that one looked to one's own interests and simply sat out papal censures or even ecclesiastical punishments. In the past the pope, who had often not been unchallenged even in his own immediate surroundings, had not been powerful enough to impose his will on the central and northern Italian episcopate, and many tried at first to ignore the growing energy with which the papacy made its will known. The king, usually a distant figure, could reckon with support if he set himself to conciliate princes and bishops. The Milan affair must have appeared to the pope to be a test case for his authority in Italy. Quite apart from that it served to bring fundamental differences to the surface where they had previously been buried.

Henry IV's inheritance

Before an open conflict could grow out of these differences, Henry's kingship had long been threatened and weakened from other quarters. The German kingdom had already entered into a crisis before Henry came to the throne, whose origins had nothing to do with the ecclesiastical problems of the time. Henry IV had to defend his position on two fronts, and Gregory VII found himself with allies for whom his ideals and aims were only of secondary importance. It is impossible to comprehend the epoch-making conflict between the two without taking this into account.

Under the year 1057 Lampert of Hersfeld reported that Saxon princes had come together frequently and complained about the injustices they had suffered at the hands of the emperor (Henry III). It would be good, they said, to deprive his son of the kingship while he was still young enough for this to be done easily, and they had decided to kill him should a favourable opportunity present itself.[150] The historian was probably allowing his inventive genius to run away with him when he set this down some twenty years later.[151] But his account is true to the extent that

---

[150] Lampert, *Annales*, s.a. 1057, p. 71. Giese, *Stamm der Sachsen*, 32f., talks of early plans for a revolution in Saxony, Schneider, *Sacerdotium*, 182, of a deposition party.

[151] According to Lampert, *Annales*, s.a. 1066, p. 102, the boy king was faced with the alternatives 'ut aut regno se abdicaret aut archiepiscopum Bremensem a consiliis suis atque a regni consortio amoveret'.

the hostility shown by some of the Saxons to the Salian rulers dated to before Henry IV's reign[152] and was not connected with the great dispute between papacy and kingship.

Henry II, although a member of a junior line of the Liudolfing royal house, had already had to accept a separate confirmation of his succession by the Saxons, and was evidently not able to secure the Ottonian demesne in Saxony without question. He built the royal palace in Goslar, where he resided frequently, as in 1019 when an important synod was held there.[153] The first two Salian rulers considered the Harz and its surroundings to be a *Königslandschaft*, a region rich in royal lands and rights and of central importance for the kingdom; it was at this time that Goslar began to flourish.[154] It was frequently visited by the rulers, who often celebrated high church feasts there.[155] Henry III founded the collegiate church of St Simeon and Jude, endowed it richly and made it into a 'prominent point on the royal itinerary' and one of the central elements in the imperial church.[156] These attempts by the kings to base their lordship on key localities reflected a general change in the structure of aristocratic lordship found elsewhere in Europe in more or less advanced form at this time.[157]

---

[152] According to T. Schmidt, 'Hildebrand, Kaiserin Agnes und Gandersheim', *NSLG*, 46/7 (1974–5), 299–309 a long pent-up resentment against the royal house did indeed come to the surface during the empress's regency.

[153] Hirsch, Pabst, and Bresslau, *Jahrbücher Heinrichs II.*, III.51 and n. 1; also *ibid.*, 213, 256, 298; Rothe, *Goslar*; Berges, 'Werla-Goslarer Reichsbezirk', 151ff., where the hostility between the rulers and the Billungs is identified as having begun under Henry II. See Leyser, 'Crisis', 417, 434ff., and 440ff. Leyser rightly points ut that the 'Investiture Contest' broke over a kingdom which had long been in a state of crisis; see also his *Rule and Conflict*, especially pp. 97ff.

[154] Bresslau, *Jahrbücher Konrads II.*, I.308 and II.361 n. 1, 382: 'the newly acquired royal palace at Goslar'; Steindorff, *Jahrbücher Heinrichs III.*, I.54.

[155] B. Heusinger, 'Servitium regis in der deutschen Kaiserzeit', *AUF*, 8 (1923), 26–159; Klewitz, 'Königtum, Hofkapelle und Domkapitel', 102–56; H. J. Rieckenberg, 'Königstraße und Königsgut in liudolfingischer und frühsalischer Zeit', *AUF*, 17 (1941), 32–154.

[156] Steindorff, *Jahrbücher Heinrichs III.*, II.99f., 116f., 356ff. For Goslar and Speyer as burial-places see Rothe, *Goslar*, 36ff.

[157] On this see Tellenbach, 'Vom karolingischen Reichsadel', 57, with reference to the building up of noble lordships by extending the autonomy originally attached to their houses and the movement towards independence of particularist circles from the tenth century which affected not only the kingdom but also the duchies; p. 68: 'Their desire for power, their striving for independent political activity led these same aristocratic circles to set themselves apart from the kingdom and to found and expand autonomous lordships directed against the king.' The premature death of Henry III meant that the other player was out of the game, and when Henry IV began to try to dam the flood the nobility had found in the papacy an ally which had declared war on the crown for quite different reasons. With similar arguments see the important recent study by Leyser, 'Crisis', 409–43.

If there had been no shortage of opposition from lay and ecclesiastical magnates in the tenth century, there was an increase under the first two Salians.[158] One only needs to recall the uprising by Duke Godfrey of Lotharingia, which kept Henry III occupied for the whole of his lifetime and found supporters not just among the lay nobility but also among the episcopate.[159] Bishop Wazo of Liège, who is well-known for having said to Henry III that he owed fidelity to the emperor but obedience to the pope, aroused Henry III's suspicions by concluding an agreement too favourable to Godfrey.[160] In the last years of Henry's reign there was a rebellion in Bavaria, where the deposed duke Conrad tried to defend his position with the help of an external power, the king of Hungary. This became still more dangerous when the rebellion was joined by Duke Welf III of Carinthia and even by the king's relative Bishop Gebhard of Regensburg.[161] Henry had just managed to suppress the rebellion when news came, shortly before his death, that the Liutizi had annihilated a Saxon army. It is said that there was widespread dissatisfaction with the emperor in those years.[162]

What this dissatisfaction meant can perhaps be seen more clearly in the history of the interregnum which followed. Henry IV was not quite six years old on his father's death. He was less than fourteen-and-a-half when he received the arms which symbolised his entry into adulthood and thus became, in name at least, capable of ruling. His political independence perhaps dates from around 1069–70.[163] The decade and a half between

---

[158] See above, pp. 51f.

[159] H. Glaesener, 'Les Démêlés de Godefroid le Barbu avec Henri III et l'évêque Wazon', *RHE*, 40 (1944–5), 141–70.

[160] Steindorff, *Jahrbücher Heinrichs III.*, II.23.   [161] See above, pp. 52–3.

[162] Hermanni Augiensis, *Chronicon*, s.a. 1053, MGH SS V.152; on these conflicts see Boshof, 'Reich in der Krise', 266–87.

[163] In many cases contemporary and slightly later writers already made Henry IV responsible for all the real or alleged mistakes or abuses of his early years, even for the schism of 1061 which began at the council of Basle when Henry was not quite eleven years old. Even recent literature occasionally contains misjudgements for similar reasons. Thus the assessment of the young Henry IV by Fenske, *Adelsopposition*, must in my opinion be rejected, e.g. his statement on p. 38 that the young king Henry IV, who ruled more and more independently from 1065, was personally responsible for the crown's loss of resources. See for a recent example Fried, 'Laienadel', 396: 'When Henry IV took the government into his own hands, created confusion by his policy towards the imperial church and pre-pared to take a firmer line with the pope as well, the archbishops of Cologne, Mainz and Salzburg as well as Otto of Northeim, Rudolf of Rheinfelden and Berthold of Zähringen soon demanded a reorientation of the policy towards Rome.' That was in Tribur in January 1066, at a time when the king was fifteen years and two months old and had ruled, since his assumption of the weapons of manhood on 29 March 1065 at the age of less than fourteen and a half, for nine months! Can the boy really have done so much damage in so short a time, and was the kingdom really in a flourishing condition before then?

1056 and 1070 must have been a period of rapid decline in royal reputation and royal power. It is instructive to compare the minorities of Otto III and Henry IV. In the years after 983 also a great part of the nobility and the episcopate were disloyal to the young elected ruler. Henry the Quarrelsome gained many adherents, though it should be noted that he was of royal blood. But a loyalist party soon formed under the skilled leadership of Archbishop Willigis of Mainz and the Saxon duke Bernard.[164] The empresses Adelheid and Theophanu were competent politicians with a high reputation. Thus Otto III's kingship was established without severe disturbance of the kingdom. In Henry IV's case, Pope Victor II seems to have kept faithfully his promise to Henry III to look after the young king for the short period for which he survived the emperor. Only cautious judgements are possible about the four-and-a-half years' regency under the empress Agnes which followed. The court routine continued: the royal itineration; the public celebration of high church feasts; the granting of privileges. The empress seems not to have been involved in the disputes among princes such as those between Archbishop Adalbert of Bremen and the Billungs,[165] or between Archbishop Anno of Cologne and the Rhenish count palatine, Henry.[166] On the other hand she probably did play a significant part in the appointment of Rudolf of Rheinfelden as duke of Suabia in 1057.[167] He may already have been betrothed to the princess Mathilda, whom he married at the end of 1059. She also played a part in the decision to give a refuge to her other daughter Judith and her husband, the exiled king Solomon of Hungary. It is not known whether she had doubts about having Cadalus of Parma elected as Honorius II against Alexander II, but it is not likely that she did. About the life led by the young king at her court and the upbringing he received one can only speculate; most of what is reported is tendentious gossip.[168] What tells most heavily against her reputation and

---

[164] See above, pp. 54f.

[165] Meyer von Knonau, *Jahrbücher Heinrichs IV.*, 1.157ff.

[166] Jenal, *Anno vol Köln*, 110ff. For our purposes the statement in n. 18 on p. 141 is particularly important: 'The whole thing looks by contrast more like a dispute aimed at pursuing territorial interests.' On Jenal's book see R. Schieffer, 'Neue Literatur über Anno von Köln', *Rheinische Vierteljahresblätter*, 40 (1976), 255.

[167] Meyer von Knonau, *Jahrbücher Heinrichs IV.*, 1.48, 168. Mathilda died only a year later. Rudolf's second marriage – its date is uncertain – was with Adelheid, the sister of Queen Bertha (*ibid.*, 567 n. 61), whom he repudiated in 1069, alleging infidelity. After she had cleared herself before Alexander II (Meyer von Knonau, *Jahrbücher Heinrichs IV.*, II.27) he is said to have been reconciled with her.

[168] See above, pp. 159f.; the fact that Paul of Bernried's partisanship was unbounded is shown by his accusation that Henry IV was responsible for the erection of Cadalus of

her abilities as a regent was the *coup d'état* of Kaiserswerth: the fact that it could be attempted at all; the feeble way in which she tolerated it afterwards; and the absence of any opposition from lay and ecclesiastical magnates. The prestige of the crown must have been low indeed if it was possible for Archbishop Anno of Cologne and his fellow-conspirators to snatch the king and the sacred royal insignia with cunning and brutality without meeting any resistance to speak of![169] The leap into the Rhine by the young king (he was eleven years and four months old) is the first independent act of his that we know of. Was it a panic fear of an attempted assassination which drove him to it, or a sense of offended royal majesty? Only one man seems to have shown his contempt for Anno, the empress's former adviser, Bishop Henry of Augsburg. When the archbishop of Cologne came to Augsburg with the court in the October following the disgraceful scene at Kaiserswerth, evidently with the intention of coming to terms with Henry, the latter left his episcopal city and took refuge in Regensburg.[170]

After Kaiserswerth it became apparent just how unrestrainedly the individual magnates sought to build up their own lordships. There was no one willing or able to check this; the instance which could build up centres of lordship on which the kingdom's reputation rested and through which the kingdom's government could be carried out had effectively

Parma as antipope, *Vita Gregorii VII* c. 61, p. 567. At the time the boy was two weeks off his eleventh birthday. In spite of this, Vollrath, 'Kaisertum und Patriziat', 43, still says that Henry had elected Cadalus in his capacity as *patricius*. Still more astonishing is her statement about his behaviour after he had come of age: 'he confined himself to insisting from a distance on his rights as determined by the patriciate and "royal paragraph" of the papal election decree'; all this was previously unknown.

[169] Everything which has been said about the shortcomings of his education has been invented. Particularly rash is the statement by Oediger, *Bistum Köln*, 117: 'In one respect, perhaps the most important respect, the conspirators of Kaiserswerth had no success. King Henry was no longer educable.' Oediger, like the rest of us, knows almost nothing about the education and educability of the boy, who was eleven years and four months old at the time of his abduction. Chuno, the *minister et nutritor regis* (*Annales Altahenses s.a.* 1069, p. 76), *serviens regis* (MGH Dipl. Henry IV., no. 21 [1057]), *nostre iuventutis pedissequus* and husband of the *nobilis femina* Mathilda (*ibid.*, no. 137, [1064]), might have been able to tell us, as might the young Liutpold of Merseburg and his brothers Berthold and Arnold. For Liutpold, who died after an unfortunate fall, his royal friend arranged a solemn burial (*ibid.*, no. 243 [1071]). What could the little king have learned after Kaiserswerth from people of the stamp of the archbishop? Faithlessness, brutality, and greed? On Anno's cruelty see Lück, 'Anno', 21.

[170] *Annales Augustani s.a.* 1062, MGH SS III.127.

ceased to exist.[171] It is probably a reasonable assumption that royal rights in Saxony now also lay defenceless and were either diminished or completely alienated. We hear much gossip about Henry IV, but we have no reliable information about independent actions until 1069, when with the thoughtlessness of youth he expressed a wish to be rid of his newly wedded wife, though he treated her nobly and did not reproach her with anything; he also had to pronounce on the affair of Bishop Charles of Constance, which he did with dignity.[172]

At the time of the dangerous Saxon uprising of 1073 the young king had only had a few years' experience of acting and planning independently. In this brief span, according to the bitterly hostile depictions written after the civil war which followed, he is supposed to have deprived the Saxons of their ancient rights, to have established a cruel and exploitative lordship, and to have built numerous castles.[173] It is more probable that he made attempts to consolidate the imperial territory around Goslar, following the example of his father and grandfather.[174] This necessarily entailed the recuperation of old royal rights and

---

[171] Deér, *Papsttum*, 96, rightly speaks of the corruption and impotence of the regency government; Fried, 'Laienadel', thinks that the princes acted in the interests of the kingdom in 1066. I cannot follow him here, any more than in his theory that the nobility sought a legitimacy from the pope which was not derived from the king (p. 398). It should also be noted that 'the nobility' was not a monolithic entity with unitary political intentions. The miserable behaviour of the episcopate between 1068 and 1076 even leads me to question the claim made by Fleckenstein, 'Heinrich IV.', 224, that Henry III succeeded in surrounding himself with an episcopate of high quality: 'Henry could indeed see his bishops as the most reliable supporters of his rule.'

[172] See above, pp. 179 and 201.

[173] Lampert, *Annales*, s.a. 1073, p. 151; *Brunos Buch vom Sachsenkrieg*, c. 25, p. 28f, with the speech by Otto of Nordheim; *Annales Altahenses*, s.a. 1073, p. 84f.

[174] K. Jordan, 'Goslar und das Reich im 12. Jahrhundert', *Niedersächsisches Jahrbuch für Landesgeschichte*, 35 (1963), 50ff.; S. Wilke, *Das Goslarer Reichsgebiet und seine Beziehungen zu den territorialen Nachbargewalten* (Göttingen 1970), 20, acknowledges the importance of the palace of Goslar for Conrad II and Henry III but rejects the theory that they had already begun to set up a new kind of royal region based on Goslar, as Henry IV wanted to do later. Nevertheless, she concedes on pp. 27f. that Saxon ethnic separatism probably revived during the minority of Henry IV and that the king was the most threatened by this and had to defend himself against it. Nitschke, 'Ziele Heinrichs IV.', 59ff., exaggerates the novelty of Henry IV's policies, which allegedly had as their model not those of his father but those of the 'Normans' and of Adalbert of Bremen. But Henry can only be understood in the context of the general changes in forms of government in Europe between the tenth and the twelfth centuries. The argument that Henry IV never claimed for himself a sacral position like that of the Ottonians and hence could not have lost it (p. 63) I find unacceptable. 'The new rulers, interested in subjects and territories, no longer referred to the religiously based characteristics of their predecessors' (p. 56); his other bold hypotheses are in my view also unconvincing.

possessions unlawfully alienated during the regency as well as attempts to acquire new ones. This was bound to irritate those affected, who in turn began to stir up the lower orders. It turns out that there were only six of the castles which were supposedly so numerous and which afflicted the people so severely, and it is far from clear whether these were rebuilt or newly erected.[175] The attempt to win back the power-base which his ancestors had enjoyed provoked unexpectedly fierce resistance. The king's position became so dangerous that he had to flee from Goslar to the Harzburg. When this too was surrounded and besieged he could take refuge only in flight. From that point on the Saxon wars broke out again and again. Both sides enjoyed periods of good fortune, but the net effect was that the Salians lost control of this *Königslandschaft*.[176]

Following his flight from the Harzburg the king hoped for assistance from the lay and ecclesiastical magnates. These, however, refused to take part in an immediate attack on Saxony; they demanded negotiations and sought to postpone decisions. Henry, whom the Saxon revolts had apparently surprised and frightened, rightly saw his position as seriously endangered. He left the Harzburg on 11 August, and already on 18 August he had to learn at an assembly in Cappel near Hersfeld that the magnates would not support him.[177] It was in August or September 1073 that he wrote his famous humble letter to Gregory VII.[178] It has been suggested, probably correctly, that Duke Rudolf of Suabia had a hand in this.[179] He, the king's brother-in-law twice over and the future antiking, was with

---

[175] That was already worked out by Meyer von Knonau, *Jahrbücher Heinrichs IV*. 2, Appendix 2; see Kost, *Östliches Niedersachsen*, 18. According to Berges, 'Werla-Goslarer Reichsbezirk', 141, Henry IV's efforts went well beyond a mere revindication of imperial territory.

[176] The map of Henry's itinerary in Brühl, *Fodrum, Gistum, Servitium Regis*, is particularly revealing; Henry stayed thirty-two times in Goslar up to 1076, then never again before his death in 1106.

[177] On Cappel near Hersfeld see Meyer von Knonau, *Jahrbücher Henirichs IV*., ii.257. The conflicts between Henry and the ecclesiastical and lay magnates are often said to have had their roots in differences over 'church reform'. This is only possible if one unthinkingly accepts the standard clichés about church reform and fails to distinguish properly between monastic and church reform. Anno of Cologne can perhaps be described as a monastic reformer, but one can hardly say of him that he was 'at all times a supporter of church reform' as does T. Schieffer, 'Anno als Erzbischof', *Monumenta Annonis* (Cologne 1975), 26. In contrast to J. Vogel, 'Rudolf von Rheinfelden', 17, I do not think it likely that Anno, Siegfried of Mainz, and Rudolf of Rheinfelden 'came into conflict with the king because of their ideas and policies of reform', especially at such an early date (around 1070); I think it impossible that they did so.

[178] *Registrum* I 29a.

[179] Meyer von Knonau, *Jahrbücher Heinrichs IV*., ii.270 and n. 142.

the king at the time the letter was sent, and he was in contact with
Gregory VII. The tensions between king and pope, in particular over the
king's contacts with the excommunicated counsellors, must have lowered
the king's reputation with many of the princes. Hence it is understandable
that Henry, after the experiences of the weeks immediately preceding,
should have tried by giving way to take off the pressure on at least one of
his fronts.[180] He sought to end the conflict begun in Alexander II's
pontificate by yielding to papal wishes in the Milanese affairs, and he
humbled himself in an unconditional and curiously exaggerated confession of guilt.[181] It cannot be determined now how sincerely he, who
had grown up in an atmosphere of insincerity, meant all that he said. The
whole of his reign was marked by his attempts to defend the power and
dignity of his kingship with all the means at his disposal against all
comers; we shall see shortly how he drew in doing this on the sources of
tradition and faith.

The phases of the conflict

Gregory's pontificate can be easily divided into sections marked by
changes in the relations between the pope and the German king. This
produces four periods: the early years from the pope's accession up to the
beginnings of the conflict in January and February 1076; the following
eleven months up to Henry's submission at Canossa; the period between
Canossa and the second excommunication and deposition of Henry IV
(2 February 1080); and the years of schism up to Gregory's death in
Salerno (25 May 1085). During the first two periods Gregory seems to
have been able to develop his ideas of the government of the church by
the pope and to put them into practice in spite of opposition. After
Canossa and the election of a German antiking he was no longer able to
impose his will on the situation. He continued to maintain his principles
uncompromisingly but his political and ecclesiastical power in Germany

---

[180] Giese, *Stamm der Sachsen*, 150, says of the revolt of 1073 that the rebellion merged with
the so-called 'investiture contest', a statement which is true only of the period which
followed. He rightly terms the alliance between the Saxons and the ecclesiastical
opponents of Henry IV a marriage of convenience.

[181] Z. N. Brooke, 'Lay Investiture', 291, also explains Henry's giving way by his difficulties
with the Saxons; C. Schneider, *Sacerdotium*, 49ff., thinks that Henry IV was already
showing signs of a change of heart and of a desire to be reconciled with the pope at the
Whitsun assembly in Augsburg. He bases his argument among other things on the
addition of the word *umillimus* to the dating-clause of six diplomata of this time. But
he also (pp. 65ff.) acknowledges the importance of the crisis in Saxony for Henry's
decisions; see Erdmann and von Gladiß, 'Gottschalk', 131.

and Italy crumbled. His death was not a decisive event in the history of the church.

After Gregory had received Henry's humble letter he wrote to the Milanese leader Erlembald that the king had sent him words full of sweetness and obedience of a kind which neither he himself nor any of his predecessors had received, so far as he could remember (I 25). Gregory must have been not a little surprised by the letter, especially since all that he had heard of or experienced from the young king would not have led him to suppose that Henry was a particularly significant force either for good or for evil. Presumably he hoped for Henry's willingness to compromise on the important issues, in particular the Milanese question and the related matter of communion with the excommunicated counsellors, though he may have had his doubts. The king was indeed absolved after Easter 1074 by papal legates in Nürnberg; he did penance and received absolution for his 'disobedience'. The counsellors may have been absolved at the same time.[182] At the end of the year Gregory seems to have been reasonably confident about the king. He asked him to send legates to the next Lenten synod to settle the Milanese affair – it is noteworthy that this had still not been resolved – and reported that 50,000 warriors were preparing to cross the sea under his (Gregory's) leadership, with the aim of aiding the Christians in the East, ending the schism in the church and journeying to the Holy Sepulchre.[183] During his absence he was entrusting the Roman church to the king, who should guard her and her honour as if she were his own mother. In spite of all his continuing worries and doubts, Gregory was perhaps at his most optimistic in 1074. In that year and early in the year 1075 he reckoned with open or concealed resistance more from the episcopate than from the royal court.

The crisis which the Saxon rebellion had meant for Henry had deepened after he had been driven from Goslar and the Harzburg. His loyal followers, Liemar of Bremen and Benno of Osnabrück, had been forced to leave their bishoprics. No help was to be expected from many of the ecclesiastical and lay magnates. Archbishops Anno of Cologne and Siegfried of Mainz vacillated between the parties. An attempt by Gregory to have his legates arbitrate in the dispute (I 39) was unsuccessful. The Saxons besieged and destroyed several royal castles. Henry was forced to give up the Lüneburg, which he had occupied, and to release Duke Magnus Billung, whom he held as a hostage, in order to rescue the loyal

---

[182] Similarly Fleckenstein, 'Heinrich IV.', 231; for Gregory's firm and comparatively optimistic mood in his early years see C. Schneider, *Sacerdotium* 42ff. and 86ff.

[183] *Registrum* II 30 and 31, pp. 163ff.; for Gregory's plans for the Orient see Erdmann, *Entstehung*, 149ff.; Goez, 'Erhebung', 124, calls the letter naive.

garrison of the Harzburg. He had to promise to raze a number of his castles. He was able to hold an assembly once more at Goslar but he felt so unsafe there that he retired to Worms. Shortly after that, in March 1074, the Harzburg was completely destroyed; its buildings had survived the previous destruction of the fortifications. Even the churches and altars were burnt and the graves of the members of the royal family were desecrated. Contemporaries ascribed these outrages to the anger of the common people in order to exonerate the role played by the ecclesiastical and lay magnates, a version which has been accepted up to the present. A letter of Archbishop Werner of Magdeburg to his colleague Siegfried of Mainz, written at the end of 1074 or the beginning of 1075, shows that even then the Saxons reckoned with a new attack by the king.[184] Both he and other magnates repeatedly offered to settle the matter before a court. In the course of 1074 Henry was able to consolidate his power and win more and more support. In the summer of 1075 he was able to defeat the Saxons decisively at a battle on the Unstrut (9 June). Demoralisation and division among the Saxons enhanced the effects of the defeat; at the end of October the Saxons submitted and most of their leaders were taken into custody as hostages.

Henry's successes and the laborious restoration of his royal authority inevitably if gradually affected his relations with the pope. We have already seen that the Milanese question was still not settled at the end of 1074, in other words that the king had been able to delay matters. It was this which led to the repeat of the threat of excommunication against five of the king's counsellors at the Lenten synod in 1075, allegedly because they had advised the sale of churches, something about which we otherwise know nothing. Gregory's letters of 1075 which concern the king are full of contradictions. It must have pleased him that Henry had dropped Bishop Hermann of Bamberg, who had been accused of simony. On 20 July he instructed the king to find a new bishop with the advice of devout men. In this letter (III 3) he even managed to praise the king for his resistance to simonists and his zeal for enforcing clerical chastity. At about this time Henry had sent three nobles, Radbod, Adelprecht, and Gottschalk (III 10) to the pope as ambassadors bearing a message in which the king showed his willingness to reach an agreement (III 9). Gregory's letter to Henry of September 1075 contained, besides restrained congratulations on his victory over the Saxons and renewed advice on the appointment to Bamberg, a declaration of the pope's willingness to accept

---

[184] *Brunos Buch vom Sachsenkrieg* c. 42, p. 41 and n. 1; K. Heidrich, 'Die Datierung der Briefe in Brunos Sachsenkrieg, *NA*, 30 (1905), 117.

the king as brother and son and to give him assistance, though this was coupled with the condition that the king should not refuse to listen to warnings for the good of his soul (III 7). In a letter to the margravines of Tuscany sent almost at the same time, which had a copy of Henry's letter of July (III 9) attached to it, Gregory showed more annoyance and mistrust: he even expressed the fear that the king did not actually wish to reach a peace settlement (III 5). It is very noteworthy that the pope complained about the breach of the discretion which had been promised; we must assume that there were secret contacts and hence that we cannot just reconstruct events from those letters which have survived, which enjoyed wide circulation. It seems likely that the expressions of friendliness of 1075, especially after the counsellors had been excommunicated, represented diplomatic and tactical attempts to reach a reconciliation in spite of everything; they can scarcely be interpreted as showing that Gregory thought that one could be reached without new conflicts.[185] It was only after the breach at the beginning of 1076 that Gregory referred to Henry IV in wholly negative fashion (*EC* 14), speaking of his depravity and his criminal acts. Had he restrained himself before for diplomatic reasons? It seems plausible to suppose that his opinions were influenced by contacts with Henry's enemies, starting with Anno of Cologne and his nephew Burchard of Halberstadt.

In the autumn of 1075 the tensions between Gregory, the German episcopate, and Henry IV grew rapidly. At the beginning of September the pope had expressed to Siegfried of Mainz his dissatisfaction over the laxity of the German episcopate (III 4) and renewed his demands for a synod to be held to deal with simony and clerical incelibacy. The archbishop did not dare to refuse the pope his obedience, but in October met with the outraged resistance of his clergy, and drew back. According to Lampert of Hersfeld he decided to leave the matter to the pope, who had brought it up so often without profit.[186]

At the same time the conflict over the church of Milan reached its height. The king retracted the half-promises he had made previously, sent a legation to Italy, and in September or October appointed the cleric Thedald as new archbishop of Milan at the request of the anti-Patarene party. He presumably thought that he could get away with this after his victory over the Saxons. Besides the Milanese appointment he also presumed to name new bishops in Fermo and Spoleto.[187] Understandably,

[185] See above, pp. 231f.
[186] Lampert, *Annales*, s.a. 1075, p. 226f.
[187] Meyer von Knonau, *Jahrbücher Heinrichs IV.*, II.576, n. 165.

Gregory took this intervention in Italy very badly, and reacted with threats. Disputes with distant kings could be treated in a relaxed and unhurried manner, but in Italy the core of his political and ecclesiastical reputation was at stake.

The famous and momentous letter of 8 December 1075 (III 10) showed a new sharpness of tone. The formula of apostolic blessing was given only on condition that Henry bore himself as befitting a Christian king, a qualification justified by Henry's having communicated with excommunicates, 'as it is said'.[188] Henry was further accused of having shown himself recalcitrant in matters which were of the greatest benefit to *ecclesiastica religio* and disobedient in his attitude and in his actions to apostolic and canonical commands, in contrast to his humble and obedient letters. Gregory came immediately to the point: quite apart from anything else, Henry's interventions in Milan, Fermo, and Spoleto had earned such condemnation. It must be stressed that even here there was no explicit reference to the king's right of investiture, though the qualification 'in so far as a church can be conferred by human hand at all' was intended to be a fundamental statement of principle, and the accusation that Henry had given the bishoprics to persons completely unknown to the pope was equally programmatic. There then follows a long passage in which obedience to God and St Peter are identified with compliance with papal instructions: *veluti si ab ore ipsius apostoli accepisset* (as if he had accepted them from the mouth of the apostle himself). The decisions of the last Lenten synod were also stressed. These were described as neither new nor Gregory's own invention; they were intended simply to eliminate error and restore the first and only rule of ecclesiastical order. Gregory offered to discuss with the king's representatives ways and means by which changes in a depraved custom (*prave consuetudinis mutatio*) could be made without too much hardship. He concluded with brutal harshness by reminding Henry of what had happened to Saul, who had failed to observe the injunctions of the prophet, and of the grace which had been shown to King David, who had humbled himself. At the end of the letter there is a reference to secret messages which the pope had transmitted through the three royal legates who had brought

---

[188] It must be stressed that Gregory makes the accusation concerning the excommunicated counsellors only with reservations: 'excommunicatis communionem tuam scienter exhibere diceris. Quod si verum est . . . '. Presumably Gregory had long known that the counsellors were still at the court. His cautious way of expressing himself was intended to leave room for further negotiations with the king. The sharpness of the letter in other respects is characterised by Paul of Bernried, *Vita Gregorii VII.*, c. 65, p. 510.

the letter back to Germany. These will have contained imperious threats, though they probably did not go as far as Gregory himself claimed in a letter to his German supporters of May or June 1076 (*EC* 14).[189]

The letter and its accompanying messages turned into an open breach the conflict which had smouldered from Alexander II's time between the papacy on the one hand and the royal court and German episcopate on the other hand. Paul of Bernried, Gregory's biographer, rightly wrote of *acriores litterae*. Henry summoned an assembly to Worms for 24 January 1076 – at the request of the magnates of the kingdom, as he explicitly stated.[190] The decisions reached there were communicated to the pope in the two famous letters from the king and the bishops. These did not spend much time on the tensions and disagreements of the months which had immediately gone before; rather, they criticised the pope's earlier actions. It was clear that it was no longer a matter of misunderstandings which could be cleared up, of merely coincidentally arising differences or of groundless enmity. It was a question of fundamentals. Historians have taken too little notice of the repeated declarations in Henry's letter that he had held himself back up until then,[191] which implies that he had long been aware of what was at stake. He had, he wrote, obeyed the pope in all things, much to the displeasure of his magnates. He had borne with patience, which the pope had misinterpreted as cowardice, everything that the latter had done to him. Three specific charges were made: the pope had robbed him of his hereditary dignity (probably a reference to the Roman patriciate); he had sought to rob him of the kingdom of Italy through evil machinations; and contrary to divine and human law he had afflicted the venerable bishops, the king's dearest companions, with overbearing insults and bitter jibes, as they themselves had testified. The bishops also did not go into details. They went to the heart of the matter as they saw it: Gregory had tried as far as possible to deprive the bishops of their power, which had been conferred on them by God through the Holy Ghost, in particular through consecration. 'Who is not amazed at the outrageous manner in which you have usurped to yourself a new and inappropriate kind of power by

---

[189] Meyer von Knonau, *Jahrbücher Heinrichs IV.*, II.579 and p. 699 n. 176. On Saul and Samuel see Arquillière, *Saint Grégoire VII*, 234f.

[190] 'Generalem conventum omnium regni primatum ipsis supplicantibus habui'; Erdmann, *Briefe Heinrichs IV.*, nos. 11, 14. According to Bonizo, *De damnatione.* ep. III, MGH LdL II.49f., the bishops advised the king to anticipate the expected excommunication.

[191] 'Tibique in omnibus magna fidelium nostrorum indignatione obedirem.'

destroying the rights which pertain to the whole brotherhood of the episcopate?'[192]

Eckhard Müller-Mertens had offered important new insights into the growing tensions of the year 1075.[193] In his view the pope intended not just to take away the kingdom of Italy from the king, as Henry complained, but also by the repeated and underlined use of the term *regnum Teutonicum* for the part of Henry's realm north of the Alps to deprive it of its traditional 'imperial' character: 'The concept of a *rex Teutonicorum* was used to challenge Henry's claim to be an imperial king and an emperor before coronation and by calling him king of the Germans to set him on the same level as the king of the Hungarians.' It was a 'reduction which Gregory practised and articulated by defining Henry IV as *rex Teutonicorum*': 'he wanted to reduce him to the level of a *rex terrenus* and a king of the Germans'. It had been frequently observed before that that Gregory saw the *mundus Christianus* as divided into equal kingdoms. A king, such as the king of Hungary, was in his opinion reduced to the status of a *regulus* should he accept his kingdom as a fief from another king. Robert Guiscard took on Gregory's point of view when he rejected Henry's offer to let him hold his conquests in southern Italy as a fief on the grounds that he could only do so from the vicar of the prince of the apostles, since he held his land from the All-Highest.[194] Admittedly, it is improbable that Henry IV and his advisers fully grasped the distinctly secular political strategy employed by Gregory to establish the pope's unique position – which was normally understood in a religious sense – in practice in the world. But it could no longer be doubted that he wished to use increasingly harsh measures to force the king to obey and to submit.[195]

It is characteristic that at the Lenten synod of 1076 Gregory did not answer any of the accusations or claims made at Worms. He did not even give reasons for his decisions in the cases of the bishops, except for the

---

[192] MGH BDK v.48, no. 20; these statements made at Worms show that, as Fuhrmann, 'Gregor VII.', 160, acutely observes, Gregory's opponents sometimes understood the pope better than his fellow-travelling supporters. However, Fuhrmann, *Deutsche Geschichte*, 102, also thinks that Henry IV hardly appreciated the spitirual depth of reform; similarly E. Werner, *Zwischen Canossa und Worms*, 67.

[193] Müller-Mertens, *Regnum Teutonicum*. See the reviews by H. Wolfram, *MIÖG*, 80 (1972), 416ff.; H. Krause, *ZRGGA*, 90 (1973), 296ff.; H. Beumann, 'Regnum Teutonicum und rex Teutonicorum in ottonischer und salischer Zeit', *AKG*, 55 (1973), 215ff.; F. Graus, *BDLG*, 110 (1974), 608ff.

[194] See below, pp. 331–2, and the literature cited there, especially *Registrum* III 15, pp. 276–7.

[195] Szabó-Bechstein, 'Libertas', 162: 'This stress on the role of the ruler in the scheme of salvation makes it evident that it had become clear to Henry IV and his entourage in the meantime just where the papal demands were really leading.'

judgement against Siegfried of Mainz, who had presided over the Worms
assembly and had attempted to divide the bishops and abbots of the
German kingdom from the holy Roman church, their spiritual mother.
The sentence on the king began its justification with a simple reference to
the pope's power to bind and to loose; only in a relative clause did
Gregory say of Henry 'who in unheard of pride has raised himself against
Your [St Peter's] church'. The only specific charge was that of communion with excommunicates, but even this was turned into an issue of
fundamental religious principle by representing it as rebellion against God
(III 10a). Gregory derived from his power of binding and loosing not only
the right to excommunicate the king, which followed from his power to
impose penances and to absolve penitents, but also the right to depose him
and to release his subjects from their oaths of obedience. This last point
was the most extreme demonstration of Gregory's conviction that his
actions were merely an expression of the will of God.

A comparison of the actions and statements of the two parties shows
that Gregory's were clearly superior both in their political judgement and
assessment of the situation and in their theological clarity and stylistic
brilliance. But it is also apparent that Henry IV, his advisers, and the
majority of the episcopate had grasped what was at stake: a fundamental
change in the relationship between pope and bishops and the strict subordination of the king to a pope who claimed to be the incorporation of
the will of God and of St Peter.

The events of 1075–6 were the consequence of the idea of a church
ruled centralistically by the pope, to whom all its members both lay and
ecclesiastic owed obedience, as this had evolved from around the middle
of the century. The behaviour of Henry IV and of the German bishops
was a demonstration of how conscious and deeply rooted was the resistance offered by traditional religious conceptions. It was to have
decisive influence on the history of the church for the long period which
followed, leading as it did to a redefinition and intensification of the
tension between the two highest powers within the church.[196]

The king's (and the German episcopate's) unheard-of measures and the
no less extreme reaction by the pope evidently did not at first have the
sensational effect one might have supposed. Gregory was at the time

---

[196] *Contra*, Nitschke, 'Wirksamkeit Gottes', 168, who says simply: 'The struggle between
Gregory and Henry IV was Henry's fault'; see by contrast the telling remarks of
Schneider, *Prophetisches Sacerdotium*, 157ff., about the 'literary and theological defence of
Henry IV against the pope's actions grounded on the sacramental basis of kingship',
which as he points out has been less taken note of by scholars than the king's spectacular
journey to Canossa and the critical negotiations in Tribur and Oppenheim in October
1076.

supported by the Romans, but the majority of the Italian episcopate had long been cool and distant. An assembly in Piacenza at Easter 1076 even excommunicated Gregory.[197] Voices of doubt and concern must have reached Gregory from Germany, and he answered them at length in a letter of May or June 1076.[198] Gregory had already divided the German bishops into two groups at the Lenten synod depending on whether they had given their consent to the schism voluntarily or not. Even those who had were only to be suspended should they continue in their rebellion; the others were given a date by which they were to show their repentance. In other words, Gregory was willing to meet everyone halfway. It is not possible to assess what contacts he had with most of them. What did arouse attention was a letter from Gregory in April (III 12) to Archbishop Udo of Trier and Bishops Dietrich of Verdun and Hermann of Metz, in which he enjoined them to make amends and also to persuade Pibo of Toul to do the same.

Pibo, who had been charged with publicly excommunicating Gregory at the royal court at Easter, avoided the dangerous situation by flight, in which he was joined by Dietrich of Verdun. Neither wished to break with the king, any more than did Udo of Trier. Udo journeyed to Rome, where he received absolution and even permission to speak with the excommunicate king. Two royal assemblies held at Worms and Mainz in May and June respectively were still frequented by an impressive number of bishops and magnates; Hildebrand's excommunication was repeated there. But in the course of the summer Henry's position deteriorated rapidly. Godfrey of Lower Lotharingia, his close ally, had been murdered in the winter and his successor was tied down by local feuds. The dukes of Bavaria and Saxony had long stood in opposition to the king, as had Archbishop Gebhard of Salzburg, Patriarch Sigehard of Aquileia, and Bishops Altmann of Passau, Adalbero of Würzburg, Adalbert of Worms, and Hermann of Metz. The last-named had released Saxon captives who had been entrusted to him, an open breach of his oath of fidelity. Other Saxons, such as Burchard of Halberstadt, were also released or able to escape. The king hoped to secure useful intermediaries by releasing high-ranking Saxon hostages such as Archbishop Werner of Magdeburg or Bishops Benno of Meissen and Werner of Merseburg, but in this he was disappointed. An expedition which the king had led against the Saxons with the support of Duke Vratislav of Bohemia failed. Equally important was the defection of Otto of Northeim, who had been entrusted with

---

[197] Meyer von Knonau, *Jahrbücher Heinrichs IV.*, II.628f.; J. Vogel, *Gregor VII. und Heinrich IV.*, 20ff.; see also p. 103 on the situation in 1078.
[198] *EC* 14, pp. 535ff.

representing the king in Saxony. By the autumn of 1076 the greater part of the Saxons were as hostile and threatening to the king as they had been before his victory at the Unstrut.[199] In September the dukes of Bavaria and Saxony had a meeting in Worms with Bishops Adalbero of Würzburg, Adalbert of Worms, and Altmann of Passau.[200] These had been opponents of the king long before his conflict with the pope. They were joined by Bishop Otto of Constance. At the meeting there were discussions about the election of another king, as there had already been earlier, and a full-scale assembly was fixed for mid October in Tribur. It was noteworthy that a great number of the king's Saxon enemies also appeared there, led by Otto of Northeim to general rejoicing.

Gregory VII had showed intelligence and circumspection in his actions following the Lenten synod of February. The year, which had begun so badly, seemed to reveal him at the height of his powers as a politician, a religious leader, and a man. There is a fair number of letters to German and Milanese recipients from this period which show how the pope defended his cause and what aims he pursued. He showed clearly and repeatedly that he was prepared to forgive those who had deserted him, provided that they did penance and above all were prepared to show obedience in the future. He tried to justify the steps he had taken, in particular the excommunication of the king. Although he wrote (and probably spoke) more openly than before about the king's supposedly evil character, he also stressed again and again his own desire for peace, his willingness to receive the king and his supporters back into communion and to forgive them if they were only willing to do penance, to obey, and to give guarantees for their future behaviour. The argument that the king should not defend evil customs contrary to the liberty of the church is repeated, a reference perhaps to the need for canonical elections as formerly understood or even perhaps an attack on the practice of investing bishops before their consecration.[201] Noteworthy is the fact that within a few days he repeatedly reserved to himself the absolution of the king from excommunication; evidently he was worried that bishops might, either in good faith or in bad, do something for which only the

---

[199] Giese, *Stamm der Sachsen*, 168, thinks that Henry 'would certainly have been well-advised' if he had followed Otto of Northeim's demand that he should capitulate. He might thus have 'been able to prevent the setting up of an anti-king'. But these are all *ex post facto* speculations. Henry wanted to conciliate the pope, not the Saxons.

[200] Lampert, *Annales*, *s.a.* 1076, p. 273; their decision was communicated to the princes of all the duchies, and is supposed to have led many to desert Henry.

[201] *Registrum* IV 3: 'Non inflatus spiritu elationis consuetudines superbiae contra libertatem ecclesiarum inventas defendat, sed observet sanctorum patrum doctrinam, quam pro salute nostra eos docuit potestas divina.'

vicar of St Peter possessed the authority.[202] At stake was what he saw as an exclusive papal right. Already in early September Gregory was also saying that another king must be found should Henry not return to God. If an election should be needed, he asked to be informed of it; he would examine both election and elected and confirm the action by apostolic authority.[203] Evidently he knew of the plans of the opposition magnates; by the end of October he wrote to his supporters in Milan about the struggle against the king and the growth of the papal party in Germany.[204] He had already named Sigehard of Aquileia and Altmann of Passau as his representatives and these did indeed appear at Tribur and played a decisive role there.[205]

From late summer onwards Henry IV had been forced to realise that his power in Germany was declining. The most recent defection to the enemy camp was the leading archbishop of the kingdom, Siegfried of Mainz. Nevertheless, his support was still considerable. Many of the bishops were either his confirmed supporters or else sought to manoeuvre between the two parties.[206] He could not hope for much from the latter, but he also did not have much to fear from them. The high nobility of the duchies included countless enemies of the dukes; they were the king's supporters, as were many free men and townsmen. He thus did not have to capitulate unconditionally; he could choose whether he should risk a conflict or seek a compromise.[207] His opponents were still

---

[202] *EC* 15 (29 August); *Registrum* IV 2 (25 August); *Registrum* IV 3 (3 September).

[203] *Registrum* IV 3.

[204] *Registrum* IV 7.

[205] Sigehard, who as papal legate at Tribur was still in the camp of Henry's opponents, was in April at Pavia with Henry, following the dramatic events at Canossa, received a significant privilege there (MGH Dipl. Henry IV, no. 293) and afterwards accompanied the king to Germany. Such a prominent change of party was not common at that time.

[206] The behaviour of the German episcopate following its bold stand at Worms is remarkable. Fleckenstein, 'Heinrich IV.', 234, thinks that the king had already alienated a great part of the episcopate years before Worms. But had there not been tensions between kings and bishops long before Henry IV, which increased with the decline of royal authority during the regency? Fleckenstein also points (pp. 229, 231) to grave mistakes in the choice of bishops; but most of the bishops who took part in the events of 1076 were in office long before Henry IV can be said to have been responsible for their appointment.

[207] Henry's position at that time was the object of a spectacular controversy between Johannes Haller and Albert Brackmann. The literature dealing with this is cited in Tellenbach, 'Zwischen Worms und Canossa'. Haller's thesis, that 'the only proper description' of Henry's actions is 'capitulation, unconditional surrender' is now hardly accepted by anyone, with the exception of E. Werner, *Zwischen Canossa und Worms*, 72, who refers to Henry's desperate position. The results of the negotiations are generally

frightened, and tried to secure themselves by mutual pledges of support. Henry's basic political idea was now to divide his opponents. It is possible that he thought it more promising to try to settle with the pope than with his German enemies, as he had done in 1073. But before that he needed to reach agreement with those assembled threateningly at Tribur, who included the papal representatives. The court assembled at Oppenheim and the negotiations between the two camps lasted for several days in October 1076. Those at Tribur were divided. A radical minority had perhaps aimed at the immediate election of a new king, but even this group was probably handicapped by rivalries between Rudolf of Suabia and Otto of Northeim. The greater part of those present did not want to push things to the limit, and the papal legates were committed to reserve the final judgement to the pope. In the end the king's opponents were satisfied when the king promised that he would make amends to and obey the pope, announced this to bishops, magnates, and nobles of all ranks, and urged them to follow his example.[208] A number of sources also report that after the negotiations with Henry were over the magnates came to an agreement that they would not recognise him as king beyond February of the following year, should he continue excommunicate.[209]

The pope received the representatives of both parties shortly after the conclusion of the negotiations of Tribur and Oppenheim and took the momentous decision to travel to Germany as soon as possible. He announced this in two letters to the political community:[210] he intended to be in Mantua on 8 January (and he was indeed in Florence by the end of December), while the princes had invited Gregory to an assembly at Augsburg fixed for 2 February, at which he was to reach his decision.[211] His aim was thus not to receive the king in Italy for Henry's fulfilment of

---

seen as a compromise. I pointed in particular to the different groupings within the episcopate. See also H. Beumann, 'Tribur, Rom und Canossa', 33–60; Hlawitschka 'Zwischen Worms und Canossa', 25–45; C. Schneider, *Sacerdotium*, 185f.

[208] Erdmann, *Briefe Heinrichs IV.*, no. 14, pp. 20f.; see also Appendix B, 69; Codex Udalrici no. 53 = Jaffé, *BRG*, v.111; fundamental on the events at Tribur is the new and detailed investigation by C. Schneider, *Sacerdotium*, 171–87; see also Hlawitschka, 'Zwischen Worms und Canossa', 25ff.

[209] Meyer von Knonau, *Jahrbücher Heinrichs IV.*, II, Appendix VI, 888ff.

[210] *Registrum* IV 1 and 2; *EC* 20; see also Paul of Bernried, *Vita Gregorii Septimi Papae* c. 82, p. 523.

[211] On the thesis of H. Beumann, 'Tribut, Rom und Canossa', that an earlier date had really been envisaged for the meeting at Augsburg, which was then postponed until 2 February in the course of the negotiations with the German embassy, see the in my opinion convincing arguments by Hlawitschka, 'Zwischen Worms und Canossa'.

his promise to do penance and promise obedience, but to keep him under the pressure of excommunication until Gregory could achieve his complete submission in the presence of all parties.

The king and his advisers recognised the dangers of such a proceeding, which would have mixed the religious and political aspects of the affair and allowed the radicals to exert their influence. Henry decided to cross the Alps as quickly as possible in order to meet the pope in Italy and be restored to communion before all else. Countless attempts have been made to interpret the dramatic events of Canossa, the motives (religious, political and personal) of pope and king, the historical preconditions and consequences. None of these interpretations, in many cases contradictory, have been able to go beyond surmises. How far were Henry and his contemporaries seriously worried by the excommunication: were they really afraid for their salvation? Was the pope really concerned simply to convert and to save the sinful man in Henry, as he so often claimed? What role – subsidiary or principal – did political and tactical considerations play for the two men? Was the king's symbolic humiliation a real sacrifice or was he primarily concerned to find a way out of his impasse by doing penance?[212] It should be noted that Henry, even when he stood before the castle at Canossa with naked feet, always made his agreements with his opponents *as king*, just as he had done at Oppenheim.[213] Even in his most desperate moments he did not accept the papal sentence of deposition or the freeing of those bound to him from their oaths of obedience. And was the option of refusal really open to Gregory? Could he deny the demonstratively penitent king forgiveness and absolution? Would he not, had he refused, have struck at the roots of his own office as supreme shepherd, particularly in a world in which he had numerous sceptically or critically inclined enemies, especially in Italy? It was essentially the logical consequence of his own position that he should accept Henry's promise to follow the pope's judgement either by doing justice to his opponents

---

[212] One can discuss all these questions endlessly; they cannot be resolved from the sources, especially since this impressive act led to the formation of a rich legend. From among the more recent literature see in particular W. von den Stein, *Canossa. Heinrich IV. und die Kirche*, 2nd edn (Darmstadt 1969); Morrison, 'Canossa', 121–48; C. Schneider, *Sacerdotium*, 201ff.; R. Schieffer, 'Von Mailand nach Canossa', 333–70; Zimmermann, *Der Canossagang von 1077*; Capitani, 'Canossa', 359–81. Henry IV by no means degraded himself in Canossa by accepting the priestly power over penance, as Laudage, *Priesterbild*, 20, thinks. He repeatedly stresses that the king was termed a layman by 'reformers' (see e.g. p. 60); but with the exception of a few passages of poetic exaggeration no one had ever doubted this.

[213] MGH Const. I.115 no. 66, 114 no. 64; Jakobs, *Kirchenreform*, 27, rightly says that 'Henry's kingship was not the subject of negotiation at Canossa'.

within a period to be fixed by the pope or by granting them peace on terms set by the pope.[214]

After the events of Canossa Gregory only had the chance of making the authority of Peter's successor felt in the German quarrels; he could no longer expect to sit in judgement over an excommunicate. Henry's most determined opponents met in mid February 1077 in Ulm and fixed the date of a further assembly to be held in Forchheim for 23 March, probably already with the intention of electing a new king.[215] The pope also intended to be there, but in the end he did not come. The king himself did not return to Germany until April, by which time Rudolf of Rheinfelden had been elected as antiking in Forchheim and crowned in Mainz. Gregory's legates, the cardinal deacon Bernard and Abbot Bernard of Saint-Victor in Marseilles had appeared at the assembly and according to the later account by Paul of Bernried had tried on papal instructions to get the decision postponed, if this could be done without danger.[216] Three years later in 1080, when he again excommunicated Henry, Gregory said explicitly that Rudolf had been elected without his agreement.[217] Once the election had taken place, however, he accepted it in so far as from then on he treated Rudolf as one of two kings (see IV 23 of 31 May 1077: *utrumque regem, Heinricum atque Rodulfum commoneatis*) whose case he would investigate and decide.[218] After he himself had received the legitimate king back into the church he also allowed another to be elected in opposition to him. Convinced of his own divinely conferred fullness of power, he claimed the right to decide which of the two was held by justice to be the most suitable to govern the empire. By half recognising

---

[214] This period of the conflict has been dealt with exhaustively and often clarified by J. Vogel, *Gregor VII. und Heinrich IV.*

[215] Meyer von Knonau, *Jahrbücher Heinrichs IV.*, II.775 n. 50 and III.3f.; both in Ulm and in Forchheim only a few bishops were present, which is characteristic of the splintering within and indecision among the German episcopate.

[216] *Vita Gregorii Septimi Papae* c. 94, pp. 529f.

[217] *Registrum* VII 14a: 'sine meo consilio vobis testibus elegerunt sibi Rodulfum ducem in regem'.

[218] Robinson, 'Pope Gregory VII and Episcopal Authority', 729; J. Vogel, *Gregor VII. und Heinrich IV.*, 6 and the literature cited in n. 29. Until then there had been two kings only when an elected and consecrated king's son was seen as a successor or co-ruler. Rudolf is the first antiking in German history, symptomatic of the decline in royal authority since the time of Henry III. See Kern, *Gottesgnadentum*, 173 and n. 318 (= Appendix 19); Mitteis, *Staat*, 297; Giese, *Stamm der Sachsen*, 45, points out that the Saxons were also outraged at Gregory's recognition of two kings, at the fact that 'he did not declare unequivocally for Rudolf but continued to give Henry his title as king'; see also *ibid.*, 40, on the danger of a schism in the kingdom according to Paul of Bernried, and 50, citing Berthold, *Annales, s.a.* 1077, p. 294; *s.a.* 1078, p. 208; *s.a.* 1080, p. 314.

the newly elected king the pope went well beyond the right he claimed for himself of excommunicating a king, which was after all a purely spiritual action in traditional understanding. Since he had not explicitly annulled either the deposition or the dispensation from oaths of fidelity even after releasing Henry from excommunication he felt able to decide between the two kings, showing once again how high were the powers he claimed for himself. But if he wished to decide the case of the two kings he would have to give a hearing to the mutual accusations and denunciations of the two sides; this naturally entailed the risk that he would be dragged down into the depths of the all too human.

Henry IV and his advisers clearly recognised what the election at Forchheim meant for his kingship. For them the king was, as he had been in the centuries before, not just the highest defender of the church and of the country and the ultimate guarantor of justice. As a consecrated person he was a figure with spiritual and liturgical character who united the people entrusted to him, whatever the defects of government as it could be carried out at the time and however much the peace he enforced might be broken. Henry could accept papal judgement on the accusations made by his opponents before the election at Forchheim at most in so far as this concerned spiritual matters. He did not see it as a political decision by the pope between him and another man who also claimed to be king and was acknowledged as such by the pope. It was logical and internally consistent when Henry demanded from Gregory that he should excommunicate Rudolf. In the years between Canossa and Henry's second deposition it was clearer than at any other time that this was a clash between two irreconcilable views of the right order in a Christian world and of the powers possessed by king and pope.[219]

It is hard to assess what moved Gregory VII repeatedly to put off reaching a decision between the two German parties in the years 1077 to 1080; there is probably no certainty to be reached in the matter. His supporters, especially in Saxony, were in a difficult position and began to lose confidence in him. They did not understand his attitude. Gregory could certainly have achieved substantial concessions in ecclesiastical

---

[219] When Bruns, *Gegenkönigtum*, 26, says that Gregory wanted to reach an agreement, this cannot be denied. The same is true of Henry, but the precondition for the agreement which each desired was that the other should accept their point of view unconditionally. Bonizo of Sutri's claim that Henry's legates even threatened to have an antipope set up is accepted by J. Vogel, *Gregor VII. und Heinrich IV.*, 187f., and also in his study 'Gottschalk von Aachen', 55. Without holding this interpretation to be impossible I have doubts. Bonizo's statement is unsupported, and we do not know how the threat was phrased. It is noteworthy that Gregory never referred to such a threat. See also the reserved assessment by D. Jasper in his review, *DA*, 42 (1986), 302.

matters from Henry IV in these years had he been prepared to accept him as sole king. It was perhaps the only time when Henry might have been willing to discuss the question of investitures, though as yet neither side had really thought through what was involved.[220] But Gregory could not accept the essentially religious character of kingship, at whose core lay a sacral and liturgical character and the conviction that the king's power was immediately conferred by God. Instead he stuck to his plan of arbitrating between Henry and his German opponents, in order to establish the subordination of the king to the pope once and for all. It was only the demand by Henry and his supporters that Gregory should excommunicate Rudolf, perfectly understandable from their point of view, that led him to give up his hesitations after years of delay and excommunicate Henry once again. Here concern over Henry's growing power may also have played a role, as this threatened to make Gregory's wish to act as arbitrator irrelevant. It must probably be conceded that Gregory's attitude in the period after Canossa was risky if not doomed to failure, seen from the point of view of political calculation. It is only explicable on the assumption that the pope, who was otherwise highly flexible politically, was led by his own proudly religious self-confidence to refuse to accept compromises which threatened his fundamental conception of a comprehensive papal primacy. It was a logical consequence of this that the core of the theocratic idea of office, kingship by the grace of God, found no place in his view of the world.[221]

At the Lenten synod of 1080, on 7 March, Henry was excommunicated for the second time. Once again Gregory deprived him of royal power and released everyone from the oaths of fidelity which had been taken to

[220] If Gregory had really intended to push reform through Germany with the help of a strong king, as J. Vogel, *Gregor VII. und Heinrich IV.*, 109, thinks – concurring, F. Kempf's review in *AHP*, 21 (1983), 302 – then he could only have joined forces with Henry, not with Rudolf, in the situation at the time. But he was certainly more interested in the role of arbitrator than in 'reforms', and it was of this that the rising power of the Salian threatened to deprive him. His judgement did not depend on who was willing and able to support reforms, but on obedience. In view of the dogged tactics with which Gregory pursued his aims between 1077 and 1080 I would not speak with Fuhrmann, 'Gregor VII.', 171, of a 'three-years' standstill'.

[221] Morrison, 'Canossa', concerns himself like most other historians only with the convictions and principles for which Gregory stood, and ignores on the other hand the fact that Henry IV and his supporters also defended a position with a religious basis. The causes of the second breach between pope and king in 1080 are in my view not properly assessed by Morrison, 'Canossa', 129. Nor can I agree with what he says in *Tradition and Authority*, 393. On the gossip about Bishop Udalrich of Padua, see above, p. 174., It is not true that Henry's legates were excommunicate, nor that it was the king who had bribed the papal legates.

him. This time the reaction was swift and decisive. Immediately after
the Lenten synod, episcopal assemblies in Mainz and Bamberg issued
declarations against Hildebrand, and at the end of June a synod in Brixen,
well attended by German and Italian bishops, pronounced Gregory's
deposition. Archbishop Wibert of Ravenna was nominated as (anti)-
pope, and took the name Clement III (1080–1100).[222]

In the years after 1080 Gregory continued the effects of the decades
before in the struggle against simony – whatever that might mean – and
against clerical incontinence as well as for the 'free' election of bishops and
abbots. No new ideas are discernible, nor were his successes any greater
than before. At most there was perhaps a new decisiveness perceptible
in his attitude to bishops who had received royal investiture before
consecration; but in Gregory's time there was no real change here.[223]
Tensions between the pope and the German episcopate generally
remained latent during the period before Henry's second excommunication. No bishop lost office in this period, regardless of whether he
tended more to the pope or to the king. The only one whom one might
consider as an antibishop was Wigold of Augsburg, invested by Rudolf of
Rheinfelden.[224] Many of the Saxon bishops were on the side of the
antiking: Archbishop Werner of Magdeburg and his successor Hartwig;
Burchard of Halberstadt; Benno of Meissen; Werner of Merseburg; Eppo
and Gunther of Zeitz-Naumburg; Richbert of Verden. None lost office.
Henry did not appoint a new archbishop even in the case of Siegfried of
Mainz, who had been driven from his city by an uprising of the burghers
after crowning Rudolf. Rudolf's episcopal supporters in southern
Germany – Archbishop Gebhard of Salzburg and Bishops Adalbero of
Würzburg, Adalbert of Worms, Hermann of Metz, and Altmann of
Passau – remained without replacements for a long time, even though
they were unable to hold on to their dioceses. It was not until shortly
before Gregory's death in April 1085 that a synod at Mainz deposed two
archbishops and nine bishops (including four antibishops).[225] Several of

---

[222] On the question of when Wibert became for his party the rightful pope see Ziese,
Wibert, 55ff.; I. Heidrich, *Ravenna unter Erzbischof Wibert (1073–1106)* (Vorträge und
Forschungen, Sonderband 32, Sigmaringen 1984), 53f.
[223] See above, pp. 180–1 and 214.
[224] Tellenbach, 'Gregorianische Reform', 110f.
[225] Meyer von Knonau, *Jahrbücher Heinrichs IV.*, IV.547ff., Appendix III; J. Vogel, 'Zur
Kirchenpolitik', 164, 185; on p. 191 he says that the king saw himself compelled to
compromise with some of the bishops. But was it not rather the bishops who had to
compromise with him? C. Brühl, 'Die Sozialstruktur des deutschen Episkopats im 11.
und 12. Jahrhunderts', *MCSM*, 7 (1977), 47, calculates that there were not in fact very
many antibishops in Germany.

these submitted to Clement III and Henry IV, and a number of new bishops were nominated; it was only as late as this that the famous 'gemination' of bishops took place, and only in a small number of dioceses. At the beginning of the schism the majority of the German episcopate – about two-thirds of it – were on the side of Henry and the antipope.

What was it which moved the minority to take up a position against the king? The most prominent among them had been invested by the king and then consecrated, as tradition demanded.[226] Their attitude to simony and clerical celibacy did not distinguish them from the other bishops, as far as we know. Like the majority, they agreed with the criticism of these abuses without taking particularly energetic steps to abolish them.[227] There were a few bishops who were rather close to Gregory – Altmann of Passau, Adalbero of Würzburg, and Hermann of Metz – and these might perhaps be called 'Gregorians'.[228] But for most of them one hesitates to use the term. The Saxon bishops were by and large caught up in the uprising of their people against Henry IV and were more Saxon than 'Gregorian'.[229] Their party preference was determined to

---

[226] Adalbero of Würzburg (1045), Eppo of Naumburg (1045), Anno of Cologne (1056), Burchard II of Halberstadt (1059), Werner of Merseburg (1059), Siegfried of Mainz (1060), Gebhard of Salzburg (1060), Richbert of Verden (1060), Werner of Magdeburg (1063), Benno of Meissen (1066), Adalbert of Worms (1070). Six of these 'reform bishops', incidentally, subscribed the proclamation of the bishops against Gregory VII in 1076. The king, or his regents, who had invested these bishops, were not for that reason anti-reformers, any more than were the bishops who accepted investiture. 'Lay investiture' only became objectionable to Gregory from the mid 1070s on. What J. Vogel 'Rudolf von Rheinfelden', 1–30, has to say suffers, like so much recent work, from the use of a vague and undefined concept of reform; for criticism of this see above, pp. 157ff.

[227] Kost, *Östliches Niedersachsen*, 50, and accurately 67f., on Werner of Magdeburg's 'lack of contact' with and 'lack of interest' in the pope. He is also to be agreed with when he says (p. 170), that the Saxons were distinctly cool towards Rudolf of Rheinfelden.

[228] See Bruns, *Gegenkönigtum*, 52: 'Spiritual motives can be attributed only to the two bishops Gebhard of Salzburg and Altmann of Passau, and here only because we have no information about their secular interests'. Fundamental on the genuinely Gregorian position of a circle based on Constance is the study by Autenrieth, *Domschule* and Autenrieth, 'Bernold von Konstanz', where good reasons are given for supposing that Bernold was the author of the appendix to the *Collection in 74 Titles* which deals with the question of excommunication, crucial for the Gregorians. See also Robinson, 'Zur Arbietsweise', 101ff.: 'the circle of south German Gregorians'; 112: 'the existence of a Gregorian friendship circle of German scholars'; Robinson, 'Bible', 67: 'These writers from a South German circle'. Few indeed understood and promulgated Gregory VII's ideas as well as did the Constance clerics Bernhard, Adalbert, and Bernold. See also Weisweiler, 'Päpstliche Gewalt', 129–42.

[229] On Gregory VII's criticism of the laxity of those bishops who counted as reformers see above, pp. 172, 186, and Kost, *Östliches Niedersachsen*, 136ff.

some extent by personal or territorial motives. Burchard of Halberstadt, for instance, was a nephew of Anno of Cologne and Werner of Magdeburg, who pursued so successfully their policy of family aggrandisement.[230] Archbishop Gebhard of Salzburg, who was a consistent opponent of Henry IV, deserves particular attention. Henry seems to have sought a reconciliation with him in the autumn of 1077. There was a meeting at Regensburg at which the archbishop demanded the restitution of all the lands alienated from the church of Salzburg during the troubles and strict punishment of the 'robbers of the church'. No agreement was reached, and Gebhard, who no longer felt safe, is said to have decided on flight in the course of his journey back to Salzburg. He then lived for many years in exile, mostly in Saxony. Even he was not deposed until 1085, however, and it is noteworthy that his demands in Regensburg were for restitution of church property, not for 'church reform'.[231]

In general the king had more difficulty in dealing with his secular than with his ecclesiastical opponents. Battles and skirmishes were more frequent than was usual in the high middle ages. The royal armies generally came off worst, but the conflict was not decided on the battlefield. Besides this there were long periods of more or less peaceful coexistence; the Salian sphere of influence was much greater than that of pope and antiking. Apart from the Saxon Otto of Northeim, Welf of Bavaria and the Zähringer Berthold of Carinthia were also in the camp of the king's opponents after the election at Forchheim. At a royal assembly at Ulm in May 1077 the south German dukes were declared to have forfeited their duchies and fiefs. Liutold, a member of the Eppensteiner family, had already driven Berthold out of Carinthia; it was not until 1079 that Suabia received a new duke in the person of the Staufer, Frederick. Bavaria remained vacant until 1096, when it was returned to Welf IV after the reconciliation between his family and Henry IV. The dukes were allies of

---

[230] Anno's politics in favour of the Steusslinger family betray the politician concerned with power. Berges, 'Werla-Goslarer Reichsbezirk', 145, remarks on the clash of territorial interests between Burchard of Halberstadt and Hezilo of Hildesheim: 'all that has nothing to do with "Gregorianism" or "Antigregorianism"'. Robinson, 'Pope Gregory VII, the Princes and the Pactum', 756, accurately notes the ideological differences between Gregory and his Saxon followers, though I cannot follow him in his assessment of the Saxons' motives; see also the remarks by T. Reuter, *DA*, 38 (1982), 283.

[231] Meyer von Knonau, *Jahrbücher Heinrichs IV.*, III.167 n. 104; J. Vogel, *Gregor VII. und Heinrich IV.*, 90, thinks that a reconciliation broke down in the face of fundamental differences in ecclesiastical issues; J. Vogel, 'Rudolf von Rheinfelden', 19, deduces Gebhard's 'deep religiosity' from the foundation of the bishopric at Gurk and the monastery at Admont.

the pope, certainly, but they had their own aims, namely to consolidate and extend their power. Were they 'Gregorians'? What significance did the ecclesiastical movements of the period have for them? And were the aristocratic circles which hoped to profit from the deposition and forfeitures suffered by the dukes 'anti-Gregorians' or 'anti-reformers'? Were they advocates of simony and clerical marriage, or defenders of the royal right of investiture?

The tragedy of Gregory VII's pontificate became clearer and clearer as it drew to its end. His ideas of the pope as the representative of Christ and St Peter on earth, of a purification of the church from old corrupt customs, of eliminating royal influence on spiritual matters, did not create a great unified movement which he could lead and steer. He must have been shocked to discover that his claims to obedience were seldom challenged but frequently ignored. Ecclesiastical punishments often had little effect, especially when they were repeatedly and summarily imposed. Even expulsion from the church often had little or no effect. How many magnates, bishops, clerics, and laymen showed themselves for years to be unconcerned by excommunication, still more so after the schism broke out in 1080, when the two parties excommunicated one another!

Gregory seems to have continued in a firm belief that justice would prevail in the years after 1080. Several sources with quite different tendencies report that on the second day of the Easter feast of 1080 he prophesied that Henry would meet his doom within the year should he not do penance by the feast of Peter's Chains (1 August). It must have been a severe blow to him that it was in fact the antiking who was to die in October,[232] after he had lost in battle the hand with which he had sworn fidelity to Henry. But even then he showed no signs of discouragement. There are many signs that both pope and king held a reconciliation to be possible even at this stage, and some of their supporters worked towards one. But Henry's position in Germany gradually consolidated, and Gregory could expect no aid from that quarter. He did reach a final reconciliation with Robert Guiscard in 1080,[233] but the latter could give no real assistance as long as he was tied up by operations in the eastern Mediterranean. He sent money to Gregory's supporters in Rome, just as Henry IV's supporters were

---

[232] Meyer von Knonau, *Jahrbücher Heinrichs IV.*, III.278 n. 46 argues for the authenticity of the reports given of this prophecy by Bonizo and Sigebert of Gembloux; already in 1076 Henry IV had written to Altwin of Brixen that Gregory had threatened to deprive him of *regnum et animam* (Codex Udalrici no. 49 = Jaffé, *BRG*, v.109). Cowdrey, *Age*, 138, observes that Gregory really thought in 1080 that he could eliminate Henry.

[233] See above, p. 222 and Cowdrey, *Age*, 149.

financed by the Byzantine emperor Alexius. At the end of his pontificate Gregory had to experience the same uncertainty and threats in Rome and the papal patrimony that had afflicted so many of his predecessors and were to afflict so many of his successors. His high-flown plans and activities stood on a very shaky footing, and the trivia of local and regional politics presented continual problems. Gregory long enjoyed good relations with the Romans, but at the end, when foreign powers intervened for and against Gregory, a peace party formed in the city, while others sought to make common cause with his enemies against the pope.

Henry IV had appeared again in Italy in the spring of 1081, for the second time since his journey to Canossa. On 21 May he stood before Rome for the first time. The inhabitants still supported Gregory, and the royal army was forced to retreat in the face of the fierce summer heat. At the beginning of 1082 the king again marched on Rome, and again besieged it unsuccessfully. However, he was able to arrange a meeting with Prince Jordan of Capua in Albano, and even the cardinal abbot Desiderius of Monte Cassino came to this meeting after some toing and froing.[234] It was not until June 1083 that the Leonine city was taken, and the antipope was able to move into St Peter's, but once again the king suffered a setback. After he had retreated (again in the face of the summer heat) the garrison he had left behind was almost completely wiped out by an epidemic. Henry finally came to an agreement with the Romans shortly before Easter 1084 and was able to enter the city ceremoniously through the Porta San Giovanni. Clement III was enthroned in St Peter's on Palm Sunday, and Henry was crowned emperor on the first day of Easter (31 March).

Gregory still held out in the Castel Sant'Angelo with his supporters, but he was threatened by further defections. Even thirteen of the cardinal priests and deacons renounced their allegiance.[235] When his position seemed hopeless the news came that Robert Guiscard was approaching the city in force. It was Abbot Desiderius who told the pope of his

---

[234] *Chronicon Montis Casinensis* III 50, MGH SS XXXIV.433f.: he avoided contact with the excommunicated king and his entourage, but in the end he allowed himself to make promises to the king in the presence of the prince of Capua. Cowdrey, *Age*, 163f. thinks that Desiderius's negotiations were not unknown to the pope and he rejects later comments by Archbishop Hugo of Lyons as misrepresentations. But it is hardly possible to decide whether either side thought at this time that a reconciliation could still be reached, as Cowdrey, *Age*, 164ff., thinks.

[235] A list of names is given in the *Gesta Romanae aecclesiae contra Hildebrandum* c. 1, MGH LdL II.369f.; it is also reported there that Gregory forced the cardinal bishops with the assistance of laymen to swear never to make concessions as far as the king was concerned.

coming rescue and the king of the coming danger. The behaviour of one of the most loyal and distinguished supporters of the Roman church was characteristic of many at the time who hoped that the worst could be avoided. The emperor abandoned the city shortly before the arrival of the Normans, and Clement III shifted to Tivoli. On 28 May the Normans were able to break into the city; after a few days it came to a battle between them and the inhabitants which resulted in one of medieval Rome's worst disasters. After Robert Guiscard had left Rome the pope, pursued by the hatred of the sorely afflicted population, was no longer able to stay there. He travelled via Monte Cassino and Benevento to Salerno, where he arrived at the end of June;[236] he was to stay there until his death on 25 May 1085.

Following Canossa and the election of Rudolf of Rheinfelden, which he accepted even if he had not brought it about, Gregory's politics had lost much of their decisiveness and dynamism.[237] The mark he made on history was due more to the actions of his early years, to the retreat by the episcopate after it had at first offered moderate and then fierce resistance, to the episode at Canossa itself and the legends which grew up around it. It owed little to the second excommunication of Henry, who was able to defend himself and establish Wibert as schismatic antipope.

It is hardly possible to say how far Gregory was conscious of his own failure. His conception of the 'right' ordering of the Christian world had a profound influence on the course of history, but it could never be fully realised. Kingship, for example, could not be 'desacralised' as long as there were monarchies at all. Again, Gregory played a decisive part in the spread of the term 'German', but the aims he pursued in doing so were soon to be forgotten so completely that only in our own time have they been reconstructed by the scholarship of Eckhard Müller-Mertens.

Much has been written about Gregory's last days. How much of what is reported was legend and how much reality is hard to decide. The words Gregory spoke on his death-bed, a transformation of Psalm 45: 8, are

---

[236] Cowdrey, *Age*, 172, contradicts those historians who describe Gregory's retreat to Salerno as a 'shameful journey' and his last months 'as a period of weakness and bitterness'. But nothing certain can be said about the pope's inner feelings. However, it cannot be overlooked that his influence was at that time weak, even if he 'exercised papal authority with vigour'; this can be seen above all from the desperate position in which his successors found themselves at first. Fuhrmann, 'Gregor VII.', 173, writes of Gregory's 'miserable end', but he does not mistake Gregory's certainty that he 'stood and suffered for God's justice'.

[237] Just how much contemporaries were already aware of this is shown by the *Vita Heinrici IV.*, c. 6, p. 22: 'Sed non magni ponderis ille bannus habebatur' (that is, the excommunication of Henry IV).

famous: 'I have loved justice and hated iniquity; therefore I die in exile.'[238] Was this a bitter summary by a man who otherwise subordinated everything to his certainty about his vocation and his knowledge of God's will? It seems unlikely. Urban II's report of Gregory's end, recorded in a fragment of a letter preserved only in Hugo of Flavigny's chronicle, seems to us to fit Gregory's view of himself better. Asked about the excommunicates, he declared: 'I absolve them all and bless them provided only that they believe without doubt that I have this spiritual power as the representative of St Peter', making an exception only for Henry IV, Wibert of Ravenna, and their immediate supporters.[239] This shows more clearly than anything else could that Gregory was not concerned with individual reform precepts or political conflicts, nor even with the moral failure of his opponents; his concern was the religious origin and validity of papal authority.

[238] Borino, 'Note Gregoriane 7', 403ff.; the interpretation of Hübinger, *Letzte Worte*, in which Cowdrey, *Age*, 174 and Goez, 'Toscana', 215 concur, is enlightening. See also J. Vogel, 'Gregors VII. Abzug aus Rom und sein letztes Pontifikatsjahr in Salerno', *Festschrift für Karl Hauck* (Berlin 1982), 341–9; Nitschke, 'Gregor VII.', 269, thinks by contrast that the famous words were said in bitterness.

[239] MGH BDK v.75 no. 35; on this see Erdmann, *Studien*, 171. Morrison, 'Canossa', 140 n. 99 cites only Paul of Bernried, of whom Giesebrecht, *Kaiserzeit* III.1175 already noted that he had made a fairly arbitrary use of the text. By writing *praeterea* instead of *praeter* he indeed reversed the sense of the report; only by using Paul can Morrison claim that Gregory had also absolved Henry and Wibert.

7

CONTINUING CONFLICTS BETWEEN
ESTABLISHED PRINCIPLES

Gregory VII had left the Roman church and the papacy in a state of deep confusion; the various national churches were in a state of either opposition or sceptical neutrality. True, the antipope was able to establish himself only in parts of Germany and Italy, and could not maintain his position in Rome; but it took a whole year before the Gregorians managed to elect a new pope. Victor III (1086–7), previously Abbot Desiderius of Monte Cassino, never succeeded in pacifying Rome, and was so fiercely attacked by the radical supporters of Gregory VII for his previous attempts at mediation between the parties, in particular by Richard of Saint-Victor in Marseilles and by Hugo of Lyons, that he, the peacemaking pope, was finally forced to excommunicate them. On his death in September 1087 there was again a delay of half a year until the election of Urban II, which could be held only outside Rome, in Terracina. Even after this it was many years before Gregory's successor could gain the upper hand over his opponents.

THE SCHISM AND ITS CONSEQUENCES

The election of Odo of Ostia as Pope Urban II in Terracina by the majority of the cardinal bishops together with representatives of the cardinal priests and cardinal deacons led to a gradual recovery in the fortunes of those groups within the church who wished to continue Gregory's policies and oppose Henry IV and Clement III. Urban (1088–99), who had been proposed as a successor by both Gregory VII and Victor III, was a talented politician, who maintained strict adherence to Gregory's principles in theory while displaying a high measure of flexibility in fighting for his cause as well as a willingness to use any means that came to hand.[1]

Like his predecessor Urban had to rely at first on his Norman allies, and for the whole of his pontificate he treated them accommodatingly. Only in alliance with them was he able to carry any weight or get anything done in Rome. He resided in Rome for only a third of his pontificate, and spent almost as much time in southern Italy.[2] At first Clement III's support in Rome was greater, but what weakened Urban's position there throughout his pontificate was not so much the schism as local opponents in Rome and in the Campagna. For a long period he had to take refuge in hiding-places, either in the island of the Tiber or in a castle belonging to the Frangipani near S. Maria Nuova. Only from 1093 on did he make slow progress, after Clement III had had to abandon the city. Even then, Clement's supporters were not without power and influence. In Lent 1094 Urban was able to buy his way into the Lateran, bribing a corrupt supporter of Clement III with money provided by Abbot Godfrey of Vendôme to do so.[3] In 1098 he won the Castel Sant'Angelo – again by bribery, according to Otto of Freising's later account[4] – and later still Paschal II won the city of Albano, which Clement III had had to abandon.[5] The cost of this operation was met by Roger of Capua. But it is characteristic of the continuing uncertainty of Urban's position that on his death his corpse could be buried in St Peter's only under cover of darkness.

---

[1] As for example in the use for propagandistic purposes of the salacious accusations made against Henry IV by the dubious Eupraxia at the synod of Piacenza in 1095; Mathilda of Canossa also exploited these for the same purpose. See Meyer von Knonau, *Jahrbücher Heinrichs IV.*, IV.423, 444, and Overmann, *Gräfin Mathilde*. Urban's close relationship with Berengar Raimund II 'el fratricida' of Barcelona was also characteristic; see Mehr, *Katalanischer Prinzipat*, 32, 34. See the characterisation of Urban by Becker, *Urban II.*, 98: 'From his first day of office he carried himself as pope with dignity and certainty – but also with the ruthlessness of a man who saw himself as dependent on his own resources alone in a difficult situation, and lived in an unbearable tension between the sublimity of his calling and pitiful impotence'. See also Becker, 'Urban II. und die deutsche Kirche', 242f. – hardly anyone in the middle ages was the target of so many and such crude accusations of immorality as Henry IV. Most of them have been exposed by recent scholarship as tendentious lies or at least as unprovable; but in spite of this some of the mud has stuck.

[2] Becker, *Urban II.*, 98f., n. 302.

[3] Godfrey of Vendôme, *Epistolae* I 8, Migne, *PL,* 157, col. 31ff.; Meyer von Knonau, *Jahrbücher Heinrichs IV.*, IV.422 n. 9.

[4] Otto of Freising, *Chronicon* II.6, p. 315: 'corruptis qui castrum Crescentii servabant muneribus'.

[5] Meyer von Knonau, *Jahrbücher Heinrichs IV.*, v.81.

His successor Paschal II (1099–1118) was elected swiftly and without much resistance. The schism had already lost much of its danger before Clement III's death in September 1101. But even after this there were still Clementines in Rome, who elected two further antipopes without consulting the emperor, though these were soon dealt with. But this did not cure the Romans of rebellion, and they had learnt the value of antipopes as a weapon in dealing with their papal opponents. In 1105 Paschal's enemies elected the archpriest Maginulf as Pope Silvester IV with support from the imperial *ministerialis* Werner, who administered the royal demesne in Ancona and Spoleto. Silvester's supporters were defeated and Silvester himself had to flee to Werner's protection, but it was not until 1111 that he resigned, as part of the arrangements made in connection with the imperial coronation between Paschal II and Henry V. Paschal's position in Rome was endangered once more in the last years of his pontificate by the dispute over the succession to the exiled prefect of the city. He had to leave the city once more, and on his death on 21 January 1118 only a minority among the Romans were on his side. His successor Gelasius II (1118–19) fled to his home city of Gaeta after only a few weeks when Henry V arrived on the scene. After he had refused Henry's offer of peace negotiations the Romans once again elected an antipope with the emperor's connivance, Archbishop Maurice of Braga, who took the name of Gregory VIII.[6] Gelasius, who was not bound by the oaths which his predecessor had taken in 1111, excommunicated Henry from Gaeta after the antipope had been set up. With Norman support he was able to return to Rome once more, but soon had to flee again and journeyed via Pisa and Genoa to France, where he died at Cluny. His successor Calixtus II (1119–24), who was elected on 2 February 1119 in Cluny, was able to enter Rome in June 1120. Even then St Peter's remained in the hands of supporters of Gregory VIII, though he himself had long since fled to Sutri. It was not until the end of 1120 that Petrus Leonis was able to bribe them into supporting Calixtus II.[7] In 1121 Gregory VIII, abandoned by all, fled into Calixtus's hands; for a long time he led a miserable existence as a prisoner in a series of castles and monasteries.

The schism which had begun with the election of Clement III and continued with interruptions into the pontificate of Calixtus II was linked in Rome and in the papal patrimony with more local conflicts between

[6] Erdmann, 'Mauritius Burdinus', 205–61.
[7] *Annales Romani* 1116–1121 in *Liber Pontificalis*, ed. L. Duchesne (Paris 1893) II.347: 'Sed accepta pecunia tradiderunt eam Petro Leonis, qui fidelis est Calixti papae cum omnibus suis munitionibus.'

the popes and their immediate opponents. These were small-scale power-struggles. The fact that from a dogmatic point of view a division within the Roman church is intolerable, that only one of the parties can be orthodox and the other must be heretical, was of only secondary importance for these local or regional disputes.[8]

The principal danger from the schism for Gregory VII and his successors lay in the fact that Clement III was supported by Henry IV and enjoyed some obedience within the lands of the empire. After Clement's death the antipopes enjoyed only modest support, but the schism continued under the last two Salian rulers in the sense that their numerous supporters were either opposed to or not in favour of the legitimate popes. The other lands of Europe did not join in the schism, but their defection was sometimes a threat when conflicts arose, and often led the popes to make concessions which stood in opposition to their real aims.[9]

The Normans of southern Italy had attacked the papal patrimony frequently enough and infringed papal rights, besides being averse to any intervention in the affairs of the churches in their own territories. But they had also often helped in critical situations by providing money or military support, and they had never come to terms with the Salian emperors and their antipopes. Hence the popes could accept them, for, as Urban II wrote to Bishop Wimund of Aversa in 1088, it was possible to have dealings with sinners and robbers but not with schismatics, with whom there could be no communion.[10] The popes refrained from putting pressure on them; they even, though reluctantly, abstained from sending papal legates when these were unwelcome to the Normans. This policy was carried so far that Urban II granted Roger of Sicily the privilege of representing the pope (the apostolic legation) in 1098,[11] a grant which was essentially incompatible with the whole tendency of papal principles.[12] Paschal II could not risk either taking any action against Roger's isolationist church policy or revoking the privilege granted by his predecessor.[13]

---

[8] See below, pp. 263f. n. 40.   [9] See below, p. 260.

[10] JL 5363; see Becker, Urban II, 115.

[11] JL 5706 = Italia Pontificia VIII.25 no. 81; Caspar, 'Legatengewalt', especially 99ff.; Deér, 'Anspruch', 171ff.

[12] Cantor, Church, Kingship, 118: 'Urban's grant of jurisdiction over the Sicilian church, legati vice, to Roger was a flagrant contradiction of the policy of the reforming papacy from the beginning of the pontificate of Gregory VII'; Holzmann, 'Papsttum, Normannen', 74: 'an arrangement which was a slap in the face for the principles of the Gregorian reform period'; Deér, 'Anspruch', 179: 'this profoundly unecclesiastical claim'.

[13] C. Servatius, Paschalis II., 93f.; Deér, 'Anspruch', 131ff., who notes the connection between the Sicilian and the English conceptions of the role of papal legates and the imitation of these practices by Geza II of Hungary.

In England there was a similar tendency towards isolationism as far as the papacy was concerned, and this could be sustained the more easily because of the distance involved. There was the same remote veneration of the papacy as had existed in earlier centuries, before the time of Leo IX and his successors;[14] pre-Gregorian attitudes continued, and after Gregory died his successors were in the main no more acknowledged than were the antipopes. Papal claims to lead or determine church affairs met with either rejection or incomprehension. In general king and episcopate showed a united front and managed church affairs without reference to the popes or the legates, in a manner which had to be accepted in Rome given the prevailing circumstances. It was not possible to enforce strict compliance with the decrees of papal councils. English bishops did not appear at foreign councils; they were not even present at the council of Clermont in 1095.[15] The popes had to content themselves with the payment of Peter's Pence. Wibert's attempts to make contact met with little success, but Urban II also encountered neutrality rather than support. Apparently Urban was able to draw William II more and more on to his side from 1096 by making the concession that no papal legate would be sent to England except at the king's request. This was an anticipation of the somewhat later arrangements for the rulers of Sicily.[16] The English king and bishops were treated diplomatically; the popes avoided putting pressure on them. The fact that the English might recognise the antipopes, or withhold payment of Peter's Pence or influence the Normans of southern Italy unfavourably suggested caution as the best policy.[17] Even when Anselm, who had succeeded Lanfranc on his death in 1089, came into conflict with king and episcopate, Urban had to show great skill in preventing the archbishop's strict principles from creating serious friction or even leading to a breach between England and the papacy. Paschal II, who was less ready to compromise, had to face a more acute risk that England would defect, but this was removed within a few years after Henry I and the pope had been able to reach agreement on the issue of investitures.[18]

The schism scarcely affected the churches of the Spanish peninsula;

---

[14] Brett, *English Church*, 34; Cantor, *Church, Kingship*, 31.

[15] Barlow, *English Church 1066–1154*, 111.

[16] Becker, *Urban II.*, 182 and n. 667.

[17] Barlow, *English Church 1066–1154*, 275; Deér, 'Anspruch', 131, describes the Sicilian government of the church as one 'which in arbitrariness, ruthlessness, and crass usurpation of church rights was exceeded in the contemporary world only by the kings of England, if at all'.

[18] See below, pp. 272ff.

Urban's policy towards Spain was in general successful.[19] He was able to continue the energetic policy of intervention pursued by Gregory VII and his important legates. As a Cluniac he was able to smooth over the differences which had arisen between his predecessor and Cluny over Spain and in general he was intelligent enough to leave the arbitration of local disputes to the Spanish themselves. Pope, rulers, and episcopate all had a common interest in the success of the *reconquista*. When the Almoravids began their counter-attack against the Christians at the end of Urban's pontificate the pope could do little materially, but his moral support helped to stiffen the will to resist. Alfons Becker has demonstrated the connection between Urban's interventions in the various regions where there was war with Islam: Spain, Sicily, and Asia Minor.[20] All other aims of previous papal policy were played down under Urban. The elimination of the remaining traces of the Mozarabic rite continued, but in a noticeably conciliatory manner. Rome's authority was unchallenged in Spain at the beginning of the twelfth century, in spite of the independence of kings and bishops. Paschal II's threat to excommunicate Alfonso I of Aragon for his unlawful marriage to Uracca, the heiress of Alfonso VI of Castile, did not seriously trouble relations.[21]

Clement III found no support in France. The high reputation of Cluny, which supported Gregory VII and his successors without wavering though without abandoning its own traditions, was here of decisive importance.[22] Especially in the parts of France where the king had only nominal influence the popes were able to achieve recognition without difficulty; it was here that the papal legates were chiefly active. In the area more intensively governed by the king there were not infrequent conflicts between the popes and their legates on the one hand and the kings and individual bishops on the other, but both sides avoided taking these to extremes.[23] It is characteristic that the severest conflict between Urban II and Philip I was not over a difference of opinion in matters of religion, or over principles of canon law or church reform, but over a gross breach of generally accepted norms of conduct by the king. This was something more than the normal harmless miscalculation of the degree in which spouses were related; it was his repudiation of his queen, Bertha, and his

[19] Becker, *Urban II.*, 242ff.
[20] *Ibid.*, 229f.
[21] Servatius, *Paschalis II.*, 126; Kehr, *Navarra und Aragon*, 40ff.
[22] On the relationship between Gregorianism and Cluniac monasticism see below, p. 342.
[23] For the distinction between royal and seigneurial France see Becker, *Urban II.*, 201f.

liaison with Bertrada of Montfort, the wife of Count Fulco of Anjou, which ran counter to all current ideas of morality.[24] The affair became still more dangerous because the scandal and even the king's excommunication were to a large extent ignored in France.[25] Urban II did all he could to limit the damage; at first he would not even confirm the excommunication imposed by his legate Hugo of Lyons, and for a long time he clung to the hope that the king would keep his promises to mend his ways. In the end he could not avoid excommunicating the adulterous king at the council of Clermont in 1095 and laying an interdict on any place where he might be present. But the scandal dragged on; it came to a dangerous head in 1098, when Philip I threatened to withdraw his obedience from Urban if he were not absolved. This was the only time when the schism affected French ecclesiastical politics; but both sides muddled through during the years that followed until the conflict was ended under Paschal II, less because of the efficacy of ecclesiastical censures than because of the mortal enmity between Philip's heir Louis and Bertrada.[26]

From the end of July 1095 until the end of August 1096 Urban lived in France. By contrast with his often-threatened position in Italy he met with general recognition and reverence in France. The high-point of his stay was his preaching of the crusade at Clermont on 26 November 1095, the beginning of a movement which was to inspire large numbers of men and have momentous consequences. The pope visited numerous other cities, but avoided the regions under direct royal rule. The first crusade was by no means an affair involving the whole of Europe; it was carried out by and large by the nobility of France, Lotharingia, and southern Italy. Germany, England, and most of Italy ignored it. Spain was preoccupied with its struggles against its own Islamic opponents, and the pope, who saw the crusade as part of a general movement against Islam, wanted the Spaniards to concern themselves with their own problems in any case. In the lands reached by Urban's preaching of the crusade large numbers were mobilised, but no Christian kings were won for the enterprise. The crusade slipped more and more out of the hands of the pope himself. The original intention of bringing help to the eastern church against the attacks by the Turks was counteracted by the tendency of the aristocratic leaders of the crusade to seek the extension of their own power, and by the

---

[24] *Ibid.*, 193ff.

[25] *Ibid.*, 204; according to Ivo of Chartres, *Epistola* 84, Migne, *PL* 162, col. 105, French bishops placed the crown on Philip I's head on the death of Urban II 'tamquam mortuo praecone iustitiam mortuam esse crediderint'.

[26] Becker, *Studien*, 113f.

barbaric lust for plunder shown by the lesser men on crusade. Yet Urban's moving words had helped to enhance papal authority in large parts of the West.[27]

In the lands dealt with so far the schism was seldom a real danger for Gregory VII's successors; but it was always a tedious burden. The mere danger of defection forced them and their supporters to make repeated concessions in the face of behaviour by kings in matters of morality and canon law which they should not really have tolerated, and in the face of breaches of canon law by ecclesiastics. Offences against the repeated prohibition by synods of the practice of lay investiture had to be accepted or forgiven after only nominal penance had been done.

In the empire and the neighbouring lands to the north and east the schism led to long struggles and much suffering. In general, Clement III's supporters were more numerous; only in eastern Saxony did his opponents control a substantial area exclusively, and even here there was some fragmentation after Gregory VII's death.[28] Several of the most powerful lay princes of southern Germany were for a time opponents of Henry IV and hence of Clement III, for example the Welfs, Zähringer, and Rheinfeldener. Later Bishop Gebhard of Constance was to create a successful coalition of the supporters of Urban II and Paschal II. The great majority of the German episcopate was opposed to them, however, and those who supported them through thick and thin were in an even smaller minority.[29]

In Italy Margravine Mathilda of Tuscany was the most reliable supporter of the Roman popes.[30] Otherwise the lay nobility contained both supporters and opponents. The bishops of northern Italy were preponderantly on the side of Clement III, though their ranks were not so closed as they had been against Gregory VII.[31] The archbishops of Milan, who had abandoned Clement III after Thedald's death, had to be consecrated by foreign bishops, for their own suffragans had almost all been excommunicated for their support of Clement III. In central Italy the 'imperial' bishops were rarer, but they were not wholly absent even

---

[27] The crusading movement, initially confined to the West, did not do much to overcome the schism.

[28] Giese, *Stamm der Sachsen*, 173, 180; Fenske, *Adelsopposition*, 154.

[29] Of the bishops described by Fenske, *Adelsopposition*, 95, as particularly true to their convictions, three – Adalbero of Würzburg, Hermann of Metz, and Burchard of Halberstadt – had subscribed the German bishops' renunciation of Gregory VII in 1076.

[30] Overmann, *Gräfin Mathilde*, especially Reg. 35 and 75 and pp. 239f.

[31] Schwartz, *Besetzung*, 7ff.; an examination of the second, detailed section of the work allows more precise judgements.

in the regions immediately around Rome. Probably one ought not to visualise the struggle between the two obediences as having been particularly fierce. Even in Italy, which had a fairly dense network of bishoprics, it was rare for an Urbanist bishop to intervene in the diocese of a Clementine or vice versa. If the one had been excommunicated by Clement and the other by Urban, neither needed to take much notice so long as they were sure of their own diocesans. The traditional life of the church went on much as before at local and regional level, in spite of the schism. Many bishops even managed to adopt an intermediate position between the two obediences.[32]

The cases in which a bishop moved from one obedience to the other are particularly instructive. Sometimes they show the spiritual and material reasons which led to the change and allow us to guess at the consequences which such decisions had inside and outside the diocese. We can here discuss only a few selected examples. The history of the Milanese change of obedience is noteworthy. Thedald's successor Anselm had been elected in 1086, invested by the emperor and consecrated by the only suffragan bishop who was not excommunicate. He had been deposed by a legate of Urban II for this breach of the prohibition of investiture and had retired to a monastery. At this point it was the pope who by con-ciliatory treatment of the prelate, now his supporter, persuaded him to resume his office. At the request of the new archbishop he even sent him the pallium without Anselm's having performed the prescribed visit to Rome.[33] In 1093 Anselm crowned Conrad, who had broken with his father Henry IV, in Milan. Soon afterwards he died and Arnulf was elected archbishop. Though he was consecrated in a dubious manner, he nevertheless recognised Urban II, and at Piacenza in 1095 the pope consequently ordered German bishops to repeat the consecration in the correct manner.[34] The election of the next archbishop also seems to have

[32] See Fenske, *Adelsopposition*, 202. The most remarkable case is probably that of Benno II of Osnabrück, whom Gregory still hoped to win over in 1081 (*Registrum* IX 10). His behaviour in Brixen in 1080 as Gregory VII was being condemned is described by Norbert's *Vita Bennonis* cc. 18, 25, ed. H. Bresslau (MGH SRG, Hanover 1902). See also Becker, 'Urban II. und die deutsche Kirche', 256: 'it was evidently still possible for German bishops to combine loyalty to the emperor with obedience to Urban'.

[33] JL 5359 and 5378; Meyer von Knonau, *Jahrbücher Heinrichs IV.*, IV.200f.

[34] *Ibid.*, 328. Bernold, *Chronicon*, s.a. 1095, MGH SS v.463, names Thiemo of Salzburg, Udalrich of Passau, and Gebehard of Constance as the consecrators. In the German version of this book I overlooked the fact that the older assumption that Conrad had invested Arnulf in 1093 had long been refuted; see most recently S. Beulertz, *Das Verbot der Laieninvestitur im Investiturstreit* (Hanover 1991), 110 and n. 383.

been irregular. Landulf was the candidate of the 'Milanese multitude', but Anselm of Buis was elected by the influence of Margravine Mathilda and under Patarene pressure. He received the staff of office from Mathilda and the archiepiscopal stola from a papal legate.[35]

It is hardly possible to form a clear picture of the motives which lay behind Milan's change of obedience. Tensions within the populace played a part, but here as elsewhere the relative importances of religious motives (including the 'reform position' of those concerned), political aspects and personal emotions remain unclear. When Welf IV sought a reconciliation with Henry IV in 1091, for example, he appears to have demanded (in vain) that the emperor should give up his pope.[36] When the reconciliation really did come about, in 1096, there was no longer any question of this; of decisive importance was the fact that the politically inspired marriage alliance between the seventeen-year-old Welf V and the 43-year-old Mathilda of Canossa had failed, understandably enough. The separation of this unnatural bond between the young man and the ageing woman may also have had something to do with disappointed hopes of inheritance. In the case of Bishop Gebhard of Constance, a son of Berthold of Zähringen, and a former monk of Hirsau, one is naturally inclined to assume that it was his support for reforming monasticism which determined his allegiance.[37] He did not follow his lay relatives in accepting reconciliation with Henry IV, but one finds with some surprise that under Henry V he raised no objections to the royal right of investiture. This 'reform demand' can thus hardly have been a question of principle with him beforehand either.[38]

In 1098 or 1102 Archbishop Ruthard of Mainz wrote to the clergy of Halberstadt that they should abandon the schism: he himself has gone from his earlier life, which he now condemns, to a new one in Christ. He does not blush to confess that he has become a new man since breaking with the emperor, and thanks God for the conversion He has brought about: 'I confess, I confess, and gladly I confess that I have taken my familiar seat in the bosom of Holy Mother Church, with all my soul.'[39]

---

[35] Meyer von Knonau, *Jahrbücher Heinrichs IV.*, v.12.

[36] Meyer von Knonau, *Jahrbücher Heinrichs IV.*, iv.338 n. 11, following Bernold.

[37] Miscoll-Reckert, *Kloster Petershausen*, 131ff.

[38] See below, p. 276 n. 91; P. Diebolder, 'Bischof Gebhard III. von Konstanz und der Investiturstreit in der Schweiz', *Zeitschrift für schweizerische Kirchengeschichte*, 10 (1916), 194 and 205.

[39] Jaffé, *BRG*, iii.374ff. no. 31 = *Mainzer Urkundenbuch*, ed. M. Stimming (Darmstadt 1932) 1.302 no. 398; P. Rassow, 'Über Erzbischof Ruthard von Mainz (1089–1109)',

Such religious pathos is astonishing when one considers the archbishop's past and the immediate causes of his transfer of obedience to Urban II. In the summer of 1089 he had received the archbishopric of Mainz from Henry IV. In 1093 he still supported his Trier colleague Egilbert, whose suffragans of Toul and Verdun had renounced their metropolitan, who had been excommunicated by Urban II. They summoned the papal legate Hugo of Lyons to consecrate the bishop-elect Poppo of Metz, which he came to do with a large following.[40] It was a dramatic conflict, in the course of which Ruthard protested against the violation of the rights of the Trier metropolitan by a papal legate. The whole thing is reminiscent of similar cases under Gregory VII.[41] Ruthard showed himself here as an exponent of a position deeply rooted in canon law and tradition, that of episcopalism. What persuaded him to change his obedience was quite different. When passing crusaders massacred the Mainz Jews in 1098 the archbishop left the Jews without protection, even those to whom he had explicitly promised help. Henry IV and Clement III as well as, probably, the Mainz burghers reproached him severely for this. The archbishop had to flee to Thuringia for safety and was deposed by Clement III. It was at this point that he joined Urban's obedience. Only when Henry V rebelled against his father was Ruthard restored to his see, in 1105. Until his death in 1109 he was one of the most influential ecclesiastical princes.[42] His relations with Paschal were not troubled by the fact that – like the majority of the German episcopate – he did not share the pope's views on investiture.[43]

We are rarely able to determine whether the subjective reasons for such decisions were more governed by religious and moral convictions than by opportunistic considerations. Often the two will have mingled or alternated. Each bishop had to try to justify and defend the decision he took. And since schism was in principle heresy, that is, a deviation from the true faith, it was necessary to paint the members of the other camp in as dark colours as possible. Tolerance was unthinkable when the yardstick was the absolute one of religion. Hence Clement III's camp also included

---

Festschrift für B. A. Stohr (Mainz 1960), II.162. For the dating of the letter see Fenske, *Adelsopposition*, 141 n. 237.

[40] Jaffé, *BRG*, v.168f. no. 86: 'asserentes enim se solos iustos solosque cum suo Urbano catholicos episcopos, ceteros papae Clementi adherentes, excommunicatos habentes aspernantur'.

[41] See above, pp. 210f. and 216f.

[42] Meyer von Knonau, *Jahrbücher Heinrichs IV.*, v.28ff. and 252f.

[43] See below, p. 276 n. 91.

many men of good faith who held Gregory VII and his successors to be heretics and schismatics.[44]

From around 1100 onwards it was still not possible to do without a belief in the absolute righteousness of one's own cause but the desire for peace was growing. Clement III was by no means wholly defeated when he died. There were even stories of miracles which had occurred at his tomb.[45] True, the schisms which followed were in general determined by political interests, especially in Rome itself. But as late as 1120 the antipope Gregory VIII, who had been abandoned by Henry V, could write that 'The Highest is witness of our conscience . . . that we suffer . . . for the true faith and the defence of justice what seems intolerable, so that the false faith of the heretics may not be granted victory, or the truth be defeated by lies and the authority of the holy fathers destroyed, or the dignity of your Empire, which God has created for the defence of the church, be set at naught.'[46]

THE INVESTITURE CONTEST

The vision Gregory and Humbert had had of the right order in the Christian world was magnificent, naive, and unrealistic. In their view the higher rank assigned in the scheme of salvation by Gelasius I to priestly authority was also valid in secular affairs. It was only logical that the part played by laymen as long as men could remember in a church where there was no conceptual division between the spiritual and the secular should come to seem offensive. On such a view, not only lay ownership of churches and monasteries but also royal appointments to bishoprics and the political, military, and economic services rendered by bishops to their rulers were deviations from an older ecclesiastical order. The prohibitions against receiving churches from the hands of a layman and against the investiture of bishops by kings and princes were radical attacks on practices of long standing. Gregory and his circle left the question of what should take the place of such supposed abuses vague, undecided, and

---

[44] Grégoire, 'Pomposa', 18; I. S. Robinson, 'The Friendship Network of Gregory VII', *History*, 63 (1978), 17: both Wibert and Manasses of Rheims were 'friends of reform'. Clement III's letter to the inhabitants of Mainz directed against Archbishop Ruthard is also characteristic, Jaffé, *BRG*, III.377 no. 32 (July 1099): 'ad inimicos regni et sacerdotii et divinae legis contemptores se ipsum totum contulit; in dominum suum hostes quos potuit concitavit et coronae suae insidiator extitit'.

[45] Ziese, *Wibert*, 266ff.

[46] Giesebrecht, *Kaiserzeit*, III.1271.

unregulated,[47] showing in doing so a lack of realism which is barely credible. The principle was clear and bold; but a real division between clergy and laity within Christendom was naturally inconceivable. Nor did Humbert and Gregory envisage that the church should give up its huge secular possessions. Unity was to be secured by subordinating the laity to the clergy. Kings and wealthy laymen were to continue to endow churches and monasteries and to protect their rights; they were to obey the bishops and content themselves with such services as these were willing to do voluntarily. How this was all to be regulated in detail was left an open question.[48]

It is understandable that decrees of such revolutionary content and such undefined consequences remained at first strange and incomprehensible. Proprietary churches and monasteries had indeed had to suffer from their owners at times, but in other times of need it was the owners who were the first to provide help. Who was to replace them? The bishops belonged to the political élite of the kingdoms with which their sees were so closely linked. They needed royal support against their opponents in the lay nobility, against their fellow bishops and against their diocesans; it was not always reliable, but it was the first port of call, and it could not be replaced by the still less reliable influence of provincial councils or distant popes. It was this which led to the mistrustful or at least wary attitude found among the episcopate to the demands made by Gregory and his successors and their close supporters, and perhaps this as well which was responsible for the surprising lack of response to the first prohibitions of investiture.[49]

Gregory's successors reaffirmed his fundamental decisions. Urban II asserted in a letter addressed to Bishop Gebhard of Constance as well as Duke Welf and several other bishops and abbots: 'Continue to trust in me

---

[47] Benson, *Bishop Elect*, 218f.; Minninger, *Von Clermont*, 80f.: 'In the decrees of prohibition issued during his pontificate a vague terminology conceals Gregory VII's precise intentions.

[48] *Registrum* v 5, p. 353, with the parallel passages noted there in n. 1; Paschal II, characteristically, could still write on 11 November 1105 to Ruthard of Mainz (JL 6050 = *Mainzer Urkundenbuch*, ed. M. Stimming (Darmstadt 1932), I.329 no. 432): 'Habeant in ecclesia primatum suum, ut sint ecclesiae defensores et ecclesiae subsidiis perfruantur.' See Becker, *Studien*, 106: 'Gregory VII himself had evidently not yet thought about the political significance and the legal consequences of this prohibition of investitures.'

[49] See above, p. 181, and also Cantor, *Church, Kingship*, 33: 'Gregorian reform ideas would be coldly received and even strongly opposed by them'; R. Schieffer, *Entstehung*, argued from the absence of resonance in 1075 and after against an early date for the prohibition of investitures, but even the later pronouncements were not too widely noticed. Jakobs, *Kirchenreform*, 27, also notes that the events of the year 1076 'rapidly outstripped contemporaries' capacity to understand them.'

as much as in our holy father Pope Gregory, in whose footsteps I wish to
tread. All that he rejected I reject; all that he condemned I condemn; what
he held I embrace wholeheartedly; what he considered rightful and
catholic I confirm and strengthen.'[50] Many of the synods of Urban II and
Paschal II repeated the prohibitions against receiving churches from the
hands of laymen and against the investiture of bishops and abbots by the
king.[51] In addition, from the council of Clermont (1095) onwards clerics
of all grades were forbidden to do homage or fealty to a layman.[52] This
had a religious justification which shows that the reserve shown by the
early church towards the world had not ceased to exist. According to the
report by Eadmer, Urban II had threatened with anathema all those who
took oaths of homage to laymen for their ecclesiastical dignities and
possessions. The hands of priests, which are so exalted that through their
service they create God, the creator of all things, are desecrated when they
are enclosed in hands which are soiled day and night by obscene contacts
and stained by robbery and the shedding of blood.[53] There is no shortage
of similar judgements.[54]

It has often been noted that the popes continued to hold strictly to the
principles laid down in Gregory's pontificate, even to formulate additional
ones which went even further, but at the same time to show tolerance
and a readiness to compromise in their political practice.[55] This was true
even of Gregory VII, especially in his final years when he had to take
account of the schism, and it was still more true of Urban, who had

[50] JL 3548 = Migne, *PL* 151, cols. 283f.
[51] Although Victor claimed to continue the work of his predecessor, no prohibition of
investitures by him has survived; see Meyer von Knonau, *Jahrbücher Heinrichs IV.*, IV.185
and n. 40. By contrast, Urban II and Paschal II prohibited investitures repeatedly: at
Melfi in 1089, at Piacenza and Clermont in 1095, at Tours in 1096, at Bari in 1098, at
Rome in 1099, at Guastalla in 1106, at Troyes in 1107, at Benevento in 1108, at Rome
in 1110.
[52] S. Williams, 'Concilium Claromontanum', 41, xvi–xviii; see W. Schwarz, 'Investiturstreit',
108; Becker, *Urban II.*, 189 and n. 694; Minninger, *Von Clermont*, 84f.; Classen,
'Wormser Konkordat', 418 n. 32.
[53] Eadmer, *Historia novorum*, 114; for a similar though more moderate formulation by
Paschal II, see below, p. 339 n. 155.
[54] Minninger, *Von Clermont*, 85 and 95f.
[55] Becker, *Studien*, 83f.; Becker, *Urban II.*, 147f.; Becker, 'Urban II. und die deutsche
Kirche', 253ff., especially p. 258: 'The restoration of church unity . . . evidently seemed
more important to Urban II than the rigorous enforcement of the reformist prohibition
of investitures.' To this we only need to add that Gregory VII had already often shown
himself conciliatory in the question of investitures. Nitschke, 'Wirksamkeit Gottes', 194,
thinks that Gregory's ideas on investitures underwent a change in the course of his
pontificate. Sprandel, *Ivo*, 120, brings some striking examples of Urban's conciliatory
attitude towards invested bishops.

inherited the schism from his predecessor. Neither made any concessions in the matter of the schism, which was after all a question of the unique succession to St Peter. Compared with this, breaches of the prohibition against investiture were easier to forgive. The idea of the papacy, which had to be defended against schismatics, clearly took precedence over the struggle against lay investiture. Only from the time of Paschal II onwards, that is, following the death of Clement III, the only antipope who was really dangerous, did the well-known themes of lay investiture and its symbols come to the foreground.[56] But what did his practice look like? At first sight one is inclined to identify a new rigour in it. At the council of Troyes for example he suspended such prominent supporters of the papal cause as Frederick of Cologne and Ruthard of Mainz, even the distinguished Gebhard of Constance, not only because they had not come to the synod but also because of their various breaches of apostolic prohibitions.[57] But Paschal was just as ready to forgive as his predecessors, as long as those guilty in his eyes were prepared to acknowledge his principles and to do penance. Characteristic of this is the way in which Bishop Reinhard of Halberstadt, who had been severely criticised for receiving royal investiture, was addressed nevertheless as bishop, brother, and friend, as well as the way in which Paschal accepted Reinhard's feeble excuse that as he had not been summoned to the council of Troyes he had not known about the prohibition of investitures decreed at the council![58] As late as 1107 a bishop who was ready to submit to the pope could thus use the same excuse as had some of his colleagues forty years previously.[59] This was probably not even cynicism; rather, there was a genuine ignorance about the theological meaning of the prohibition of investiture.

The relationship between the purely sacramental and pastoral functions of ecclesiastical office on the one hand and the rights and duties associated with the office's endowment on the other when a bishopric was conferred by a king or a proprietary church by a layman or ecclesiastic seems to have long remained a subject about which there was little reflection. For

---

[56] W. Schwarz, 'Investiturstreit', 117; Z. N. Brooke, 'Lay Investiture', 219, divides the conflict into two periods: 'one contest ended in 1106 and another, a different one, began'.

[57] The fullest is *Annales Patherbrunnenses*, ed. P. Scheffer-Boichorst (Innsbruck 1870) *s.a.* 1107, p. 117f.; see also Ekkehard, *Chronicon*, *s.a.* 1107, MGH SS VI.242: 'Tunc etiam nonnullos nostrates episcopos eo quod eidem concilio non intererant, officii suspensione dominus papa multavit, quos tamen non multo post satisfacientes clementer absolvit.' See K. Bogumil, *Das Bistum Halberstadt im 12. Jahrhundert* (Cologne 1972).

[58] *Urkundenbuch des Hochstifts Halberstadt*, ed. K. Jänicke (Berlin 1896), I.89f.; see on this Fenske, *Adelsopposition*, 170. [59] See above, p. 182.

monasteries and lesser churches, unless they enjoyed special privileges, canon law required that the diocesan bishop should examine, consecrate, and oversee abbots and clerics, though this requirement was not always observed. This was true even when a monastery or proprietary church belonging to a bishop lay in a different diocese; there was then a perfectly straightforward distinction between the rights and functions of one bishop in his capacity as owner and those of the other as spiritual superior. Even the participation of king or prince in appointments to bishoprics, although it had its justification in a theocratic view of royal office, was constrained by the need for canonical election and still more by the necessity of consecration by the consecrated. Thus even the old order of things knew certain distinctions.

Once the accusation of simony came to be made against those kings, princes, and the proprietors of churches who demanded or accepted more than conventional gifts in return for bestowing churches, and still more against those applicants who made such gifts or payments, people seem here and there to have tried to get round the problem by offering the justification that the giving and taking occurred only in connection with the material endowment of the church, something which could be separated from its spiritual functions and prerogatives. Abbo of Fleury had argued against this interpretation as early as the end of the tenth century,[60] and after that there was a growing discussion about whether the temporalities and spiritualities of churches formed a unity or could be separated, though the old naivety about the issue predominated for a long time.

From the middle of the eleventh century the traditional right of kings to participate in the appointment of bishops was called in question on the grounds that they were laymen; the argument for doing so was at first and long afterwards given as the danger of simony, though this argumentation became more and more schematic and formulaic. It was not without a certain justification, especially after the notion of simony had been extended to cover such things as favours as well as cash payments; certainly no king would have been likely to have engaged himself for the election of a candidate unless he could assume that the man possessed the necessary qualities for the office but also a readiness to do the king's will.

The problems which were to carry more weight in the history of the church arose from the fact that the king, who was a layman, bestowed churches, whose essence lay in the service of the sacraments. Was it not an affront to Christ himself, who through his presence in the sacrament of consecration bound the cleric to his church, if a layman should decide in

[60] See above, p. 170 n. 133.

advance who was to receive his blessing? Had such a layman not trans-
gressed the generally accepted boundaries set for him? Humbert of Silva
Candida had already directed his polemical attacks against the arguments
of those who tried to distinguish between the *invisibilis Spiritus Sancti
gratia* present in the sacraments from the *visibiles ecclesiarum res*, arguments
which must thus have been current in his time.[61] Humbert defended the
unity of the two passionately and stubbornly; but was not his theory
curiously bound up with its own time, originating as it did in criticism of
traditional assumptions and customs? There had simply not been any
earlier consideration of the question of how the relationship between the
church's spiritual function and its material possessions was to be defined.
The need to provide a living for those who performed the sacraments and
material support for their services to the poor and the sick was not seen as
an ecclesiological problem. Whether estates, meadows, woods, and mills
took on a sacred quality when they belonged to churches was a question
which probably concerned theologians and members of the hierarchy
more than it did the average Christian.

At all events both opponents and defenders of the traditional state of
affairs proceeded from the assumption that the church and the property
with which it had been endowed belonged together. The supporters of
the king referred to the rights which he had always enjoyed over
episcopal appointments, and as far as the consecration of bishops was
concerned they did not need to make any concessions, for the king had
never interfered in this. When in the famous Ravenna forgeries of the
1080s Hadrian I's conferring of the right of investiture on Charles the
Great and Leo VIII's on Otto I were invented, what was at issue was the
bishopric as a not very precisely defined whole, not just its rights and
property,[62] though it was admittedly a terrible anachronism to ascribe to
the popes of the eighth and tenth centuries the ability to confer such
privileges.[63] But the forgeries had considerable effect, though only at a
subsidiary level; the king's rights here were seen primarily as issuing from
his position as God's elect. This, of course, presupposed that the king
ruled by the grace of God, an idea which no Christian ruler could ever
dispense with and which was, then and later, to stand in the way of a
complete submission to papal power.

[61] See above, p. 171 n. 134.
[62] MGH Const. I.657ff. no. 446; 663ff. no. 448f.; 674ff. no. 450; see F. Schneider, 'Eine
antipäpstliche Fälschung des Investiturstreits und Verwandtes', *Festschrift für H. Finke*
(Munich 1925), 84–122; Jordan, 'Kaisergedanke', 105ff.; Jordan, 'Ravennater
Fälschungen', 426–8; Benson, *Bishop Elect*, 39 and 233; Fried, 'Laienadel', 486 n. 118.
[63] See above, pp. 65ff.

The contrasting views of the position of clergy and laity within the church each had a religious foundation, which meant that an understanding between the two camps was impossible. In the matter of investitures, which was closely linked with the theocratic view of office, there were for this reason *rapprochements* but not solutions. In the key issue, the relationship between 'spiritual' and 'secular' power, men had, as so often in history, to live on the basis of a coexistence between essentially irreconcilable standpoints after Gregory VII had produced his fundamental modifications of the two powers doctrine as proposed by Gelasius I.[64] King and episcopate, clergy and laity, lay and spiritual élites were so dependent on one another that their members were forced in practice to accept a provisional *modus vivendi* in spite of the innovations promulgated by the popes and their supporters and in spite of the renewed defence of tradition by kings and the lay and ecclesiastical élites who supported them. The results were not the same in all countries, but there were similarities, nevertheless. The ways in which they came about, on the other hand, varied according to the historical preconditions and the characters of the principal actors: it has often been noted that the question of investitures in England, Spain, and France did not lead to long-drawn-out disputes, but merely to episodic crises, in sharp contrast to the dramatic and emotion-laden struggle within the empire.[65]

In France, where the king was weak and exercised traditional royal rights in only a part of the bishoprics, and where the king's authority was diminished by his much-criticised way of life, there was no really powerful opponent who could face up to the pressure from the curia. The power of unconsecrated princes to appoint clerics to churches was still more vulnerable, while the popes had supporters who made up in devotion and fanaticism what they lacked in numbers. Even Gregory VII had not shown himself particularly rigorous here, and because of the schism Urban II was still more diplomatic. The affair of the election of

---

[64] *Registrum* VIII 21, p. 553, where it is shown in n. 3 that Gregory shortened the text of Gelasius's statement. Such modifications are characteristic of Gregory; there is an interesting parallel in a prayer for the feast of Peter's throne, see H. Volk, 'Gregor VII. und die oratio "Deus qui beato Petro"', *Jahrbuch für Liturgiewissenschaft*, 3 (1923), 116ff. and Tellenbach, *Libertas*, 181f. and n. 29.

[65] Böhmer, *Kirche und Staat*, 159; Cantor, *Church, Kingship*, 168: the investiture controversy lasted half a century in Germany and half a decade in England; Vincke, *Staat und Kirche*, 257; Kehr, *Katalanischer Prinzipat*, 23 and 63; L. Della Calzada, 'La proyección del pensamiento de Gregorio VII en los reinos de Castilla y León', *StGreg*, 3 (1948), 50; Becker, *Studien*, 74 and 139ff. The difference was already apparent to contemporaries, for example Wenrich of Trier c. 8, MGH LdL 1.297: 'cum his qui sub aliis regibus degunt, mitius agatur'.

Archbishop Daimbert of Sens, in which Bishop Ivo of Chartres played an important role, was particularly characteristic. The whole business was unusually long drawn out because Archbishop Hugo of Lyons not only demanded from Daimbert that he recognise the primacy of Lyons before his consecration but also claimed – with what justification is not clear – that Daimbert had received investiture from the king. When the new archbishop appeared in Rome the pope himself consecrated him and gave him the pallium, without making any declarations of principle.[66] Paschal II also intervened from time to time in disputed elections.[67] But in the land of the peace of God the longing for peace and the willingness to compromise were very marked. Gradually, though earlier than elsewhere, new forms of episcopal appointment came into use, without any official negotiations or declarations. Investiture, where it had been practised, went out of use, and canonical election was recognised everywhere, though the king (or prince, depending on the bishopric) was still able to exercise considerable influence and preserve the feudal hierarchy. The king was still entitled to give consent (*concessio*) to the use of the church's property and to demand the services of the bishop.[68] As early as 1097 Ivo of Chartres, one of the most learned and unprejudiced theologians of his time, wrote: 'whether this *concessio* is given by investiture, a gesture, a nod, a word or a staff, what does it matter?'[69] There were for a long time to be clashes over episcopal appointments, but these never led to the kind of dispute about principle that they produced in Germany and Italy.

In the Spanish kingdoms, which had many ties with the Roman church, the part played by the king in appointment to, defence of, and control over the bishopric was scarcely a matter for debate. There were no clashes between spiritual and secular authority; only a really crude infringement of episcopal rights such as occurred with Diego Pelaez of Santiago could cause Urban II to intervene. The bishop may have been involved in an aristocratic conspiracy. At all events Alfonso VI took steps against him. With the help of the papal legate Richard, abbot of Saint-Victor in Marseilles, who had already been recalled, the bishop was deposed, imprisoned, and replaced by Abbot Peter of Cerdaña. The pope was evidently brought into the matter by the archbishop of Toledo.

---

[66] Becker, *Studien*, 99f.; Becker, *Urban II.*, 192: 'the only genuine investiture dispute in France during the whole pontificate of Urban II'.

[67] Becker, *Studien*, 114ff. and 123; C. Servatius, *Paschalis II.*, 313ff.

[68] Becker, *Studien*, 107ff., 121ff., 162ff.

[69] *Epistola* 60, ed. Leclercq, 246; on the interpretation see especially H. Hoffmann, 'Ivo', 407.

Cardinal Rainer of S. Clemente (later to become Paschal II) took steps
against Peter as papal legate, and the affair dragged on for years before it
was ended by a compromise: each side renounced its claim and the
Cluniac Dalmatius was appointed in Santiago.[70]

In the era of William the Conqueror and Lanfranc of Canterbury the
pope had exercised little influence in England. William II at first recognised neither Urban II nor Clement III. The attempt to instrumentalise
the king's conflict with Bishop William of Durham for papal purposes
proved futile; so did the attempt to use Bishop Herbert of Thetford and
Winchester to bring about a *rapprochement*.[71] Even the great Anselm had
at first acknowledged the special conditions prevailing in England by
allowing himself to be appointed and invested by the king and doing fealty
and homage. After only a short time, however, he had broken with the
king and was isolated among the episcopate.[72] Only then did William II's
hopes of dealing with his difficulties with Anselm with the help of the
pope lead to contacts with Rome. Anselm, who was present at the
Lateran synod of 1099, became an upright and determined exponent of
the papal cause. The early years of Henry I's reign were marked by
serious tensions over the question of episcopal investiture and homage,
though these were eased by the pope's tactical flexibility and by the
courteous respect Henry I and Anselm showed to one another.[73] In the
treaty of L'Aigle of the summer of 1105 the king agreed to renounce
investiture conditionally. But at the end of the year Anselm could still
write to his friend Hugo of Lyons that 'the whole difficulty in the conflict
between the king and me seems to lie principally in the fact that the king,
although (as I hope) convinced that the apostolic decrees prevent him
from investing, is (so he says) not yet ready to renounce the homage of
prelates, and asks the apostolic see to agree to this'. Anselm asked what he
should do should this request be granted and a devout prelate-elect
subsequently refuse to become the king's man for a bishopric or a
monastery.[74] In a letter to Anselm from Benevento dated March 1106 the
pope released the archbishop in person from Urban II's prohibition
against receiving investiture and from the excommunication which he felt
he had incurred. The archbishop was also authorised to receive those
prelates back into the church who had accepted investiture, or had
consecrated the invested, or done homage. 'But if in future candidates

---

[70] Becker, *Urban II.*, 233ff.
[71] *Ibid.*, 173ff.
[72] *Ibid.*, 176ff.; Cantor, *Church, Kingship*, 34ff.; Tillmann, *Legaten*, 19.
[73] *Epistolae* 318 and 319, *S. Anselmi opera omina*, v.246ff.
[74] *Ibid.*, ep. 389, pp. 333f.

should accept prelacies without investiture, they shall not be excluded from the blessing of consecration, even if they perform homage to the king, until such time as the grace of almighty God and the rain of your prayers soften the king's heart so that he gives up' the practice of demanding homage.[75] This was the basis of the so-called Concordat of London agreed on in August 1107 at the royal palace in London. The king renounced investiture, but retained decisive influence over episcopal elections, which were to take place in the chapel of the palace; he also retained the right to demand homage from the new bishop and to put him into possession of the bishopric before he was consecrated.[76] It was still a compromise, and one which was not, unlike that in France, arrived at by the development of custom; it was an agreement worked out in considerable detail and one which surrendered a good part of the papal claims in order to accommodate the English king.

In the empire the moves made under Gregory VII to put the prohibitions of investiture issued at his synods into practice in individual cases were not numerous, and they were still fewer under Urban II. Vacant bishoprics were generally filled using the old forms, and Henry IV's supporters among the episcopate were in the overwhelming majority. But even his opponents had been invested with their offices, with the exception of Hartwig of Magdeburg and Gunther of Naumburg, who had been appointed by Rudolf of Rheinfelden with Gregory VII's participation.[77]

The supporters of Gregory and Urban were succeeded in part by supporters of Henry. Here and there antibishops were set up against those invested in the usual manner, but only a few of these were of any real importance. Ulrich of Passau was able to preserve the enclave in the eastern part of the diocese created by his predecessor Altmann. Only in Constance was Gebhard III able to establish himself, and he had been elected in Gregory VII's time. As papal vicar he was one of the leaders of the opposition, but even in his own diocese he was not without opposition: the antibishop Arnold of Heiligenberg, elected in 1092, was able to drive him out of his diocese in 1103, and it was not until two years later that he was restored by Henry V.[78]

The changing balance of power frequently affected the position in

---

[75] *Ibid.*, ep. 451, p. 397; Barlow, *English Church 1066–1154*, 287; Böhmer, *Kirche und Staat*, 161.

[76] *Ibid.*, 160; Cantor, *Church, Kingship,* 222ff.; Classen, 'Wormser Konkordat', 417; Minninger, *Von Clermont*, 222ff.

[77] Tellenbach, 'Gregorianische Reform', 111.

[78] Becker, *Urban II.*, 144f., and 148f.; Miscoll-Reckert, *Kloster Petershausen*, 131ff. and the literature noted there in n. 11.

individual dioceses. Old supporters of Gregory VII like Siegfried of
Mainz, Gebhard of Salzburg, Adalbert of Worms, Adalbero of Würzburg,
and Altmann of Passau all had to spend years in exile, though when the
imperial cause suffered setbacks they were able to return temporarily.
Urban II was at first not able to influence German affairs much. His main
supporter was Gebhard of Constance, who was joined one after the other
by the suffragans of the imperialist archbishop Egilbert of Trier.[79] Urban
was willing to make concessions to those who were prepared to acknowledge him as the rightful pope. In France in 1096 he accepted the
submission of Emehard of Würzburg and even of Otto of Strasbourg, the
brother of Frederick of Swabia, without imposing heavy penances. This
has been interpreted as a change of sides by the two prelates, and the fact
that the two were found shortly afterwards in Henry's entourage has
occasioned some surprise,[80] though it is probable that we are dealing
here with ecclesiastics who managed to adopt a position of neutrality.
Similarly, the Gregorian Hartwig of Magdeburg consecrated Albuin of
Merseburg, nominated by the king.[81] Ruthard of Mainz and Anselm of
Milan really did change sides, as we have already seen.[82] But the Milanese
example in particular shows clearly that Urban II did not regard having
accepted royal investiture as a particularly serious offence against canon
law, let alone as heresy, an offence against the faith. It could be forgiven,
if the guilty prelate was prepared to atone for the much greater crime of
having supported the schism.

Henry IV was never sounded out on the possibility of putting an end
to the old and embittered conflict. So long as Clement III lived and the
schism still existed there could be no negotiations about reconciliation, for
the king remained loyal to the pope whom he had recognised. Only at the
end of 1100 were such negotiations considered by the princes and at the
imperial court.[83] But in a letter to Gebhard of Constance which cannot
be dated more precisely than to the early years of his pontificate Paschal
showed his brusque rejection of such ideas: 'do not let yourself be
disturbed by foolish rumours or by the empty prattle of those who boast
that we shall soon reach an agreement with Henry and his followers. For
with God's help we shall strive to the end to secure that their corruption

[79] Becker, *Urban II.*, 152f.
[80] *Ibid.*, 161; Meyer von Knonau, *Jahrbücher Heinrichs IV.*, IV.470; V.5.
[81] *Ibid.*, V.3, and see the important observations by Becker, *Urban II.*, 146ff.: 'in the period
that followed, many bishops, including imperial ones, sought to adopt as colourless and
non-committal an attitude of neutrality between the parties as possible'.
[82] See above, pp. 261f.
[83] Meyer von Knonau, *Jahrbücher Heinrichs IV.*, V.103.

and their power shall be rooted out by the merits of the apostles.'[84] The curia made no demands – for example, for the renunciation of investiture – in this phase, and the emperor rejected none. Urban II had apparently discussed the question of investitures, if not with Henry IV, then at least with the latter's rebellious son Conrad. There is a brief notice about his meeting with the pope in Cremona in April 1095. Here the young king gave oaths of security and received in turn promises of help, 'saving the rights of the church and the apostolic decrees, especially those on investiture'.[85] Probably Conrad, who was in a weak position, had accepted the prohibitions with fewer conditions than those insisted on later by the kings of France and England. How far he was prepared to go can be seen from the mention of the marshal service (leading the pope's horse) which he performed on his first meeting with the pope,[86] something which had not been done for more than two hundred years since the times of Louis II and Nicholas I. Urban II evidently had plans for this 'son of the Roman church'. He and Mathilda of Tuscany pushed through Conrad's marriage with a daughter of the Sicilian ruler; perhaps this was done with the intention of making Conrad into an Italian vassal of the papacy?

What lay behind the inflexibility shown by the curia towards Henry IV – especially when we consider that it was by no means so intransigent towards other rulers – can only be a matter for surmise. It was probably not so much his stubborn defence of the rights of his predecessors or his character, painted in such dark colours by the papalists, or his alleged crimes, or the slanders spread about him, as his resistance to the consequences of the new ideas of papal power and to the restrictions these implied for his own theocratic rulership. It was this which made him the head of the schism, and thus a figure with whom Gregory's successors could not be reconciled, even after his death.[87]

Only after Henry V's rebellion did serious contacts between curia and royal court become both possible and desirable. As early as the Mainz

---

[84] Paschal II to Gebhard of Constance, 18 January 1100 (JL 5817 = Pflugk-Harttung, *Acta*, II.169).

[85] 'salva scilicet ipsius ecclesiae iusticia et decretis apostolicis, maxime de investituris': MGH Const. I.564 no. 394.

[86] R. Holtzmann, *Der Kaiser als Marschall des Papstes* (Schriften der Straßburger Wissenschaftlichen Gesellschaft in Heidelberg NF 8, Berlin 1928), 8; Fried, 'Regalienbegriff', 513 and n. 214.

[87] It was not the details of the 'reform programme', such as canonical elections, prohibition of clerical marriage, simony, or lay investiture which created the irreconcilable differences but the resistance of Henry and his supporters to the demands of the popes for absolute obedience which led to schism and made the conflict unresolvable.

assembly of January 1106 an embassy was sent to Paschal. It consisted of Archbishops Bruno of Trier and Henry of Magdeburg, together with Gebhard of Salzburg and three other bishops.[88] On their journey they were taken prisoner by the local count in Trent, and only a few of the bishops actually reached the pope; it is not known whether they engaged in any political discussions with him. But in October a German delegation with a composition similar to that of January again appeared before Paschal in Guastalla. It is not known what they negotiated about at the curia. It is noteworthy, however, that the leader of the delegation, who was once again the archbishop of Trier, was deposed for three days because he had accepted investiture from the old emperor. After that he was received into the pope's grace again and given the pallium. The pope thus saved his face,[89] but this by no means solved the question of investitures, for Henry V exercised the right of investiture with no more qualms than his father had shown. The whole issue of investitures can scarcely have been the reason for the breach between father and son. Even before Henry IV's death his son had already invested several bishops in the usual manner. It is still more remarkable that the German bishops did not put up any resistance to this, and even supported him.[90] The old leader of the opposition to Henry IV, Gebhard of Constance, consecrated the new bishop, Gottschalk of Minden, while Archbishop Ruthard of Mainz consecrated Ruotpert of Würzburg, set up in place of the deposed Erlung, and Reinhard of Halberstadt, invested by Henry V. Gebhard of Constance had also been invited to the ceremony; he excused himself on the grounds of pressure of business and frailty, but agreed to Reinhard's appointment without reservation. The participants showed no hesitation about the investiture, and it is not likely that they felt any.[91] The German

---

[88] Meyer von Knonau, *Jahrbücher Heinrichs IV.*, v.283 and 294.

[89] Meyer von Knonau, *Jahrbücher Heinrichs V.*, vi.25f. and 31; Blumenthal, 'Some Notes', 61–77.

[90] As early as 1105 Henry V performed investiture in the usual manner: Gebhard of Speyer, Gottschalk of Minden, Ruotpert of Würzburg, Hartwig of Regensburg. At the beginning of 1106 Conrad of Salzburg was appointed in the same way: only later did he come to change his opinion. See his *Vita*, c. 5, MGH SS xi.65: 'Ea res postea dolorem cordis perpetuum ei peperit. Abhorrebat siquidem vir ille venerabilis, et medullitus detestabatur hominii et iuramenti prestationem, quam regibus exhibebant episcopi et abbates vel quisdam ex clero pro ecclesiasticis dignitatibus, eo quod nefas et instar sacrilegii reputaret ac predicaret occulte et publice, manus chrismatis unctione consecratus sanguineis manibus, ut ipse solebat dicere, subici et homini exhibitione pollui'; see Benson, *Bishop Elect*, 40 and n. 76.

[91] Fenske, *Adelsopposition*, 164ff., where the important explanations of his absence made by Gebhard (*Mainzer Urkundenbuch*, ed. M. Stimming (Darmstadt 1932), I.338 no. 431) and Paschal's rebuke (*ibid.*, 339f. no. 433) are discussed at length. Fenske's conjecture that

episcopate was also to support Henry V in the subsequent disputes over investitures which culminated in the dramatic events of 1111. As early as Albert Hauck's time it was realised that the attitude of the episcopate to the question of investitures in effect continued that shown in the time of Henry IV. They had never objected seriously to the traditional rights of the king,[92] and in so far as they were or later became his opponents this had other causes.[93]

It is thus quite understandable that the tensions between the pope on the one hand and the king and the imperial church on the other could not be resolved. In mid May 1107 a distinguished deputation led once more by Bruno of Trier and including the powerful royal chancellor Adalbert of Saarbrücken appeared before Paschal in Châlons-sur-Marne. Here again there was no *rapprochement*, but there was a significant exchange of views noted by the young Suger and recalled at a distance of some thirty years when he was a distinguished abbot of Saint-Denis, in a report which modern scholarship has generally regarded as trustworthy. Suger, who did not care for the way in which the Germans presented themselves, praised the archbishop of Trier alone as a man of distinction and good humour, well endowed with eloquence and wisdom. The speech reported by Suger showed a certain tactical flexibility, for although it defended royal rights in episcopal elections it allowed consecration to follow election with the king's consent but precede investiture with the *regalia*. The pope was still not prepared to listen to this and allowed a bishop speaking on his behalf to reject it utterly;[94] nevertheless one has the impression from now on that in spite of all the theatrical displays of inflexibility in the

Ruthard and Reinhard had objected to the form of the nomination is not supported by the sources. The judgement on Gebhard is also contradictory. On the one hand Fenske acknowledges that Gebhard had explicitly approved of Reinhard's appointment; on the other hand the sincere apologies for absence and the silence about the king's role are seen as objections. Bogumil, *Bistum Halberstadt*, 20, also deduces from Gebhard's silence that he ignored the king's influence on the appointment. In my opinion this overworks the argument from silence. Fenske, *Adelsopposition*, 45, finds it most surprising 'that Henry V began to take up his father's position on the disputed question of episcopal investiture'. He rightly notes that the 'bishops close to reform' did not hold a renunciation of lay investiture to be essential, and explains this, not very convincingly in my opinion, by saying that 'they were no longer governed by that strictness of principle which charac- terised many of the opponents of Henry IV among the German episcopate'. But who had ever been opposed to royal investiture as a matter of principle?

[92] Hauck, *Kirchengeschichte Deutschlands*, III.89.
[93] See below, p. 282 n. 111.
[94] Suger, *Vita Ludovici Grossi regis*, ed. H. Waquet (CHF 11, Paris 1929), 56f.; cf. H. Schlechte, *Erzbischof Bruno von Trier* (Diss. Leipzig 1934), 38ff.; Hoffmann, 'Ivo', 422; Benson, *Bishop Elect*, 242ff.; Classen, 'Wormser Konkordat', 426 and n. 40; Fried, 'Regalienbegriff', 468 and n. 57; Minninger, *Von Clermont*, 134ff. and 143 with n. 232.

negotiations both sides regarded an agreement as both possible and unavoidable.

The Germans stayed away from the council held at Troyes soon afterwards, however, and several bishops had severe penalties inflicted for this, though in the usual manner these were soon relaxed.[95] It was not until 1109 that a new embassy appeared in Rome; once again it included Bruno of Trier, Frederick of Cologne, and the chancellor Adalbert. The state of the controversy over investitures current at that time is reflected in a tract *De investitura episcoporum* which probably appeared shortly before and has been seen with good reason as in effect a set of instructions for the embassy written by the monk Sigebert of Gembloux.[96] The Germans again insisted on investiture, and that before consecration, though they were not so concerned with the precise form it took. Evidently the question of the symbols of investiture was to be passed over; this was the extent to which the Germans were prepared to compromise.[97] Investiture itself was defended as a practice which had not only existed time out of mind but had also been sanctioned by earlier popes and in particular made the object of privileges issued by Popes Hadrian I and Leo VIII.[98] A crucial substantive argument was the claim that the protection of the church's property against tyrants and robbers must be seen to by those who had donated it in the first place.[99] On this occasion as on previous ones no agreement was reached. The embassy returned in March 1110 bearing a statement from the pope that he claimed only that which was sanctioned by canon and church law and did not intend to reduce the extent of royal rights in the slightest. This left everything open.[100]

The negotiations were also intended to prepare the way for Henry V's Italian expedition and imperial coronation. The fact that both sides expected the coronation to take place suggests that they were prepared to make more serious efforts to reach an agreement and also that the differences of opinion were no longer seen as irreconcilable, as they had been in Henry IV's time. In mid August 1110 the king marched into Italy with an unusually powerful army; by the end of the year he was in Arezzo. During the course of the expedition there had been several exchanges of messengers between pope and king. From Aquapendente the chancellor

[95] See above, pp. 267f.
[96] J. Beumann, *Sigebert von Gembloux*, 93 with n. 394 and especially 100: ' . . . this work had indeed more of the nature of a statement of the royalist standpoint'.
[97] Krimm-Beumann, 'Traktat', 77; on the agreement in form with Ivo of Chartres see above, p. 271 and n. 69.
[98] On the so-called Ravenna forgeries see above, p. 269 and n. 62.
[99] Krimm-Beumann, 'Traktat', 73; see Fried, 'Regalienbegriff', 471.
[100] *Annales Patherbrunnenses, s.a.* 1110, p. 122.

Adalbert, archbishop-elect of Mainz and at that time the king's most powerful and trusted adviser, set out for Rome with a number of lay magnates. In the church of S. Maria in Turri a sensational agreement was confirmed on oath between the royal ambassadors and the pope's pleni-potentiary, Petrus Leonis.[101] The relationship between king and churches was to be radically altered. Henry was to promise that on the day of his coronation that he would renounce his rights of investiture into the pope's hands publicly before clergy and people and set the churches free with their rights of offerings and their possessions, in so far as these did not obviously belong to the realm. Besides this he also promised to return and confirm the patrimonies and possessions of St Peter, as Charles, Louis, Henry, and the other emperors had done, and to help the pope to retain them as far as he was able.[102] In return the pope agreed to command the bishops to give back the *regalia* to the king and realm, in other words to renounce the greater part of their possessions and the basis of their power as princes of the empire. Specifically listed as *regalia* were towns, duchies, marches, counties, mints, tolls, markets, imperial advocacies, hundreds, and estates with appurtenances such as *ministeriales* and castles. Paschal gave an extensive justification of his intentions. The servants of the altar had become servants of the court. The bishops would be able to devote themselves to pastoral care after they had renounced the *regalia* and would no longer be absent from their dioceses for long periods.[103] The curia had finally grasped that it would be impossible to deprive the king of both

---

[101] MGH Const., 1.137ff. no. 83ff.

[102] Blumenthal has put forward noteworthy observations in her articles 'Patrimonia', 9–20, and 'Paschal II', 67–92. She rightly draws attention to the second promise made by Henry V, on the restoration of the papal patrimony, which she says has not been properly taken note of in the previous literature. But probably she considerably over-estimates its potential efficacy, as e.g. in the statement in 'Patrimonia', 10: 'the days of political weakness and of abject poverty of the papacy would have been over'. People at the curia were perfectly well aware of the fact that the kings only stayed for short peri-ods in Rome and its environs and how unreliable their support was; for Henry V see my table in 'Kaiser, Rom', 251. Besides this, Henry's promise was made advisedly with the reservation *secundum suum posse*. Such a conditional promise could scarcely have made a difference to papal power and certainly not have prevented the synod of 1112 ('Paschal II', 79, 81). The essential royal concession was the renunciation of investitures; the essential papal one was the pope's command to the prelates concerned to renounce their *regalia*.

[103] MGH Const., 1.141, no. 90; Blumenthal, 'Patrimonia', 15, explains this as follows: 'The reason for the disagreement between the two parties is a different understanding of the concept of *regalia* at the German court on the one hand, and the papal curia on the other.' In my opinion it was not a question of different understandings of the concept of *regalia* but the pope's excessive willingness to make concessions which brought the majority to oppose the treaty.

influence over episcopal appointments and his rights to episcopal services without any compensation. The result was a religiously motivated attempt to deal with the problem by severing at a stroke the involvement of bishops in worldly affairs and thus completely transforming their political and financial situation.[104] It is hardly possible to imagine the consequences the planned action would have had for the government and for the economy. Even though one may assume a divergence between the curial and the royal conceptions of *regalia*, the narrower curial definition would still have meant a radical intervention in the church's political and material existence.[105]

Henry V was to declare later that his negotiators had stressed that the king did not want to do violence to the churches and sacrilegiously deprive them of everything.[106] In the end they agreed to the renunciation of the right of investiture which had been demanded, so long as the pope had fulfilled his promises; but they knew, as Henry noted in parenthesis, that he could not do so. Each side was quite clear that the agreement would have revolutionary consequences, but each was prepared to take the risk in order to break the deadlock of decades, though the king and his advisers were perhaps more sceptical. One may perhaps note in favour of Paschal II and the curia that the prohibition of investitures and the claims to rule made by the popes since the time of Gregory VII were still bolder and more revolutionary, and yet had not been realised. It had been

[104] P. Zerbi, 'Pasquale II e l'idea della povertà della Chiesa', *Annuario dell'Università cattolica del Sacro Cuore, Anno accademico 1964/65* (Milan 1965), 207–29. Zerbi's view has been partly rejected, partly modified; see Fried, 'Regalienbegriff', 473 n. 72, and also Blumenthal, 'Patrimonia', 10: 'Paschal had no intention of impoverishing the Church.'

[105] The problem of the *regalia* has been re-opened in recent years. See Ott, 'Regalienbegriff', 234–304. For the explanation of the events of 1111 the question of different concepts of the *regalia* at the curia and the royal court has been important; the reflections of Fried, 'Regalienbegriff', 472ff., have been particularly fruitful. Nevertheless it must be emphasised that it was not such differences but the concessions made by the pope which brought about the failure of the treaty.

[106] MGH Const. 1.150 no. 100: 'Ad haec cum nostri responderent nos quidem nulle ecclesiae violentiam inferre nec ista substrahendo tot sacrilegia incurrere.' In spite of the later claim by Gerhoch of Reichersberg (see Meyer von Knonau, *Jahrbücher Heinrichs V.*, VI.381 n. 47) it is unlikely that the royal side set a cunning trap for the pope; *contra*, Hausmann, *Reichskanzlei*, 23: 'Adalbert on the other hand knew very well that the pope would not be able to prevail in this matter, but he accepted the proposals in a spirit of cool calculation.' Minninger, *Von Clermont*, 161, 279, says that the agreement was not utopian but failed simply because it conflicted with the interests of the nobility and of the imperial church. But it is difficult to imagine how the episcopate could have lived without *regalia* or what the king could have done with them. Perhaps there was some idea of granting out the *regalia* to the bishops again?

shown that complete freedom of the church from all lay influence was not possible without freeing it from established economic and political ties. It is noteworthy, however, that the curia was still not willing to accept compromises such as those worked out for France and England.

The reading of the papal command to renounce the *regalia*, which had up till then been kept secret, in St Peter's on 12 February 1111 provoked an uproar.[107] The majority of the bishops and prelates present were taken unawares and protested loudly. The preparations for the imperial coronation were interrupted, and confusion and indecision spread; attacks by Romans on Germans outside the church helped to increase the panic. In the evening the king left St Peter's; the pope, together with many of the cardinals and their followers, was quartered under strict guard in the vicinity of the church. After fighting which lasted several days the Germans left the city with their prisoners. Two months later the pope, concerned by the sufferings of the prisoners, the desolate state of the Roman church, and the danger of a new schism, agreed to the treaty of Ponte Mammolo on 11 April. This conceded the right of investiture to the king, renounced all thought of vengeance for what had been done, and promised never to excommunicate Henry. Henry in return granted indemnity for all that had been done to him and his followers during the fighting in Rome, and guaranteed once more the patrimony of St Peter and the possessions of the Roman church.[108] The report, which Paschal had entered in the papal registers, shows besides this that Henry declared in the course of the negotiations that he conferred by his investiture not the churches themselves or any ecclesiastical office but only the *regalia*.[109] As noted, he renewed his promise to restore the patrimony and to do his best to preserve it; even this treaty, negotiated under duress, showed a certain willingness on the part of the king to compromise. The pope had to confirm his promises in the form of a privilege, which would frequently be condemned as a 'pravilege' in the years to come.

Although the courageous (or desperate) attempt to separate the episcopal churches from the German and Italian crown had ended in failure, it was an event of immense importance in the history of the church. It tackled the problem of the relationship between Christianity and the world, which has existed from the time of the early church up till the present; this was made explicit by Paschal II, and the king's representatives, whatever their scepticism, had at least grasped the point. Had the

---

[107] MGH Const. I.151 no. 100: 'universis in faciem eius resistentibus et decreto suo planam heresim reclamantibus'.
[108] MGH Const. I.143f. no. 94.   [109] MGH Const. I.149 no. 99.

proposal been practicable it could have been termed a genuine church reform.

The following years up to the agreement of the so-called Concordat of Worms were full of contradictions and tensions. The pope, burdened with feelings of guilt, struggled on grimly, in spite of having been compromised, until his death in 1118. The attacks on him went so far as to accuse him of heresy, though others offered intelligent if somewhat unenthusiastic defences. Since he would not publicly break his promise never to excommunicate Henry, though his behaviour was not always free of ambiguities, others, in particular French ecclesiastics, took it upon themselves to pronounce damnation on Henry at synods.[110] The events of 1111 were scarcely noticed in Germany and did not harm the emperor's reputation. Only from 1115 onwards did some lay and ecclesiastical princes exploit the church's opposition to Henry for their own territorial aims.[111]

Paschal's successors, who were not bound by the oath he had taken, once more took up the leadership in the struggle against the emperor, a role which after the short pontificate of Gelasius II fell to Calixtus II in particular, who as Archbishop Guido of Vienne had already in 1112 in his capacity as papal legate held a great French synod at which Henry V was condemned as a second Judas for treachery, perjury, and desecration of the temple.[112] The synod declared the 'pravilege' extorted from Paschal in captivity to be null and void. One has the impression that the bitter propaganda directed against pope and emperor, because it treated the question of lay investiture and its associated problems in isolation, could no longer sustain the old level. The insights gained in the course of settling these matters in England and France were lost to sight in the passions aroused by the struggle.

Nevertheless, the ground must have been slowly prepared for the

[110] See below, n. 112.

[111] Henry V's main opponent was, from 1112 on, Adalbert of Saarbrücken, from 1110 archbishop-elect of Mainz, who had played a key part in negotiating the treaties of 1111 and was one of those who had sworn them. Archbishop Frederick of Cologne, who had already been invested by Henry IV, did not become an enemy of the emperor until 1114 in connection with a conspiracy by the burghers of Cologne. It was also in 1114 that Archbishop Adelgot, who had received the pastoral staff from Henry in 1107, fled the royal camp. These and other opponents of the king were motivated by considerations not so much of ecclesiastical as of territorial politics. They then found willing allies in the popes and still more in their legates. On Adalbert see Hausmann, *Reichskanzlei*, 42; Büttner, 'Erzbischof Adalbert', 398; Classen, 'Wormser Konkordat', 426 and 431; on Frederick of Cologne and Adelgot of Magdeburg see Meyer von Knonau, *Jahrbücher Heinrichs V.*, VI.298ff. and 310f.

[112] Mansi, XXI, col. 74ff.

compromise reached in the Concordat of Worms. In 1117 Henry repeated almost word for word the statement recorded by Paschal II in his report on the treaty of Ponte Mammolo that in conferring investiture he did not confer the church or ecclesiastical office but only the *regalia*, when three cardinals in Rome reproached him with the argument that investiture was the *summa dissensionis* which rocked and imperilled the church.[113] It was thus no longer disputed that the emperor did not claim to confer churches, only their possessions, and a step had been taken towards the Concordat. It may be assumed that there were several such discussions, both at formal and informal levels. In 1117, for example, Archbishop Ralph of Canterbury spent a week in talks with the emperor, with the pope's agreement.[114] It is possible that Ralph explained the customs of the English king, who had since 1114 been Henry's father-in-law. In the autumn of 1119 the famous discussion between Abbot Pontius of Cluny and the learned bishop of Châlons, William of Champeaux, on the one hand and Henry V on the other took place in Strasbourg; we have an extensive account of this in the report of the *scholasticus* of Rheims, Hesso.[115] We can see at last how both sides were looking for a more nuanced approach to the question and were prepared to discuss details. William of Champeaux made it clear that Henry could still expect all the services of the church even if he should renounce the right of investiture completely, just as was the case in France. Agreements were reached, and the two intermediaries returned to the pope in Paris. Calixtus sent them back to the emperor to discuss more precise agreements and the promises made by each side were recorded in writing. They were laid before the pope and the council which had been opened in Rheims on 18 October. Pope and emperor had already set out for a meeting arranged in Mouzon, when the negotiations collapsed. The assembly at Rheims found the formulation in the draft treaty 'I renounce all investiture of churches' too vague and it demanded a more precise definition of the church's property.[116] Henry was not prepared to agree to this without consulting the princes, and made several requests for more time, which evidently increased the already considerable mistrust felt by the pope and his entourage. Memories of the coup of 1111 perhaps led them to flee from Mouzon and return to Rheims. At the end of the

[113] Jaffé, *BRG* v.315 no. 178; see above, p. 251 and n. 109 and also Minninger, *Von Coermont*, 176.
[114] Meyer von Knonau, *Jahrbücher Heinrichs V.*, VII.35 and n. 1; Eadmer, *Historia novorum*, 243.
[115] Hesso Scholasticus, *Relatio de concilio Remensi*, MGH LdL III.22ff.
[116] The record of the promises made by pope and king is also in MGH Const. I.157 nos. 104, 105. See T. Schieffer, 'Mouzon', 324–41.

council Henry V and his supporters were once again excluded from the church.[117]

Yet in spite of harsh words and ecclesiastical sanctions the following three years were no longer marked by an atmosphere of bitter conflict. There was no shortage of tensions or of local feuds in the empire, but the desire for peace between emperor and pope dominated, though it was usually expressed as a desire to preserve the honour of the kingdom.[118] In February 1122 the pope sent the excommunicated emperor a conciliatory letter through Bishop Azo of Acqui, who had long taken up the role of intermediary, in which he urged the emperor to see reason.[119] The emperor and the princes sent Bishop Bruno of Speyer and Abbot Erlolf of Fulda about this time to the pope. They returned together with three papal legates: Cardinal Bishop Lambert of Ostia and Cardinal Deacon Gregory of S. Angelo, who were to become pope as Honorius II and Innocent II, and Cardinal Deacon Saxo of S. Stefano Rotondo. On 8 September the legates met with emperor and princes in Worms. Agreements were reached which were defined in declarations by emperor and pope and on 23 September were read to a great crowd before the city. The emperor renounced the right to investiture with ring and staff and conceded the right of canonical election and unhindered consecration within his realm (regno vel imperio). In return the pope allowed the emperor to be present at the election and to decide disputed elections with the advice of the metropolitan and the bishops of the province. In Germany the prelate-elect (not the consecrated prelate) was to receive the

---

[117] It is by no means the case, as Hesso (p. 26) would have us believe, that the king was merely not prepared to keep his promises; there was a genuine and unresolved difference between the parties. Hesso himself shows (p. 25) that the members of the synod saw in the formulation 'Dimitto omnem investituram omnium ecclesiarum' both investiture and possession of churches, and suspected that the king had the intention, 'ne forte aut possessiones antiquas ecclesiarum sibi conetur vendicare aut iterum episcopos de eisdem investire'. T. Schieffer, 'Mouzon', 339, quite justifiably posed the question: was there really no talk of a secular investiture in Strasbourg? Chodorow, 'Ecclesiastical Politics', 613–46, gives an acute analysis of the differing factions present at the council; note his description of Henry's request for a delay as injudicious (p. 633).

[118] The princely assembly at Würzburg in September or October 1121 decided among other things to seek a solution to the investiture question, 'ut in hoc regnum honorem suum retineat'; MGH Const. I., 158 no. 106.

[119] JL 6950 = Migne, PL 163, col. 1232. Just how much the climate of opinion had changed can be seen from a comparison with 1112 (above, n. 112). Calixtus II now pleads with the king: 'obtineat ecclesia quod Christi est, habeat imperator, quod suum est.' Stroll, 'New Perspectives', 92–115, tries to explain the abrupt change between Guido's attitude in 1112 and Calixtus II's attitude before the concordat; see also her 'Calixtus II: A Reinterpretation of his Election and the End of the Investiture Contest', Studies in Medieval and Renaissance History, N.S. 3 (1980), 1–53.

regalia by investiture with a sceptre before consecration. In the other parts of the empire this was to take place within six months of consecration.[120] This distinction between the countries which made up the empire was an important gain for the papacy and shows once again that the popes from the time of Gregory VII onwards felt threatened by royal influence much more in Italy than elsewhere. The demand that the emperor should renounce any intervention in episcopal elections within the Roman church province had long been conceded.[121]

The fundamental religious conflicts which, especially in Germany, had grown with the increase in the practical realisation of papal claims and with a new sensibility towards the relationship of clergy and laity within the church, receded slowly into the background from the beginning of the new century. The political, economic, and legal problems took on greater priority as a result of a new realism and of the development of new forms for the life of the church. The way in which the question of investitures, which from Gregory VII's time had been handled with a good deal of flexibility in practice, came to the fore once the schism had ended, shows how the dispute had become a more superficial one, dominated by tactical issues. The claim that the worldly possessions of the church had a sacral character could not be maintained; the distinction between the spiritualities and the temporalities of the church came to be generally accepted. It was a partial success for the ideas promulgated by Humbert and Gregory that the rights of the king, which in all countries had originally applied to churches without differentiation, came to be restricted to the temporalities. But the higher churches were drawn into the feudal system after the failure of Paschal's attempt to preserve the issue of principle by renouncing the churches' temporalities. In consequence

---

[120] MGH Const. I.159ff., no. 107f. A. Hofmeister, *Das Wormser Konkordat*, new edition with foreword by Roderich Schmidt (Darmstadt n.d.) is still fundamental; the foreword discusses recent scholarship critically. Ott, 'Regalienbegriff', 241: 'Following the death of Henry IV begins that phase of the investiture contest in which the dispute over principles is replaced by the attempt to seek a practical solution.' Note especially Kempf, 'Kanonistik', 18: 'The reformers had already from the beginning of the century begun to realise that the previously valid fundamental position on the indivisible unity of church office and church possessions . . . would have to be revised' and p. 31: 'churchmen had become more realistic in the post-Gregorian era' and 'typical Gregorian ideas had suffered a fracture in the course of the investiture contest'. But the assumption (see Müller-Mertens, *Regnum Teutonicum*, 375, citing K. Jordan in B. Gebhardt, *Handbuch der deutschen Geschichte*, 9th edn (Stuttgart 1970), I.361) that investiture which followed consecration had only a formal character goes too far. It long remained a constitutive element in the relationship between the king and the invested prelate, and the former preserved very substantial rights.

[121] See above, pp. 233f.

the attempts made from the time of Urban II to ward off feudalisation by prohibiting fealty and homage had to be dropped. The churches thus came to be more than ever tied to the 'world' through their fiefs.

The recognition of a feudal link between kings and bishops meant that kings had to be allowed some participation in episcopal appointments, something which had been long and fiercely opposed. In the English and German concordats this was even explicitly defined. That was perhaps the bitterest consequence of the papal retreat, for the election was the election of a bishop not simply as holder of a fief but also as the possessor of the highest power of consecration and as supreme shepherd within his diocese.

The renunciation of investiture with ring and staff, which was achieved everywhere sooner or later, was a success for the movement towards a clearer demarcation of lay influence within the church, for the renunciation made clear that the residual rights of the laity were not of a spiritual nature. But it should not be overlooked that both investiture and its symbols had come about as a historical development and were transitory things. Considered in the context of the whole history of the church they were something more than a mere episode, but they represented only a phase in the history of the relationship between Christianity and the world, a problem which has had to be faced ever anew from the time of the early church up to the present day.

THE STRUGGLE AGAINST RIGHTS OF PROPERTY IN CHURCHES AND MONASTERIES
From the church proprietors to church patrons

Cardinal Humbert's attack on lay investiture applied to bishoprics. The sixth canon of Nicholas II's Easter synod of 1059, by contrast, laid down that no cleric or priest might receive a church from the hands of a layman, whether or not a price was paid.[122] Here no distinction was made between higher and lesser churches. The prohibition was repeated in this form by Alexander II.[123] As early as 1060 a synod in Tours presided over by Cardinal Priest Stephen produced a more cautious but still decisive formulation: the prohibition applied not just to simoniacal transactions but to any conferring of a bishopric, an abbey, an archdeaconry, an archipresbytery, or any other ecclesiastical dignity, rank, office, or fief which contravened the provisions of canon law.[124] A note also written in

---

[122] See above, pp. 176f.
[123] JL 4501 = Migne, *PL* 146, col. 1,289 no. 12.
[124] Mansi XIX, col. 927.

France in 1060, which refers to the regulations laid down by Nicholas II, says: 'We know that the laity should have no rights at all in churches; but where we cannot take these away from them completely we nevertheless deny them absolutely the offerings made in connection with mass and altar.'[125] This canon was repeated word for word shortly after 1078 by a synod held in Gerona.[126] All the prohibitions of investitures from Gregory VII's pontificate also refer to churches of all kinds. According to the report of Arnulf of Milan about the Lenten synod of 1075 the pope denied the king any right to bestow bishoprics and he removed all laymen 'from the investiture of churches'.[127] The prohibition by the autumn synod of 1078 is more precise: 'We determine that no cleric may accept the investiture of a bishopric or an abbey or a church from the hand of an emperor, a king, or any lay person male or female.'[128] Already before this in January of the same year a synod in Poitiers presided over by Hugo of Die had issued an equally precise prohibition, which forbade the giving and receiving not only of bishoprics, abbeys, and churches but also of 'any ecclesiastical possessions'; this was probably a repetition of the decrees of a synod held in Autun in September 1077.[129] The prohibitions of investitures in the time of Urban II and Paschal II were equally general. One can thus not say that the lesser churches were left out of official declarations.[130]

It is a quite different question if we ask how far all these decrees were observed in practice. How unclear the position was even in Calixtus II's time can be seen from the precise account given by Hesso Scholasticus of the synod in Rheims after the collapse of negotiations between pope and emperor. The participants had agreed to the excommunication of Henry V, but the original text of a proposed prohibition of lay investiture, 'we forbid absolutely the investiture of churches and church property at the hands of laymen', met with fierce opposition from clergy and laity. On the next day the prohibition was restricted to bishoprics and abbeys and promulgated in this form.[131] In recent scholarship the correction has often been taken as having applied to church property only, but this

---

[125] *Ibid.*, 875f.

[126] Mansi xx, col. 520.

[127] 'ab investituris ecclesiarum': Arnulf, *Gesta archiepistoporum Mediolanensium* iv 7, MGH SS viii.27.

[128] *Registrum* vi 5b, p. 403, c. xxxi.

[129] 'aliquarum ecclesiasticarum rerum': c. 1, Mansi xx, col. 498. See on this above, p. 182 with n. 185.

[130] On the other hand it is equally improbable that the general formulation of 1059 was only intended to apply to lesser churches.

[131] MGH LdL iii.27.

overlooks the fact that Hesso explicitly says that it applied to the lower churches, which is naturally of some importance for the state of the debate about investitures at a point so close to the Concordat of Worms.[132] A synod under the pope himself was here able to agree about the abolition of investiture in connection with bishoprics and monasteries, but was divided over other churches and church property. This indecision was not ended by the Concordat of Worms, and it had to be dealt with by compromises.

Here and there the idea survived that the possession of churches was incompatible with their true nature. One need only remember Abbo of Fleury, who warned that 'he who would save his soul should not dare to believe that a church belongs to anyone but God', and that 'if we say this church is mine or another says that church is his we do not speak as Catholics should'.[133] This seems like a frontal attack on the proprietary church, but that was an institution which both at the time and long afterwards enjoyed an almost undisturbed dominance. Even Abbo himself, whose monastery possessed countless proprietary churches, did not for a moment consider giving them up.[134] The movement against proprietary churches which gathered momentum from the middle of the eleventh century onwards was directed not against bishops, monasteries, canonries, and priests as proprietors, but only against the rights of laity in the bestowing of churches, regardless of whether these were based, like those of the king, on a theocratic conception of office, or on the rights of proprietors.[135]

A tendency to reject the possession of churches by laymen went hand in hand with attempts to restrict or abolish the rights of kings and princes in the appointment to bishoprics. Characteristic is the injunction of the Lenten synod of 1078 that the laity must be told what dangers for their

---

[132] While Meyer von Knonau, *Jahrbücher Heinrichs V.*, VII.135, cites the passage accurately, the statement by Haller, *Papsttum*, II.1, 475 is simply wrong: 'he contented himself with a wording which forbade laymen investiture "with churches"'; see also his 'Die Verhandlungen von Mouzon (1119)', *Abhandlungen zur Geschichte des Mittelalters* (Stuttgart 1944), where the misunderstanding on p. 193 n. 2 is particularly evident. But Kempf's account, *Handbuch*, 457, 'He could not bring himself to accept the extension of Calixtus's prohibition of investiture of churches to church property' is also wrong. It was not just church possessions but the churches themselves apart from bishoprics and monasteries which were struck off the list. It is, however, noteworthy that Hesso's explanation, 'videbatur enim eis, quod sub hoc capitulo domnus papa decimas et cetera ecclesiastica beneficia, quae antiquitus laici tenuerant conaretur minuere vel auferre' did not in the least correspond to the change made in the text.

[133] Abbo of Fleury, *Liber Apologeticus*, Migne, *PL* 139, col. 465.

[134] Tellenbach, *Libertas*, 115 and n. 7; Stutz, *Papst Alexander III.*, 31f. and n. 4.

[135] For an assessment of lay rights in proprietary churches as such see above, chapter 3.

souls they incurred by holding tithes and owning churches.[136] A canon of the council of Clermont (1095) declared: 'No altars or tithes and above all no churches may remain in lay hands. Those who own them are to be warned and implored to give them up. If they do not do so after repeated warnings they are to be excommunicated.'[137] But demands as radical as this could not be put into general practice, even though the moral pressure on laymen who owned churches was not without its effect. The tanner Leo of Bari, who renounced his churches 'at the urgings of wise ecclesiastics', offers a good example of this.[138] He was one of sixty-two seamen who had brought the bones of St Nicholas from Asia Minor to Bari and joined in an association to build the church dedicated to Nicholas there; this had left him with substantial rights. But now he had learned that it was 'a sin and a breach of the laws of the church and the sacred canons, if a lay person should have lordship over a church or over its property'. He therefore handed over the share he had acquired in the rights of the seamen. But simple renunciation, as we shall see, was not the only way to eliminate lay ownership of the church or to reform it in accordance with the demands of canon law.

Laymen had long made gifts of proprietary churches to monasteries, a tendency which had increased with the growth of the movement against lay rights over churches,[139] though it is hardly possible in the current state of scholarship to give anything like a statistical survey of the practice. The transfer of churches or parts of them, of tithes, and of ecclesiastical benefices is nevertheless recorded frequently. Georg Schreiber described Cluny even in its early phase as a 'magnetic field, which drew lay proprietary churches towards it'.[140] Although this great scholar repeatedly pointed out that it was monastic piety which found echoes among the laity, that 'Cluny knew how . . . to transform reluctantly perceived inclinations into inner assent to a deed which was regarded as a moral one', he nevertheless posited an exaggerated contrast between a reform-

---

[136] *Registrum* VI 5b, 402, c. XXXII.

[137] Pflugk-Harttung, *Acta*, II.161 no. 194, c. 10.

[138] H. F. Schmid, 'Gemeinschaftskirchen', 24ff. and especially 30; Dormeier, *Montecassino*, 163 n. 456; on Nordic congregational parish churches see also K. Haff, 'Das Großkirch-spiel in nordischen und niederdeutschen Rechten des Mittelalters', *ZRGKA*, 32 (1943) sections I and II.

[139] See already Mollat, 'Restitution', 399ff., where the reservations made by donors are taken into account; Dormeier, *Montecassino*, 57ff., shows appropriate caution in assessing the views there on lay control of churches.

[140] Schreiber, 'Gregor VII.', 126; see Wollasch, 'Reform und Adel', *VuF*, 17 (1973), 292 and n. 77: 'the Cluniacs had it confirmed by the reform papacy itself that their lordship over churches and monasteries was untouchable and praiseworthy'.

minded episcopate and 'a laity entangled in the material exploitation of
the house of God and its revenues'. 'It [the episcopate] hammered and
drummed on the opposing position'; and in further military metaphors
Schreiber speaks of waves of attack by French synods against lay ownership of lesser churches, of a hail of fire, of opportunities for monastic and
canonical groups to break through and shake the front line of lay
domination of the church. 'One may see how the laity, once so proud in
its ownership, now retreats, step by step. It admits defeat. Every donation
means a further acceptance of a passive role.'[141] These sentences were
written during or shortly after the Second World War and are marked by
the military jargon that was fashionable at the time. It may be doubted
whether there was so much combat in connection with the countless
donations of proprietary churches to monasteries, even in France, for
many laymen offered their churches to monasteries, as they had always
done, not so much under duress as with the desire to support the
salvation-bringing activities of the monks in them.

In spite of extensive gifts to ecclesiastical institutions, especially to
monasteries, large numbers of churches still remained in lay hands in the
first half of the twelfth century. But both the realisation in practice of the
rights of the bishop and his assistance as defined in the old legislation on
proprietary churches and their extension had the effect of reducing the
freedom of the church proprietor. Lay rights disappeared altogether as far
as these concerned the spiritual direction of the church. The proprietor's
role in appointing and controlling the cleric of the church declined, that
of the bishop increased. Investment was now being made in pastoral care,
not just in the church as a set of resources.[142] The process was much the
same as that which affected the higher churches. The owners were
restricted to a few non-spiritual functions. They retained the right to
find a cleric for their church and to present him, but it was episcopal
ordination which was crucial. In the end it was not ownership which
came to be seen as the basis of the lay proprietor's rights but his services
as founder, donor, and protector.[143] But this transformation of owners
into patrons was only completed in the twelfth century.[144] If one

---

[141] Schreiber, 'Gregor VII.', 61; Schreiber, 'Kluny und die Eigenkirchen', 359–418: 'hail of
fire', 'a platoon eager for victory', 'activist NCOs', 'Burgundian citadel'; on the result see
Schreiber, 'Gregor VII.', 117.

[142] Wirtz, 'Donum', 131ff. and especially 137f.; Feine, *Kirchliche Rechtsgeschichte*, 395ff., on
what follows as well.

[143] Wirtz, 'Donum', 142; J. Vincke, 'Der Übergang vom Eigenkirchenrecht zum
Patronatsrecht bezüglich der Niederkirchen in Katalonien und Aragon', *StGreg*, 3 (1948),
459.

[144] Stutz, 'Gratian', 11f.

recalls that in the eleventh century there had been denials that the layman could have any rights at all over churches one can see that here too a compromise was gradually arrived at. The institution of the proprietary church was not so easily defended as the rights of the king, which were based on his rulership by the grace of God. It was done away with completely in as much as property rights in churches could no longer be freely disposed of; but the development of the institution of the patron was accompanied by the concession of individual rights which allowed the patron moral and religious influence over his churches and often even a fixed share in their incomes.[145]

It is crucial to note that the history of the ownership of churches by other churches, that is by cathedrals, priories, monasteries, and other institutions, took a quite different direction, although the law of proprietary churches was originally a unified one which applied both to ecclesiastics and to laymen.[146] There was no inherent spiritual nexus between a bishopric, priory, or monastery and the church it owned.[147] A bishop had no more rights over a proprietary church which did not lie in his diocese than did a layman, an abbot, or any other ecclesiastic.[148] Like them he had to respect the rights of the diocesan bishop and his assistants. But although there was in principle no difference between lay and ecclesiastical proprietary rights the latter were not attacked in the eleventh century. It was thus not a question of restoring ancient diocesan rights; it was a question of the relative ranking of the two great orders within the church, clerics and laymen. The clergy was placed so high above the laity that the proprietary rights of a layman over the clerics who served his churches came to be regarded as intolerable; but if a layman's church was transferred to an ecclesiastic the proprietary church as such was unexceptionable.

Nevertheless, the traditional legislation on proprietary churches was repeated at synods, often with application to ecclesiastical proprietors, and sometimes it was even tightened up. The diocesan bishop was to play a proper part in the appointment of clerics to monastic proprietary churches and those owned by other bishops. Chaplains were to be appointed to monastic churches at the bishop's decision (*arbitrium*), by his ordination and with the consent of the monks.[149] The *cura* of parishes was to be

---

[145] Stutz, 'Eigenkirche, Eigenkloster', 364ff.
[146] Stutz, 'Gratian', 21.   [147] Stutz, *Benefizialwesen*, 416.
[148] Tellenbach, *Libertas*, 112 and appendix VII. These canons were a continuation of the provisions of the Carolingian era: fundamental was Eugenius II's synod of 826, MGH Capit. I.374.
[149] Clermont c. 16, Pflugk-Harttung, *Acta* II.161 no. 194.

bestowed by the bishop on the priest with the abbot's consent; the priest was responsible to the bishop for the spiritualities, to the abbot for the temporalities of the church.[150] Bishops were to install priests but not to demand anything from the churches of monasteries except the customary dues.[151] There were thus repeated attempts to preserve the unity of the diocese; how successful these were can hardly be judged.[152] Even Anselm of Canterbury is said to have consecrated priests for his proprietary churches outside his own diocese,[153] though Pascal II had only just explained to him in 1102 that the unity of the diocese was of crucial importance. In answer to a query by Anselm the pope had declared: 'The bishop, once consecrated, may not accept churches from the hands of a layman if they lie outside his diocese, though it is lawful to do so if they lie within it. For that would seem to be not so much a giving as a taking back, since all churches within a diocese ought to be in the power of the bishop. Abbots ought to receive them from the hands of the bishop.'[154]

There must often have been abuses in connection with the transfer of proprietary churches to monasteries. Monks appear to have bought churches from laymen who did not want or were unable to defend their rights.[155] The synod of Poitiers (1078) allowed abbots, monks, and canons to make such acquisitions if the diocesan bishop agreed.[156] The new owners needed to be explicitly instructed that the priest of a donated church ought to have the same income that he had previously enjoyed;[157] but even bishops appear to have tried to get hold of the revenues of monastic churches. Urban II's council at Nîmes in 1096 deplored an ancient simonistic practice whereby bishops 'sold' altars and tithes on the death of a cleric to his successor, presumably implying that they expected a payment for investiture of the new possessor,[158] much like the practice in normal changes of ownership.[159]

---

[150] Clermont c. 4, Mansi xx, col. 902.   [151] Nîmes (1096) c. 1, *ibid.*, 931ff.

[152] According to the conciliar provisions which have survived it was essentially a question of distinguishing between spiritual and secular competence over monastic proprietary churches, as Violante, 'Monachesimo', 43, rightly stresses. This was merely to point to an old demand. However, one can definitely not deduce from these sources that popes and bishops proceeded against monastic proprietary churches in the interests of a restored diocesan structure. An investigation of regional differences might allow a more nuanced view of the matter.

[153] Böhmer, 'Eigenkirchentum', 302.

[154] JL 5909 = *S. Anselmi opera omnia*, iv.126f. no. 223.

[155] Mollat, 'Restitution', 416; Dormeier, *Montecassino*, 94ff.

[156] Poitiers (1078) c. 6, Mansi xx, col. 498.

[157] Lillebonne (1080) c. 12, Mansi xx, col. 557.

[158] C. 1 p. 931ff.; see Barlow, *English Church 1000–1066*, 186.

[159] See above, pp. 83 and 169.

In the course of the twelfth century the rights of ecclesiastics over proprietary churches at first developed along similar lines to those of laymen. The rights of the diocesan bishop were secured. The institution of the clerical patron was developed for chapels and small churches; it implied the right to present the cleric to the church and to a share of the revenues. The parish churches of monasteries and canonries could be fully incorporated once canons and the newer monastic orders had taken on the pastoral responsibilities associated with them. The older Benedictine monasteries (including Cluniacs, Hirsauans, and Cistercians) had originally rejected the servicing of parishes by their monks as incompatible with the monastic profession, but from the middle of the twelfth century full incorporation was more and more the rule, with the consequence that the bishop's rights were restricted and that the ecclesiastical foundation which owned the church was able to enjoy full use of its revenues.[160]

The transfer of churches from laymen to monasteries and canonries appears to have brought no improvement in the position of the clergy who serviced them, and indeed it often meant a worsening of their situation.[161] It was necessary to lay down that they should enjoy at least a modest proportion (*portio congrua*) of the revenues and properties of the parish. Whether the parish clergy was better educated, more devout, more conscientious in the ninth or twelfth centuries than it had been in the eleventh is a question which it is hardly possible to answer with certainty.[162]

'Monastic reform' and its connection with the wider changes within the church

Before the appearance of newer monastic movements in the late eleventh century western monasticism had been fairly uniform and more or less conservative. In France, Burgundy, and northern Spain, Cluny was both directly and indirectly a model and influence, a development which reached Germany and Italy somewhat later. In England, by contrast, native monastic traditions were on the whole preserved.[163]

What is known as monastic reform was a continuation, without decisive changes, of phenomena which can also be observed in earlier

[160] Feine, *Kirchliche Rechtsgeschichte*, 325ff.; Stutz, 'Gratian', 13ff. and 20; Wirtz, 'Donum', 150 n. 2.
[161] Böhmer, 'Eigenkirchentum', 351 and Barlow, *English Church 1066–1154*, 24, claim this of England specifically.
[162] According to Boyd, *Tithes*, 103, these conditions continued in parishes in the eleventh century.
[163] Barlow, *English Church 1066–1154*, 177ff.; Cantor, *Church, Kingship*, 310: a return to flight from the world in the twelfth century; Knowles, *Monastic Order*, 100.

eras.[164] All the measures taken towards reordering monasticism, both by
the monks themselves and by the environment which supported and
directed them, were directed to the one single end: to make possible, to
preserve, and to perfect the monastic way of life which brought salvation
to Christendom. Support was given for the monastic flight from the
world, for monastic good works in the form of asceticism and of service,
and for the monastic liturgy; abuses, where they had arisen, were
corrected. As a by-product of this there developed certain differences
in monastic customs and constitutions, but these were of secondary
importance compared with the common religious intention.[165]

The flight from the world could be realised most easily by solitary
hermits living in poverty. Monasteries could not be isolated from the
world to the same extent. They were in all essentials subject to the bishop
and his diocese and from the moment of their foundation were dependent
on material support, care, and protection by bishops, by ecclesiastical and
lay property owners, and by those who wielded public power. The richer
they were, the more indispensable was such cooperation. Abbots and their
monasteries shared interests with the founders and those of their owners
who were concerned for religion: preservation and perfection of the
internal life of the monastery and its protection from harmful influences
from without. As a rule the founders and owners of monasteries could do
more in this respect than abbots and monks.[166] Laymen had to take care
to protect their foundations from interventions by their descendants, who
sometimes saw their ancestors' foundations as having robbed them of
a part of their inheritance. Bishops had to take care that their successors
did not endanger their foundations. For reasons of this kind many
monasteries had in earlier times been donated to the king, who was seen
as a guarantor of their liberty and of their existence. Later it became
commoner to give monasteries to bishops for their security.[167] A monastery without a lord and owner seemed at first an impossibility. The
epoch-making novelty was the foundation of Cluny. Although its
founder Duke William the Pious gave it to the papacy, this was said

[164] See above, pp. 109ff.
[165] These must nevertheless be admired as the expression of a genuine striving, even if they
sometimes lost themselves in external details and in pedantry.
[166] Reforms rarely proceeded from the abbots and convents themselves. They were over-
whelmingly the result of initiatives taken by ecclesiastical and lay monastic proprietors,
who had been impressed by the exemplary monasticism of another monastery. The
popes also rarely intervened without having been asked to do so by another party.
[167] There were cases of donors retaining a right to buy back their monasteries if these should
be oppressed by their episcopal proprietor; for examples see Tellenbach, *Eigenklöster*, 40
n. 221, 42 n. 228, 48 n. 260.

explicitly to be only for its protection, not for its domination. Since the pope was a long way off and at the time powerless, the abbot and convent of Cluny had themselves to take on the functions which were elsewhere exercised by the lords of monasteries. They had to administer and protect their property and rights themselves by making use of their moral authority; in cases of conflict they frequently had to use diplomatic skills to reach an acceptable compromise.[168] Papal privileges allowed them to have those acts for which a bishop was indispensable carried out by an external bishop of their choice, without having to risk damaging interventions and claims by their diocesan bishop. The election of a new abbot could also take place without external intervention. It became customary for the abbot to designate his successor during his own lifetime and appoint him as coadjutor. The election by the convent conformed to the Rule of St Benedict, but as in proprietary and royal monasteries it was essentially a giving of consent to a decision which had already been taken. The symbolic assumption of office seems to have taken place without any external participation, if it is permissible to reconstruct Cluny's lost early customs from those monastic customs which were codified later under Cluny's influence. It would appear that from an early date the old abbot performed it by handing over his staff of office; after he had died the elect invested himself by taking the staff from the altar.[169]

Cluny was itself not a proprietary monastery, but it did not make the slightest attempt to combat the institution of property rights in churches and monasteries, whether these were in the hands of kings, bishops, or other lay or ecclesiastical magnates. Cluny possessed countless proprietary churches of its own, and from the late eleventh century onwards, as the movement against lay proprietary churches gathered momentum, it acquired many more, most of them by donation, some by purchase.[170] When lay or ecclesiastical owners of monasteries asked Cluny for abbots or monks to reform their monasteries or introduce Cluniac customs, she did not make it a precondition that the owners should renounce their ownership before fulfilling such requests. Saint-Benigne in Dijon remained a proprietary monastery of Langres even after Bishop Bruno had asked for the monk William of Volpiano from Abbot Maiolus of Cluny in 990.[171] The monastery in Dijon remained quite independent of Cluny

---

[168] See above, p. 111.
[169] De Valous, *Le Monachisme clunisien*, 90ff.; de Valous, 'Cluny', 36ff.; Mayer, *Fürsten und Staat*, 68ff.; Bulst, *Untersuchungen*, 196ff.; Jakobs, *Hirsauer*, 82ff.; Borgolte, *Klosterreform*, 56 and n. 43.
[170] See in particular Urban II., JL 5602 = Migne, *PL* 151, cols. 441f.
[171] Bulst, *Untersuchungen*, 35f.

and under its new abbot became itself the centre of a widespread monastic circle with exemplary character. Saint-Benigne in turn gave no impulses to the abolition of proprietary churches and monasteries. The monastery of Fécamp, taken over by William, remained a proprietary monastery of the dukes of Normandy, and the other monasteries he influenced themselves possessed proprietary churches. When William followed the Cluniac model shortly before his death by designating the monk Halinard as his successor with the agreement of the convent, this was not intended to diminish the rights of Saint-Benigne's owner, the bishop of Langres, who seems to have approved the election.

William of Volpiano together with his brothers and relatives founded the monastery of Fruttuaria in his home diocese of Ivrea in 1000 or 1001.[172] Fruttuaria was not donated to anyone, not even to the Roman church as Cluny had been. It was to be God's property alone. But William took great trouble to secure papal and royal protection for it. He retained the direction of the monastery, though he did not even call himself abbot. Probably it was not until 1023 that he installed the first abbot, John, with the agreement of the convent. The appointment of a new abbot had already been defined along Cluniac lines in the privilege granted by Arduin in 1005.[173] The old abbot was to designate his successor with the agreement of the convent during his own lifetime and invest him with the abbot's staff. If the predecessor was no longer alive the elect was himself to take the staff from the high altar. Fruttuaria was thus protected from the start against episcopal intervention in abbatial elections. William secured in addition a privilege of exemption from the bishop of Ivrea, which was confirmed by the pope. Abbot and monks acquired the right to ask a bishop of their own choice to perform all consecrations and ordinations in the monastery. Fruttuaria was not intended to be a criticism of the existing practice of proprietary monasteries, any more than Cluny or Saint-Benigne or other earlier monasteries which had been regarded as a pattern of the monastic virtues. Their privileges were conceived of as enhancing the freedom of the monastery concerned to pursue the religious life, not as a propagandistic model for a general reform of monastic constitutions.

From the middle of the eleventh century Fruttuaria had an important influence on monastic life in Germany. The first step was the foundation of Siegburg by Anno of Cologne, who visited Fruttuaria in 1068 and was

[172] Ibid., 115f.
[173] MGH Dipl. Arduini, no. 9; see on this H. H. Kaminsky, 'Zur Gründung von Fruttuaria durch den Abt Wilhelm von Dijon', ZKG, 77 (1966), 245f.; Jakobs, 'Cluniacenser und Papsttum', 658.

granted permission to take an abbot and twelve monks back to his home diocese. The resulting reform of Siegburg together with its diffusion and its programme have been investigated and impressively documented by Josef Semmler.[174] His work has shown that Siegburg not only remained completely independent of its mother monastery and soon lost all contact with it, but also differed sharply from it. If Fruttuaria had been founded free of all earthly lordship, Siegburg remained the proprietary monastery of the archbishop of Cologne, who had a decisive say in the appointment of a new abbot in spite of the monastery's privilege of free election. He also influenced the appointment of the monastery's advocate. Anno accepted gifts of monasteries by laymen to the church of Cologne, but the monks of Siegburg were apparently not prepared to take on monasteries which remained under lay domination.

Somewhat later we can observe the influence of the idea of a special monastic freedom – such as that of Cluny or Saint-Benigne or Fruttuaria – on a group of south German monasteries. These were mostly founded by powerful nobles, who out of concern for their monasteries' future donated them to the pope, renounced their proprietary rights over the election and appointment of abbots and reserved the advocacy for a member of their family who would be appointed by the monastery and enjoy only limited rights and revenues. These developments occurred at the same time as the popes were turning against traditional lay rights within the church and beginning their great conflict with the Salian emperors. The south German nobles supported the papal cause for their own reasons; the monastic movements affected went beyond mere movements of internal renewal and were more influenced than their older models by current political trends.[175] All this has been extensively discussed in recent scholarship. Absolute certainty is hard to achieve because the sources are patchy and often ambiguous or partisan. Since the relationship between the promulgation of new forms of monastic constitution and their realisation in practice could change over quite short periods of time it is hard to judge their influence on the history of the monasteries concerned; often we cannot go beyond hypotheses. A few exemplary and particularly well-known cases may help to illustrate this.

It is probably not possible to explain fully how St Blasien, a *cella* of Rheinau, rapidly came to be one of the most important monasteries of south-west Germany. Abbot Giselbert, in office from 1068, sent two

---

[174] Semmler, *Siegburg*, 37ff.; K. Schmid, 'Adel und Reform', 277: 'the manifestations of a Suabian reform movement and of so-called Gregorianism are not completely congruent with one another'.

[175] See below, p. 301 with n. 195.

monks to Fruttuaria, 'whence they acquired the religion of our order'. In 1074 Fruttuaria and the Black Forest monastery concluded an agreement of confraternity. Perhaps the connection was the result of a suggestion by the Empress Agnes, who had already in 1062 written to the abbot of Fruttuaria and, together with her son-in-law Rudolf of Rheinfelden, enjoyed close contacts with St Blasien, a monastery which was claimed by the bishop of Basle as his.[176] It is possible that Fruttuarian customs and practices influenced St Blasien as early as that, for they were probably known there, as can be seen from the early history of the Hirsau movement.

As early as 1043 Leo IX had persuaded his nephew, Count Adalbert II of Calw, to restore his decayed proprietary monastery in Hirsau dedicated to St Aurelius. The plan was not realised until much later, when Abbot Frederick and monks were brought from the distinguished monastery of Einsiedeln in 1065.[177] In all this the count acted like an old-style monastic proprietor. He secured privileges from pope and king; he appointed and then deposed Abbot Frederick, and secured the monk William from St Emmeram in Regensburg as his successor with the consent of the convent. The choice of the first two abbots suggests that the count was concerned to have a monastery in which genuine monastic piety was practised. When in 1075 he secured a diploma from Henry IV, the so-called Hirsau Formula, he took a quite different path.[178] He still appeared as proprietor, but as one who renounced his rights and those of his heirs; it was at his request that the king issued the unusual privilege. The convent was to elect and appoint a new abbot from its own ranks or from elsewhere on the death of the abbot; the Cluniac practice of designation by the predecessor was not envisaged. The investiture of the new abbot was to be carried out by the prior or dean, who was to take the staff of office from the altar dedicated to St Aurelius and convey it to the elect, a practice which has been appropriately termed the 'right of monastic self-investiture'.[179] Even the choice of the advocate – to be made if possible from among the family of the founder – was left to the

[176] Büttner, 'St. Blasien und das Bistum Basel im. 11. und 12. Jahrhundert', 138–48; Wollasch, 'Muri und St. Blasien', 425f.; Jakobs, *Adel*, 11ff. and 35; Borgolte, *Klosterreform*, 57; Mordek, 'Papst Urban II.', 205ff.; the source cited in the text is the *Annales Necrologici* of St Blasien, MGH Necrologia 1.329f.; see Meyer von Knonau, *Jahrbücher Heinrichs IV.*, 1.167 n. 98; for Agnes and Fruttuaria see Giesebrecht, *Kaiserzeit*, III.1255, dated to 1062.

[177] K. Schmid, *Kloster Hirsau*, 57; Jakobs, *Hirsauer*, 7.

[178] K. Schmid, *Kloster Hirsau*, 66f.

[179] MGH Dipl. Henry IV, no. 280; the quotation is taken from Borgolte, *Klosterreform*, 56 n. 43.

abbot, at whose request the advocate was to receive the right of jurisdiction from the king. The count also secured papal protection for the
monastery; in token of this the abbot was to lay a gold piece each year on
the altar of St Peter. But none of the rights renounced by the count of
Calw went to king or pope; Hirsau had achieved complete emancipation.

What led to this cannot be reliably determined. The tales in the
biography of William of Hirsau, written in the 1090s, about a dispute
between count and abbot, have a legendary flavour.[180] Adalbert of Calw,
like other lords sympathetic to reform who gave up their proprietary
rights, sincerely wanted to make possible a further degree of monastic
perfection by his act of emancipation. He was hardly in a position to force
them to become free.[181] It is more likely that such lords took advice from
abbots or monks whom they trusted. In Hirsau the new constitution of
1075 was probably drafted by Abbot William, who then won the count's
consent. He may have been influenced by the examples of Cluny, Saint-
Benigne, and in particular Fruttuaria, with which he had become familiar
while at St Blasien. What has been said about an influence of Gregory VII
on Hirsau hardly goes beyond more or less plausible hypotheses.[182] It
should not be overlooked that the count of Calw had a special relationship with the pope,[183] nor that Gregory VII in 1076 rejected lay rights
over churches in principle, though in his practice he was far from taking
this seriously.[184] On the other hand the sharpness with which Gregory in
1079 criticised a privilege issued by his predecessor Alexander II is very
noticeable: the privilege conceded the hereditary advocacy for the
monastery of All Saints in Schaffhausen to its founder, Count Eberhard of
Nellenburg. Gregory made his criticisms precisely at the point when
Eberhard's son Burchard had renounced all worldly power over the
monastery. Did he really intend to affront the count, his faithful

---

[180] *Vita Wilhelmi abbatis Hirsaugiensis* c. 2, MGH SS XII.212: the count, who had refounded
the reendowed Hirsau, is depicted not simply as the stock model of the violent layman
but as a cunning trickster. God himself, whom William begged with tears in his eyes 'ut
de terrene potestatis iugo eriperet locum', had mercy and 'ex improviso eundem
comitem tanta circumdedit adversitate, ut pene desperaret ullum evadendi aditum se
posse reperire'. The poor man sought the advice and help of ecclesiastics, who persuaded
him to set the monastery free.
[181] For a different view see Jakobs, *Hirsauer*, for example p. 98: 'Hirsau wrested' – who is
Hirsau?; p. 99: 'in 1075 Hirsau broke with the proprietary church right of the count
of Calw'; pp. 191f.: 'the reformed monasteries' fundamental concern was to wrest
proprietary monastic rights from dynastic lords' and 'this sacrifice was made by the count
of Calw in 1075 under duress'.
[182] See Borgolte, *Klosterreform*, 74 n. 112 on the differing views.
[183] See *Registrum* II 11, pp. 142f.
[184] See above p. 266.

supporter, at this point? The letter in which the criticisms were expressed is addressed to William of Hirsau. Can it be that William had persuaded Burchard to take the step and that the letter was impetrated with his consent?[185]

There were other cases where the advocacy belonging to the founding family was not just reduced in its competence but had its very right to existence denied. A famous example of this is the former Habsburg proprietary monastery of Muri. When in 1082 Count Werner invited the abbots William of Hirsau and Siegfried of Schaffhausen to reform Muri with Hirsau monks he renounced not only his property but also his hereditary rights to the advocacy, which were frequently reserved elsewhere.[186] At first Muri became completely subordinate to St Blasien and had only a prior; its advocate was chosen by the abbot of St Blasien. A few years later the monks of Muri succeeded in winning their independence and an abbot of their own, and it was realised at this point that an advocate from the founders' family was a better choice.[187] Even though attempts were made here and there to eliminate advocacies based on proprietary rights completely, the general development of the advocacy shows that for a long time it was not possible to remove all traces of the proprietary past.[188]

A great number of monasteries was influenced for shorter or longer periods by the customs or constitution of Hirsau. This did not, however, lead to the creation of an organised monastic association, and the legal position of these monasteries varied considerably. For his map of the Hirsau 'order' Hermann Jakobs used different signs to denote imperial and royal monasteries, episcopal monasteries, and dynastic monasteries which had not been donated either to the kingdom or to a bishopric.[189] This alone shows that a substantial element of proprietary rights survived within the groups of monasteries influenced by Hirsau.[190] One meets

[185] *Registrum* VII 24, pp. 502ff.
[186] Büttner, 'Wilhelm von Hirsau', 324; K. Schmid, 'Adel und Reform', 308f.
[187] Mayer, *Fürsten und Staat*, 117; Wollasch, 'Muri und St. Blasien', 422f.; Jakobs, *Hirsauer*, 157f.
[188] There are countless examples in Tellenbach, *Eigenklöster*, chapter 3; Klebel, 'Eigen-klosterrecht', 175–214, is particularly suggestive; K. Schmid, 'Adel und Reform', 315, rightly stresses that the founding families did not suffer by renouncing their proprietary rights.
[189] Jakobs, *Hirsauer* (at the end of the book).
[190] The subtle discussion in Jakobs, *Hirsauer*, 86f., of the 'rejection of self-investiture as an expression of spiritual proprietary church law' has not really convinced me. The question was hardly thought about in such a principled way in Hirsau, which like all other important monasteries of the eleventh and twelfth centuries possessed numerous proprietary churches of its own; see K. O. Müller, 'Traditiones Hirsaugienses', *Zeitschrift für württembergische Landesgeschichte*, 9 (1949–50), 28ff., who shows that at this time

curious combinations such as that found in the monastery of Komburg in the diocese of Würzburg.[191] Even before monks from Hirsau took it over it had been donated to the church of Mainz under Archbishop Wezilo. Wezilo's successor Ruthard laid down that the convent, which had adopted Hirsau's customs, should have the right of free election; but the elected abbot was to receive the staff of office only at the point of his consecration, and this was to be performed not by the diocesan, the bishop of Würzburg, but by the proprietor, the archbishop of Mainz.[192] If this interpretation is correct then the arrangement was distinctly uncanonical.[193] It led to disputes between Mainz and Würzburg with the consequence that at the beginning of the thirteenth century a papal legate determined that it should be abolished. The archbishop of Mainz was to be patron in Komburg but the bishop of Würzburg was to have spiritual jurisdiction there; this corresponded to the normal development of rights of proprietorship over monasteries into rights of patronage. In other countries as well, the older monasteries remained, in spite of increased autonomy, tied to their environment by the fact that their founders and former lords, kings, bishops, and nobles, retained restricted rights of participation in the monastery's internal affairs. Only the emergence of monastic orders in the strict sense created new forms of completely independent monasticism.[194]

Monastic reform in the eleventh and early twelfth centuries was not congruent with 'Gregorianism'.[195] It had its own special preconditions, which existed long before the impulses sent out by the papacy had begun

Hirsau possessed forty-nine churches wholly or in part. See also Bogumil, *Bistum Halberstadt*, 88: the monasteries of the reform movement initiated by Herrand possessed, acquired, and founded proprietary churches, which they viewed as a form of wealth.

[191] Mayer, *Fürsten und Staat*, 202f.; Büttner, 'Erzstift Mainz', 34ff.; Büttner, 'Wilhelm von Hirsau', 335; Jakobs, *Hirsauer*, 90.

[192] Mayer, *Fürsten und Staat*, 203, 207, 272 presumably assumed for this reason that the bishop of Würzburg retained the right of consecration. Jakobs, *Hirsauer*, 91f., justifiably argues against this that there is no mention of such a retention in the Komburg charter. Semmler, *Siegburg*, 72 and 177, notes the interesting cases of Sinsheim and Gladbach, where spiritual jurisdiction was transferred from the diocesan bishop to the proprietary bishop.

[193] Tellenbach, *Eigenklöster*, 87; Klebel, 'Eigenklosterreche', 192ff.: monasteries founded by laymen and made over to the pope or a bishop must count as family monasteries.

[194] See above, p. 110.

[195] Bultot, 'Mépris du monde', 275: 'we know that one has to distinguish the movement of monastic reform in the eleventh century . . . from the Gregorian movement'. Bishops who founded or reformed monasteries were by no means always Gregorians: see J. Vogel, 'Zur Kirchenpolitik', 162, on Wezilo of Mainz.

to take effect. Monastic reform was influenced by these but followed its
own development. In general, monks shared the traditional veneration for
the papacy as head of the church. But in the historic conflicts between
popes and secular princes they were not the popes' automatic allies. The
English monasteries would have had no opportunities to act in this way
in the face of royal dominance, nor would those in southern Italy and
Sicily. In Spain as well monasteries were scarcely able to take a position
opposed to their princes. In the great struggle between the popes and the
Salian rulers the most prominent monastic groupings took up varying
positions. The Siegburg congregation has been accurately described as
more or less neutral.[196] Monasteries often adopted the attitude of
bishops or princes with whom they had close contacts. The Hirsau
monasteries were probably in general 'Gregorian', but they were by no
means all equally radical.[197] The well-known wandering preachers
against Henry belonged to the south-western opposition movement
which included ecclesiastical and secular elements with very varying
motives and aims.[198] Admittedly, the vicious propaganda against the
king's person, which went way beyond all political or ecclesiastical
considerations, must have had its effect.[199] The behaviour of Gebhard,
abbot of Hirsau and then bishop of Speyer, towards the captured and
betrayed emperor in Bökelheim at Christmas 1105 can hardly be
explained rationally.[200]

Henry IV for his part frequently fulfilled wishes expressed by reform
monasteries. As a young man he had supported the monastic policies of
Archbishop Anno of Cologne, and he had no reservations about granting
the privilege known as the Hirsau Formula to Hirsau. There is no sign
that Henry had any objections to any form of reform monasticism, and it
is not particularly plausible to suppose that he saw in the reform of south

[196] Semmler, *Siegburg*, 135: 'The monks of Siegburg were essentially neutral in the great
dispute between *regnum* and *sacerdotium*', and p. 258: 'it cannot be overlooked that the
younger Cluniac reform of Siegburg was often supported by Henry IV's most faithful
adherents'; Semmler, 'Klosterreform und Gregorianische Reform', 171; on monasteries
and monks on both sides see already Hauck, *Kirchengeschichte Deutschlands*, III.865,
and further, among others, Büttner, 'Erzsttift Mainz', 61; Fleckenstein,'Hofkapelle
und Reichsepiskopat', 119; Robinson, 'Pope Gregory VII and Episcopal Authority',
116.
[197] Jakobs, *Hirsauer*, 212ff.; see already Hauck, *Kirchengeschichte Deutschlands*, III.873.
[198] Zerfass, *Laienpredigt*, 131ff.
[199] See above, p. 275.
[200] The former abbot of Hirsau was certainly a quite deliberate choice as the merciless guard
of an emperor who was to be finally eliminated. See Meyer von Knonau, *Jahrbücher
Heinrichs IV.*, v.264ff.

German aristocratic monasteries a dangerous attack on the imperial church and on imperial interests.[201]

[201] For another view see Jakobs, *St. Blasien*, 272, who in my opinion overestimates the interest shown by the king for or against the reform of a particular monastery. A similar line is taken by J. Vogel, 'Rudolf von Rheinfelden', 30, who ascribed Henry's mistrust of Rudolf in the last resort to the duke's reforming activities, especially in respect of the monastery of St Blasien; against this see K.-U. Jäschke's review in *Hessisches Jahrbuch für Landesgeschichte*, 19 (1969), 528f. Nor would I risk with Jakobs the hypothesis that the monks in imperial monasteries prayed for the emperor, the empire, and for the king and his followers in the church and the world, whereas Cluniac monks prayed for nobles in their own right in the church and the world. What can we know about this?

8

POPE, CHURCH, AND CHRISTENDOM

•

The unity of the church has its origins essentially in the belief in the omnipresence of Christ in the sacraments, in the liturgy, and in prayer. Its organisational forms by contrast are rooted more in specific communities which coexist with one another – individual churches and parishes, dioceses, provinces, patriarchates, and synods held within them – than in the great overriding community of faith. The great turning-point under Constantine the Great and the subsequent Christianisation of the Roman empire produced a temporary and fairly superficial unification, whose problems soon became apparent. Gelasius I's doctrine of the two powers, for centuries the theoretical basis of unity, showed reservations in the way it recognised that *sacerdotium* and *regnum* belonged to 'this' world. In any case, reality did not correspond to this famous theory; often enough we can observe the old feeling that the realm of Christ and that of the world were alien to one another, something which was either to be rejected militantly or accepted humbly.

The unifying effects of the Roman empire did not long survive. The particular kingdoms which emerged and gradually subordinated the churches with their territories came on the whole to be a hindrance to contacts between the churches, which nevertheless still occurred here and there. The national and regnal churches were to a greater or lesser extent autonomous and not easily influenced from outside. The high religious authority of the Roman church and the pope did not change this situation much. Only exceptionally did popes play a significant role beyond their own region before the middle of the eleventh century. They were normally active only when called upon to be so, not on their own initiative; their advice or judgements were not compulsory; they could be accepted, ignored, or rejected at will. The popes did not have the power to command, except perhaps in their own immediate vicinity: in the churches of the city of Rome and in their church province they could act like a bishop or metropolitan, and within the *patrimonium Petri*, the area of their secular lordship, to the same extent as could other large proprietors and princes. Their means of enforcing their will militarily, judicially, and financially did not extend further than those of a medium-ranking prince. For this reason also their political and social significance for the lands and peoples of the West was not great, and it was distinctly unstable. The possibilities open to them of using a universalistic ideology to bind the particular churches together, either politically, judicially, or institutionally, were also very limited.

Only from the time of Henry III, Leo IX, and Victor II did the popes and their assistance make increasingly effective and determined attempts to exercise real leadership within the western church. Both the claim and the wish to issue instructions to all churches, not just to those in their immediate sphere of influence, was a novelty. The churches, up to then united only in a spiritual fashion, came gradually to be united by the fact that there now existed an instance on earth which commanded and judged. Christ had always been their monarch; the pope now became a representative of the heavenly lord who was present not just in the sacred mysteries but in real historical time, commanding and demanding obedience. As their head he had the effect of forging the churches in this world, in spite of all their divergences, into a unity, and thus realising their catholicity.

The new idea of a hierarchically organised church bound to obedience to the pope was not realised suddenly. It took on significance only gradually, and the higher clergy, especially the bishops, clung more or less determinedly to the customary order, in a resistance which took the forms of an inability to understand the new, a rigid traditionalism, and a conscious resistance to the pope's authoritarian interventions in matters of law and religion which were either rejected or even attacked as unlawful. Moreover, once the popes had come to claim a right to command and discipline laymen as members of the church, there were severe conflicts from the pontificate of Gregory VII onwards, which led to more rapid changes in western Christianity. The controversies which arose out of these gave a powerful impulse to the exposition and development of the ancient religious ideas on which the popes claimed to base their

authority. The growing activities of the popes as pastors and rulers
corresponded to the development and the justification of the theory of
papal primacy and its ecclesiological significance.

The expansion and realisation of the papal claim to lead the whole
church as its superior were based on the old notions of the Roman church
as the guarantee of the true faith and of Peter as the prince of the
apostles.[1] The popes themselves frequently referred straightforwardly and
explicitly in their official writings to the way in which they represented St
Peter or the Roman church. A pope like Gregory VII could call himself
the vicar of St Peter, *qui nunc in carne vivit* (who is now alive in the flesh).[2]
When Gregory claimed in the *Dictatus Papae* that the Roman pontifex was
sanctified by the merits of St Peter this was probably meant to be taken
quite literally.[3] This sanctity was the expression of a miraculous closeness
to the prince of the apostles, but it too gave the activities of the pope
within the church universal an exclusive character. Gregory showed
inconsistency and ambiguity in his pronouncements on the relationship
between the pope and his apostolic or divine lord. Often he made a clear
distinction between St Peter and himself, as for example in his first letter
to Bishop Hermann of Metz: 'if only the blessed Peter could answer
through me, who is often venerated or injured in the person of myself, his
servant'.[4] In despair he prayed to God: 'Either You Yourself with Your
Peter must steer the papacy or else You must look on while I am defeated
and the papacy is covered in confusion.'[5] The prayers in which Gregory

---

[1] There was not as yet a complete definition of dogma, but rather a certain tendency to
'religious indeterminacy' had been preserved – the expression comes from H. Dombrois,
Hierarchie. Grund und Grenze einer umstrittenen Struktur (Vienna 1971), 13. C. Violante
speaks of indeterminacy in a similar sense at a crucial point of his conference summing-
up, 'La riforma Gregoriana', *StGrat*, 13 (1989), 427: 'This ecclesiological indeterminacy
seems to me to be the characteristic of his pontificate.' S. Kuttner, 'Urban II and the
Doctrine of Interpretation', *StGrat*, 15 (1972), 55–85, rightly notes that 'Gregory VII was
by no means an unbending doctrinaire'. Morrison, 'Canossa', 142: 'For Gregory
there was a close relationship between the comprehensive power of St Peter and papal
authority, the two were not identical.'

[2] *Registrum* IX 3; on Petrine mysticism and Petrinity see Goez, 'Reformpapsttum', 211f.;
on Gregory's conviction that he as pope was as one with the prince of the apostles see
Nitschke, 'Wirksamkeit Gottes', 152ff.; on his belief that he was identical with St Peter
see Nitschke, 'Gregor VII.', 277f. For a summary of the role in Gregory's makeup of the
historical figure of Peter, its tradition, its theology, its ecclesiological significance, see
M. Maccarone, 'I fondamenti "petrini" del primato romano in Gregorio VII', *StGreg*, 13
(1989), 55–128, especially 96ff., where Maccarone brings out the immediate and very
untraditional personal devotion shown by Gregory towards St Peter.

[3] *Registrum* II 55a c. 23, p. 207; see H. Fuhrmann, 'Über die Heiligkeit des Papstes',
Jahrbuch der Akademie der Wissenschafte zu Göttingen (1980), 78ff.

[4] *Registrum* IV 2.   [5] *Registrum* V 21.

pronounced his excommunications and depositions of Henry IV all have St Peter as their addressee.[6] Admittedly, this reverent sense of distance towards the prince of the apostles had no effect on the absolute obedience which Gregory demanded for his commands: 'Therefore I believe that it is through your mercy, not through my deeds, that it has pleased and pleases you that the Christian people, which is specially entrusted to you, should obey me, especially by virtue of your vicariate which is entrusted to me. And through your grace God has given to me the power to bind and to loose.'[7] He saw his plenitude of power as so comprehensive that it made him a judge even of the highest on earth, something we shall return to.

Gregory did not identify himself completely with St Peter, but he did identify his commands with those of the prince of the apostles or even of God, his verdict with that of the Holy Ghost,[8] the obedience due to him with that owed to St Peter. In consequence, disobedience could be called idolatry.[9] And when disobedience to the pope counted as deviation from the true faith, as heresy, we can see that papal authority, in spite of the expressions of humility we have noted, was taken as being divine.[10] Gregory's environment, in reacting against him, produced still more explicit if less sublime interpretations of his beliefs. As early as 1076 the German episcopate accused Gregory of having 'arrogated to himself a certain new and unseemly power'. As far as he could he had taken from the bishops all the power which they had been granted by God through

---

[6] *Registrum* III 10a, VII 14a.

[7] *Registrum* III 10a; C. Schneider, *Sacerdotium*, sees, besides a consciousness of being Peter's vicar and of exercising the power to bind and loose, a prophetic vocation as fundamental to Gregory's religiosity. It seems questionable to me whether the frequent reference to prophets in Gregory's writings are simply literary and stylistic in origin or a genuine revival of the prophetism of the Old Testament (this with reference especially to Schneider, 118f.).

[8] *Registrum* v 8: 'iudicio Sancti Spiritus et auctoritate apostolica'; VIII 19: 'nostrum potius vero Spiritus Sancti iudicium'. This view was shared by many of Gregory VII's supporters, see Sprandel, *Ivo*, 82: 'The strict Gregorians drew the shortest line connecting the will of God and the commands of the pope.'

[9] One of the biblical passages most frequently cited by Gregory is 1 Samuel 15: 23; see the list given by Caspar in his edition of the *Registrum*, 602 n. 2, and Blaul, 'Studien', 196.

[10] The question of obedience and disobedience to the pope was not an acute one before Gregory VII's pontificate; see Congar, 'Platz des Papsttums', 202. Robinson, *Authority and Resistance*, 22f., compares the concept of obedience as found in Gregory I's writings with that held by Gregory VII; see also his 'Pope Gregory VII and Episcopal Authority', 111: 'To Gregory I *obedientia* signified the voluntary subjection of the human will to the divine will. To Gregory VII however, *obedientia* had come to mean the subjection of the bishops and the clergy to the commands of the pope.' *Registrum* IX 20, addressed to Lanfranc of Canterbury, is a particularly drastic example.

the grace of the Holy Ghost.[11] At about the same time Henry IV reacted
to the papal threat to deprive him of royal power: 'As if we had received
the *regnum* from you, as if *regnum* and *imperium* lay in your and not in
God's hands.'[12] Among the opponents of Gregory and his successors there
was a widespread criticism of his unheard-of arrogance, expressed forcefully in the *Liber de unitate ecclesiae*: 'While the Lord Christ, united with
God, himself changes the times and gives and takes kingdoms, keeping the
hearts of kings in his right hand, Pope Hildebrand is said to have taught
that he himself possesses power over kings and their kingdoms and can
make kings, though the Psalmist teaches that only God can do this.'[13] The
quotation in this work from Ezekiel 28: 2 directed against Gregory is a still
more drastic formulation: 'because thine heart is lifted up, and thou hast
said, I am a God, I sit in the seat of God, [in the midst of the seas, yet thou
art a man, and not God, though thou set thine heart as the heart of
God].'[14]

If the head of the church is owed obedience like that due to God
himself, what becomes of the old attitude of Christianity towards the
world of which Christ himself said 'my kingdom is not of this world'? The
question may be posed but not definitively answered. Obedience in
suffering was demanded towards God's will, as in the times of the early
church, and even now in the face of divinely sent trials: death, plague,
war, natural disasters, harvest failure, and hunger. But men may see in
the most savage afflictions and injustices the hand of either God or the
Devil. They may be taken to be either the punishment for sins or the
unfathomable expression of divine will which must be accepted in
humility. But disobedience towards the commands of the church,
disturbances of the right order of things, were in the opinion of Gregory
and his successors and their supporters not to be suffered but to be
combated, since the church possessed the exalted powers enjoyed by the
papacy. Resistance could and should be offered. Since this was not always
possible peacefully, it followed that to resist the enemies of the church,
heretics and heathens, warriors prepared for sacrifice and witnesses
prepared to testify to the church's truth must be found.

The claim of the Roman bishops on the basis of the old idea of papal
primacy to be in all respects the true leader of the church produced a
fundamental change within the church. There were gradual shifts of
emphasis away from the loosely organised episcopal churches and the

---

[11] 'novam quandam indebitamque potentiam usurpando arrogasti': MGH Const. I.107,
no. 58.
[12] MGH Const. I.111, no. 62.
[13] II 1, MGH LdL II.212.   [14] II 7, MGH LdL II.218.

national and regnal churches towards the Roman church as the religious and jurisdictional centre. Ecclesiastical centralism took on greater importance compared with the previous tendencies to ecclesiastical particularism and autarchy. The church, previously a mere spiritual unity, was now to become a real unity. Even the defenders of conservative views and structures had to come to terms with the ecclesiological theories they opposed. They were attracted to them even in the act of opposition. On the other hand it should not be overlooked that the thousand years of tradition in the pre-Gregorian church were strong enough to prevent the idea of a powerful centralism from achieving complete spiritual and political domination, as can be seen in the history of a number of developments in the late eleventh and early twelfth centuries.

Popes, bishops, synods, canon law, theology

In the eleventh and twelfth centuries there seems to have been an intensification of those forms of human hierarchy which had in theory always been present, and a tendency for them to take on a more objective shape, one which expressed itself less as mere personal ties; these were developments which were not confined to the ecclesiastical sphere. There was also a tendency towards rounding off and defining the boundaries of spheres of influence and control, seen in kingdoms and principalities with their transpersonal elements, aristocratic lordships, urban and rural communes, 'feudal hierarchies', parishes, and dioceses. Individual fraternities of monastic communities of prayer, liturgy, and ascetic togetherness were replaced by monastic orders with a strict organisation covering many monasteries. In all these areas clearer forms were accompanied by sharper legal definitions.[15]

These tendencies were manifest throughout the ecclesiastical sphere. The existence of the church universal had previously been defined in the service of the sacraments, in the power to consecrate possessed by bishops and priests, over and above this in the judicial and dogmatic decisions made by synods, and finally in the spiritual authority of the bishop of Rome. There now developed a strong tendency to give the spiritual hierarchy a more concrete form, one of command from higher to lower accompanied by obedience from lower to higher, and hence to give expression to the existence of the church universal on earth as well. The decisive development here was the way in which the pinnacle of the

---

[15] Bernold, *Liber Apologeticus*, c. 20, MGH LdL II.84: it is not within the pope's discretion to decide whether to proceed against unrighteousness. He is obliged to do so; see Weisweiler, 'Päpstliche Gewalt', 133.

hierarchy, the bishop of Rome, came in practice to acquire those powers of lordship and justice which in a distant and idealised manner he had long been recognised as possessing.

An early and powerful expression of these epoch-making tendencies can be found in the *Dictatus Papae* (II 55a) composed by Gregory at the height of his power (probably around 1075). Scholars are now agreed that scarcely a single one of the twenty-seven theses was the product of Gregory's spontaneous invention, but in spite of their loose organisation they have rightly been seen as the quintessence of 'Gregorianism', even though their influence in practice was less strong than might have been expected. For although they were rooted in traditional theology and earlier canons the way in which they were put together shows that the intention was to realise them in practice; they were programmatic declarations of the principles needed for the functioning of the Roman church and the pope within the *ecclesia universalis*.[16] It opens *fortissimo*: the Roman church alone is founded by God, and the Roman pontifex alone is rightly called universal. The priority of its prerogatives over those of all other churches is stressed repeatedly (cc. 8–11, 23). Papal legates, even those in minor orders, take precedence in synods over bishops (c. 4). Since the Roman church has never erred and will never err, its teaching is binding on the whole church and only those in agreement with it may be called catholic (cc. 22, 26). The power to bind and loose is not given Gregory's usual emphasis but the right to depose bishops and reconcile them with the church (c. 3) is based on it. A synod may only be called universal with the pope's consent (c. 16). The majority of the theses deal with the pope's precedence over other bishops. He can depose them in their absence (c. 6) and without a synodal bearing (c. 25). He can transfer them to another bishopric; he can divide rich bishoprics and join poor ones together. He can intervene within the diocese; he can ordain clerics from any church (c. 14); he can permit inferiors to accuse their superiors (c. 24); no one may condemn a person who appeals to the apostolic see (c. 20); all important matters in all churches should be referred to the pope (c. 21).

The *Dictatus Papae* is an epoch-making expression of the idea of the pope's universal episcopacy. Its first thesis says nothing about who had founded those other churches which were not, unlike the Roman church, founded by God, and which were not, unlike her, to be called

---

[16] *Registrum* II 55a. Cf. Hofmann, *Dictatus papae Gregors VII.*; Hofmann, '"Dictatus Papae" als Index', 531ff.; Fuhrmann, 'Reformpapsttum', 185f. and n. 26; Gilchrist, 'Reception', 35–80 and 192–227; Mordek, 'Kanonistik", 80f. and n. 81; Mordek, 'Dictatus Papae', *Lexikon des Mittelalters* (Munich 1985), III, cols. 978ff.

universal. Petrus Damiani had taken a straightforward historical view here and made emperors, kings, and others responsible. Although his statement was adopted by many later canonists including Deusdedit, Anselm of Lucca, and Bonizo of Sutri, they did not ascribe the merit of having founded the other churches to princes but to the Roman church.[17] A similar transformation was applied to a famous declaration made by Leo the Great to the apostolic vicar for the Illyrian provinces, Anastasius of Thessalonica, who in Leo's view had exceeded his powers. He said that Anastasius had been called only to administer a 'part of the pope's responsibilities, not to the fullness of power'.[18] Canon law collections of the late eleventh century applied this classic formulation no longer merely to apostolic vicars but to all bishops, who were said to possess not the fullness of power (*plenitudo potestatis*) of the Roman bishop but a part of his cares (*pars sollicitudinis*) with which he had entrusted them.[19] The most decisive definition of the pope's universal episcopacy was given by Bernold of St Blasien: no bishop has so great a power over the flock entrusted to him as does the apostolic superior, who, though he has delegated care and control to individual bishops, has in so doing not robbed himself of any of his superior power, just as no king deprives himself of royal power by delegating it to dukes, counts, and judges.[20]

Gregory VII himself did not yet write in this manner about the pope's *plenitudo potestatis*,[21] but it is noteworthy that the episcopal letter of renunciation written from Worms in January 1076 already seems to contain a response to papal measures and claims, of a passion, comprehensiveness, and principle seldom found later. Although it is not certain whether the *Dictatus Papae* already existed at that time, and it is very improbable that it was known to the assembly at Worms, Gregory's manner was already perceived as an attack on the traditional form of the church. The conflicts of the preceding years must have made the bishops conscious of the deep changes taking place in the relationship between pope and episcopate.[22] Gregory was accused of disturbing the peace of the church: 'You have in your raging madness torn asunder all the limbs of the church, which according to the Apostle should lead a "quiet and peaceful life" (1 Timothy 2: 2) . . . throughout Germany, Gaul, and

---

[17] Tellenbach, *Libertas*, 139 n. 28; Kempf, 'Eingliederung', 70.
[18] 'in partem sollicitudinis, non in plenitudinem potestatis': Caspar, *Geschichte des Papsttums* (Tübingen 1930), I.455; Rivière, 'In partem Sollicitudinis', 210–31; Benson, '"Plenitudo Potestatis"', 193–214; Szabó-Bechstein, 'Libertas Ecclesiae', 114.
[19] Benson, '"Plenitudo potestatis"', 206ff.
[20] Bernold, *Apologeticus* c. 23, MGH, LdL II.87f.
[21] Benson, '"Plenitudo potestatis"', 205 and n. 40.
[22] See above, pp. 267ff.

Spain.' For he had taken the power from all bishops which had been
granted to them by the grace of the Holy Spirit and arrogated to himself
a new and unlawful power in order to destroy those rights which
belonged to the whole confraternity of bishops.[23] This violent and open
dispute between papalism and episcopalism soon came to an end,
however. Those who had subscribed the letter came to an understanding
with the pope, and most of them reserved their position after Canossa.
Admittedly, following the renewed excommunication of Henry IV by
Gregory in March 1080 the majority swung back behind the king, but the
condemnation of Gregory in Brixen in June 1080 was no longer marked
by such fundamental discussions of the rights of pope and bishops. There
then followed a schism lasting twenty years, in the course of which the
popes avoided carrying disputes with bishops to extremes and were
concerned to make contact even with those who belonged to the
opposing obedience. But even in those lands which rejected Clement III
there was rarely any attempt to treat bishops in the manner laid down in
the *Dictatus Papae*. The popes had no enthusiastic supporters in England
in this period, and only a handful elsewhere. The majority of bishops
seems to have been concerned to run their dioceses in the traditional
manner and with as little innovation as possible, to extend their church's
property, to fulfil their obligations within their church province and the
political unit to which they belonged and reap the benefits of doing
so. There can be no question of their having followed the doings
and proclamations of pope and curia with attention, let alone with
enthusiasm. Yet in spite of this the authority and power of the popes grew
steadily between the pontificates of Leo IX and Calixtus II, though they
could not as yet exercise a power of government which was capable of
intervening everywhere and passing over the traditional regional
instances. There were few differences of opinion in this period about the
theoretical aspects of the relationship between pope and bishops; the
extreme opinions found in some of the tracts of the so-called Anonymous
of York are a rare exception, and their author was still more isolated in
denying the existence of the pope's primacy altogether.[24]

The forum in which the popes made their commands known most
effectively was the synods over which they presided in person; the
number of these held between 1041 and 1122 has been estimated at over

[23] MGH Const. I.107, no. 58.
[24] *Tractatus Eboracenses*, especially III (MGH LdL III.656ff.) and also V (pp. 680ff.) and
VI (pp. 686f.) = Pellens, *Texte*, J 4, pp. 35ff.; J 28, p. 214ff.; J 29, pp. 226ff., and in
particular Böhmer, *Kirche und Staat*, 437ff., 457ff., 475ff. = Pellens, *Texte*, J 2, pp. 7ff.;
J 12, pp. 84ff.; J 23, pp. 125ff.

a hundred.[25] Admittedly, the majority of those attending the synods held in Rome itself were, as they had always been, drawn from the city of Rome and its suburbs, and from the Roman church province. But even here there were often distinguished visitors, ambassadors, and representatives who might be impressed by what they saw; pilgrims too may have been present, though the majority would hardly have understood what was going on. When the popes held their synods in other parts of Italy or more distant countries the composition of the meetings was quite different. The synods held by Leo IX in Rheims and Mainz in 1049 were attended by only a few prelates from Italy, most of whom were drawn from the pope's entourage. German and Burgundian bishops were present in Rheims, which compensated for the gaps in the attendance of the French episcopate (six of the seven archbishops were absent); in Mainz the majority of the German episcopate was present.[26] The famous synod held by Nicholas II in April 1059 was attended by 113 fathers, almost all of whom came from Italy.[27] The participation at the important synods held by Gregory VII was described using general formulae, as for example in the protocol of the Lenten synod of 1076, 'where a multitude of bishops and abbots was present together with countless laymen and clergy of diverse orders' (III 10a). Occasionally numbers are given – Bonizo speaks of 110 bishops for the synod just mentioned and of about 100 for the Lenten synod of 1078, whereas the autumn synod of the same year, probably the most influential of Gregory's synods, had a much smaller attendance. Deusdedit, using similar formulae, speaks of fifty bishops at the Lenten synod of 1080.[28] The note in the register on the November synod of 1083 mentions the participation of archbishops, bishops, and abbots from Campania, 'the principalities', and Apulia, plus 'a few also from Gaul'.[29] Henry IV was at that time in a position to prevent participants from travelling. The king of France sent an embassy to the well-publicised synod of Urban II in Piacenza (March 1095), and a few of Urban's faithful supporters appeared from Germany: Archbishop Thiemo of Salzburg, Bishops Ulrich of Passau and Gebhard of Constance. Abbot Udalrich of the Reichenau was consecrated at the synod by the pope in person. Urban's most impressive synod in Clermont is said to have been very fully attended, but there were probably no participants

[25] Zema, 'Reform Legislation', 22.

[26] Steindorff, *Jahrbücher Heinrichs III.*, II.87.

[27] Boye, 'Synoden Deutschlands', 166 n. 4.

[28] Meyer von Knonau, *Jahrbücher Heinrichs IV.*, I.134f.; II.636 n. 26 (correcting 607 to 667 in the reference for the quotation from Bonizo); III.104 n. 16, 163 n. 106, 247 n. 20. See R. Somerville, 'The Councils of Gregory VII', *StGreg*, 13 (1989), 33–53.

[29] *Registrum* IX 35a, p. 627.

from England or the empire.[30] Following the end of the schism and the
death of Henry IV Paschal II was able to gather round him at the synod
of Guastalla in October 1106 not only numerous French and Italian
bishops but also once again a few representatives of the German
episcopate, though these were missing once more from the synod of
Troyes after the tension between papacy and empire had increased.[31] The
synod of 1112 was the most important of the remaining ones held by
Paschal, but once again this consisted largely of Italians, with a few French
bishops.[32] Calixtus II's first great synod in Rheims in 1119 had a substantial attendance, including Spanish, Italian, English, and German
bishops as well as French ones, and the great Lateran synod of 1123 also
brought together representatives from many countries.[33]

It is clear from this survey that the primary significance of these
numerous papal synods did not lie in the extent of their international
attendance. They undoubtedly helped to spread the legal and ecclesiological views of the popes and their entourages, but the impulse they gave
to centralisation was more important. The canon law of the early church
had rightly been called 'episcopal and conciliar': it was episcopal law, not
papal law.[34] In essence synods were liturgical gatherings, through which
Christ himself worked.[35] The legitimacy of the decrees issued by synods,
whether large or small, was determined by the extent to which these were
observed within the regional divisions of the church; it was this which
made synods ecumenical.[36] Diocesan and provincial synods also took
decisions on local and current issues. The last of the great councils which
was counted as ecumenical, Constantinople IV in 869, was, like its
predecessors, essentially a council of the east Roman or Byzantine empire.

[30] Meyer von Knonau, *Jahrbücher Heinrichs IV.*, IV.457.
[31] Meyer von Knonau, *Jahrbücher Heinrichs V.*, VI.25f., 50; see above, pp. 275ff.
[32] *Ibid.*, VI.232.
[33] Meyer von Knonau, *Jahrbücher Heinrichs V.*, VII.124f., 228.
[34] Andresen, 'Legitimierung', 45: 'The law of the old church was episcopal law made in
synods' and 'The canon law of early Christianity was bishops' law, not popes' law';
Vicaire, 'Pastorale', 90: 'up to the middle of the eleventh century the southern councils
were purely local or at best provincial'; G. Roethe, 'Zur Geschichte der römischen
Synoden im 3. und 4. Jahrhunderts', in *Forschungen zur Kirchen- und Geistesgeschichte*, 11
(1937), 1: 'Outside Italy and one or two neighbouring regions there was no higher
ecclesiastical authority than the great episcopal assemblies.'
[35] Congar, *Ecclésiologie*, 177; Fransen, 'Papes', 207, speaks of the 'prophetic function of the
council'.
[36] A. Hauck, 'Die Rezeption und Umbildung der allgemeinen Synode im Mittelalter',
Historische Vierteljahresschrift, 10 (1907), 466; on this see A. M. Wittig, 'Konzil und
Rezeption', *Annuarium Historiae Conciliorum*, 20 (1988), 24ff., and the recent literature
there cited.

After that, synods in the west were confined to dioceses, provinces, and countries, the most comprehensive being those of the empire. But whereas the greater synods held at provincial or national level declined in frequency and significance,[37] the papal ones grew in authority, even though the circle of those attending was by no means universal. Even the Lateran council of 1123 is not counted among the ecumenical councils on the grounds that it was attended by bishops from all countries, but because it was summoned, presided over, and confirmed by the pope, which also holds for the following ecumenical councils. The view spread gradually from Rome that the pope stood above the synod, a doctrine whose kernel is already found in the *Dictatus Papae* of Gregory VII: only the pope can recognise a synod as ecumenical (c. 16); he can depose and reconcile bishops without a synod; no one, and that means no synod, may presume to revise his judgement, something he alone may do for all (c. 18); there is no instance which may judge him (c. 13).

Canon law, however, long remained based on old traditions renewed by synods with a more or less regional character. The synodal decrees transmitted from century to century long outnumbered papal decrees. There were periods, like the pontificate of Nicholas I, when papal influence on the development of canon law was considerable, but for long stretches of time it was much less so. There can be no question as yet of Rome's having controlled the transmission of canon law or taken a conscious part in the process, even in the second half of the eleventh century. Gregory VII and his successors made use of the sources available to them, but they were no lawyers, and only a few members of their entourages appear to have had a really profound knowledge of secular and ecclesiastical law.[38] It has rightly been stressed that Gregory's thought was not rigidly doctrinal and was by no means free from contradictions, just as the popes of the early middle ages cannot be said to have lived with a law-book tucked under their arm.[39] Important collections of canon law such as that in Seventy-Four Titles and those composed by Cardinals Deusdedit and Atto, by Bonizo of Sutri, and by Anselm of Lucca, were certainly affected by contemporary trends and by the development of the papal primacy, but none was commissioned by the curia, and the collections of the twelfth century, up to and including that of Gratian,

[37] Feine, *Kirchliche Rechtsgeschichte*, 245; Kempf, 'Primatiale und episkopal-synodale Struktur', 28; Sieben, 'Konzilien', 134, shows that Bernold nevertheless did not 'completely reduce conciliar law to papal law . . . [he] perceived a further component . . . the consent of the universal church'.

[38] Caspar, 'Gregor VII. in seinen Briefen', 13; Fuhrmann, 'Reformpapsttum', 187f.; Mordek, 'Kanonistik', 67, 80; Morrison, 'Canossa', 122.

[39] Fuhrmann, 'Provincia constat', 398; Fuhrmann, 'Reformpapsttum', 185.

were the result of private scholarship.[40] It should also be noted that older collections continued to be copied and used. The *Decretum* of Burchard of Worms, for example, was repeatedly transcribed in the eleventh and twelfth centuries and circulated very widely.[41] Whether or not the increased importance of the papal primacy was reflected in the collection, the techniques of collecting and arranging remained the same, whether in Deusdedit's collection or in that of Burchard. The sources were copied out, put into some kind of order and given rubrics; this in itself constituted a remarkable achievement, rightly considered. Interpretation, comparison, noting of contradictions were still rare, let alone attempts to resolve such contradictions. Rational juristic thought had its predecessors, as we can see in the correspondence between Bernold and Adalbert and still more in the canonical collections and letters of Ivo of Chartres;[42] but only from Gratian onwards did canon law become a science, and the pope's supremacy in matters of canon law was a development completed still later.

Yet the statement in the *Dictatus Papae* that the pope alone is empowered to make new laws according to the needs of the times already represents a decision in his favour and against tradition. If his power was there justified on the grounds of *temporis necessitas*, another statement by Gregory, made in a letter probably addressed by Wimund, later bishop of Aversa, goes deeper.[43] Quoting John 14: 6: 'I am the way, the truth and the life', Gregory said: 'He does not say "I am custom", but "I am truth".' Ivo of Chartres, who preserves the letter fragment, cites it under the rubric 'A usage contrary to truth is to be abolished.'[44] *Usus* is a neutral term; *consuetudo* has in Gregory's writing more negative overtones (*antiqua et pessima, execranda, nefanda, nova, pestifera, prava*), but it also has

---

[40] Stickler, *Historia*, 160ff., lists the collections which he terms *collectiones reformationis Gregorianae*; Fuhrmann, 'Reformpapsttum', 200: 'Although the number of collections originating in the immediate circle of the papacy is astonishing, there is nowhere a reference to a direct commissioning of such a work by a pope'; Mordek, 'Kanonistik', 73; Kempf, 'Kanonistik', 13.

[41] Stickler, *Historia*, 159: in spite of the *collectiones Gregoranae reformationis* the *decretum Burchardi* continued to enjoy a high reputation and was widely used; H. Mordek, 'Handschriftenforschungen in Italien', *QFIAB*, 51 (1971), especially 630ff.; Mordek, 'Kanonistik', 73, and see his remarks in *St Grat* 20 (1976), 240 n. 33.

[42] Fried, 'Römische Kurie', 158ff. On the Hildesheim (formerly Constance) *scholasticus* Bernhard and the Constance *scholastici* Adalbert and Bernold see Robinson, 'Bible', 63f.; on Ivo see Sprandel, *Ivo*, 31ff.

[43] On the question of date see *Italia pontificia*, ed. P. Kehr, 10 vols. (Rome and Zurich 1906–75), VIII.282; Ladner, 'Two Gregorian Letters', 226.

[44] 'Usum qui veritati contrarius est, abolendum esse': JL 5277 = Ivo of Chartres, *Decretum* IV, c. 213 (Migne, *PL* 161, col. 311 and also Jaffé, *BRG*, v.576 no. 50).

the traditional positive one of usage sanctified by tradition when referring to the canons of councils and the decrees of former popes. The bishop of the infallible Roman church decides what is truth, what is *usus*, and what is *consuetudo*. This power had the same fundamentally religious roots in the Petrine commission as the claim to the obedience of all Christians. Nothing could demonstrate more clearly the suprahuman and divine character claimed by the papacy.[45]

A remarkable modification of the absoluteness of canon law can be found in a statement made by Urban II, in which he distinguished between two kinds of laws: those common to all (*publica*) and those which are individual and affect only a private person (*privata*). *Publica lex* is the law laid down by the fathers, for example the *lex canonum*. *Lex privata*, the inspiration of the Holy Spirit, is written in the heart; he who is guided by it may follow it with our authorisation, even if his bishop should contradict.[46] Here too the pope claimed to stand above canon law. He is to decide what is *veritas*, what is *consuetudo*, what is the inspiration of the Holy Spirit and what is canon law. Occasionally it does seem to have been assumed that this freedom of decision had its limits, as for example in the discussion of the papal election decree of 1059 and the 'pravilegium' of 1111.[47]

---

[45] It is certainly true that Gregory regarded tradition as deeply binding. Morrison, *Tradition and Authority* speaks repeatedly of a 'Janus complex' in connection with the dialectic between tradition and discretion; see pp. 78, 199, 253, 265, 277, 290, 318, 346. The pope possesses not just the power to temper traditional law but to make new law. We must agree with Fuhrmann, 'Reformpapsttum', when he says on the one hand (p. 190) that 'Gregory as pope was the defender of tradition' and on the other (p. 191) that 'papal privilege takes precedence over the law of the universal church'. This contradiction reveals once more the 'religious indeterminacy' noted above, p. 306 n. 1. On the dictum of Gregory VII transmitted by Ivo of Chartres see the literature cited by Fuhrmann, 'Reformpapsttum'', 190 n. 35; the arguments of De Lubac, 'Pouvoir l'Eglise', 340, are to be taken very seriously: 'Necessity does not make law. The end does not justify the means. There may perhaps be a raison d'état . . . but there is certainly no raison d'église.' See most recently H.-W. Goetz, 'Tradition und Geschichte im Denken Gregors VII.', *Historiographia medievalis. Festschrift für Franz-Josef Schmale*, ed. D. Berg and H.-W. Goetz (Darmstadt 1988), 138ff., especially 140.

[46] JL 5760 = Mansi, xx, col. 714; see Tellenbach, *Libertas*, 31 n. 43; Mordek, 'Kanonistik', 72f.; H. Fuhrmann, 'Das Papsttum zwischen Frömmigkeit und Politik. Urban II. (1088–1099) und die Frage der Selbstheiligung', in *Deus qui mutat tempora. Festschrift für Alfons Becker*, ed. E.-D. Hehl, H. Seibert, F. Staab (Sigmaringen 1987), 118ff.

[47] Deusdedit, *Libellus contra invasores et schismaticos* c. 11, MGH LdL II.309; Godfrey of Vendôme, *Libelli* I, MGH LdL II.682, on which see Morrison, *Tradition and Authority*, 308ff. But these objections are hardly to be seen as 'several checks upon the Gregorians' lofty doctrine of unlimited power', as objections of principle to the doctrine of papal plenitude of power; they were pragmatic correctives in individual cases. Nevertheless we can see here also the continuing ambivalent relationship between tradition and authority.

The influence of the pope on the dogmatic controversies of the time can no more be described in simple and unambiguous terms than can that on canon law. It has already been noted that theological controversies were infrequent in the tenth and early eleventh centuries, and that the life of the church was not deeply affected by them. Not until Berengar of Tours's (d. 1088) renewal of the ninth-century controversy over the nature of the Eucharist did such a dispute affect wider circles, especially in Germany and Italy.[48] The dispute provoked occasional interventions by popes and their legates. Under Leo IX synods in Rome and Vercelli had already condemned the scholasticus of Tours's spiritualistic interpretation of the Eucharist, and in 1054 Berengar was compelled to recant at a synod in Tours presided over by the papal legate Hildebrand. The epoch-making synod held by Nicholas II at Easter 1059 also concerned itself with the question of the Eucharist.[49] During Gregory VII's pontificate Berengar's case was dealt with on several occasions, though with long gaps between; finally at the Lenten synod of 1079 Berengar was forced to accept the definition that the body and blood of Christ were after their transformation in the Eucharist 'not just by the sign and virtue of the sacrament but in the properties of its nature and the truth of its substance' his body and blood. The pope thereupon forbade Berengar ever again to dispute with anyone on the body and blood of the Lord or to teach on the subject.[50]

In spite of the pope's unambiguous position the synod of Brixen of 1080 which renewed the sentence of deposition on Gregory VII denounced him as the 'former student of the heretic Berengar'.[51] Up to our own times there have been differing opinions as to whether Hildebrand/Gregory consistently rejected Berengar's doctrines or whether he was prepared to meet him halfway, at least for a time. The most important recent stage in the controversy was a dispute between Carl Erdmann and Ovidio Capitani, though here the main question at issue was whether certain documents which appear to be favourable to Berengar were forged by him or genuine.[52] Nevertheless there is agreement that Hildebrand/Gregory's attitude to Berengar 'was completely

---

[48] See above, pp. 1 and 139f.

[49] Steindorff, *Jahrbücher Heinrichs III*, II.121ff., 131ff.; Meyer von Knonau, *Jahrbücher Heinrichs IV*, I.139f. 237 n. 13; Erdmann, 'Gregor VII.' 60ff., 67ff.

[50] 'non tantum per signum et virtutem sacramenti, sed in proprietate naturae et veritate substantie': *Registrum* VI, 17a.

[51] MGH Const. I.119 no. 70.

[52] Erdmann, 'Gregor VII.', 52ff.; MGH BDK v.148 no. 7; Capitani, 'Studi per Berengario', 67–173; O. Capitani, 'La lettera di Goffredo II Martello conte d'Angiò a Idebrando', *StGreg*, 5 (1956), 19–31; Capitani, 'Rapporti', 99–145.

consistent over twenty-five years . . . Hildebrand gave Berengar a hearing, but never agreed with him.'[53] But neither as archdeacon nor as pope did he consider it his duty to intervene in person in the dogmatic dispute, but rather to have the question settled by theologians such as Bishop Hugo of Langres, Abbot Lanfranc of Bec, the fathers of the Roman synod, and later the circle around Alberic of Monte Cassino. There was never a dialogue between Gregory and Berengar over dogma.[54] Gregory saw it as his main concern to make sure that the theological issue, which had created a considerable stir, did not lead to undesirable political and ecclesiastical confrontations on a wider scale. He did not claim that as pope he could decide the matter independently of a synod, though the *Dictatus Papae* might be taken to have implied that this was in principle conceivable.[55]

The theological dispute of the eleventh century about the doctrine of the Eucharist was a revival of old dogmatic differences which had already existed in Augustine's and Ambrose's time and were very much alive in the ninth century. The ecclesiastical transformations of the eleventh century, with the gradual realisation of papal primacy which accompanied them, were thus not the trigger for the disputes, and there was no immediate connection between the two complexes. Berengar of Tours, a man of deep piety, certainly did not for a moment suppose that his doctrine could lead to a 'diminishing of the position of the priest', whose exaltation was the aim of the 'Gregorian revolution'.[56] 'Church reform' was just as compatible with Berengar's rational and symbolic interpretation of the Eucharist as with the primitive realism of his opponents.[57]

---

53 Erdmann, 'Gregor VII.', 62, 74; Capitani, 'Rapporti', 122 n. 48, only brings a different motivation for the forgeries.

54 *Ibid.*, 142: 'A meeting, even if a polemical one, always presupposes a certain common ground, the possibility of a dialogue, the existence of identical interests. All that never existed between Gregory and Berengar.'

55 *Ibid.*, 124; Kempf, *Handbuch*, 535f.: the dispute as such was not produced by the reform movement and it was the theologians who carried it out, while Rome merely supervised its course'; *contra*, Macdonald, *Authority and Reason*, 112.

56 I do not agree with the view of Erdmann, 'Gregor VII.', 48, on the 'divergence between Berengar's doctrines and the spirit of Gregorian church reform', nor with the opinion expressed by Steindorff, *Jahrbücher Heinrichs III.*, II.122, that the doctrine of transubstantiation attacked by Berengar 'was closely woven with the dominant hierarchical system'.

57 The judgement of Geiselmann, *Eucharistielehre*, 445, goes beyond contemporary controversies: 'the prescholastic doctrine of the eucharist was thus in a most fundamental sense a struggle to understand and to reconcile the views of Augustine and of Ambrose on the sacraments'.

There was no direct connection between the eucharistic question and another theological controversy, that over the validity of the sacraments received and dispensed by unworthy bishops and priests. This too went back to the time of the fathers, had been fought over bitterly by the Formosians and their opponents around 900, and was revived once more by the struggle against simony.[58] Pope Leo IX had not succeeded in pushing through the idea that simoniac ordinations were generally invalid. In general it was acknowledged only in theory that the consecrations performed by uncanonically chosen bishops and priests were invalid. This is true both of simonists and of schismatics, who were also seen as heretics, as well as of all excommunicates.[59] The question whether the sacraments dispensed by simonists, schismatics, and excommunicates were effective for their recipients was much debated. Petrus Damiani took a mild line, Humbert a stricter one.[60] The popes were not very rigorous here, being willing to make concessions, especially when the recipients of sacraments claimed not to have known that their dispenser's ordination was defective. As a matter of theology it was agreed in principle that such ordinations were valid, though a ceremony of reconciliation was required, for example by laying on of hands. But there was no decision that reordinations were necessary, though the argument was occasionally offered that an ordination performed by a heretic was as if it had never been.[61]

The affirmation of the validity of the sacraments dispensed by unworthy clerics had a religious basis. Reflections on the matter had led here and there to deep uneasiness among the faithful. But the theological issue was often obscured. In the struggles of the period it was usual to condemn opponents without much scruple as simonists, schismatics and heretics.[62] Theological theory could be interpreted according to convenience and applied in a partisan fashion. For a petty country priest it was natural to claim that he had known nothing of the simoniacal consecration of the bishop who had ordained him. Who was to decide whether or not he was telling the truth? And if he had indeed rejected ordination by a bishop on the grounds that he was a simonist or schismatic it would not have gone well for him either with the bishop or with the owner of the church entitled to present him or with the parish.

This is not the place for a comprehensive history of theology in the

---

[58] Tellenbach, 'Gregorianische Reform', 106.
[59] Schebler, *Reordinationen*, 219ff.
[60] *Ibid.*, 223 and 235, where Schebler describes Gregory VII as vacillating on the issue.
[61] *Ibid.*, 249.
[62] See above, p. 173 n. 147.

tenth and eleventh centuries,[63] but after having touched on the question of how a papacy newly conscious of its primacy affected synods, canon law, and such important issues as the doctrine of the Eucharist and the validity of the sacraments of unworthy clerics, we must at least ask what part the popes played in the dispute between the representatives of the older and younger waves of scholastic theology. Prescientific theology lived from the currently available tradition of the great facts of salvation as recorded in the Bible.[64] It was oriented towards Holy Scripture, which was simply read and recited. The explanations offered by the church fathers were accepted. Independent exegesis was confined to grammatical issues and to the allegorical and moral sense of Scripture.[65] Theologians, like monks, wanted to 'seek God, not discuss Him'.[66] In monastic and cathedral schools eloquence was the highest form in which understanding and mediation could be offered; in the church it was the sermon. In the course of the tenth and eleventh centuries dialectic moved out from the schools in which liberal arts were taught into theology.[67] The beginnings were marked by rhetorical and intellectual experimentation, but this was soon applied to the discussion of religious traditions. Only gradually did a disciplined and scientific questioning emerge from this phase and become the basis for scholastic theology. The new methods soon led to resistance on several levels by conservative theologians.[68] The representatives of both tendencies, progressive and conservative, were equally distant from the popes and their entourages. It is startling to read a work like Petrus Damiani's *De divina omnipotentia in reparatione corruptae et factis infectis reddendis*, which plays with both rationalism and with agnosticism.[69] But

---

63 See M. A. Schmidt, *Scholastik* (Die Kirche in ihrer Geschichte G 2, Göttingen 1969) especially pp. 81ff., 86, and K.-V. Selge, *Kreuzzüge und Stauferzeit* (Die Kirche in ihrer Geschichte F 1, Göttingen, forthcoming).

64 Congar, *Ecclésiologie*, 18: 'prescientific theology'; Grabmann, *Geschichte der scholastischen Methode*, I.181.

65 De Ghellinck, 'Dialectique', 82f.; E. Gilson, 'Le moyen âge comme saeculum modernum', in *Concetto, Storia Miti e Immagini del Medio Evo*, ed. V. Branca (1979), 3: 'I do not think I deceive myself when I say that the whole of the early middle ages, up to the eleventh century, is oriented towards the past, or rather towards a future which will continue the past'; B. Smalley, *The Study of the Bible in the Middle Ages* (Oxford 1952), 43.

66 J. Leclercq, *L'Amour des lettres et le désir de Dieu* (Paris 1957), 196; Riché, *Ecoles*, 137ff.

67 Grabmann, *Geschichte*, I.215; Riché, *Ecoles*, 261ff.

68 Grabmann, *Geschichte*, I.231; de Ghellinck, 'Dialectique', 89f.

69 It turns around the problem, much discussed from the time of the fathers onwards, whether God's omnipotence can make events which have happened unhappen – to take an extreme example, whether he could restore virginity to a fallen virgin. The text is in Migne, *PL* 145, cols. 595–622, newly edited by P. Brezzi and B. Nardo (Edizione nazionale dei classici del pensiero Italiano 5, Florence 1943).

Petrus was not only a devoted supporter of papal church policy but quite independently of this a highly talented and original writer and thinker.[70]

The decisive development for the future was probably the fact that conservative and progressive theology could often be found in the same author: use of the authors of antiquity together with their rejection; the ability to indulge in dialectical subtleties and to stress the authority of the simple word of the Bible.[71] It was precisely this tension which was an essential precondition for the rise of scholastic theology. The great popes from Leo IX to Paschal II were probably more rooted in pre-scientific theology. None of them shows any sign in their writings, speeches, and measures of having been influenced by early scholastic thought. At an unconscious level, however, they and their actions helped to bring about the rise of early scholasticism, in as much as these led to many of the great controversies discussed in the scholarly literature of the late eleventh and twelfth centuries.

THE MEANS AND INSTRUMENTS OF POWER AT THE PAPACY'S DISPOSAL

As the popes from Leo IX onwards set out to claim a new form of leadership for the universal church the 'structural changes' in the organisation of the Roman church soon set in; these were to continue over a long period until the 'massive bureaucratic machinery' – in Paul Kehr's opinion the essential feature of the Roman curia from the twelfth century onwards – had been fully developed.[72] The existing ecclesiastical arrangements, the existing forms of urban and territorial administration were too restricted to serve the popes' needs. It is significant that from Leo IX's time the local members of the papal entourage were complemented by important personalities from distant lands.[73]

The college of cardinals, which by the time of Paschal II had consolidated its position as the body which elected the popes and had first claim to advise them, developed slowly and not linearly.[74] The first group to achieve prominence was the order of the cardinal bishops. After the election of Nicholas II only five out of seven of these were available, for

[70] On Petrus Damiani as a lively thinker and a realistic observer of the world see above, p. 164 n. 103.
[71] See for example the impressive exposition by W. Hartmann, 'Manegold von Lautenbach und die Anfänge der Frühscholastik', *DA*, 26 (1970), 47–149.
[72] Jordan. 'Entstehung', p. 153; Barlow, *English Church 1066–1154*, 269: 'The pope had no jurisdictional or coercive power'; Kehr, *Katalanischer Prinzipat*, 66.
[73] See above, pp. 146f.
[74] Pásztor, 'Pier Damiani', 324.

one had been elected as antipope and another had supported him. Nevertheless the electoral decree of 1059 was evidently intended to determine their leading role for the future.[75] It did not do so, however; the elections which followed all ignored the provision of 1059 that the cardinal bishops had first voice in the papal election, and by the time of Paschal II's election all three orders of the college of cardinals already carried equal weight.[76]

The bishops were joined by the second order, that of the priests of the ancient titular churches of Rome. These too changed from performing traditional liturgical functions in the Roman city regions to being participants in papal government, though only a few of them achieved the same importance in the internal administration and the foreign policy of the popes as did the cardinal bishops.[77] Around 1100 a third order joined the college, the deacons of the palace and the city regions, in a process which has not yet been fully explained.[78] The development appears to have been accelerated during the schism by the rival popes, who each tried to win over the clergy of the city regions. The cardinals were already of considerable importance by the end of the pontificate of Gregory VII, though Gregory is said not to have allowed them much influence.[79] That may be one of the reasons why the majority of the cardinals deserted Gregory for Clement III in 1084, when Gregory was besieged and under great pressure in the Castel Sant'Angelo.[80] Their behaviour probably cannot be explained simply as opportunism in the face of Gregory's impending defeat; it was also due to the relations between pope and cardinals, which had long been cool. Already in 1082 a group of the Roman urban clergy had turned against the exploitation of the lands of the church to satisfy the needs of the struggle against Henry IV,[81] a group

---

[75] See above, p. 146.
[76] Ganzer, *Auswärtiges Kardinalat*, 7; Fürst, *Cardinalis*, 118; Alberigo, 'Origini', 43; Hüls, *Kardinäle*, 5.
[77] Klewitz, 'Entstehung', 64.
[78] Hüls, *Kardinäle*, 38ff., though it should be noted that for a long time to come 'the whole terminology used for the concept of cardinal was in flux'; see Fürst, *Cardinalis*, 101. The observation is of importance for the arguments of Jasper, *Papstwahldekret*, 74ff., 81.
[79] Mirbt, *Publizistik*, 562; Gaffrey, *Hugo der Weisse*, 60; Klewitz, 'Entstehung', 68; Fürst, *Cardinalis*, 106; Fürst, 'Gregorio VII, cardinali e amministrazione', *StGreg*, 13 (1989), 31.
[80] See above, p. 250 and n. 235; Hauck, *Kirchengeschichte Deutschlands*, III.833; Meyer von Knonau, *Jahrbücher Heinrichs IV.*, III.523ff.; Gaffrey, *Hugo der Weisse*, 64; Sydow, 'Untersuchungen', 23.
[81] Previous work on this has been made obsolete by Zaffarana, 'Sul "conventus"', 399ff., using a newly discovered version in Vat. Lat. 586 (eleventh century). This also mentions that the Margravine Mathilda had the treasure of the church at Canossa melted down to help the pope; see also Jasper, *Papstwahldekret*, 73.

which included cardinals who remained loyal to Gregory until the end.[82] These circles may well have been moved by genuine concern for the fate of the Roman church.

During the schism there were of course two colleges of cardinals.[83] Some of Wibert's supporters held out in Rome years after his death.[84] Then the concessions made by Paschal II to Henry V in 1111 led to new conflicts within the college of cardinals. The investiture privilege he issued was universally condemned, but with varying degrees of intensity. The antipope Gregory (VIII) was supported by only a few cardinals; the basis of his support was the Roman urban party around the Frangipani. It has rightly been said that this was no longer a schism within the church, but rather a dispute between Roman factions; in consequence, the cardinal college was not seriously divided.[85]

Even in the period of its formation the college of cardinals could be seen as being something more than simply the group of those who elected, advised, and assisted the popes; it had a comparatively independent position within the Roman church. At the beginning of the twelfth century the ecclesiological significance of the college of cardinals, its character as a divine institution, its function within the Roman church, and its relationship to the prince of the apostles, to the pope, and to the bishops were all things which had still to receive full theoretical clarification, and they were to be the object of controversy much later; there is a corresponding uncertainty in modern scholarship.[86] In terms of church politics the college was already an important element within the Roman church. The popes would in the future not infrequently have to face diverging groupings within the college. The schism of 1130 was essentially the product of tensions between the cardinals, and the problems of the early period came to the surface again and again in the later medieval history of the institution.

The groups of persons who saw to the correspondence, the financial administration, and the liturgical needs of the papal court were directly subject to the pope. Collectively they formed what by 1100 was termed

[82] Zaffarana, 'Sul "conventus"', 401; the valuable biographical data given by Hüls, *Kardinäle*, 88–254, allow us to see who went over to the antipope and who merely objected to the use of church property for military purposes. The defections should thus not be seen simply as personal aversion to Gregory or pure opportunism.
[83] Klewitz, 'Entstehung', 70.
[84] See above, p. 202.
[85] See above, p. 202 with nn. 6f.; Klewitz, 'Entstehung', 108f.; see especially Erdmann, 'Mauritius Burdinus', 240, 246.
[86] Alberigo, 'Origini', 39ff.; Alberigo, *Cardinalato*, 48.

the *curia*.[87] From Leo IX to Alexander II the papal entourage included a small number of personalities who exercised a decisive influence on papal politics – one need only think of Humbert and Hildebrand. Hildebrand himself, however, as pope certainly decided all important issues himself;[88] and the pontificates of Urban II and Paschal II also do not seem to have had any *eminences grises*,[89] though some cardinals emerged from the ranks of the scribes and chaplains to take on something of an independent role.

The pope and his court had multifarious contacts with lay and ecclesiastical dignitaries both near and far. Many came to the papal court to ask for and receive privileges, to bring letters, to convey or receive messages, to win papal support or defend themselves against accusations; in doing so they made acquaintances, they brought back more or less reliable information and they related their curial experiences at home. Apart from the legates – those who were sent from Rome and those bishops and abbots who acted in distant countries as papal representatives – letters and written communications were the most important instruments of papal government, though one should not overestimate the influence which could be exercised by such means.

The correspondence of the popes was not equally intensive from year to year. Those written to were only a restricted selection from among the ecclesiastical and lay dignitaries of Europe, and not all of these were equally receptive. For those letters which set out the fundamental principles of papal policy it would be of decisive importance whether or not they were read by anyone except their recipient. We can get some idea of this kind of dissemination by looking at the notes in Erich Caspar's edition of Gregory VII's register on the manuscript transmission of his letters derived from the recipients' versions. The most frequently mentioned sources are Hugo of Flavigny and Cardinal Deusdedit, followed by Paul of Bernried, the *Codex Udalrici*, Bruno's *Book of the Saxon War*, and the *Annalista Saxo*.[90] Bruno includes six letters from the register in full and four more from among the *epistolae vagantes*.[91] Both historical and propagandistic writings include some quotations and allusions. The

---

[87] Jordan, 'Päpstliche Verwaltung', 134; Jordan, 'Entstehung', 150; Pásztor, 'Curia Romana', 503; S. Haider, 'Päpstliche Kapelle', 38–70.

[88] Caspar, 'Gregor VII. in seinen Briefen', 4.

[89] The one who comes closest is the chancellor, John of Gaeta; see H. Bresslau, *Handbuch der Urkundenlehre für Deutschland und Italien* (Leipzig 1912), I.239f.

[90] Caspar, *Registrum*, 651.

[91] *Brunos Buch vom Sachsenkrieg*, c. 69, pp. 60ff. = *Registrum* III 6; cc. 105 and 106, pp. 93ff. = *Registrum* IV 23 and 24; c. 113, pp. 105ff. = *Registrum* VI 1; c. 70, pp. 61f. = *Registrum* III 10a; c. 73, pp. 66ff. = *Registrum* VIII 21; c. 72, pp. 62ff. = *EC* 14; c. 118, pp. 111ff. = *EC* 25; c. 119, p. 112 = *EC* 26; c. 120, pp. 113f. = *EC* 27.

present state of research does not yet allow us to make definitive statements about the extent to which papal letters were disseminated. It would
seem that canon law collections offered only a feeble echo of Gregory's
letters and decretals. Deusdedit alone used a copy of his register.[92] Out of
thirty-eight collections which have been examined, thirty contain
between none and ten chapters drawn from Gregory and only eight have
more (between eleven and thirty-nine chapters).[93] It has already been
mentioned that these collections were put together independently of the
pope and the curia and had a more or less private character.[94] The letter-
collections of the post-Gregorian era occasionally included papal letters,
less with the intention of preserving them or of making use of them for
contemporary political propaganda than out of literary interest.[95] So far it
has not been possible to demonstrate a connection with the curia, or with
an 'imperial archive' for any of these collections.[96] What can be shown is
that such letter-collections drew upon one another, as happened with
other literary genres; and certainly they reflected the intense attention
paid to the startlingly novel papal statements and to the reactions to them.

The papal court was also governed by propagandistic considerations, to
the extent that this was possible at that time. In the *Gesta Romanae
Ecclesiae* Gregory is even accused of having spread his writings throughout
the globe.[97] Nevertheless, we must keep in mind just how restricted the
public which could be reached by this kind of publicity was at this time.
There were no flysheets or open letters which could be distributed in their
hundreds, though the second letter of Gregory to Hermann of Metz was
circulated in a number of versions, a fact reflected in its comparatively
broad surviving manuscript transmission.[98] But the majority of papal
letters were addressed to a single recipient or to a few recipients. Often
they went to the bishops of a church province, or the clergy and people
of a diocese, to the abbot and monks of a monastery, or the clergy of a
church. Relatively few were addressed to a wider circle. The letters

---

[92] Gilchrist, 'Reception', 73; R. Schieffer, 'Tomus Gregorii papae', *AfD*, 17 (1971), 170ff.

[93] Gilchrist, 'Reception', 69ff.; in the continuation of his studies, *ZRGKA*, 66 (1980),
he arrives at different figures but at essentially the same conclusion; see Mordek,
'Kanonistik', 80 n. 81.

[94] See above, pp. 315f.

[95] Erdmann, 'Bamberger Domschule', 36; Erdmann, *Briefliteratur*, 1f.; Erdmann, in
Wattenbach–Holtzmann–Schmale, *Deutschlands Geschichtsquellen im Mittelalter* II.415ff.

[96] Erdmann, 'Bamberger Domschule', 40ff.

[97] MGH LdL II.375; but anti-Gregorians also wanted their writings spread, as MGH LdL
II.419 shows.

[98] *Registrum* VIII 21; see Erdmann, 'Anfänge der staatlichen Propaganda', 504; Arquillière,
Saint Grégoire VII, 216: 'this piece contains a complete theology of the relations between
church and state'.

contain information, tasks, orders, threats, punishments, and rewards, more rarely appeals. Often they refer to the pope's exalted position and rights. Sometimes they include more or less exhaustive polemics, which were intended to function as propaganda and did so.

The fact that this aim was achieved can be recognised most clearly in the echo the letters had in the so-called pamphlet literature of the time, though it should be noted that this began slowly and reached substantial proportions only gradually.[99] The events of 1076 were not discussed in them straightaway, but it was soon realised what epochal significance these had. It is characteristic that these writings had the form of letters or theological tractates,[100] and their authors were naturally almost all clerics. They were often intended to be read by the persons to whom they were addressed or dedicated, not by a wider audience, and this is reflected in the fact that most of them have survived in only a few copies. One of the most famous and substantial, the *Liber de unitate ecclesiae*, has only survived because Ulrich of Hutten had it printed (the manuscript he used is now lost); such chance survivals suggest that there must have been a rich pamphlet literature, especially by comparison with what had previously been known in this genre, much of which has now been lost.[101] True, many of these works show their authors' restricted horizons, but others, on both sides of the divide, were remarkably clear sighted and reveal a profound understanding not only of the principles enunciated with such passion by Gregory VII and his successors, but also of the conception of the rightly ordered Christian world which their opponents held and developed.

In order to carry through their comprehensive ideas of church government the popes needed material backing. As ever, they had to protect themselves from their enemies in the city of Rome and in the Campagna; they had to prevent the alienation of church property and to recover property which had been alienated; and they needed to defend their interests in Italian politics. This involved them in precisely those secular affairs condemned by the apostle in the command, 'A soldier on active service will not let himself be involved in civilian affairs' (2 Timothy 2: 4): the old dilemma of the Christian on earth.

Until the time of Urban II there seem to have been few changes in the

---

[99] They come largely from Germany and Italy, the two lands most affected; France and Spain add little, Cluny and at first Rome as well add nothing; see Mirbt, *Publizistik*, 83, 86, 91.

[100] *Ibid.*, 12, 83.

[101] MGH LdL II.173; R. Holtzmann, in Wattenbach–Holtzmann–Schmale, *Deutschlands Geschichtsquellen im Mittelalter* (1978), II.406ff.

central financial administration of the papacy.[102] Hildebrand was occasionally referred to as *oeconomus* during his time as archdeacon, but this should not be conceived of as the title of an independent office.[103] The renders due to the pope in money and in kind were delivered to the Lateran palace. An apostolic *camera* was first set up for the papal finances under Urban II, who followed the example of Cluny's financial administration: the first chamberlain was the Cluniac monk Peter.[104] The links between Roman and Cluniac financial administration lasted for some twenty-five years: Gelasius II still had a French chamberlain,[105] but under Calixtus II we find an Italian, Alfonsus.[106]

It is hardly possible to get a precise picture of income and expenditure of the apostolic see in this period of transformation of its financial administration. It is still a matter of dispute whether Gregory VII was a competent or a not-very-competent financier.[107] He probably needed a lot of money, both to keep the inhabitants of Rome happy and to pay for mercenaries. Nothing is known of any building activities in Rome during his pontificate. From 1080 his financial difficulties must have increased, for Gregory met with the resistance of some of the Roman clergy when he used (and probably had to use) some of the lands of the papacy to finance the struggle against Henry IV.[108] Urban II must also have spent most of his pontificate in dire financial straits, for a large part of the normal papal incomes will have flowed into the coffers of the antipope. It is reported by a number of sources that he was very willing to accept money, understandably enough in the circumstances. The exiled Greek metropolitan Basileos of Reggio claimed in a letter to Patriarch Nicholas of Constantinople that Urban had given his archbishopric to a φράγγος (Frank, meaning a Norman), who had paid him and Duke Roger 10,000 gold pieces for it.[109] The cardinals too were said to be very receptive to gifts of money.[110] It is hard to say what foundation there was for such claims; but they were evidently widely believed, as is

[102] Jordan, 'Päpstliche Verwaltung', 126.
[103] *Ibid.*, 122f.
[104] J. Sydow, 'Cluny und die Anfänge der apostolischen Kammer', *SMGBO*, 63 (1951), 55f.; Jordan, 'Päpstliche Verwaltung', 128ff.
[105] Sydow, 'Untersuchungen', 56f.
[106] Jordan, 'Päpstliche Finanzgeschichte', 100.
[107] Sydow, 'Untersuchungen', 24; Jordan, 'Päpstliche Finanzgeschichte', 65f.; Zema, 'Economic Reorganisation', 144 n. 21; on Gregory VII in particular see Goez, 'Toscana', 197.
[108] See above, p. 323 n. 81.
[109] W. Holtzmann, 'Die Unionsverhandlungen zwischen Kaiser Alexios I. und Papst Urban II. im Jahre 1089', *Byzantinische Zeitschrift*, 28 (1928), 54f.
[110] Sydow, 'Untersuchungen', 59.

shown by the famous satirical piece written by Garcia of Toledo, *De Albino et Rufino*, probably during Urban's lifetime.[111] Paschal II is said to have inherited an improved financial administration and increased revenues from his predecessor,[112] and with the death of Clement III the financial competition from the antipopes was effectively ended.

The papal incomes came from a number of sources. Archbishops and some bishops had to pay for their pallia; princes gave presents; charges were made for privileges; some monasteries had to pay a *census*; England and Poland paid Peter's Pence; other territories whose princes had become vassals of the holy see made similar payments in token of their tributary status.[113] All these things were uncertain, however. The payments were often delayed, and had to be reclaimed, more or less successfully. A substantial proportion vanished into other people's pockets on its way from the payer to the curia.

It is probably justifiable to assume that the greater part of the pope's revenues came from the great estates of the *patrimonium Petri*: rents, the profits of justice, and the services of vassals.[114] It has rightly been noted that one can hardly speak of a 'papal state' before the thirteenth century.[115] It was more a bundle of highly privileged estates together with isolated governmental rights, not a consolidated and coherent territorial lordship. It was difficult to collect in all the payments and services due and bring them to the curia without loss, and besides this parts of the *patrimonium* were often enough threatened by enemies from without or from within by factions or rebellious magnates. Two examples may serve to illustrate this. At the end of 1052 the duchy of Benevento came to the papacy by way of a treaty between Henry III and Leo IX. Leo, however, promptly lost the battle of Civitate, and the popes exercised influence in Benevento only intermittently until well into the twelfth century. The curia had to deal with a variety of partners: with Normans, with Lombard princes who at times succeeded in recovering their positions, with urban factions, with the archbishop of Benevento, with a noble family which for a time achieved princely status, then with rectors some of whom were installed by the pope and some of whom were elected by the

---

[111] MGH LdL ii.423; see P. Lehmann, *Die Parodie im Mittelalter*, 2nd edn (Munich 1963), 626ff.

[112] Sydow, 'Untersuchungen', 41.

[113] See above, p. 87 n. 45.

[114] Halphen, *Etudes*, especially on the city prefect and the judges, pp. 16ff., 39ff., and the lists at the end; Jordan, 'Päpstliche Finanzgeschichte', 62.

[115] Toubert, *Structures*, 935.

Beneventans.[116] The situation in the Sabina was quite different. Here the greatest difficulties were created by branches of the Roman family of the Crescentii and by the imperial abbey of Farfa, which had more property in the area than did the holy see. Paschal II was able to dominate the area for a time, but it is significant that Henry V sent Paschal to Tribuco, near Farfa, after he had captured him in 1111. Only after the Concordat of Worms did the Sabina come into papal hands.[117]

It is important to have a sense of the uncertainty of the papal revenues and the fragile nature of the popes' territorial rule in order to appreciate their spiritual and political leadership in western Europe. It should also be noted, however, that their position did not differ greatly in this respect from that of other great rulers, of the emperor and most kings. All these rulers practised 'high politics' against a background of permanent resistance and petty quarrels in their own immediate vicinity and with a power-base which was often restricted and insecure, though their public obligations, by contrast, were negligible, apart from church building and the financing of military campaigns.

The relations of the popes with the Norman princes were governed by principles but equally by tedious border skirmishes and local struggles with the various lay and ecclesiastical magnates of the region. Much is reminiscent of the equally exhausting struggles with the local powers within the papal territories. But the attempts of the papacy to establish its position as suzerain in southern Italy were also a part of the struggle which began in the pontificate of Alexander II to intensify its influence within all the western kingdoms, to provide a religious justification and legal definition for it.[118]

The attempt to persuade William the Conqueror to receive England in 1066 as a fief from the holy see failed. By contrast, Sancho Ramirez of Aragon made his land over to the Roman church in 1068 and received it back as a fief; but attempts to establish suzerainty over Castile and León failed. In Urban's time Berengar Raimund of Barcelona, 'el fratricida', gave his hereditary lands to the holy see. In 1075 Gregory VII held out to King Svein Estridson the prospect of a kingdom for one of his sons,

---

[116] O. Vehse, 'Benevent als Territorium der Kirchenstaates bis zum Beginn der avignonesischen Epoche', *QFIAB*, 22 (1930–31), 87ff.

[117] O. Vehse, 'Die päpstliche Herrschaft in der Sabina bis zur Mitte des 12. Jahrhunderts', *QFIAB*, 21 (1929–30), 157ff.; Hüls, *Kardinäle*, 259, notes that the Crescenzi-Ottaviani were the main opponents of the reform papacy in the Sabina.

[118] K. Jordan, 'Das Eindringen des Lehenswesens in das Rechtsleben der römischen Kurie', *AUF*, 12 (1932), 71ff.; Erdmann, *Entstehung*, 204ff.; Zema, 'Economic Reorganisation', 149ff.

probably as a vassal of the Roman church.[119] A year later Zwonimir-Demetrius of Croatia had himself elected and crowned king in the presence of a papal legate, and he is said to have taken an oath of fealty to Gregory VII.[120] The pope tried to establish closer links with Russia and Serbia. He claimed rights of superior ownership for the kingdom of Hungary, and reproached King Solomon for having accepted his kingdom as a fief from the German king.[121] The formula for an oath of fidelity which Gregory sent to Germany for the election of a king in 1078 shows his intentions, as does his claim that Saxony had been granted to the Holy See by Charles the Great.[122] One can hardly say that Gregory intended to establish a feudal overlordship of the papacy over all states; rather he aimed at strengthening papal influence by making flexible use of opportunities as they arose.[123]

Recent scholarship has offered diverging opinions on the justification offered by Gregory for his claims over certain kingdoms and states. The discussion has concentrated on the question of the rights of the popes to invest the Norman princes with the lands they had conquered. It has generally been assumed that ancient imperial rights were being usurped here. The question is whether this was justified by the Donation of Constantine or by the papal vicariate of the apostles understood in a purely religious sense. The protocol of the Roman Lenten synod of 1080 seems to derive the fullness of spiritual power over kingdoms and principalities simply from the power to bind and loose: if you can bind and loose in heaven, you can on earth grant empires, kingdoms, principalities, duchies, marches, counties, and all human possessions to anyone according to his merits, and take them away again.[124] It has been questioned whether such a claim was already the basis of the papal enfeoffment of 1059; instead, it has been suggested, the papal action was based on the Donation of Constantine.[125] But according to Amatus of Monte Cassino the Normans themselves explicitly justified their decision to accept the status of papal vassals with the argument that the pope was the vicar of St Peter and St Paul. When Robert Guiscard rejected Henry IV's offer to enfeoff him with the conquered lands he argued in this way. God had through the victory over the Saracens given him fame and the land itself and so made him greater than anyone in his people,

[119] See above, pp. 162 and 176f.
[120] P. Kehr, 'Rom und Venedig bis ins. 12. Jahrhundert', *QFIAB*, 19 (1927), 107f.
[121] *Registrum* II 13, 63, 70; Tellenbach, *Libertas*, 232; Tellenbach, 'Zusammenleben', 54.
[122] *Registrum* VIII 23, and see Caspar, *Registrum*, 567 n. 3.
[123] Tellenbach, *Libertas*, 186 and n. 35; Tellenbach, 'Zusammenleben', 34f.
[124] *Registrum* VII 14a.
[125] Deér, *Papsttum*, 51, and 78ff.

hence it was only proper that he should have the land which the king now wished to grant him only from the All-Highest himself.[126] It is striking how Robert is here made to equate subjection to the vicar of the apostles with subjection to God. This purely religious and idealistic justification, however, could be combined with other legally based claims; Gregory VII and his successors did not see religious, historical, or juristic arguments as alternatives, here or elsewhere.

The dependence of kingdoms and principalities, whatever its formal justification, would play a certain political role in the centuries to come,[127] but it rarely had practical political consequences either for the popes or for the territories and rulers concerned. The military assistance given by the Normans in the eleventh century was probably the most important result, but the popes could not rely on this, and in the period which followed the Normans and their successors were dangerous neighbours. The greatest advantage – though this too should not be overestimated – probably came from the gifts and tributary payments made to the popes by their vassals, even if these were frequently in arrears.[128]

The popes demanded obedience to their commands from Christendom and justified this demand by reference to their exalted mission. But what power did they have to back up their orders or to compel obedience to them? The power to open or close the heavens was the strongest means at their disposal. Through excommunication they could threaten with the loss of eternal salvation, and certainly many Christians were moved to obedience by this. But it was often found, especially when the conflicts were with kings or peoples, that excommunications were ignored, that the prohibition of contacts with the excommunicated was circumvented, and that it was almost always possible to find clerics who were prepared to dispense the sacraments to the excommunicate. Such contempt for the church's ban reached its height when there were schisms and two popes condemned each other and each other's followers.[129]

---

[126] Amatus, *Ystoire de li Normant* VII 27, pp. 298ff.; see also V. de Bartholomeis, *Fonti per la storia d'Italia* 76 (Rome 1935), 320f. and Deér, *Papsttum*, 28f. with Erdmann, *Entstehung*, 120; Tellenbach, 'Zusammenleben', 54; Deér, *Papsttum*, 92, 100; Cowdrey, *Age*, 129, on which see the objection raised by Hoffmann in his review, *DA*, 39 (1983), 663, though this does not deprive the text in Amatus of its significance in any way, even if we leave open the question of the authenticity of the words ascribed to Robert Guiscard.

[127] Tellenbach, 'Zusammenleben', 34ff.

[128] The same consciousness of the pope's superordination to kingdoms and the papal claim of imperial rights and insignia led to the papal practice of creating kings from the eleventh century onwards; see H. Hirsch, 'Das Recht der Königserhebung der Kaiser und Päpste im hohen Mittelalter', *Festschrift für E. Heymann* (Weimar 1940), I.209–49.

[129] See above, p. 249.

It was disputed whether the popes were allowed to use physical force against those who resisted them. As lords of the patrimony of St Peter the popes had of course long used earthly means of compulsion on the modest scale and within the modest compass open to them. They had given diplomatic and financial assistance to wars against the heathen, even against Christians, and had occasionally led these themselves. In general it was held that the spiritual power should where necessary summon the secular power to support it with coercive force, in the case of stubborn resistance to purely ecclesiastical commands by bad Christians, heretics and schismatics and in the case of political and military conflicts with secular opponents. When Henry III refused to provide the military assistance against the Normans that had been asked for, Leo IX himself led the campaign against them. Norman troops were assembled under Nicholas II with the intention of eliminating the antipope and his supporters; later on there were further military operations against schismatics using allies or vassal and mercenary forces. Gregory VII asked the king of Denmark in 1075 what help he might expect should the Roman church call in the king for help 'in the matter of soldiers and of the material sword' (II 51). The Normans freed him with fire and sword in 1084 when he was no longer able to hold out in the Castel Sant'Angelo against his domestic enemies and against Henry IV.

Already in the eleventh century objections were raised to such use of secular means of coercion. Petrus Damiani expressed doubts about Leo IX's Norman campaign.[130] Later on it became the usual practice for the opponents of Gregory VII and his successors to criticise the ecclesiastical *ius gladii* (right to use the sword), while their defenders justified it.[131] Bernold of St Blasien and Anselm II of Lucca offered a well-worked-out justification of the pope's use of coercive force.[132] Gregory VII's own actions were simultaneously rooted in religion and in power politics. As Henry Xaver Arquillière put it, 'Gregory may not have formulated the theory of the two swords, but he practised it energetically.'[133] Only later were its theological and legal consequences to be fully worked out.

But there was still a great gap between theoretical claims and their practical realisation. Gregory's plan of 1074 to bring military help to the Christians of the East, hard pressed by pagans, could not be carried out;

---

[130] Erdmann, *Entstehung*, 131f.; Stickler, 'Potere coattivo', 275.

[131] Erdmann, *Entstehung*, 245; Stickler, 'Potere coattivo', 281.

[132] *Ibid.*, 282 and n. 176: 'thus the main work of Anselm of Lucca was not just a mirror of Gregorian coercive power but over and beyond that its fulcrum and vehicle, not only in its own time but in the centuries to come'.

[133] 'Origines des deux glaives', *StGreg*, I (1947), 508.

he himself had intended to take part in the campaign.[134] Urban II set the
First Crusade in motion with his inflammatory preaching in Piacenza and
Clermont, but he soon lost control over it.[135] Nor were the later crusades
genuinely papal undertakings; frequently enough they developed their
own aims, which diverged from those which the popes had intended
for them. Nevertheless the church's attitude to warfare had undergone
fundamental changes in the course of the eleventh century, both in
theory and in practice: the exalted privileges of the heirs of St Peter
seemed to make even their use of military power lawful and unavoidable.

ECCLESIA AND *CHRISTIANITAS*
Popes and kings

From the time of Gelasius I onwards a higher rank had been claimed for
the priesthood as against the laity, even as against its head the king; and
the claim was generally accepted. All Christians needed the help of the
ordained, who alone could perform the sacraments, to achieve salvation.
It was the priest who at the last judgement would have to give an account
of his stewardship for the laity.[136] From this responsibility Gregory VII
derived, more energetically and comprehensively than had been done
before, a duty of obedience towards the vicar of St Peter. This was in
essence of course meant to apply to the areas of religious and moral
conduct; but in the reality of earthly life *all* deeds and thoughts have a
religious and moral aspect, so that the claim to obedience took on
unexpected dimensions. The consequence was that it became ever more
difficult to observe straightforwardly the warning of St Paul 'A soldier on
active service will not let himself be involved in civilian affairs', which
Pope Gelasius had taken to be the reason why God had created secular
authority to relieve the burden on that of the priesthood.[137]

The Roman church had long been compelled to undertake political
and economic activity in the context of its local and regional connections.
From the middle of the eleventh century these activities expanded
concomitantly with its spiritual influence. They affected above all the

---

[134] *Registrum* I 46, 49; II 31; see Erdmann, *Entstehung*, 149ff.
[135] See above, p. 259.
[136] See above, pp. 123–4.
[137] Recent authors find it difficult to accept the medieval indivisibility of religious and
political activity. Szabó-Bechstein, 'Libertas Ecclesiae', 47, claims that 'Gregory's
intention was not to exercise secular power himself', and cites *Registrum* I 62, p. 91. But
this says precisely the opposite: 'portamus . . . non solum spiritualium set et secularium
ingens pondus'. On p. 175 she rightly stresses the fact that Gregory was not a systematic
thinker capable of grasping a fundamental division between this world and the next.

higher clergy, kings, and princes. The expenditure of much energy and diplomatic skill was needed to accustom these to the Roman see's new claims. Tensions had to be endured, conflicts fought through. There were fundamental debates about the relations of the pope, who was the successor to the prince of the apostles, with the bishops, who were the successors to the remaining apostles, and still more about the pope's relations with the kings, who seemed by virtue of their unction to be set high above all other laymen and were charged with a consciousness of having received their power by the grace of God.

The reciprocal recognition of each other's dignity by kings and popes continued even after popes had begun to complain about inadequate obedience and kings had begun to ignore or react against unaccustomed papal interventions. In spite of the bitter struggles involving popes and antipopes the nature of the papal office remained unchallenged, with a few rare exceptions. Equally, the conviction that the king had his office from God, to whom he owed an account of his actions, also continued to exist. But the office of king became a problematic one when the pope's claim to be obeyed as the representative of St Peter led to judgement on and correction of the actions and way of life of kings even on earth.

In most western countries, however, there were no serious conflicts between popes and kings on such issues.[138] The relations between the popes and distant kings or princes such as those of Denmark, Norway, Russia, Poland, Croatia, or Hungary were particularly untroubled. These rulers listened respectfully to the doctrines announced to them about the obedience due to St Peter, but these did not disturb their loose and intermittent contacts with Rome. There were often tensions in the relations with the kings of England, France, and Spain, but the demands of 'church reform', for the abolition of simony or the elimination of clerical marriage or the renunciation of lay investiture, never led to a complete breach. Gregory VII came nearest to this with Philip I of France. In 1074 he threatened to deprive him of the kingdom of France, for Philip was not a king but rather a ravening wolf and an unjust tyrant. Urban II was finally driven, much against his will, to excommunicate Philip for his moral shortcomings, in particular the scandal of his marriage. Although Count Berengar Raimund II of Barcelona had murdered his brother and co-heir this did not prevent Urban from accepting the fratricide's homage and alliance when in 1090 the count offered his land to St Peter.[139] Robert Guiscard was for many years under a papal sentence of excommunication, but his stubborn disobedience did not prevent a reconciliation.

---

[138] On what follows see also above, pp. 203ff.   [139] Kehr, *Katalanischer Prinzipat*, 32.

Only with Henry IV, the king of Germany and Italy, did an irrevocable breach come about. In the course of this fundamental questions about the divinely willed relationship between papacy and kingship were raised anew. What led to the conflict is a question which has been much discussed since the time of the conflict itself. Gregory may have been aware of the rumours about the young king's way of life, of which a number were going the rounds. But these were not mentioned in the early years of his pontificate – although some expressions of concern suggest a certain inner distance – and Gregory also made very positive statements about the king. Only after the break in 1076 did he come to talk of the unheard-of depravities and of the manifold injustices of the king, who had raised his heel against St Peter and planned to destroy Holy Church. Already in his time as a deacon the questionable and highly dishonourable reputation (*sinistra et multum inhonesta fama*) of the young king had come to his attention. As he grew older his immorality (*iniquitas*) had grown, until Gregory had warned him through three devout men to do penance for his crimes (*sceleribus*).[140] After Canossa we hear no more of such harsh judgements, until after Brixen Henry once more became the despiser of Christian laws, the destroyer of churches and the kingdom, the supporter and companion of heretics (VIII 21). It is thus conceivable that Gregory held Henry to be morally reprehensible before 1076, but this was hardly a reason for the pope, who had experience of the world and was well aware of the average level of morality of his contemporaries, to proceed against Henry. More serious was undoubtedly Henry's refusal to separate himself from counsellors of whom Gregory disapproved, even when these had been excommunicated. But, once again, to ignore excommunication was by no means an unforgivable offence at the time. Resistance to the demands of church reform can hardly have brought about the conflict, especially as simony was much less important in Germany than in other countries; it was the bishops and clergy rather than the king who were responsible for the lack of success in combating clerical incelibacy, and the problem of lay investiture had not been resolved anywhere at that time. Probably it was the Milanese affair, which he rightly regarded as scandalous,[141] which led Gregory to take a strict line and issue the threats he did; even then, he probably did not expect that his harshness would provoke such a violent reaction at the royal court.

What led king and bishops to adopt their radical attitude can only be guessed at, but the pope's lordly behaviour was certainly responsible for their making fundamental declarations on the religiously correct view of

[140] *EC* 14, pp. 535ff.   [141] See above, pp. 180f.

the relationship between royal and episcopal office. The rapidity of Gregory's counter-attack, with its excommunication and deposition of Henry and its release of Henry's subjects from their oaths of obedience, led to an intensification of the theocratic elements in Henry's defence of his conduct: he set the divine origins of his own office against Gregory's usurpation of divine power.[142] Gregory in turn was much concerned to defend his conduct, which he justified not on the grounds that his opponents had offended against individual norms of morality or canon law, but on the grounds that they were guilty of heretical disregard for the exalted vicariate of the pope.

Gregory VII must have been disappointed by the ineffectiveness of the measures he took against Henry IV. In 1076 and again in 1080 he devoted much energy to explaining and defending them. His arguments contain ideas and claims which often seem aggressively polemical and not particularly in accord with convictions he expressed on other occasions. What he wrote about the origins of kingship received much attention. Of those kings who were well disposed towards him he was always willing to allow that they had their office from God, especially if they respected the pope's superior vocation and did not deny him their obedience. If a king resisted him he could in his anger go so far as to incriminate royal power as such, by recalling the fact that it was invented by human pride before Christ had appeared on earth and had its origins in those who did not know God and, driven on by the prince of this world, the devil, lusted in blind greed and intolerable arrogance to rule over men like themselves (IV 2, VIII 21). Gregorians were capable of expressing this idea more moderately: Bernold said that kingship was a human invention; Deusdedit argued that God had permitted but not willed it. A learned anti-Gregorian, Wenrich of Trier, offered the formulation that the name of king had been invented at the world's beginning and subsequently confirmed by God.[143]

Characteristic of Gregory's attitude to the world was the argument 'if the apostolic see may decide on and judge spiritual things by virtue of the powers conferred on it by God, how much more may it judge worldly things?' 'If St Peter binds and looses heavenly and spiritual things, how

---

[142] *Briefe Heinrichs IV.*, ed. Erdmann, 16 no. 12; see Maccarone. 'Teologia del primato Romano', 93.

[143] Bernold, *Libelli* XII, MGH LdL II.147; Deusdedit, *Liber contra invasores simoniacos* c. 12, MGH LdL II.383; Wenrich, *Epistola* c. 4, MGH LdL I.289. For a recent comprehensive study see W. Stürner, *Peccatum und Potestas. Der Sündenfall und die Entstehung der herrscherlichen Gewalt im mittelalterlichen Staatsdenken* (Beiträge zur Geschichte und Quellenkunde des Mittelalters, Sigmaringen 1987), especially 131ff. on Gregory VII's views on the origins of secular dominion.

much more then earthly and secular things?'[144] In a prayer to the Apostles
Peter and Paul he said: 'Act now, I beg you, most holy fathers and princes,
so that the world may see and recognise that if you can bind and loose in
heaven you can also on earth give and take kingdoms, principalities,
duchies, counties and all men's possessions according to their deserts'
(VII 14a). 'He to whom power has been given to open and close the
heavens, shall he be not allowed to judge the earth? Surely not!' Since St
Peter, and hence his vicar the pope, has been given power over heavenly
things, it follows *a fortiori* that he must have power over earthly, secular
matters.[145] This deduction from the higher to the lower is by no means
self-evident, however, and the argumentation has rightly been described
as 'idiosyncratic and logically not quite in order'. At the very least it is not
compelling. Gelasius I himself, while stressing the higher rank of the
priesthood, had laid down that the clergy should not intervene in worldly
affairs, where they were to be subject to the ruler. He was still governed
by the concern felt in the early church that 'spiritual activity should be
distant from the drives of the flesh'.[146] Nicholas I had held fast to this
principle, and Hincmar of Rheims, like many theologians, had repeatedly
recalled St Paul's injunction to obey worldly authority.[147] In spite of the
dominance of Gregorian thinking this tradition long survived. Cardinal
Beno, for example, cited the famous passage of Gelasius I on the two
powers, which Christ in His wise prescience of human frailty had so
separated that the Christian emperors needed bishops to attain eternal life
and the bishops needed imperial ordinances while on earth.[148] The *Liber
de unitate ecclesiae* accused Hildebrand and his supporters impassionedly of
usurping the office of both powers: 'He who contradicts the Gospels and
despises the teaching of the apostles is neither Christian nor catholic', and
there then follow the biblical texts which govern the relationship of the
Christian to the world.[149] An antagonism had arisen between irreconcilable standpoints, each fundamentally rooted in the Christian faith.

Value-distinctions between clergy and laity

The antagonism between spiritual and secular power was at its sharpest
and most fundamental, both in theory and in practice, where convictions
were attacked which had for centuries governed the life of the regionally

[144] *Registrum* IV 2 and 24; see also I, 22, p. 38 n. 1.
[145] Blaul, 'Studien', 124.
[146] 'spiritualis actio a carnalibus distaret actibus': Thiel, *Epistolae*, 567.
[147] Tellenbach, *Libertas*, 82ff.
[148] Beno, *Gesta* III 17, MGH LdL II.403.   [149] *De unitate* II 15, MGH LdL II.230f.

organised church: the doctrine of the two powers and the idea of the king's divinely appointed mediatory position between clergy and laity. If the church was to be united under the leadership of the highest priest on earth it was necessary to decide what competence the kings were still to be allowed. It was now that the idea that the king was something more than a layman was called in question.[150] The tendency to downgrade the laity, who had in reality long been the followers within the church, and to stress the superiority of the clergy, was much more widespread.[151]

Gregory VII's remarks on the unholy origins of worldly power or Urban II's references to lay hands dripping with blood in which no cleric might place his own hands to swear homage, might perhaps be dismissed as rhetorical overstatement.[152] But Gregory's famous words about the exorcist, one of the lowest grades of cleric, who as spiritual emperor had been given a higher power – that to drive out demons – than that given to any layman for secular authority, reflect his high opinion of the clergy and his low opinion of the laity.[153] Urban II is said to have claimed in a sermon that the least of clerics was greater in the church than any mortal king.[154] Paschal II's pronouncements on the difference in dignity between clergy and laity had a similar tone. It is unworthy, he wrote for example of Anselm of Canterbury, that a cleric who has thrown in his lot with God and taken on a higher rank than that of the laity should do homage to laymen for mere worldly gain.[155]

When objection was first taken to the traditional constitution of the church it was directed only against the participation of kings and princes in the nomination and appointment of bishops and abbots, and against the possession by laymen of rights in churches. There was at first no objection to clerics – bishops, abbots, and other clergy – having rights of property in churches.[156] It was thus a question not so much of the restoration of an older diocesan organisation as of the elimination of traditional rights of laymen over churches. To allow clerics to possess what was denied to

---

[150] See above, pp. 172f.
[151] The idea of a church based on the clergy in particular can be found as early as John VIII, JE 3030 = MGH Epp. VII.332 no. 5: 'ecclesia nihil aliud est nisi populus fidelis, sed praecipue clerus censetur hoc nomine'. A decisive point in the history of the clericalisation of the church was the creation of a highest instance in the form of the cardinal bishops and in the restrictions on the rights of the king and of the Romans in papal elections, see Kempf, 'Pier Damiani', 86, 88f.
[152] See above, pp. 266, 337.
[153] The clerical hierarchy seemed to him, according to Arquillière, *Saint Grégoire VII*, 235, 'like a direct emanation of Christ'.
[154] Landulf, *Historia Mediolanensis* c. 40, MGH SS XX.37.
[155] JL 5909 = *S. Anselmi opera omina* V/1, 125 no. 223.
[156] See above, pp. 176 and 178f.

laymen made the distinction of rank between the two groups clear; for the proprietary rights of clerics were no more bound up with spiritual functions than those of the laity. In spite of this, that which was energetically rejected for the laity was found acceptable for clerics. The attempt, only partially successful, to eliminate lay proprietary rights was a characteristic expression of the general tendency to put a greater distance between clergy and laity. Subsequent developments, however, led to a certain assimilation between lay and clerical rights in churches. A layman as patron of a church was once again able to take an honourable and influential part in church life, and the influence of congregations on the election of priests, the administration of church property, and the building of churches was still more considerable. After the first partial successes in restricting what was felt to be an excessive weight given to the laity, there seems to have been a tempering of the opposition of the first revolutionary era against any lay element in the control of the finances and personnel of individual churches.[157]

A clearer distinction between the *ordo clericorum* and the *ordo laicorum* was well advanced from the second half of the eleventh century; modern scholarship has pointed repeatedly to the increasing 'clericalisation' of the church from this period on.[158] The term *ordo laicorum* took on a derogatory tone, with the twin biblical concepts of the spiritual and the fleshy man seeming to prove the inferiority of the *ordo laicorum*. Once the distinction had been moved from the spiritual to the jurisdictional plane the clergy came to identify itself with the church as such.[159] The socio-legal element in the life of the church grew stronger; clericalisation meant juridification.[160] General consideration of the course of church history does indeed make it seem plausible that the conception of the church as something which primarily concerned the hierarchy, the body of the clergy, became more important at this time. But in what sense are we to understand the enhanced importance of the clergy within this clericalised church? P. A. Häussling has offered helpful explanations here: 'Concern for salvation is an expression of personal concern in the face of the [priestly] task; it intensifies the need to match up to the task. Such a

---

[157] See above, p. 290 n. 142.

[158] Congar, *Laie*, 90; T. Schieffer, 'Cluny', 55: 'clericalisation of the church – a character-istic trait of the Gregorian era'; Barlow, *English Church 1066–1154*, 269; Prosdocimi, *Chierici e laici*, 112f., speaks of a 'separation' of clerics and laymen and on p. 120 cites Hugo of Saint-Victor: 'laici . . . pars corporis Christi sinistra sunt'. The greater value placed on the difference between clergy and laity can be taken as one of the main char-acteristics of 'church reform'.

[159] Zerfass, *Laienpredigt*, 187ff.

[160] Congar, *Laie*, 60f., 68.

concern only becomes "clerical" when – to put it exaggeratedly – the distinction between the clergy and the remaining people of God is seen as one of essence, not of function . . . when the celebration of masses was for the clergy no longer the fulfilling of their function within the liturgy of the whole church but rather the expression of their distinct status as those through whom alone God might be approached.' In this sense Gregory VII was the first to formulate the sociological notion of 'clericalism'.[161]

It is noteworthy that the more recent interpretations of the church as a clerical church have been offered with cautions and qualifications, not to say some hesitations. There have been calls for investigation of the influence of Gregorian reform on the understanding of the liturgy.[162] It has been stressed that the division between clergy and laity still stood in the service of the integration of the laity into the unitary 'church society' of the middle ages[163] and that men remained theoretically aware of the fact that divine service was an act of the whole church and the liturgy a matter for all.[164] The papacy still sought after the participation of the laity within the life of the church, merely pushing them back from positions of influence.[165] We have also been rightly reminded of the distinction between ecclesiological theory and the practical life of the Catholic church, in which the simple experience of the faithful preserved much of traditional unitarism.[166]

A crisis in western monasticism

Before the rise in papal activity the religious thought and hope of western Christendom had been influenced most by monasticism and the monastic life, which turned simultaneously to the early church and the last judgement. Crucial here was the solidarity shown by the monks with the whole church. Ascetic penance, performance of the liturgy, devout prayer were all regarded as helpful not just for the individual souls of those who performed them but for those of all fellow-Christians. They were particularly beneficial to those who were closely connected with the individual monasteries, either as founders and benefactors or as relatives of the monks and nuns who served God in them. The gratitude of those who sought and found links with monasteries secured these a high reputation and made them rich.[167]

[161] Häussling, *Mönchskonvent*, 269f.   [162] *Ibid.*, 358 n. 19.
[163] Zerfass, *Laienpredigt*, 182.   [164] Häussling, *Mönchskonvent*, 271.
[165] Congar, *Ecclésiologie*, 96.   [166] Congar, *Laie*, 85.
[167] See above, pp. 301f.

In their flight from the world, monks perceived both clergy and laity as the 'world' in which they had not only to serve spiritually but to which they also had, in spite of its alienness, to render what belonged to it, following biblical precept. They thus as a matter of principle had no intention of winning it over, improving it or changing it. They accepted the fact that not all Christians could renounce the world. In general they were not the initiators or in the vanguard of the struggles against moral deficiencies or breaches of the church's laws. Italian groups like those around Camaldoli and still more Vallombrosa, German ones like the more radical members of the Hirsau movement, were notable exceptions. Monastic reform, which was concerned with the perfection of the coenobitic way of life, was usually something rather different from what is known as church reform.[168]

The relationship of monastic movements to the popes was determined on the whole by the general belief in the special religious position of the Roman church and its bishop. The increased realisation of papal primacy in practice from the time of Henry III and Leo IX onwards was approved of and supported by monks, without their becoming either active companions of or fighters for the papal cause. In some countries, monasteries and monastic groupings adopted the line taken by their kings and bishops. In Germany it was possible for important monasteries to remain bound to the king and his supporters in spite of their veneration for the Roman church. There was a certain tendency towards peace which corresponded to the original monastic impulse to flee the world.

We do not know precisely what kind of monasticism Gregory VII had practised. Two of his successors came from Cluny, two from Monte Cassino. It is all the more remarkable that in spite of their monastic origins they showed no traces of quietism; all followed the great Gregory and his predecessors in their intense efforts to subordinate the clerical hierarchy and secular rulers to the command of Peter's vicar and to ride out the conflicts which ensued from this.[169] The responses of the leading figures of contemporary monasticism were equally remarkable.

Hugo of Cluny was in his lifetime probably the most revered man in western Christendom. Gregory VII also showed his reverence for Hugo by seeking his advice and his help, though occasionally he reproached him. The great abbot was a loyal supporter of the popes. With monastic restraint he never sought to check or correct them, but he served their aims with some reserve. As papal legate in France he generally took up a

---

[168] See above, pp. 105f.

[169] Hoffmann in his introduction to Dormeier, *Montecassino*, 8, rightly observes that Victor III and Gelasius II were not popes after the hearts of the Gregorian radicals.

reconciliatory and mediatory position. He was close to Henry III and the empress Agnes; he was Henry IV's godfather. For this reason he seems to have tried where possible to mediate between pope and king and try to settle their differences. His appearance at Canossa is well known; he seems to have taken part in the preparations for the meeting there and had to be absolved because he had had personal contact with the excommunicate Henry IV.[170] Later he seems to have developed a more reserved attitude to Henry IV. According to the life of Hugo of Cluny written by Rainald he met the king once more in person in 1083, when he came from the pope, besieged and in great need in the Castel Sant'Angelo, to Sutri, and tried to mediate.[171] There can be no doubt of his loyalty to the popes, of whom Urban II was probably closest to him. The radical Gregorian Hugo of Lyon accused him of having included the excommunicated Henry in the Good Friday prayers; Hugo is said to have excused himself by saying that he had prayed 'for whatever emperor',[172] but may we not assume that he really did pray quietly for his godson? Henry IV called on Hugo for help and mediation several times in the final desperate period of his life,[173] and so must have believed in his neutrality at least.[174] But there is no reason to suppose that Hugo supported his cause either then or earlier.

Hugo of Lyons's attacks on Desiderius of Monte Cassino (Victor III) were still sharper than those on Hugo of Cluny. He reproached himself with having together with the brothers of the Roman church agreed to Victor's election, in a momentary weakness and taking more thought for his reputation with men than with God, whereby he had sinned gravely against God. Who would have believed, had they not heard it from Victor's own mouth, that he had given his word to the so-called King Henry to aid him in securing the imperial crown.[175] But Desiderius had never really deserted Gregory, and when he agreed after a long delay to accept election as his successor he reaffirmed his belief in him. His

[170] Berthold, *Annales*, *s.a.* 1077, MGH SS v.289; see Meyer von Knonau, *Jahrbücher Heinrichs IV.*, ii.741 with n. 199, 892.

[171] Meyer von Knonau, *Jahrbücher Heinrichs IV.*, iii.490f.; Diener, 'Itinerar', nos. 100, 101 (see *ibid.*, 418, 426).

[172] 'pro imperatore quolibet': see the letter of Hugo of Lyons to the Margravine Mathilda, Mansi xx, cols. 635–6, and Meyer von Knonau, *Jahrbücher Heinrichs IV.*, iv.179 n. 31.

[173] *Briefe Heinrichs IV.*, ed. Erdmann, nos. 31, 37, 38, 39f., and 46ff.

[174] I agree with Hoffmann, 'Von Cluny', 202, that there can be no question of Hugo's having been neutral. His mediatory behaviour is ascribed by Hoffmann to his own personality; but are we not here confronted with the expression of a fundamental kind of monastic piety and indifference to the world?

[175] Hugo of Flavigny, *Chronicon*, MGH SS viii.466; see Meyer von Knonau, *Jahrbücher Heinrichs IV.*, iv.177f.; Loud, 'Abbot Desiderius', 306f.

appearance before Henry in Albano at Easter 1082 may have been
motivated partly by the hope of being able to mediate between pope and
king as well as by fear of an attack by Prince Jordan of Capua on his
monastery.[176] But evidently the abbot did indeed make some conditional
promises at that point. He was not among the cardinals who abandoned
Gregory in 1084. How much he tried to prevent a fatal clash between
Gregory and Henry can be seen from the fact that in 1083 he let each of
them know about Robert Guiscard's approach, something which for the
one was a promise of rescue and for the other a threat of great danger.[177]
When Gregory left Rome after its sack by the Normans he first went
straight to Monte Cassino. Desiderius is said to have supported him and
the cardinals who followed him until his death.[178]

The two great monasteries of European rank continued to uphold their
attitude to the papacy into the early twelfth century; but there were
internal tensions. From 1109 Cluny was ruled by Abbot Pontius, a man of
high reputation whom Hugo himself had nominated. Pontius had
condemned Paschal's 'pravilegium' of 1111 but had then supported the
pope against the radicals, and in 1115 had been prepared to mediate
between Paschal and Henry V.[179] He received Gelasius II in Saint-Gilles
when the pope had fled from Rome, and conducted him to Cluny, where
the pope soon died. He played an important part in the election of
Calixtus II, which also took place in Cluny,[180] and on behalf of the pope
he made repeated attempts, together with William of Champeaux, to
reach an agreement with Henry V.[181] Not until 1122 did it become
openly known that the convent of Cluny was divided into two factions,
and probably had been for some time; a schism broke out, which ended
with the scandalous end of the great abbot in a Roman prison.[182]

Differences of opinion also became apparent within Monte Cassino.
Bishop Bruno of Segni, who was from 1107 also the abbot of the mother
abbey of Benedictinism, attacked the pope vigorously over the 'pravilege'
of 1111. Paschal II, who saw him as the leader and standard-bearer of the

[176] See above, p. 250 n. 334.
[177] Meyer von Knonau, *Jahrbücher Heinrichs IV.*, III.458.
[178] Leccisotti, 'L'incontro di Desiderio', 307–19; on p. 319 Leccisotti calls Desiderius a lover
of peace and equilibrium; *Chronicon Montis Casinensi* III 53, MGH SS XXXIV.435. Loud,
'Abbot Desiderius', 326, says: 'It was inconceivable that the abbot should wish to destroy
the fruits of a lifetime's work dedicated to St Benedict for the sake of a pope whose
ideals he did not share.' I do not dare to follow this assumption.
[179] Tellenbach, 'Sturz', 40.
[180] On the relationship between Calixtus II and Pontius see Cowdrey, 'Two Studies', 219.
[181] See above, p. 283 and n. 115.
[182] Tellenbach, 'Sturz', 13ff.

opposition, commanded him to be content with his bishopric and ordered an election to be held in Monte Cassino. The convent rejected the candidate whom Bruno sought to impose upon them by force and insisted on their right of free election.[183] Another former monk of Monte Cassino, John of Gaeta, was Paschal's main supporter and Bruno's main opponent here. He was papal chancellor from the pontificate of Urban II and himself became pope as Gelasius II in succession to Paschal II; like Pontius of Cluny he took on a mediatory position.[184] It is also worth remembering that Honorius II also deposed an abbot of Monte Cassino, Oderisius II, who nevertheless remained a cardinal and was to become a supporter of the antipope Anacletus II.[185]

Tensions were very apparent within the convents of these two ancient and venerable Benedictine monasteries. In addition to this, Cluny seems to have got into financial difficulties as a result of its almost unbearable obligations of commemorative prayer,[186] while Monte Cassino lay in the middle of a political constellation subject to rapid change, and hence was exposed to multifarious dangers. More important for the development of Benedictine monasticism in many places was the dissatisfaction of the diocesan bishops about the tendency shown by monasteries to secure exemption from diocesan jurisdiction and to acquire proprietary monasteries and other ecclesiastical rights and revenues. The popes, who from Calixtus II onwards were only rarely former monks, became less and less willing to back the monasteries in these struggles. At the start of his pontificate Calixtus II still supported the two great Benedictine abbeys. As early as the council of Rheims in 1119 there were outraged complaints by the bishops of the province of Lyons, especially the bishop of Mâcon, in whose diocese Cluny lay: Pontius had injured and insulted him and his church, withdrawn churches with their tithes and other obligations from him, refused to acknowledge the rights due to him or to have the clerics of his churches ordained by the bishop. Numerous bishops, monks, and clerics shouted vociferous support for these accusations.[187] At the Roman synod of 1123 there was an exact replay of these scenes.[188] This time it was

---

[183] *Chronicon Montis Casinensis* IV 42, p. 511; Cowdrey, *Age*, 220.

[184] See above, p. 325 n. 89 and Meyer von Knonau, *Jahrbücher Heinrichs V.*, VII.52ff.

[185] Tellenbach, 'Sturz', 37f.; Cowdrey, *Age*, 223ff.

[186] G. Duby, 'Le Budget de l'abbaye de Cluny entre 1086 et 1155', *Economies, Sociétés, Civilisations*, 7 (1952), 155–71; J. Wollasch, 'Gemeinschaftsbewußtstein und soziale Leistung im Mittelalter', *FMSt*, 9 (1975), 280ff.; Hoffmann, 'Petrus Diaconus', 80ff.

[187] Tellenbach, 'Sturz', 31f.; Hoffmann, 'Petrus Diaconus', 16f.; Cowdrey, 'Two Studies', 221f.

[188] Tellenbach, 'Sturz', 36ff.; Hoffmann, 'Petrus Diaconus', 98f.

about Monte Cassino that archbishops and bishops complained: they had no choice but to lay down their staves of office and serve the monks, for these retained for their own use churches, estates, castles, tithes, and the oblations of the living and the dead. Forgetful of their heavenly obligations they lusted insatiably after the rights of the bishops. In response to the charges Pontius of Cluny had pointed to the fact that his abbey belonged to the Roman church and to the pope;[189] Oderisius II also argued from the privileges of the Roman see.[190] Calixtus supported the Benedictines at first, but under pressure from the episcopate he gradually reduced their privileges, which had been greatly extended, especially under Urban II.

At the beginning of the twelfth century the Benedictines had by no means become unfaithful to their old ideals, but through their liturgical services, their prayers for the living and for the dead, their care of the poor and sick and their administration of high privileged monastic estates they had become entangled in many worldly matters. In consequence there grew up, as so often before in the history of monasticism, a longing within the ranks of the monks themselves for a stricter form of monastic and eremitical life. At the end of the eleventh and beginning of the twelfth centuries new monastic centres emerged, which aroused more enthusiasm within a changing western Christendom than the old Benedictine monasteries could do. The most decisive development was the later division of the Benedictine order through the powerful expansion by the Cistercians, whose beginnings go back to the turn of the century. Through their criticism of Cluniac monasticism they achieved much publicity and their tight and unified organisation in the form of an order initiated a new chapter in the history of western monasticism.

The rise of the canons regular had already begun in the eleventh century, and these too often appeared as rivals to traditional Benedictinism. On the other hand there was also a growth of unrest in religious communities which no longer found full satisfaction with an institutionalised and clericalised church, were unhappy even in questions of faith and in the pursuit of apostolic poverty, and ran the risk of being perceived and persecuted as heretics.

The crisis in the relationship between church and monasticism which set in after the turn of the century thus had a number of causes. Monasticism in all its various forms still had a great future before it. But it

---

[189] Ordericus Vitalis, *Historia ecclesiastica* XII 21, ed. Chibnall, VI.268ff.

[190] The parallels between Pontius and Oderisius and between Cluny and Monte Cassino have been impressively set out and explained by Hoffmann, 'Petrus Diaconus' and by Cowdrey, 'Two Studies', 267.

was never again to hold as significant a place in the religious thought and feeling of western Christendom as it had towards the end of the eleventh century.

EPILOGUE

Gregory VII, with his precursors and companions, had given decisive impulses towards change in the life of the church and of Christendom. Yet their ideas could not be realised in pure form and their aims could not be fully reached; the first attempt to do so failed.[1] The structures of the preceding period turned out to have a remarkable capacity for survival, and the prevailing values of the earlier period continued to influence the course of events under the surface. It would in any case run counter to all historical experience to assume that the traditions of centuries might have just rapidly faded away. And can we in any sense suppose that an older period of church history can be completely superseded or made obsolete by a younger one? The judgements of recent scholarship about the changes in the relationship between clergy and laity, between spiritual and secular power, have often relied too one-sidedly on the statements of great popes and theologians and on the doctrines of canon lawyers. It is important to take into account historical reality at the same time, to note both the practice of government and the survival of a monarchistic view of the world and of a continuing belief in the direct relationship of the king by the grace of God to God himself, all things which emerged rather later and found less literary articulation than the much-discussed ideologies of popes and canonists.

---

[1] See above, p. 253.

Gregory's successors and their supporters continued faithful to the ideals of their revered predecessor, but their sense of realism grew,[2] and of necessity they were compelled to take account both of the religiously based claims of their opponents and of historical forces. They thus had to settle for what could be realised in their own time and to hope that changes might be possible in the future. The influence of the popes on the heads of the individual churches, the bishops, was strengthened not just in theory but in practice. But there can be no question of the bishops' having been loosened from their previous embedding within regional churches.[3] True, the old intermediate instances between pope and bishops had lost a good deal of their importance. But the individual bishop's conduct of office in day-to-day matters continued for the time being to be determined at least as much by the prevailing local powers – his episcopal colleagues, the king and his court, local magnates – as by the distant pope and his only intermittently functioning apparatus of curia and legates.[4] One should also remember that even after the compromises which had been reached kings in general still participated in the selection of bishops; these in turn were largely drawn from the families of the lay nobility. One would be hard put to it to show that there were general qualitative differences between the episcopate of the eleventh century and that of the twelfth in religiosity, morality, or education.

In the Gregorian view of things kings were to be subject to the pope like all other Christians and to obey him. It is not apparent that Gregory saw kings as having a sphere in which they were to function independently. If the world was to be taken to be the sphere of influence of Christianity, then the highest responsibility had to be borne by the pope. The formula used to justify this was *ratione peccati* ('by reason of sin'); only the pope himself could determine how this was to be applied. What resulted was thus a decisive turning towards the world; it was by no means a distancing of the church, with its mission of salvation, from the world.[5]

---

[2] Kempf, 'Kanonistik', 20.

[3] Kempf, 'Primatiale und episkopal-synodale Struktur', 61; Kempf, 'Eingliederung', 62.

[4] Congar, 'Platz des Papsttums', 25, sees the whole church by contrast as one vast diocese; R. Manselli, *Studi sulle eresie del secolo XII°*, 2nd rev. edn (Studi Storici 5, Rome 1975), 18, takes the opposite view: 'the ecclesiastical organisation of the western church still remained essentially episcopal, not centralised'.

[5] Ladner, 'Aspects', 416 and n. 45, rejected the opinion I expressed in *Church, State and Christian Society*, 157f. In his view Gregory did not think in terms of a 'maximum program of world conversion' but rather of a guarantee of protection for the priestly and hierarchical nature of the church in its doctrine and liturgy. His objections only confirm me in my opinion. By demanding from all members of the church, clerical and lay, the

In the preceding period the church had not suffered under the oppression of the king as a layman; it had enjoyed the helpful protection of kings responsible to God for the conduct of their theocratically rooted office. Of course it is true that he was 'earthbound', however high his ideals.[6] But was this not equally true of clerical office-holders within the church? One cannot properly understand how unresoluble was the tension between popes and kings if one fails to recognise the fact that both sides saw their divine legitimation as indisputable and as an indispensable component of their dignity.[7] No one disputed these things for the pope, while the 'desacralisation' of Christian rulership was in historical reality a failure.[8] As long as a Christian monarchy existed, a direct relationship between the king and God would continue to be posited in the face of all attempts to deny it. Indeed, it was the equality of all kings in their relation to God that was the basis for the idea and reality of the sovereign state.[9]

It has often been assumed that from the time of Gregory VII and Humbert onwards there was not only a devaluation of the role of the laity within the church but a clericalisation of the church. The distance between clergy and laity and the different valuations put upon them go back to a very early period of church history. They increased in the course of the centuries; one should note especially the changes in the way

same obedience to the pope as was due to God, Gregory secured the rights of the church by subjecting the world to her. There is no room here for the flight from the world of early Christians or early monasticism. We see here once more the erroneous interpretation of *libertas ecclesiae*; it is not freedom from the world but absolute superordination to it. Incidentally, the 'wicked world' had never 'rashly' sought to identify itself with the church. I had already in *Libertas*, 20, defined the medieval concept of 'privilege' as a positive term for freedom; see now Szabó-Bechstein, *Libertas Ecclesiae*, 146ff. and 157f., who offers the felicitous definition of Gregory's conception of *libertas ecclesiae* as a privilege conferred on the whole church by Christ in person.

[6] Kempf, 'Problem', 107.

[7] Congar, *Laie*, 132.

[8] Those who talk of desacralisation in spite of this follow the literary hierarchical theory too one-sidedly and ignore reality. See for example W. Kölmel, *Regimen Christianum. Weg und Ergebnisse der Gewaltenverhältnisse und des Gewaltenverständnisses (8.–14. Jahrhundert)* (Berlin 1970), 117, or Kempf, 'Kanonistik', 29: 'deposed from their theocratic position, rulers confined themselves to willing in a secular political sense'. Occasionally views like mine have been expressed, for example by Schwineköper, 'Christus-Reliquien-Verehrung', 183f., 281 and by Carozzi, 'D'Adalberon', 83: 'But the extreme nature of this ecclesiastical position which reduced kingship to the level of a simple human invention explains why it was almost impossible for the Gregorians to triumph completely.'

[9] Tellenbach, 'Zusammenleben', 55ff.

laymen participated in the celebration of the Eucharist and the growing stress on the priestly power to bind and loose.[10] What resulted was not simply an emancipation of the clergy, which entailed an increased emphasis on its superior rank and a reduction in status for the previously dominant laity, but rather the idea of a church of the clergy, which had as its counterpart the whole group of lay Christians.[11] Whereas within the church in its still undivided form the clergy had been a privileged group within the whole, they now formed collectively a new unity, and the church took on conceptually the new form of a closed spiritual hierarchy; the old unity was now represented by the word *Christianitas*. 'The church' could not be considered as an institution, a partner for other sociologically definable entities, capable as never before of practical political decisions. However, the notion of the church as an autonomous part of a total society is so much a current one today that it is often applied unreflectingly to periods in which it was only possible for individuals as holders of clerical offices and dignities to act, not for 'the church'. The relation between the church as the body of all clergy to the community of the faithful, which some sought to distinguish from the church as *Christianitas*, is in any case a distinctly problematic one.[12] Can the distinction be more than a theoretical construct? Was the 'church of the clergy' not a part of *Christianitas*? Does the *ecclesia* not include *Christianitas*? It has been said that *Christianitas*, being rooted in earthly things, was a vague and indefinite entity compared with the supernaturally organised hierarchy of the *ecclesia*; essentially it was only the living link between the papal leader and his Christian followers. This is to fall back once again on the justified objection that no real distinction can be made between *Christianitas* and church.[13] In the same way, it could be said of Gregory VII that he was not a master of theory and that for him 'church

---

[10] Congar, *Ecclésiologie*, 96, 148: 'the questions of binding and loosing took on here a real importance greater even than that of the Eucharist and the mystical unity it brought about'.

[11] Ladner, 'Concepts', 54; Ganzer, 'Kirchenverständnis Gregors VII.', 107.

[12] The problematic nature of the distinction can be seen in R. Seeberg, *Lehrbuch der Dogmenteschichte*, 5th edn (Graz 1953), 293: 'The idea that the church of the faithful is the city of God is transformed into the idea that the church ruled by the pope is the city of God'.

[13] Kempf, 'Problem', 119ff. and n. 44. See on this O. Köhler, 'Unitatis redintegratio. Die Christianitas und das Problem der Einheit der Kirche und der Einheit des Menschengeschlechts', *Festschrift für Friedrich Kempf*, ed. H. Mordek (Sigmaringen 1983), 481ff.

and Christianity are distinct, although for Gregory the distinction remains hidden within the totality of his ideas'.[14]

It has been much discussed whether in medieval history Christianity in all its manifestations existed simultaneously in two orderings, those of priestly and royal government, how these two related to each other, whether a unified government was ever called for or realised. This is not just a matter of the relation between the church and the world. It is also a question of the relation between the two powers founded by God, priesthood and kingship, as defined by Pope Gelasius I, and of whether either of the two ever succeeded in mediatising the other or whether each remained functionally independent. The alternatives have often been summed up in the terms monism and dualism.

It is absurd to suppose that the kingly office, even at its most exalted moments in the early middle ages, ever completely absorbed the priestly power, even though it was seen as a divinely founded office and whatever dominance it achieved as a matter of fact. The exalted service of the sacraments was always treated with reverence, and kings, although it could be said of them that they shared in the office of bishops and priests, never claimed to be able to confer the sacraments. A judgement as to whether the papacy either claimed or realised an exclusive right to lead church and Christianity is much less certain, much more controversial, and must be much more cautiously made. It has sometimes been assumed that a papal hierarchy really did come into existence, a clerical church with powers over *Christianitas*, a view expressed most forcibly by Walter Ullmann.[15] Even a theologian like Friedrich Kempf tended in spite of his own more dualist view of things to concede the existence of an inherent tendency towards a unitary and exclusive leadership of Christianity: 'The development moved in the direction of a papal system integrating everything under it', and Gregory VII showed a 'monistic impetus'. But he also noted that 'Gregorian ideas were fractured in the course of the Investiture Contest'; Gregory's successors had to 'reconcile his radically religious

---

[14] Van Laarhoven, '"Christianitas"', 80, 96. It is understandable that W. Ullmann in his review in *HZ*, 191 (1960), 624, of F. Kempf, 'Die päpstliche Gewalt in der mittelalterlichen Welt. Eine Auseinandersetzung mit W. Ullmann', *Saggi storici intorno al papato dei Professori della Facultà di Storia Ecclesiastica* (Miscellanea Historica Pontificia 21, Rome 1959), should speak of the 'dogmatically slippery distinction between *christianitas* and *ecclesia*'; but it is possible to react less irritatedly and use more friendly terms to describe such inconsequentialities in matters of faith.

[15] Ullmann, *Growth of Papal Government*. For a critical assessment see H. Barion's review of the piece by Kempf cited in the previous note, in *ZRGKA*, 46 (1960), 481–501, where Barion's response to Kempf is particularly noteworthy.

idealism, which thought only in terms of church and pope, with reality'.[16]

We do not here have to show how the coming era tried to shape and theoretically define the relationship between 'spiritual' and secular' power. The dialectic between monism and dualism continued in the new and rapidly developing sciences of canon law and dogmatic theology.[17] But in the last resort it was not one-sided and debatable theories which determined the church's form and history, but 'life as it is lived', and this was made up much more of revealed belief, ancient tradition, and recourse to the roots of the early church, in the form of picture, myth, legend, and symbol, than of ideological dispute.[18] The great conflict between monism and dualism over the distance between pope, Peter, and Christ, over the question of whether the emperor held his power from the pope or from God himself, could be resolved, in the wise opinion of a learned canonist from Bamberg writing at the beginning of the thirteenth century, only by faith, not by dogmatic norms. 'It is a dispute which has no judge, only an executor; but it is devout to believe that the emperor has his sword from the pope.'[19]

---

[16] Kempf, 'Eingliederung', 62; Kempf, 'Problem', 112; Kempf, 'Kanonistik', 31.

[17] Kempf, 'Kanonistik', 28, terms it decisive in assessing the monistic or dualistic nature of doctrines to see 'whether they take account of an autonomous secular political willing in cases of conflict or posit a spiritual political willing as a norm to which all must be subordinated'. But if it is really necessary to indulge in such an artificial and theoretical distinction between forms of willing then the question must be raised whether it is not necessary to allow the king not just a secular political will but a religiously legitimated right of participation, if monism or 'hierocracy' are to be seriously challenged.

[18] Congar, *Laie*, 85.

[19] 'quaestio ista iudicem non habet, sed solum executorem, tamen pium est credere, quod imperator gladium habeat a Papa': Stickler, 'Sacerdozio e regno', 4.

SELECT BIBLIOGRAPHY

A systematic bibliography covering the whole of the available scholarly literature would have taken up too much room. Reference may be made to the excellent bibliographies in F. Kempf, H.-G. Beck, E. Ewig, and J. A. Jungmann, *Handbook of Church History* III, ed. H. Jedin and J. Dolan (London 1968 = English translation of *Handbuch der Kirchengeschichte* III/1, Berne 1965) and in a number of recent surveys: U.-R. Blumenthal, *The Investiture Controversy* (Philadelphia 1988); H. Jakobs, *Kirchenreform und Hochmittelalter 1046–1215* (Munich 1984), 165–226; B. Schimmelpfennig, *Das Papsttum, Grundzüge seiner Geschichte von der Antike zur Renaissance* (Grundzüge 56, Darmstadt 1984), 289–333; E. Hlawitschka, *Vom Frankenreich zur Formierung der europäischen Staaten- und Völkergemeinschaft 840–1046* (Darmstadt 1986), 239–87. The following list is confined to titles cited in shortened form in the notes which are either quoted in the text or are contributions to a debate or offer discussion of specific problems. Works and sources referred to only once in the notes are cited there in full.

Adam of Bremen. *Gesta Hammaburgensis ecclesiae pontificum*, ed. B. Schmeidler (MGH SRG, Hanover 1917)

Addleshaw, G. W. *The Beginnings of the Parochial System* (York 1953)

Aimé (Amatus). *Ystoire de li Normant*, ed. O. Delare (Rouen 1892)

Alberigo, G. 'Le origini della dottrina sullo ius divinum del cardinalato', in *Reformata Reformanda. Festschrift für Hubert Jedin*, vol. 1 (Münster 1965)

   Cardinalato e collegialità. Studi sull'ecclesiologia tra l'XI^mo ed il XIV^mo secolo (Florence 1969)

Amari, M. *Storia dei Musulmani in Sicilia*, 2nd edn by C. Nellino (Catania 1933–9)

Andersson, I. *Schwedische Geschichte (Sverige historia)*, German translation by A. Brandt (Munich 1950)

Andresen, C. 'Die Legitimierung des römischen Primatsanspruchs in der alten Kirche', in *Das Papsttum in der Diskussion*, ed. G. Denzler (Munich 1974)

Andrieu, M. (ed.). *Le Pontifical Romain au moyen âge* (Studi e Testi 86ff., Vatican 1938ff.)

Angenendt, A. 'Religiosität und Theologie. Ein spannungsreiches Verhältnis im Mittelalter', *Archiv für Liturgiewissenschaft*, 20/21 (1978–9)

'Die Liturgie und die Organisation des kirchlichen Lebens auf dem Lande', *Settimane*, 28 (1982)

Annales Altahenses maiores, ed. E. L. B. von Oefele (MGH SRG, Hanover 1891)

S. Anselmi Opera Omnia, ed. F. S. Schmitt. 6 vols. (Edinburgh and Rome 1940–61)

Anton, H. H. *Der sogenannte Traktat De Ordinando Pontifice* (Bonner historische Forschungen 48, Bonn 1982)

Arnaldo, G. 'Papato, arcivescovi e vescovi nell'età postcarolingia', in *Vescovi e diocesi in Italia nel Medio Evo (sec. IX–XII)* (Padua 1964)

Arquillière, H. X. *Saint Grégoire VII. Essai sur la conception du pouvoir pontifical* (Paris 1934)

Autenrieth, J. *Die Domschule in Konstanz zur Zeit des Investiturstreites* (Stuttgart 1956)

'Bernold von Konstanz und die erweiterte 74 Titel-Sammlung', *DA*, 14 (1958)

Bardach, J. 'L'Etat Polonais aux Xme et XIme siècles', in *L'Europe aux IXme–XIme siècles. Aux Origines des états nationaux. Actes du Colloque international à Varsovie et Poznan* (Warsaw 1968)

Barion, H. *Das fränkisch-deutsche Synodalrecht des Frühmittelalters* (Kanonistische Studien und Texte 5/6, Bonn 1931)

Barlow, F. 'Edward the Confessor's Early Life, Character and Attitudes', *EHR*, 80 (1965)

The English Church 1000–1066. A Constitutional History, 2nd edn (London 1966)

Edward the Confessor (London 1970)

The English Church 1066–1154 (London 1979)

Beck, H.-G. *Geschichte der orthodoxen Kirche im byzantinischen Reich* (Die Kirche in ihrer Geschichte D, Göttingen, 1980)

Becker, A. *Studien zum Investiturproblem im Frankreich* (Schriften der Universität des Saarlandes, Saarbrücken 1955)

Papst Urban II. (1088–1099), vol. I (Schriften der MGH 19/1, Stuttgart 1964)

'Urban II. und die deutsche Kirche', *VuF*, 17 (1973)

Benson, R. L. '"Plenitudo Potestatis": Evolution of a Formula from Gregory IV to Gratian', *StGrat*, 14 (1967)

The Bishop Elect. A Study in Medieval Ecclesiastical Office (Princeton 1968)

Berges, W. 'Zur Geschichte des Werla-Goslarer Reichsbezirks vom neunten bis elften Jahrhundert', in *Die deutschen Königspfalzen* (Veröffentlichungen des Max-Planck-Instituts für Geschichte 11/1, Göttingen 1963)

Beumann, H. 'Zur Entwicklung transpersonaler Staatsvorstellungen', *VuF*, 3 (1963)

'Tribur, Rom und Canossa', *VuF*, 17 (1973)

Beumann, J. *Sigebert von Gembloux und der Traktat de investitura episcoporum* (VuF Sonderband 26, Sigmaringen 1976) (see also J. Krimm-Beumann)

Blaul, O. 'Studien zum Register Gregors VII.', *AUF*, 4 (1912)

Bloch, M. *Les Rois thaumaturges. Etude sur le charactère attribué à la puissance royale* (Paris 1924); English translation as *The Royal Touch* (London 1973)

Blumenthal, U. R. 'Patrimonia and Regalia in 1111', in *Law, Church and Society, Festschrift for Stephan Kuttner* (Philadelphia 1976)

'Some Notes on Papal Politics at Guastalla', *StGrat*, 19 (1976)

'Paschal II and the Roman Papacy', *AHP*, 16 (1978)

Böhm, L. 'Rechtsformen und Rechtstitel der burgundischen Königserhebungen im neunten Jahrhundert', *HJb*, 80 (1961)

Böhmer, H. *Kirche und Staat in England und der Normandie im elften zund zwölften Jahrhundert* (Leipzig 1899)

'Das Eigenkirchentum in England', in *Festschrift für F. Libermann* (Halle 1921)

Böhmer, J.-F. *Papstregesten 911–1024*, edited by H. von Zimmermann (Vienna 1969), cited by number

Boglioni, P. (ed.). *La Culture populaire au moyen âge* (Montreal 1979)

Bogumil, K. *Das Bistum Halberstadt im zwölften Jahrhundert* (Mitteldeutsche Forschungen 69, Cologne 1972)

Borgolte, C. *Studien zur Klosterreform in Sachsen im Hochmittelalter* (Freiburg 1976)

Borino, G. B. 'L'elezione e la deposizione di Gregorio VI', *Archivio della Società romana di storia patria*, 139 (1916)

'Note Gregoriane 7. Storicità delle ultime parole di Gregorio VII.', *StGreg*, 5 (1956)

'Odelrico vescovo di Padova (1064–1086) legato di Gregorio VII in Germania 1079', in *Miscellanea in onore di Roberto Cessi*, vol. 1 (Rome 1958)

Boshof, E. 'Das Reich in der Krise. Überlegungen zum Regierungsstil Kaiser Heinrichs III.', *HZ*, 228 (1979)

'Bischof Altmann, St. Nikola und die Kanonikerreform', in *Gedenkschrift für J. Riederer* (Passau 1981)

Bouquet, H. and M. Brial. *Recueil des Historiens des Gaules et de la France* (Paris 1738–)

Boyd, C. E. *Tithes and Parishes in Medieval Italy. The Historical Roots of a Modern Problem* (Ithaca, N.Y. 1952)

Boye, M. 'Quellenkatalog der Synoden Deutschlands und Reichsitaliens von 922–1059', *NA*, 48 (1929)

'Die Synoden Deutschlands und Reichsitaliens von 922–1059', *ZRGKA*, 18 (1929)

Bresslau, H. *Jahrbücher des deutschen Reiches unter Konrad II.*, 2 vols. (Leipzig 1879–84)

Brett, M. *The English Church under Henry I* (Oxford 1975)

Die Briefe Heinrichs IV. (see Erdmann)

Brommer, P. 'Die bischöfliche Gesetzgebung Theodulfs von Orléans', *ZRGKA*, 60 (1974)

'Benedictus Levita und die "Capitula episcoporum"' *Mainzer Zeitschrift*, 70 (1975)

'Die Quellen der "Capitula" Radulf von Bourges', *Francia*, 5 (1977)

Select bibliography 357

Brooke, C. N. L. 'Gregorian Reform in Action. Clerical Marriage in England 1050–1200', *Cambridge Historical Journal*, 12 (1956)
Brooke, Z. N. 'Lay Investiture and its Relations to the Conflict of Empire and Papacy', *PBA*, 25 (1939)
Browe, P. *Die eucharistischen Wunder des Mittelalters* (Breslauer Studien zur historischen Theologie, new series 4, Breslau 1938)
Brühl, C. *Fodrum, Gistum, Servitium Regis*, 2 vols. (Kölner Historischer Forschungen 14, Cologne 1968)
Brüske, W. *Untersuchungen zur Geschichte des Liutizenbundes* (Münster 1955)
Brunos Buch vom Sachsenkrieg, ed. H.-E. Lohmann (MGH Deutsches Mittelalter 2, Leipzig 1937)
Bruns, H. *Das Gegenkönigtum Rudolfs von Rheinfelden unds seine zeitpolitischen Voraussetzungen* (Diss. Berlin 1940)
Büttner, H. 'Das Erzstift Mainz und die Klosterreform des elften Jahrhunderts', *Archiv für mittelrheinische Kirchengeschichte*, 1 (1949)
'St. Blasien und das Bistum Basel im 11. und 12. Jahrhundert', *Zeitschrift für schweizerische Kirchengeschichte*, 44 (1950)
'Wilhelm von Hirsau und die Entwicklung der Rechtsstellung der Reform-klöster im elften Jahrhundert', *Zeitschrift für württembergische Landesgeschichte*, 25 (1966)
'Die Mainzer Erzbischöfe Friedrich und Wilhelm und das Papsttum im zehnten Jahrhundert', in *Festschrift für J. Bärmann* (Geschichtliche Landeskunde 3, Wiesbaden 1966/67)
'Friedrich Barbarossa und Burgund', *VuF*, 12 (1968)
'Erzbischof Adalbert von Mainz, die Kurie und das Reich in den Jahren 1118–1122', *VUF*, 17 (1973)
Bulst, N. *Untersuchungen zu der Klosterreform Wilhelms von Dijon (962–1031)* (Pariser Historische Studien 11, Bonn 1973)
Bultot, R. 'Mépris du monde au XIme siècle', *Annales ESC*, 22 (1967)
Cantor, N. F. *Church, Kingship and Lay Investiture in England, 1089–1135* (London 1958)
Capitani, O. 'Studi per Berengario di Tours', *BISI*, 69 (1957)
'Per la storia dei rapporti tra Gregorio VII e Berengario di Tours', *StGreg*, 6 (1959–61)
'Motivi di spiritualità clunicacense e realismo eucaristico in Odone di Cluny', *BISI*, 71 (1960)
'Immunità vescovili ed ecclesiologia in età pregregoriana e Gregoriana', *StMed*, 2 (1962) and 6 (1965)
'La figura del vescovo in alcune collezioni canoniche della seconda metà del secolo XI', in *Vescovi e diocesi in Italia nel Medioevo (sec. IX–XII)* (Padua 1964)
'Canossa: una lezione da meditare', *RSCI*, 32 (1978)
Carozzi, C. 'La Géographie de l'audelà et sa signification pendant le haut moyen-âge', *Settimane*, 29 (1983)
'D'Adalberon de Laon à Humbert de Moyenmoutier', *MCSM*, 10 (1983)
Caspar, E. 'Die Legatengewalt der normannisch-sizilischen Herrscher im zwölften Jahrhundert', *QFIAB*, 8 (1904)

'Gregory VII. in seinen Briefen', *HZ*, 130 (1924)

Chalandon, F. *Histoire de la domination Normande en Italie et en Sicile* (Paris 1907)

Chenu, M.-D. 'Moines, clercs, laïcs au carrefour de la vie évangelique et le reveil évangelique', in *La théologie au douzième siècle* (Paris 1957); English translation as *Nature, Man and Society in the Twelfth Century* (Chicago 1968)

Chodorow, S. 'Ecclesiastical Politics and the Ending of the Investiture Contest. The Papal Election of 1119 and the Negotiations of Mouzon', *Speculum*, 46 (1971)

    Christian Political Theory and Church Politics in the Mid-Twelfth Century. The Ecclesiology of Gratian's Decretum (Berkeley 1972)

Classen, P. 'Das Wormser Konkordat in der deutschen Verfassungsgeschichte', *VuF*, 17 (1973)

Claude, D. *Geschichte des Erzbistums Magdeburg bis in das zwölfte Jahrhundert*, vol. 1 (Cologne 1972)

Congar, Y. M. J. *Der Laie, Entwurf einer Theologie des Laientums* (Stuttgart 1957)

    'Der Platz des Papsttums in der Kirchenfrömmigkeit der Reformer des elften Jahrhunderts', in *Sentire ecclesiam, Festschrift für K. Rahner*, ed. J. Daniélou and H. Gorgrimler (Freiburg 1961)

    L'Ecclésiologie du haut moyen âge (Paris 1968)

    'Les Laiques et l'ecclésiologie des "ordines" chez les théologiens du XIme et XIIme siècles', *MCSM*, 5 (1968)

Cowdrey, H. E. J. *The Cluniacs and the Gregorian Reform* (Oxford 1970)

    'Two Studies on Cluniac History 1049–1126', *StGreg*, 11 (1978)

    The Age of Abbot Desiderius. Monte Cassino, the Papacy and the Normans in the Eleventh and Early Twelfth Centuries (Oxford 1983)

Darlington, R. R. 'Ecclesiastical Reform in the Late Old English Period', *EHR*, 51 (1936)

Deanesly, M. 'Early English and Gallic Minsters', *TRHS*, 4th series, 23 (1941)

    Sidelights on the Anglo-Saxon Church (London 1962)

    The Pre-Conquest Church in England, 2nd edn (*An Ecclesiastical History of England*, ed. J. C. Dickinson, London 1963)

de Berthelier, S. 'L'Expansion de l'ordre de Cluny, *Revue Archéologique*, 6th series, 11 (1938)

de Clercq, C. *La Législation religieuse franque. Etudes sur les actes de conciles et les capitulaires, les statuts diocésains et les règles monastiques*. 2 vols. (Louvain 1936–58)

Deér, J. 'Der Anspruch der Herrscher des zwölften Jahrhunderts auf die apostolische Legation', *AHP*, 2 (1968)

    Papsttum und Normannen (Cologne 1972)

de Gaiffier, B. 'L'Hagiographie et son public au XIme siècle', *Miscellanea Historica in honorem Leonis van Essen* (Brussels 1947)

    Etudes critiques d'hagiographie et d'iconologie (Subsidia hagiographica 43, Brussels 1967)

Delehaye, H. *Sanctus. Essai sur le culte des Saints dans l'antiquité* (Subsidia hagiographica 17, Brussels 1927)

Les Origines du culte des martyrs, 2nd edn (Subsidia hagiographica 20, Brussels 1933)

de Lubac, H. 'Le Pouvoir de l'Eglise en matière temporelle', *Revue des Sciences Réligieuses*, 12 (1933)
    Corpus Mysticum. L'Eucharistie et l'église au moyen âge (Paris 1944)

Demm, E. 'Die Rolle des Wunders in Heiligkeitskonzeptionen des Mittelalters', *AKG*, 57 (1975)

Dereine, C. 'Vie commune, règle de St. Augustin et chanoines réguliers au XIme siècle', *RHE*, 41 (1946)
    'Chanoines', *DHGE*, 12 (1953)

de Valdeavellano, L. G. *Historia de España*, 2nd edn (Madrid 1955)

de Valous, G. *Le Monachisme clunisien des origines au XVme siècle* (Paris 1935)
    'Cluny', *DHGE*, 13 (1956)

Dhondt, J. *Etudes sur la naissance des principautés territoriales en France (IXme et Xme siècles)* (Paris 1948)

Dickinson, J. G. *The Later Middle Ages. From the Norman Conquest to the Eve of the Reformation (An Ecclesiastical History of England*, ed. J. C. Dickinson, London 1979)

Diener, H. 'Das Itinerar des Abtes Hugo von Cluny', in G. Tellenbach (ed.), *Neue Forschungen über Cluny und die Cluniacenser* (Freiburg 1959)
    'Das Verhältnis Clunys zu den Bischöfen vor allem in der Zeit seines Abtes Hugo', in G. Tellenbach, *Neue Forschungen über Cluny due die Cluniacenser* (Freiburg 1959)

Dormeier, H. *Montecassino und die Laien im 11. und 12. Jahrhundert* (Schriften der MGH 27, Stuttgart 1979)

Douglas, D. C. 'Rollo of Normandy', *EHR*, 57 (1942)
    'The Rise of Normandy', *PBA*, 33 (1947)

Duby, G. *La Société aux XIe et XIIe siècles dans la région mâconnaise* (Paris 1953)
    Frühzeit des abendländischen Christentums 900–1140 (n.p. 1967)
    'Aux origines d'un système de classification sociale', in *Mélanges en l'honneur de F. Braudel* (Paris 1973)
    'Gérard de Cambrai, la paix et les trois fonctions sociales (1024)', *Comptes rendus des séances de l'Académie des Inscriptions et Belles Lettres* (1976)
    Les trois Ordres ou l'imaginaire du féodalisme (Paris 1978)

Duchesne, L. *Les premiers Temps de l'Etat pontifical* (Paris [1898] 1911)

Dümmler, E. *Jahrbücher des ostfränkischen Reiches*, 3 vols., 2nd edn (Leipzig 1887–8)

Düwel, K. 'Die Bekehrung auf Island', *Kirchengeschichte als Missionsgeschichte 2. Die Kirche des frühen Mittelalters, 1. Halbband*, ed. K. Schäferdiek (Munich 1978)

Dufourcq, C. E. 'La coexistence des Chrétiens et des musulmans dans Al-Andalus et dans le Maghrib au Xe siècle', in *Occident et Orient au 10e siècle* (Paris 1979)

Duine, F. *La Métropole de Bretagne. Chronique de Dol composée au XIme siècle* (La Bretagne et les pays Celtiques, ser. in 8° 12, Paris 1916)

Dupré-Théseider, E. 'Ottone I e l'Italia', in *Renovatio Imperii. Atti della Giornata Internazionale di Studio per il Millenario* (Faenza 1961)
    'La grande rapina dei corpi Santi dell'Italia al tempo di Ottone I', *Festschrift für Percy Ernst Schramm*, vol. 1 (Wiesbaden 1964)

Eadmer, *Historia novorum*, ed. M. Rule (Rolls Series 81, London 1884)

Eichmann, E. 'Die sogenannte Römische Königskrönungsformel', *HJb*, 45 (1925)

Elze, R. 'Das "Sacrum Palatium Lateranense" in zehnten und elften Jahrhundert', *StGreg*, 4 (1952)

Pontificale Romano Germanicum, see C. Vogel and R. Elze

Erdmann, C. 'Mauritius Burdinus (Gregor VIII.)', *QFIAB*, 19 (1927)

Kaiserfahne und Blutfahne (Sitzungsberichte der preußischen Akademie der Wissenschaften, phil.-hist. Klasse, Berlin 1932)

'Die Anfänge der staatlichen Propaganda im Investiturstreit', *HZ*, 154 (1935)

Die Entstehung der Kreuzzuggedankens (Stuttgart 1935); English translation as *The Origin of the Idea of Crusade* (Princeton 1977)

'Die Bamberger Domschule im Investiturstreit', *ZBLG*, 9 (1936)

(ed.). *Die Briefe Heinrichs IV.* (MGH Deutsches Mittelalter 1, Leipzig 1937)

'Der ungesalbte König', *DA*, 2 (1938)

Studien zur Briefliteratur Deutschlands im elften Jahrhundert (Schriften der MGH 1, Leipzig, 1938)

'Gregor VII. und Berengar von Tours', *QFIAB*, 28 (1938)

Erdmann, C. and von Gladiß, D. 'Gottschalk von Aachen im Dienst Heinrichs IV.', *DA*, 3 (1939)

Fasoli, G. *I re d'Italia* (Florence 1949)

Fauroux, M. *Recueil des Actes des ducs de Normandie de 911 à 1066*, Mémoires de la Société des Antiquaries de Normandie 36, 4th series, vol. VI (Rouen 1961)

Fawtier, R. *Histoire des institutions françaises au moyen-âge*, vol. II (Paris 1958)

Fechter, J. *Cluny, Adel und Volk (910–1154)* (Diss. Tübingen 1966)

Feine, H. E. 'Die genossenschaftliche Gemeindekirche im germanischen Recht', *MIÖG*, 58 (1960)

Kirchliche Rechtsgeschichte, vol. 1, fifth edn (Weimar 1972)

Fenske, L. *Adelsopposition und kirchliche Reformbewegung im östlichen Sachsen. Entstehung und Wirkung des sächsischen Widerstandes gegen des sächsische Königtum* (Göttingen 1977)

Fichtenau, H. 'Zum Reliquienwesen im frühen Mittelalter', *MIÖG*, 60 (1952)

Finucane, R. C. 'The Use and Abuse of Medieval Miracles', *History*, 60 (1975)

Fischer, F. M. *Politiker um Otto den Großen* (Berlin 1938)

Fleckenstein, J. *Die Hofkapelle der deutschen Könige*, 2 vols. (MGH Schriften 16/I–II, Stuttgart 1959 and 1966)

'Rex Canonicus. Über Entstehung und Bedeutung des mittelalterlichen Königskanonikates', *Festschrift für Percy Ernst Schramm*, vol. 1 (Wiesbaden 1964)

'Heinrich IV. und der deutsche Episkopat in den Anfängen des Intestiturstreits. Ein Beitrag zur Problematik von Worms, Tribur und Canossa', in *Adel und Kirche. Festschrift für Gerd Tellenbach*, ed. J. Fleckenstein and K. Schmid (Freiburg 1968)

'Hofkapelle und Reichsepiskopat unter Heinrich IV.', *VuF* 17 (1973)

'Zum Begriff der ottonisch-salischen Reichskirche', *Festschrift für C. Bauer* (Berlin 1974)

'Zum Problem der Abschließung des Ritterstandes', *Festschrift für W. Schlesinger*, ed. H. Beumann, vol. II (Cologne 1974)

Foreville, R. *L'Eglise et la royauté en Angleterre sous le règne de Henri II Plantagenet (1154–1189)* (Paris 1943)
'Les Statuts synodaux et le renouveau pastoral du treizième siècle', *Cahiers de Fanjeaux*, 6 (1971)
'Royaumes, métropolitains et conciles provinciaux', *MGSM* (1974)
'The Synods of the Province of Rouen in the Eleventh and Twelfth Century', in *Festschrift for Christopher Cheney* (Cambridge 1976)

Fournier, P. and Le Bras, G. *Histoire des collections canoniques en Occident*, vol. I (Paris 1931)

Fransen, G. 'Papes, conciles généraux et oecuméniques', *MCSM*, 7 (1974)

Fried, J. 'Die römische Kurie und die Anfänge der Prozeßliteratur', *ZRGKA*, 59 (1973)
'Der Regalienbegriff im elften und zwölften Jahrhundert', *DA*, 29 (1973)
'Laienadel und Papst in der Frühzeit der französischen und deutschen Geschichte', in *Aspekte der Nationbildungen im Mittelalter*, ed. H. Beumann and W. Schröder (Nationes 1, Sigmaringen 1978)

Fürst, C. G. *Cardinalis. Prolegomena zu einer Rechtsgeschichte des römischen Kardinalskollegiums* (Munich 1967)

Fuhrmann, H. 'Studien zur Geschichte der mittelalterlichen Patriarchate', *ZRGKA*, 39 (1953); 40 (1954); 41 (1955)
'Die pseudoisidorischen Fälschungen und die Synode von Hohenaltheim', *ZBLG*, 76 (1957)
'Pseudoisidor in Rom', *ZKG*, 78 (1967)
'Provincia constat duodecim episcopatibus. Zum Patriarchatsplan Erzbischof Adalberts von Hamburg', *StGrat*, 11 (1967)
Einfluß und Verbreitung der pseudoisidorischen Fälschungen, 3 vols. (MGH Schriften 24, Stuttgart 1972–4)
'Reformpapsttum und Rechtswissenschaft', *VuF*, 17 (1973)
'Pseudoisidor, Otto von Ostia (Urban II.) und der Zitatenkampf von Gerstungen', *ZRGKA*, 68 (1982)
'Gregor VII., "Gregorianische Reform" und Investiturstreit', in *Das Papsttum*, ed. M. Greschat, vol. I (Stuttgart 1985)
Deutsche Geschichte im hohen Mittelalter. Von der Mitte des 11. bis zum Ende des 12. Jahrhunderts (2nd edn, Göttingen 1983); English translation as *Germany in the High Middle Ages, c. 1050–1200* (Cambridge 1986)

Gaffrey, B. *Hugo der Weisse und die Opposition im Kardinalkolleg gegen Gregor VII.* (Diss. Greifswald 1914)

Ganzer, K. *Die Entwicklung des auswärtigen Kardinalats im hohen Mittelalter* (Bibliothek des deutschen Historischen Instituts in Rom 26, Tübingen 1963)
'Das Kirchenverständnis Gregors VII.', *Trier Theologische Zeitschrift*, 78 (1969)

Gay, J. *L'Italie méridionale et l'Empire Byzantin* (Bibliothèque des Ecoles françaises d'Athène et de Rome 90, Paris 1904)

Geary, P. G. 'L'Humiliation des Saints', *Annales ESC*, 34 (1979)

'La Coercition des Saints dans la pratique réligieux médiévale', in *La culture populaire*, ed. P. Boglioni (Montreal 1979)

Geary, P. J. *Furta sacra. Thefts of Relics in the Central Middle Ages* (Princeton 1978)

Geiselmann, J. *Die Eucharistielehre der Vorscholastik* (Forschungen zur christlichen Literatur- und Dogmengeschichte 15, Paderborn 1926)

Gerhardt, M. *Norwegische Geschichte* (Bonn 1963)

de Ghellinck, J. 'Dialectique et dogma au Xme–XIIme siècles', in *Studien zur Geschichte der Philosophie. Festschrift für C. Baeumker* (Münster 1913)

Giese, W. *Der Stamm der Sachsen in ottonischer und salischer Zeit* (Wiesbaden 1979)

Giesebrecht, W. *Geschichte der deutschen Kaiserzeit*, vol. III (Leipzig 1890)

Gilchrist, J. 'Simoniaca Haeresis and the Problem of Orders from Leo IX to Gratian', *Proceedings of the Second International Congress of Medieval Canon Law*, ed. S. Kuttner and J. J. Ryan (Vatican City 1965)

The Church and Economic Activity in the Middle Ages (London 1969)

'The Reception of Pope Gregory VII into the Canon Law, 1073–1141', *ZRGKA*, 59 (1973) and 66 (1980)

Godfrey, C. J. *The Church in Anglo-Saxon England* (Cambridge 1962)

Goez, W. 'Zur Erhebung und ersten Absetzung Gregors VII.', *RQ*, 63 (1968)

'Papa qui et episcopus', *AHP*, 8 (1970)

'Reformpapsttum, Adel und monastische Erneureung in der Toscana', *VuF*, 17 (1973)

'Rainald von Como (1061–1084). Ein Bischof des elften Jahrhunderts zwischen Kurie und Krone', in *Festschrift für W. Schlesinger*, ed. H. Beumann (Cologne 1974)

Grabmann, M. *Geschichte der scholastischen Methode* (Freiburg 1909)

Grant, R. M. *Miracle and Natural Law in Graeco-Roman and Early Christian Thought* (Amsterdam 1956)

Graus, F. *Volk, Herrscher und Heiliger im Reich der Merowinger* (Prague 1965)

Grégoire, R. 'Pomposa et la réforme de l'Eglise au XIme siècle', *Analecta Pomposiana*, 1 (1965)

Groten, M. 'Von der Gebetsverbrüderung zum Königskanonikat', *HJb*, 103 (1983)

Grundmann, H. *Ketzergeschichte des Mittelalters*, 2nd edn (Die Kirche in ihrer Geschichte G 1, Göttingen 1967)

Guilleman, B. 'Les Origines des évêques en France aux XIme et XIIme siècles', *MCSM*, 7 (1974)

Guttmann, B. 'Die Germanisierung der Slaven in der Mark', *Forschungen zur Brandenburgisch-Preussischen Geschichte*, 9 (1897)

Haase, K. *Die Königskrönungen in Oberitalien und die 'eiserne' Krone* (Diss. Strasbourg 1901)

Haendler, G. *Geschichte des Frühmittelalters und der Germanenmission* (Die Kirche in ihrer Geschichte E, Göttingen 1961)

Häussling, A. A. *Mönchskonvent und Eucharistiefeier. Eine Studie über die Messe in der abendländischen Klosterliturgie des frühen Mittelalters und zur Geschichte des Meßhäufigkeit* (Liturgiegeschichtliche Quellen und Forschungen 58, Münster 1973)

Haider, S. 'Zu den Anfängen der päpstlichen Kapelle', *MIÖG*, 87 (1979)

Hallinger, K. *Gorze und Cluny*, 2 vols. (Studia Anselmiana 22–5, Rome 1950–1)

'Zur geistigen Welt der Anfänge Clunys', *DA*, 10 (1953–4)

Halphen, L. *Etudes sur l'administration de Rome au moyen-âge* (Paris 1907)

Hartmann, L. M. *Geschichte Italiens im Mittelalter*, 4 vols. (Leipzig 1897–1915)

'Grundherrschaft und Bürokratie im Kirchenstaat vom 8. bis 10. Jahrhundert', *VSWG*, 7 (1909)

Hartmann, W. 'Der rechtliche Zustand der Kirchen auf dem Lande. Die Eigenkirche in der fränkischen Gesetzgebund des 7.–9. Jahrhunderts', *Settimane*, 28 (1982)

Hauck, A. *Kirchengeschichte Deutschlands*, 5 vols., 4th edn (Leipzig 1911–29)

Hausmann, F. *Reichskanzlei und Hofkapelle unter Heinrich V. und Konrad III.* (MGH Schriften 14, Stuttgart, 1956)

Hellmann, M. 'Die Synode von Hohenaltheim', *HJb*, 73 (1954)

Hermann-Mascard, N. *Les Reliques des saints. Formation coutumière d'un droit* (Paris 1975)

Hessel, A. 'Cluny und Mâcon', *ZKG*, 22 (1901)

Hiestand, R. *Byzanz und das Regnum Italicum im 10. Jahrhundert* (Diss. Zürich 1964)

Higounet, C. *Histoire de l'Aquitaine*, vol. 1 (Toulouse 1971)

Hinschius, P. *Das Kirchenrecht der Katholiken und Protestanten in Deutschland* (Berlin 1878)

Hirsch, H. 'Untersuchungen zur Geschichte des päpstlichen Schutzes', *MIÖG*, 54 (1942)

Hirsch, S., H. Pabst, and H. Bresslau. *Jahrbücher des deutschen Reiches unter Heinrich II.*, 3 vols. (Leipzig 1862–75)

Hlawitschka, E. 'Zwischen Worms und Canossa', *HJb*, 94 (1974)

Hödl, L. 'Die lex continentiae. Eine problemgeschichtliche Studie über das Zölibat', *Zeitschrift für katholische Theologie*, 83 (1961)

Hoesch, H. *Die kanonischen Quellen im Werk Humberts von Moyenmoutier. Ein Beitrag zur Geschichte der vorgregorianischen Reform* (Cologne 1970)

Hoffmann, H. 'Ivo von Chartres und die Lösung des Investiturproblems', *DA*, 15 (1959)

'Französische Fürstenweihen des Hochmittelalters', *DA*, 18 (1962)

'Von Cluny zum Investiturstreit', *AKG*, 45 (1963)

Gottesfriede und Treuga Dei (MGH Schriften 20, Stuttgart 1964)

'Petrus Diaconus, die Herren von Tusculum und der Sturz Oderisius' II. von Monte Cassino', *DA*, 27 (1971)

'Der Kirchenstaat im hohen Mittelalter', *QFIAB*, 57 (1977)

'Langobarden, Normannen, Päpste', *QFIAB*, 58 (1978)

Hofmann, K. *Der dictatus Papae Gregors VII.* (Paderborn 1933)

'Der "Dictatus Papae" Gregors VII. als Index einer Kanonessammlung', *StGreg*, 1 (1947)

Hofmeister, P. 'Mönchtum und Seelsorge bis zum 13. Jahrhundert', *StMGBO*, 65 (1953–4)

Holtzmann, W., 'Laurentius von Amalfi', *StGreg*, 1 (1947)

'Papsttum, Normannen und griechische Kirche', *Miscellanea Bibliothecae Hertitianae*, vol. I (Munich 1961)

Hóman, B. *Geschichte des ungarischen Mittelalters*, vol. I (Berlin 1940)

Hübinger, P. E. *Die letzten Worte Papst Gregors VII*. (Rheinisch-Westfälische Akademie der Wissenschaften, Geisteswissenschaftliche Vorträge 185, Opladen 1973)

Hüls, R. *Kardinäle. Klerus, Kirchen Roms 1049–1130* (Bibliothek des deutschen Historischen Instituts in Rom 48, Tübingen 1977)

Hunt, W. *The English Church from the Foundation to the Norman Conquest* (London 1931)

Imbart de la Tour, P. *Les Paroisses rurales du IIme au XIme siècles* (Paris 1900)

Jacob, L. *Le Royaume de Bourgogne sous les empéreurs Franconiens* (Paris 1906)

Jaffé, P. *Bibliotheca rerum Germanicarum*, 6 vols. (Berlin 1860–9)

Jakobs, H. *Die Hirsauer* (Cologne 1961)

  Der Adel und die Klosterreform in St. Blasien (Cologne 1968)

  'Rudolf von Rheinfelden und die Kirchenreform', *VuF*, 17 (1973)

  'Die Cluniacenser und das Papsttum im 10. und 11. Jahrhundert', *Francia*, 2 (1974)

  Kirchenreform und Hochmittelalter 1046–1215 (Oldenbourgs Grundriß der Geschichte 7, Munich 1984)

Jasper, D. *Das Papstwahldekret von 1059. Überlieferung und Textgestalt* (Beiträge zur Geschichte und Quellenkunde des Mittelalter 12, Sigmaringen 1986)

Jenal, G. *Erzbischof Anno von Köln*, 2 vols. (Stuttgart 1974–5)

John, E. 'The King and the Monks in the Tenth-Century Reform', *Bulletin of the John Rylands Library*, 48 (1959–60)

Jones, G. *A History of the Vikings* (London 1969)

Jordan, K. 'Zur päpstlichen Finanzgeschichte', *QFIAB*, 25 (1933–4)

  'Der Kaisergedanke in Ravenna zur Zeit Heinrichs IV.', *DA*, 2 (1938)

  'Ravennater Fälschungen aus den Anfängen des Investiturstreits', *AUF*, 15 (1938)

  'Die Entstehung der römischen Kurie', *ZRGKA*, 59 (1939)

  'Die päpstliche Verwaltung im Zeitalter Gregors VII.', *StGreg*, 1 (1947)

Kahl, H.-D. 'Compellere intrare. Die Wendenpolitik Bruns von Querfurt im Lichte hochmittelalterlichen Missions- und Völkerrechts', *Zeitschrift für Ostforschung*, 4 (1955)

  'Das altschonische Recht als Quelle der Missionsgeschichte des dänisch-schwedischen Raumes', *WaG*, 17 (1957)

  'Bausteine einer missionsgeschichtlichen Phänomenologie des Hochmittelalters', *Miscellanea Historiae Ecclesiasticae*, vol. I (Stockholm 1961)

  'Heidnisches Wendentum und christliche Stammesfürsten. Ein Blick in die Auseinandersetzungen zwischen Gentil- und Universalreligion im abendländischen Hochmittelalter', *AKG*, 44 (1962)

Kaiser, R. *Bischofsherrschaft zwischen Königtum und Königsmacht* (Pariser Historische Studien 17, Bonn 1981)

Kantorowicz, E. H. *Laudes regiae. A Study in Liturgical Acclamations and Medieval Ruler Worship* (Berkeley 1946)

The King's Two Bodies (Princeton 1957)

Selected Studies (Locust Valley, NY 1964)

Kehr, P. F. *Das Papsttum und der katalanische Prinzipat bis zur Vereinigung mit Aragon* (Abhandlungen der preußischen Akademie der Wissenschaften, phil.-hist. Klasse 1, Berlin 1926)

Das Papsttum und die Königreiche Navarra und Aragon bis zur Mitte des zwölften Jahrhunderts (Abhandlungen der preußischen Akademie der Wissenschaften, phil.-hist. Klasse 4, Berlin 1928)

Wie und wann wurde das Reich Aragon ein Lehen der römischen Kirche? (Abhandlungen der preußischen Akademie der Wissenschaften, phil.-hist. Klasse 1, Berlin 1928)

Die Belehnung der süditalienischen Normannenfürsten durch die Päpste 1059–1192 (Abhandlungen der preußischen Akademie der Wisschechaften, phil.-hist. Klasse 1, Berlin 1934)

Vier Kapitel aus der Geschichte Kaiser Heinrichs III. (Abhandlungen der preußischen Akademie der Wissenschaften, phil.-hist. Klasse 3, Berlin 1936)

Keller, H. 'Pataria und Stadtverfassung, Stadtgemeinde und Reform. Mailand im Investiturstreit', *VuF*, 17 (1973)

Kemp, E. W. *Counsel and Consent. Aspects of the Government of the Church Exemplified in the History of the English Provincial Synods* (London 1961)

Kempf, F. 'Das Problem der "Christianitas" im zwölften und dreizehnten Jahrhundert', *HJb*, 79 (1960)

'Kanonistik und kuriale Politik im zwölften Jahrhundert', *AHP*, 1 (1963)

'Pier Damiani und das Papstwahldekret 1059', *AHP*, 2 (1964)

'Primatiale und episkopal-synodale Struktur der Kirche vor der Gregorianischen Reform', *AHP*, 16 (1978)

'Die Eingliederung der überdiözesanen Hierarchie in das Papalsystem des kanonischen Rechts von der Gregorianischen Reform bis zu Innozenz III.', *AHP*, 18 (1980)

Kempf, F., H.-G. Beck, E. Ewig, and J. A. Jungmann, ed. H. Jedin and D. Dolan. *Handbuch der Kirchengeschichte*, 3 vols. (Berne 1965); English translation as *Handbook of Church History* (London 1968)

Kern, F. *Gottesgnadentum und Widerstandsrecht im frühen Mittelalter* (Leipzig 1914); English translation as *Kingship and Law in the Middle Ages* (Oxford 1939)

Kienast, W. *Die Herzogstitel in Frankreich und Deutschland (9.–12. Jh.)* (Munich 1968)

Studien über die französischen Volksstämme des Frühmittelalters (Pariser Historische Studien 7, Stuttgart 1968)

'Der Wirkungsbereich des französischen Königtums von Odo bis Ludwig VI. (888–1137) in Südfrankreich', *HZ*, 209 (1969)

Deutschland und Frankreich in der Kaiserzeit (900–1270), 3 vols. (Stuttgart 1974)

Klauser, R. 'Zur Entwicklung des Heiligsprechungsverfahrens bis zum dreizehnten Jahrhundert', *ZRGKA*, 71 (1954)

Klauser, T. 'Die Liturgie der Heiligsprechung', in *Heilige Überlieferung, Festschrift für J. Herwegen* (Münster 1938)

Kleine abendländische Liturgiegeschichte (Bonn 1965)

Klebel, E. 'Eigenklosterrecht und Vogteien in Bayern und Österreich', *MIÖG*, Ergänzungsband 14 (1939)

Klewitz, H.-W. 'Die Entstehung des Kardinalskollegiums', *ZRGKA*, 25 (1936)
'Cancellaria. Ein Beitrag zur Geschichte des geistlichen Hofdienstes', *DA*, 1 (1937)
'Königtum, Hofkapelle und Domkapitel im zehnten Jahrhundert', *AUF*, 16 (1939)

Kloczowski, J. 'Les Structures ecclesiastiques en Europe du IXme au XIme siècles', in *Europe aux IXme–XIme siècles* (Warsaw 1968)
'La Province ecclésiastique de la Pologne et ses evêques', *MCSM*, 7 (1971)

Knowles, D. *The Monastic Order in England 940–1216*, 2nd edn (Cambridge 1963)

Köhler, O. *Das Bild der geistlichen Fürsten in den Viten des zehnten, elften und zwölften Jahrhunderts* (Abhandlungen zur mittleren und neueren Geschichte 77, Berlin 1935)
'Die ottonische Reichskirche. Ein Forschungsbericht', in *Festschrift für G. Tellenbach* (Freiburg 1968)

Kölmel, W. *Rom und der Kirchenstaat im zehnten und elften Jahrhundert* (Abhandlungen zur mittleren und neueren Geschichte 78, Berlin 1935)

Köpke, R. and Dümmler, E. *Jahrbücher des deutschen Reiches unter Otto I.* (Leipzig 1876)

Kost, O. H. *Das östliche Niedersachsen im Investiturstreit* (Studien zur Kirchengeschichte Niedersachsens 13, Göttingen 1962)

Krause, H. G. 'Das Papstwahldekret von 1059 und seine Rolle im Investiturstreit', *StGreg*, 7 (1960)

Krimm-Beumann, J. 'Das Traktat "De investitura episcoporum" von 1109', *DA*, 33 (1977) (see also J. Beumann)

Kroener, A. *Wahl und Krönung der deutschen Kaiser und Könige in Italien (Lombardei)* (Diss. Freiburg 1901)

Kuhn, H. 'König und Volk in der germanischen Bekehrungsgeschichte', *Zeitschrift für deutsches Altertum und deutsche Literatur*, 77 (1940)
'Das Fortleben des germanischen Heidentums nach der Christianisierung', *Settimane*, 15 (1971)

Kurze, D. *Pfarrerwahlen im Mittelalter* (Forschungen zur Rechtsgeschichte und zum Kirchenrecht 6, Cologne 1966)

Kuttner, S. 'Cardinalis. The History of a Canonical Concept', *Traditio*, 3 (1945)

Ladner, G. B. *Theologie und Politik vor dem Investiturstreit* (Baden bei Wien 1936)
'Aspects of Medieval Thought on Church and State', *Review of Politics*, 9 (1947)
'Die mittelalterliche Reformidee und ihr Verhältnis zur Idee der Renaissance', *MIÖG*, 60 (1952)
'The Concepts of "Ecclesia" and "Christianitas" and their Relation to the Idea of Papal "Plenitudo potestatis" from Gregory VII to Boniface VIII', in *Sacerdozio e regno da Gregorio VII a Bonifacio VIII* (Miscellanea Historiae Pontificiae 18, Rome 1954)
'Two Gregorian Letters. On the Sources and Nature of Gregory VII's Reform Ideology', *StGreg*, 5 (1956)

The Idea of Reform. Its Impact on Christian Thought and Action in the Age of the Fathers (Cambridge 1959)

'Gregory the Great and Gregory VII. A Comparison of their Concepts of Renewal', *Viator*, 4 (1973)

Lammers, W. 'Formen der Mission bei Sachsen, Schweden und Abodriten", *BDLG*, 106 (1970)

Lampert of Hersfeld. *Annales*, ed. O. Holder-Egger in *Lamperti monachi Hersfeldensis Opera* (MGH SRG, Hanover 1894)

Lange, W. *Studien zur christlichen Dichtung der Nordgermanen 1000–1200* (Palaestra 222, Göttingen 1958)

Larson, L. M. *Canute the Great* (New York 1912)

Laudage, J. *Priesterbild und Reformpapsttum im 12. Jahrhundert* (Cologne 1984)

Le Bras, G. 'Les confréries chrétiennes', in *Etudes de sociologie religieuse*, vol. III (Paris 1956)

Leccisotti, T. 'L'incontro di Desiderio di Monte Cassino col re Enrico IV ad Albano', *StGreg*, I (1947)

Leclercq, J. (ed.). *Ives de Chartres, Correspondance*, vol. I (CHF 22, Paris 1949)

'L'Idéal monastique de Saint Odon', in *A Cluny. Congrès scientifique* (Dijon 1950)

'Cluny fut elle ennemie de la culture?', *Revue Mabillon*, 47 (1957)

L'Amour des lettres et le désir de Dieu (Paris 1957); German translation as *Wissenschaft und Gottverlangen. Zur Mönchstheologie des Mittelalters* (Düsseldorf 1963); English translation as *The Love of Letters and the Desire for God* (London 1963)

'Le Monachisme du haut moyen âge, VIIIme–Xme siècles', *Théologie de la vie monastique*, 49 (1961)

'La Spiritualité des chanoines réguliers', *MCSM*, 3 (1962)

Leclercq, J., F. Vandenbrucke, and L. Bouyer. *Histoire de la spiritualité*, vol. II (Paris 1961)

Leitmaier, C. *Die Kirche und die Gottesurteile. Eine rechtshistorische Studie* (Wiener rechtsgeschichtliche Arbeiten 2, Vienna 1953)

Lemarignier, J. F. *Etudes sur les privilèges d'exemption et de jurisdiction ecclésiastiques des abbayes normandes depuis les origines jusqu'en 1140* (Archives de la France monastique 44, Paris 1937)

'Structures monastiques et structures politiques dans la France de la fin du Xe siècle et des débuts du XIe siècle', *MCSM*, 4 (1957) = *Settimane* 4 (1957)

'Les Institutions ecclésiastiques en France de la fin du Xme au milieu du XIIme siècle', in *Histoire des institutions françaises au moyen âge*, vol. III (Paris 1962)

'Aspects politiques des fondations des collegiales dans le royaume de France au XIme siècle', *MCSM*, 3 (1962)

Le Gouvernement royal aux premiers temps Capétiens (987–1108) (Paris 1965)

La France médiévale. Institutions et société (Collection U, Série Histoire médiévale, Paris 1978)

Lerner, F. 'Kardinal Hugo Candidus', *HZ*, Supplement 22 (1931)

Lesne, E. *La Hiérarchie épiscopale. Provinces, Métropolitains, Primats en Gaule et Germanie 742–882* (Mémoires et Travaux des Facultés Catholiques de Lille 1, Lille 1905)

Histoire de la propriété ecclésiastique en France, vol. 1 (Lille 1910)

Letonnelier, G. 'L'Abbaye exempte de Cluny et le Saint-Siège', *Archives de la France monastique*, 22 (1923)

Levi-Provençal, E. *Histoire de l'Espagne Musulmane*, vol. 11 (Paris 1950)

Leyser, K. J. 'The German Aristocracy from the Ninth to the Early Twelfth Century', *Past and Present*, 41 (1968)

Rule and Conflict in an Early Medieval Society. Ottonian Saxony (London 1979)

'The Crisis of Medieval Germany', *PBA*, 69 (1983)

L'Huillier, A. *Vie de saint Hugues, abbé de Cluny 1024–1109* (Solesmes 1888)

Liebermann, F. *The National Assembly in the Anglo-Saxon Period* (Halle 1913)

Lintzel, M. *Die Beschlüsse der deutschen Hoftage 900–1125* (Berlin 1924)

Lippelt, H. *Thietmar von Merseburg. Reichsbischof und Chronist* (Mitteldeutsche Forschungen 72, Cologne 1973)

Little, L. K. 'Formules monastiques de malediction aux IXme et Xme siècles', *Revue Mabillon*, 58 (1970–5)

'The Personal Development of Peter Damiani', in *Order and Innovation in the Middle Ages. Essays in Honour of J. R. Strayer*, ed. W. C. Jordan, B. M. Nab, and T. F. Ruiz (Princeton 1976)

'La Morphologie des malédictions monastiques', *Annales ESC*, 34 (1979)

Löwe, H. 'Pirmin, Willibrord und Bonifatius. Ihre Bedeutung für die Missionsgeschichte ihrer Zeit', in *Kirchengeschichte als Missionsgeschichte 2. Die Kirche des frühen Mittelalters, 1. Halbband*, ed. K. Schäferdiek (Munich 1978)

Loewenfeld, S. *Epistolae Pontificum Romanorum ineditae* (Leipzig 1885)

Lortz, J. *Die Geschichte der Kirche in ideengeschichtlicher Betrachtung*, vol. 1 (Münster 1962)

Lot, F. *Les Invasions barbares et le peuplement de l'Europe*, vol. 1 (Paris 1942)

Lotter, F. 'Bemerkungen zur Christianisierung der Abodriten', *Festschrift für W. Schlesinger*, ed. H. Beumann, vol. 11 (Cologne 1974)

Der Brief des Priesters Gerhard an Erzbischof Friedrich von Mainz. Ein kanonistisches Gutachten aus frühottonischer Zeit (VuF Sonderband 17, Sigmaringen 1975)

'Ein kanonistisches Handbuch über die Amtspflichten des Pfarrklerus als gemeinsame Vorlage für den Sermo synodalis "Fratres presbyteri" und Reginos Werk "De synodalibus causis"', *ZRGKA*, 93 (1976)

Loud, G. A. 'Abbot Desiderius of Monte Cassino and the Gregorian Papacy', *JEH*, 90 (1979)

Loyn, H. R. 'The King and the Structures of Society in Late Anglo-Saxon England', *History*, 42 (1957)

Anglo-Saxon England and the Norman Conquest (London 1962)

The Vikings in Britain (London 1972)

Lück, D. 'Erzbischof Anno II. von Köln, Standesverhältnisse, verwandtschaftliche Beziehungen und Werdegang bis zur Bischofweihe', *AHVN*, 172 (1970)

Maccarone, M. 'La teologia del primato Romano del secolo XIme', *MCSM*, 7 (1974)

Macdonald, A. J. *Authority and Reason in the Early Middle Ages* (London 1933)

Mackinney, L. C. 'The People and Public Opinion in the Eleventh Century Peace Movement', *Speculum*, 5 (1930)

Manaresi, C. *I Placiti del regnum Italiae*, vol. II, part 1 (Fonti per la Storia d'Italia 96, Rome 1957)

Manselli, R. 'La Christianitas medioevale di fronte all'eresia', in *Concetto, storia, miti e immagini el medio evo*, ed. V. Branca (Florence 1973)

La Religion populaire du moyen âge. Problèmes de méthode et d'histoire (Montreal 1975)

Mansi, J. D. *Sacrorum Conciliorum Nova et Amplissima Collectio* (Venice 1757–98)

Maurer, K. *Die Bekehrung des norwegischen Stammes zum Christentum*, 2 vols. (Munich 1855–6)

Mayer, G. *Fürsten und Staat* (Weimar 1950)

Meersseman, G. G. 'Die Klerikervereine von Karl dem Großen bis Innozenz III.', *ZKG*, 46 (1952)

'L'eremitismo e predicazione itinerante dei secoli XI e XII', *MCSM*, 4 (1965)

'I penitenti nei secoli XI e XII', *MCSM*, 5 (1968)

'Per la storiografia delle confraternite laicali nell'alto Medievo', in *Storiografia e Storia. Studi in onore di Eugenio Dupré-Theseider*, vol. I (Rome 1974)

Ordo Fraternitatis, Confraternite e pietà dei laici nel medievo, in collaboration with Gian Piero Pacini, 3 vols. (Italia Sacra 24–6, Rome 1977)

Mehne, J. 'Cluniazenserbischöfe', *FMSt*, 11 (1977)

Menéndez Pidal, R. *Das Spanien des Cid*, 2nd edn (Madrid 1936); English translation of the first edition as *The Cid and his Spain* (London 1934)

Meulenberg, L. F. *Der Primat der römischen Kirche im Denken und Handeln Gregors VII.* ('s-Gravenhagen 1965)

Meyer, O. 'Überlieferung und Verbreitung des Dekrets des Bischofs Burchard von Worms', *ZRGKA*, 24 (1935)

Meyer von Knonau, G. *Jahrbücher des deutschen Reiches unter Heinrich IV. und Heinrich V.*, 7 vols. (Leipzig 1890–1909)

Miccoli, G. *Chiesa Gregoriana* (Florence 1966)

Migne, J. P. *Patrologia Latina* (Paris 1841–64)

Minninger, M. *Von Clermont zum Wormser Konkordat* (Forschungen zur Kaiser- und Papstgeschichte des Mittelalters, Beihefte zu J.-F. Böhmer Regests Imperii 2, Cologne 1978)

Mirbt, C. *Die Publizistik im Zeitalter Gregors VII.* (Leipzig 1894)

Miscoll-Reckert, J. J. *Kloster Petershausen als bischöflich-konstanzisches Eigenkloster* (Freiburg 1973)

Mitteis, H. *Der Staat des hohen Mittelalters*, 2nd edn (Weimar 1958); English translation as *The State in the High Middle Ages* (Amsterdam 1975)

Mollat, M. 'La Restitution des églises privées au patrimoine ecclésiastique en France du IXme au XIme siècle', *Revue d'histoire du droit français et étranger*, 4th series 28 (1949)

Moorman, J. R. H. *A History of the Church in England* (London 1953)

Mor, C. G. *L'età feudale*, 2 vols. (Milan 1952–3)

Mordek, H. 'Papst Urban II., St. Blasien und die Anfänge des Basler Klosters St. Alban', *ZGO*, 131 (1983)

'Kanonistik und Gregorianische Reform', in *Reich und Kirche vor dem Investiturstreit*, ed. K. Schmid (Sigmaringen 1985)

Morrison, K. F. 'Canossa. A Revision', *Traditio*, 18 (1962)

Tradition and Authority in the Western Church 300–1140 (Princeton 1969)

Moulin, L. *La Vie quotidienne des religieux au moyen âge X–XVme siècles* (Paris 1978)

Müller-Mertens, E. *Regnum Teutonicum* (Berlin 1970)

Mundó, A. 'Moissac, Cluny et les mouvements monastiques de l'Est de Pyrénées du Xme au XIIme siècles', *Annales du Midi*, 75 (1963)

Munier, C. 'L'"Ordo romanus qualiter concilium agatur" d'après le cod. Colon. 138', *Recherches de théologie ancienne et médiévale*, 29 (1962)

Musset, L. 'Relations et échanges d'influences dans l'Europe du Nord-Ouest, Xme et XIme siècles', *CCM*, 1 (1958)

'La Naissance de la Normandie', in *Histoire de la Normandie*, ed. M. de Bouard (Toulouse 1970)

Neunhäuser, B. 'Der Gestaltwandel liturgischer Frömmigkeit', in *Perennitas. Festschrift für T. Michels* (Münster 1963)

Nicol, D. M. 'Byzantium and the Papacy in the Eleventh Century', *JEH*, 13/14 (1962–3)

Nitschke, A. 'Die Wirksamkeit Gottes in der Welt Gregors VII. Eine Untersuchung über die religiösen Äußerungen und die politischen Handlungen des Papstes', *StGreg*, 5 (1956)

'Die Ziele Heinrichs IV. Beobachtungen zum Wandel einer Staatsform', *Festschrift für W. Treue* (Munich 1969)

'Gregor VII.', in *Die Großen der Weltgeschichte*, ed. K. Kissmann and U. Bill, vol. III (Zurich 1973)

Norden, W. *Erzbischof Friedrich von Mainz und Otto der Große* (Berlin 1912)

Nottarp, H. *Gottesurteile. Eine Phase im Rechtsleben der Völker* (Bamberg 1949)

Gottesurteilstudien (Munich 1956)

Nussbaum, O. *Kloster, Priestermönche und Privatsmessen* (Bonn 1961)

'Der Standort der Liturgen am christlichen Altar vor dem Jahre 1000', *Theophaneia*, 18 (1965)

Nylander, J. *Das kirchliche Benefizialwesen Schwedens während des Mittelalters* (Münster 1953)

Oediger, F. W. *Das Bistum Köln von seinen Anfängen bis zum Ende des zwölften Jahrhunderts*, 2nd edn (Geschichte des Erzbistums Köln 1, Cologne 1972)

Oexle, O. G. 'Memoria und Memorialüberlieferung im frühen Mittelalter', *FMSt*, 10 (1976)

'Die funktionale Dreiteilung der "Gesellschaft" bei Adalbero von Laon', *FMSt*, 12 (1978)

'Die mittelalterlichen Gilden. Ihre Selbsdeutung und ihr Beitrag zur Sozialordnung', *Miscellanea Medievalia*, 12/1 (1979)

'Liturgische Memoria und historische Erinnerung. Zur Frage nach dem Gruppenbewußtsein und dem Wissen der eigenen Geschichte in den mittelalterlichen Gilden', *Festschrift für K. Hauck* (Berlin 1982)

Oleson, T. T. *The Witenagemot in the Reign of Edward the Confessor* (Toronto 1955)

Onasch, K. *Russische Kirchengeschichte* (Die Kirche in ihrer Geschichte M 1, Göttingen 1967)

Ordericus Vitalis. *Historia ecclesiastica*, ed. M. Chibnall (Oxford 1969)

Ott, I. 'Der Regalienbegriff im zwölften Jahrhundert', *ZRGKA*, 35 (1948)

Otto of Freising. *Chronica sive Historia de duabus civitatibus*, ed. A. Hofmeister (MGH SRG, Hanover 1912)

Overmann, A. *Gräfin Mathilde von Tuszien* (Innsbruck 1895)

Pascher, J. *Die Liturgie der Sakramente*, 3rd edn (Freiburg 1961)

Pásztor, E. 'La curia Romana', *MCSM*, 7 (1974)

'San Pier Damiani. Il cardinalato e la formazione della curia Romana', *StGreg*, 10 (1975)

Paul of Bernried, *Vita Gregorii Septimi Papae*, in J. M. Watterich, *Pontificum Romanorum . . . vitae*, vol. II (Leipzig 1862)

Pellens, K. *Die Texte des normannischen Anonymus* (Wiesbaden 1966)

Pflugk-Harttung, J. von. *Acta Pontificum Romanorum inedita*, 3 vols. (Tübingen 1881–2)

Plöchl, W. M. *Geschichte des Kirchenrechts*, 2nd edn, vols. I and II (Vienna 1960–1)

Poggiaspalla, F. 'La chiesa e la participazione dei chierici alla guerra nella legislazione fino alle decretali di Gregorio IX', *RSCI*, 32 (1959)

'La vita comune del Clero dalle origini alla riforma Gregoriana', *Uomini e Dottrine*, 14 (1968)

Pontal, O. *Les Statuts synodaux* (Typologie des sources du moyen âge occidental 11, Turnhout 1975)

Poschmann, B. *Die abendländische Kirchenbuße in spätrömischer und frühmittelalterlicher Zeit* (Bresslau 1930)

Buße und letzte Ölung (Handbuch der Dogmengeschichte IV 3, Freiburg 1951)

Poupardin, R. *Le Royaume de Provence sous les Carolingiens 855–933* (Bibliothèque de l'école des hautes études 131, Paris 1901)

Le Royaume de Bourgogne 888–1038 (Bibliothèque de l'école des hautes études 163, Paris 1907)

Prentout, H. *Essai sur les origines et la fondation du duché de Normandie* (Paris 1911)

Prosdocimi, L. 'Chierici e laici nella Società occidentale del secolo XII^mo', *Proceedings of the Second International Congress of Medieval Canon Law, Boston College 1963*, ed. S. Kuttner and J. J. Ryan (Vatican City 1965)

Rehfeldt, B. *Todesstrafen und Bekehrungsgeschichte* (Berlin 1942)

König, Volk und Gefolgschaft im nordischen Altertum (Berlin 1942)

Reindel, K. *Die bayerischen Luitpoldinger 893–989* (Quellen und Erörterungen zur bayerischen Landesgeschichte 11, Munich 1953)

Reuter, T. 'The "Imperial Church System" of the Ottonian and Salian Rulers. A Reconsideration', *JEH*, 33 (1982)

Riché, P. *Les Ecoles et l'enseignement dans l'occident chrétien de la fin du Vme au milieu du XIme siècles* (Paris 1979)

Rivière, J. 'In partem Sollicitudinis. Evolution d'une formule pontifical', *Revue des sciences religieuses*, 5 (1925)

Robinson, I. S. *Authority and Resistance in the Investiture Contest* (Manchester 1978)
'Zur Arbeitsweise Bernolds von Konstanz und seines Kreises', *DA*, 34 (1978)
'Pope Gregory VII and Episcopal Authority', *Viator*, 9 (1979)
'Pope Gregory VII, the Princes and the Pactum 1077–1080', *EHR*, 94 (1979)
'The Bible in the Investiture Contest. The South German Gregorian Circle', in *The Bible in the Medieval World. Essays in Memory of Beryl Smalley* (Oxford 1985)
Rodulfus Glaber. *Historiarum Libri Quinque*, ed. M. Prou as *Les cinq Livres de ses histoires (900–1040)* (Collection de textes 1, Paris 1886)
Rossetti, G. 'Il matrimonio del clero nella società altomedievale', *Settimane*, 24 (1977)
Rothe, E. *Goslar als salische Residenz* (Diss. Berlin, 1940)
Rouche, M. 'De l'orient à l'occident. Les origines de la tripartition fonctionelle et les causes de son adoption par l'Europe chrétienne à fin du Xme siècle', *Occident et Orient au Xme siècle* (Dijon 1979)
Sackur, E. *Die Cluniacenser in ihrer kirchlichen und allgemeingeschichtlichen Wirksamkeit bis zur Mitte des elften Jahrhunderts*, 2 vols. (Halle 1892–4)
Säbekow, G. *Die päpstliche Legationen nach Spanien und Portugal bis zum Ausgang des zwölften Jahrhunderts* (Diss. Berlin 1940)
Santifaller, L. *Zur Geschichte des ottonisch-salischen Reichskirchensystems*, 2nd edn (Vienna 1964)
Sauer, H. *Theodulfi Capitula in England. Die altenglischen Übersetzungen zusammen mit dem lateinischen Text* (Texte und Untersuchungen zur englischen Philologie 8, Munich 1978)
'Zur Überlieferung und Anlage von Erzbischof Wulfstans Handbuch', *DA*, 46 (1980)
Sawyer, P. H. *The Age of the Vikings* (London 1962)
Kings and Vikings. Scandinavia and Europe, AD 700–1100 (London 1982)
Scharnagl, A. *Der Begriff der Investitur in der Literatur des Investiturstreits* (Kirchenrechtliche Abhandlungen 56, Stuttgart 1908)
Schebler, A. *Die Reordination in der 'altkatholischen' Kirche* (Bonn 1936)
Scheffer-Boichorst, P. *Die Neuordnung der Papstwahl durch Nikolaus II.* (Strasbourg 1879)
Schieffer, R. 'Von Mailand nach Canossa', *DA*, 28 (1972)
Die Entstehung des päpstlichen Investiturverbots für den deutschen König (MGH Schriften 28, 1981)
'Heinrich III.', in *Maisergestalten des Mittelalters*, ed. H. Beumann (Munich 1984)
Schieffer, T. *Die päpstlichen Legaten in Frankreich vom Vertrag von Meersen (870) bis zum Schisma (1130)* (Historische Studien 262, Berlin 1935)
'Heinrich II. und Konrad II. Die Umprägung des Geschichtsbildes durch die Kirchenreform des elften Jahrhunderts', *DA*, 8 (1951)
'Nochmals die Verhandlungen von Mouzon', *Festschrift für E. Stengel* (Münster 1952)
'Kaiser Heinrich III. 1017–1056', in *Die großen Deutschen*, vol. 1, 2nd edn (Berlin 1956)
'Cluny et la querelle des Investitures', *RH*, 225 (1961)

Schimmelpfennig, B. 'Der Zölibat und die Lage der Priestersöhne', *HZ*, 127 (1978)

Schlesinger, W. *Kirchengeschichte Sachsens im Mittelalter*, 2 vols. (Mitteldeutsche Forschungen 27, Cologne 1962)

Schmale, F. J. 'Die Absetzung Gregors VI. in Sutri und die synodale Tradition', *AHC*, 11 (1979)

Schmid, H. F. 'Gemeinschaftskirchen in Italien und Dalmatien', *ZRGKA*, 77 (1960)

Schmid, K. *Kloster Hirsau und seine Stifter* (Freiburg 1959)
'Neue Quellen zum Verständnis des Adels im zehnten Jahrhundert', *ZGO*, 108 (1960)
'Die Thronfolge Ottos des Großen', *ZRGGA*, 81 (1964)
'Adel und Reform in Schwaben', *VuF*, 17 (1973)
'Gedenk- und Totenbücher als Quellen', in *Beiträge der Monumenta Germaniae Historica zum 31. Historikertag Mannheim 1976* (Munich 1976)
'Bemerkungen zum Konstanzer Klerus der Karolingerzeit', *Freiburger Diözesan-Archiv*, 100 (1983)

Schmid, K. and O. G. Oexle, 'Voraussetzungen und Wirkung des Gebetsbundes von Attigny', *Francia*, 2 (1974)

Schmid, K. and J. Wollasch, 'Die Gemeinschaft der Lebenden und Verstorbenen in Zeugnissen des Mittelalters', *FMSt*, 1 (1967)

Schmid, P. *Der Begriff der kanonischen Wahl in den Anfängen des Investiturstreits* (Stuttgart 1926)

Schmidt, T. *Alexander II. (1061–1073) und seine Zeit* (Stuttgart 1977)

Schmitz, G. 'Das Konzil von Trosly', *DA*, 33 (1977)

Schneider, C. *Prophetisches Sacerdotium und heilsgeschichtliches Regnum im Dialog 1073–1077. Zur Geschichte Gregors VII. und Heinrichs IV.* (Münstersche Mittelalter-Schriften 9, Munich 1972)

Schneider, G. *Erzbischof Fulco von Reims (883–906) und das Frankenreich* (Münchner Beiträge zur Mediävistik und Renaissance-Forschung 14, Munich 1973)

Schramm, P. E. *Geschichte des englischen Königtums im Lichte der Krönung* (Weimar 1937); English translation as *A History of the English Coronation* (Oxford 1937)
Der König von Frankreich. Das Wesen der Monarchie vom neunten zum sechzehnten Jahrhundert, vol. 1 (Weimar 1939)
Herrschaftszeichen und Staatssymbolik. Beiträge zu ihrer Geschichte vom dritten bis sechzehnten Jahrhundert, 3 vols. (MGH Schriften 14, Sutttgart 1954–6)

Schreiber, G. *Kurie und Kloster im zwölften Jahrhundert* (Kirchenrechtliche Abhandlungen 65–68, Stuttgart, 1910)
'Kirchliches Abgabenwesen an französische Eigenkirchen aus Anlaß von Ordalien', *ZRGKA*, 5 (1915)
'Mönchtum und Wallfahrt', *HJb*, 55 (1935)
'Kluny und die Eigenkirchen', *AUF*, 17 (1942)
'Mittelalterliche Segnungen und Abgaben', *ZRGKA*, 32 (1943)
'Gregor VII., Cluny, Citeaux, Prémontré zu Eigenkirche, Parochie, Seelsorge', *ZRGKA*, 34 (1947)

Schröder, I. *Die westfränkischen Synoden von 888–987 und ihre Überlieferung* (MGH Hilfsmittel 3, Munich 1980)

Schwartz, G. *Die Besetzung der Bistümer Reichsitaliens unter den sächsischen und salischen Kaisern* (Leipzig 1913)

Schwarz, W. 'Der Investiturstreit in Frankreich', *ZKG*, 42 (1923) and 43 (1924) 'Jurisdictio und Conditio', *ZRGKA*, 45 (1959)

Schwineköper, B. 'Christus-Reliquien-Verehrung und Politik. Studien über die Mentalität der Menschen des frühen Mittelalters, insbesondere über die religiöse Haltung und sakrale Stellung der frühmittelalterlichen deutschen Kaiser und Könige', *BDLG*, 117 (1987)

Seegrün, W. *Das Papsttum und Skandinavien bis zur Vollendung der nordischen Kirchenorganisation (1164)* (Quellen und Forschungen zur Geschichte Schleswig-Holstein 51, Neumünster 1967)

Segl, P. *Königtum und Klosterreform in Spanien* (Kallmünz 1974)

Selge, K.-V. *Kreuzzüge und Stauferzeit* (Die Kirche in ihrer Geschichte F 1, Göttingen, forthcoming)

Semmler, J. 'Traditio und Königsschutz', *ZRGKA*, 45 (1959)
Die Klosterreformen von Siegburg, ihre Ausbreitung und ihr Reformprogramm in elften und zwölften Jahrhundert (Rheinisches Archiv 56, Bonn 1959)
'Klosterreform und Gregorianische Reform', *StGreg*, 6 (1959–61)
'Mönche und Kanoniker im Frankreich Pippins und Karls des Großen', in *Untersuchungen zu Kloster und Stift* (Veröffentlichungen des Max-Planck-Institut für Geschichte 68, Göttingen 1980)

Servatius, G. 'Kirche und Staat im Mittelalter. Auf dem Weg nach Canossa', in *Kirche und Staat auf Distanz. Historische und Aktuelle Perpsektiven*, ed. G. Denzler (Munich 1977)
Paschalis II. (1099–1118). Studien zur seiner Person und seiner Politik (Stuttgart 1979)

Sieben, H. J. 'Konzilien in der Sicht des Gregorianers Bernold von St. Gallen', *AHC*, 11 (1979)

Southern, R. W. *Kirche und Gesellschaft im Abendland des Mittelalters* (Berlin 1976); originally appeared as *Western Society and the Church in the Middle Ages* (Harmondsworth 1970)

Sprandel, R. *Ivo von Chartres und seine Stellung in der Kirchengeschichte* (Pariser Historische Studien 1, Stuttgart 1962)

Steindorff, E. *Jahrbucher des deutschen Reiches unter Heinrich III.*, 2 vols. (Leipzig 1874–81)

Stickler, A. 'Il potere coattivo materiale della Chiesa nella Riforma Gregoriana secondo Anselmo di Lucca', *StGreg*, 2 (1947)
Historia Juris canonici Latini I (Turin 1950)
'Sacerdozio e regno nelle nuove Ricerche attorno ai secoli XII e XIII nei Decretisi e Decretalisti fino alle decretali di Gregori IX', in *Sacerdozio e regno da Gregorio VII a Bonifacio VIII* (Miscellanea historiae Pontificiae 18, Rome 1954)

Stöckl, G. *Geschichte der Slawenmission* (Die Kirche in ihrer Geschichte E 1, Göttingen 1961)

Stroll, M. 'New Perspectives on the Struggle between Guy of Vienne and Henry V', *AHP*, 18 (1980)

Stürner, W. 'Salvo debito honore et reverentia. Der Königsparagraph im Papstwahldekret von 1059', *ZRGKA*, 54 (1968)

'Der Königsparagraph im Papstwahldekret von 1059', *StGreg*, 9 (1972)

'Das Papstwahldekret von 1059 und die Wahl Nikolaus II.', *ZRGKA*, 59 (1973)

Stutz, U. *Geschichte des kirchlichen Benefizialwesens von seinen Anfängen bis auf Alexander III.* (Berlin 1895)

Die Eigenkirche als Element des mittelalterlich-germanischen Kirchenrechts (Berlin 1895)

'Lehen und Pfründe', *SRGGA*, 20 (1899)

'Das karolingische Zehntgebot', *ZRGGA*, 29 (1908)

'Gratian und die Eigenkirchen', *ZRGKA*, 1 (1911)

'Eigenkirche, Eigenkloster', *PRE*, 22 (1913)

'Kirchenrecht', in *Enzyklopädie der Rechtswissenschaft*, ed. F. Holtzendorff and J. Kohler, vol. v, 7th edn (Munich 1914)

Papst Alexander III. gegen die Freiung langobardischer Eigenkirchen (Abhandlungen der preußischen Akademie der Wissenschaften, phil.-hist. Klasse, Berlin 1936)

Sydow, J. 'Untersuchungen zur kurialen Verwaltungsgeschichte im Zeitalter des Reformpapsttums', *DA*, 11 (1954–5)

Szabó-Bechstein, B. 'Libertas ecclesiae', *StGreg*, 12 (1985)

Szaivert, W. 'Die Entstehung und Entwicklung der Klosterexemtion', *MIÖG*, 59 (1951)

Tellenbach, G. *Die bischöflich-passauischen Eigenklöster und ihre Vogteien* (Berlin 1928)

Römischer und christlicher Reichgedanke in der Liturgie des frühen Mittelalters (Sitzungsberichte der Heidelberger Akademie der Wissenschaften, phil.-hist. Klasse, Heidelberg 1934–5, 1)

Libertas. Kirche und Weltordnung im Zeitalter des Investiturstreits (Stuttgart 1936); English translation as *Church, State and Christian Society at the Time of the Investiture Contest* (Oxford 1938)

'Zwischen Worms und Canossa', *HZ*, 162 (1940)

'Über Herzogskronen und Herzogshüte im Mittelalter', *DA*, 5 (1941)

'Vom karolingischen Reichsadel zum deutschen Reichsfürstenstand', in *Adel und Bauern im deutschen Staat des Mittelalters*, ed. T. Mayer (Leipzig 1943)

'Vom Zusammenleben der abendländischen Völker im Mittelalter', *Festschrift für G. Ritter* (Tübingen 1950)

'Zum Wesen der Cluniacenser. Skizzen und Versuche', *Saeculum*, 9 (1958)

(ed.). *Neue Forschungen über Cluny und die Cluniacenser* (Freiburg 1959)

'Der Sturz des Abtes Pontius von Cluny und seine geschichtliche Bedeutung', *QFIAB*, 42/43 (1963); a French version appeared in *Annales du Midi*, 76 (1964)

'Zur Erforschung des hochmittelalterlichen Adels (IX.–XII. Jh.)', in *XIIme Congrès internationale des sciences historiques. Rapports 1* (Vienna 1965)

'Liber Memorialis von Remiremont. Zur kritischen Erforschung und zum Quellenwert liturgischer Gedenkbücher', *DA*, 25 (1969)

'Servitus und libertas nach dem Traditionen der Abtei Remiremont', *Saeculum*, 21 (1970)

'irdischer Stand und Heilserwartung im Mittelalter', *Festschrift für H. Heimpel* (Göttingen 1972)

'Zur Translation einer Reliquie des heiligen Laurentius von Rom nach Lüttich im 11. Jahrhundert', *Storiografia e Storia. Studi in onore di Eugenio Dupré-Theseider*, vol. 1 (Rome 1974)

'Die geistigen und politischen Grundlagen der karolingischen Thronfolge', *FMSt*, 13 (1979)

'Kaiser, Rom und Renovatio', *Festschrift für K. Hauck* (Berlin 1982)

'Die abendländische Kirche im 10. und 11. Jahrhundert im Ganzen der Kirchengeschichte', *Festschrift für F. Kempf* (Sigmaringen 1983)

'Die historische Dimension der liturgischen Commemoratio', *Memoria* (Münstersche Mittelalter-Schriften 48, Munich 1984)

'Zur Geschichte der Päpste im 10. und 11. Jahrhundert', *Festschrift für J. Fleckenstein* (Sigmaringen 1984)

'Gregorianische Reform. Kritische Besinnungen', in *Reich und Kirche von dem Investiturstreit*, ed. K. Schmid (Sigmaringen 1985)

Thiel, A. (ed.). *Epistolae Romanorum pontificum genuinae et quae ad eos scriptae sunt a Hilario usque ad Pelagium II*, vol. 1 (Brunsbergae 1868)

Thietmar of Merseburg. *Chronicon*, ed. R. Holtzmann (MGH SRG N.S. 9, Berlin 1935)

Tillmann, H. *Die päpstlichen Legaten in England bis 1218* (Bonn 1926)

Töpfer, B. *Volk und Kirche zur Zeit der beginnenden Gottesfriedensbewegung in Frankreich* (Berlin 1957)

Toubert, P. 'La Vie commune des clercs au XIᵐᵉ–XIIᵐᵉ siècles. Un questionnaire', *RH*, 231 (1964)

Les Structures du Latium méridional et la Sabine du IXᵐᵉ siècle à la fin du XIIᵐᵉ siècle, 2 vols. (Rome 1973)

Uhlirz, K. and M. *Jahrbücher des deutschen Reiches unter Otto II. und Otto III.* (vol. I, Leipzig 1902; vol. II, Berlin 1954)

Ullmann, W. *The Growth of Papal Government in the Middle Ages. A Study in the Ideological Revolution of Clerical to Lay Power* (London 1955; 3rd edn 1970)

van Laarhoven, J. '"Christianitas" et Reforme Grégorienne', *StGreg*, 6 (1959–61)

Vesper, E. 'Der Machtgedanke in den Bekehrungsberichten der isländischen Sagas', *Zeitschrift für Religions- und Geistesgeschichte*, 7 (1955)

Vicaire, M. H. 'La Pastorale des moeurs dans les conciles languedociens, fin du XIᵐᵉ–debut du XIIIᵐᵉ siècle', in *Le Credo, la Morale et l'Inquisition* (Cahiers de Fanjeaux 6, Toulouse 1971)

Villada, Z. G. *Historia Ecclesiastica de España*, vol. 2/2 (Madrid 1933)

Vincke, J. *Staat und Kirche in Katalanien und Aragon während des Mittelalters*, vol. 1 (Bonn 1931)

Violante, C. *La società Milanese nell'età precomunale* (Rome 1953; 2nd edn 1974)

La pataria Milanese e la riforma ecclesiastica I (Rome 1955)

'Il monachesimo Cluniacense di fronte al mondo politico ed ecclesiastico. Secoli X^mo e XI^mo', in *Spiritualità Cluniacense, Convegno del Centro di Studi sulla spiritulaità medioevale*, vol. II (Todi 1960) reprinted in his *Studi nella Cristianità medioevale. Società, istituzioni, spiritualità* (Milan 1972)

Vita Heinrici IV. imperatoris, ed. W. Eberhard (MGH SRG, Hanover 1899)

Völker, K. *Kirchengeschichte Polens* (Grundriß der slavischen Philologie und Kulturgeschichte, Berlin 1930)

Vogel, C. and R. Elze. *Le Pontificale Romano-Germanique*, vol. III (Studi e Testi 269, Vatican City 1972)

Vogel, J. 'Zur Kirchenpolitik Heinrichs IV. nach seiner Kaiserkrönung und zur Wirksamkeit der Legaten Gregors VII. und Clement (III.) im deutschen Reich 1084/85', *FMSt*, 16 (1982)

Gregor VII. und Heinrich IV. nach Canossa (Arbeiten zur Frühmittelalterforschung 9, Berlin 1983)

'Gottschalk von Aachen (Adalbero C) und Heinrichs IV. Brief an die Römer 1081/82', *Zeitschrift des Aachener Geschichtsvereins*, 90/1 (1983–4)

'Rudolf von Rheinfelden, die Fürstenopposition gegen Heinrich IV. im Jahre 1072 und die Reform des Klosters St. Blasien', *ZGO*, 132 (1984)

Vogel, W. *Die Normannen und das Fränkische Reich bis zur Gründung der Normandie 799–911* (Heidelberg 1906)

Vollrath, H. 'Kaisertum und Patriziat in den Anfängen des Investiturstreits', *ZKG*, 85 (1974)

von Harnack, A. *Christus praesens – vicarius Christi* (Sitzungsberichte der preußischen Akademie der Wissenschaften, phil.-hist. Klasse, Berlin 1927)

Waitz, G. *Jahrbücher des deutschen Reiches unter König Heinrich I. 919–936*, 3rd edn (Leipzig 1883)

Wattenbach, W. *Deutschlands Geschichtsquellen im Mittelalter. Vom Tode Kaiser Heinrichs V. bis zum Interregnum*, rev. edn by F.-J. Schmale (Darmstadt 1976)

Wattenbach, W. and R. Holtzmann. *Deutschlands Geschichtsquellen im Mittelalter. Die Zeit der Sachsen und Salier*, rev. edn by F. J. Schmale, 3 vols. (Darmstadt 1967–71)

Watterich, J. M. *Pontificum Romanorum . . . Vitae*, 2 vols. (Leipzig 1862)

Weisweiler, H. 'Die päpstliche Gewalt in den Schriften Bernolds von St. Blasien und der Investiturstreit', *StGreg*, 4 (1952)

Wemple, S. F. *Atto of Vercelli. Church, State and Christian Society in Tenth Century Italy* (Temi e Testi 27, Rome 1979)

Wenskus, R. *Studien zur historisch-politischen Gedankenwelt Bruns von Querfurt* (Münster 1956)

Werner, K. F. 'Untersuchungen zur Frühzeit des französischen Fürstentums', *WaG*, 18 (1958)

Williams, J. R. 'Archbishop Manasses of Reims and Pope Gregory VII', *American Historical Review*, 54 (1949)

Williams, W. 'Concilium Claromontanum 1095', *StGrat*, 13 (1967)

Wipo. *Gesta Chuonradi*, ed. H. Bresslau in *Wiponis Opera* (MGH SRG, Hanover 1915)

Wirtz, H. 'Donum, investitura, conductus ecclesiae', *ZRGKA*, 35 (1914)

Wolf, A. *Olav Tryggvason und die Christianisierung des Nordens* (Innsbrucker Beiträge zur Kulturwissenschaft 6, Innsbruck 1959)

Wollasch, J. 'Muri und St. Blasien. Perspektiven schwäbischen Mönchtums in der Reform', *DA*, 17 (1961)

   Mönchtum des Mittelalters zwischen Kirche und Welt (Münstersche Mittelalterschriften 7, Munich 1973)

   'Reform und Adel in Burgund', *VuF*, 17 (1973)

Wollasch, J. with W. D. Heim, J. Mehne, F. Neiske, and D. Poeck. *Die Synopse der cluniacensischen Nekrologien*, 2 vols. (Münstersche Mittelalterschriften 39, Munich 1982)

Zaffarana, Z. 'Sul "conventus" del Clero Romano nel maggio 1082', *StMed*, 7 (1966)

Zema, D. B. 'Reform Legislation in the Eleventh Century and its Economic Import', *Catholic Historical Review*, 27 (1942)

   'Economic Reorganisation of the Roman See during the Gregorian Reform', *StGreg*, 1 (1947)

Zerfass, R. *Der Streit um die Laienpredigt* (Freiburg 1974)

Ziese, J. *Wibert von Ravenna. Der Gegenpapst Clemens III. (1084–1100)* (Stuttgart 1982)

Zimmermann, H. *Papstabsetzungen des Mittelalters* (Graz 1968)

   Der Canossagang von 1077. Wirkungen und Wirklichkeit (Akademie der Wissenschaften und der Literatur zur Mainz. Abhandlungen der geistes- und sozialwissenschaftlichen Klasse Wiesbaden 1975 5)

INDEX

Abaelard, Peter, 166

abbots, 104, 108–13, 125, 129, 169, 294–300; *see also* elections, abbatial; investiture, of prelates by rulers

Abbasids, 5

Abbo of Fleury, 43, 88, 118, 125; *collectio canonum*, 31; on church and its property, 170, 268, 288

Abd ar-Rahman III, caliph of Cordoba, 3, 5

Abodrites, 4, 15

Abraham, bishop of Freising, 53

abuses, ecclesiastical, 32, 78, 138, 161, 169, 175, 209, 247, 264–5, 292–4; *see also* marriage, clerical; proprietary churches; simony

Adalbero, archbishop of Rheims, 69

Adalbero, bishop of Laon, *Carmen ad Robertum regem*, 113, 126

Adalbero, bishop of Metz, 53

Adalbero, bishop of Würzburg, 213, 238–9, 246–7, 260, 274

Adalbert, archbishop of Bremen, 162, 223, 226, 228; plans for patriarchate, 18, 34, 65, 200

Adalbert, archbishop of Magdeburg, 20, 55

Adalbert, bishop of Worms, 238–9, 246–7, 274

Adalbert of Constance, canonist, 247, 316

Adalbert, count of Calw, 208, 298–9

Adalbert, king of Italy, 48, 71

Adalbert of Saarbrücken, royal chancellor, archbishop of Mainz, 277–9, 282

Adalbert, St, bishop of Prague, 20

Adalward, bishop of Verden, 20, 51

Adam of Bremen, historian, 8, 11, 17, 162

Adela, countess of Flanders, 208

Adelgot, archbishop of Magdeburg, 202

Adelheid, empress, 54, 226

Adelheid, margravine of Turin, 202

adoptionism, 22

advocate, advocacy, 279, 297–300

Ælfric, abbot of Eynsham, 25, 125

Ælnoth, hagiographer, 8

Æthelred II, king of England, 16, 62

Æthelstan, king of England, 14, 61, 63

Æthelwold, archbishop of Winchester, 61

Africa, 47

Agapetus II, pope, 66, 69

Aghlabites, 3, 47

Agnes, empress, 142–3, 195, 204, 343; as regent, 226–7; and Cadalan schism, 226; and 'reform', 159–60; and St Blasien, 298

agnosticism, 96, 321

Aimo, archbishop of Bourges, 127

Alan, duke of Brittany, 85

death, 230, 246, 251; death-bed words,
251–2; deserted by entourage, 250, 323;
difficulties of last years, 249–51; effects
of pontificate on papacy and church,
251, 253, 348; papal administration and
finances, 323–6, 328; and Romans, 238,
249–50, 323; *see also* Canossa, meeting
at; Gregory VII, pope, attitude of
successors to
Gregory VII, pope, programme and
doctrines of: as theoretician not fully
coherent, 315, 338, 352; claims absolute
obedience from all Christians, 25, 307–8,
311, 334, 337; claims to feudal
overlordship, 331–2; flexibility and
realism of, 202, 205, 208–10, 238, 245,
252, 266, 285; not primarily concerned
with reform, 160, 252; pope as successor
of St Peter, 205, 237, 249, 306–7, 334;
radicalism of, 187, 264–5, 348, 352;
reception of in canon law, 326; sees
disobedience as rebellion or heresy, 307,
337; on canonical election, 207; on
clerical marriage, 165–6, 207–8; on
excommunication, 206, 252, 336; on
kingship and secular power, 245, 270,
333, 337, 339, 349, 352; on lay
investiture, 177–84, 214, 234, 246,
264–5, 273, 285, 287; right order in the
world, 25, 251, 264, 327, 337–8, 349; on
simony, 207, 214–16, 232–4, 246; on
truth and custom, 316; and crusade, 231,
333; and eucharistic controversy,
318–19; *see also Dictatus Papae*
Gregory VII, pope, relations with churches
and rulers outside the empire: England,
200, 205, 207, 209, 218, 220–1; France,
180, 208–11, 221, 335; Normans of
southern Italy, 221–2, 249, 333;
northern and eastern Europe, 201,
217–20, 331; Spain, 196–7, 219–20, 258,
335
Gregory VII, pope, relations with churches
of the empire, *see* Gregory VII, pope,
and Henry IV
Gregory VII, pope, and bishops, 178–81,
205–18 *passim*; consecrates bishops,
180–1; objections of principle to

treatment of, 217–18, 307, 311–12, 337;
treats bishops as stewards, 218; views on
position of, 207, 310–11, 315–16; and
French episcopate, 209, 221; and
German eipscopate, 213–18, 231, 233,
235, 237–8, 246, 274, 307, 337; and
Italian episcopate, 174, 211–13, 238, 260
Gregory VII, pope, and Henry IV, 222–52
passim; depositions and
excommunications of Henry IV, 237,
242, 244–5; reasons for breach, 232–5,
337; relations before the breach, 213–18,
229–35; relations in period between
Worms and Canossa, 235–42; relations
after Canossa, 242–52; Gregory justifies
position, 237–9, 306, 326; Gregory's
attitude to Rudolf, 173, 243–5, 251;
Gregory's support varied and unreliable,
187, 223, 247–9; Milanese conflict, 180,
211, 223, 239–40, 336; attitude of
Italian church, 212, 223, 231, 234–6,
238, 260; attitude of Italian margravines,
206, 211–12, 216, 260; attitude of
Saxons, 173, 187, 231, 244; attitude of
German lay magnates, 229–30, 240–9,
297–302; attitude of German episcopate,
208, 213–18, 233–8, 246–7; *see also*
Canossa; Clement III, antipope;
Gregorians; Rudolf of Rheinfelden;
Worms
Gregory VII, pope, attitude of successors
to: desire for peace, 264, 283; greater
realism and flexibility, 266, 285, 349,
352; reaffirm his principles, 265, 274–5,
349
Gregory VIII, antipope, 255, 264, 324
Gregory, cardinal deacon, papal legate, 216
Gregory, cardinal deacon of S. Angelo,
284; *see also* Innocent II, pope
Gregory, bishop of Vercelli, 156
Guibert of Nogent, 174
Guido, archbishop of Vienne, 282, 284; *see
also* Calixtus II, pope
guilds, religious, 130–1
Gundechar, bishop of Eichstätt, 54
Gunther, bishop of Regensburg, 84
Gunther, bishop of Zeitz-Naumburg, 273,
316

228–9, 231–2, 239, 243, 247; *see also*
Gregory VII, pope, and Henry IV;
patricius; regency government
Henry V, emperor: excommunications of,
255, 282, 284, 287; imperial coronation,
255, 281; practises investiture, 262–3,
276–7, 283; rebellion against father, 263,
275; and antipopes, 255, 264; and
Calixtus II, 282–5, 344; and Germany,
273, 282; and Paschal II, 276–81, 324,
330, 344
Herbert, bishop of Thetford-Norwich,
175, 272
hereditary priests, 90, 163
heresy, heretics, 128, 131, 138, 140, 143,
256, 264, 274; accusations of as polemic,
2, 139, 165, 211, 263–4, 282;
disobedience to pope as, 165, 263–4,
307, 320, 333, 336–7; links with reform,
138, 140; treatment of, 7, 9, 138, 308;
nicolaitism as, 143; simony as, 82, 167–9,
173, 211
Heriger, archbishop of Mainz, 51–2
Herimar, abbot of Saint-Rémi, Rheims,
188
Heriold, king of Denmark, 13
Hermann, bishop of Bamberg, 186,
213–16, 232
Hermann, bishop of Metz, 214, 238,
246–7, 260, 306, 326
Hermann, bishop of Volterra, 168
Hermann Billung, Saxon margrave, 6, 55
hermits, 101, 140, 294, 346; Italian, 120,
144
Herold, archbishop of Salzburg, 53, 56
Hersfeld, monastery, 86
Hesso Scholasticus, 283, 287–8
Hezilo, bishop of Hildesheim, 218
hierarchy, ecclesiastical, 26, 86, 90, 131,
151, 309, 339, 340; indeterminate nature
of, 122, 306; structure of, 33–5, 37–8,
151; and papacy, 187, 305, 309–10, 342,
351–2
Hildebrand, monk and archdeacon: career
of, 146, 155, 158, 193, 202, 222, 318–19,
328; influence of on popes, 149, 193,
198, 204, 325; and Humbert's views,
183–4; *see also* Grevory VII, pope

Hincmar, archbishop of Rheims, 34, 338
Hirsau, monastery, 110, 293, 298–302; and
papacy, 128, 299, 302, 342; Hirsau
Formula (royal privilege), 298, 302
Holy Land, 100, 215, 231
homage, prohibited to clerics, 266, 272–3,
339; *see also* feudalisation of church
Honorius II, antipope, 155, 159–60, 172,
193, 200, 203, 212, 226–7; *see also*
Cadalus, bishop of Parma; schism,
Cadalan
Honorius II, pope, 284, 345
Hrabanus Maurus, archbishop of Mainz, 1,
92, 139
Hubert, cardinal bishop of Palestrina, 215,
217
Hubert, subdeacon, papal legate, 209
Huesca, bishop of, 220
Hugo, archbishop of Besançon, 210
Hugo, archbishop of Rheims, 69–70
Hugo, bishop of Die, archbishop of Lyons,
166, 174, 181–2, 207, 209–11, 220, 250,
253, 259, 263, 271–2, 287, 343
Hugo, bishop of Langres, 189, 319
Hugo Candidus, cardinal priest of S.
Clemente, 146; and election of Gregory
VII, 155–6; as papal legate, 196–9
Hugo, St, abbot of Cluny, 119, 188, 193,
206, 210; and Gregory VII, 342; papal
legate, 342; and Henry IV, 107, 343
Hugo of Arles, king of Italy, 45, 48
Hugo of Flavigny, historian, 325
Humbert, archbishop of Lyons, 180
Humbert, cardinal bishop of Silva Candida:
career, 146, 325; and schism of 1054,
191–2; as radical, 187, 264–5, 285, 320,
350; on eucharist, 139; on lay
investiture, 184, 285–6; on simony
(*Adversus Simoniacos*), 168–9, 171, 177–8,
183–4, 264–5, 269; on three orders, 126
Hunfrid, archbishop of Ravenna, 190
Hungary, Hungarians, Magyars: threat to
Christendom, 2, 4–5, 12, 16, 26, 47,
127; Christianisation of, 2, 9, 11–12, 18;
church in, 35, 65, 67; and papacy, 220,
236, 331, 335
Huzman, bishop of Speyer, 182, 208

Liudprand, bishop of Cremona, historian,
47, 49, 71
Liutizi, Slav confederation, 4, 9–10, 15;
defeat Saxons, 225
Liutold, duke of Carinthia, 248
Liutpold, archbishop of Mainz, 190
Lodi, 202, 208
London, concordat of, 273, 286
Lorsch, monastery, 86
Lothar I, emperor, 13
Lothar, king of France, 43
Lothar, king of Italy, 48
Lotharingia, 41, 43, 50–2; reform and, 146
Louis II, emperor, 87, 275
Louis the Blind, king of Provence, 45–7
Louis the Child, king of east Francia, 50
Louis the Pious, emperor, 13, 121, 279
Louis the Stammerer, king of west Francia,
41
Louis IV, king of France, 43
Louis VI, king of France, 259
Lübeck, 10
Lund, province, 65
Lüneburg, castle, 231
Lyons: primacy, 211, 271; province, 46,
115, 345

Mâcon, bishop of, and Cluny, 115, 117,
345
Magdeburg, archbishopric: as missionary
centre, 18; foundation, 53–4, 56, 58, 72
magic, 39, 97–9
Maginulf, *see* Silvester IV, antipope
Magnus Billung, duke of Saxony, 231
Mainz, archbirhopric, 35, 52, 86; province,
18, 50–1
Mainz, assembly (1080), 246
Maiolus, abbot of Cluny, 295
Manasses, archbishop of Rheims:
deposition, 186, 210–11, 221, 264; and
Hugo of Die, 174, 182
Mantua, meeting at, 241
Marinus, papal legate, 70
markets, 81, 279
Marozia, duke of Theophylact, 70
marriage, clerical, 80, 161–7, 175, 188,
193–4, 197–8, 208, 213, 220, 249, 335–6;
and reform programme, 80, 161, 166;

and sacraments, 165, 208; defenders of,
165–6, 207; economic necessity of,
89–90; status of children, 90, 163; *see also*
celibacy, clerical; nicolaitism
Marseilles, Saint-Victor, monastery: as
centre of monastic reform, 110
marshal service, 275
martyrs: heathen and Christian, 19;
missionary, 20; generation of, 96–9; *see
also* saints
mass, *see* eucharist; liturgy
Mathilda, margravine of Tuscany, 206,
211–12, 216, 233, 254, 260, 262, 275,
323
Mathilda, wife of William the Conqueror,
199
Maurice, archbishop of Braga, *see*
Gregory VIII, antipope
Melrichstadt, battle of (1078), 127
memoria, see libri memoriales
Menfö, battle of (1044), 143
Merseburg, bishopric, 27, 54
Methodius, missionary, 20
metropolitans: and king, 34, 43, 200;
authority and rights of, 18, 23, 33–6, 43,
45, 50, 55, 65, 72, 88, 151, 174, 177,
182, 201–2, 207, 216, 221, 263, 284, 305;
see also legates, papal; pallium
Michael Cerullarios, patriarch of
Constantinople, 192
Michael, king of Serbia, 219
Miesco I, duke of Poland, 14
Milan, archbishopric: province, 35, 48–9,
180; and papacy, 34, 68, 194, 240,
260–2, 274
Milan, ecclesiastical disputes at, 140, 180,
194, 198, 201–4, 211, 213, 222–3, 231–4,
336; *see also* Patarenes
Minden, bishopric, 49, 51
ministeriales, 255, 279
minsters, 28
miracles: miraculous, 19–20, 91, 97–101,
264, 306; eucharistic, 98; healing, 101;
see also magic; supernatural
mission, missionaries, 2–21, 27, 64–5, 71–2,
94, 104, 219; rivalries among, 18, 65
monasteries, *see* abbots; bishops: and
monasteries; Cluny; customs, monastic;